The Sociology of Migration

The International Library of Studies on Migration

Series Editor: Robin Cohen
        Department of Sociology, University of Warwick, UK

1. Theories of Migration
     Robin Cohen

2. Geography and Migration
     Vaughan Robinson

3. The Sociology of Migration
     Robin Cohen

4. Migration in European History (Volumes I and II)
     Colin Holmes

5. The Politics of Migration
     Zig Layton-Henry

6. Law and Migration
     Selina Goulbourne

The Sociology of Migration

Edited by

Robin Cohen

Professor of Sociology
University of Warwick, UK

THE INTERNATIONAL LIBRARY OF STUDIES ON MIGRATION

An Elgar Reference Collection
Cheltenham, UK • Brookfield, US

Published by
Edward Elgar Publishing Limited
8 Lansdown Place
Cheltenham
Glos GL50 2HU
UK

Edward Elgar Publishing Company
Old Post Road
Brookfield
Vermont 05036
US

A catalogue record for this book is available from the British Library.

Library of Congress Cataloging in Publication Data
The sociology of migration / edited by Robin Cohen.
    p. cm. — (The international library of studies on migration
; 3) (Elgar reference collection)
  Includes bibliographical references and index.
  1. Alien labor. 2. Aliens—Social conditions. I. Cohen, Robin,
1944–   . II. Series. III. Series: Elgar reference collection.
HD6300.S64 1996
304.8—dc20

96–12607
CIP

ISBN 1 85898 000 3

Printed in Great Britain by Galliard (Printers) Ltd, Great Yarmouth

Contents

Acknowledgements

The editor and publishers wish to thank the authors and the following publishers who have kindly given permission for the use of copyright material.

American Sociological Association for article: Alejandro Portes and Alex Stepick (1985), 'Unwelcome Immigrants: The Labor Market Experiences of 1980 (Mariel) Cuban and Haitian Refugees in South Florida', *American Sociological Review*, **50** (4), August, 493–514.

Asian and Pacific Migration Journal for articles: Ronald Skeldon (1992), 'International Migration Within and From the East and Southeast Asian Region: A Review Essay', *Asian and Pacific Migration Journal*, **1** (1), 19–63; Paul M. Ong, Lucie Cheng and Leslie Evans (1992), 'Migration of Highly Educated Asians and Global Dynamics', *Asian and Pacific Migration Journal*, **1** (3–4), 543–67.

Blackwell Publishers Ltd for article: Elizabeth Petras (1980), 'The Role of National Boundaries in a Cross-National Labour Market', *International Journal of Urban and Regional Research*, **4** (2), 157–94.

Berliner Institut für Vergleichende Sozialforschung and Dr Nermin Abadan-Unat for article: Nermin Abadan-Unat (1988), 'The Socio-Economic Aspects of Return Migration in Turkey', *Migration: A European Journal of International Migration and Ethnic Relations*, **3**, 29–59.

B.S.A. Publications Ltd for article: Philip Corrigan (1977), 'Feudal Relics or Capitalist Monuments? Notes on the Sociology of Unfree Labour', *Sociology*, **II** (3), September, 435–63.

Center for Migration Studies for articles: Pang Eng Fong and Linda Lim (1982), 'Foreign Labor and Economic Development in Singapore', *International Migration Review*, **XVI** (3), Fall, 548–76; Saskia Sassen-Koob (1984), 'Notes on the Incorporation of Third World Women into Wage-Labor Through Immigration and Off-Shore Production', *International Migration Review*, **XVIII** (4), Winter, 1144–67; Monica Boyd (1989), 'Family and Personal Networks in International Migration: Recent Developments and New Agendas', *International Migration Review*, **XXIII** (3), Fall, 638–70.

Elsevier Science Ltd for article: Sharon Stanton Russell (1986), 'Remittances from International Migration: A Review in Perspective', *World Development*, **14** (6), 677–96.

International Organization for Migration for articles: J.S. Birks, I.J. Seccombe and C.A. Sinclair (1988), 'Labour Migration in the Arab Gulf States: Patterns, Trends and Prospects', *International Migration*, **XXVI** (3), September, 267–85; T.K. Oommen (1989), 'India: "Brain Drain" or the Migration of Talent?', *International Migration*, **XXVII** (3), September, 411–25.

International Socialism Journal for article: Nigel Harris (1980), 'The New Untouchables: The International Migration of Labour', *International Socialism*, **2** (8), Spring, 37–63.

Plenum Publishing Corporation for article: Calvin Goldscheider (1987), 'Migration and Social Structure: Analytic Issues and Comparative Perspectives in Developing Nations', *Sociological Forum*, **2** (4), 674–96.

Royal African Society for article: Barbara B. Brown (1983), 'The Impact of Male Labour Migration on Women in Botswana', *African Affairs*, **82** (328), July, 367–88.

Sage Publications Ltd for articles: Anthony H. Richmond (1988), 'Sociological Theories of International Migration: The Case of Refugees', *Current Sociology*, **36** (2), Summer, 7–25; Janet L. Abu-Lughod (1988), 'Palestinians: Exiles at Home and Abroad', *Current Sociology*, **36** (2), Summer, 61–9.

University of California Press and the Society for the Study of Social Problems for article: Alejandro Portes (1979), 'Illegal Immigration and the International System, Lessons from Recent Legal Mexican Immigrants to the United States', *Social Problems*, **26** (4), April, 425–38.

University of Chicago Press for articles: Michael Burawoy (1976), 'The Functions and Reproduction of Migrant Labor: Comparative Material from Southern Africa and the United States', *American Journal of Sociology*, **81** (5), March, 1050–87; Kenneth L. Wilson and Alejandro Portes (1980), 'Immigrant Enclaves: An Analysis of the Labor Market Experiences of Cubans in Miami', *American Journal of Sociology*, **86** (2), September, 295–319.

Every effort has been made to trace all the copyright holders but if any have been inadvertently overlooked the publishers will be pleased to make the necessary arrangement at the first opportunity.

In addition the publishers wish to thank the Library of the London School of Economics and Political Science and the Marshall Library of Economics, Cambridge University for their assistance in obtaining these articles.

Introduction

Robin Cohen

Migration is at the heart of early sociological concerns. Auguste Comte's view that human-kind gradually evolved from a theological, to a metaphysical and finally to a scientific ('positive') state was based on the idea that greater concentrations of people led to higher and higher stages of civilization. Although his notions were largely abstract, they drew from the increasing nineteenth-century knowledge of the great ancient riverine civilizations like Mesopotamia. There the first cities were built and the first elaborated system of writing, cuneiform, was developed. Comte's eminent successor, Emile Durkheim, was also concerned with the break-up of rural, 'mechanical' solidarity consequent on the migration to the cities. Urban concentrations produced a new and more specialized division of labour. But, he argued, the Utilitarians had over-emphasized economic changes at the expense of under-standing the moral and legal basis of the new order. Instead of mechanical solidarity, based on blind obedience to custom and tradition, urbanized societies required 'organic' solidarity, rooted in a mutual need for each other's services.

Durkheim was sensitive to the dangers of unrestrained, hedonistic individualism which, he saw, could never produce social cohesion or a beneficial moral order. But Comte and Durkheim saw the changes they described in peaceful, evolutionary terms. Marx was probably the first of the great nineteenth-century thinkers to see migration as a more violent process. Detaching the peasant from the soil for industrial purposes was a traumatic business. As he saw it: 'great masses of men [were] suddenly and forcibly torn from their means of subsistence, and hurled on to the labour market as free, unprotected and rightless proletarians'.[1] The expression 'free' proletarians alluded to Marx's idea that labourers were now free from their own means of production and subsistence and 'free', but of necessity required, to sell their remaining possession, their labour power, in the market.

The Peculiarity of Migrant Labour

Subsequent sociologists have questioned the extent to which modern capitalism required 'free' labour in the sense Marx understood and indeed have suggested that many forms of modern production used 'unfree labour' successfully and profitably.[2] The most evident example of this proposition is the deployment of slaves from West Africa in the plantations of the New World, the first important example of mass forced migration in the modern world. However, as Corrigan (Chapter 1) shows, slavery by no means exhausted the types of unfree labour utilized by modern industry and agriculture. (Corrigan's account provides a comprehensive list of sources on this question at the date of publication.) Burawoy (Chapter 2) extends this account conceptually, temporally and geographically. By focusing on two apparently divergent settings, apartheid South Africa and the southwestern states of the United States, he is able to demonstrate that forms of unfree labour survive to the present day. They are seen, notably but not exclusively, in the system of rotating labour in the two settings he examines.

Such systems provide considerable benefits to the employers as the 'social wage' (which Marxists call 'the cost of reproduction') is met outside the workplace and often outside the wider urban and industrial milieu. What is meant by such a notion? Essentially the employers avoid most, if not all, of the following costs – which are met characteristically by the peasant household: prenatal and post-natal care, early socialization and training, education, employment insurance, disability and medical care, the 'family' (as opposed to the individual) wage, holiday allowances, health care and pension entitlements. It is a formidable list and one can see why many employers might prefer to use temporary migrants rather than permanent, stabilized workers. However, as Burawoy makes clear, there are associated costs – including the transport of workers, their housing and, because a pure model of labour circulation is ultimately unstable, to do with the policing of the system of rotating labour itself.

The Dynamics of International Labour Migration

I have already suggested that some states and employers have sought to update the migration of quasi-free and unfree labour in order to deploy it in a new context. Nigel Harris (Chapter 3) addresses the dynamic of international labour migration as a whole, showing how dispossessed peasants from poor countries are forced through poverty and lack of alternative to seek work in rich countries. After the Second World War, two countries in Europe, Switzerland and Germany, tried to implement and perfect a *gastarbeiter* model of rotating labour. These countries hoped thereby to avoid social wage costs, prevent settlement, deny civic rights to foreign workers and head off what can usefully be described as 'welfare chauvinism' on the part of the local population – who were all too easily swayed by populist allegations that foreigners were stealing their jobs, housing and benefits. Despite the rigour with which these policies were implemented, they were ultimately unsustainable. Employers retained good workers, migrants organized themselves to advance their human rights and long-term settlement took place, particularly in Germany.

The end of labour recruitment in Europe was closely matched by the beginning of extensive recruitment of Arab and Asian workers in the Gulf states. The massive hike in oil prices after 1973 allowed a number of the states in the region to commence public works, hospital, school and university building and the provision of infrastructure on a gigantic scale. Birks and his colleagues (Chapter 4) tell the story of this recruitment at its heyday. Labour recruitment to the Gulf was, however, to experience a sudden reverse as a result of the Gulf War when many Asians had to be repatriated and many Palestinians and Yemenis were deported because they appeared too sympathetic to Saddam Hussein's regime.[3]

Women Migrants and the Women Left Behind

It was said by early feminist writers that women were 'hidden from history'. This was certainly true of women's migration which has remained curiously under-researched despite the long reach of feminist-inspired studies in so many other areas of social life.[4] One reason why they have often remained hidden from migration history is that immigration policies often insisted on 'family migration'. In several settings (Caribbean migrants to Britain, for example) it is clear that independent women migrating for their own reasons were passing themselves off as married in order to secure admission. Another reason for the relative neglect of women, is that many were often 'left behind' in systems of male-dominated contract labour, such as those obtained in apartheid South Africa. However, such women were by no means always turned into victims. On the contrary, as is shown by Brown (Chapter 5), some were able to use their male spouse's absence to try to gain a toehold in land ownership.

The remaining reading in the section (Chapter 6) is concerned with the three areas where women are active participants in the global labour force – as domestic workers,[5] in the newly-industrializing countries and in the so-called 'global cities', where service labour (including domestic labour) is still in high demand. The rise of independent women's migration is both a reflection of increasing demand and, probably, the loosening grip of patriarchal relations in the rural areas of many countries.

Enclaves and Labour Markets

Like economists, sociologists are vitally interested in the role of migrants in the labour market and in the economic life of the countries of settlement. One thesis that gets constantly replayed, refined or rejected in new entrepreneurial settings is Weber's notion of the 'complex affinity' between Protestantism and capitalism. Clearly he spotted something very important, which might be generalized as saying that an appropriate cultural precognition is central to the entrepreneurial impulse. Successful capitalists have to be 'driven' or 'compelled' in some deep-seated psychological sense. However, this driving ambition is found in a great variety of settings – amongst the Chinese in Singapore and Malaysia, the Lebanese in West Africa, the East African Asians in Britian and, as our contributors show in Chapters 7 and 8, amongst the Cubans in Florida. Given these examples, it is difficult to argue that Protestantism is the key variable. Instead, it might be hypothesized that Weber mistook the religious trees for the migrant woods. In other words it may be that migration itself confers a special sociological advantage in allowing outsiders to spot niches and opportunities that locals overlook through over-familiarity.

The literature on immigrant labour markets has been heavily dominated in recent years by 'dual labour market theory' – the idea that there is limited competition for certain '3D' (dirty, dangerous and difficult) jobs in one segment of the market because they are handed to the next cohort of unskilled immigrants. This issue is probed in Chapter 7 as is the related question of whether particular niches are colonized by particular immigrant groups (and with what effect). Labour markets are also somewhat artificially driven by political circumstances. How welcome were Cuban and Haitian refugees? Was there a displacement effect of local labour? These issues are usefully explored in Chapter 8.

Effects of Return Migration and Remittances

A number of countries (Bangladesh, the Philippines, Lesotho to name but three) are crucially dependent on remittance income from migrants abroad. In 1995, the Philippines had over three million nationals working in other countries. The export of labour is both its most valuable export and the largest single source of foreign exchange earnings. In Chapter 9 Russell reviews the literature. It is worth emphasizing that the level of earnings through remittance income is very mercurial. As in the Gulf War, workers can suddenly be sent home, while their relationship with their home country might slowly diminish. It is also sometimes necessary for the home government to seek to protect its workers abroad – the governments of India, Mexico and the Philippines have all had to intervene to protect their workers against human rights abuses in other countries.

What happens when migrant workers come home? Abadan-Unat (Chapter 10) investigates this in the case of Turkey, one of the most illustrative cases. It is perhaps only natural that a considerable proportion of the income of migrant workers is spent on consumer goods and on acquiring or improving property. In general, economists would regard this as a 'non-productive' investment. Foreign consumer goods use up foreign exchange and might encourage similar imports. House-building might provide a little employment and stimulate the production of construction materials, but that income does not directly produce goods and commodities. Trying to use returnee migrants to promote development has proved more difficult in practice than it is in theory. Some skills are repatriated certainly, but more needs to be done to encourage productive investment if returnees are to act as innovators and stimulators of their home economy.

Migration and Social Structure

What happens to the sending family, household and community when migration occurs? The answer depends on a good number of variables – the scale of the process, whether the migrants return or stay away, how long they are gone, whether remittances are significant and continuous, and what the opportunity cost of their departure has been for the family concerned. In some cases a process of complex adaptation to migration occurs (Chapter 11) and old rules of generational deference, patriarchy and male dominance have to give way to the necessity to sustain the unit by seeking work elsewhere. There are a host of possible illustrations, but one poignant example that comes to mind is described by Seddon in the case of Nepal.[6] There male migration was traditionally to take up service in the British army in the famous Gurkha regiments. With the end of empire and the end of the Cold War the demand for Gurkha soldiers has dramatically decreased. Alternative opportunities are scant, so many Nepalese women are forced into the international and regional sex industry with enormous consequences for the Nepalese social structure. Migration scholars are also increasingly beginning to appreciate how migration decisions are taken not only individually but collectively as families and households jointly seek to mitigate misfortunes or advance the interests of their members (Chapter 12). The role of the family and kin group in sustaining migration once it has commenced has also been identified as a key phenomenon in perpetuating movement.[7]

Refugees and Displaced Persons

Refugees have always been part of the story of human migration. Flight from natural disasters, adverse climatic changes, famine, and territorial aggression by other communities or other species is as old as social organization. Biblical figures sought refuge in sanctuary towns, Mohammed fled Mecca for Medina in AD 622. Despite the long history of flight migration, refugees have never been formally integrated into sociological theories of the causes and nature of migration. In this respect Richmond's article (Chapter 13) represents a brave attempt at an original synthesis.

We have become very much more aware of refugee migration at the end of the twentieth century. This is partly because of the large numbers involved. (In 1995, the United Nations High Commission for Refugees estimated the number of refugees and 'other people of concern' to the organization at 27.4 million.) However, unease and anxiety at how to cope with the scale of migration is also complemented by a sense of horror at the manner in which displacement occurs – often through what is described as 'ethnic cleansing'. Taking a slightly longer view of this distasteful phenomenon, we can recognize that mass displacements often arise at the moment of nation-state formation or when modernizing nation-builders seize control of the state. Armenians were 'cleansed' by Turkey in the First World War, Hindus and Muslims crossed from India to Pakistan in 1947/8 (eight million in either direction). This is not to excuse, but rather to give context to, the case covered here, namely the displacement of the Palestinians in 1948 and their consequent exile (Chapter 12).

The 'Brain Drain'

The migration of peasants into cities and unskilled workers further afield has constituted the principal focus for sociologists of migration. However, there are at least two other major forms of migration that need discussion – that of entrepreneurs and highly skilled professionals. Such migration has often been described as a 'brain drain' (Chapter 15). The implication is obvious. Skilled people in poor countries are being lured by salaries and professional opportunities to rich countries. There is certainly an echo of 'disloyalty' implied, even 'exploitation'. One can, to be sure, see the viewpoint of a poor taxpayer in India (say) whose tax has been used to subsidize the expensive education of a doctor in an Indian medical school, only to find the doctor has taken off to Houston on graduation. Equally, one can see that a rich and powerful country might choose to go 'immigration shopping', hoovering up the best-trained professionals worldwide at no cost to itself. The images of 'disloyalty' and 'exploitation' are thereby confirmed.

However, one should not run away with this line of argument. Asian countries can, in fact, benefit from having a large and powerful diaspora[8] abroad (Chapter 16). Far from being a 'drain', a diaspora can act as an advance guard – a form of mini-colonization. The diaspora demands food, clothing and fondly-remembered goods from the home country. Relatives and good causes at home are supported, often with a remarkable generosity, induced perhaps by the charms of nostalgia. The national airline labours to keep up with the demand for family and festival visits generated by the members of the diaspora, their families and friends. The diaspora can effect trade links, foster cultural and diplomatic links and act, in the last instance, as a powerful lobby group which will protect the country of origin's interests in the country of settlement. This more benign outcome rests, of course, in seeking to maintain and develop affective, transnational links with one's nationals abroad. Certainly it would be shooting oneself in the foot if the home country were so unwise as to raise issues of loyalty.

Migration in Asia

As an editor, I would normally not have considered an article on a particular region for a general publication of this kind. Certainly, it would be unnecessary to carry a specialized article on, say, Latin American or African migration. However, Skeldon's chapter (17) on Asia covers a development of global significance. On the 1 May 1984 there were said to be more planes above the Pacific than the Atlantic. This is a signal (though of course more data are needed) that the international migration system is slowly shifting from one based on the Atlantic to one based in the Pacific basin. We all know about the 'hothouse' or 'tiger' economies of East Asia, starting with Japan, then Hong Kong, Taiwan, Singapore and South Korea, and now including countries as diverse as Malaysia, Thailand, China and Indonesia. In each instance – with the partial exception of Japan which is exhibiting some of the sclerosis characteristic of a mature economy – growth rates of nearly three times the OECD-countries' average were being recorded in the early 1990s. With economic development has come a demand for labour, often recruited from diverse parts of the region. The poorer parts of Asia are also still sending considerable numbers of migrants to the Middle East, North America and Western Europe. Skeldon documents these flows and comments on the literature in a comprehensive and insightful article.

The State-System and Migration

In his treatise on *Eternal Peace* Immanuel Kant (1795) argued that all 'world citizens' should have a right to free movement, a right which he grounded in humankind's common ownership of the earth. One can hardly imagine a supposed 'right' that has been so extensively violated, such that nearly two hundred years after Kant's book John Lennon, of Beatle's fame, wrote a plaintive song entitled 'Imagine There's No Countries' – a plea for universality and internationalism. The fact is that the nation-state system has arrogated to itself the right to determine who shall enter and, in some cases like the Soviet Union, who shall leave. In one way or another the three remaining chapters (18, 19 and 20) deal with the consequences of this assertion of state power.

In one sense, the illegal migrant is the unconscious bearer of Kant's message, the small social actor who challenges the mighty Leviathan. How effective is the international state system in policing immigration (Chapter 18)? Should foreign labourers be tolerated so long as they do not seek citizenship? How significant are they in helping to generate the impressive growth rates in the 'hothouse' economies of East Asia (Chapter 19)? How are national boundaries formed and policed and what effect do they have on the international labour market (Chapter 20)?

A Concluding Note to the Student

As this introduction is little more than a short guide to the articles reprinted here, no formal conclusion is necessary. However, I would like to emphasize that this series is intended to give students an opportunity to have access to first-class research published in a number of highly-regarded scholarly journals. Even the best equipped library will not have all the journals used, many may have only one or two. Faced with a shortage of library materials, students are often tempted to buy a simple textbook or to try to read one or two 'key' articles. The sociology of migration is a difficult and complex area and is unlikely to be adequately covered in this way. So this collection of articles presents a challenge and an opportunity to use 'the real thing' – the articles and journals that professional scholars themselves use. Taste it slowly and savour the flavour. Bon appetit!

Notes

1. Karl Marx (1976), *Capital: A Critique of Political Economy*, Volume 1, Harmondsworth: Penguin, p. 876 [first published 1867].
2. See Robin Cohen (1987), *The New Helots: Migrants in the International Division of Labour*, Aldershot: Gower; and Robert Miles (1987), *Capitalism and Unfree Labour: Anomaly or Necessity?* London: Tavistock.
3. Nicolas Van Hear (1995), 'Displaced People after the Gulf Crisis' in Robin Cohen (ed.), *The Cambridge Survey of World Migration*, Cambridge: Cambridge University Press, 424–30.
4. See, however, Gina Buijs (ed.) (1993), *Migrant Women: Crossing Boundaries and Changing Identities*, Oxford: Berg; Annie Phizacklea (ed.) (1983), *One Way Ticket: Migration and Female Labour*, London: Routledge; and R.J. Simon and C.B. Brettall (eds) (1986), *International Migration: The Female Experience*, Totowa, NJ: Rowman & Allenheld.
5. See also Noeleen Heyzer et al. (1994), *The Trade in Domestic Workers: Causes, Mechanism and Consequences of International Migration*, (Volume 1), London: Zed Press.
6. David Seddon (1995), 'Two-way Migration between India and Nepal' in Robin Cohen (ed.) *The Cambridge Survey of World Migration*, Cambridge: Cambridge University Press, 367–70.
7. Douglas S. Massey et al. (1993), 'Theories of Migration: A Review and Appraisal', *Population and Development Review*, **19** (3), 431–66. This article is also reproduced in an Elgar Reference Collection, viz. Robin Cohen (ed.) (1996), *Theories of Migration*, Cheltenham: Edward Elgar.
8. For more on the contemporary understandings of this term, see Robin Cohen (1995), 'Rethinking "Babylon": Iconoclastic Conceptions of the Diaspora Experience', *New Community*, **21** (1), 5–18.

Part I
The Peculiarity of Migrant Labour

[1]

FEUDAL RELICS OR CAPITALIST MONUMENTS? NOTES ON THE SOCIOLOGY OF UNFREE LABOUR*[1]

PHILIP CORRIGAN

Abstract Through examining bonded service relations in Britain; slavery and neo-slavery in the U.S.A., Tsarist Russia, and Southern Africa; and what is normally perceived as 'migration', it is shown that ascriptive constraint and non-wage coercion *increases* with the expansion of capitalism and, moreover, that this is not a feature of 'early stages' but crucial to such 'high technology' areas as the European motor car industry. Closes by arguing for the recognition of 'migration' as the circulation of a commodity (labour power) and for the primacy of relations of production, in the combination of relations and forces which define particular production modes.

Introduction

Three quotations may help to elucidate the intention of these notes. In 1968, Matthew warned that: 'To emphasize the differentiated character of modern institutions and neglect their grounding in persistent networks of ascriptive relationships is to court the danger of prematurely concluding that modern society has solved its problems.'[2] Five years later, Aufhauser wrote: 'The preoccupation with the presence or absence of contradictions within the slave mode of production has left unexplained some striking, if discouraging similarities which modern economies bear to slavery.'[3] In a recent review of the work of Fogel and Engerman, Laslett emphasizes that 'It is a revelation to have shown that the success in production, which has made our civilisation the strongest and the richest that there has ever been, in material things, may indeed be a matter of compulsion.'[4]

My notes concern the theoretical problems to which these remarks direct attention. I am particularly concerned with the significance of:

'Bonded' service relations, and their expansion at the same time as 'free wage labour' in Britain.
Slavery, and 'neo-slavery', in the United States, and elsewhere, particularly Tsarist Russia and Southern Africa, including forms of debt-peonage.
What is commonly called 'migration', historically and in contemporary Europe (the 'guestworker' phenomenon).

Taken by themselves, these notes attempt only a connection, linking the works cited and a number of puzzles and restrictions which haunt the paradigms of

*Accepted: 30.5.76

sociology and Marxism. I attempt to make these connections through the structured relations of the different 'pictures' exhibited by the sources; and I try to
elucidate what their common logic makes evident.

Wallerstein, in a recent review of this area, argued: 'the key intellectual bottle-
neck at the moment is theoretical . . . to rethink and restate the conceptual frameworks we have inherited . . .'[5] Worsley, similarly, clarifies one such 'bottle-neck'
when he remarks:

The inability of sociology to integrate the theory of 'race relations' with class analysis, or to situate
interactionist and community studies within a framework of political economy, has meant that the
implications of massive immigration for the overall economies of both the host and exporting societies
are rarely spelt out.[6]

In general terms what has happened is that we have failed to understand the
contribution of 'Labour' to production, in all the varieties possible. This is gradually being recomprehended in an assessment of what 'really happened' in the early
stages of capitalization.[7] Moreover, the paradigms which we currently employ
scatter the phenomena we need brought together. This is not a new occurrence.
Going by appearances what I am discussing is *obviously* the phenomenon of population, employing the insights of *demography*. As has been recently urged:

Theoretically . . . the population variable has an important part to play in the process of economic development. In view of this it is surprising to note how little attention historians have paid to the actual *role* of
demographic change in English economic experience over the last two hundred years or so.[8]

But, as Marx argued over a century ago,

It seems to be correct to begin with the real and the concrete, with the real precondition, thus to begin, in
economics, with e.g. the population . . . However, on closer examination this proves false. The population is an abstraction if I leave out, for example, the classes of which it is composed. These classes in turn
are an empty phrase if I am not familiar with the elements on which they rest. E.g. wage labour, capital,
etc. These latter in turn presuppose exchange, division of labour, prices, etc. For example, capital is
nothing without wage labour, without value, money, price etc.

And a few pages further on:

In all forms of society there is one specific kind of production which predominates over the rest, whose relations thus assign rank and influence to the others.
It is a general illumination which bathes all other colours and modifies their
particularity . . . Capital is the all-dominating economic power of bourgeois
society.[9]

The paradigms which dominate Marxist analysis at this time are as much the
subject of my critical remarks as those of sociology or history. That the same kind
of constraints apply is nowhere better illustrated than in a recent, and highly-
praised, work by Perry Anderson which, nevertheless, does not escape bewitchment

FEUDAL RELICS OR CAPITALIST MONUMENTS 437

by paradigms of evolutionary necessity. He is thus able to 'bracket off' varieties of coercion (unfree labour) as indispensable in 'the early modern epoch'; he then emphasizes that

All modes of production in class societies prior to capitalism extract surplus labour from the immediate producers by means of extra-economic coercion. Capitalism is the first mode of production in history in which the means whereby the surplus is pumped out of the direct producer is 'purely' economic in form— the wage contract: the equal exchange between free agents which reproduces, hourly and daily, inequality and oppression. All other previous modes of exploitation operate through *extra-economic* sanctions—kin, customary, religious, legal or political.[10]

He universalizes one tendency, thereby downgrading the equal, if less tidy, fact that (a) capitalism is also the first world-market system of production, with 'world' classes and relations; (b) within this market, capitalism 'fights' and 'dominates' through competition and subordination; (c) the latter frequently (empirically) leads to the preservation and even the creation of pre- and non-capitalist modes, methods, and mentalities, as the works I cite make evident. Anderson makes all too solid the boundaries of 'the nation': the essential axiom from which all the discussions of e.g. 'migration', 'race relations', working-class 'affluence', and so on flow.

There is a strong sense in which the general Marxist paradigm shares much with its apparent theoretical adversary in a consensus concerning the invariant nature of the single path to modernity, involving most efficient (i.e. technical) solutions to standard problems. All agree on the subservience of social relations to productive forces, which are themselves understood as 'technology' plus 'economics', governed by 'the laws of world economy'.[11] In this framework: (i) politics, the State, and class struggle are separated from economics, the enterprise and production (of course they *are* related, but only contingently and externally); (ii) ideas (whether of one writer or of the masses) are 'forcibly abstracted' from the real relationships which sustain them; (iii) revolution becomes a matter of *taking* power or control and never of *transforming* (circumstances and people) and creating; and (iv) the emancipation of labour is effectively postponed by taking the division of labour as a resource, even as a necessary accompaniment, of 'being modern', not as the limiting (empirically 'crippling') constraint internal to *one* mode of production. Recalling remarks of Mannheim in 1936, T. H. Marshall recently stressed:

'Capitalism'—or the market—lives by recognizing and rewarding inequalities and depends on them to provide the motive force that makes it work . . . Democracy, one might say, legitimized inequality (since you do not tax stolen goods), with the help of the trade unions . . . The trouble is that no way has been found of equating a man's value in the market (capitalist value), his value as a citizen (democratic value), and his value for himself (welfare value) [women of course being valueless !].[12]

Marshall poses 'poverty' against 'inequality'; the former—and he stresses 'in theory' —can be removed, the latter is *how social relations work*. In what follows, I wish to make the same distinction between 'brutality' and varieties of being 'unfree' in labour relations; the former (as Stokely Carmichael first established clearly with regard to 'race relations'), as individual acts by particular employers, are theoretically eliminable, the latter is how the capitalist world market *circulates its defining commodity*: labour power. Unfree labour is not a feudal relic, but part of the essential relations of capitalism. If we do not grasp this, but keep to our partial visions, we shall only understand the phenomena I mention as 'residuals'. In fact we are discussing the majority; why should they be thought of as 'residuals' of the minority amongst the working classes of Europe, Japan, or North America?

Bondage and Service in nineteenth- and twentieth-century Britain

It is right to begin the sociology of unfree labour by reconceptualizing a document which has been taken as a benchmark for the creation of that 'free wage labour' which Anderson makes central: the 1834 Royal Commission on the Poor Laws in England and Wales.[13] In recognizing that this text celebrates the dictatorship of money and markets, a necessary illusion is at work.[14] This normally makes of capitalism in nineteenth-century Britain, a singular struggle between *laissez-faire* and 'State intervention'. Whilst it is true that there was a widespread dismantling of much legislation which regulated the labour market this was not the result of arbitrary power and cumulative *ad hoc* decisions: it was the manner in which the relevant (new) State apparatuses were made. The ground was never simply cleared away: new procedures were enforced that continue to regulate the markets of the British economy to this day.[15]

The same narrow focus has obscured certain defining empirical regularities of the historical experience of the British working class. Most important is the *de jure* and *de facto* status of most workers as servants until 1875[16] and the *de facto* dominance of service relationships until after the 1914–18 War.[17] The statistically dominant forms of service were the in- or domestic servants, and the out- or agricultural servants. I shall begin with domestic servants, *the* working-class occupational group without equal over time. Leonore Davidoff has calculated:

In 1881, servants of both sexes represented one in 22 of the whole population ... numerically they grew from 751,541 in 1851 to a peak of 1,386,167 in 1891 and never fell below one million until the late 1930s. They were 34% of all women employed in 1891, and still 23% in 1930.[18]

Further,

... all service positions shared certain characteristics. The master was expected to provide total support: food, housing and a small cash wage. The servant reciprocated by being entirely at the disposal of the master, to obey his personal authority including directions as to the way in which the work was to be performed.[19]

This complex diffusion of service relations and constraints pervades both the British working class *and* the servant-keeping classes. A range of specific institutions was created to attend to 'the servant problem': moral, as in the case of the Girls'

FEUDAL RELICS OR CAPITALIST MONUMENTS   439

Friendly Society, and straightforwardly labour oriented.[20] In the 1920s and 1930s, for example, the number of servants in absolute terms increased; in the latter decade, in County Durham alone (and apart from the regular *hawking* of paupers at various hiring fairs) there was both a private and a State agency to train servants and send them South. As the special commissioner noted in 1933, 'Durham girls have now acquired such an excellent reputation as domestic servants that the demand exceeds the supply . . .'[21] It is relevant here to stress Davidoff's important point that 'fewer girls went into service wherever there was alternative employment. For this reason many girls in mining districts went into service.'[22]

Before examining the out-servants, I wish to sketch the significance of the bonding system for miners in Britain. Mining entails moving labour to the raw material which can only be turned into a commodity through extraction and processing;[23] when the commodity is no longer profitable, the communities created by these conditions are either left to subsist somehow (especially if the 'slackness in trade' is temporary), or actually cleared away, relatively quickly; although the long withering through neglect is perhaps empirically as common.[24]

In eighteenth-century Scotland, there prevailed what T. S. Ashton calls the 'Scottish collier-serf' relationship through which whole families were fixed to a particular pit (not to the owner or lessee). The man acted as 'cautioner' for his 'bearer' (often, but not necessarily his wife, although usually a woman), and both accepted that any children would be enserfed through a practice known as 'arling' whereby the acceptance of a baptism gift, by custom, tied that child to that pit.[25] Adam Smith, amongst others, compared these collier-serfs to the slaves of the plantations and also remarked how colliers would flee to Tyneside, even though their earnings there would only be 10d. or 1s. a day, compared with 2s. 6d. in Scotland. A very clear theoretical account is provided in the *Edinburgh Review*, in 1899, in a discussion of the replacement of enserfment by the bond. The pitmen, it argues,

were emancipated in the same great cause they were enslaved in—the cause of low wages . . . [The owners] had come to realise that slavery had been a sad economic mistake. It had made coal-mining such an unpopular employment that nobody could be induced to enter it except for exorbitant remuneration, and even their own slaves had to be coaxed into work by extremely high rates of wages.[26]

As with so many other instances, the first 'Emancipation' of these serfs was no liberation at all, resulting in debt slavery. When the second 'Emancipation' of 1799 came, the *Edinburgh Review* writer notes that it 'did not, as was expected, immediately increase the supply of colliery labour or reduce its wages. On the contrary, one of its first effects was a remarkable flight of colliers to other occupations . . . to the work of common labourers at half their original wages.'[27]

In two major pit counties in England, the Miners' Bond[28] fixed labour power to a place and at a price for a year at a time until 1845 in Northumberland, and 1875 in Durham. In the accounts cited, the overlapping of servant and employee

440   PHILIP CORRIGAN

statuses through until the 1939–45 War is evident; long after the bonding ceremony
had ceased, pitmen continued to be housed in specially built mining villages; the
very plans and street names of which displayed the subordination of the non-work
life to the coal-master and his agents. In this, of course, coal mining exhibits the
familiar patterns of paternalism, as with the Ironmasters, like Crowley of Winlat-
on.[29] T. S. Ashton argues that 'it was natural for the landowning coal-masters to
apply to the underground workers the same rules of hiring as were associated with
agricultural employment'.[30] The evidence is not clear—and certainly there is
nothing 'natural' about any of this; but we do know that the hiring constraints
continued much longer for agricultural servants.

    Many would place what follows as a pre-1914, or at the latest pre-1939, account:

At each Christmas each worker on the Estate is given a brace of pheasant (shot by the Squire's friends and
gamekeepers on a hunting, shooting weekend) and a hunk of beef from a fat bullock butchered specially
for the occasion: 'We all stand in a row—most of us puts ties on—and we each go forward in turn and
shake the Squire's hand, and his Lady gives us the meat, wishing us a Merry Christmas.'

In fact it is 1974, and the county Northumberland, England.[31] Agrarian production
relations show how facile are the conventional separations and linearity of most
schema. There are few better starting points than Thomas Hardy's careful essay of
1883, which serves as a reminder of how different labour markets coalesce and
overlap through the mechanisms of hiring, particularly the hiring fair. Hardy notes
how a shilling 'is passed to bind the bargain'; Jack Studholme recalls, in the 1910s,
and Cumberland rather than Hardy's Dorset, that 'they'd give you a shilling. That
was to bind you to six months' employment.'[32] This service relation (and, of
course, the deference was dialectical and *not* passive subordination[33]) persisted until
the 1939–45 War, as is documented in *Akenfield*.[34] And 'tied cottages' continue to
constrain and render 'impure' the wage labour of agricultural (amongst other)
workers; perhaps that is why *The Times* considers them a 'feudal relic'.[35]

    There is a final facet of these complex relations which is worthy of note: the
provision of allotments by paternalistic employers. The reasons for such provision
are various: to increase 'commitment'; to lower the reproduction costs of these
particular units of labour; and, for reasons of complex moral regimen. With regard
to the latter point, the *Penny Magazine* of 1845 (p. 88) argued that 'the object of
making such allotments is moral rather than economic; [cultivation of the land]
has a tendency to keep a man at home and from the ale house . . .'[36] Regarding the
other two reasons, there is considerable unanimity between J. S. Mill, V. I. Lenin,
and the Select Committee of Inquiry into Allotments, in Britain in 1969. In the
latter's word: 'Throughout their history, allotments and allotment gardens have
been provided primarily for the relief of poverty.' They had earlier illustrated this
point by a quotation from J. S. Mill which concludes that allotments are a 'method
of making people grow their own poor rate'.[37] That they also had a direct relation
to wage-rates is evident from Lenin's observation on the *otrabotochni* system in
Tsarist Russia:

Words like bondage, usury, extortion, etc. merely describe the form and character of the transaction, but they do not describe its economic substance. How can a peasant over a number of years [referring to an example he has just worked through] perform work that is worth 10·69 rubles for 6 rubles? He is able to do it because his allotment covers part of the expenditure of his family and makes it possible for his wages to be forced down below the 'free wage worker's' level.[38]

Slavery, Labour Reserves, and Capitalism

Much of the above does not challenge directly the paradigms which I am criticizing; it can be dismissed as 'the early stages' of what is now *obviously* a free wage-labour situation. Above all it leaves the prism of 'nation' unquestioned, thereby obscuring the fact that capitalism is a world-market phenomenon, with an international division of labour and 'world-historic' classes. Only within that reality can one make judgements about the validity or otherwise of Marx's 'general laws' of capitalism. The recent work on slavery, and 'neo-slavery' (for example, serfdom in Tsarist Russia, the *inquilino* in South America, labour reserves in Southern Africa) is thus crucial to the case I am making. These forms of coercion should not be conceptualized as residuals from former modes of production, and essentially irrational; but as indications of capitalism's expansion. Such a reconceptualization makes a modification of the linear model essential and makes visible the supporting paradigms which much current analysis assumes correct.

What recent discussions provide is a means of understanding a variety of forms of constrained labour relations as crucial supporting machinery for free wage-labour. This exposes the error of those, such as Barrington Moore[39] for example, who can describe the conditions of democracy in Britain, relating this to the lack of certain forms of agrarian production (e.g. the plantation), by simply 'thinking away' the world structure of capitalism and, central to that, the British Empire. The expansion of capitalism, in fact, hinges on the introduction, on a very large scale, of unfree forms of labour which whole generations of historians have seen as simply feudal relics, the sociological equivalent of cultural lags. In reality, to take the cases of serfdom in Eastern Europe;[40] of early factory and cash-crop production in Tsarist Russia;[41] or of the apparent establishment of a free labour market in the latter formation,[42] we find that we cannot explain or understand the dynamics of the unfree labour relations as other than the specific effects of capitalism's expansion.

There is an important connection to be made between the latter studies and those which criticize the dualist version of the linear theory of modernization.[43] This holds that certain kinds of social formations (underdeveloped) become modern (developed) through the expansion of the 'modern' sector (characterized in terms of a free wage-labour market, forms of democracy, and so on) and the diminution and eventual disappearance of the 'feudal' sector. This, within individual countries, creates the same separation that the prism of 'nation' accomplishes for world relations: it makes it impossible to understand 'peasantization' phenomena as expressions of capitalist expansion; it makes it difficult to understand the entrepreneurial power of landed and fiscal wealth. Apart from the *inquilinos* of Chile, already mentioned, one should examine here the specific forms of debt peonage established in Brazil, noting the 'delicacy' of the differentiating activity of labour markets for 'natives' and 'ex-Slaves'.[44] Recently, Obregon has shown how capitalism's penetration is registered by changes in 'mechanisms of absorption, exclusion and depression of the labour force'; and 'a clear modification of the structure of the labour market' both from a quantitative and qualitative viewpoint.[45]

Finally, this theoretical convergence may be detected in various accounts of apparently post-slavery situations, since the developments which follow an 'Emancipation' often make clear both the previous structure and the reasons for the alleged liberation.[46] The crushing burden of debt imposed on former slaves or neo-slaves is one of the dominant features of such accounts. There are also other connections, for example with hiring periodization. 'Peonage in the Southern United States grew out of the labor settlement following emancipation . . . a contract system emerged as one way to create a stable labor force . . . Most blacks signed annual contracts.'[47]

All I have space to accomplish here are the implications of U.S. slavery for my general thesis and certain structural features, not least those connected with the nature of State power, which are analogous to the Southern African labour regimes of the 1960s and 1970s. I am aided in this by a complementary survey by Burawoy. Barrington Moore noted some years ago that plantation slavery in the South 'was not an economic fetter upon industrial capitalism. If anything the reverse may have been true; it helped to promote American industrial growth in the early stages.'[48] Once again, we need to extend such a grasp through 'the concept of a semi-peripheral area (like the U.S. North), at once exploiting and exploited, and seeking to break loose and become a core nation by snapping the economic umbilical cord of the U.S. South to Great Britain'.[49] As Marx noted, in a polemic against Proudhon's dualist notion of 'good' and 'bad' aspects of capitalism,

Direct slavery is just as much the pivot of bourgeois industry as machinery, credit, etc. . . . Modern nations have been able to only disguise slavery in their own countries, but they have imposed it without disguise upon the New World.[50]

Twenty years later, he insisted that 'the veiled slavery of the wage-workers in Europe needed, for its pedestal, slavery pure and simple in the new world'.[51]

It is to that pedestal I now wish to turn; in so doing I do not seek to obscure U.K. involvement in slavery which provided 'the sinews of Empire' for so long, and continues to do so in that 'reverse imperialism', imported contract labour.[52] I do not seek to enter into the various debates about methodology (cliometrics versus empathy) because, like Wallerstein, and others, I see the theoretical issues as crucial.[53] It remains of significance, for sociologists of knowledge, to contrast the enormous publicity given to Fogel and Engerman's work, with the relative silence surrounding works by Daniel, on peonage, or by the late Robert Starobin on *industrial* slavery. Starobin showed that slaves were used, efficiently and effectively,

FEUDAL RELICS OR CAPITALIST MONUMENTS 443

within manufacturing and mineral working in order to sustain a higher rate of profit than free wage-labour could produce. The alleged incompatibility between slavery and rational economics does not exist; industrial slavery did not decrease either labour mobility, or investment flows. Starobin argues that the Civil War was a socio-political event focused upon the expansion and clash of differing kinds of labour and product markets in the 'new lands' of the western and north-western United States.[54]

Engerman has condensed a number of the theoretical implications of his clio-metrics in a single article, in which he—as does Aufhauser, at greater length and with more force[55]—erases the distinctive nature of the socio-legal demarcation between slave and free labour by stressing that

the choice between working and starving faced by a legally free individual seems no more attractive than a similar choice faced by a slave, and the ruling class may be able to impose legislation which can provide themselves with the same economic benefits under either legal system of labor.

He notes three benefits which slave-owners obtain from their property rights:

One, the pleasure of conspicuous consumption, has been shown to be unimportant as an explanation of the demand for slaves in the antebellum South. Second, there is possible economic exploitation in the textbook sense of the provision to the laborer of a consumption basket with value below his marginal product. Third, the rights of ownership permit the forcing of laborers off what would be their desired supply curve if choice were voluntary, leading to a larger input than would be voluntarily provided at a market-clearing wage.[56]

Engerman also shows, by contemporary materials, how these high participation rates, taken with economies of scale, render substantial savings through a general lowering of the reproduction costs of labour. This point has great force when examining the two giant labour reserve economies of South Africa and the E.E.C.

It is important to draw attention to the continuities in unfree labour in the United States.[57] Daniel, for example, reports in the preface to his revised edition, how

Two men were arrested in March 16, 1973, by local authorities in Homestead, Florida, for allegedly holding twenty-eight migrant workers in peonage. Labor contractor Joseph L. Brown, who was indicted by a federal grand jury the next day, was 'seized as he walked to his car, a 1973 Cadillac, clutching a bag containing $43,786 in cash'.[58]

Daniel's work brings out the shadowy compliance of law enforcement agencies with unfree labour requirements; together with the consequent formation, by the Communist Party of the U.S.A., of the International Labor Defense, in 1925, to fight Klu Klux Klan. The I.L.D. later assisted in the formation of the Abolish Peonage Committee in 1939. We are now fortunate in having the work of Rosen-garten displaying the struggles of Nate Shaw and others against peonage.[59]

Relatedly, articles such as that of Ransom and Sutch draw attention to the con-trols over local markets exercised by coalitions of landlords and merchants (who

444 PHILIP CORRIGAN

also acted as bankers) which restricted labour movement and determined products. In short, they demonstrate the local version of cartel power which forms a significant aspect of several discussions: in the case of bonding pitmen in north-east England, the cartel of the Coal Owners is crucial (the Newcastle Upon Tyne Coal Office registered labour); in the case of serfdom in the East, as Blum and Kahan stress, the monopoly over the grain trade, and related activities, is similarly decisive. Meyer, in a comment on three other papers I have cited, tries to establish the general form of this cartel or monopoly situation with regard to labour as follows:

Any kind of growing economy wherein labor commands a good price combined with a political environment within which one man can enslave other men, will be sufficient to create the institution of slavery in some form or other . . . slavery if it can be instituted, is highly profitable or economically beneficial to those who are politically powerful enough to be among the owners . . . it is difficult to identify any invisible hand that automatically eliminates the economic privileges of slavery once these are established.[60]

This is, of course, State control that is being made visible. State control of this character is crucial to the dynamics of both the 'national' and international systems I have indicated. Within, for example, one such system, the British Empire, the control exercised by politically instituted monopolies or semi-monopolies like the Chartered Companies, on the one hand, and the naval and military strength which guarantees the shipping of labour units from one country to another; substantially reduce the cost of labour at the point of production.[61] We are dealing with the same kind of power when we learn that in August 1973, Bloemfontein Municipal Council clamped 'hard plastic rings, nearly impossible to remove without a hacksaw, on the wrists of its 2,400 African workers. The bands are colour coded so white overseers can tell the wearer's status, African homeland, and place of work . . .'[62]

As John Rex has argued,

What needs to be disputed here is Max Weber's contention that free wage labour was the only form of labour compatible in the long run with the logic of rational capitalism . . . What we see in fact from the case of plantation slavery, as we do from the case of African labour in South Africa, both of which we might call world historical systems to be set alongside free wage labour as alternatives, is that capitalism is compatible with a variety of forms of labour.[63]

In these papers, Rex clarifies a number of points which have been implicit in these notes so far. Perhaps most important is his demonstration of the subtlety and sophistication of the methods for sustaining particular forms of unfree labour in Southern Africa:

The function of reserve policy is not merely to act as a compulsion to peasants to become workers. It has also to ensure that the employers are not left with those responsibilities which, in the absence of a welfare state guaranteeing unemployment benefits and family support, they would have to assume. The reserve has to be . . . an economic and social system which will supplement wage earning employment as a means of support for the native.[64]

In the same year, Harold Wolpe drew out from this the relations which this paper has reiterated throughout:

When the migrant labourer has access to the means of subsistence, outside the capitalist sector, as he does in South Africa, then the relationship between wages and the cost of production and reproduction of labour-power is changed. That is to say, capital is able to pay the worker below the cost of his reproduction.[65]

Which is what we have found with bonding, allotments, serfdom, and slavery. Furthermore,

The Monopolization of State power is the lynchpin on which white economic privilege depends; if the settler bloc loses control of the State, it loses all else as well. For it is through the use of State power that, inter alia, the ownership of 87% of the land and most of the natural resources is declared to be white, that black labour is kept cheap, and that white labour is kept dear.[66]

This violence, as Legassick details, is not 'explicable in terms of "archaisms", but in terms of the specific form that capitalism has taken', particularly regarding the simultaneous dissolution-conservation of subordinated social structures, modes of working, and ideologies.[67] To close with a final 'structural simile': in the 1840s, there was a slogan of the capitalists in the southern States: 'Take the factories to the fields.' Now, in Southern Africa, the factories have been taken into the homelands; furthermore, in the Transkei, garden allotments have been provided for these 'free wage workers' so they can grow their own food. In this way the total production costs are further reduced.

Migration of labour or circulation of labour-power?

Much of the situation just described turns on *forced* migration. In 1973 and 1974 (until May of the latter year, at least) Southern African plantations and mines 'pulled in' over one million labourers supplied by the Portuguese colonialists. Engerman has stressed that slavery in the New World was similarly 'forced international migration'; it followed attempts at voluntary migration, indenturing convicts, and enslaving native populations.[68] It is time to show how migration-as-coercive-circulation is a continuing (and not merely a preliminary constituent) of advanced capitalism; how it is an ingredient within, and not an external support for, such advanced technological production as exemplified by the European motor car industry.

It may well be that the *major* form of labour's contribution to the making and remaking of capitalism as a world market system is large scale circulation. We shall never grasp 'the facts' if we fail to appreciate labour theoretically as it is itself treated (in practice, in accounts, in State policies) *as a commodity which is circulated.* In this way we shall also be true to the historical experience of the millions thus circulated. We have to subsume 'motivational' approaches to an historical and

446 PHILIP CORRIGAN

materialist explanation of recurring movements of this magnitude, just as we have done for capital itself.[69] In a neglected paper of twenty years ago, Vilar suggests this when he argues that

the exploitation of colonial areas by means of slavery, forced labour, or quasi-feudal methods [is not merely] more important than price movements, they may provide clues to them. Thus the so-called 'long waves of prices and economic activities'—the price-rise of the sixteenth, the deflation of the seventeenth centuries . . . might we not see them in terms of a historic alternation between an increase in the exploitation of colonial and European labour . . .[70]

Providing we understand 'alternation' as of the same character as the alternating electrical current: simultaneous and concurrent, cumulatively beneficial to that specifically capitalist illumination to which Marx directed our attention in 1858. This is the framework within which to understand migration: as the circulation (whether 'sucked' or 'pushed') of labour. If we use this approach we shall find that all the economic 'miracles' of our era will have their very *secular* suffering exposed to view.

Most studies of migration are still either statistical or purely motivational, although recent work on emigration from Britain has begun to recognize some of Marx's fundamental insights.[71] The danger is always present, additionally, even in otherwise subtle accounts, of allowing one change (say, a major population shift) to obscure another; thus the very specific changes in a mode of production which take place during an apparently general slump or depression are lost from theoretical grasp. For example, studies of one coercive removal of population—the Highland clearances—have ignored the simultaneous creation of a specific form of labour reserve economy, the crofting system.[72] It is also relevant to take a large-scale view, both over space and time: the work of E. Hunt indicates the advantages to be gained (although even here the lack of systematic attention to international flows is a weakness). He detects such patterns as the following:

In the coal industry [in Britain] no less than 316,000 jobs were lost in twelve years after 1955 but 309,000 were created in the twelve years before 1914. Similarly the contraction of the labour force on the railways by a quarter between 1960 and 1964 was impressive [from 514,500 to 399,000] but not more impressive than the 200,000 men gathered together with 'considerable ease' in the course of the year or so before 1846.[73]

He also draws attention to 'switching'—Northumbria, for example, had a net inflow of 8·7 per cent of population from 1861 to 1871; and a net outflow of 9·2 per cent in 1921–31.[74]

In the case of the United States, Paolo Cinanni has advanced the following argument:

In 1850 the U.S. had scarcely 23 million inhabitants and occupied a rather modest position in the world economy. But from 1850 to 1950, with the arrival of some 36,970,000 immigrants, they obtained a natural increase of 114 million inhabitants instead of 64 million . . . In my opinion this is one of the fundamental factors that has enabled the American economy to exploit its enormous resources making the rise to world supremacy possible.[75]

FEUDAL RELICS OR CAPITALIST MONUMENTS   447

But we should recognize quite specific flows within this overall tide; particular kinds of labour-power, moreover, which no melting pot ever rendered down to some standard 'free wage labour' unit as Gutman has shown.[76] Once in the United States there are particular kinds of 'friction' and 'easiness' of movement which are scrutinized in the work of various historians and theorized in the work of Harvey.[77] The links which these notes attempt to make are also made in the accounts collected of letters of migrants, whether 'free' or 'slave'.[78]

Cinanni's statement also obscures the range and variety of flows within Europe itself. To take the case of France, although 47,000 people left in the decade 1880–9, over 100,000 immigrated; in the case of Germany, inflows of Italian and Polish workers were common before 1914 by which years seasonal flows had grown to over 700,000. It is as well to keep these distinctions in mind when we turn to 'Europe's "new proletariat"—the total of more than ten million foreign workers who man the garbage trucks and building sites of industrialised Europe . . .'.[79] Although I challenge the stereotype drawn here, Bellini's article, like that of David Stephens, recognizes the scale and the historical roots of this phenomenon, which is linked to the flows *from* Europe. Stephens argues that in the case of Britain, in a contrast between ideological reasoning employed by different 'justifications', the immigration of former colonial black subjects has always been discussed as a moral obligation

never as the economic migration which it fundamentally was, at least in origin. West Germany is perhaps the opposite of Britain, in the sense that the recruitment of foreign workers has long been regarded as a temporary and necessary expedient. Germany has long received immigrant workers . . . In 1907, foreign workers numbered 873,000, of whom 128,300 were Italians. After the second World War, ten million refugees entered West Germany. By mid-1955 only 80,000 foreign workers remained. Since 1958, however, there has been an increase in immigration and by the year 1972 there were in the region of 2·3 million foreign workers in West Germany.[80]

Clive Jenkins, in a recent statement on the 'guestworker' phenomenon has shown that, despite severe controls operating in all 'host' countries by 1975,[81] he could identify more than 6,000,000 people from fifteen countries who had been made nomadic by the 'powerful and wealthy multi-national companies . . . It is civilized to take work to the people, but here we see people being taken to the marketplace as though they were dumb commodities.'[82] It is usual to segregate, in theoretical discussions, multi-national companies (with a high organic composition of capital) from the stereotypical guestworker. In fact, to take the case of the motor-car industry, there is a direct dependence upon the *attraction* and *holding* of a particular labour force for assembly-line work. This was made clear by James Ensor's interviews with major bosses of car plants in 1973. Kaj Holmelius, of Saab-Scania, for example, stated baldly 'In another ten or twenty years we won't be able to use the production line in Sweden; though it will still be possible for Swedish firms to set up production lines in Africa.' And,

M. Pierre Dreyfus, director general of Renault . . . points out that the world motor car industry is now relying increasingly on 'colonial' labour—the French on Algerians; the Germans on Turks; Yugoslavs on Italians [sic]; the Americans on Puerto Ricans and [n.b.] Negroes from the Deep South—and questions whether the industry may not eventually have to move its plants from Europe or the U.S. to the home countries of these workers.[83]

The theoretically most valuable work remains that of Castles and Kosack, who show the range of means available to employing enterprises for the lowering of their costs of production.[84] As Gorz explains,

a large proportion of immigrant workers (90 per cent in Germany and Switzerland) are not accompanied by their families [this] brings the country of immigration an additional and substantial saving on social capital (housing, schools, hospitals, transport and other infra-structural facilities).[85]

The leading enterprises within the E.E.C. countries have thus converted whole countries into labour reserves; driving down their costs of production by minimalizing the reproduction costs of labour. But the migrants also serve political ends; lacking the most elementary 'civil rights', denied membership of a trade union—what better vanguard against the organized labour movement could be found? In an exactly contrary way, *white* migration to Southern Africa also serves political ends.[86]

As the slaves of the U.S.A. have found their poet in Genovese; so also have the migrants of Europe in the 'book of images and words' created by John Berger and Jean Mohr: *A seventh man*.[87] This shows the contact between contemporary large-scale historical experiences and others I have mentioned; perhaps most directly with the lives of former slaves in the U.S.A. and former serfs in Tsarist Russia. A work like this is much more of a challenge to contemporary paradigms than the somewhat static, inevitably sequential, set of images I have tried to offer.

Marios Nikolinakos has attempted a general theory of migration: a critique of neo-classical *assumptions*.[88] The latter never move beyond the phenomena at best (at worst they simply ignore the range of empirical data). Thus, whilst a recent attempt at a general theory correctly argues that 'the majority of movements are replacement movements. They arise to fill vacancies . . . there come into being long or short *movement chains*',[89] it fails to grasp the relations that effect such chains, about which Vilar was so illuminating twenty years ago.

Ascription and the division of labour

The argument of these notes is congruent with that advanced by several economists, since the early 1970s;[90] like them I demand a sociology of the 'real world', analytical attention to the large scale enduring 'social facts' of our era. There is an equally strong sense in which we cannot simply take 'the facts' as our units of analysis. Consider, briefly, the notion of dualistic or segmentary labour markets: another instance of those dichotomous bifurcations that pervade our paradigms. Such studies, whether of 'race' relations; 'sex' relations, i.e. women workers; or, badly paid homeworkers, are all marked by limitations.

Recent work in the U.K. and the U.S.A. has 'discovered' that 'both women and coloured workers are disproportionately represented in low wage employment'.[91] With a flourish, 'dual labour markets' are produced: *primary*, with high-wage, high-production, high-skill, and high-consumption indices, and *secondary*, with low indices; moreover there are 'workers with distinct work habits and social-psychological profiles'.[92] These allegedly distinctive strata, as Max Weber recognized some time ago, *share* their market position with any member of the working class. Their unfree or ascriptive economic and social relations are the precise pedestal for the (relatively) more free, seemingly 'achieved', relations of others within the working class. Ascription is not, as it were, antagonistic to effective social or technical division of labour (the rationalist thesis in brief); but *is the manner in which* that division and circulation is accomplished. Status relations are the mode of achieving contractual relations; the contradiction between formal and substantive rationality is permanent and coextensive with capitalism.

William Lovett, the moral force Chartist, depicts these relations in the case of women with great clarity:

Woman stands on a footing of social equality with man; as her labours and co-operation, in her sphere, are as essential to the production of the wealth of society as his more hardy, and, it may be, laborious [sic] portion of the work. For without her solace and domestic aid he would have less inclination to labour, and less of his time to devote to it.[93]

'Housewifery' is part of the necessities—those *faux frais* of Marx—of a certain kind of wage labouring. The unfree labour of housework (however unproductive dogmatists show it to be; and notwithstanding that it is not paid for) relates directly to the highest productivity/consumption sections of the working class. Without that labour, the reproduction cost of labour power would be substantially increased through private, company, or social expenditure replacing this domestic, private, labour-service. Moreover, these particular qualities fit perfectly the requirements of the current phase of the outworking system, which has recently been 'exposed' (again) in Britain.[94]

The same strictures hold for relations of skin colour. An excellent corrective to withering attention to the puzzle of colour is provided in the work of Castles and Kosack, Nikolinakos, and Sheila Allen. Instead of the typical commitment to solve riddles concerning the 'consistency' or 'rationality' of ideological justifications, work needs to continue on the sustained logic of practices; which is another version of the shift from motivational to materialist studies I recommended in the case of migration. In their differing ways Thomas and Nikolinakos agree, in the latter's words, that 'racism, which in the era of colonialism justified the economic exploitation of the indigenous peoples in the colonies by the imperialist countries, has been transplanted to within the metropolis, within the capitalist countries themselves'.[95]

The continued exploitation of the whole working class depends upon the marked (i.e. visible) oppression of its weakest members. This is one tendency in contradiction with another: 'No management can afford to neglect any section of his potential labour force through prejudice alone. Equality of opportunity is an integral part of the battle for the maximum utilisation of manpower.'[96]

I am not, however, spotlighting some temporary 'adjustment problem', or 'moral dilemma'; this is not an obstacle to efficiency, but how capitalist efficiency operates. It *is* logical. No greater 'truth' about labour relations has ever been told than that relating to the Burakumin 'caste' of Japan. There were about 300,000 when they were 'emancipated' and the caste *abolished* in 1871; there were well over a million in 1974.[97]

It is here, to recapitulate, that Aufhauser's demonstration of the structural analogy between slavery and Taylorism is relevant; particularly his comparison of the author of *Sociology for the South*, George Fitzhugh, and F. W. Taylor. The former recognized how the poor whites could 'constitute our militia and our police' when he urged.

Educate all Southern whites, employ them not as lackeys, ploughmen, and menials, but as independent freemen should be employed, and let the negroes be strictly TIED DOWN TO SUCH CALLINGS as are unbecoming to white men, and peace would be established between blacks and whites. (my capitals)[98]

This was written in 1854, thirteen years later, Marx declared that the contradiction at the heart of capitalism is never more 'glaring than that . . . there is a complaint of the want of hands, whilst at the same time many thousands are out of work, because the division of labour CHAINS THEM TO A PARTICULAR BRANCH OF INDUSTRY' (my capitals).[99]

Two recent works—Braverman's *Labor and monopoly capital*, and Wallerstein's *Modern world system*—together with earlier more fragmentary attempts should return attention to the validity and the veracity of Marx's 'general theory' concerning the sociology of capitalism.[100] This is most concisely presented as 'The General Law of Capitalist Accumulation' (*Capital*, ch. 25) and is particularly relevant in the distinctions made of 'Different forms of the relative surplus population'. As Marx phrased it in his draft for *Capital*, the *Grundrisse*,

society in its fractional parts undertakes for Mr. Capitalist the business of keeping his virtual instrument of labour—its wear and tear—intact as a reserve for later use. He shifts a part of the reproduction costs of the working class off his own shoulders and thus pauperizes a part of the remaining population for his own profit.[101]

In *Capital* itself, Marx argues that

along with the surplus population, pauperism forms a condition or capitalist production, and of the capitalist development of wealth. It enters into the *faux frais* of capitalist production; but capital knows how to throw these, for the most part, from its own shoulders on to those of the working-class and the lower middle class.[102]

Indeed, what Marx italicized as '*the absolute general law of capitalist accumulation*' co-ordinates all I have mentioned.

It establishes an accumulation of misery, corresponding with an accumulation of capital. Accumulation of wealth at one pole is, therefore, at the same time accumulation of misery, agony of toil, slavery, ignorance, brutality, mental degradation, at the opposite pole, i.e. on the side of the class that produces its own product in the form of capital.[103]

To stay within the terrain of one country (and even there to survey with one eye closed), or to focus upon this or that exchange between two countries, is to deny, in advance, the relevance of this theory. Empirically it also shuffles off the agenda the millions in the labour reserves whose 'misery', now as in Marx's time, 'is in inverse ratio to its torment of labour'.[104]

At some times, it *is* more efficient literally (*de jure*) or practically (*de facto*) to enslave work populations—even though this means taking over some costs of feeding, clothing, and so on. At other times it *is* more efficient to marginalize large numbers of potential work units on their own land, in their own communities, as storage, and to draw from them—by filiations which are both long range and extremely complex, differing qualities and quantities of labour power as required for purposes of making profits.[105]

Moreover, these experiences lead to contradictory forms of proletarian consciousness; another area which has been the site of dualist notions recently criticized by Cousins and Davis.

The existence of commodity-production follows from the social division of labour. Labour is concentrated in great masses thus potentially becoming aware of its great strength; it is also specialized in separated tasks and this diversity of tasks appears in an institutionalized and reified form as separate occupations and industries with competing claims over tasks and rewards, and as different labour markets. In short, both concentration and homogeneity *and* division and fragmentation result.[106]

This *is* the central unfree aspect of wage labour, its extra-economic social and ideological coercion. Gorz, furthermore, has shown how such a division of labour works to the benefit of capital. He points to the 'outcasts', at the *centre* of any capitalist social formation; on his estimation there are 20 per cent who are not marginal but central.

The existence of this mass of outcasts facilitates . . . [the subtraction of a] significant proportion of the labor force from the prevailing laws of the labor market and thus to deny it the *historic* price of its labor. This historic price would be extremely high for all the exhausting, unhealthy, dirty and dangerous jobs society cannot dispense with . . .
In other words, paying manual at its historic price would be incompatible with the present wage scale and income distribution . . . [and] with the present scale of social values and the social hierarchy of capitalist society . . .[107]

Here the much vaunted 'liberation' accomplished by the Great Transformation is put into historical and sociological perspective. The 'free wage labour' relation of capitalism is subordinated to the ascriptive constraints of a division of labour and social relations which enable the circulation of people as commodities. It is this modal quality which has prompted Wallerstein to ask whether capitalism should not be seen 'as a system that combines within its economic arena *some* firms largely based on contractual wage-labor and *some* (even most) firms based on one variant or another of coerced or semi-coerced semi-wage labor'?[108] Except—and one must stress the point—this runs the danger of making dualism (' some firms . . . and some firms . . .') world-wide. Rather, *all* enterprises rely upon the use of coercion; some are more brutal than others.

Conclusion

It is time to try to indicate the theoretical significance of these notes. Although many Marxists are as bewitched by evolutionary and dichotomous thinking as any other social scientists, there are some who have freed themselves (because they observe how certain practical liberations have been accomplished). They emphasize the primacy of social relations. The most rigorous critique of the errors which follow from basing analysis of capitalism's imperialism on 'countries' is provided by Charles Bettelheim in his 'Theoretical comments' on the work of Emmanuel.[109] Bettelheim relates the law of value and the capitalist world economy; stressing the twofold character of the international division of labour. Unsurprisingly, his most direct critique of the 'theory of productive forces' (upon which all varieties of linear development theory ultimately base themselves), has come in his work on the differentiating qualities of *socialist* construction.

In the combination productive forces/production relations the latter play the dominant role by imposing the conditions under which the productive forces are reproduced. Conversely, the development of the productive forces never really determines the transformation of production relations; this transformation is always the focus of intervention by the contending classes—that is, of class struggle.[110]

After all, 'Machines, on closer inspection, turn out to be the embodiments of the relations between men [and women], and the same can be said for the biological justifications for the division of labour.'[111]

I can offer no better conclusion, than Martin Nicolaus's critical comments on the work of Mandel. He, as I do, depicts the *universal contradiction*.

The entire world has had to be explored, charted, crisscrossed, paved, railed, mined, sown, flown, piped, riveted and wired; every human being upon this earth has had to be uprooted, transplanted, educated and re-educated, pushed and pulled, organized and re-organized; every idea and invention has had to be thought and invented, tested and discarded, picked up and reformulated, sifted through a hundred languages and applied a million different ways—before one single person could insert bolt A into nut B for the 479th consecutive time in one day and say 'Basta! Enough of this! There are no more 'local' contradictions, and no more 'economic' contradictions in the sense that is usually meant; all of our contradictions, and the deeper they are, the truer this is, have universal causes and universal effects: one baby in one room in one town who cries from hunger throws the entire history of the world into question . . . we cannot retreat into the provinces of our nationalist or disciplinary specialties; our analysis and our action must be at the least—at the minimum—as universal as the power of Capital itself.[112]

FEUDAL RELICS OR CAPITALIST MONUMENTS 453

Notes and references
1. This is a revised version of a paper given to the Political Economy Group, Durham, 13 May 1975. I would like to thank members of that Group, particularly Gavin Williams, for their assistance. The revised version has also benefited from discussions with Jason Ditton and Val Gillespie, and editorial comments from Philip Abrams. Eric Wolf originally encouraged me to revise the first version.
2. L. Matthew, 'Ascription in Modern Societies', *Sociological Inquiry*, 38 (1968), 120.
3. R. Aufhauser, 'Slavery and Scientific Management', *J. Economic Hist.* 33 (1973), 812.
4. P. Laslett, 'The Balance Sheet of Slavery', *Listener*, 4 July 1974, 25.
5. I. Wallerstein, 'American Slavery and the Capitalist World Economy', *American J. Sociology*, 81 (1976), 1200.
6. P. Worsley, 'Proletarians, Sub-proletarians, Lumpenproletarians, Marginalidados, Migrants, Urban Peasants and Urban Poor', *Sociology*, 10 (1976), 133.
7. Cf. P. Deane, 'The role of Capital in the Industrial Revolution', *Explorations in Economic Hist.*, 10 (1973), 363 f.; F. Mendels, 'Proto-industrialisation: the first stage of the industrialisation process', *J. Economic Hist.* 32 (1972), 261; F. Weaver, 'Relative backwardness and cumulative development: a comparative approach', *Studies in Comparative Int. Development*, 9 (1974), 71 f. Two excellent critiques of 'rationality' are: R. Cameron, 'The Unbound Prometheus', *Explorations in Economic Hist.* 7 (1970), 233 f., and A. Portes, 'Rationality in the Slum', *Comparative Studies in Society and Hist.* 14 (1972). A survey of how false models of capitalism persist is D. Horowitz, 'Textbook models of American economic growth', *Hist. Political Economy* 7 (1975), esp. 247 f.
8. N. Tranter, *Population since the Industrial Revolution* (Croom Helm, 1973), p. 137; cf., M. Burawoy, 'The Functions and Reproduction of Migrant Labour: Comparative Material from Southern Africa and the United States', *American J. Sociology* 81 (1976), 1050–1054.
9. K. Marx, *Grundrisse*, trans. M. Nicolaus (Penguin, 1973), pp. 100, 106–7. My method here follows the explanation of 'critique' given by D. Sayer, 'Method and Dogma in Historical Materialism', *Sociological Rev.* 23 (1975). Cf. P. Corrigan and D. Sayer, 'Moral relations, political economy and class struggle', *Radical Philosophy*, 12 (1975).
10. P. Anderson, *Lineages of the Absolutist State* (New Left Books, 1974), 403. He echoes here an earlier argument that the creation of the 'weekly wage earning class' is one of the 'prime achievements of industrial society'; T. S. Ashton and J. Sykes, *The Coal Industry in the Eighteenth Century* (Manchester University Press, 1929), 99.
11. For preliminary criticisms of the 'theory of productive forces' see, P. Corrigan, 'On the historical experience of the People's Republic of China', *J. Contemporary Asia* 4 (1974) and 'On the politics of production', *J. Peasant Studies* 2 (1975); also Sayer, 'Method and Dogma', and the recent work of C. Bettelheim. A different comment on the same consensus comes in R. Bendix, 'Tradition and Modernity Reconsidered', *Comparative Studies in Society and Hist.* 9 (1967), part III.
12. T. Marshall, 'Value problems of welfare capitalism', *J. Social Policy* 1 (1972), 29–30, cf. K. Mannheim's discussion of how the bourgeois depiction of equality *must* fail to 'notice' the market inequalities of class; *Ideology and Utopia* (Routledge, 1960), 249 f.
13. The Poor Law Report is available in a corrected text edited by the Checklands (Penguin, 1974). For a critique of ahistorical sociology see J. Ditton 'Perks, Pilferage and the Fiddle', *Theory and Society* (1976); on vagrancy, W. Chamblis, 'A sociological analysis of the law of vagrancy', *Social Problems*, 12 (1964); and on the creation of the labour market J. Saville, 'Primitive accumulation and early industrialisation in Britain', *Socialist Register* (1969), O. Hammen, 'Marx and the agrarian question', *American His. Rev.* 77 (1972), and W. Lazonick, 'Karl Marx and enclosures in Britain', *Rev. African Political Economy* 6 (1974).

14. Cf. Marx, *Grundrisse, Capital*, vol. iii (Lawrence & Wishart, 1972), ch. 50, and vol. i (Lawrence & Wishart, 1967), 539 f.; Sayer, 'Method and Dogma'.

15. e.g. the Poor Employment Act, 1817. The Commissioners who administered the Act were converted into the Commissioners of the Public Works Loan Board in 1875 which has been used as an instrument of economic management ever since. Cf. M. Flinn, 'The Poor Employment Act of 1817', *Economic His. Rev.* 14 (1961), 'A Policy of "Public Works" ', *New Society*, 18 Nov. 1971. For similar longevity see D. Blelloch, 'A Historical Survey of Factory Inspection in Great Britain', *Int. Labour Rev.* 38 (1938), and V. Allen, 'The Origins of Industrial Conciliation and Arbitration', *Int. Rev. Social Hist.* 9 (1964).

16. I refer here to the 1875 Employer and Workman Act; for the prior situation see D. Simon 'Master and Servant', 160–200 in J. Saville (ed.), *Democracy and the Labour Movement* (Lawrence & Wishart, 1954), and note the reports of attempted returns to *pre*-1875 in the furnishing trade of 1910 or later in S. Harrison, *Alex Gossip* (Lawrence & Wishart, 1962). On management: R. Bendix, *Work and Authority in Industry* (Harper, New York, 1963); J. Child, *British management thought* (Allen & Unwin, 1969); on work discipline, S. Pollard, 'Factory discipline in the industrial revolution', *Economic His. Rev.* 16 (1963), *The Genesis of Modern Management: A Study of the Industrial Revolution in Great Britain* (Penguin, 1968), and E. P. Thompson, 'Time, Work-Discipline and Industrial Capitalism', *Past & Present*, 38 (1967).

17. In 1851 '. . . more than a quarter of all men over the age of twenty were still employed in agriculture. Twice as many men and women worked in domestic service as in the cotton trade, the largest of the industrial occupations', R. K. Webb, *Modern England, from the Eighteenth Century to the Present* (Allen & Unwin, 1969), 112–13. In 1881 service occupations accounted for around a third of the paid employed population, about the same as manufacturing. The last three groups to be recognized as independent wage workers (all in the mid- or late-thirties of this century) were young workers, agricultural workers, and domestic servants. Until such recognition they were precisely of 'the family' as they are in the statistical profiles of King, 1688 and Coloquhoun, 1801.

18. L. Davidoff, 'Mastered for Life: Servant and Wife in Victorian and Edwardian England', *J. Social Hist.* 7 (1974), 410. The figure only falls below 20 per cent in that *annus mirabilis* for British workers, 1940, when unemployment fell below one million for the first time since 1919, thus neatly confirming Marx's point about the interconnectedness of active and surplus populations, *Capital*, i. 640 f.

19. Davidoff, 'Mastered for Life', and consider the following remark by an official in the Registrar General's Department in a preface to a Census volume: in 1851 'the English family, in its essential type, is composed of husband, wife, children and servants; or less perfectly but more commonly, of husband, wife and children.'

20. B. Harrison, 'For Church, Queen and Family: the Girl's Friendly Society, 1874–1920', *Past and Present*, 61 (1973), and 'State Intervention and Moral Reform', ch. 12 in P. Hollis (ed.), *Pressure from Without* (Leeds, Arnold, 1974).

21. Qu. N. Branson and M. Heinemann, *Britain in the 1930's* (Weidenfeld & Nicholson, 1971), 65.

22. L. Davidoff, 'Domestic Service in the Working Class Life Cycle', *Bull. Soc. for the Study of Labour Hist.* 26 (1973), 12. Cf. the important data in *Bulletin* of the North East Group for the Study of Labour History, 15 (1971); and for shopworkers W. Whittaker, *Victorian and Edwardian Shopworkers . . .* (Newton Abbot, David & Charles, 1973).

23. Cf. the two surveys by M. Bulmer, 'Policy, Society and Economy in County Durham, 1918–1972', *Durham University J.* 65 (1973), and 'Sociological Models of Mining Communities', *Sociological Rev.* 23 (1975).

24. On the mining labour market in Britain see Marx, *Capital*, i. 665 f; and B. Duckham's

FEUDAL RELICS OR CAPITALIST MONUMENTS 455

Introduction to the reprint of R. Galloway, *History of Coal Mining in Great Britain* (Newton Abbot, David & Charles, 1969).

25. Cf. Ashton and Sykes, *Coal Industry*, ch. 5; B. Duckham, 'Life and Labour in a Scottish Colliery, 1698–1755', *Scottish Hist. Rev.* 47 (1968); J. Barrowman, 'Slavery in the Coalmines of Scotland', *Trans. of the Mining Institute of Scotland* 19 (1897). The relevant debate here is whether this serfdom continued agrarian serfdom or was of a new type; Barrowman argues the latter view.

26. 'Slavery in Modern Scotland', *Edinburgh Review* 189 (1899), 144.

27. Ibid. 148, quoting Bald's studies of 1803.

28. On this Northern Bond see Ashton and Sykes, *Coal Industry*, ch. 6; H. Scott, 'The Miners' Bond in Northumberland and Durham', *Proc. of the Society of Antiquaries of Newcastle upon Tyne*, 4th ser., 11 (1947); P. Hair, 'The Binding of the Pitmen in the North East, 1800–1809', *Durham University J.* 27 (1965)—all give examples of the texts of such bonds. For organisations of the Coalmasters cf. P. Sweezy, *Monopoly and Competition in the English Coal Trade, 1550–1850* (Harvard, University Press, 1938).

29. Cf. M. Flinn (ed.), *The Law Book of the Crowley Iron Works* (Durham, Andrews for the Surtees Society, 1957). As late as 1926 miners and their families in Britain constituted 10 per cent of the total population. In 1936 only 55 per cent of British coal was machine produced, compared with the Ruhr's 97 per cent or the Pas de Calais' 88 per cent. As late as 1930 there were only forty pithead baths for the whole of Britain. For local statistical profiles cf. D. Rowe "Occupations in Northumberland and Durham, 1851–1911', *Northern Hist.* 8 (1973); and for an excellent internal account see J. Davison, *Northumberland Miners, 1919–1930* (Newcastle upon Tyne, Harold Hill for the National Union of Mineworkers, 1973).

30. Ashton and Sykes, *Coal Industry*, p. 84. Davison, *Northumberland Miners*, p. 202, refers to the miners' coal company houses as 'tied cottages'.

31. B. Mooney, 'A Letter from the Squire', *New Statesman*, 20 Dec. 1974, p. 887. Cf. H. Newby, 'Agricultural Workers in the Class Structure', *Sociological Rev.* 20 (1972), 'Deference and the Agricultural Worker', *Sociological Rev.* 23 (1975), and C. Bell, 'Sources of Variation in Agricultural Workers' Images of Society', *Sociological Rev.* 21 (1973); and I. Carter, 'Agricultural Workers in the Class Structure: A Critical Note', *Sociological Rev.* 22 (1974).

32. T. Hardy, 'The Dorsetshire Labourer', *Longman's Magazine*, 2 (1883), 259; M. Bragg, 'To be a Ploughman: The Way Things Were', *Listener*, 13 Mar. 1975, p. 333. Agricultural labour regimes are well displayed in R. Samuel (ed.), *Village Life and Labour* (Routledge, 1975). Cf. R. Williams, *The Country and the City* (Paladin, 1973), ch. 25, and the exchanges between D. Craig and I. Carter in *J. Peasant Studies* 2 (1974–5). The equivalent of the Scots collier-serf's 'bearer' was the Northumbrian hind's 'bondager', similarly acquired with the man at the hiring. Cf. L. Hindmarsh, 'On the State of Agriculture and the Condition of Agricultural Labourers of the Northern Division of Northumberland', *J. Statistical Society* 1 (1838), 404–9; J. Grey, 'A View of the Past and Present State of Agriculture in Northumberland', *J. Royal Agricultural Society of England* 2 (1841), 183–90; and the full account in J. J. Henley's report and evidence to the Royal Commission, *Parliamentary Papers* 1867–8 (4068) xvii. 52–71 and 219 f. Photographic evidence is available in R. Gard, *Northumberland at the Turn of the Century* (Newcastle upon Tyne, Oriel, 1970).

33. Cf. H. Newby, 'The Deferential Dialectic', *Comparative Studies in Society and Hist.* 17 (1975); S. Yeo, 'On the Uses of "Apathy"', *Archives Européenes de Sociologie*, 15 (1974).

34. R. Blythe, *Akenfield* (Penguin, 1972); for a critical comment see H. Newby, letter, *Sunday Times*, 2 Dec. 1974.

35. D. Leich, 'Can the Government ever settle the "feudal relic" of tied cottages?', *The Times*, 14 Mar. 1975.
36. On allotments: Lord Fortescue, 'Poor Men's Gardens', *Nineteenth Century*, 23 (1888); J. Wilkinson, 'Pages in the History of Allotments', *Contemporary Rev.* 65 (1894); F. Green, 'The Allotment Movement', *Contemporary Rev.* 114 (1918); D. Barnett, 'Allotments and the Problem of Rural Poverty' in E. L. Jones and G. Mingay, *Land, Labour and Population in the Industrial Revolution* (Methuen, 1967) who give data on the extent of allotments and allotment gardens in Northumbria.
37. Ministry of Housing and Local Government, *Report* of the Committee of Inquiry into allotments, H.M.S.O. Cmnd 4166, 1969, Ss. 358, 15. Note: 'The readiness of the mining companies to provide allotments was due to a number of factors. Most of the rows of terrace houses provided for the miners had little or no garden space and the provision of land for allotments was the obvious alternative' (ibid. Ss. 331). Why 'obvious'? Consider mill-towns, dockworkers' housing, etc. Empirically the statement is also false; long rows of houses with ample gardens can be seen, e.g. in Cambois, North Blyth, Northumberland. As late as 1906 allotments were used to keep wages as low as $2\frac{1}{2}d$. an hour in the High Wycombe furniture industry; Harrison, *Alex Gossip*, p. 19.
38. V. Lenin, 'The Agrarian Question in Russia . . .', *Selected Works*, vol. i (Moscow, Marx-Engels-Lenin Institute, 1936), p. 54. This text was *not* published until 1918; although it was written in 1908.
39. B. Moore Jr., *The Social Origins of Dictatorship and Democracy* (Penguin, 1969), ch. 7.
40. J. Blum, 'The Rise of Serfdom in Eastern Europe', *American His. Rev.* 62 (1957); A. Kahan, 'Notes on Serfdom in Western and Eastern Europe', *J. Economic Hist.* 33 (1973).
41. Cf. e.g. V. Yatsunsky, 'Industrial Revolution in Russia', *Voprosi Istorii*, 12 (1952); T. Kemp, 'The Modernisation of Tsarist Russia' in his *Industrialisation in Nineteenth Century Europe* (Longmans, 1969); S. Baron, 'The Transition from Feudalism to Capitalism in Russia', *American Hist. Rev.* 77 (1972); G. Yaney, *The Systematization of Russian Government, 1711-1905* (Urbana, University of Illinois, 1974), ch. 4. One aspect of the world relations I have been trying to make visible is exemplified in the contradictory impact within Tsarist Russia of the repeal of two pieces of *British* legislation: in 1842 on the *export* of textile machinery, and in 1846 on the *import* of cheap corn.
42. Cf. T. von Laue, 'The State and the Economy' in C. Black (ed.), *The Transformation of Russian society* (Harvard, University Press, 1960), and 'Russian Peasants in the Factory, 1892-1904', *J. Economic Hist.* 21 (1961); G. Rimlinger, 'Autocracy and the Factory Worker in Early Russian Industrialisation', *J. Economic Hist.* 20 (1960), and 'The Expansion of the Labour Market in Capitalist Russia, 1861-1917', *J. Economic Hist.* 21 (1961); and R. Zelnik, 'The Peasant and the Factory', in W. Vucinich (ed.), *The Peasant in Nineteenth Century Russia* (Stanford, University Press, 1968). For general accounts E. Wolf, *Peasant Wars of the Twentieth Century* (Faber, 1971), ch. 2; G. Grossman, 'The Industrialisation of Russia' in C. Cipolla (ed.), *The Emergence of Industrial Societies*, vol. ii (Fontana, 1973); and P. Anderson, *Lineages of the Absolutist State* (New Left Books, 1974), part II, ch. 6. The latter, taken with the work of N. Harding, 'Lenin's Early Writings—the Problem of Context', *Political Studies*, 23 (1975), and A. Hunt, 'Lenin and Sociology', *Sociological Rev.* 24 (1976), provides a perceptive location of Lenin's *Development of Capitalism in Russia*.
43. e.g. A. Frank, 'Destroy Capitalism not Feudalism', in *Latin America* (Monthly Review Press, 1969), ch. 23; R. Stavenhagen, 'Seven Fallacies about Latin America' in J. Petras and M. Zeitlin (eds.), *Latin America* (New York, Fawcett, 1968), ch. 1; E. Laclau, 'Feudalism and Capitalism in Latin America', *New Left Rev.* 67 (1971). Dualism is only a special case of 'either/or' thinking which bewitches the Left as much as the Right. Cf. A. Frank, *Capitalism and Underdevelopment in Latin America* (Penguin, 1971), pp. 73 f.; A. Obregon,

FEUDAL RELICS OR CAPITALIST MONUMENTS 457

'Contemporary Peasant Movements', in S. M. Lipset and A. Solari (eds.), *Elites in Latin America* (Oxford University Press, 1967); G. Huizer, *Peasant Rebellion in Latin America* (Penguin, 1973), and R. Stavenhagen 'Peasant Movements and Land Reform in Latin America', in H. Landsberger (ed.), *Rural Protest* (Macmillan, 1974); and D. Preston, 'Geographers on the Peasants', *Progress in Geography*, 6 (1974).

44. Cf. E. Wolf and E. Hansen (eds.), *The human condition in Latin America* (Oxford University Press, 1972), pp. 145 f.; J. Quartin, *Dictatorship and Armed Struggle in Brazil* (New Left Books, 1971), pp. 117 f.; E. Feder, *The Rape of the Peasantry* (New York, Anchor, 1971), pp. 114 f.

45. A. Obregon, 'The Marginal Pole of the Economy and the Marginalised Labour Force', *Economy and Society*, 3 (1974); criticized in advance by Frank, *Capitalism and Underdevelopment*, pp. 135 f.

46. C. Goldin, 'The Economics of Emancipation', *J. Economic Hist.* 33 (1973). On the dynamic situation of the wage worker under capitalism as a form of debt slavery cf. K. Marx, *Capital*, ii (Lawrence & Wishart, 1970), 377 f.

47. P. Daniel, *The Shadow of Slavery* (New York, Oxford University Press, 1973), p. 19. He stresses (pp. 82 f.) how this applies to migrant labour in general whether from Mexico, Puerto Rico, or Europe. Cf. Burawoy, 'The Functions and Reproduction of Migrant Labour' for similar emphasis.

48. Moore, *Social Origins*, p. 112: note the critical praise of this work in E. Genovese, *In Red and Black* (New York, Vintage, 1972), pp. 345 f.

49. Wallerstein, 'American Slavery', p. 1211; this is a review of R. Fogel and S. Engerman, *Time on the Cross*, 2 vols. (Boston, Little Brown, 1974), and E. Genovese, *Roll, Jordan, Roll* (New York, Pantheon, 1974).

50. K. Marx, *Poverty of Philosophy* (New York, International Press, 1963), pp. 111–12: as to credit, see Marx, *Capital*, i. 754 f.

51. Marx, *Capital*, i. 760. The slavery in Europe is only *veiled*. A term like 'free wage slavery' is more accurate and realistic. Cf. K. Marx, interview in New York, *World*, 18 July 1871, reprinted in *Labour Monthly*, 54 (1972).

52. Cf. M. Craton, *The Sinews of Empire* (Temple Smith, 1975); D. Davis, *The Problem of Slavery in Western Culture* (Penguin, 1970); E. Williams, *Capitalism and Slavery* (Deutsch, 1967); R. Sheridan, *Sugar and Slavery* (New York, Bowker, 1974); H. Bernstein and M. Pitt, 'Plantations and Modes of Exploitation', *J. Peasant Studies* 1 (1974); J. Grace, *Domestic Slavery in West Africa* (Muller, 1975); A. Zable, 'Neocolonialism and Race Relations', *Race*, 14 (1973). Particular significance attaches to the relationship between the *size* of the Indian market and the rate of English capital growth.

53. For criticisms of Fogel, *Time on the Cross*, see T. Haskell, 'Were Slaves more Efficient?', *New York Rev. of Books*, 19 Sept. 1974. Note also R. Fogel, 'From the Marxists to the Mormons', *Times Literary Supplement*, 13 June 1975, and the subsequent exchange of letters between Thompson and Fogel, ibid., 4 and 11 July 1975, concerning H. Gutman, *Slavery and the Numbers Game* (Urbana, University of Illinois Press, 1975), which began life as a special issue of the *J. Negro Hist.* (1975).

54. R. Starobin, *Industrial Slavery in the Old South* (New York, Oxford University Press, 1970). Much of his account invites comparison with, e.g., serfdom in Tsarist Russia.

55. Aufhauser, 'Slavery and Scientific Management'; S. Engerman, 'Some Considerations Relating to Property Rights in Man', *J. Economic Hist.* 33 (1973). Cf. D. Montgomery, 'Immigrant Workers and Scientific Management', paper to Immigrants in Industry Conference, November 1973.

56. Engerman, 'Some Considerations', pp. 45–6. In 1970, in an unpublished paper to a B.S.A. Conference meeting John McGreal and I drew attention to almost identical formulae

458   PHILIP CORRIGAN

regarding the neo-slavery of inverted imperialism within the U.K. in work wherein
Peston remarks that 'it would seem unlikely . . . that the full value of their marginal pro-
duct would accrue to the /black/ immigrants in Britain. The 'it would seem' is as revealing
as the rest. J. McGreal and P. Corrigan, 'Ideology in "Colour and Citizenship" ', paper to
B.S.A. Conference (group meeting), 1970; E. Rose (ed.), *Colour and Citizenship* (Oxford
University Press, 1969), p. 652.

57. Goldin, 'Economics of Emancipation', cf. E. Bonacich, 'Abolition, the Extension of
    Slavery and the Position of Free Blacks, 1830–1863', *American J. Sociology* 81 (1975); R.
    Ransom and R. Sutch, 'Debt peonage in the cotton South after the Civil War', *J. Economic
    Hist.* 32 (1972); N. Brown and M. Reynolds, 'Debt Peonage Re-examined', *J. Economic
    Hist.* 33 (1973).
58. Daniel, *Shadow of Slavery*, p. xiii. Cf. D. Harper, 'Exploitation in Migrant Labour Camps',
    British J. Sociology 25 (1974); Burawoy, 'Functions and Reproduction of Migrant Labour';
    H. Wolpe, 'The "white working class" in South Africa', *Economy and Society*, 5
    (1976).
59. T. Rosengarten, *All God's Dangers; The Life of Nate Shaw* (New York, Avon, 1973).
60. J. Meyer, 'Comment' (on Engerman, Goldin, and Kahn), *J. Economic Hist.* 33 (1973), 105.
61. Cf. R. Roberts, *Chartered Companies* (Bell, 1969); H. Tinker, *A New System of Slavery* . . .
    (Oxford University Press, 1974); J. Banaji, *Modes of Production* (Dar-es-Salaam, Depart-
    ment of Sociology, 1975); H. Alavi, 'India and the colonial mode of production', *Socialist
    Register* (1975).
62. *Sunday Times*, 26 Aug. 1973, p. 6.
63. J. Rex, 'The Plural Society: The South African Case', *Race*, 12 (1971), 404; cf. M. Cham-
    berlain, *The Scramble for Africa* (Longmans, 1974); E. Morel, *The Black Man's Burden* (New
    York, Monthly Rev. Press, 1969); L. Oliver, *White Capital and Coloured Labour* (Hogarth
    Press, 1929); H. Blumer, 'Industrialisation and Race Relations' in G. Hunter (ed.), *Indus-
    trialisation and race relations* (Oxford University Press, 1965); and H. Wolpe, 'White
    Working Class'.
64. J. Rex, *The Compound, the Reserve and Urban Location* (British Sociological Association
    Conference, 1972), p. 7.
65. H. Wolpe, 'Capitalism and Cheap Labour Power in South Africa', *Economy and Society*, 1
    (1972), 434; cf. H. Wolpe, 'Industrialisation and Race in South Africa', in S. Zubaida (ed.),
    Race and Racialism (Tavisock, 1971), and the changes made in his 'White Working Class'
    which is complemented by the theoretical discussion at the start of Burawoy, 'Functions
    and Reproduction'.
66. R. Davies, 'The White Working Class in South Africa', *New Left Rev.* 82 (1974) 56; cf. S.
    Mhlongo, 'Black Workers' Strikes in South Africa', *New Left Rev.* 83 (1974); R. First *et
    al.*, *The South African Connection* (Penguin, 1973). The latter taken with almost any issue of
    The Times or *Sunday Times* (e.g. 16 May 1976, p. 9), reminds us that we can no more
    understand this peculiarity *within* Southern Africa than we could by considering slavery
    in the antebellum South a home-grown product. With respect to *white* migration I repeat
    this point below.
67. M. Legassick, 'South Africa: Capital Accumulation and Violence', *Economy and Society*, 3
    (1974), 287; cf. Wolpe, 'White Working Class'.
68. Engerman, 'Property Rights in Man', p. 49. Cf. Marx's polemic against Wakefield's *The
    Modern Theory of Colonisation* in *Capital*, i, ch. 33.
69. L. Jenks, *The Migration of British Capital to 1875* (Nelson, 1971); cf. B. Thomas, *Migration
    and Urban Development* (Methuen, 1972).
70. P. Vilar, 'Problems in the Formation of Capital', *Past and Present*, 10 (1956) 34; and see,
    e.g., I. Malhotra, 'Taking the Beggars to the Jobs', 'Beggars Beg to Differ', *Guardian*, 2

FEUDAL RELICS OR CAPITALIST MONUMENTS 459

and 15 Mar. 1976. I am grateful to Jason Ditton for drawing these items to my attention.

71. H. Johnston, *British Emigration Policy, 1815–1830* (Oxford, Clarendon Press, 1972); K. Marx, 'Forced Emigration', *New York Daily Tribune*, 22 Mar. 1853; Cf. A. Redford, *Labour Migration in England, 1800–1850* (Manchester, University Press, 1964); R. Taylor, 'Migration and Motivation', in J. Jackson (ed.), *Migration* (Cambridge University Press, 1969); L. Stone, 'Social Mobility in England, 1500–1700', *Past and Present*, 33 (1966); J. Patten, *Rural-Urban Migration in Pre-Industrial England*, Oxford, School of Geography, Research Paper, 6 (1973); D. Preston, *Rural-Urban and Inter-Settlement Interaction* Leeds, Department of Geography, Working Papers, 9 (1974); and contrast Burawoy, 'Functions and Reproduction'.

72. K. Marx, 'The Duchess of Sutherland and Slavery', *New York Daily Tribune*, 9 Feb. 1853, and *Capital*, i. 726 f.; L. Levi, 'On the Economic Condition of the Highlands and Islands' *J. Statistical Society* 27 (1865); A. MacKenzie, *The History of the Highland Clearances* (Glasgow, MacLaren, 1966); M. Gray, 'The Consolidation of the Crofting System', *Agricultural Hist. Rev.* 5 (1956); T. Smout, 'Scottish Landowners and Economic Growth, 1650–1850', *Scottish J. Political Economy* 11 (1964); I. Carter, 'The Highlands of Scotland as an Underdeveloped Region' in E. de Kadt and G. Williams (eds.), *Sociology and Development* (Tavistock, 1974); and E. Richards, 'Structural Change in a Regional Economy: Sutherland and the Industrial Revolution, 1780–1830', *Economic Hist. Rev.* 26 (1973).

73. E. Hunt, 'How Mobile was Labour in Nineteenth Century Britain?', *Exeter Papers in Economic Hist.* 6 (1972), 42; and cf. E. Hunt, *Regional Wage Variations in Britain, 1850–1914* (Oxford, Clarendon Press, 1973); H. Lind, 'Internal Migration in Britain', in Jackson, *Migration*.

74. There were, by about 1850, some half a million Irish men and women in England. In the 1971 *Census* it is shown that there were 480,000 Irish born and 653,000 'new /i.e. black/ Commonwealth' born amongst the economically active population. Since 1945 Britain has been a net exporter of people; in some years the outflows were at the proportional level of Italy.

75. P. Cinanni, 'The Backgrounds of Migrating Labour', in N. van Houte and W. Melgert (eds.), *Foreigners in our Community* (Amsterdam, Keesing, 1972), p. 29; cf. Wallerstein, 'American Slavery'. Between 1715 and 1800 the 'European' population of British America rose from 250,000 to 5 million (1·5 million being from the British Isles); between 1801 and 1840 1·5 million moved from Europe to North America; between 1841 and 1880 1·3 million so moved (from 1845 to 1850 no less than 80 per cent of them came from Britain and Ireland; from 1851 to 1875, 50 per cent so); between 1881 and 1900 a further 13 million moved from Europe to the U.S.A., and between 1900 and 1914 another 18 million. Of the 34 million or so who thus moved between 1871 and 1914 25 million became permanent settlers; A. Armengaud, 'Population in Europe' in Cipolla, *The Industrial Revolution*; but cf. O. Grada, 'A Note on Nineteenth Century Irish Emigration Statistics', *Population Studies*, 29 (1975); M. Fullam, 'Provisional Providers', *New Society*, 1 Jan. 1976.

76. H. Gutman, 'Work, Culture and Society in Industrialising America', *American Hist. Rev.* 78 (1973). Cf. M. Reich, 'The Evolution of the US Labour Force' in R. Edward, *The Capitalist System* (New Jersey, Prentice Hall, 1972), Harper, 'Exploitation'; Montgomery, 'Immigrant Workers'; S. Terkel, *Working* (New York, Avon, 1975).

77. S. Thernstrom, *Poverty and Progress* (Harvard, University Press, 1964); 'Class and Mobility in a Nineteenth Century City', in R. Bendix and S. M. Lipset (eds.), *Class, Status and Power*, 2nd edn. (Routledge, 1965); 'Working Class Mobility in Industrial America' in M. Richter (ed.), *Essays in Theory and History* (Harvard, University Press, 1970); D.

460   PHILIP CORRIGAN

Montgomery, 'The Working Classes of the Pre-Industrial American City, 1780–1830', *Labor Hist.* 9 (1968); D. Harvey, *Social Justice and the City* (Leeds, Arnold, 1973); J. Eyles, 'Social Theory and Social Geography', *Progress in Geography*, 6 (1974).

78. R. Starobin, *Blacks in Bondage* . . . (Croom Helm, 1974); C. Erickson, *Invisible Immigrants* . . . (Coral Gables, Florida, University of Miami Press, 1972).

79. J. Bellini, 'European Migrant Labour: Present and Future Conditional', *New Community*, 4 (1975), 8. Changes in this area are both subtle and rapid; cf. the section 'Migrant workers' in *Social and Labour Bulletin* of the I.L.O.; the statistical series *MN* issued by O.P.C.S. Monitors covering both inter- and intranational movements.

80. P. Stephens, 'West Europe and its Migrants', *New Society*, 13 Jan. 1974, p. 629; a chart on the same page details German *Gastarbeiter*: 497,000 Turks, 471,000 Yugoslavs, 422,000 Italians, 269,000 Greeks, and 184,000 Spaniards; other groups being less than 100,000. Cf. data in *Europa*, 4 Feb. 1974, p. vi.

81. There have been increasing controls in Britain since the early 1960s, see the work of S. Allen: 'Immigrants or Workers?' in Zubaida, *Race and Racialism*; 'Race and the Economy', *Race*, 13 (1971); 'Black Workers in Britain', in van Houte, *Foreigners*; for suspensions or restrictions in West Germany, see *The Times*, 24 Nov. 1973; France, *The Times*, 5 July 1974; Netherlands, S. Masterman, 'Chaos and Racialism as Holland Prepares to Close the Door on Immigrants', *The Times*, 17 Sept. 1975; there have been two referenda in Switzerland, in 1970 and 1974, neither of which achieved the repatriation sought for. In 1974 there were 1,100,000 migrant workers out of a total population in Switzerland of 6,400,000.

82. Reported, *The Times*, 30 May 1975, p. 2. Of course, as Worsley argues, 'Proletarians, Sub-Proletarians . . .', official figures are unreliable, not least because of the illegal migration—which is massive in France for example; for West Germany, S. Paine, *Exporting Workers; The Turkish Case* (Cambridge University Press, 1974); P. Pringle, 'Paying Guests', *Sunday Times Magazine*, 26 May 1974; S. Castles and G. Cosack, 'How the Trade Unions Try to Control and Integrate Migrant Workers . . .', *Race*, 15 (1974); M. Nikolinakos, 'Economic Foundations of Discrimination in the Federal Republic of Germany', in van Houte and Melgert, *Foreigners*; for France, B. Chatwin, 'Fateful Journey to Marseilles', *Sunday Times Magazine*, 5 Jan. 1974; P. Brogan, 'A Foreign Legion of Workers in French Industry', *The Times*, 15 May 1972; G. Merritt, 'Renault Hold a Mirror to France's Social Unrest', *Financial Times*, 30 Apr. 1973; for Europe, J. Power, 'Future Conditional for Immigrant Workers', *The Times*, 30 July 1973, 'A Trojan Horse Full of Migrant Workers Inside Europe's Walls', *The Times*, 1 Aug. 1973, 'At Last Europe Faces up to the Social and Economic Costs of Immigrant Labour', *The Times*, 11 June 1974; M. Westlake 'Creating the Helots of Europe', *The Times*, 23 May 1973, 'Distributing the Profits of Migrant Labour', *The Times*, 30 May 1973.

83. J. Ensor, 'Car Plants . . .', *Financial Times*, 12 Mar. 1973. On 21 Sept. 1973 *The Times* editorialized on both the fact that 'American automobile chiefs' had been impressed by lower costs and higher profits in Continental Europe in the 1960s and the link between this and 'non-unionized immigrant labour'. For the *slavery* of high technology see H. Beynon, *Working for Ford* (Penguin, 1973).

84. S. Castles and G. Cosack, 'The Function of Labour Immigration in Western Europe', *New Left Rev.* 73 (1972), *Immigrant Workers and the Class Structure in Western Europe* (Oxford University Press, 1973). Cf. M. Nikolinakos, 'Notes on an Economic Theory of Racism', *Race*, 14 (1973), 'Notes towards a General Theory of Migration in Late Capitalism', *Race and Class*, 17 (1975).

85. A. Gorz, 'Immigrant Labour', *New Left Rev.* 61 (1970), 29; his *Socialism and Revolution* (Allen Lane, 1975), pp. 11 f., is as close to my 'general theory' as any text. Marx noted

FEUDAL RELICS OR CAPITALIST MONUMENTS 461

similar internal relations when he quoted from the Medical Officer's Report to the Privy Council (1863): 'The young people migrate to the eastern mining districts of Glamorgan and Monmouth. Carmarthenshire is the breeding ground of the mining population and their hospital', *Capital*, i. 681 f.

86. There is a clear analysis in CETIM, *White Migration to Southern Africa* (Geneva, Centre Europe, Tiers Monde, 1975), and *Sunday Times*, 19 May 1974.

87. J. Berger and J. Mohr, *A Seventh Man; a Book of Images and Words about the Experience of Migrant Workers in Europe* (Penguin, 1975). Cf. J. Berger, 'Directions in Hell', *New Left Rev.* 87-8 (1974); E. N'goumou and J. Power, 'The Clandestine Traffic', *The Times*, 15 June 1974; and the exceptional film *Shaft in Africa*.

88. Nikolinakos, 'Notes towards a General Theory'.

89. T. Hagerstrand, 'On the Definition of Migration', in E. Jones, *Readings in Social Geography* (Oxford University Press, 1975), p. 208.

90. e.g. F. Hahn, 'Some Adjustment Problems', *Econometrica*, 28 (1970); W. Leontieff, 'Theoretical Assumptions and Non-observed Facts', *American Economic Rev.* 61 (1971); T. Balogh, *New Society*, 7 Oct. 1971, p. 675, and 'An Economics for the Real World', *Times Literary Supplement*, 18 Jan. 1974; cf. P. Worsley, 'The State of Theory and the Status of Theory', *Sociology*, 8 (1974).

91. N. Bosanquet, 'Is there a Dual Labour-Market in Britain?', *Economic J.* 83 (1973), 426. On the realities of the British labour market see: K. Roberts, 'The Entry into Employment . . .', *Sociological Rev.* 16 (1968); D. Ashton, 'The Transition from School to Work', *Sociological Rev.* 23 (1973). The actual structure of state provision—in a reified form, the network of 'unfree labour markets'—can be seen in Department of Employment, *Into Action; Plan for a Modern Employment Service* (1972), and the 'Jobs on the Fence' supplement, *The Times*, 24 Apr. 1975, on the Manpower Services Commission. Participant observation during spells of unemployment verifies the rigidity of the segmentalization practised by special offices for different qualities of labour-power.

92. B. Silverman and M. Yanowitz, 'Radical and Liberal Perspectives in the Working Class', *Social Policy*, 4 (1974), 48. R. Lekachman, 'Unemployment in America', *New Society*, 24 Apr. 1975, p. 192, notes that 'real' unemployment in the U.S.A. may have been 14 per cent in 1975. Cf. C. Cramer, *American Enterprise* . . . (Elek, 1973); C. Degler, *The Age of Economic Revolution, 1876-1900* (San Francisco, Scott, 1967); E. Bonacich, 'Abolition' and 'Advanced capitalism and Black/White Race Relations in the United States: A Split Labor Market Interpretation', *American Sociological Rev.* 41 (1976); D. Montgomery, 'The Shuttle and the Cross . . .', *J. Social Hist.* 5 (1972); and the studies in W. O'Neill, *Insights and Parallels* (Minneapolis, Burgess, 1973), especially that by Grimsted.

93. W. Lovett, *Social and Political Morality* (Simpkin, 1953), p. 90. Cf. N. McKendrick, 'Home Demand and Economic Growth . . .' in *Historical Perspectives* . . . (Europa, 1974); J. Scott and L. Tilly, 'Women's Work and the Family in Nineteenth Century Europe', *Comparative Studies in Society and Hist.* 17 (1975).

94. Cf. T. Forester, 'The Home Workers', *New Society*, 4 Sept. 1975; C. Adam, 'Mayhew's London Survives', *New Statesman*, 17 Oct. 1975; E. Wigham, 'Protecting the Army of Home Workers from Exploitation', *The Times*, 4 May 1976.

95. M. Nikolinakos, 'An Economic Theory of Racism', p. 378; cf. Thomas, *Migration and Urban Development*, p. 197. That is, 'black workers in Britain are bearers of the under-developed economies from which they have come .˙. . an inverted form of imperialism', McGreal and Corrigan, 'Ideology in "Colour and Citizenship" '. Cf. Marx on slavery in the context of 'The genesis of the industrial capitalist', *Capital*, i. ch. 31. As he says, p. 752, n. 1, 'This subject one must study in detail, to see what the bourgeoisie makes of itself and the labourers, wherever it can, without restraint, model the world after its own image.'

96. M. Meth, *Here to Stay* (Runnymede Trust, 1969), p. 17. Cf. The House of Lords debate on Rose, *Colour and Citizenship, Hansard* (Lords), 16 Dec. 1969; and recent data in *New Society*, 10 and 17 Apr. 1975.

97. H. Wagatsuma, 'The Pariah Caste in Japan', in A. de Reuck and J. Knight (eds.), *Caste and Race; Comparative Approaches* (J. & A. Churchill, 1968); P. Hazelhurst, 'Slow Advance by Japan's Untouchables', *The Times*, 11 June 1974. The *Eta* fraction of the Burakumin exemplify much of what my remarks are about. On 'caste' see C. Meillassoux, 'Are there castes in India?', *Economy and Society*, 2 (1973).

98. Fitzhugh in 1854 quoted in Starobin, *Industrial Slavery*, p. 209. Aufhauser, 'Slavery and Scientific Management', p. 820, is right to stress that both the lash and the *threat* of firing 'result from a violation of established rules . . .'; in other words, 'the practical content of discipline does not vary much between labour regimes.'

99. Marx, *Capital*, i. 641. Cf. A. Gorz (ed.), *Critique de la division du travail* (Paris, Ed. du Seuil, 1973).

100. H. Braverman, *Labour and Monopoly Capital; The Degradation of Work in the Twentieth Century* (Monthly Rev. Press, 1974), ch. 17; I. Wallerstein, *The Modern World System* (Academic Press, 1974). Cf. T. Sowell, 'Marx's "increasing misery" doctrine', *American Economic Rev.* 50 (1960); D. Hodges, 'Marx's general law of capitalist development', *Cahiers de l'ISEA*, 10 (1966); D. Thorner, 'The Marxian Theory of Development', *Int. Social Science J.* 14 (1962), and 'The Principal Modes of Production of Karl Marx', in C. Mitra (ed.), *Economic Theory and Policy* (Delhi, Oxford University Press, 1974). Contrast B. Hoselitz, 'Karl Marx on Secular and Social Development', *Comparative Studies in Society and Hist.* 6 (1963), a paper read to the conference on which Thorner, 'Marxian theory', reports.

101. Marx, *Grundrisse*, pp. 609–10.

102. Marx, *Capital*, i. 644: see his discussion of the floating, the latent, the stagnant, and the nomad fraction of the world 'surplus population', ibid., ch. 25. Cf. R. Mishra, 'Marx and Welfare', *Sociological Rev.* 23 (1975).

103. Marx, *Capital*, i. 645. See also the discussion in *Grundrisse*, pp. 281 f., and in *Wage Labour and Capital* (Moscow, Progress Press, 1952).

104. Marx, *Capital*, i. 644. Note how Marx describes the *real* accumulation of capital as '*stock-piling*: the stockpiling of workers, along with their instruments, at particular points', *Grundrisse*, p. 508. On the circulation of labour as a commodity, cf. *Capital*, ii, ch. 5, and on the coercion of 'free' wage labour, iii, part vii.

105. Cf. Y. Lacoste, 'General Characteristics and Fundamental Structures of Medieval North African Society', *Economy and Society*, 3 (1974); S. Amin, 'Development and Structural Change', *J. Int. Affairs* 24 (1970), 'Underdevelopment and Dependence in Black Africa', *J. Modern African Studies* 10 (1972), and 'Accumulation and Development', *Rev. African Political Economy* 1 (1974); H. Hill, 'Peripheral Capitalism . . .', *Australian and New Zealand J. of Sociology* 11 (1975).

106. J. Cousins and R. Davis, 'Working Class Incorporation', in F. Parkin (ed.), *The Sociological Analysis of Class Structure* (Tavistock, 1974), p. 285; cf., M. Bulmer (ed.), *Working Class Images of Society* (Routledge, 1975), and Gorz, 'Immigrant Labour'.

107. Gorz, *Socialism and Revolution*, pp. 12 f. One group of apparently outcast producers is examined in R. Rehfisch, *Gypsies, Tinkers and Other Travellers* (Academic Press, 1975). Cf. Nikolinakos, 'Towards a General Theory'.

108. Wallerstein, 'American Slavery', p. 1212.

109. C. Bettelheim, 'Theoretical Comments', in A. Emmanuel, *Unequal Exchange* (New Left Books, 1972), pp. 293 f.

110. C. Bettelheim, *Cultural Revolution and Industrial Organisation in China* (Monthly Rev.

FEUDAL RELICS OR CAPITALIST MONUMENTS 463

Press, 1974), pp. 91–2; and of his 'State Property and Socialism', *Economy and Society*, 2 (1973), 400 f.; Corrigan, 'Historical Experience', 'Politics of Production', Corrigan and Sayer, 'Moral relations'.

111. R. Young, 'Darwinism and the Division of Labour'; *Listener*, 23 Nov. 1972, p. 205; cf. R. Williams, 'Social Darwinism', *Listener*, 23 Nov. 1972.

112. M. Nicolaus, 'The Universal Contradiction', *New Left Rev.* 59 (1970), 18. For an articulation of the view criticized, see E. Mandel, *Europe versus America?* (New Left Books, 1970), *Late Capitalism* (New Left Books, 1975); Oxfam's *Whose Right to Work?* (May 1976) also wishes to enforce the international division of labour.

Biographical note; PHILIP R. D. CORRIGAN, born 1942. Librarian (F.L.A., 1967) and lecturer, 1960–9; studied sociology at L.S.E., 1969–70; Lecturer, Newcastle upon Tyne Polytechnic, 1970–1; B.A., Sociology, Durham University, 1973; S.S.R.C. Senior Research Fellow, Durham University, 1973–7; Ph.D., Durham, 1977; currently Lecturer, Department of Sociology, North East London Polytechnic.

[2]

The Functions and Reproduction of Migrant Labor: Comparative Material from Southern Africa and the United States[1]

Michael Burawoy
University of Chicago

For a capitalist economy to function, its labor force must be maintained; that is, workers must receive a historically determined minimal day-to-day subsistence. It must also be renewed; that is, vacancies must be filled. A system of migrant labor is characterized by the institutional differentiation and physical separation of the processes of renewal and maintenance. Accordingly, migrant labor entails a dual dependence upon employment in one place and an alternate economy and/or state in another. In addition, the separation of migrant workers from their families is implied. It is enforced through specific legal and political mechanisms which regulate geographical mobility and impose restrictions on the occupational mobility of migrants. These mechanisms in turn are made possible by the migrant workers' powerlessness in the place of employment, in the labor market, and under the legal and political systems where they are employed. One consequence of a system of migrant labor is the externalization, to an alternate economy and/or state, of certain costs of labor-force renewal—costs normally borne by the employer and/or state of employment. This framework is developed and applied to migrant farm workers in California and migrant mine workers in South Africa. The differences between the two systems are highlighted and analyzed in terms of the broader features of the respective social structures. Finally, the implications of the theoretical scheme are discussed and extended to an interpretation of race relations.

Traditionally, studies of labor migration have adopted the perspective of the individual migrant. This has involved the examination of two questions: the reasons for migration and its consequences at the level of the individual or group. In answer to the first question, it has generally been assumed that individuals respond to the "push" and "pull" factors associated with the market. With regard to the second question, attention is directed to prob-

[1] This paper originated with the ideas and work of Jaap van Velsen and was later stimulated by Harold Wolpe. I owe the greatest debt to Adam Przeworski, who read and criticized successive drafts and helped in placing the analysis in a broad theoretical framework. I am also grateful to a number of persons who were kind enough to comment on various versions of the paper, forcing me to reformulate many aspects of the problem: Manuel Castells, William K. Cummings, Terence Halliday, Ida Susser, William J. Wilson, and two anonymous referees.

Migrant Labor: Functions and Reproduction

lems of adaptation, assimilation, and acculturation of the newly arrived migrant. In each instance, individuals are conceptualized as actively responding to environmental forces, maximizing their individual interests, and in this sense exercising control over their own destiny. Although these formulations are important, they are too restricted to clarify the functioning of a *system* of migrant labor either in its broader social, political, and economic contexts or where the flow of labor is regulated to a greater or lesser extent to suit dominant political and economic interests.

The shortcomings of conventional analysis are particularly apparent with regard to migrant laborers in the fields of California or the gold mines of South Africa, where specific political mechanisms regulate their movement between industry and "home." Accordingly, what is of interest is not how migrants adapt to their new environment but how structural, particularly political and legal, constraints make permanent "integration" impossible. The issues are not ones of assimilation and acculturation but of enforced segregation through such "total" institutions as the compound and labor camp and the corresponding persistence of race and ethnic differentiation. The individual cannot be conceived of as a rational actor maximizing interests under market forces. Instead, the flow of labor is directed by supramarket institutions beyond the control of an individual or even a group of migrants. For these reasons, the analysis of such systems of migrant labor requires a different perspective: one focusing on the nature of external coercive institutions and their mode of organization. The development of such an approach is the purpose of this paper.

THEORETICAL INTRODUCTION

For an economy to function, a labor force has to be maintained and renewed. In other words, workers have to subsist from day to day, and vacancies created by their departure from or by the expansion of the labor force must be filled by new recruits. Under capitalism the distinction between these two elements of the reproduction of labor power is normally concealed.[2] The same institutions simultaneously perform both renewal and

---

[2] The concept of "reproduction" is central to this paper and will be used in two empirical contexts, those of labor power and systems of migrant labor. In each context, reproduction presupposes the existence of what is being reproduced. It expresses a preoccupation with continuity, persistence, and above all repetition. The concept is motivated by the view "that nothing which exists is natural (in the nonhabitual sense of the word), but rather exists because of the existence of certain conditions, whose disappearance cannot remain without consequences" (Gramsci 1971, p. 158). Social relations, labor power, systems of migrant labor, etc., do not merely exist but have to be produced again and again—that is, *reproduced*. Analysis of the conditions of reproduction entails examining how different levels or regions of the social structure interconnect so as to ensure the repetition of the particular process of "producing" labor power,

maintenance functions. For example, the distinction between the rearing of children and the day-to-day sustenance of the productive worker is not normally inscribed in the organization of the family. On the contrary, domestic work simultaneously provides for both maintenance and renewal requirements of the labor force. Equally, in the provision of welfare, housing, and urban amenities such as transportation, the state simultaneously performs both maintenance and renewal. Only in a few institutions such as the school are renewal processes clearly separated from those of maintenance. As indicated in the distribution of family welfare benefits, even the industrial enterprise tends to treat the day-to-day maintenance of the labor force and the creation of a future one as though they constituted a single process.

By contrast, the organization of migrant labor not only makes the distinction apparent but is even defined by the separation of the processes of maintenance from those of renewal. How does this separation manifest itself? First, the two processes take place in geographically separate locations. Second, at the level of the institutions of reproduction, the institutions of maintenance may be very different from those of renewal, or a single institution may continue to engage in both processes. To take the family as an example of the latter possibility, geographical separation of the two processes is reflected in a corresponding division of labor and internal differentiation of the family unit. Thus, for Mexican migrants, processes of renewal are organized under the Mexican state in the Mexican economy and those of maintenance in the United States. Yet the kinship group remains a single cohesive unit despite its internal differentiation. What is important for this paper is that the activities of maintenance and renewal are separated.

They remain, however, indissolubly interdependent, as reflected in the oscillatory movement of migrants between work and home. Under capitalism the binding of production and reproduction is achieved through economic necessity: for the laboring population, work is necessary for survival; under feudalism the unification is achieved through coercive regulation. A system of migrant labor contains elements of each. On the one hand, renewal processes are dependent on income left over from maintenance, which is remitted home by the productive worker. On the other hand, productive workers require continued support from their families engaged in renewal

systems of migrant labor, etc. While what is being reproduced has invariant characteristics, the conditions for its reproduction may have to be modified. Thus, as we shall see, while the definition of a system of migrant labor entails the specification of a set of invariant features, the conditions of reproduction will vary between societies and over time. In addition to Marx's treatment in *Capital,* an important discussion of reproduction is to be found in Balibar (1970, chap. 3).

Migrant Labor: Functions and Reproduction

at home, because they have no permanent legal or political status at the place of work. In other words, the state[3] organizes the dependence of the productive worker on the reproductive worker, while the economy organizes the dependence of the reproductive worker on the productive worker. The interdependence establishes the cohesion of the family. Similar ties link the state supplying labor and the state employing labor: the former requires revenue and employment for its population, the latter requires labor at low wage rates.

In the following sections, I explore two implications of the separation of the maintenance and renewal processes. The first concerns the functions of migrant labor. Under such a system costs of renewal, normally borne by the employing state and economy, are to a considerable degree borne by another economy or another state or a combination of the two. Furthermore, the employer of migrant labor is neither responsible politically nor accountable financially to the external political and economic systems. In other words, a proportion of the costs of renewal is externalized to an alternate economy and/or state. The second implication concerns the conditions for the reproduction of a system of migrant labor—namely, the reproduction of its defining characteristic, the separation of maintenance and renewal processes.

The two systems of migrant labor were chosen not for their similarity but for their contrast, with a view to highlighting the invariant characteristics they share. Furthermore, I hope to show that an analysis founded on examination of the conditions for the reproduction of the invariant characteristics leads to a better understanding of the peculiarities of the individual system; that is, differences arise out of the interplay between the under-

---

[3] The notion of the capitalist state used here derives from Poulantzas (1973) and Przeworski. For our purposes, the capitalist state is constituted of formal institutions, each with an internal coherence and relative autonomy, which in combination possess the monopoly of universally binding rules to which force may be applied. Throughout the paper I associate the state with the organization of the reproduction of systems of migrant labor, thus unavoidably conferring upon it a monolithic quality it does not in practice possess. Although this is no place to elaborate on a theory of the capitalist state, two points are in order. First, I do not regard it as necessary that the capitalist state be an "instrument" of the economically dominant class. Though there are instances, particularly in the case of migrant labor in California, in which the state does indeed appear to be an instrument of the economically dominant class, this is not *implied* by our definition of the capitalist state. On the contrary, it is the relative autonomy of the capitalist state which is central to its operation. Indeed, the discussion of migrant labor in South Africa mentions significant occasions when the state clearly acted in opposition to the interests of the mine owners. Therefore, I propose a tentative formulation of the function of the capitalist state: in normal times it preserves the cohesion of a society as a whole. Second, it is a state in which a society is divided into classes; therefore, it reflects to some extent the interests and struggles of *all* classes, if only to preserve the stability of the whole.

American Journal of Sociology

lying structure and the particular political and economic context. More specifically, I argue that observed patterns of relations among races, classes, and fractions of classes emerge out of an interaction between the organization of the separation of maintenance from renewal processes and certain features of the particular industry and the particular state.

MINE WORKERS IN SOUTH AFRICA

The South African gold mines, first commercially exploited in the last decade of the 19th century, have relied on two types of migrant labor. On the one hand, unskilled tasks have been and continue to be performed by African labor recruited from the rural hinterland and surrounding territories (see Wilson 1972*a*, p. 70, for exact distribution by geographic location). Once cajoled into selling their labor power by expropriation of land, imposition of taxation, and similar nonmarket inducements, African workers became attracted to wage employment as a way of making up or supplementing their means of subsistence (Horwitz 1967, chap. 2). On the other hand, white labor, initially recruited from Britain, was employed in skilled and supervisory positions. Just as craft unions at that time had a powerful monopoly of a sector of the British labor market, so the white workers of South Africa, in part influenced by their experience at home, formed a union to protect their positions from competition from black labor (Simons and Simons 1969, chap. 3). Although mine owners wished to advance blacks into more skilled occupations, their efforts were obstructed as early as 1893 by the legal enforcement of the color bar which reserved a range of jobs for white workers. As the mining industry expanded, the color bar became an entrenched feature of the occupational structure, barring blacks from advancement into skilled and even semiskilled jobs and stipulating an upper limit to the employment ratio of blacks to whites (Wilson 1972*a*, pp. 110–19). On a number of occasions, most notably during the Rand Revolt of 1922, management attempted to breach the color bar, but the power and determination of white workers to protect their monopolistic position proved insurmountable.

Once the color bar was accepted as irrevocable, management sought to offset the costly protection of white labor by externalizing the costs of renewal of a black labor force. This process was made possible by the reproduction of the system of migrant labor. Initially a response to the insecurity of employment in industry and the lack of provision for permanent settlement near the place of work under colonial rule, migrant labor continues to be an institutionalized feature of the mining industry. Just how the system has been perpetuated and how certain labor costs are reduced under it will be examined in subsequent sections.

Migrant Labor: Functions and Reproduction

The Economic Functions of Migrant Labor

Earlier I was careful to define a system of migrant labor in institutional terms. Others have defined it in economic terms, and I now propose to consider some of the difficulties of these formulations. Wolpe (1972), Castells (1975), and, with some qualifications, Castles and Kosack (1973, chap. 9) all assert that a system of migrant labor lowers the cost of the reproduction of labor power; Wolpe goes so far as to claim that it constitutes a system of cheap labor power. However, the assessment of the costs and benefits of migrant labor and of its effects on the rate of profit is far more complicated than even Castles and Kosack (pp. 374–75, 422) indicate and requires considerably more substantiation than any of the writers provide.[4] First, they fail to distinguish among the institutions whose costs are reduced, preeminently between the state and the employer—though, of course, the·two sets of costs are not unrelated. In other words, they do not address the question, Cheap for whom? (Castles and Kosack, however, do discuss the implications for domestic labor.) Second, they do not adequately examine which aspects of the costs of the reproduction of labor power—maintenance or renewal—are reduced. Third, while it is true that migrant labor does lead to some economic savings for employer and state, the reproduction of a *system* of migrant labor in itself represents a cost which may outweigh the economic benefits based on the externalization of renewal. None of these writers considers the costs (political as well as economic) of the reproduction of a system of migrant labor.

What evidence is there to suggest that black mine workers receive little more than the costs of maintaining themselves from day to day? Virtually all black workers in the gold mines migrate between the reserves[5] or surrounding black countries and their places of employment. In other industries, migrant labor is less prevalent, and Wilson writes, "The mining industry would have to double the wages if they hoped to compete with the manufacturing sector for labor" (1972a, p. 153). His calculations appear to be based on the average earnings of Africans in different sectors, and while they do not take into consideration skill differential and pay-

---

[4] When migrant labor is referred to as "cheap," the issue is not whether a single migrant worker costs less to hire than a single domestic worker in any specific context, although that meaning is frequently conferred upon the term. Like the other writers cited here, I am considering the cost of the *system* of migrant labor. I am concerned with an institutional rather than a marginal economic analysis.

[5] The reserves are those geographical areas where the black three-quarters of the South African population are allowed to acquire permanent domicile and landed property. They represent approximately one-tenth of the area of South Africa. Bantustans are the theoretically self-governing reserves. In practice, however, the degree of self-government is so limited by their poverty that, except concerning some internal matters, Bantustans depend upon the South African government in Pretoria.

American Journal of Sociology

ments in kind, these factors alone cannot account for the observed difference. The mining industry pays less by virtue of its access to isolated labor supplies, because some proportion of the costs of renewal is assumed to be borne by a subsistence economy. But it should be noted that people in these subsistence economies (particularly the reserves) may be so poor that they are largely dependent on income remitted by kinsmen working in urban areas. Through a frugal existence in town, savings are made from what are essentially maintenance wages.

While the extraction of produce from a precapitalist mode of production redounds to the benefit of the employer of migrant labor, reliance on an alternate state or its functional equivalent redounds to the benefit of the South African state. Functions normally performed by the state, such as provision of welfare facilities, education, and social security, are transferred to the communal context of the precapitalist economy. The provision of urban amenities is therefore limited to those necessary for the single productive worker.

But pointing to the existence of "excessive exploitation" and the externalization of costs of labor-force renewal is not the same as demonstrating the existence of cheap labor. In one sense all labor is cheap simply because it is exploited.[6] In another sense, it is a more difficult concept to grapple with. *Cheap with respect to what?* It is conceivable, for example, that the reduction in the costs of reproducing labor power through access to a subsistence economy would be outweighed by the latter's replacement by a capital-intensive argicultural economy. (In fact, given the state of soil erosion in the reserves, this is unlikely, but it is the sort of question involved in examining whether a particular system of labor is cheap.) So far, I have highlighted the *economic* benefits for state and capital of a system of migrant labor, but there are also political benefits. A series of political costs are externalized to the reserves, costs associated with the residence of a large, stable black population under a white supremacist state. Indeed, the system of migrant labor is often perceived in political terms.

We cannot, however, ignore the *costs* associated with migrant labor, such as high rates of turnover, recruitment expenses, and the more general set of costs experienced by the state and arising from the political and legal conditions for the reproduction of a system of migrant labor. When all these are introduced, many of them intangible, the balance sheet becomes so complex that the notion of cheap labor, in practice if not in principle, may become impossible to handle.

[6] "Exploitation" refers to the existence of a "surplus value" remaining when the value of a worker's wage and the value of the means of production consumed by a worker are subtracted from the value of a worker's produce. The rate of exploitation is the ratio of this surplus value to the value of the wage.

Migrant Labor: Functions and Reproduction

One way of circumventing the problem is to dispense with the notion of cheap labor altogether. An alternative approach is to adopt the tautological argument that migrant labor exists because it is cheap and it is cheap because it exists. This is not as unenlightening as it might appear, for tautologies are useful if they lead to the formulation of important questions. For example, we may be led to ask what is cheap about migrant labor and thus to generate new insights.

Finally, it may be that "Cheap with respect to what?" is less appropriate than *"Cheap for whom?"* While migrant labor may be cheap for industries that rely extensively on unskilled labor and have facilities for the recruitment of migrant laborers, the smaller industry which uses skilled labor and has little access to isolated labor supplies finds a system of migrant labor more expensive. If industry bears a small minority and the state the majority of the costs of organizing a system of migrant labor, the former may find it cheap compared with other systems of labor, while the latter may find it more expensive than systems relying more on market institutions for the regulation of labor supplies. Yet at the same time, one must not forget that the state does not finance itself but relies on industry to support its activities. Thus the question of whether migrant labor is cheap for a particular industry involves not only an examination of the direct costs experienced by that industry but also secondary costs, such as taxation appropriated by the state. While "Cheap for whom?" may appear to simplify the problem, it still remains inordinately complex, and the problems of comparison—that is, Cheap for whom with respect to what and under what conditions?—are still with us.

I have argued elsewhere (Burawoy 1974) that the appearance of migrant labor in South Africa must be sought, not in its specific or general cheapness, but in the historically concrete circumstances of the articulation of different modes of production and the corresponding superstructures. At the level of function, there is nothing necessary about the system of migrant labor. It is not what Castells (1975) refers to as an "organic" part of capitalism at a particular stage in its development. Instead, it is a conjunctural feature which acts as a functional substitute for other modes of organizing labor under capitalism.

Dependence on a Capitalist Economy

I turn now to examine the conditions for the reproduction of a system of migrant labor. They naturally revolve around the separation of the means of renewal from the means of maintenance of a labor force. Two aspects of the reproduction of this separation can be delineated. First, there is the reproduction of a twin dependency upon the capitalist economy on the one hand, and upon a subsistence economy and/or alternate state on the other.

American Journal of Sociology

Second, there is the (coercive) separation of the family from the worker (in such a manner as to preserve their mutual dependence) through a series of legal and political measures and institutions.

What is the basis of a dependence on the capitalist economy, and how is it reproduced? Originally, the imposition of taxes upon the Africans living in the rural areas dislocated them from their subsistence livelihood and required them to seek employment in the emerging extractive industries. This was so, for example, for Malawians who trekked to the South African gold mines and the Zambian copper mines. In South Africa, the movement of blacks to the towns was further compounded by the state's expropriation of land, making subsistence existence increasingly difficult and reliance on an additional source of income increasingly necessary. With regard to Mozambique, Harris (1959) shows how the colonial administration forced ablebodied males into the system of migrant labor by conscription, where necessary. Even where subsistence livelihood could still be eked out, Africans have supplemented it with income from employment in the urban areas. Arrighi (1973) shows how Africans who began to respond to the demand for agricultural produce with the development of Southern Rhodesia at the beginning of this century were priced out of the market through discriminatory subsidies favoring the European farmer. Accordingly, the rewards of remaining in the rural areas and accumulating surplus produce were arranged to be less than those of entering wage employment. In this way, the colonial administration managed to generate a commitment to and, to a certain degree (taxes still had to be paid in cash), a dependence on the capitalist economy. In all these cases, Africans who engaged in productive activities in the towns were able to send home a portion of their income out of which taxes could be paid and on occasion "luxury" items bought. The broadening commitment to the South African wage economy and in particular the gold mines stems largely from the inability of the reserves in South Africa and, to a lesser extent, the rural areas of Malawi and Mozambique to support the reproduction of a labor force.

Dependence on a Subsistence Economy

Wages earned by African mine workers on the Rand are calculated on the assumption that they supplement the produce of a subsistence economy (Bettison 1960; Harris 1959). To provide some material basis for such an assumption and to ensure continuing dependence on a subsistence economy, the economy must be capable of providing for some needs. It must be continually recreated in the face of the eroding tendency of capitalism (Lenin 1960, pp. 40–41). It is necessary in this discussion, there-

Migrant Labor: Functions and Reproduction

fore, to examine the impact of an industrial economy upon the subsistence economy in the surrounding rural areas.

The rural economy in the South African reserves has been under continual decay, as soil erosion and overpopulation make the extraction of a viable existence there increasingly difficult. The South African government's recognition of this fact and its desire to prevent the further decline of the rural black economy lead Wolpe (1972) to interpret the policy of "separate development" as an endeavor to re-create the subsistence base of the migrant labor force. So far, the actual resources invested in the Bantustans are meager compared with what will be necessary to reverse the trend. One factor in the slowing down of the accumulation of land in the hands of a few Africans in the reserves and the dispossession of the majority has been the government's active policy of reproducing a system of communal land tenure and the corresponding precapitalist relations of production. How much the reserves are able to produce is a matter for some debate. In any event, the numerous prosecutions under the pass laws suggest that the dependence is more an artifact of the legal and political institutions forcing Africans back into the reserves than a result of a commitment to a viable economy.

The situation in surrounding black territories like Malawi is somewhat different. While the impact of migrant labor in some areas has contributed to the erosion of the subsistence economy, in others it has reinforced that economy. The crucial variable would appear to be the reliance of the subsistence economy on ablebodied males. Where the economy is such that the absence of males does not prevent the cultivation of crops, the earnings remitted by those absent serve to bolster the rural political economy (van Velsen 1961; Harris 1959; Watson 1958). By contrast, those economies relying on male labor for cultivation, as in "slash and burn" techniques, have tended to be adversely affected by the system of migrant labor (Richards 1939).

The Regulation of Circulation

The twin dependency on two modes of production does not reproduce itself without recourse to noneconomic institutions. We have already noted how attachment to the capitalist economy was generated by the intervention of colonial administrations in the subsistence economies and how dependency on the latter is perpetuated by preventing their erosion through supramarket intervention. The thesis I am about to outline is that the twin dependency can be better seen as a *reflection* of a set of political and legal arrangements designed to separate the means of renewal from those of maintenance and at the same time to ensure a continued connection between the two.

American Journal of Sociology

The separation of family from worker is organized through a set of laws restricting urban residence, with few exceptions, to those who are gainfully employed. The enforcement of pass laws externalizes the supplies of unemployed labor and the processes of labor-force renewal to areas where those not gainfully employed are legally permitted to reside—namely, the reserves or Bantustans and the surrounding black territories. Influx control and pass laws also ensure that, on termination of a contract with an employer, a worker returns to the "home" area before being allowed to gain further employment in the urban area. Should a worker become unemployed owing to retirement, physical disability, or simply scarcity of opportunity, he can have no legal residence outside the reserves or wherever his home may be. Such arrangements compel the worker to maintain close ties with the remainder of the family in the reserves or surrounding territories. Equally, these measures lead to the remittance of a proportion of wages earned in town and thereby supply the domestic unit with necessary commodities for the renewal of the labor force. In other words, influx control and pass laws preserve the separation of renewal and maintenance functions, prevent the stabilization of families in the urban areas and the surrender of subsistence existence in the reserves, uphold the continued interdependence of worker and family, and, finally, regulate the circulation of labor between the place of work and "home."

Restrictions on Occupational Mobility

Participation in a system of migrant labor has tended to be incompatible with employment in skilled positions (Arrighi 1973, pp. 216–18) for at least two reasons. First, for jobs requiring both training and experience for their effective performance, high rates of labor turnover could be prohibitively costly.[7] Second, entry into the more skilled occupations in any considerable numbers could result in the development of power based on the possession of a relatively scarce resource. We may conclude, therefore, that the preservation of the color bar is not merely a matter of safeguarding the interests of white workers but also represents a major factor in the reproduction of a system of migrant labor.

In this condition, we have the possible seeds of the erosion of a system of migrant labor. With its superior recruitment facilities and extensive use of unskilled labor, the mining industry has successfully adapted itself to the exigencies of a system of migrant labor. However, as manufacturing assumes an increasingly important role in the South African economy, and as the color bar is removed from increasingly higher skill levels, a greater

[7] This need not be so when the turnover arises from fluctuations in the level of employment, e.g., in the case of migrant coke workers in England at the turn of the present century (Hobsbawm 1964, chap. 9).

Migrant Labor: Functions and Reproduction

number of Africans will be engaged in skilled and supervisory positions. This is perhaps the major contradiction between the reproduction of a system of migrant labor and the development of the South African economy.[8]

Migrant Labor Powerlessness

The reproduction of a system of migrant labor hinges on the inability of the migrants, as individuals or as a group, to influence the institutions that subordinate them to the other fractions of the labor force as well as to the employer. Domination of the migrant labor force takes place in three arenas: the labor market, the industrial organization, and the state.

I shall deal with the state first. Under the capitalist state, the migrant is treated as an alien without rights of citizenship. In the South African colonial superstructure, the differential incorporation of races leaves the subordinate race with no formal power to modify fundamental institutions. The migrant has no significant political rights and only limited legal rights in the urban areas. Only in the Bantustans or reserves can Africans exercise rights of citizenship, and because of their very limited resources such participation is unable to affect their lives materially. Protest by blacks directed at the South African state has been dealt with violently, and the rise of a police state makes combination almost impossible (see, e.g., Simons and Simons 1969; Roux 1964; Kuper 1957).

In cementing the system of migrant labor, the role of ideology is not unimportant. The coincidence of racial characteristics and participation in a system of migrant labor has a number of consequences. All dominant ideologies under capitalism tend to conceal the underlying class structure; if an ideology has a strong component of racial supremacy, class differentiation is masked by the prevailing racial perspectives. This remark applies equally to the consciousness of the dominant and the dominated classes. As a result, the dominant ideology pays little attention to the economic role of migrant labor and the manner in which its exploitation is organized. Behavioral characteristics due to participation in a system of migrant labor are portrayed by the dominant ideology as racial characteristics. Migrant labor is seen as a voluntaristic form of participation in the South African economy, upholding the integrity and indigenous culture of the African people. It is considered the natural and

[8] In this connection it is interesting to note the emergence of the border industry program (Bell 1973). The South African government has tried to promote the movement of capital to labor, rather than the reverse. Industries established near the borders of the reserves enable black laborers to commute to work. Mayer (1971, "Postscript") describes the development of a township in the reserve near East London and the government's attempt to reunify productive worker and family. The Border Industry Program promoted by the Mexican government (Baerresen 1971; Briggs 1973, pp. 44–47) represents a similar movement of American capital to an external labor reservoir.

American Journal of Sociology

inevitable form of black labor. It purportedly reflects the strength of
tradition pulling the African from the foreign and corrosive urban area
to his natural environment and thereby solidifying his so-called tribal
allegiances. Instead of there being an inherent conflict between the dominant ideology and the system of migrant labor, the former reinforces and
legitimates the coexistence of two structurally different modes of organization of labor distributed according to racial characteristics.

Domination within industry is enforced with the cooperation of the
state, as when strike action is suppressed. Though not actually illegal,
trade union organization among blacks has been thwarted through "racial
discrimination in the law and in labor practices; government obstruction
and intimidation; and colour prejudice among white workers" (Hepple
1971, p. 72). Only 2% of black workers in South Africa are organized
into trade unions. The structural conflict between migrant labor and organized nonmigrant white workers redounds to the advantage of the employer. The conflict is based on competition over the distribution of
income *within* the working class. Concessions extracted from the mine
owners by one group are granted, to a considerable extent, at the expense
of the other group. For example, the restrictive practices and development
of a strong white trade union led to the institutionalization of a system of
migrant labor incorporating an ever-increasing earnings gap between
black and white workers (Wilson 1972a, p. 46). Not surprisingly, white
workers have assisted management in the subordination of black workers
within industry, for example, through the breaking of strikes. Equally,
white workers are ever conscious of management's interest in breaching
the color bar and advancing black workers into more skilled positions.
This reinforces divisions within the working class. In addition, the black
labor force has been the victim of collusion among the different mining
companies in wage fixing. With the development of the Chamber of Mines
to coordinate policies of the industry in areas of common interest to the
various companies, there arose a common wage policy based on the principle of "maximum average" (Horwitz 1967, p. 27). Such industrywide
policies prevented competition for labor from redounding to the advantage
of the black migrant workers.

Finally, I turn to the domination of black workers in the labor market.
The superior recruitment organizations of the mining industry give it
monopolistic access to such labor reservoirs as Malawi and Mozambique
and even more distant territories. In 1973 foreign labor accounted for
80% of the blacks employed. Since pass laws preclude the development of
a labor reservoir within the urban areas, they favor industries with effective recruitment organizations which employ black labor in primarily
unskilled occupations. With a weaker recruitment capacity, manufacturing
industry has to restrict itself to a labor supply from the reserves, for which

Migrant Labor: Functions and Reproduction

it competes with all other employers of black labor. Overpopulation in the reserves and diminishing subsistence levels have led to increases in earnings necessary to supplement rural incomes. Being less dependent on South African labor and drawing extensively on foreign labor reservoirs where subsistence levels have not declined, the mining industry has managed to maintain the real earnings of its black workers at approximately the same level over the past 60 years (Wilson 1972a, table 5).

A System of Migrant Labor Which Failed to Reproduce Itself

So far I have argued that the distinguishing feature of a system of migrant labor is the separation of processes of renewal from those of maintenance. Further, this separation is not a natural or voluntaristic phenomenon but must be enforced through a set of political and legal mechanisms which presuppose that the migrant is without citizenship rights and has only limited power in the state of employment. Therefore, when the specific mechanisms that enforce the circulation of labor, restrict its upward mobility, and establish the migrant's powerlessness are relaxed or disappear, if my thesis is correct, we should then expect the system to fail to reproduce itself. In this context the decline of migrant labor in Zambia is pertinent.[9]

Prior to the Labour Government's assumption of power in Britain after the Second World War, the pattern of migrant labor between the Northern Rhodesian (now Zambian) copper mines and the rural hinterland followed that just described for South Africa. Until the postwar period, the colonial administration actively organized the political and legal mechanisms that separated the worker from his family. Subsequently, the administration retreated from the performance of these functions for reasons related to Zambia's status as a British protectorate. First, Africans were not merely allowed to organize trade unions but in some instances were actively encouraged to do so. Later in the 1950s, political parties representing the African population began to appear. At the same time, the colonial government became less resolute in defending the color bar in industry (particularly the copper industry). Without support from the colonial administration, white workers were unable to prevent the removal of the color bar from jobs which they had previously monopolized. As restrictions on African advancement were being relaxed, regulations on the geographical movement of black workers began to disappear also. Significantly, in the early 1950s the mining companies began to dispense with their "pole-and-dagga" huts and to build family accommodations for their black employees.

[9] Epstein (1958) and Burawoy (1972, chap. 2) describe these changes as they occurred on the Northern Rhodesian copper belt.

American Journal of Sociology

Thus, the separation of renewal and maintenance functions was being slowly and even deliberately undermined. Finally, shifts in ideology from white supremacy to evolutionary movement to African self-determination further weakened the legitimacy of migrant labor and the regulatory mechanisms necessary for its reproduction. Therefore, we may tentatively conclude that, unless separated by a specific set of political and legal institutions, the processes of maintenance and renewal tend to coalesce. In other words, economic factors by themselves cannot enforce the separation of worker from family but must be supplemented by structures of coercion.

Systems of migrant labor, as they have existed or continue to exist in southern Africa, may be regarded as "pure" types. State organization of the separation of maintenance from renewal is transparent. Further, I have shown how a system of migrant labor dissolves when the state no longer performs this function. But the framework developed is of limited interest if it can be applied only to southern Africa. The question before us now is: Can the framework be extended to shed light on the nature of migrant labor in other, radically different countries?

FARM LABOR IN CALIFORNIA

The discussion here is complicated by the more variegated history of seasonal agricultural labor in California. I will endeavor to highlight the aspects most relevant to comparison with South African mine workers and to the development of a more general framework for the analysis of systems of migrant labor in capitalist societies.

Because California is the United States's largest agricultural producer, farm labor has assumed a critical role in its development. The history of farm labor is the history of a succession of labor reservoirs. Each group entered as a domestic migratory or alien migrant labor force, but, before stabilizing, voluntarily left agriculture for employment in other sectors of the economy or was removed forcibly and succeeded by a new group of migrants.

The Chinese were the first immigrant group to respond to the seasonal demands of California agriculture. They were rendered occupationally immobile by discriminatory practices, and their stabilization coincided with increasing demands for Chinese exclusion by domestic labor during the last two decades of the 19th century (McWilliams 1964, chap. 2). With the eclipse of Chinese labor, whites affected by the depression of the 1890s were recruited for work in the fields; but with the return of economic prosperity, a new reservoir was tapped—the Japanese (ibid., chap. 4). By the end of the first decade of this century, the Japanese had superseded every other group, only to lose their dominance to Mexicans by 1915. After the First World War and increasingly until the Second, white domestic

Migrant Labor: Functions and Reproduction

labor was again recruited for farm work. Although attempts to settle the dust bowl migratory workers of the 1930s into camps were made, they were never very successful (McWilliams 1971, chap. 16). Many laborers were recruited from the skid rows of California cities for temporary jobs in agriculture (Fisher 1953, pp. 51–57; Anderson 1923; Parker 1920).

The wartime demand for labor outside agriculture threatened the supply of domestic labor. The governments of Mexico and the United States signed an agreement providing for the use of Mexican labor under contract in farm employment. Known as the bracero program, this was the first governmentally administered system of migrant labor in agriculture. At the same time as braceros entered legally under contract, illegal migrants, referred to as "wetbacks," were also crossing the border from Mexico in search of employment. Their numbers have varied according to such factors as the state of the Mexican economy (Gamio 1930, chaps. 1, 12), the stringency of border controls (Samora 1971), and the availability of jobs in the United States (see Frisbie [1975] for a statistical analysis of economic push and pull factors). Although the actual number of illegal Mexican entrants is not known, the number apprehended annually rose steadily from the early 1940s to a peak of over a million in 1954 (Galarza 1964, chap. 8). Recent studies indicate that with the termination of the bracero program in 1965 the number of illegal entrants has again risen, while commuters who live in Mexico and work in the United States have assumed a new prominence in the border states (North 1970, chaps. 1, 3). Meanwhile, domestic labor has organized itself in an attempt to prevent competition from labor recruited legally or illegally from foreign labor pools.

The Economic Functions of Migrant Labor

Castells (1975) indicates that, in addition to suffering excessive exploitation, migrant labor functions as a regulator of capitalist crises, cushioning the impact of the expansion and contraction of capital. When industry faces a recession, for example, migrant workers are particularly easy to lay off. The nature of agricultural production, rather than capitalist crises, gives rise to fluctuations in the demand for farm labor. Nonetheless, migrant labor performs the same "regulatory" function in California agribusiness, providing for seasonal labor requirements.

> The basic dilemma faced by farm employers, particularly those with farm operations requiring seasonal hands in large numbers, is this: They want a labor supply which, on the one hand, is ready and willing to meet the short-term work requirements and which, on the other hand, will not impose social and economic problems on them or on the community when work is finished. This is what is expected of migratory workers. The de-

1065

American Journal of Sociology

> mand for migratory workers is thus twofold: To be ready to go to work
> when needed; to be gone when not needed. [U.S. President's Commission
> on Migratory Labor 1951, p. 16]

The more generic function of a system of migrant labor—namely, the
externalization of the costs of labor force renewal and low wage labor—is
complicated by the coexistence of three different labor systems in California. First, there are migrants who circulate between Mexico and
California. They constitute a system of external migrant labor. Second,
there are aliens who reside in California throughout the year. They constitute a system of internal migrant labor. Finally, there is a domestic labor
force which migrates from place to place in search of employment. It does
not constitute a system of migrant labor as defined here. I shall refer to
this fraction of the labor force as migratory labor. At different periods in
the history of California agriculture, different systems have been dominant.

The migrants from Mexico bear the closest resemblance to Africans from
Malawi or the reserves working in the South African mining industry. In
both cases the system of migrant labor facilitates the externalization of
the costs of renewal and the provision of earnings at a level commensurable
with the day-to-day existence of the farm laborer.[10] A system of internal
migration has no obvious parallel with the South African situation. Japanese, Chinese, and many Mexican aliens who worked in the fields during
the harvest period did not return "home" in the off-season but eked out
an existence in California towns. As a result, they became a potential
burden upon the state where they were employed. At the same time, because they were mainly single, ablebodied men, the processes of maintenance were separated from those of renewal, which took place in their
country of origin (see, e.g., Fuller 1940, p. 19824).

Domestic migratory labor distinguishes itself from migrant labor by the
fusion of the functions of labor-force renewal and maintenance. The employer and/or state must bear all the costs of reproducing labor power.
Other techniques are adapted to compensate for the inability to externalize
costs in the case of domestic migratory workers. The prevailing adaptation
has been the exploitation of family labor in picking crops, so that earnings
of the *individual* can be maintained at inordinately low levels. If we look

[10] According to the 1960 census, over half the Chicano families living in the rural areas
had an income below $3,000 and 14% received less than $1,000 (Briggs 1973, p. 23).
Another survey showed that commuters from Mexico were being paid average hourly
rates of $1.65 (if they were Mexican nationals, i.e., "green card" commuters [see n. 12])
and $1.45 (if they were U.S. citizens) (North 1970, p. 114). The corresponding annual
incomes were, respectively $3,910 and $2,984 (ibid., p. 117), both falling below the
poverty line. Illegal migrants from Mexico were paid at rates between those of green
card commuters and U.S. citizen commuters (ibid., p. 116). According to Samora (1971,
pp. 98–102), in the El Paso region in 1969 the going wage for wetbacks was between
$0.75 and $1.10 per hour—far below the national minimum wage of $1.60.

Migrant Labor: Functions and Reproduction

upon wages as the costs of maintaining and renewing the family, the greater the number employed within each family, the less each individual member has to be paid. In this way, the earnings of domestic labor are kept at the level paid to internal and external migrants. However, with domestic labor the state of employment has to bear a set of costs, such as welfare for the old and young and education, even though these may be small as compared with costs for other sectors of the national labor force.

Although there is evidence to suggest that growers prefer a system of migrant labor to a system of migratory labor (U.S. President's Commission on Migratory Labor 1951, p. 16), there have been periods in California history, particularly during economic depressions, when migrant labor barely existed. More recently, the organization of migratory labor in the United Farm Workers Union and the eclipse of the bracero program have led to an increase in the use of domestic labor. Clearly the interests of the state, as defined by such factors as the level of employment and the political power of domestic groups, interact with the interests of the growers to determine the relative importance of each system of labor.

The issue of cheap labor arises in the California context, just as it did for South Africa. The immediate economic gains to growers from the use of migrant labor may be more apparent in the case of farm labor. First, migrant labor is a common form of adaptation to seasonal fluctuations in the demand for unskilled work. For example, in the first half of the 19th century, Irish migrants traveled to England to work as farm laborers during harvest periods and returned to Ireland during the slack seasons (Redford 1926, pp. 122–29). They were also paid less than domestic labor. Second, the system of migrant labor is not such a "total" institution in California as it is in South Africa, and it may require fewer resources for its reproduction. It appears to be less a response to government intervention than a direct reflection of the economic interests of the growers. It may be argued that in South Africa political costs as well as economic costs are being externalized, whereas in California the economic costs are paramount. So long as migrant labor was readily available, the need for capital substitution was not urgently felt. But with moves in the direction of effective union organization of domestic migratory workers and the dissolution of the bracero program, growers have turned increasingly to picking by mechanization.

Twin Dependency

In discussing South Africa, I noted that a system of migrant labor involved a twin dependency on two separated economies. This is also true, but in a weaker sense, in California. External migrants—essentially Mexicans—

American Journal of Sociology

depend on their own state and to a lesser extent on employment in the United States. In the case of internal migrants, there is an overriding dependency on employment in the United States; and, like external migrants, they have tended to be restricted to such marginal occupations as farm labor. In both instances, there is a separation of the processes of labor-force maintenance from those of renewal, but the connection between the two is stronger for external migrants.

With respect to the migrant's dependency on employment in the South African economy, I noted the deliberate policies of the colonial administration to force the African population off the land and into the labor market to create an industrial work force and also remove competition with white farmers in the commodity market for agricultural products. These goals were achieved through the expropriation of land and the levying of taxes. The dependency of Mexicans on the United States economy cannot be reduced to such terms. The availability of Mexican labor has been contingent upon such factors as the state of the Mexican economy and political change, as in the revolutionary period between 1910 and 1930 which led to the release of many Mexicans from peonage in the haciendas.

However, at a more general level the proximity of the United States has been a factor in the persistent underdevelopment of Mexico, making it difficult for that nation to absorb the full potential of its labor force or to compete with wages available in the United States. Furthermore, the very sale of labor power by an underdeveloped country, such as Malawi or Mexico, to an economically advanced nation serves only to reinforce the relations of economic subjugation and domination. This is so despite protestations by the South African and United States governments that in employing nationals of underdeveloped countries they are doing these countries a service. In a narrow sense, they are doing just that by absorbing surplus labor that could present a political threat to the underdeveloped nation and by providing rural workers with "their only real opportunity for economic self improvement" and the possibility of remitting income home (Hancock 1959, p. 122). In a broader context, however, migrant labor exists only because of the uneven development of capitalism and reflects the economic dependence of Mexico on the United States and Malawi on South Africa.

It should be noted that some Mexicans who cross the border to work do not in fact return to Mexico on the termination of their employment, just as there are many Malawians residing illegally in South Africa. Many Mexicans attempt to find jobs elsewhere in the United States. Being illegal residents in the United States makes them much more vulnerable to arbitrary exploitation by employers. In many respects their position is akin to that of the internal migrant who faces limited employment opportunity and discriminatory practices. The Chinese and Japanese during those

Migrant Labor: Functions and Reproduction

periods when they dominated farm labor were dependent on finding employment in marginal occupations. Unlike Mexicans, they could not easily return home and become the responsibility of another state. However, because they are single, internal migrants can subsist on relatively small incomes.

Finally, brief mention should be made of attempts to establish a system of migrant labor among domestic workers when they dominated the farm-labor force in the interwar period. Apart from increasing exploitation through the employment of family labor, there were moves among growers to create subsistence economies so as to reduce the burden of the work force on the state and to stabilize its movement. Such programs for "land colonization" stemmed from the potential shortage of labor and the costs of armies of unemployed during the slack season, but they achieved little success before growers discovered alternative external labor reservoirs (McWilliams 1971, pp. 92–96, 200–210; U.S. Congress 1940, pp. 230–31, 240, 250). In effect, the programs were efforts to set up a system of "reserves" as in South Africa or a system of workhouses like those which provided a pool of labor for English employers in agriculture and industry during the 18th century (Redford 1926, pp. 21–23).

More common has been the technique of engendering dependence through the distribution of relief. Unemployed domestic labor is maintained during the slack season by the judicious provision of relief immediately suspended when openings appear in the fields. This ensures the availability of labor in the busy season (McWilliams 1971, pp. 285–96). Similar mechanisms for the distribution of relief appeared in England at the end of the 18th century: ". . . the perpetuation of the Speenhamland and 'roundsman' systems, in all their variety, was ensured by the demand of the larger farmers—in an industry which has exceptional requirements for occasional or casual labor—for a permanent cheap labor reserve" (Thompson 1968, p. 244). As the study of Piven and Cloward (1971, chaps. 1, 4) suggests, the distribution of poor relief is designed to meet the conditions for dual dependency upon the state on the one hand and the employer on the other, so that labor may be mobilized and distributed to accommodate the changing demands of the economy. Poor relief, therefore, may be regarded as a functional equivalent of migrant labor, in that both perform the same regulatory function, cushioning the seasonal labor requirements of the agricultural industry.

The Regulation of Circulation

Poor relief and land colonization are designed to control the movement of *domestic* labor, so that it is available where and when it is needed and does not constitute a liability where and when it is not needed. What mechanisms are available to control the movement of external migrants such as those from Mexico? The work contract, defining the relationship between migrant workers and growers or intermediaries, is by its very nature only for temporary employment; after it has expired, the workers have no alternative but to leave the agricultural areas. They may leave for their homes across the border, move into a California town, or migrate to some other part of the United States.

Just as influx control enforces the separation of maintenance and renewal functions while regulating the return of labor to its home, similar mechanisms operate to regulate the movement of Mexican migrants. Thus, border patrol (Samora 1971, chaps. 1, 2) attempts to restrict illegal immigration into the United States. Immigration laws are designed to separate workers from their families, so that the costs of labor-force renewal are borne in Mexico while the United States employer and government, either at the federal or regional level, are responsible only for maintaining workers during the period of employment (North 1970, pp. 92–93).

Immigration laws and their enforcement by border patrol and other government agencies aim to prevent the emergence of pools of unemployed Mexicans liable to become public charges. At the same time, they provide growers and other employers with adequate supplies of labor. The consolidation of the bracero program in the 1950s was accompanied by more stringent policies of influx control. During this period, immigration authorities attempted to restrict migration across the border to workers contracted for agricultural employment by agencies established in Mexico. At the same time, legislative measures in the United States were introduced to prevent braceros from "escaping" from farm employment and seeking jobs elsewhere. Accordingly, each worker was given a card bearing a contract number, an employer's name, and the names of counties in which it was valid (Galarza 1964, p. 83). In other words, it was a species of the notorious South African pass. These types of restriction on migrant employment in the United States and the removal of migrants from the country when the contract expired ensured their continuing reliance on Mexico and a binding connection to the processes of labor-force renewal.

Restrictions on Occupational Mobility

The return of migrants to their homes after the termination of the employment contract serves to restrict them to unskilled occupations in particular sectors of employment. Under the system of migrant labor found in South Africa, the color bar broadly defines the boundaries between jobs monopolized by migrants and those held as the preserve of domestic white labor. Structural conflict within the working class of the mining industry occurs in a vertical dimension between a white labor aristocracy and black migrant

Migrant Labor: Functions and Reproduction

labor. By contrast, within California agriculture there is no need for the counterpart of a color bar, because virtually all jobs are unskilled. At the same time, the equivalent of a color bar does operate to prevent mobility out of agricultural employment.

The result is that conspicuous conflicts have occurred in the horizontal dimension between migrant workers (Chinese, Japanese, Mexicans, etc.) and domestic workers (white depression victims, Chicanos, etc.). Differing relations to the means of production have not been the axis of manifest conflict; on the contrary, the working class has been internally divided as a result of differing relations to superstructural elements—that is, differences of legal and political status in the place of employment. Though weak in comparison with organized labor, domestic farm labor is potentially more powerful than are migrant workers. Thus, during the last decade of the 19th century, domestic labor successfully resisted displacement by Chinese labor. Growers continued to employ Chinese labor after legislation had been passed to provide for the exclusion from employment of Chinese not legally resident in the country. The refusal of growers to bow before pressure from labor organizations led to riots throughout the state between 1893 and 1896, eventually forcing the removal of Chinese from the fields (McWilliams 1971, pp. 74–80; Fuller 1940, pp. 19814–15). Since then, domestic labor has had only limited success in establishing itself as a permanent farm-labor force, reflecting its vulnerability to the political power of agribusiness.

The Vulnerability of Farm Labor

In discussing the reproduction of the system of migrant labor in South Africa, I contrasted the strength of the domestic white workers with the powerlessness of black migrants who confront a state organized for their repression. The perpetuation of the system turns on the ability of white workers to maintain the color bar at a skill level consistent with migrant labor. In California, the situation is reversed. There the reproduction of the system of migrant labor rests, not on the strength, but on the weakness of domestic labor, its inability to prevent growers from drawing upon foreign supplies of labor. We take it for granted that the migrant—internal or external—has little or no power, few if any rights, and virtually no means of appealing against infringements of his labor contract.[11] There-

[11] This is not entirely correct. Particularly in the case of braceros there is a long history of attempts by the Mexican government, under pressure from organized labor in Mexico and anti-American interests, to protect the rights of Mexican nationals employed in the U.S. Southwest. This has sometimes involved blacklisting employers who failed to comply with the terms of the agreement signed between the two governments concerning the working conditions and rights of braceros. For a period during the Second World War, the Mexican government refused to authorize braceros for work in Texas

American Journal of Sociology

fore, what is of interest is the manner in which *domestic* laborers have been systematically prevented from forcing the growers to employ them and them alone, under minimum wage conditions.

Farm labor has traditionally been excluded from labor legislation (Briggs 1973, chap. 5; Myers 1959). For example, the National Labor Relations Act of 1964 excluded farm workers from unemployment compensation. From 1910 to 1956, farm wages ranged from 40% to 75% below factory wages (Hancock 1959, p. 25). In 1966 farm wages were half the average of those in industrial employment as a whole. When domestic labor has threatened to organize, it has been either displaced by migrant labor— external or internal—or violently repressed. Thus, Galarza (1964, pt. 4) describes in detail how the bracero program fostered the replacement of domestic labor with Mexican labor paid at prevailing rates, ones which domestic workers found unacceptable since they were based on labor-force maintenance rather than maintenance and renewal. In this way the braceros came to dominate the picking of a number of crops. The segmentation of the farm-labor force into migrants (legal or illegal) and domestics has obstructed the development of effective union organization. As recently as 1973, strike activity by the United Farm Workers Union was unable to prevent the gathering of the harvest crop by labor recruited from foreign countries.

In other words, the ability of domestic labor to organize itself is severely circumscribed by the power of the growers, who have gained monopolistic access to external labor reservoirs. In achieving these ends, there has been a long history of collaboration between farmers and immigration authorities (Greene 1969) and of collusion between farmers and state police in suppressing labor organizations and labor protest. Where police efforts have been inadequate or ineffectual, growers have shown no hesitation in recruiting "citizen armies" and vigilante groups to combat resistance from farm labor (see, e.g., McWilliams 1971, chaps. 14, 15; U.S. Congress 1940, which was devoted to these issues). While the federal government has been aware of the collaboration of the rich and powerful in California and of the use of the state as an instrument for protecting the economic

---

because of instances of extreme racial discrimination. In practice, growers either ignored many conditions of the bracero contract or chose to use illegal migrants when they were available. A historical treatment of attempts by the Mexican government to secure reasonable conditions for contract labor working in the United States under the bracero programs may be found in Scruggs (1960, 1963). The U.S. Labor Department has also tried to enforce conditions laid down in the bracero program. However, in the early 1960s such attempts in the Texas cotton harvest led to court cases in which growers entered suits against the Department of Labor. Where the court's ruling upheld the government, growers rapidly introduced cotton harvesting by mechanization, and the plight of domestic labor was exacerbated (Jones 1965, pp. 131–52). The severity of the growers' reaction attests to the infrequency with which conditions of employment of Mexicans were actually regulated.

Migrant Labor: Functions and Reproduction

interests of large-scale farmers, the strength of the farm lobby in Washington has managed to prevent any effective intervention (Galarza 1970). As recently as 1974, despite opposition from organized labor, the Supreme Court sanctioned the use of foreign migrants on the basis of the administrative fiction that they are legal residents of the United States.[12]

The power of the growers is reflected in their ability to establish common wage rates, and even in times of labor scarcity, these have prevented competition from redounding to the advantage of farm labor. Fisher (1953), McWilliams (1971), Galarza (1964), and others have documented the collaboration of growers in employer associations to define what is in effect a "maximum average," though it is referred to as the "prevailing wage." In theory, the prevailing rates are to be fixed by the free play of the market. In fact, they are established unilaterally by the growers according to the same criteria followed by the South African Chamber of Mines: ". . . a wage which is fair to one's neighbor in that it is no higher, and a wage which is fair to oneself in that it is no lower" (Fisher 1953, p. 110).

Unilateral wage fixing, monopolistic recruitment, militant antiunionism, and powerful lobbies in central government imply an inordinate concentration of power. For some time commentators have viewed the low wage levels and unhealthy working conditions of farm labor as a consequence of the concentration of land ownership and the vertical integration with the cannery industry, which has engaged in price fixing (McWilliams 1971, pp. 279–80). With the concentration of ownership and the absorption of agriculture into a national food industry, recent years have witnessed the entry of large corporations and industrial conglomerates into large-scale farming. Thus, one discovers that the four leading private owners of agricultural land are Southern Pacific Company, Tenneco Incorporated (the large oil and chemical conglomerate), Tejon Ranch Company (half owned by the *Los Angeles*

[12] Farm workers brought a suit for "declaratory and injunctive" relief with respect to the practice of the Immigration and Naturalization Service in permitting some aliens living in Mexico and Canada to commute to work in the United States on a daily and seasonal basis (October 17, 1974). The Supreme Court ruled (November 25, 1974) by a margin of five to four that "both the daily and seasonal commuters were immigrants who were lawfully admitted for permanent residence and were returning from temporary visit abroad when they entered the United States and were different from those groups of aliens which could be admitted only on certificate by the Secretary of Labor" (*Supreme Court Reporter* 1974, p. 272). The declaration supported the long-standing administrative practice of allowing migrants from Mexico to enter the United States for temporary work (42,000 daily commuters, of whom 25,000 are involved in agriculture, and 8,300 seasonal commuters), on the grounds that such migrants were permanent residents of the United States and therefore not subject to either quota restrictions or certification by the Secretary of Labor (such immigrants use the green card as a reentry permit in lieu of an immigrant visa). Dissenting judges felt the ruling was based on an "administrative construction of a statute which conflicts with the express meaning of the statutory terms" (ibid., p. 283), but it has provided growers with unrestricted access to an external labor supply and as a result has constituted a major obstacle to the effective unionization of domestic workers.

American Journal of Sociology

Times Mirror Corporation), and Standard Oil of California (see Fellmeth 1971, vol. 1, chap. 1; vol. 2, appendix 1B; Agribusiness Accountability Project 1972). If this were not enough, the problems facing the United Farm Workers Union have been compounded by the intervention of the International Brotherhood of Teamsters, which has signed "sweetheart" contracts with many of the growers.

Does the dominant ideology exercise a moderating influence on the arbitrary use of this power and in particular on the reproduction of the system of migrant labor? Whereas the South African ideology of white supremacy legitimates the colonial superstructure (Burawoy 1974) that organizes the conditions of reproduction of the system of migrant labor and institutionalizes migrant powerlessness, the dominant ideology in the United States is conditioned by notions of "equality," "justice," and "citizenship." Accordingly, the United States government has frequently appeared to resist the use of migrant labor in agriculture, particularly when subjected to pressures from organized labor concerned to protect domestic farm workers (Hawley 1966; Scruggs 1960). The various bracero programs since 1942 have required growers to provide evidence of a shortage of domestic labor and to make visible attempts to recruit such labor. The agreement between the United States and Mexico also stipulated that braceros had to be paid at prevailing rates, and employers were required to make contributions to insurance schemes, housing, and nonprofit canteen facilities and to offer each worker a minimum number of hours of work every week (see, e.g., Galarza 1964, pts. 2, 3).

While these provisions are to be found in the agreements signed between the governments of the United States and Mexico, their execution has been quite a different matter. To supervise the scheme, the United States government appointed bodies sympathetic to the interests of the growers. Together with associations of farm employers, these bodies worked out ways to circumvent the provisions (Fisher 1953, chaps. 4, 5; Galarza 1964, pts. 4, 5). It was in the administration of the program that the government was able to conciliate the powerful growers opposed to restrictions imposed on their employment practices.

If the dominant ideology does not exercise much constraint over the practices of growers, it does tend to conceal those practices. First, it presents United States agriculture as composed of a large number of small-scale independent farmers who work on their own land. This hides the decline in the numbers of such independent farmers and the fact, particularly significant in California, that the overwhelming proportion of land is owned by industrial consortiums and worked by a migrant or migratory labor force. Second, the dominant ideology tends to obscure the typical conditions of migrant-labor exploitation. Just as in South Africa the racial perspectives of separate development have tended to conceal the position of

Migrant Labor: Functions and Reproduction

particular groups with respect to the means of production, in the United States the combination of an ideology which stresses ethnic pluralism with the coincidence of ethnicity and occupation has had a similar effect. Whereas in South Africa conflict between migrants and nonmigrants is highlighted but seen in racial terms, in California conflict between migrant and domestic labor is masked by their common Mexican heritage.

CONCLUSION

We have learned that one condition for the separation of maintenance and renewal processes lies in the political status of migrant laborers. It is their relation to the state—the denial of legal, political, and civil rights—that distinguishes migrant workers from domestic workers. The distinction holds for both mine workers on the Rand and farm laborers in California. At the same time, we have observed a marked contrast in relations between domestic and migrant workers in the two areas. In South Africa a caste division in the form of a color bar separates the two sectors of the labor force, while in the United States competition between domestic and migrant labor prevails. In the former country, domestic labor has access to considerable resources of political power, while in the latter it appears relatively weak. What does this discrepancy signify?

The State and Its Bearing on the Reproduction of Migrant Labor

The fact that unbridled competition between migrant and domestic labor is as ubiquitous in the United States as it is restricted and regulated in South Africa, *irrespective* of the particular industry, indicates that the skill differentials found in the mining industry and absent in agriculture cannot explain the different patterns of relations between migrant and domestic workers in our two case studies.[13] On the contrary, it suggests that we must turn to broader characteristics of the two societies in order to understand the differences alluded to in the previous paragraph.

First, there is the simple demographic fact that migrant labor, legal and illegal, is *relatively* insignificant in the United States (though not as insignificant as is commonly supposed) as compared with its central role in the South African labor system. Second, domestic labor in South Africa constitutes a minority segment of the total labor force and as a result is *relatively* undifferentiated as compared with the domestic labor force in the United States. The simple dichotomy between domestic workers with rights of citizenship and migrants with no rights may be a useful simplifi-

[13] Outside the context of gold mining, there is the added complication in South Africa that not all black labor is obviously migrant labor (see, e.g., Wilson 1972*b*, chap. 4).

American Journal of Sociology

cation in the South African context, but it is too crude for the United States, where such marginal fractions of the domestic labor force as migratory farm workers are incomparably weaker than organized labor in other sectors of the economy.

At the same time, the numerical and functional significance of migrant labor is contingent upon the state's capacity to reproduce a system of migrant labor. I have emphasized repeatedly that the volume of migrant labor is not something to be taken as given but is *created and recreated by the state*. Within a single nation, the *state* determines the relative importance of migrant and domestic labor. Accordingly, changes in the organization of the state, as in Zambia, can go so far as to transform a numerically dominant sector of the labor force from migrant to domestic status and at the same time deny a minority sector its domestic status. Similarly, in contrast to other European countries, Britain has until recently awarded full citizenship rights to immigrants from other parts of the Commonwealth. Whereas immigrants to France, Germany, and Switzerland have tended to assume the status of migrants, in Britain they became part of the domestic labor force (Castles and Kosack 1973, chap. 11). To what extent the political status of immigrants actually affects their economic status has been an issue for debate, with some playing down the importance of differences (Castles and Kosack 1973) and others giving them greater emphasis (Rex 1974). The point is, however, that the state determines whether an immigrant is to be a migrant or a domestic worker. Therefore, the first two factors considered above—the demographic importance of migrant labor and the differentiation of the domestic labor force—are contingent upon a third: the nature of the state, its organization and in particular the relative autonomy of the economy with respect to the political system.

In South Africa a dual labor market is organized by a monolithic state, so that one sector is largely composed of migrant workers and the other of domestic workers. In the United States, on the other hand, with its less centralized state apparatus, the dual labor market is defined in terms of relation to the economic structure. Low-profit service and competitive industries with an unstable nonunionized or weakly unionized labor force produce the lower income strata of the working class, while high-profit monopoly industry with stable unionized labor accounts for the higher income strata (O'Connor 1973, chap. 1; Harrison 1972). The dominant division in the South African labor market is based on relation to the state, whereas that in the United States is based on industry of employment, that is, relation to the economy. In one instance, migrant labor constitutes the basis of an entire segment of the labor force; in the other, it forms but a fraction of a segment. Yet in both instances, although for different reasons, the reproduction of migrant labor deepens the division

Migrant Labor: Functions and Reproduction

between the two segments. We may conclude, therefore, that the relevant differences between South Africa and the United States turn on the relative autonomy of the economy with respect to the state. In South Africa an overarching state intervenes in the organization of productive and market relations, whereas in the United States productive and market relations are reproduced with significantly less intervention from the state.

What, then, has this analysis of reproduction requirements accomplished? I have assumed that, although the conditions of reproduction may vary over time and between societies, what is being reproduced is defined by certain invariant structures. In the case of migrant labor, the invariant structure was found to be the separation of maintenance and renewal processes. Furthermore, the unique characteristics and consequences of a given system of migrant labor emerge out of the interplay between the invariant structure and a specific economic and political context. In other words the marked dissimilarity of the systems of migrant labor in South Africa and the United States may be attributed to the differing political, ideological, and economic situations in which the separation of maintenance and renewal processes is organized. Thus, reproduction analysis is a powerful tool in comparative analysis, between societies and over time, because it accounts simultaneously for similarity and diversity. Yet the very strength of such analysis is also its major weakness, as is apparent in my treatment of labor power. Throughout, I have assumed that labor power itself is invariant. This is implied by limiting the reproduction of labor power to two processes—maintenance and renewal. The treatment ignored the possibility that labor power, like machinery, may be adapted to the changing demands of capital and technological innovation. In my examples of migrant labor, adaptation is not a significant factor, because the jobs performed remain the same over time. But extending the analysis of reproduction of labor power to an entire labor force over a long period shows that requisite skills, education, and socialization in the broadest sense, that is, the content of labor power, undergo considerable change (Braverman 1974). Changes in the structure of capitalism, such as the consolidation of the dual economy, have repercussions for processes of labor force adaptation (Bowles 1972). In other words, a diachronic rather than synchronic analysis of the reproduction of labor power cannot, in general, restrict itself to the processes of maintenance and renewal but must be extended to include processes of adaptation.

The Rise and Fall of Systems of Migrant Labor

So far, I have established the conditions for the reproduction of a system of migrant labor, but a complete theory of reproduction should embrace a characteristic dynamics (Cortés, Przeworski, and Sprague 1974, pp. 279–

1077

American Journal of Sociology

80). The reproduction of any system in and of itself creates tendencies toward its change and persistence. Moreover, these tendencies can be deduced from the "laws" or conditions of reproduction. Are there any rudimentary processes which might constitute a theory of the dynamics of a system of migrant labor? Or are the changes brought about by the internal structure of the system, that is, by its dynamics, swamped by external exigencies which impinge in an unpredictable fashion upon the system?

I noted that the system of migrant labor in Zambia dissolved primarily because the colonial state disengaged itself from the organization of the separation of the maintenance and renewal processes. To what extent was this the product of a dynamics immanent in the structure of the system of migrant labor and its reproduction? To what extent was it the result of external forces? The expansion of the Northern Rhodesian (Zambian) economy required the expansion of the system of migrant labor. The increased involvement of Africans in wage employment led to their organization initially into tribal associations but also into embryonic and, later, strong trade unions. Organized economic class struggles inevitably led to increased remuneration and consequently undermined the foundations of the system of migrant labor and precipitated its dissolution. Advancing with economic struggles, political struggles eroded another central requirement of the reproduction of a system of migrant labor—migrant-labor powerlessness. In other words, the expansion of the system of migrant labor stimulated and structured class struggles which ultimately forced the breakdown of the system itself. At the same time, however, intertwined with such a "bottom up" view of the dynamics of the system of migrant labor are the "top down" concessions by the colonial government prompted by political changes in Britain and by the general climate in the colonized world. To disentangle the intricate interaction of concessions and struggles in the decline of the system of migrant labor in Zambia would be a worthwhile and challenging task. Suffice it to say here that internal dynamics are but a partial explanation of the dissolution of the system in Zambia.[14]

---

[14] The system of migrant labor has not completely dissolved. In a survey I conducted among a carefully selected sample of 218 mine workers in 1969, I found that 39% had returned to their home villages within the preceding two years and 71% within the preceding five. Breaking these figures down by age and length of time spent in urban areas (urban experience), I found that the older a worker (controlling for urban experience), the more frequently he returned to his home village, and the greater his urban experience (controlling for age) the less frequently he returned to it. Zambian workers have never had their land expropriated in the manner of the enclosure movement in England. Therefore they retain ties to the rural areas as a form of security, particularly for retirement. This may involve remitting a part of their income home—though very few (7%) claim to do so on a regular basis—or entertaining visiting kinsmen from the home area, as well as returning periodically to the rural areas. As an increasing proportion of the work force is born in the urban areas, with no home village,

Migrant Labor: Functions and Reproduction

Nonetheless, Zambia does illustrate dynamics arising in the place of employment—namely, the weakening of the colonial state and the advance of the political and economic status of the migrant worker. By contrast, for South Africa we stressed the dynamics of the interaction of capitalist and precapitalist economies and the way in which the expansion of the former tended to erode the latter. In its reproductive role, the South African state organizes counteracting influences designed to re-create the precapitalist mode of production. But it is becoming increasingly apparent that, although the system of migrant labor contains its own contradictions that continually threaten to undermine the system, the major threat to the system, particularly as it affects the gold mines, is from relatively autonomous external sources.

Prior to 1950, southern Africa constituted a relatively coherent political unit bound together by various forms of colonial rule and organized around certain focal points of industrial development. The peripheral areas served as labor reservoirs and were made subservient to the economic interests of the extractive industries, most notably the copper mines of Northern Rhodesia, the coal mines of Southern Rhodesia, and the gold mines of South Africa, as well as agriculture in all these territories. Struggles for political independence in Malawi, Tanzania, and Zambia led to the "autonomization" of the foreign reservoirs that supplied labor for the gold mines. The ban on recruitment for South African industry imposed by the Zambian and Tanzanian governments meant that South Africa would have to become increasingly reliant on its own internal system of migrant labor. Hence there emerged renewed interest in the reserve areas and the creation of Bantustans. With no major industry of its own, Malawi continued to serve as a major foreign labor reservoir for South African industry, particularly the gold mines, reinforcing its own underdevelopment and its dependency on South Africa.

The sporadic but very definite success of guerrilla movements in Portuguese Africa led to a coup d'état in the metropolitan country and to the demise of Portuguese colonialism in Africa, precipitating disturbances throughout southern Africa. The white minority regime of Southern Rhodesia is now under pressure to negotiate with black nationalist leaders, and in 1974 Malawi declared a ban on the supply of migrant labor to South

---

and as pension and welfare schemes improve in the economy as a whole, the retention of linkages between urban and rural communities should be expected to decline further. But the most telling statistics concerning the dissolution of the system of migrant labor are to be found in commitment to employment in industry: in 1969 the average length of service of Zambian mine workers was 9.4 years (as compared with 4.3 years in 1955), with a corresponding turnover of 6.4% per annum—an extremely low turnover by any standards.

Africa. With the independence of Mozambique, there is the possibility of another major source of labor withdrawing its supply to South Africa. The reaction of the South African Chamber of Mines has been as follows:

> Energetic steps have been taken to attract South Africans and the proportion has increased from 22 per cent at 31st March, 1974 to 32 per cent at 30th April, 1975. It is hoped that it will be possible to increase this proportion even further, and it will therefore be necessary to compete for labour with other sectors of the economy and to provide more housing accommodations for South African workers. Inevitably the bulk of mining labour will remain migratory for many years to come but it is hoped that a core of stable South African employees can be built up on longer-life mines. . . . [South African Chamber of Mines 1975]

The South African state is now faced with the dilemma of choosing either the expanded reproduction of the system of migrant labor within its own boundaries or the dissolution of the system. (For further details, see South African Institute of Race Relations 1975, pp. 281–88; Leys 1975.)

The South African example demonstrates that a system of migrant labor is placed in jeopardy as soon as the external labor reservoir gains political autonomy. The study of Mexican migrant workers in the United States lends some support to such a conclusion. The utilization of Mexican labor to bolster the United States economy has been the subject of considerable political debate within Mexico, from time to time leading the Mexican government to impose controls and conditions on the use of such labor. The bracero program, with its elaborate although rarely entirely enforced system of regulations, reflected just such a concern for the treatment of Mexican nationals. In practice, however, political control over the supply of labor is only a minor factor in the determination of the ebb and flow of migrant labor across the border. Indeed, it may be argued that in this instance it is unrealistic to speak of a system of migrant labor at all, because any characteristic dynamics of the system are overwhelmed by a wide range of external factors, such as the state of the economy on either side of the border.

Parallels with slavery are intriguing and deserve brief mention. In its purest form, slavery is an extreme version of migrant labor in which processes of renewal take place in a distant country (insofar as male workers only are involved) and maintenance takes place on the plantation; the severance between maintenance and renewal is total and final. Indentured labor stands somewhere on the continuum between systems of slavery and the systems of migrant labor examined in this paper. Under a system of worldwide colonialism, such as existed in the 18th century, slaves could be procured readily; but with economic, political, and ideological changes in the system of world capitalism, the movement for abolition established itself. As a result, the survival of the system became

Migrant Labor: Functions and Reproduction

contingent upon the organization of labor-force renewal *alongside* its maintenance. Wallerstein (1976) argues that increased "costs" of slavery in the decades before the American Civil War noted by Fogel and Engerman (1974) and Genovese (1974) were a result of American prohibition of international slave trade in 1807. Further, he argues, slavery was a viable system of labor only so long as a substantial proportion of the costs of renewal were borne in external labor reservoirs, and therefore their collapse spelled the downfall of slavery.[15] In other words, the *specific* cheapness of slavery is to be found, neither in the powerlessness of slaves (though this is an inevitable and necessary condition) nor in their efficiency, but (if it is to be found at all) in the characteristic mode of reproduction of labor power. When monopolistic access to external labor reservoirs is lost, systems of slavery and migrant labor have to be reconstituted or transformed. It remains to be seen whether the South African system of migrant labor is to be successfully resurrected through the intervention of the state or whether it will follow the historic road of slavery in the United States.

Beyond Migrant Labor

What light does our conceptual distinction between maintenance and renewal shed on systems of labor that are not migrant and in which internal differentiation of the domestic labor force is prominent? One approach to these broader issues is a reformulation of our analysis of the costs of reproduction of labor power. Earlier, the savings generated by a system of migrant labor were expressed in terms of the *externalization* of certain costs. That is, certain processes normally financed by the employer and the state of employment are externalized so that the employer and the employing state assume no responsibility. However, such savings could be viewed in terms of the *reduction* of certain renewal costs rather

[15] Although the heyday of American slavery appears to have come after the importation of slaves became illegal, with the slave population quadrupling in 50 years as a result of natural increase, the increase must be regarded as a consequence of the incorporation of renewal processes into plantation society. The reproduction of a system of slavery involves the reproduction not merely of slaves but also of slave owners. Thus, to show that slavery is a viable labor system at any point in time, it is not enough to show that the "break-even age"—when "the accumulated expenditures by planters on slaves were greater than the average accumulated income which they took from them" (Fogel and Engerman 1974, p. 153)—is less than life expectancy. It must also be shown that the difference reflects earnings greater than the costs of the life-style of the slaveholders. Although Fogel and Engerman (1974, p. 155) do note that the break-even age rose in the decades before the Civil War and imply that life expectancy also increased, they neither tell us the trend of the difference between these two values nor relate the difference to the costs of the reproduction of the style of life of the slaveholders. In other words, the data of Fogel and Engerman do not speak directly to the hypothesis presented here.

American Journal of Sociology

than their externalization. That is, it is cheaper to educate and bring up
a family, and so forth, in a Bantustan or a Mexican shantytown than in
Johannesburg or California, where the reproduction of labor power is
organized for higher-income groups and where, as a result, lower-income
groups are penalized. Luxuries superfluous to the basic processes of renewal in the Bantustan or Mexican town or village become necessities
in Johannesburg or California. In other words, the requirements for a
minimal standard of living vary from place to place, according to the level
of industrial development. Increases in the level of consumption or, more
broadly, the rise of the cost of reproduction of labor power, is a consequence of and a condition for the economic expansion of capitalist societies (Gorz 1967, chap. 4).

Against this background, the significance of migrant labor lies in the
separation of the processes of maintenance and renewal, so that renewal
takes place where living standards are low and maintenance takes place
within easy access of employment. Thus, wages earned by migrant workers
are lower than those of domestic workers, because the former require
fewer resources to sustain the renewal process than the latter. Where a
supply of migrant labor is not available, industry itself may migrate to
areas where the costs of the reproduction of labor power are lower. Indeed,
the migration of industry may be a more attractive proposition for capitalists, as it relieves them of responsibility for the social and political costs
of the maintenance of migrant labor. On the other hand, when a host
country assumes responsibility for the regulation and domination of the
labor force, the capitalist enterprise is frequently subjected to political and
economic uncertainties beyond its control.

Expressing economic benefits in terms of reduction rather than externalization of costs allows us to go beyond migrant labor and examine various ways of organizing the reproduction of labor power within a single
economy. The question becomes: Are there areas or institutions within a
given society which organize the process of labor-force renewal at reduced costs? If there are, what specific mechanisms perpetuate the coexistence of differing modes of organizing labor-force renewal? Thus, one
might ask whether the urban ghetto in the United States is a functional
equivalent of the Bantustan in South Africa. Although an adequate treatment would involve a careful comparison of the political economies of
Bantustan and ghetto, a few remarks may be made in passing. One striking resemblance between the two places is the importance of the female-
dominated household. Liebow (1967), for example, shows how the "matri-
focal" family of the urban ghetto is a product of "the inability of the
Negro man to earn a living and support his family" (p. 224). Marriages
do not last long, and women of the ghetto, like women of the Bantustan
and of the villages in British Guiana (Smith 1956), are forced to extend

1082

Migrant Labor: Functions and Reproduction

their sources of income by whatever means they can muster and through alliances with a succession of mates. Liebow's observations suggest that ghetto life is characterized by the separation of the processes of renewal, engaging the mother and her children, from those of maintenance, which concern the "marginal" or temporarily employed lower-class male.

My argument would be that the ghetto, like the Bantustan and the Mexican town or village, is a definitely located institution whose function for the capitalist economy is the allocation of the renewal processes to areas where renewal costs are low. As one exposition of the dual labor market thesis for the United States points out, the reproduction of a differentiated labor force rests on the reduction of renewal costs through segregation in housing, education, and welfare (Baron and Hymer 1968). "Institutional racism" (Wilson 1973, p. 34) or "internal colonialism" (Blauner 1972, pt. 1) may then be understood as the apparatus, coercive where necessary, for the regulation of renewal processes of a particular segment of the labor force and their allocation to specific institutions and areas. In other words, I am suggesting that racism be interpreted as a particular mode of reproduction of labor power and that "powerlessness" is not so much the defining as a necessary condition for racism. Furthermore, distinctions between different types of race relations, such as van den Berghe's (1967) distinction between competitive and paternalistic ones, may be understood in terms of particular articulations of productive and reproductive processes. Thus, where the same elements of the dominant class organize both production of commodities and reproduction of labor power, a system of paternalistic relations emerges, whereas when the two processes are separated, with one organized by the employer and the other by the state, a different system—competitive race relations—emerges.

One may ask one further question: What is the importance of the variation in the costs of labor-force renewal? Low-profit industry is dependent on the existence and perpetuation of institutions which reduce the costs of labor-force renewal for segments of the working class. At the same time, the economy as a whole, but particularly high-profit monopoly industry, is dependent on increasing levels of demand and therefore on increasing the costs of labor-force reproduction. This opposition of short-term need for reducing the cost of labor and long-term need for increased demand is partially resolved through the bifurcation of the working class (both in South Africa and the United States). With the expansion of capital, the opposition develops and the schism within the working class widens (Fuchs 1968, pp. 53, 61; Bluestone 1972). One segment of the labor force devotes more time and money to renewal processes, while the other struggles to maintain itself from day to day. The consequences may be observed in the diverse forms of family organization measured in terms of the relationship between renewal and maintenance activities.

1083

American Journal of Sociology

I introduced race into the discussion and could equally well have extended the argument to relations between the sexes[16] to defend the thesis
that it is not just the "powerlessness" which certain minority groups
share but also their different modes of insertion into the reproduction of
labor power which determines their group characteristics. That blacks
have had less political power than whites means that they are more vulnerable to excessive exploitation, but this has been realized only through
specific modes of reproduction of labor power on the plantation and in the
ghetto. What differentiates women from blacks and both from migrants can
ultimately be reduced to the different modes of reproduction of labor power
in which they are engaged or their different relations to a single mode of
reproduction. Interpreting the significance of these various modes of
reproduction of labor power thrusts the discussion back to the relationship
between the rate of exploitation and the rate of profit. I have repeatedly
pointed out that the relationship between exploitation and profit is mediated by an ensemble of structures that reproduce not merely labor power
but also the social relations characterizing capitalist production. Intensi-
fying exploitation does not appear spontaneously but has to be created
and re-created by modes of enforcement; it requires a more elaborate and
costly apparatus of reproduction, or more specifically the expansion of the
state, which in turn eats away at profits. Yet at the same time, a reduction in the rate of exploitation may generate greater consent, thereby
allowing a relative contraction of the state and conceivably leading to an
increase in the rate of profit. Here I can only raise what is a complex
empirical and theoretical problem.

REFERENCES

Agribusiness Accountability Project. 1972. *A Profile of California Agribusiness*. Washington, D.C.: Government Printing Office.
Anderson, N. 1923. *The Hobo*. Chicago: University of Chicago Press.

[16] First, the family facilitates the expansion and contraction of capital through its dual
function as labor reservoir and reproductive unit. Increased labor demands, as occa-
sioned, for example, by wartime emergency, lead to the expansion of the state's role in
the renewal process, as reflected in the increase in day-care centers (Kleinberg 1974)
and the release of women for participation in the labor force. The allocation of women
to low-paying jobs is premised upon the costs of maintenance and renewal in a family
with two sources of income. Second, as with race relations, I would argue that relations
between men and women are the *effects* of the articulation of primarily two types of
structures: modes of production and modes of reproduction. To be sure, people can be
distinguished by their anatomy or their color, but these only become socially significant
when they are the basis of the allocation of individuals to specific sets of roles. What
are perceived as characteristics of blacks or women are, not some primordial givens, but
the effects of the particular positions they occupy in the social structure. A theory of
relations between sexes or between races is first and foremost a theory of empty places
in the structures of production and reproduction and only secondarily a theory of the
allocation of individuals to those places.

Migrant Labor: Functions and Reproduction

Arrighi, G. 1973. "Labor Supplies in Historical Perspective: A Study of the Proletarianization of the African Peasantry in Rhodesia." Pp. 180–234 in *Essays on the Political Economy of Africa*, by G. Arrighi and J. Saul. New York: Monthly Review Press.

Baerresen, D. W. 1971. *The Border Industrialization Program of Mexico.* Lexington, Mass.: Heath-Lexington.

Balibar, E. 1970. "The Basic Concepts of Historical Materialism." Pp. 201–308 in *Reading Capital*, by L. Althusser and E. Balibar. New York: Pantheon.

Baron, H. M., and B. Hymer. 1968. "The Negro Worker in the Chicago Labor Market." Pp. 232–85 in *The Negro and the American Labor Movement*, edited by J. Jacobson. New York: Anchor.

Bell, T. 1973. *Industrial Decentralisation in South Africa.* London: Oxford University Press.

Bettison, D. G. 1960. "Factors in the Determination of Wage Rates in Central Africa." *Human Problems in British Central Africa*, no. 28 (December), pp. 22–46.

Blauner, R. 1972. *Racial Oppression in America.* New York: Harper & Row.

Bluestone, B. 1972. "Capitalism and Poverty in America: A Discussion." *Monthly Review* 24 (2): 65–71.

Bowles, S. 1972. "Unequal Education and the Reproduction of the Hierarchical Division of Labor." Pp. 218–28 in *The Capitalist System*, edited by R. C. Edwards, M. Reich, and T. E. Weisskopf. Englewood Cliffs, N.J.: Prentice-Hall.

Braverman, H. 1974. *Labor and Monopoly Capital.* New York: Monthly Review Press.

Briggs, V. M. 1973. *Chicanos and Rural Poverty.* Baltimore: John Hopkins University Press.

Burawoy, M. 1972. *The Colour of Class on the Copper Mines: From African Advancement to Zambianization.* Zambian Papers, no. 7. Manchester: Manchester University Press, for the Institute of African Studies, Zambia.

———. 1974. "Race, Class and Colonialism." *Social and Economic Studies* 23 (4): 521–50.

Castells, M. 1975. "Immigrant Workers and Class Struggles in Advanced Capitalism: The Western European Experience." *Politics and Society* 5 (1): 33–66.

Castles, S., and G. Kosack. 1973. *Immigrant Workers and Class Structure in Western Europe.* London: Oxford University Press, for the Institute of Race Relations.

Cortés, F , A. Przeworski, and J. Sprague. 1974. *Systems Analysis for Social Scientists.* New York: Wiley.

Epstein, A. L. 1958. *Politics in an Urban African Community.* Manchester: Manchester University Press.

Fellmeth, R. C., ed. 1971. *Power and Land in California.* Washington, D.C.: Center for the Study of Responsive Law.

Fisher, L. H. 1953. *The Harvest Labor Market in California.* Cambridge, Mass.: Harvard University Press.

Fogel, R. W., and S. L. Engerman. 1974. *Time on the Cross: The Economics of American Negro Slavery.* Boston: Little, Brown.

Frisbie, P. 1975. "Illegal Migration from Mexico to the United States: A Longitudinal Analysis." *International Migration Review* 9 (1): 3–14.

Fuchs, V. R. 1968. *The Service Economy.* New York: National Bureau of Economic Research.

Fuller, V. 1940. "The Supply of Agricultural Labor as a Factor in the Evolution of Farm Organization in California." Pt. 54 in U.S. Congress, Senate, Committee on Violations of Free Speech and Rights of Labor, *Hearings before a Subcommittee of the Committee on Education and Labor, United States Senate.* Washington, D.C.: Government Printing Office.

Galarza, E. 1964. *Merchants of Labor.* Santa Barbara, Calif.: McNally & Loftin.

———. 1970. *Spiders in the House and Workers in the Field.* Notre Dame, Ind.: University of Notre Dame Press.

Gamio, M. 1930. *Mexican Immigration to the United States.* Chicago: University of Chicago Press.

American Journal of Sociology

Genovese, E. 1974. *Roll, Jordan, Roll: The World the Slaves Made.* New York: Pantheon.
Gorz, A. 1967. *Strategy for Labor.* Boston: Beacon.
Gramsci, A. 1971. *Prison Notebooks.* New York: International.
Greene, S. 1969. "Immigration and Rural Poverty—the Problems of the Illegal Entrant." *Duke Law Journal* 69 (3): 475–94.
Hancock, R. H. 1959. *The Role of the Bracero in the Economic and Cultural Dynamics of Mexico.* Stanford, Calif.: Stanford University Hispanic American Society.
Harris, M. 1959. "Labor Migration among the Mozambique Thonga: Cultural and Political Factors." *Africa* 29 (1): 50–64.
Harrison, B. 1972. "Public Employment and the Theory of the Dual Economy." Pp. 41–76 in *The Political Economy of Public Service Employment,* by H. L. Sheppard, B. Harrison, and W. J. Spring. Lexington, Mass.: Heath-Lexington.
Hawley, E. W. 1966. "The Politics of the Mexican Labor Issue, 1950–1965." *Agricultural History* 40 (3): 157–76.
Hepple, A. 1971. *South Africa: Workers under Apartheid.* London: Christian Action Publications, for the International Defence and Aid Fund.
Hobsbawm, E. J. 1964. *Labouring Men: Studies in the History of Labour.* London: Weidenfeld & Nicolson.
Horwitz, R. 1967. *The Political Economy of South Africa.* New York: Praeger.
Jones, L. 1965. "Mexican-American Labor Problems in Texas." Ph.D. dissertation, University of Texas.
Kleinberg, J. 1974. "Public Child Care: Our Hidden History." Pp. 27–36 in *The Day Care Book,* edited by V. Breitburt. New York: Knopf.
Kuper, L. 1957. *Passive Resistance in South Africa.* New Haven, Conn.: Yale University Press.
Lenin, V. I. 1960. *Collected Works.* Vol. 3, *The Development of Capitalism in Russia.* Moscow: Foreign Languages Publishing House.
Leys, R. 1975. "South African Gold Mining in 1974: 'The Gold of Migrant Labour.'" *African Affairs* 74 (295): 196–208.
Liebow, E. 1967. *Tally's Corner.* Boston: Little, Brown.
McWilliams, C. 1964. *Brothers under the Skin.* Boston: Little, Brown.
———. 1971. *Factories in the Field.* Santa Barbara, Calif.: Peregrine.
Mayer, P. 1971. *Townsmen or Tribesmen.* London: Oxford University Press.
Myers, R. 1959. *The Position of Farm Workers in Federal and State Legislation.* New York: National Advisory Committee on Farm Labor.
North, D. S. 1970. *The Border Crossers: People Who Live in Mexico and Work in the United States.* Washington, D.C.: Trans-Century Corp.
O'Connor, J. 1973. *The Fiscal Crisis of the State.* New York: St. Martin's.
Parker, C. 1920. *The Casual Laborer and Other Essays.* New York: Russell & Russell.
Piven, F. F., and R. A. Cloward. 1971. *Regulating the Poor: The Functions of Public Welfare.* New York: Random House.
Poulantzas, N. 1973. *Political Power and Social Classes.* London: New Left.
Redford, A. 1926. *Labour Migration in England: 1800–1850.* Manchester: Manchester University Press.
Rex, J. 1974. "Ethnic and Class Stratification: Their Interrelation and Political Consequences—Europe." Paper delivered to the International Sociological Association, Toronto, August 19.
Richards, A. 1939. *Land, Labour and Diet in Northern Rhodesia.* London: Oxford University Press.
Roux, E. 1964. *Time Longer than a Rope: A History of the Black Man's Struggle for Freedom in South Africa.* Madison: University of Wisconsin Press.
Samora, J. 1971. *Los Mojados: The Wetback Story.* Notre Dame, Ind.: University of Notre Dame Press.
Scruggs, O. M. 1960. "Evolution of the Mexican Farm Labor Agreement of 1942." *Agricultural History* 34 (3): 140–49.

Migrant Labor: Functions and Reproduction

————. 1963. "Texas and the Bracero Program, 1942–1947." *Pacific Historical Review* 32 (3): 251–82.

Simons, H. J., and R. E. Simons. 1969. *Class and Colour in South Africa: 1850–1950.* Harmondsworth, Middx.: Penguin.

Smith, R. T. 1956. *The Negro Family in British Guiana.* London: Routledge & Kegan Paul.

South African Chamber of Mines. 1975. *Presidential Address.* Advertisement in *Wall Street Journal.*

Supreme Court Reporter. 1974. Vol. 95, no. 4 (December 15).

Survey of Race Relations in South Africa 1974, A. 1975. Johannesburg: South African Institute of Race Relations.

Thompson, E. P. 1968. *The Making of the English Working Class.* Harmondsworth, Middx.: Penguin.

U.S. Congress, Senate. Committee on Education and Labor. 1940. *Report on Violations of Free Speech and Rights of Labor.* 77th Cong. 2d Sess. Washington, D.C.: Government Printing Office.

U.S. President's Commission on Migratory Labor. 1951. *Migratory Labor in American Agriculture.* Washington, D.C.: Government Printing Office.

van den Berghe, P. L. 1967. *Race and Racism.* New York: Wiley.

van Velsen, J. 1961. "Labour Migration as a Positive Factor in the Continuity of Tonga Tribal Society." Pp. 230–41 in *Social Change in Modern Africa,* edited by A. Southall. London: Oxford University Press, for the International African Institute.

Wallerstein, I. 1976. "American Slavery and the Capitalist World-Economy." *American Journal of Sociology* 81 (March): 1199–1213.

Watson, W. 1958. *Tribal Cohesion in a Money Economy.* Manchester: Manchester University Press, for the Rhodes-Livingston Institute.

Wilson, F. 1972a. *Labour in the South African Gold Mines 1911–1969.* Cambridge: Cambridge University Press.

————. 1972b. *Migrant Labour in South Africa.* Johannesburg: South African Council of Churches and SPRO-CAS (Study Project on Christianity in Apartheid Society).

Wilson, W. J. 1973. *Power, Racism and Privilege.* New York: Macmillan.

Wolpe, H. 1972. "Capitalism and Cheap Labour-Power in South Africa: From Segregation to Apartheid." *Economy and Society* 1 (4): 425–55.

Part II
The Dynamics of International Labour Migration

[3]

The new untouchables: the international migration of labour

NIGEL HARRIS

The rise of imperialism is also the rise of the modern State. The manifestation of the power of the State is in the first instance its tight control of one patch of very clearly defined territory and the population trapped within its boundaries. The imposition of this pattern on humanity by the first group of modern States, those of Europe, produced a defensive reaction by the ruling classes of the rest of the world. They in turn were obliged to establish the same type of tight control over whatever territories could be appropriated. The pattern which emerged is reminiscent of the enclosure movement in Britain: the appropriation of common lands by private owners to the point where all territory within Britain was officially parcelled up among a category of "owners". The process both within the territory of any given State and internationally eliminated all "free lands" and all free men and women: all who do not officially belong to one or other local ruling class (and can, in principle, acquire a valid passport to prove that they actually exist).

By now almost all inhabitable territory in the world has been demarcated, and humanity corralled within licensed national pens. Indeed, the division is so all-embracing, its sheer novelty is no longer apparent; most people cannot conceive of a world not divided into national patches, not dominated by baronial fiefs.

The development of the internal control of States over their respective territories and populations – the increased "nationalization" of the globe – is the other side of the coin to increased "internationalization". For what is meant by internationalization is increased interaction between increasingly defined national patches. The growth of the one necessarily presupposes the increase in the other.

Now, each national patch is almost equally related in economic terms to every other one – a condition in sharp contrast to the imperatives of political or military interaction where geographical proximity is of primary significance. This interaction ensures increased synchronization of the world system, or rather, its increased subordination to the dominant centres of world power. Yet such subordination should not conceal the necessary parallel process of "internal colonization", the attempt by particular States to subordinate all areas within their control to a single centre, usually the capital city.

Thus, the obverse of increased nationalization of the areas of the world is increased interdependence of the national patches. It is a contradictory process, for the interests of individual States are in collision with the imperatives of a world economy, with capital accumulation on a world scale.

The State's primary interest is in retaining and extending its territorial control, not assisting the development of an international economic order outside its control. In slump, the contradiction emerges so sharply, the accumulation is sacrificed to the maintenance of the power of the State, of the local ruling class, over its inhabitants.

The "internationalisation" of labour is one element in these processes. Throughout the history of capitalism, workers have moved in search of work, or been driven to work, in areas other than those where they were raised. This comon phenomenon however becomes remarkable only when national boundaries are laid down and become of sufficient importance to impede, block or shape the international movement of workers. That is, political controls are imposed in the attempt to break a movement impelled by the operation of a world labour market. To put it in another way, growth in the world system prompts the ruling classes of growing and dominant economies to despatch raiding parties to capture part of the labour force belonging to a weaker ruling class. Then the passport and visa, with the whole complex of subsidiary controls, become an instrument for the control and direction of the marginal labour force[1].

Whether the system is expanding or contracting determines the precise form of the contradiction between the interests of the State and those of the world economy. In expansion, the world labour market acts like acid upon territorial controls, other things being equal; either ruling classes are obliged to dismantle trade, finance and labour movement controls, or black markets in each area threaten the structures of control: "liberalization" is the product, rather than – as is frequently claimed – the cause of expansion. Nonetheless, although in the 1950s and 1960s many labour importing countries liberalized entry procedures, the essential formal controls were retained, and with the onset of contraction, strengthened. Protectionism in trade was matched by a protectionism in labour, and both exaggerate the severity of contraction.

The unprecedented expansion in the world economy after 1948 was a highly uneven process, producing disproportionate growth at certain key points in the advanced capitalist countries as well as in particular regions in the backward countries. This disproportionate growth was reflected in an increased concentration of the demand for labour. The two most important centres of the world system, the core zones of the American and European economies, attracted a sustained inflow of workers from abroad. But many other smaller centres, at various times, also attracted inflows – in the 1970s, the Middle Eastern oil producing States; South Africa, Ghana, Nigeria, Ivory Coast, Venezuela, Singapore etc. The legal movement was accompanied to a greater or lesser extent, depending upon the restrictions in force and the powers of the local State to enforce them, by both a black market in labour, illegal migration, and the "unscheduled" movements of refugees – for example, the large scale movements in Africa, the flight of Cubans, Argentinians, Cambodians, Vietnamese, Bengalis, and now Afghanis.

The concept of a crude undifferentiated "labour" is quite inadequate to understand the process of official worker movement. Those who move tend to be in the most active age groups, eighteen to thirty five years of age, and in terms of ability and skills, to be above the average for the sending

THE NEW UNTOUCHABLES 39

area. The jobs they move to are restricted, although they range across the spectrum from temporary seasonal work to permanent highly skilled jobs (for example, doctors). Each stratum of occupations has a separate dynamic.

For relatively unskilled workers, the areas of recruitment have often been geographically close – Eire for Britain, the Mediterranean countries for Germany and France, Mexico and Central America for the United States. But it is also true that European labour demand stretches far into West Africa, to Turkey and Iran, British demand to India, Malaysia and the Philippines, and American to Korea, Taiwan and the Philippines on the opposite side of the Pacific. Territorially, each national labour market expands and contracts geographically with the rhythms of growth. There are also countries now which supply unskilled or semi skilled labour globally; for example, the Philippines. As the level of skill in demand rises, so the extent of the catchment area expands, until a world labour market operates, as for example with doctors.

Where labour exporting countries are geographically close to the place where labour demand is increasing rapidly and the controls on movement are weak, the emigration of workers can be proportionally very large. North Yemen, adjacent to Saudi Arabia, has some 44 per cent of its adult labour force working abroad. Lesotho supplies to South Africa some 21 per cent of its domestic labour force; Algeria and Tunisia at one time had between 11 and 12 per cent of their workers abroad. In the heyday of movement, emigration amounted to 70 per cent of the increase in Portugal's labour force, and, before 1962, to over 100 per cent of Eire's.

Since emigrants are not drawn uniformly from a country as a whole but from particular districts, these national figures conceal the much greater effect on particular sending districts. For example, Indian migration to Britain is drawn from one medium sized state State, Gujerat, and a small State, Punjab, and within Punjab, largely from one district, Jullundur; Indian migration to the Gulf is drawn mainly from another small State, Kerala, while the largest State in India, Uttar Pradesh (with a population of around 100 million) provides few emigrants.

The movement is not just one way. Most countries export and import labour at the same time. Greece, with over two million workers abroad, imports workers from Egypt and Pakistan. Jordan, a major supplier of Palestinian labour to the oil producing countries, uses labour also from Egypt and Pakistan. Sicilians move to North Italy and Germany, leaving their harvests to be collected by Senegalese. Mexicans move north for the harvest in the United States, while Guatemalans enter southern Mexico for the harvest there. The United States and Britain supply highly skilled labour to the Middle East. The movement of labour is thus an exchange of skills, a continual redistribution of a margin of each national labour force in response to changes in the geography of capital accumulation.

The price of labour power

The orthodox explanations of worker movement usually turn on the "overproduction" of labour in some countries (the backward) and a "scarcity" of labour in others.[2] But there is never a "scarcity" of labour, only a scarcity of

40   *International Socialism 2:8*

workers willing to sell their labour at a given price. In so called "population surplus" countries, there is rarely a real surplus; for example, in both India and China, a good harvest produces full employment, a "labour scarcity" and rising agricultural day labourers' wages. The problem is employing people at an adequate wage all the year round; but so far as the system is concerned, the existing labour force is only the "right size" for producing the existing output.

In the advanced capitalist countries, a number of factors have reduced the physical availability of labour power, the number of labour hours on offer per year, in the postwar period: a decline in the birth rate (reflected fifteen years later in the new entrants to the labour force); a decrease in the number of hours worked per week; an increase in the holidays per year; an increase in the number of years of full time education, or the conversion of apprenticeships to part time education; earlier retirement, and, perhaps, the continued process of the decasualization of the labour force[3]. On the other hand, there are factors working in the opposite direction – the end of the National Service in Britain or the draft in the United States, the remarkable increase in the number of women entering paid employment, immigration and temporary workers entering work from abroad; at certain times, the considerable increase in part time work by the pensioned (off-setting the earlier retirement); the expansion in second and third jobs ("moonlighting"). How are we to explain these different changes, and the creation of specific "labour scarcities"?

The price of labour power is determined by what Marx calls the socially necessary cost of maintaining and reproducing labour power; by "repro-duction", we mean, not the biological creation of a baby, but the process of creating an adult worker from the age of 0 to, say, between 12 and 15 years of age. Marx's statement is applicable collectively, not necessarily indivi-dually – that is, the return to the working class for its labour power is determined by the costs of maintaining the working class and reproducing it. What is determined here is the value of labour power; actual collective wages may, to a greater or lesser degree diverge from value, but will ultimately remain in some definite relationship to value.

What determines the "socially necessary costs"? There are obviously many factors, but one of the most important for modern capitalism, is the need to attain a given level of productivity by the labour force. Defining what is "necessary" is obviously difficult, for the productivity of labour is a function not simply of the more obvious training and educational inputs, the quality of diet ensuring consistent concentration and discipline, the quality of housing ensuring the worker does not spend much of his or her attention worrying or seeking a roof, the condition of the worker's family, parents and children, so that he is or she is "free" to work fully, etc. There are factors relating to the possible exhausting or psychologically debilitating results of work – and an adequate level of recreation and leisure, and the facilities to pursue these etc. Which of these elements are necessary, which optional extras?

In some backward countries, levels of productivity in particular plants can be pushed up to roughly the same level as those pertaining in an advanced economy, even though the labour force in the plant does not

THE NEW UNTOUCHABLES 41

receive wages remotely comparable to similar workers in an advanced country, nor does he or she have access to anything matching the services available there. Does this mean the wages received and services available in advanced capitalism are not necessary? It does not. For while particular plants may emulate the same level of productivity, the society as a whole cannot; it can utilize a particular range of technical innovations, but it cannot generalize them, nor itself innovate.

Average labour productivity in the advanced capitalist countries has increased enormously over the past century. There has been a substantial but much smaller increase in the absolute level of real wages required to sustain the worker at these rising levels of average productivity. If we took the return to labour as a whole which, today, is much more than simply the wage, we could divide it into two elements: (i) the cost of maintaining the workers at a given level of productivity; and (ii) the cost of reproducing the workers' children so that, when they enter the labour force, they can attain a given level of productivity. While the first element has increased considerably over the past century, the increase is dwarfed by the growth in the second element. Leaving aside the family-bourne cost of rearing, the growth in the public sector inputs – through the expansion in educational, housing, welfare and medical services – has been very considerable, particularly in the postwar period (in practice, of course, it is exceedingly difficult to separate "maintenance" and "reproduction" in looking at the public sector services, and to separate these elements from the costs of the control and supervision of the population).

To deal with the average for a class is misleading. For much of the history of capitalism, the bottom third of the workforce has not been paid enough to meet the costs of reproduction at the average level of productivity then prevailing. Some sections of the workforce have not been paid sufficient to meet the bare minimum costs of reproduction (the infant mortality rate, like the rate of deaths to women in childbirth, is a partial index of this). And at certain times, the wages of the lowest categories of labour has been insufficient even to maintain the worker, a factor producing increasing levels of malnutrition and, during epidemics, a very high death rate.

So far as the world labour force is concerned, this situation has not changed very much. For example, a recent study of Calcutta small firms shows that, if we assume the going day labourer's wage rate is the minimum subsistence and reproduction price of labour power, then both small capitalists and the family labour employed in their firms receive returns which are some 41 per cent below what they should be – they are, as it were, "committing suicide" by working[4].

Thus, the labour force is a highly differentiated object. If we could imagine a national capitalism as an unchanging entity – output and employment, both absolutely and relatively, remaining constant – then the hierarchy of skill grades would persist indefinitely. Reproduction would consist in replacing a set number of workers of given skill by exactly the same number with the same skills. If reproduction costs were entirely bourne from the wage paid out to the worker through the family, then household incomes would form a hierarchy exactly corresponding to the hierarchy of skills and the hierarchy of productivities. Each skill stratum of workers would reproduce its successors in the stratum at the average costs of reproduction of labour at the level of productivity appropriate to the stratum. Of course, instability would arise at the base of the hierarchy if the price of labour power there was too low to ensure the reproduction of the numbers required. Nonetheless the main idea of a stable pyramid in which maintenance and reproduction expenditures are proportional to the size and productivity of each stratum is the important element. In practice, there are no stable strata; the essence of capitalism is change, the continuous transformation of relationships and productivities so that the literacy of today is the illiteracy of tomorrow.

The public sector

The only purpose of the abstract exercise at the end of the last section is to allow us to identify more clearly what happens when the State intervenes to meet a major part of reproduction costs directly. Then the link between the wage received by the worker, the productivity on which we assume the wage is based, and the outlays incurred by the worker's family to meet reproduction costs is broken. Variations in productivity and wages are no longer directly reflected in variations in family expenditure on reproduction.

By necessity, the State must now set some average minimum standard for the provision of its services to ensure the proper reproduction of the labour force. Leaving aside social and political factors, it can only do so in relationship to some notional average level of productivity for the labour force as a whole. Even if it endeavoured to tailor its services to a more complex structure of productivities, since there is no guarantee that a given worker would work at the trade for which he or she had been raised – and in conditions of rapid change, the trade itself may have disappeared altogether by the time the child enters the labour force – setting an average minimum standard is the sole method available. Alternatively, the State could identify a special category of people for high productivity jobs and concentrate reproduction expenditure here. To a greater or lesser extent, in reality this does happen in particular services (for example, education), but there are political constraints on how far such a discriminatory system can be generalized.

The State assumes this role for a variety of reasons, one of which is that the speed of change and the nature of the skills required mean that the skills can only be transferred collectively, on a standarized basis; as capitalism develops, parents become increasingly poor instruments for transferring skills required in the future.

A powerful factor in determining what average the State chooses is competition. States compete with each other – indeed, the State is the single most important agency of competition in the world system. A factor identified as important in the State's ability to compete is the quality of its labour force. Public welfare programmes in Britain begin with an official report on the quality of troops recruited for the Boer War – that is, the ability of the British State to compete in military terms with its nearest rivals was jeopardized by the poor physical quality of its young men[5]. In modern times, the output of graduates or toolmakers in the United States or the Soviet Union, as proportions of the labour force of those countries, become

THE NEW UNTOUCHABLES 43

standards for all lesser powers. The argument was explicit in the British Labour Party's propaganda for the 1964 general election, and provided the justification for the Wilson government's programme to expand higher education rapidly. Thus, the level of labour productivity on the basis of which a programme for higher educational expansion was based was not the actual level of 1964, but an aspired level – the level thought to be necessary to keep up with or overtake the leading industrial powers of the world. Of course, the *intention* of the State is not the same thing as the actual performance; the British new universities may have been intended to produce engineering graduates, but in fact, produced many more sociologists! Nor does the fact that the State had the intention mean that what it proposed is correct; it can and does make major errors of judgement.

The potential for mistakes when the State endeavours to establish a minimum requirement for reproduction costs is enormous. Such errors are compounded by the conflicts and rivalries rife within the public sector itself, by the competition for funds. For example, educational standards are not simply the product of a cool appraisal of what is required to meet certain levels of productivity (that is difficult enough); they are weapons by which, for example, the Ministry of Education endeavours to capture a larger share of finance and defeat rival agencies. There are pressure groups pressing on all sides: building contractors for hospital construction, universities for expanding higher education, MPs seeking favour for the constituencies, for their brothers and mates. Bribes and threats bend decisions for paradoxical conclusions. And beyond the narrow circle of power, from time to time, the class struggle itself reshapes government priorities.

In periods of growth and relative optimism, the State gambles by setting standards at high levels, even though, on strict calculations, this is not justified relative to the needs of the system at that time. In fact, the decisions may be errors even though expansion continues. In a number of backward countries, decisions to expand higher education in order to expand economic growth have merely produced an excess of graduates and the problem of educated unemployment.

But there are other problems which arise. First, State intervention in this field imposes a rigidity upon the system which renders it much more inflexible when expansion changes into contraction. Expenditure on reproduction could, when the family was the primary spender, be varied with fluctuations in economic activity – wage cuts were reflected in a decline in family nutrition, for example. But public expenditure is an issue of public debate and public employment, issues discussed in conditions for a competitive political party system where, for example, demands for more housing are weapons in the battle to win elections. Large changes in public expenditure to stabilize the profit rate under the pressures of slump cannot be secured speedily without economic disaster, nor without political challenge. There are other rigidities in particular sectors; for example, if workers hang on to their houses when local unemployment rises, even though jobs are available in other areas where housing is not.

Second, the State's assumption of an *average* standard for the whole labour force is, from the viewpoint of the interests of the system, enormously wasteful. Advanced capitalist economies exhibit great uneveness of development. Parts of the economy operate at levels of labour productivity far below the average. It follows that the bottom strata of the workforce are "over educated" or physically "over maintained" for their role in the economy. This contradiction receives subjective expression in the unwillingness of workers, trained to work at an approximation to the average level of productivity, to work for wages well below the average. The price of labour power in the sectors where there are vacancies is below the rate of return which is appropriate to the costs of reproduction of the unemployed. For the unemployed to work at such a price would permanently jeopardize the chances of them ever working at the appropriate price. Thus, in the Greater London Council area in 1979, with the unemployment total standing at 130,000, there were severe labour shortages on London Transport, in the clothing, timber, metal goods, and electrical engineering trades, not to mention in the case of school canteen supervisors.

Third, the State institutes regulations to prevent the employment of minors, in part to protect the quality of the subsequently available adult labour force. This in turn reduces the contribution of child labour to household income, thus weakening the economic incentive to families to have children. The introduction of pensions for the aged removes another element in that incentive – that is, reduces the need to have a sufficient number of children to support the worker's old age. The results of this, in conjunction with the introduction of birth control techniques, have been a decline in average family size – and, in due course, a decline in the number of new entrants to the labour force (this decline has been partly compensated by an increase in the survival rate of children, a decline in infant mortality). There is a further factor, however, in the decline in family size. The intervention of the State produces not only standardization of the publicly borne reproduction costs. The costs have been further increased by the transformation of household activity since the second World War. The capital intensity of household activity has been advanced very rapidly, enormously boosting the productivity of household labour at the same time as considerably increasing the costs of the family unit. It appears that adult male wages have not increased commensurately with this process, so that today, the adult wage male wage cannot, as it was supposed to do in the nineteenth century, cover the costs of a wife and two children. Two adult wages now appear to be necessary to meet family based reproduction and maintenance costs. One result of this process has been the expulsion of housewives from the home to pursue paid – albeit, very low paid – employment. It should be noted in passing that the family can be no wiser than the State in assessing what is a socially necessary level of costs; parents perforce must, like the State, gamble. "Keeping up with the Jones" is thus not an eccentricity, but a primary mechanism of capitalist competition relative to the household.

In practice, the system heavily qualifies its commitment to an average standard for all. The labour supply to low paid worker sectors is identified by using special social criteria, by instituting a kind of "caste identified" labour supply – certain occupations are reserved as temporary, for "amateur workers" – the aged, school students (for example, newspaper delivery, Saturday morning shop assistants etc.), students on vacation or looking for work, housewives. As is well known, there are whole strata of "women's jobs". In the United States, a special category exists of "native immigrants", that is, those who are by all ordinary legal criteria fully natives, but are treated as if they were not: blacks, Puerto Ricans, Chicanos etc. However, the more sustained the process is to reproduce the whole population to a particular average level of competence, the more such groups resist the typecast employment, preferring to remain unemployed rather than jeopardize their long term job prospects. Nor is this preference simply a function of the availability of social security support for the unemployed. Educated unemployment in Calcutta illustrates that people will fight to the bitter end to prevent their occupational downgrading, preferring starvation to indignity.

Sectors of "labour scarcity"

What types of employment are affected by a general upgrading of the labour force? The factors at stake are not simply questions of the price of labour power if by that we mean the take home pay. It is rather the price of labour power relative to the intensity and conditions of work (which includes the danger, the physical hardship, the cleanliness, the noise, the tedium of work, the provision for paid holidays, the hours and shifts, the health and safety conditions, how good local facilities – housing, medical services, schools, creches etc. -- are, and so on). Industries with old plants and poor conditions exist everywhere, and survive because the overall costs of upgrading (as opposed to simply investing in a new machine) are higher than the expected rate of profit. Parts of the textile industry and plants in the old areas of engineering exemplify some of these factors.

There are other activities where price competition is severe and the workers poorly organized because of the structural conditions at work. Take, for example, catering, hotels and restaurants. If we assume for the sake of argument that in 1979 Britain, the Supplementary Benefit rate of £55.90 per week for a couple with two children represented a benchmark for the "maintenance and reproduction" costs, a worker would have to earn £61.75 in gross earnings to reach this level. The lowest grade of non-service hotel workers received a weekly minimum rate of £40.40, rising to £42.80 (with, for London workers, an allowance of £2.40). Younger workers, employed on a seasonal basis, could expect £36 for a six day, 40 hour week in London (out of London young cleaners might expect £27.30). There are between half and three quarters of a million workers in this activity, 63 per cent of them full time, with average gross earnings in 1978 of £59.60 per week (or 8.5 per cent below the "socially necessary" level).

In construction and agriculture, seasonal work produces short term demands for labour which cannot be met if the workforce is being simultaneously upgraded. In construction, as in the coalmines in Belgium and West Germany, the key factor is less the price of labour power alone, and more its relationship to the danger and hardship of the work.

At its base, the labour market fades away into outworkers; people, usually housewives, working at home at rates where there is no pretence at all to meet even the lowest maintenance wages, let alone an element for family reproduction. There are estimated to be a quarter of a million home workers in Britain. In Nelson in Lancashire, some 6,000 mainly Asian women sew ribbons and bows for the textile trades at rates equivalent to 10p per hour. Garment workers on a rate of 9 to 35p per garment can expect weekly pay of £20 to £25. Nineteenth century conditions continue to flourish in modern capitalism.

Migration

When the system grew rapidly, masses of native workers were drawn into sectors where the price of labour power was relatively higher, sectors we have identified – somewhat oversimply – as those of higher productivity. Thus, agricultural workers in France, Germany, the United States and Japan, moved in the 1950s and 1960s into urban industrial and service jobs. In the sectors vacated, equipment was substituted for labour on a considerable scale but without this eliminating labour scarcities. It is here that labour demand was created for workers from abroad.

Immigrant labour has been reproduced at costs below the average for the destination country. It was therefore subjectively willing, at least initially, to work for wages well below the average, or work at average wages in conditions inferior to the average. The picture is more complicated than this because in many cases, the immigrant worker was drawn from that minority in the backward country which had been reproduced at costs well above the local average. The wages on offer to the worker in his or her home country were fixed relative to the local average level of productivity, but were below those appropriate for his or her costs of reproduction, as assessed by the open world market. Thus, the excesses of the rivalries between States – the underproduction of "low productivity labour" in the advanced, and the overproduction of "high productivity labour" in the backward – receive some partial equilibration by the international movement of workers.

There are also important socio-psychological factors at work. Workers who grow up in a particular social environment, tend to absorb the defensive ethics developed by preceding generations to protect themselves from the ravages of capital. There are jobs they will not do, paces or hours or conditions of work they will not accept, moves from one locality to another that they will not make for the sort of wages and terms on offer. A worker torn out of this environment is much more appropriate to the needs of capital, much more ruthlessly driven to earn at whatever the wages on offer are. Such a worker is less able to support himself or herself during unemployment by borrowing from local networks of relatives and friends, and less likely to have reserves on which to fall back in hard times, less likely to have possessions that can be sold or pawned. Such workers are likely to be much more responsive to differences in wages – regardless of conditions – and, lacking local social ties, much more geographically mobile in response to changes in the labour market. This – as well as overt discrimination – is a factor in the general picture of immigrants working longer hours, working more night shifts, doing more piece-work, with a higher rate of job changing and of geographical mobility than native workers. It is also a factor in explaining what seems to be a more extreme mismatch between the qualifications of immigrant workers and the jobs they actually do. If the natives refuse to be downgraded even if this means the misery of longterm unem-

THE NEW UNTOUCHABLES   47

ployment, the immigrants start in grades well below what the natives, with the same qualifications, would accept (of course, it is also true that at least at first foreign workers are more uninformed about what is locally considered reasonable, what alternatives exist etc.; they may also be consoled by the fact that a poor job in an advanced country offers better returns and conditions often than a good job in a backward country). Some employers recognise this factor: migrants make the best workers; and they always try to recruit new immigrants since those who have lived for some time in the country are likely to have become "spoiled", ie conform to local working class standards.

Moveable jobs

The import of labour is necessary where the price of labour power is too low to induce a sufficient number of workers to work in "immoveable" jobs: that is, jobs which cannot, at least in the short term, be relocated abroad. For example, local coal mines cannot be mined abroad, nor can local dustbins be emptied, local houses built, and local soils cultivated abroad, although in almost all cases, alternative supplies from abroad can be found., There is however no permanently fixed boundary between moveable and immoveable jobs; changes in comparative wage costs, in technology and so on can radically shift the boundaries.

Capital can gain access to labour power at prices well below those governing in its home territory where jobs are moveable. Parts of manufacturing (for example, in the recent past, labour intensive links in textiles, electronic components, television sets etc.), some agricultural tasks, tourism, conform to this. States, recognizing the dangers implicit in the dispersion of activity, sometimes impose regulations to prevent jobs moving; the US government, for example, does not permit US aircraft manufacture to move (but does permit imports). Export processing zones in South Korea, Malaysia, Brazil, the Caribbean etc. have attracted industrial activities from the advanced countries, at the same time as these countries have exported labour. On Mexico's northern border In-Bond plants have been permitted, set up by United States companies to manufacture consumer goods with raw materials and equipment imported from the States and Mexican labour; all the output is exported back to the United States. The In-Bond plant areas have thus been expropriated by the US labour market. At the same time, US nationals have started horticultural farms in northern Mexico to produce foodstuffs for the United States market. Finally, Mexico is a major exporter of labour to the States for farmwork and employment in textiles and services.

There are other examples of this kind, although not on such a large scale. Thus, India exports labour to the Gulf States, and Saudi Arabia finances vegetable farming in the Indian State of Andhra Pradesh, the produce being flown to Riyadh.

Firms with equipment and productivity standards derived from the advanced capitalist countries are able to transplant activities as isolated colonies to backward countries, providing the political context is right. Capital in the backward countries can then emulate the activity. But while productivity in the plants can be sustained at high levels, the general social average remains low. The workers in such plants are, as it were, "home based emigrants".

The theoretical significance

Access to foreign workers makes possible the continued growth of certain national capitals for three main reasons. Firstly it allows more workers to be utilized by a given capital stock: the small farmer in the Punjab produces much more surplus value when he is imported to work in a foundry in Wolverhampton, and in doing so he is benefitting the capitalist class as a whole.

Secondly, the costs of reproduction of such labour are, as we have seen, less than those of the average labour in the advanced countries. Utilizing it enables the capitalist to increase the proportion of the working day that goes in surplus to him rather than in the maintenance of the worker. Ideally then, from the point of view of profit maximization, the native workers would be expelled to permit the lower cost immigrants to take the jobs. The absurdity of this idea illustrates clearly why the State cannot, in slump, pursue directly the accumulation of capital; on the contrary, it must sacrifice accumulation to social stability. The State consists of people, linked by social bonds to the rest of the population. Attempts to expel the natives would involve the State in political self-destruction. On the contary, the State must do the opposite, stressing the inviolable rights of the natives in order to direct blame at the foreigners.

Finally, apart from the effect of the import of labour on the long run decline in the profit rate, it constitutes a net subsidy from one national capital to another. The sending country bears the cost of reproduction of the worker from its domestic product; the destination country receives adult labour power without the costs that would be needed to raise and train the worker. The higher the skill level, the greater the subsidy involved in the transfer. The subsidy is between national capitals (it could also be called "theft"), between countries. It does not necessarily benefit any individual employer who may employ the immigrant worker at the same rates as native labour. How far the destination country in fact is able to realize the full value of the subsidy varies, in particular with the terms of entry. Immigrants who settle and establish families, who draw on local public "maintenance" services (including ultimately old age pensions) will, in time, reduce the net subsidy. The subsidy is maximized for single adult workers on temporary contracts without any right to participate in local reproduction and maintenance services.

Russia and Japan

The framework presented here does not have the same application to all movements of workers internationally. For example, in the oil producing States of the Middle East, some of the relationships are reversed. Backward Saudi Arabia imports labour from more advanced Egypt, as well as from Europe and the United States (but it also imports labour from more backward North Yemen). Reproduction costs for an important part of the Egyptian labour force were certainly much higher than those in Saudi

THE NEW UNTOUCHABLES 49

Arabia at the beginning of the migratory movement. The "raiding operation" is much more extreme – the loss to Egypt is the same as it would be in emigration to an advanced country, but the gain to Saudi Arabia is much greater.

The Soviet Union has a very highly educated labour force but poor levels of labour productivity. Does this refute the general argument presented here? First, a high level of reproduction costs is a necessary but not a sufficient condition for attaining high levels of productivity. There are many other factors at stake in productivity, including the volume and quality of equipment available to the workforce, the organization of the capitalists (in this case, the State bureaucracy) and so on. Second, as the earlier discussion noted, the components of the conditions required for sustaining high productivity are very varied and cannot simply be reduced to education; they include adequate and easily available housing conditions, recreational facilities, and perhaps a given measure of "social freedom", all elements notoriously poor in the Soviet Union. High educational levels alone would not make up for the generalized poor quality of existence for the average Russian worker.

The case of Japan is an interesting one. First, its public services are much inferior to other advanced capitalist countries, but the levels of productivity attained in its leading industries are well in advance of its nearest rivals. Second, its rates of economic growth have been spectacularly high without this generating the sort of specific demands for labour which impel immigration. There is virtually no immigration to Japan, although there is a significant minority of Korean immigrants in the country (left over from the second World War and the partition of Korea, formerly a Japanese imperial possession).

Japan has reached the position of an advanced capitalist country very recently. Far from exhibiting labour scarcities, as recently as the early 1960s, the government was endeavouring to increase Japanese emigration by subsidizing migrants to leave. In the mid-1950s, some 15,000 emigrated each year under agreements between the Japanese government and those of Brazil, Bolivia, Paraguay and Argentina, as well as those who moved to the United States (much as the Netherlands Government encouraged emigration up to the mid-1950s in the belief that the country had too many workers). In the last half of the 1950s, 75,000 departed; in the first half of the sixties, 43,000; in the second half, 25,000 (there are said to be now 630,000 people "of Japanese origin" in the States, 760,000 in Brazil). Second, the reserves of agricultural labour in Japan have remained intact until relatively recently as can be seen in this comparative table:

PERCENTAGE OF THE LABOUR FORCE IN THE PRIMARY SECTOR

	1960 %	1970 %	1975 %
Japan	33	20	12.5
United States	—	4	3.8
France	22	14	10.8
West Germany	—	8	6.6
USSR	42	26	—
United Kingdom	—	3	2.5

(— = *not available*)

I.S. D

Thirdly, Japan is alone among the advanced capitalist countries in having a decrease in female participation rates as income has risen (from 50.1% in 1963 to 47.1% in 1973). This suggests that Japan has not exhausted its domestic labour reserves to the point where women's employment begins to increase. The poor level of public services also tends to keep a higher proportion of women at home; home based reproduction services must replace those of the State. Even today, in many companies women are still expected to retire at the age of 40, or, in some cases, on marriage, indicating that employers are not under pressure to keep women at work.

There are other indications of "relative labour abundance". Most workers still retire at 55 (although pensions are not payable until the age of 60). There is still a low rate of turnover in the large scale sector – employers are not bidding against each other for scarce skills. To some extent, the decline in labour hours available has not matched the other advanced capitalist countries – between 1960 and 1974, West German hours worked per week in manufacturing declined by 20% (from 48.8 to 39.1), Japan's by 5% (from 45.7 to 43.3 hours).

Japan's economy is, in comparison to its rivals, a fractured one – between a bloc of very high productivity modern industries of enormous scale, and a fluctuating mass of small enterprises, many of them subcontractors to the large firms, with relatively low productivity, low pay, little security of work and poor conditions. The high growth of the leading companies is purchased at the cost of the small enterprises.

In general, Japanese growth is achieved by a high concentration on certain key sectors, not by attempting to generalize performance on all fronts. The increase in reproduction costs required to support the advanced sector is not spread through society and there is much heavier reliance on the family (but not, of course, in education). The low level of public intervention in the provision of maintenance and reproduction services is thus much more characteristic of a backward economy than an advanced. There is no supplementary benefits system, unemployment pay is very low. Hospital and medical services are notoriously bad for the majority. There are few homes for the invalided or elderly. Housing is very poor and extraordinarily expensive; a 1978 survey showed that a quarter of households lived in tiny one room flats; a quarter of households had no bathroom; ten per cent no running water; and two thirds were not connected to the sewerage system. Parks are rare (London has 22.8 square metres of park per head of the population, Tokyo 2), as are libraries and museums.

In sum then, Japan is still arriving at the state where the State is obliged to seek to guarantee a minimum reproduction standard for the whole labour force. The obligation is also affected by the political context – the class struggle in Japan has never reached the point of forcing standardization as happened in, for example, Britain immediately after the second World War. The State in Japan has also no doubt delayed embarking upon this transformation as it observes the gambles undertaken in other advanced capitalist countries and their effect on gross investment[6] and thus the overall rate of economic growth.

Low public expenditure in Japan becomes another factor of competition in conditions of slump. The other advanced capitalist countries on the

THE NEW UNTOUCHABLES 51

one hand press Japan to raise its public spending; on the other, they are tempted to try to sacrifice reproduction expenditure and lower their own rates of spending to the Japanese level. Meanwhile, South Korea and Taiwan seek to emulate the Japanese trajectory of growth, to Tokyo's alarm.

There is a final factor worth noting in connection with "moveable" jobs. Japan's investment abroad – unlike other advanced capitalist countries – is mainly in backward countries. In particular, Japanese companies have invested heavily in certain sectors of production in South Korea, Taiwan, Singapore, Malaysia etc. (in textiles, electronics etc.). To some extent it may have widened its low priced labour pool to a greater extent than its rivals.

There are an enormous number of unanswered questions in examining the relationship between reproduction costs, labour productivity and immigration. But at least on a superficial level, Japan does not seem to defeat the main argument.

The functions of immigration in primarily destination countries

When world capitalism expanded, migration to the core zones of the system made possible the performance of low productivity jobs important for the national economies concerned. Perhaps, without the remaining structures of protection, many of those jobs would have been "exported", or, reshuffling of occupations would have made possible high growth without immigration. Be that as it may, the degree to which immigration was necessary depended upon the size of existing labour reserves (in agriculture, in home labour etc.) and the rate and pattern of growth of the particular national economy concerned.

Native labour moved upwards to jobs, the return to which more closely related to the appropriate return to average levels of productivity. Once immigrant workers had been drawn in, they were able to follow native labour, depending upon how freely they were permitted to change jobs and sectors – out of construction, agriculture, mining, to former native strongholds, metal manufacturing and assembly. This in turn created new vacancies where they had formerly worked, necessitating new immigration. By now, the foreign born are roughly 6 to 7 per cent of the population in most west European countries (the remarkably low figure for Britain – 3.3 per cent – is a mark of the poor growth rate here); and possibly 9 to 10 per cent of the local labour force (but 18.4 per cent of the Swiss population). Between a fifth and a third of the labour force in the metal trades in Switzerland, Holland and Germany are immigrant workers.[7]

The situation in the United States is more complicated since it has the largest minority of "native immigrants" (black people, Puerto Ricans, Chicanos etc.). In the case of black people, there has been a sustained movement over a long period out of southern agriculture to metal manufacturing and steel production in the old industrial centres of the north and north east. Later, the expanding new industries of the west coast, and now the south (aircraft, electronics, science based industries etc.) have attracted white skilled workers from the north and north east. Currently, the expansion of southern industry is for the first time since the Civil War attracting net black immigration. The possibility of immigrant labour moving up the hierarchy cannot be separated from the movement of "native immigrants".

Seasonal migration by agricultural workers is important in parts of Europe – for example, the movement of casual labour from southern Spain to southern France.[8] It is also important in the United States. The only contract labour system for foreign workers still remaining there brings Caribbean workers to Florida's apple orchards each year. Elsewhere, illegal seasonal workers from Mexico plug the gaps left by the upgrading of the American labour force. In this case, not only does the farmer not meet annual reproduction costs since the work is paid only in the season of employment, he does not pay annual maintenance costs. In the case of illegal migrants, the farmer can pay wages below the legal minimum by using the threat, if the worker does not accept this, of denouncing him or her to the police and immigration service. Real returns to the workers can scarcely be much above what he or she might expect to earn in Mexican agriculture – if jobs were available. It is hardly surprising that there are too few native Americans willing to work for such pay even when there are high rates of official unemployment in the district concerned. Texan farmers, in trying to strengthen their case to the Government against the imposition of fines on employers taking on illegal migrants, advertised 4,000 farm-hand jobs at the minimum legal hourly rate (then $2.20 per hour). They received only 300 applications from workers with legal status.

In Europe, it has often been argued that, in the absence of strict border controls, the flow of immigrants varies with the level of unemployment in the destination country – as unemployment rises, immigration falls. But this affects only legal movement. There are no useful figures on illegal movement. In the United States, it is argued that illegal migration has increased during the current phase of stagnation since 1974. This could represent a substitution of cheap labour for more expensive native workers. Or it could reflect changes in the structure of the labour market – a sharp contraction in the core metal using industries, without an equivalent decline in labour intensive agriculture, and possibly even an expansion in catering and restaurants (which could result from a big increase in tourism, for example). The same could be happening in Europe in the illegal sectors.

This illustrates that the demand for cheap labour power does not disappear in slump. On the contrary, it can increase. The British Government has pursued policies of deliberate discrimination against black people in the name of its immigration policies, in defiance of the needs of the British economy, but it has made consistent concessions to permit the entry of European workers on work permits. Some 120,000 permits were issued in 1978. Any increase in foreign tourism increases the pressure of the restaurants and catering trades on the Government to permit the import of labour. Nonetheless, last November the Government tightened the regulations to reduce work permits as part of its attempts to bludgeon native workers into accepting low paid jobs.[9]

The French Government has recently cut residence permits for foreign

THE NEW UNTOUCHABLES 53

workers from ten to three years, and now to one, affecting between half and one million north and west African workers. This was supposedly done to increase the job opportunities for the native unemployed. Yet a recent official report calculates that for every 150,000 foreign workers sacked, only 13,000 jobs become available for native workers. Indeed, we could go further and infer that, since French workers will not accept the wages on offer for most of these 13,000 jobs, important tasks in the economy will not be performed and one possible result will be an increase in native unemployment in other sectors dependent upon the performance of these tasks. The Government's policy has little at all to do with unemployment – it is designed to incite racialism on the one hand, and lower public expenditure by reducing the cost of maintaining the unemployed by expelling them from the country on the other.

Immigrants provide a target in slump, a measure of flexibility made necessary precisely because of the rigidity of structure of modern capitalism. The expulsion of immigrants is a substitute for increasing the level of unemployment more dramatically,[10] even though it is deleterious to the economy. Between 1974 and 1977, the number of foreign workers in West Germany fell by 19%, and in France by 16%. Or, take the example of the British merchant fleet between 1976 and 1979. Carrying capacity fell by 20%; the number of British officers fell by 5%, and of British ratings, hardly at all. The number of non-British ratings fell by 20%. Given the difference in wages between British and non-British ratings, this change must have raised labour costs per unit of freight carried – thus, the employers purchased the loyalty of British ratings at the cost of a decline in their capacity to compete internationally.

The function of immigrant labour depends on an accepted level of social discrimination; the exclusion of immigrants from the same rights as the natives is accepted by the natives without protest. It is this which makes possible the harassment of foreign workers by the State. Whether it is the obscene persecution at Heathrow airport, the manhunts in Texas or the border States, or the French police checking everyone with dark skins on the Metro, the aim is the same – to keep open the division between native and foreigner.

In the Middle East, these mechanisms are often more advanced. In Saudi Arabia, the regulations governing the mass of immigrant workers include a ban on strikes; employers are, in theory at least, fined for employing illegal immigrants; immigrants have no right to change their jobs without a passport check (drivers on intercity buses are supposed to check passenger passports). To add terror to the regulations, there are periodic mass expulsions – for example, 30,000 people called by the Government "Pakistanis" were expelled from the country *en masse* in March 1978. In the United Arab Emirates, under the July 1977 regulations, the government assumed the right to deport any foreign worker who disobeyed the orders of his or her employer, tried to organize a work stoppage, damaged production, assaulted an employer or representative, or committed any other serious misdemenour.

The aim of such regulations appears to be to force the solidarity of the native population by the continual demonstration of the "disprivilege" of the foreigner. Such demonstrations are particularly required when economic contraction is continually reminding the poorest natives of their own misfortunes. Thus the panoply of intimidatory controls has nothing to do with the specific characteristics of the foreign worker concerned, but rather is related to the need to secure the loyalty of the natives. The argument that immigrants are the cause of the native response is of the same logic as blaming the poor for their poverty, the unemployed for being jobless, and so on.

Controls can work in a slump provided there is sufficient police power. But they do so with paradoxical results. First, they have negative effects for native employment (tending to raise native unempoyment rates, and force natives into poorer paid work) and for the economy as a whole, leaving aside the waste involved in employing a bureaucracy and police force to implement the regulations. But secondly, regulations drastically reduce just that flexibility which is one of the main advantages of immigrant labour to capitalism. For example, in West Germany in the 1960s, sixty per cent of Italian workers stayed for under two years, returning to Italy after that time. If tight border controls are introduced, foreign workers will not return to Italy for fear of not regaining re-entry to Germany – they are forced into permanent settlement, exile. And it then becomes politically difficult to expel them. Similarly, if the United States succeeded in controlling the Rio Grande border with Mexico, it would no doubt curb seasonal migration but increase the numbers permanently resident in the United States.

Singapore, being a very small territory with a powerful State, has apparently succeeded in operating tight controls. The city is an industrialized economy, based upon a mass of cheap labour (but the State maintains possibly the most advanced system of publicly provided reproduction and maintenance services in Asia, restricted to natives). Every expansion in the economy produces a shortage of labour in certain sectors – construction, ship repair (for men), textiles and electronics (for women). Immigrant labour fills the gaps, but under tight control – employers are permitted to recruit abroad, but remain responsible for their labour force. The State, with the close collaboration of the trade unions, ensures control to hold immigrant wages down, to prevent the labour market operating. Immigrants are used as the lever to keep down wages in general in the city for the mass of workers. Foreign workers are permitted to enter in the first instance for six months in construction; others, many of them young women, may not change jobs for three years, hold trade union office, marry or have children; they have no right to public housing, medical services or schools; those that ultimately secure permission to marry do so only on condition of signing a bond to accept sterilization after the birth of their second child. The penalty for disobeying the rules is expulsion.

These regulations apply to those entering the city on work vouchers (granted to those earning below 750 Singapore dollars per month). They do not apply to the highly skilled, professional or business classes who are granted employment vouchers (for those earning 750 Singapore dollars or more). In 1979, the government announced a new policy to reduce or eliminate the island's dependence on immigrant labour, by trying to force an increase in the capital-intensity of production (that is, substituting equip-

THE NEW UNTOUCHABLES   55

ment for labour by changing the industrial mix of the city's output). Companies utilizing a great deal of labour are expected to leave the island, locating in the countries from which immigrants are drawn (the Singapore Government is also trying to locate labour intensive industry on the Indonesian island of Batam). To achieve this aim, the Government has proposed increasing wages for three years by 7 per cent, plus 32 Singapore dollars. In fact this is a very small increase to achieve such a change; the Singapore Manufacturers' Association estimates the wage bill for its members at between 8 and 15 per cent of total costs, so the increase will add only between 1.6 and 3 per cent to costs. Of course, consistent with its record, even this small increase is not to be paid to the workers (lest "they get used to high wages") but paid into the government Provident Fund. The payments can be stopped if the Singapore leadership decides the policy is in fact jeopardizing the city economy.

In other countries which are expanding, the controls are much weaker. In the Middle East, governments have moved from accepting general immigration to, at least officially, tolerating only temporary project-related entries (and the employer in the project is required to remove the labour force from the country at the end of the project). But the labour market continues to operate. Workers escape from the project or take second jobs. In mid-1978, 5,000 Indians working for Engineering Projects of India went on strike when the company, under government pressure, tried to prevent moonlighting. EPI asked the Ministry of the Interior to deport 250 of its workers, and made a small pay increase to the rest.

In summary then, foreign workers are necessary when the system grows to compensate for the deficiencies of national planning (whether the planning is declared or not), to straddle the contradiction between the development of the State and the growth of capital. In slump, they are also necessary, but this economic function is subsidiary to their social role: they are the anvil upon which the loyalty of the natives to the existing State can be forged.

The effects of emigration on primarily sending countries

If a State exports workers, labour power, on a significant scale in competition with other States, then the world labour market would begin to exercise an influence over the domestic production of labour, as the world market guides the domestic production of any other commodity. The more developed the export of labour, the more an exporting State would seek to control the lease or sale of labour power (to become a labour contractor or supervisory agent for labour contractors), to standardize its quality and tailor it to the specific vacancies abroad. To maximize its profits, it would need to minimize the costs of reproduction, ultimately to convert the economy to a manufacturing plant for breeding and raising workers. This might be done directly, or through the medium of the family, with State incentives and services being directed to induce the family to produce and train the numbers required (the family would then become, as it were, a private firm under the supervision of the State). It follows that such a State would have relinquished any ambition to create a diversified national economy in favour of filling one specialized niche in the world system.

At the moment, States "pillage" their domestic labour forces – or permit them to be pillaged by other States – without paying attention to sustaining future supplies, much as capitalism ransacked pre-capitalist sectors in the early phases of its growth. But exporting States do seek to control emigration, to ensure certain levels of pay and remittances, and to supervise their nationals abroad to prevent conflicts which might jeopardize their competitive position. In particular, in east and south Asia, prices are partly set in relationship to competing States in the provision of labour to multinational employers for construction work in the Middle East or merchant seamen's jobs.

What are some of the immediate crude effects of large scale emigration for work? Some of them can be listed as follows: firstly emigration is drawn from particular districts, so that an important first effect is localised depopulation – as in parts of Eire, northern Portugal, Algeria, Lesotho, North Yemen, etc. Those leaving are workers in the most active age groups, so the effect of departures is magnified in the age group 15 to 35, and often, among the most skilled. Thus, the domestic labour force is stripped of its most decisive elements. Sometimes, emigration draws heavily on one sex, producing a sex imbalance, which has maximum effects on those in the reproductive age groups, reflected in a decline in the marriage and birth rates. Thus, not only is the present generation stripped, the next generation is jeopardized.

Secondly, the resulting shortage of skills can produce considerable labour scarcities in particular trades, and wage inflation. It is reported, for example, that the daily wage rate for masons in Pakistan used to be 15 rupees, but by 1979, under the impact of emigration of building craftsmen to the Middle East as well as a local house building boom financed from the remittances of workers abroad, the daily rate was 40 rupees. In North Yemen, large scale emigration has generated such wage inflation that now child labour can work as drivers at high wages. While this is good for low paid workers, it is catastrophic for local ruling classes with any ambition to speed capital accumulation. More generally it indicates a tendency for emigration to draw wages in the sending country up towards the level in the destination country, to create a single price in an international labour market.

A sequence of events in South Korea also illustrates this. In March 1977, Korean workers were involved in a three day riot at a Hyundai project in Saudi Arabia. President Park of South Korea intervened to raise the minimum pay level to (US)$240 per month. This in turn almost certainly encouraged more workers, particularly drivers, to opt for work in the Middle East. In May 1978, Park was obliged to raise the pay of Pusan bus drivers by 70% to discourage emigration, but without success since shortly afterwards he imposed a temporary ban on the recruitment of drivers for work abroad.

Thirdly, for some exporting countries, remittances from their nationals working abroad have become very important as sources of foreign earnings. Take three countries importing labour to Europe:

THE NEW UNTOUCHABLES   57

REMITTANCES AS A PERCENTAGE OF EXPORT EARNINGS

	1970	1973	1974
Greece	54%	58%	35%
Portugal	55%	62%	50%
Turkey	46%	90%	94%

These cases are not as extreme as North Yemen which is said to be able to import one hundred times more than it exports.

Having workers abroad firmly yokes the growth of local incomes to growth in the centres of world production abroad. Contraction in the world system similarly has reverse effects. For example, the virtual end of European recruitment of Turkish workers – as well as a flourishing black market in remittance payments to Turkey – was a powerful element in the severity of the crisis in Turkey. Official remittances peaked at (US)$1.42 billion in 1974, and fell to $0.98 billion in 1978 (unofficial payments, 1973 to 1978, are put at just over $2 billion). The pressure of the Turkish government to be admitted to the Common Market and the EEC provisions for the free movement of labour are a measure of the despair of the Turkish ruling class – only by leasing its labour for exploitation by foreign capital can it retain its hold on Turkey.

Fourthly, while in theory remittances make possible industrial imports to accelerate domestic growth; in practice States have to offer incentives to persuade their nationals to return part of their earnings through the official markets. That means that the exchange rate must either give special advantages to those wishing to return remittances or permit the currency to float so that any advantage in operating on the black market is removed. Such measures make it extremely difficult to control national finance in the interests of capital accumulation. Furthermore, since workers abroad can buy foreign consumer goods, they will do so abroad unless they can buy such goods at home at the same price – thus, incentives to repatriate earnings include the 'liberalization' of the import of consumer goods. This further reduces the chances of building national industry on an import substitution basis.

Finally, in general, emigrants regard home as merely home, not somewhere where they can use their foreign earnings to set themselves up as small capitalists (an illusory aim, given the relatively small earnings they individually make). Thus, remittances converted into local currency are used to buy land for housebuilding, to build houses and buy consumer goods. One result is, as noted earlier, inflation in the construction industries. In sum, the districts of emigration become dormitory suburbs or country cottages of workplaces abroad, places where foreign earnings are consumed not where productive activities are improved.

These elements indicate some of the pressures on world labour demand that restructure labour exporting countries, making even more difficult any independent strategy for national economic development. In practice, States react empirically, adjusting policy step by step without being conscious of the overall drift until it is too late to reverse the process. Their preoccupations are more directed at supervising the return of remittances.

The power of the State over nationals outside its frontiers is limited. At most, it can withold the renewal of passports, seize property left behind or punish relatives. But abroad, no international policy yet exists to trace recalcitrants in the way, at least in principle, stolen goods can be traced. Usually, documentation is its sole power, which explains in part efforts made to enforce the necessity to travel with documents, to eliminate the possibility of undocumented movement.

Other measures are taken to strengthen control. Where local companies employ local labour on contracts abroad – as happens with Korean, Turkish or Greek construction companies in the Middle East, or Mexican construction companies in Venezuela – controls can be tight. The State can penalize the company. In turn the company handles the transport (and keeps the return ticket until the worker is instructed to return), housing, feeding and supervision of the worker. The South Koreans stiffen this control by appointing, in charge of each gang of workers, a volunteer craftsman demobilized from the army for the purpose of supervision.

Such controls require local capital to be developed enough to act as employer. For the Philippines, this is not usually the case. The government has therefore moved towards leasing labour in groups to foreign employers. Hirers of labour are required to sign a contract with the government guaranteeing certain conditions and accepting an obligation to return a certain proportion of foreign earnings to the Manila agent directly (that is, not through the worker).

Regulations on remittances vary widely, as does the power to enforce them. South Korea demands remission of 80% of foreign earnings. India requires, in theory, 10%. Filipino workers abroad are required to return 40% of earnings, and 70% if they are seamen. Pakistan demands that 20% of the earnings of professional and technical staff be paid to the State as tax, but it has little or no power to enforce this.

The People's Republic of China has recently entered the market by permitting provincial governments to offer Chinese labour to foreign employers for work abroad. Guangdong province has recently published details of its proposals in Hong Kong. It offers "unlimited numbers" of workers, aged 18 to 35, to work a 48 hour week, with three days holiday per year. The government promises that its workers will be "diligent and obedient to the employers' reasonable instructions and work assignments". Workers will receive free board and travel; they will be given 10% of their total earnings (which should be between £69 and £104 weekly) as pocket money while abroad, and 10% on the termination of the contract, the rest presumably accruing to the Guangdong or Chinese Governments.

Perhaps the Chinese are copying the Philippines Government which has developed a marketing strategy for what is known as "the export of warm bodies". The Overseas Development Board of the Ministry of Labour circulates glossy brochures to multinational companies proclaiming the superior character (and very low cost) of this "prized living export", "the best bargain in the world labour market". The government lays out its terms and promises, on signature of the contract, to "package and deliver workers to various worksites round the world".

In conclusion, then, the national organisation of the sale of labour power is, at the government level, already well organised. Private labour

THE NEW UNTOUCHABLES 59

contractors tout their wares round the globe and have done so for much of the history of capitalism, but State organisation – with a close eye on the balance of payments – is relatively new. If the process were to persist, sooner or later States would have to intervene in the reproduction process to ensure continued supplies and proper maintenance.

Conclusion

International migrants are a particular stratum of the world working class, embodying the contradiction between a world economy and its national political and social organisation. Relative to the national ideologies which dominate the world, they should not exist at all. Endeavouring to eliminate them, regardless of the damage thereby inflicted upon the world economic system, is part of the self-destructive drive of capitalism in crisis: the growth of world production is sacrificed to the maintenance of class rule.

The legal migrant is still a person. Although frequently oppressed, immigrants are still in an infinitely superior position to those who dare to move without a licence: the illegal migrant and the mass of refugees. Since these people belong to no ruling class, any barbarity may be inflicted upon them. They can be treated as cruelly as those lost peoples encompassed by the expanding modern national State: the Red Indians, the aborigines, the nomads.[11]

The ruling classes of the destination countries seek to stabilise their national power at the cost of the world system, at the same time as borrowing or stealing the labour forces of more backward ruling classes. There is a strikingly vivid model for a different method of achieving similar results. South Africa reclassified the majority of its natives as foreigners, nationals of a set of hastily run up independent States, the Bantustans. To do this, the distinction between "labourer" and "labour power" was vital, as the Minister of Mining explained in 1965: "They (black workers) are only supplying a commodity, the commodity of labour... it is labour we are importing and not labourers".[12] Apartheid, insofar as its aims in the field of labour were actually achieved, secured the purpose of offloading the costs of the reproduction of black labour to the Bantustans while retaining access to the labour power of adult workers. It also prevented black workers seeking to emulate the reproduction costs of white South Africa. Its viability depended upon being able to maintain a divided economy, between a majority low productivity sector and a minority high productivity sector. It has analogies with Japan. Insofar as this structural condition is superceded, apartheid comes to act as a powerful constraint on the growth of South African capitalism.

No issue today so sharply differentiates revolutionary internationalists and national reformists as that of the international migration of workers. The issue at stake is a challenge to the very existence of the national State and its prerogatives in the control of a territory and the inhabitants. Much of the politics of the Left is concerned with gaining control of the State and accelerating the growth of its power over its inhabitants, not with abolishing the State. Deploring the ill treatment of immigrants is seen, not as an attack on the powers of the State, but as an argument for ending all immigration. Demands for a "humane immigration policy" rival the fantasies of "send capital to the countries from which the immigrants come, not immigrants to the countries where capital exists". If the Left had power to direct capital to new locations, it has the power to abolish capital. In the United States, it is part of the Left which stresses that illegal immigrants menace only the oppressed but native groups – blacks, Puerto Ricans, women – and that, to protect these groups, illegals should be expelled. Yet to permit the expulsion of illegal immigrants is to take one step nearer to the expulsion of immigrants, which in turn is a step closer to the expulsion of selected sections of natives. That way madness lies. Accepting the right of the State to control immigration is accepting its right to exist, the right of the ruling class to exist as a ruling class, the right to exploit, the "right" to a world of barbarism.

In South Africa, the white trade unions allied with the State for immediate gains to a minority of workers at the expense of the majority. It is the AFL-CIO which campaigns more consistently for the rounding up and expulsion of illegal Mexican workers; they "permit" US business to locate across the southern border to use cheap Mexican labour, but refuse to follow them to recruit Mexican workers and establish parity of wages on both sides of the frontier (a demand which would of course bring them into direct collision with the interests not only of US business but also the Mexican ruling class, also dependent upon cheap labour). It is the British TUC which continually presses for an end to the issue of work permits, an aim which, if achieved, would rob the TUC leadership of the opportunity of banquets in expensive London hotels. While it is the labour movement which leads the attack on foreign workers, employers may sleep quietly in their beds: whatever the secondary quarrels, the unions accept "the national interest", the employers' interest, that this is the best of all possible worlds.

NOTES

1. Compare the contemporary tolerance of the passport as a means of labour control to Marx's comment on internal labour passports:

    "The excess of despotism reached in France will be apparent by the following regulations as to working men.

    "Every working man is supplied with a book by the police – the first page of which contains his name, age, birthplace, trade or calling, and a description of his person. He is therein obliged to enter the name of the master for whom he works, and the reasons why he leaves him. But this is not all: the book is placed in the master's hands and deposited by him in the bureau of the police with the character of the man by the master. When a workman leaves his employment, he must go and fetch this book from the police office; and is not allowed to obtain another situation without producing it. Thus the workman's bread is utterly dependent on the police. But this again is not all: this book serves the purpose of a passport. If he is obnoxious, the police write 'bon pour retourner chez lui' ('Valid for return home', NH) in it, and the workman is obliged to return to his parish!

    "...No serfdom of the feudal ages – no pariahdom of India has its parallel" (Karl Marx/Frederick Engels, *Collected Works*, London, 1978, Vol.10, p.578.)

2. This phenomenon is usually related to apparently accidental changes in the birth rate, reflected later in changes in the size of labour force. In fact, there is often no correlation with birth rates – for example, Greece, Spain, Portugal and

THE NEW UNTOUCHABLES 61

Yugoslavia have the same sort of birth rates as those countries to which their nationals have migrated.

"Surplus workers" is the obverse of "lack of the means to employ" (or "capital deficit"), just as "scarcity of labour" means "excess of the means to employ" (implying an excess demand for goods or services, "capital surplus"). But differences of this kind have existed for a very long time, so they can hardly account for particular movements of workers at particular times. There are many areas, in any case, with a "capital deficit" but hardly any emigration.

Furthermore, the argument implies that it is the "surplus" workers, the unemployed, who move, when frequently it is not. "Scarcity" implies a general spread of unfilled vacancies in labour importing countries, when such a situation never exists, only particular scarcities in particular trades. The argument also assumes that the existing labour force in destination countries is "fully utilized" when it never is nor could be outside the realm of theory. There are always sections of the population which could be employed if the wage and conditions offered were good enough – women working at home, people under the age of 15, the sick, invalided and retired. If the price of labour, the wage, were to rise high enough, it would induce a movement of workers out of low into higher paid jobs (as happened in Germany, France and the United States with agricultural workers in the 1950s and 1960s). Alternatively, jobs can be exported or subcontracted abroad, as today when the Lancashire millowners are trying to subcontract garment making to the Mediterranean countries (the "outward processing" system).

Thus, the occurrence of "scarcity" or "surplus" does not *explain* the movement of workers; on the contrary, it is the movement which alone gives rise to the invention of these terms.

3. In Britain, the numbers in higher education have roughly doubled every twenty five years in this century. Between 1955 and 1970, numbers were doubling every eight years. On comparative expenditure and enrolments, see:

INCREASES IN HIGHER EDUCATION
(AVERAGE ANNUAL GROWTH RATES)

	Dates	1. Expenditure	2. Enrolments
France	1958-68	13.3%	9.8%
W. Germany	1957-66	16.3%	5.0%
Italy	1950-65	15.0%	3.9%
Japan	1950-65	11.1%	6.9%
UK (England & Wales)	1950-66	9.8%	5.1%
US	1955-67	11.4%	7.5%

(*OECD Observer*, No.50, Feb. 1971, p.15.)

Decasualisation reduces the labour hours available if we assume that casual workers formerly took several jobs, and after being decasualized, remained in one job without working the same number of hours as they previously worked in more than one job.

4. The 1971 survey of 47,000 industrial units, employing between one and four workers, and covering 116,000 workers in all, showed:

1. Value added — Rs.104 million
2. Hired labour costs — Rs. 66 million (at Rs.1,375 per year)
3. Imputed wage for employers and family labour — Rs. 93 million
4. Profits — Rs. 55 million
5. Actual return to employers and family labour — Rs. 38 million (or Rs.559 per person).

(A.N. Bose, *"Calcutta and Rural Bengal"*, Minerva, Calcutta, 1978.)

5. The Report of the Inspector General of Recruiting, following the Boer War, noted "the gradual deterioration of the physique of the working classes from whom the bulk of recruits must always be drawn" (cited R.M. Titmuss, *Essays on the Welfare State*, London, 1958.)

6.

Distribution of the Gross Domestic Product, 1976

	G.N.P. per capita, 1976 US$	Public Consumption %	Private Consumption %	Gross Domestic Investment %
Japan	4910	9	57	33
US	7890	17	64	16
France	6550	13	62	23
W. Germany	7380	18	55	24
USSR	2760	—	—	—
UK	4020	19	60	17

7. One estimate of the net subsidy from immigrant homelands to West Germany puts the figure for workers who have moved between 1957 and 1966, and 1968 and 1973 (there was a net outflow of foreign workers in 1967) at US$33 bn. (1962 prices). Remittances returned to the homelands in the same period were US$8.8 bn. There are no estimates of the immigrant net contribution to West Germany's gross domestic product. Another estimate, solely for highly skilled and professional immigrants to Britain, Canada and the United States, 1961 to 1972, puts the subsidy at US$46 billion.

8. This migration increases shortages for casual labour during the harvesting in parts of Spain which encourages the larger farmers to buy labour saving equipment, which in turn increases emigration: "to their paternalist relationship with the big landlords, has been added a further dependence on the European trade cycle" (Bernard Kayser, *Manpower Movements and Labour Markets* (Report), OECD, 1971, p.196.)

9. In a study of Cologne in Germany, a writer notes:
    "the throng of foreign workers does not form a simple quantitative supplement, elastic by definition: on the contrary, it is for the most part an essential force in the economy because of the sectors of which it is in possession. For the main feature of immigrant manpower on the labour market is its practically irreversible specialization: it seems out of the question that, even in a period of crisis, nationals should demand again for themselves jobs which have become considered inferior and abandoned to the foreigners" (Kayser, *op.cit.*, p.175.)

10. It is for this reason that Böhning describes immigrant labour as a "conjunctural shock absorber" (W.R. Böhning and D. Maillat, *The effects of the employment of foreign workers*, OECD, Paris, 1974, p.18)

11. Compare Victor Serge's observation on the exiled:
    "I have witnessed the birth of the enormous category of 'stateless persons', that is, of those men to whom tyrants refuse even a nationality. As far as the right to live is concerned, the plight of these men without a country ... can be compared only to that of the 'unacknowledged man' of the Middle Ages who, since he had no lord or sovereign, had no rights and no protection either, and whose very name became a kind of insult". (*Memoirs of a Revolutionary, 1901-1941*, translated by Peter Sedgwick, [to whom much thanks for pointing out the passage], Oxford, 1963, p.373.)

12. And once their labour power was exhausted, they must carry their bodies off, out of the territory of the State. General Circular No.25 of 1967 stipulated that:
    "as soon as they become, for some reason or another, no longer fit to work or

THE NEW UNTOUCHABLES 63

superfluous in the labour market, they are expected to return to their country of origin or the territory of their national unit where they fit in ethnically (even) if they were not born and bred in the 'Homeland' " (cited in *Crossroads: A consequence of ideology or urbanization*, by M.J. Andrews, unpublished dissertation, May 1979.)

[4]

Labour Migration in the Arab Gulf States: Patterns, Trends and Prospects *

J. S. BIRKS, I. J. SECCOMBE AND C. A. SINCLAIR **

INTRODUCTION

This paper presents an analysis of recent changes in the scale and characteristics of non-national migration to, and employment in, the six Gulf Cooperation Council (GCC) member states. The paper comprises five main sections. Firstly, it examines the scale, distribution and nationality composition of the non-national workforce stock in 1985. The second section focuses on migrant worker flows in the 1980s. It begins by examining the volume of labour migration, using work permit and placement data sources. The growth of clandestine migration and employment is commented on. Changes in the nationality composition, employment by economic sector and wage rates, are appraised. The third part of the paper describes the 1986 oil price shock and details the ensuing net non-national labour outflows. Finally, the paper presents an outline projection of non-national workforces in the Gulf in the early 1990s. Statistical tables appear at the end of the text.

NON-NATIONAL WORKFORCE STOCKS IN 1985

The size of the Non-national Workforce in 1985
The total workforce in the Gulf states in 1985 was 7.1 million. Sixty-nine per cent (4.9 million) of this total was in Saudi Arabia. The GCC's workforce is overwhelmingly non-national in composition. In all six states, nationals were a minority of the workforce in 1985. In 1985 there were more than 5.1 million non-nationals in the workforces of the six GCC states. Although Saudi Arabia has the largest non-national workforce (3.52 million), some 68 per cent of the total, the degree of dependence on non-national workers is greatest in some of the smaller Gulf states. The share of non-nationals in the workforce is over 80 per cent in Kuwait and Qatar and almost 91 per cent in the UAE. Even in Saudi Arabia non-nationals account for more than 71 per cent of its workforce.

---

* Paper presented at the Round Table (organized by the Development Policy Forum of the German Foundation for International Development (DSE) and ICM in cooperation with the Government of the Republic of the Philippines) on International Labour Migration in the Philippines and South-East Asia, Manila (Philippines), 8th-11th December 1987. The views and opinions expressed in this paper are those of the authors and not necessarily those of any international agency with which the authors are or have been associated.
** Mountjoy Research Centre, Durham (U.K.).

Nationality Composition of the Non-national Workforce in 1985
In 1985, 43 per cent of the migrant workforce in these six countries came from South Asia; a further 20 per cent came from South-East Asian countries. Together, Asian labour sending countries accounted for more than 3.2 million (63 per cent) of the migrant worker stock in the Gulf in 1985. Non-national Arab workers represent only 30 per cent (1.54 million) of the total. Overall, the non-national workforce in the GCC is Asian, rather than Arab, in character. (See table 2.1 on page 274).

South-East Asian migrant workers are highly concentrated, with more than 92 per cent employed in Saudi Arabia. South Asians are spread more widely throughout the Gulf, with just over 50 per cent in Saudi Arabia, 20 per cent in the UAE, and a further 25 per cent in Oman and Kuwait.

In the lower Gulf states Asian migrant workers are strikingly dominant, accounting for 91 per cent of the migrant workforce in Oman, 84 per cent in Bahrain and 79 per cent in the UAE.

In 1985 more than one-third of all migrant workers in the GCC member states came from two labour supplying countries, India (22 per cent) and Pakistan (14 per cent). In 1985 the stock of Indian workers in the Gulf numbered more than 1.1 million. Almost half of these were in Saudi Arabia where they represented nearly 15 per cent of the migrant workforce. India's share of the migrant workforce rises to 42 per cent in the UAE, 49 per cent in Bahrain and 62 per cent in Oman. The distribution of Pakistanis is also dominated by Saudi Arabia which accounts for more than 57 per cent of the total. Pakistanis are especially prominent in the UAE where they account for over a quarter of the migrant workforce. The main South-East Asian labour suppliers are the Philippines (356,000), South Korea (325,000) and Thailand (268,000).

South-East Asians account for over 27 per cent of the non-national workforce in Saudi Arabia. Their share in other Gulf states is much smaller, ranging from less than two per cent in Oman to 11 per cent in Bahrain.

Sectoral Distribution of the Non-national Workforce in 1985
Table 2.2 (see page 275) shows the sectoral distribution of non-national workforces by country of employment in 1985. Contrary to the conventional wisdom, which sees non-nationals mainly in construction, in 1985 the largest proportion of non-nationals were employed in services. Financial services, personal and community services accounted for 1.5 million non-national workers, almost 30 per cent of the total. Construction was the second largest sector, with 1.45 million workers, just under 29 per cent of the total. Wholesale and retail trade was 14 per cent of non-national employment. Relatively small shares were employed in utilities (3.2 per cent) and mining and quarrying (1.1 per cent). Manufacturing absorbs 9.4 per cent of the total and agriculture 8.9 per cent.

These shares vary little across the Gulf countries. In Saudi Arabia and Oman however, construction was still the lead sector in 1985, accounting for 29 per cent and 47 per cent of non-national employment, respectively. In Kuwait services account for more than 46 per cent of non-national employment. The construction sector's share has fallen from 25 per cent in 1980 to under 23 per cent in 1985. Only in Saudi Arabia and Oman is agriculture a major employer of non-nationals.

Non-nationals dominate three sectors in particular: construction, manufacturing and utilities. The non-national presence is lowest in agriculture and fishing, though even here they now account for over half of the workforce. Similarly, even in services, where nationals tend to concentrate, non-nationals now account for 60 per cent of total employment, a share which rises to 72 per cent in Kuwait and 83 per cent in the UAE. The share of non-nationals in the oil sector (mining and quarrying) is also relatively low, at 55 per cent, reflecting the success of efforts at workforce localization in this prestige sector.

THE SCALE AND CHARACTERISTICS OF MIGRANT WORKER FLOWS 1980 – 1985

Migrant Worker Flows, 1980 to 1985
The phenomenal rate of growth in non-national workforces during the mid 1970s began to slow in the 1980s. In Kuwait, for example, the non-national workforce increased by 6 per cent per annum between 1980 and 1985 compared to 16 per cent per annum in the preceding five years. The decline in economic activity over the last three years (1985-87) has noticeably depressed the demand for non-national workers, though not to the extent that some popular accounts have suggested.

Table 3.1 (see page 276) shows the number of labour permits issued to non-nationals working in Abu Dhabi, Bahrain, Kuwait, Oman and Saudi Arabia over the years 1976-86. These are not stock figures since they omit employment in the public sector as well as excluding undocumented workers.

There is a consistent pattern in the trend of labour permit issues across the Gulf. Issues first peak in the late 1970s and again in 1983-84. Labour imports were booming in the early 1980s, not only because of the continued expansion of the construction sector, which drew in large numbers of South-East Asians, but also because of the surge of non-national employment in other sectors, most notably services. After 1983 there is a clear drop in new labour inflows to the Gulf. Signs of a net re-migration of workers from the GCC began to appear in 1985.

Saudi Arabia is typical of this pattern. The number of permits issued rose from 523,000 in 1977 to an initial peak of 687,000 in 1979. A small drop in 1980 was followed by a 16 per cent increase in 1981 and further small increases in 1982 and 1983 to a new peak of 790,000. In 1984 the number of permits issued fell by nearly 5 per cent.

In Bahrain, work permit issues peaked at 34,300 in 1984, and have declined by 21 per cent to 27,200 in 1986. In Kuwait, new labour permit issues peaked early in 1977 and, after declining in 1978 and 1979, rose to a new high of 86,000 in 1983. Here, labour permit issues slumped by 54 per cent in 1984 with the onset of recession and the tightening of security. Labour permit issues have remained around the same level in 1985 and 1986.

Oman shows a different pattern to the other Gulf states. Labour card issues rise throughout the 1980s, peaking at 316,000 in 1985. This reflects increased oil production with continued high levels of government expenditure as a result. In 1986, however, labour card issues were down by 4 per cent at 304,000.

The fall in new labour inflows is also evidenced by data on placements from the major South and South-East Asian labour sending countries. Although this data suffers from considerable under-reporting, particularly in the early years, and excludes those using private or unofficial recruiting agents, examination of trends is valuable.

Table 3.2 (see page 277) confirms the dramatic increase in placements since the mid 1970s. They have risen from 84,000 in 1976 to over 900,000 in 1981. In most cases 1981-82 are the peak years of official placements, thereafter the rate of growth and the number placed tail off. For example, the number of Pakistanis placed in the GCC countries has fallen from 168,400 in 1981 to 62,000 in 1986.

The picture is not, however, one of across-the-board reductions in labour placements. The timing and scale of the decline varies by sending country and by destination,

269

reflecting variations in the rate and extent of the economic slowdown in different GCC states, as well as relative wage rates, occupational composition and organization of the various labour flows.

Table 3.3 (see page 278) compares placements over the period 1983-86, by destination, from the two major labour suppliers to the Gulf: India and the Philippines.

In the Indian case worker placements have fallen from 199,000 in 1983 to 102,000 in 1986, a decline of 49 per cent. This reduction came mainly in 1985 and 1986, when the number of Indians placed in Saudi Arabia fell by 22 per cent and 39 per cent respectively. Although Saudi Arabia accounts for the greater part of the overall decline, fewer Indians have been placed in all six countries over the past four years. Only in the UAE has the decline been relatively small (less than 10 per cent). In the UAE placements of Indians show a small rise in 1986.

Placement of Filipino workers in the Gulf states have fallen from 293,000 in 1983 to 249,000 in 1986; a decline of 15 per cent. In fact the data show a slight increase in 1986. In this case the decline is confined to Saudi Arabia where placements have dropped from 253,000 to 185,000. In all other Gulf states the number of Filipino workers, although relatively small, has continued to increase.

In summary, non-national labour flows into the Gulf states, as measured by the number of labour permits issued in the GCC countries and the number of worker placements registered by the labour sending countries, have fallen since 1982-83. Before turning to the most recent changes in non-national workforce stocks we will outline other trends affecting the characteristics of the migrant workforce during the 1980s.

Clandestine and Undocumented Migrants
During the 1980s most Gulf states have made increased efforts at enforcement of labour and residence regulations. In Kuwait, the number of illegal entry cases investigated by the Ministry of Interior has risen from 55,000 in 1985 to 73,000 in 1986 and is forecast to top 100,000 in 1987. In 1986 almost 27,000 non-nationals were deported for violation of entry or labour regulations. In the UAE over 6,200 non-national workers were expelled in 1986 for similar offences.

In Saudi Arabia, Ministry of Labour officials put the number of non-nationals deported for overstaying or violating regulations at nearly 300,000 during 1985 and 1986, compared to 88,000 in 1979.

Despite increased efforts at deportation and enforcement of labour and residence regulations, the number of workers in the illegal or grey labour market has continued to grow. Estimates suggest that in Saudi Arabia the number has risen from perhaps 150,000 (4 per cent of non-national labour stocks) in 1984 to 230,000 or more in 1986/87. The grey labour market swells as non-nationals lose their jobs, with recession, in the formal sector. Many seek informal or clandestine employment, with the prospect of accruing short term savings. For the majority, remaining in the Gulf, even on an illegal basis, gives greater present income and better prospects than would result from returning home.

Changing Nationality Composition of Migrant Worker Flows
Non-Arab workers have assumed increased importance in both flow and stocks during the 1980s. In the lower Gulf states (Bahrain, Qatar, Oman, the UAE) the share of Asians, already high in 1980, has increased further during the 1980s.

Tables 3.4, 3.5 and 3.6 (see pages 279, 280, 281) show that an increased share of work permits issued in these states have been to South and South-East Asian workers. In Oman their share has risen from 93 per cent to 96 per cent. Here there has been a striking growth in the number of Sri Lankan and Bangladeshi workers. In Bahrain the Asian share has grown from 88 per cent to over 93 per cent.

Data for Kuwait also indicate an increasing share of new work permits going to Asian migrants. Unlike the lower Gulf countries, that increase is from a much lower base in the 1970s. In 1977, for example, Arab migrants accounted for 47 per cent of new work permit issues. By 1985 their share was less than 15 per cent. There has been a shift away from the traditional Asian labour suppliers (India and Pakistan) towards new South Asian (Bangladesh and Sri Lanka) and South-East Asian (Thai, Filipino and others) labour sources.

Although the Arab share of new work permits in Kuwait has fallen, their share of renewals has remained high and in 1985 was 46 per cent. Renewals account for 93 per cent of work permits issued to Arabs in 1985. Renewals are also significant for some South Asian nationals: 92 per cent of Pakistanis and 85 per cent of Indians are now on renewed work permits. As yet, more recent South and South-East Asian labour suppliers show relatively low rates of work permit renewal. Nevertheless, the proportion of Filipino migrant workers on renewed work permits in Kuwait has risen from less than 12 per cent in 1980 to 42 per cent in 1985.

In sum, during the first half of the 1980s, demand for non-national labour increasingly turned towards new supplies in South and South-East Asia notably Bangladesh, Sri Lanka, Indonesia, Thailand and the Philippines. At the same time, an increasing share of Arab and South Asian workers were renewing their work permits, often on less favourable terms.

Evidence from Kuwait suggests a growing stability in the non-national workforce. Table 3.7 (see page 282) shows that, while new work permit issues have declined by more than 50 per cent since 1983, work permit renewals have increased from under 55,000 in 1980 to 163,500 in 1985. Renewals now represent approaching 80 per cent of all work permit issues. (The absolute decline in work permit renewals in 1986 relates to the sharp fall in new issues in 1984). The scale of work permit renewals in Kuwait demonstrates the retention of non-national labour despite economic downturn. This is corroborated by the growth in the number of non-national workers transferring their sponsorship from one employer to another.

Changing Sectoral Distribution of the Non-national Workforce
Overall, non-national employment has diversified and the early dominance of the construction sector is much reduced. Analysis of work permit data by sector points to the same conclusion.

The construction sector has experienced the greater absolute decline in new labour inflows. In Kuwait, the fall in the construction sector accounts for over 53 per cent of the recent cut in new work permit issues. However, there have also been significant cuts in new work permits issued for employment in the oil sector, manufacturing and trade.

Demand for non-national workers has moved away from unskilled and semi-skilled workers in the construction sector. Nevertheless, demand for unskilled manual workers remained high and is growing in the service sector. Table 3.8 (see page 283) compares the broad occupational structure of the non-national workforce in Kuwait for 1980 and 1985. The fastest growing sector is services, which increased by 92 per cent over the five years, rising from 20 per cent to 27 per cent of non-national employment. Demand for professional, technical and skilled office workers has also been strong with increases of 66 per cent, 37 per cent and 34 per cent in the administrative, clerical and professional and technical sectors, respectively. In contrast, the number of production workers grew by only 23 per cent and their share of the workforce fell to 39 per cent.

271

Wage rates for non-national workers
The mid-1980s have seen a general decline in wage levels for non-nationals throughout the GCC. Information is scanty, but wage rates are reported to have fallen by an average of 20 to 30 per cent and up to 45 per cent since 1983. Lower wage rates for non-nationals have occurred either as salary cuts for those renewing their contracts of employment, or by the replacement of workers with new low cost labour from South and South-East Asia. As competition for opportunities in the non-national labour market intensifies, some governments in labour supplying countries have sought to maintain their market share by lowering recommended minimum wages for their nationals employed abroad. In June 1986 Pakistan announced a 15 per cent wage cut for its nationals working in the Middle East while Bangladesh lowered its recommended minimum by 20 per cent.

Both Kuwaiti and Omani work permit data show a rise in the share of lower paid non-nationals which is consistent with the switch to new labour sources and the growth of service sector employment. In Kuwait migrants paid less than $360 per month accounted for 43 per cent of new work permits issued in 1979. By 1985 this share had risen to 48 per cent.

THE 1986 OIL PRICE SHOCK: NET LABOUR OUTFLOWS
Despite efforts at economic diversification, the economies of the six Gulf states remain heavily dependent upon the production and export of oil. Through the 1980s, the oil sector has contributed an average of 50 per cent of gross domestic product (gdp) and 80 per cent of total government revenues. The deterioration in gdp seen in most of the Gulf states since 1981 is largely accounted for by declining oil prices and production. In aggregate, government revenues have declined by some 56 per cent as oil earnings slumped from $160 bn. in 1981 to under $60 bn. in 1985. Over the same period Gulf governments have reduced total expenditure by more than 30 per cent. The decline in overall government expenditure , and the switch away from investment expenditure has, as the previous section has shown, been reflected in falling demand for new non-national labour.

In 1986 oil prices deteriorated further, falling from $26 a barrel in January to $8 a barrel in July. In December OPEC agreed a benchmark price of $18 which has remained relatively firm. The fall in oil prices has sharply cut government revenues. Oil revenues for 1986 are estimated at just over $30 bn., a fall of more than one third on their 1985 value. This reduction has pushed all the GCC states further into budget deficit and has led to a marked downturn in the demand for non-national labour.

Net labour outflows occurred in both 1986 and 1987. Table 4.1 (see page 284) shows estimated changes in non-national workforce stocks in 1985-86 and 1986-87 for each of the six GCC-member states. In aggregate terms, these estimates show a net outflow of around 615,000 (12 per cent) non-national workers since 1985.

South-East Asian labour has been most acutely affected by the sharp downturn in economic activity over the past two years. Saudi Arabia, which accounts for the majority, has seen the departure of more than 360,000 South-East Asian workers. The biggest outflow has been of South Koreans, reduced by more than 75 per cent in two years who were disproportionately concentrated in the construction sector. Filipino workers, although showing a net outflow from Saudi Arabia approaching 19 per cent, have been less acutely affected because of continuing demand in sectors other than construction, notably services.

PROSPECTS FOR MIGRANT LABOUR TO 1990
The future size of the non-national workforce in the Gulf states cannot be accurately projected in detail because of the complexity of factors involved in the resolution of

272

manpower demand and supply in the Gulf. Nevertheless, an indication of likely trends over the next three years can be outlined.

The projection for the six Gulf labour importers is summarised in table 5.1 (see page 285). The projection is based on an assessment of sector-specific economic growth rates, manpower demand and indigenous labour supply, over the period 1987-90. It assumes that the oil price will stabilize at $18 a barrel (in real terms) and that oil revenues will ease upwards. As a consequence, government revenues and investment expenditure will also rise, leading to gentle economic recovery by 1990. In sectoral terms, the construction sector will continue to decline in importance, while services grow steadily.

The projection shows that by 1990 the non-national workforce will have reduced to 4.36 million, down by 3.4 per cent on the present stock (4.51 million). Outflows from Saudi Arabia will account for over 80 per cent of the total reduction. In fact the rate of outflow is likely to ease as major exports of surplus non-national labour, particularly from the construction sector, come to an end. Nevertheless substantial net outflows are projected for 1988 and 1989. By 1990, however, the non-national workforce will be increasing slowly, despite attrition and replacement by nationals.

As the migration balance returns again to one of net labour inflows, the number and share of South-East Asians in the Gulf is set to rise. South-East Asians will continue to replace more expensive, and less productive, Arab and South Asian manpower, particularly in the construction sector. Demand for South-East Asian labour will also continue to rise in the service sectors.

Settlement of the Gulf war and investment in extensive reconstruction programmes is likely to provide a major new opportunity for non-national labour, particularly in Iraq's southern cities and in the reconstruction of infrastructure for the Iranian oil industry. The experience of South-East Asian countries in the provision of contract labour for the construction sector should give them a comparative advantage in bidding for new work.

TABLE 2.1

GCC: NON-NATIONAL WORKFORCE STOCKS BY NATIONALITY GROUP AND COUNTRY OF EMPLOYMENT, 1985

	Bahrain	Kuwait	Oman	Qatar	Saudi Arabia	UAE	Total
Nationality Group:							
Arab	7,600	252,900	20,900	16,400	1,154,200	95,500	1,547,500
South Asian	70,900	242,700	280,800	46,200	1,126,300	447,700	2,214,600
South-east Asian	10,700	31,200	4,600	4,000	968,400	25,000	1,043,900
Other	7,700	17,100	7,800	4,100	273,800	30,300	340,800
Total	96,900	543,900	314,100	70,700	3,522,700	598,500	5,146,800

%	Bahrain	Kuwait	Oman	Qatar	Saudi Arabia	UAE	Total
Nationality Group:							
Arab	7.8	46.5	6.6	23.2	32.8	16.0	30.1
South Asian	73.2	44.6	89.4	65.3	32.0	74.8	43.0
South-east Asian	11.1	5.7	1.5	5.7	27.4	4.2	20.3
Other	7.9	3.2	2.5	5.8	7.8	5.0	6.6
Total	100.0	100.0	100.0	100.0	100.0	100.0	100.0

Source : State of Bahrain, Central Statistical Organization, Statistical Abstract ; State of Bahrain, Directorate of Statistics, Census of Population and Housing, 1981 ; State of Bahrain, Ministry of Labour and Social Affairs, Annual Report on Foreign Employment, 1984 ; State of Kuwait, Central Statistical Office, Annual Statistical Abstract 1986 ; State of Kuwait, Central Statistical Office, Census of Population and Housing, 1985 ; State of Kuwait, Ministry of Labour and Social Affairs, Annual Report on Expatriate Employment, 1985 ; Sultanate of Oman, Directorate General of National Statistics, Statistical Yearbook, 1986 ; State of Qatar, Central Statistical Organisation, Annual Statistical Abstract, 1986 ; State of Qatar, Central Statistical Organization, Results of Manpower Survey in the Private Sector, 1984 ; State of Qatar, Central Statistical Organization, Industrial Survey, 1984 ; Kingdom of Saudi Arabia, Central Department of Statistics, Statistical Yearbook, 1984 ; Kingdom of Saudi Arabia, Central Department of Statistics, Census of Private Establishments, 1981 ; Saudi Economic Survey (weekly) ; UAE, Central Statistics Department, Census of Population, 1980 ; UAE, Central Statistics Department, Annual Statistical Abstract, 1984 ; Emirate of Abu Dhabi, Department of Planning, Statistical Yearbook, 1985 ; Economic Commission for Western Asia, Demographic and Related Socio-economic Data Sheets, 1985.

274

TABLE 2.2

GCC: NON-NATIONAL WORKFORCE STOCKS BY SECTOR OF EMPLOYMENT, 1985

	Bahrain	Kuwait	Oman	Qatar	Saudi Arabia	UAE	Total
Economic Sector:							
Agriculture & fishing	1,150	9,800	11,000	4,450	394,550	32,300	453,250
Mining & quarrying	750	4,350	3,750	–	35,200	11,900	55,950
Manufacturing	6,900	46,800	7,200	10,850	359,300	53,250	484,300
Utilities	1,400	6,000	1,250	1,050	144,450	10,800	164,950
Construction	31,500	123,450	148,600	15,700	1,021,600	128,700	1,469,550
Trade	15,200	70,700	65,000	13,300	468,500	89,200	721,900
Transport & Communications	7,950	29,900	2,500	6,300	176,150	48,500	271,300
Financial Services	900	16,850	5,050	3,400	63,400	16,150	105,750
Services	31,000	236,050	69,750	15,500	859,550	207,700	1,419,550
Total	96,750	543,900	314,100	70,550	3,522,700	598,500	5,146,500

%	Bahrain	Kuwait	Oman	Qatar	Saudi Arabia	UAE	Total
Economic Sector:							
Agriculture & Fishing	1.2	1.8	3.5	6.3	11.2	5.4	8.8
Mining & Quarrying	0.8	0.8	1.2	–	1.0	2.0	1.1
Manufacturing	7.1	8.6	2.3	15.4	10.2	8.9	9.4
Utilities	1.5	1.1	0.4	1.5	4.1	1.8	3.2
Construction	32.6	22.7	47.3	22.2	29.0	21.5	28.6
Trade	15.7	13.0	20.7	18.9	13.3	14.9	14.0
Transport & Communications	8.2	5.5	0.8	8.9	5.0	8.1	5.3
Financial Services	0.9	3.1	1.6	4.8	1.8	2.7	2.0
Services	32.0	43.4	22.2	22.0	24.4	34.7	27.6
Total	100.0	100.0	100.0	100.0	100.0	100.0	100.0

Note: Mining and quarrying employment in Qatar is included in manufacturing.

Sources: State of Bahrain, Central Statistical Organization, Statistical Abstract; State of Bahrain, Ministry of Labour and Social Affairs, Annual Report on Foreign Employment, 1984; State of Kuwait, Central Statistical Office, Annual Statistical Abstract, 1986; State of Kuwait, Ministry of Labour and Social Affairs, Annual Report on Expatriate Employment, 1985; Sultanate of Oman, Directorate General of National Statistics, Statistical Yearbook, 1986; State of Qatar, Central Statistical Organisation, Annual Statistical Abstract, 1986; State of Qatar, Central Statistical Organization, Kingdom of Saudi Arabia, Central Department of Statistics, Statistical Yearbook, 1984; Saudi Economic Survey (weekly); UAE, Central Statistics Department, Annual Statistical Abstract, 1984; Emirate of Abu Dhabi, Department of Planning, Statistical Yearbook, 1985.

TABLE 3.1

GCC: WORK PERMIT ISSUES, 1976-86

Country	1976	1980	1983	1984	1985	1986
Bahrain	14,900	20,100	31,800	34,300	32,500	27,200
Kuwait	43,400	56,200	86,100	39,400	41,600	42,200
Oman	93,600	148,800	258,100	294,600	316,000	304,000
Saudi Arabia	n.a.	643,200	790,000	752,500	780,600	n.a.
UAE	51,700	124,800	140,900	n.a.	175,700	n.a.

Sources: State of Bahrain, Central Statistical Organization, Statistical Abstract; State of Bahrain, Ministry of Labour and Social Affairs, Annual Report on Foreign Employment, 1984; State of Kuwait, Central Statistical Office, Annual Statistical Abstract, 1986; State of Kuwait, Ministry of Labour and Social Affairs, Annual Report on Expatriate Employment, 1985; Sultanate of Oman, Directorate General of National Statistics, Statistical Yearbook, 1986; Central Statistical Organization, Kingdom of Saudi Arabia, Central Department of Statistics, Statistical Yearbook, 1984; Saudi Economic Survey (weekly); UAE, Central Statistics Department, Annual Statistical Abstract, 1984; Emirate of Abu Dhabi, Department of Planning, Statistical Yearbook, 1985.

276

TABLE 3.2

CONTRACT LABOUR PLACEMENTS FROM SELECTED ASIAN LABOUR SENDING COUNTRIES
TO THE MIDDLE EAST, 1976-86

Country	1976	1980	1983	1984	1985	1986
India	4,200	236,200	220,797	198,810	160,555	109,951
Philippines	7,812	132,044	323,414	311,517	266,617	262,758
Pakistan	41,690	129,847	128,206	88,460	101,000	62,000
Rep. Korea	21,269	124,834	140,100	116,050	n.a.	n.a.
Bangladesh	5,559	29,815	59,220	56,753	77,694	36,852
Sri Lanka	526	24,053	68,905	n.a.	n.a.	n.a.
Thailand	1,287	20,690	63,520	67,468	61,083	72,673
Indonesia	1,200	4,950	n.a.	36,582	45,129	n.a.

Sources: Ministry of Labour, New Delhi; Philippine Overseas Employment Administration, Manila; ARTEP, Impact of out and return migration on domestic employment in Pakistan; Hyunho Seok, Republic of Korea, in G. Gunatilleke, Migration of Asian Workers to the Middle East; A. M. Siddiqui, The economic and non-economic impact of Labour Migration from Bangladesh, in F. Arnold and N. Shah, Asian labour migration; Central Bank of the Philippines; Protector of Emigrants, Bombay; Ministry of Planning, Colombo; BMET Annual Reports, Dhaka; Office of Labour Administration, Seoul; Department of Labour, Bangkok; National Economic and Social Development Board, Bangkok; Department of Manpower, Jakarta.

TABLE 3.3

GCC: RECORDED PLACEMENTS OF INDIAN AND FILIPINO WORKERS BY DESTINATION
1983-86

(a) Indian				
Country	1983	1984	1985	1986
Bahrain	18,894	15,514	11,246	5,784
Kuwait	14,490	5,466	5,512	4,235
Oman	49,120	43,228	37,806	22,417
Qatar	7,772	4,362	5,214	4,029
Saudi Arabia	83,235	88,079	68,938	41,854
UAE	25,559	24,286	21,286	23,323
Total	199,070	180,935	150,002	101,642
(b) Filipino				
Bahrain	6,617	8,804	8,267	7,103
Kuwait	14,781	15,418	24,766	25,325
Oman	2,773	4,178	4,523	5,476
Qatar	2,863	3,540	3,540	3,759
Saudi Arabia	253,080	240,504	191,248	185,120
UAE	12,831	16,469	15,939	22,322
Total	292,945	288,913	248,283	249,105

Source: Ministry of Labour, New Delhi and POEA, Manila.

TABLE 3.4

BAHRAIN: LABOUR CARDS BY NATIONALITY OF HOLDER, 1980-85

Nationality Group	1980 No.	1980 %	1983 No.	1983 %	1984 No.	1984 %	1985 No.	1985 %
Arab	730	3.6	722	2.3	628	1.8	478	1.5
South Asian	14,633	72.8	25,251	79.3	26,355	76.9	24,154	74.4
South-east Asian	3,001	14.9	3,761	11.8	4,807	14.1	5,906	18.2
Other	1,746	8.7	2,111	6.6	2,471	7.2	1,920	5.9
Total	20,110	100.0	31,845	100.0	34,261	100.0	32,468	100.0

Source: Bahrain Statistical Abstract (various years).

279

TABLE 3.5

OMAN: LABOUR CARDS BY NATIONALITY OF HOLDER, 1980-84

Nationality Group	1980		1983		1984	
	No.	%	No.	%	No.	%
Arab	2,332	1.8	3,145	1.3	3,358	1.3
South Asian	121,515	91.6	224,076	95.1	255,611	94.9
South-east Asian	1,147	0.9	2,782	1.2	3,905	1.4
Other	7,624	5.7	5,642	2.4	6,536	2.4
Total	132,618	100.0	235,645	100.0	269,410	100.0

Source: Oman Statistical Abstract (various issues).

TABLE 3.6

KUWAIT: NEW WORK PERMIT ISSUES BY NATIONALITY GROUP, 1980-85

Nationality Group	1980		1983		1984		1985	
	No.	%	No.	%	No.	%	No.	%
Arab	22,530	40.1	31,379	44.4	5,474	13.9	5,639	13.5
South Asian	14,960	26.6	34,741	49.1	11,775	30.0	12,548	30.2
South-east Asian	14,075	25.1	2,083	2.9	19,835	50.4	20,764	49.9
Other	4,613	8.2	2,524	3.6	2,237	5.7	2,672	6.4
Total	56,178	100.0	70,727	100.0	39,321	100.0	41,623	100.0

Source: Ministry of Labour and Social Affairs, Report on Employment and Expatriate Labor.

TABLE 3.7

KUWAIT: WORK PERMIT ISSUES BY TYPE OF PERMIT, 1976-86
(in thousands)

Type of Permit	1976	1980	1983	1984	1985	1986
New Issues	43.4	56.2	86.1	39.4	41.6	42.5
Renewals	42.8	54.9	105.3	140.7	163.5	148.7
Cancellations	n.a.	16.9	21.8	24.6	31.4	34.1
Transfers	n.a.	11.7	10.9	21.6	n.a.	n.a.

Source: Ministry of Labour and Social Affairs, Report on Employment and Expatriate Labour.

TABLE 3.8

KUWAIT: NON-NATIONAL WORKFORCE BY OCCUPATIONAL GROUP, 1980 AND 1985

Occupational Group	1980		1985	
	No.	%	No.	%
Professional & technical	62,008	16.3	83,010	15.4
Administrative & managerial	4,036	1.1	6,717	1.3
Clerical	35,371	9.3	48,710	9.0
Sales	26,072	6.8	31,741	5.9
Services	77,026	20.2	148,213	27.5
Agriculture & related	5,982	1.6	10,409	1.9
Production, craftsmen & related	170,112	44.7	210,228	39.0
Total	380,607	100.0	539,028	100.0

Source: Ministry of Planning, Census of Population and Housing, 1980 and 1985.

283

TABLE 4.1

GCC: ESTIMATED CHANGE IN
NON-NATIONAL WORKFORCE STOCKS
1985/86 AND 1986/87

Country	1985/86	1986/87
Bahrain	- 3,900	- 6,000
Kuwait	- 16,700	- 13,100
Oman	- 21,600	- 17,100
Qatar	- 2,900	- 4,100
Saudi Arabia	-214,900	-282,900
UAE	- 18,600	- 13,500
Total	-278,600	-336,700

Source: author's estimates.

TABLE 5.1

GCC: PROJECTED NON-NATIONAL WORKFORCE STOCKS
1987 TO 1990

Country	1987	1990
Bahrain	79,550	74,100
Kuwait	502,200	495,500
Oman	275,400	260,500
Qatar	62,800	61,350
Saudi Arabia	3,025,900	2,901,700
UAE	566,450	566,300
Total	4,512,300	4,359,450
% Change		− 3.4

Source: author's estimates.

285

Part III
Women Migrants and the Women Left Behind

[5]

THE IMPACT OF MALE LABOUR MIGRATION ON WOMEN IN BOTSWANA

Barbara B. Brown

In recent years scholars have become increasingly concerned with the role women play in society. Researchers studying women in the Third World have focused particularly on the impact of development on the social and economic role of women. However, there continue to be large gaps in our understanding of women in the development process. One such gap is the impact of labour migration on women.

Labour migration is a common phenomenon today both within the Third World and between it and the industrialized countries. Yet, while numerous scholars have analyzed who migrates and what causes the migration, there has been little in-depth study of the effects of this migration on women. Most of the existing literature assumes that migration is a rational response to a given range of resources and choices and that, as such, the family as a unit, including the women members, benefits from such migration. This view, however, oversimplifies the situation. The evidence shows that high male outmigration has led to a modification in the structure of family life and has transformed women's social and economic position to their detriment.

This argument on women and migrant labour falls within the growing body of literature which holds that labour migration engenders a process of underdevelopment. According to this argument, migration discourages local development by producing a kind of 'low-level equilibrium trap' in which migrants and their families are only maintained at or near subsistence level by the low wages received. Due to manpower shortages within the sending areas and the lack of capital, productivity of the rural areas remains unchanged or declines, thus spawning further dependence on the migrant labour system.

Research on the impact of migrant labour on women brings a needed broader perspective to the underdevelopment debate which up until now has suffered from a narrow economistic approach. Many scholars have concerned themselves with analyzing the 'rate and incidence of migration'.[1] W. A. Lewis examined the conditions under which labour would leave rural areas and the impact migration would have on economic growth.[2] William Barber then

Barbara Brown, who spent 1976–8 in Botswana, is currently a Research Associate at the African Studies Center, Boston University.

1. J. Clyde Mitchell, 'Migrant Labour in Africa South of the Sahara: the causes of labour migration', *Bulletin of the Inter-African Labour Institute*, 6, (1959), *passim*.
2. W. A. Lewis, 'Economic Development with Unlimited Supplies of Labour', *The Manchester School*, London, 1954.

applied Lewis's model to southern Africa, to a study of Zimbabwe.[3]   More
recently, economists have developed more sophisticated modelling techniques
to project labour flows.   The best known examples of this approach are provided by Michael Todaro and John Harris who have shown that individuals
migrate in order to maximize the returns from perceived opportunity sets.[4]

Recently, some scholars have criticized such studies for the narrowness and
ahistorical quality of the approach.   They argue that one should focus on the
historical process of social and economic change which has created the structure
within which the decision to migrate is made.   Such scholars as André Gunder
Frank and Samir Amin have proposed that migration is the consequence of
the historical development of capitalism and the geographic concentration of
the means of production in particular regions.[5]   In research specifically on
southern Africa, a new school of Marxist historiography has grown up to
pursue this line of argument and to analyze the political and economic configuration of forces particular to the region.   Best known among the scholars
working in this vein are Giovanni Arrighi writing on Zimbabwe, and Colin
Bundy, Harold Wolpe and Martin Legassick writing on South Africa.[6]   Their
work is of interest here because of the consideration they give to the social
structure of the rural communities from which the migrants come.

These scholars argue that in southern Africa, including Botswana, a precapitalist rural sector continues to exist and is functional to the process of
accumulation and growth in the capitalist sector.   Subsistence farming permits
employers to offer a wage lower than the cost of maintaining a worker and his
family.   As a result of the traditional sexual division of labour, much of the
burden of social reproduction and agricultural production is borne by women.
Men return to the rural areas only for periods of rest or when they are too
old to work.

The principal concern of scholars working in this vein has been to analyze
the process of capital accumulation in southern Africa.   They are interested
primarily in the historically specific way this process occurred and the impact
it had on the political development of race rule.   Hence, they focus on the

3.   W. J. Barber, *The Economy of British Central Africa*, (London: Oxford University Press, 1961).
4.   Michael Todaro, 'A Model of Labor Migration and Urban Unemployment in Less Developed
Countries', *American Economic Review*, **59**, (1969) *passim* and John Harris and Michael Todaro,
'Migration, Unemployment and Development: a two-sector model', *American Economic Review*,
60, (1970), *passim*.
5.   Andre Gunder Frank, 'The Development of Underdevelopment', *Monthly Review*, **18**,
(1966), *passim*; Samir Amin, 'Introduction', in this *Modern Migrations in Western Africa*,
(London: Oxford University Press, 1974).
6.   See, *inter alia*, Giovanni Arrighi, 'Labour Supplies in Historical Perspective: Proletarianization of the African peasantry in Rhodesia', *Journal of Development Studies* **6**, (1970), pp.
197–234; Colin Bundy, 'The Emergence and Decline of a South African Peasantry', *African
Affairs*, **86**, (1972), pp. 369–388; Harold Wolpe, 'Capitalism and Cheap Labour-Power in South
Africa: from segregation to apartheid', *Economy and Society*, **I**, (1972), pp. 425–456, Martin
Legassick and Harold Wolpe, 'The Bantustans and Capital Accumulation in South Africa',
Review of African Political Economy, **7**, (1976), pp. 87–107.

coercive measures used to establish and maintain rural 'labour reserves'. While they give some recognition to the importance of the social-sexual structure of the reserves, this usually comes as a passing acknowledgement in studies whose focus remains on politics and economics. These researchers have not examined what changes in the family have occurred as a consequence of the migrancy. To use a common analogy, the rural family is seen as a black box from which the migrant leaves and to which he returns when he has finished work. The inner workings of the box are ignored.

Labour migration in the southern African context

As the economy of South Africa grew, it required a large supply of cheap labour. The easiest way of obtaining such labour was to 'semi-proletarianize' a large segment of the black population, pushing rural dwellers into wage labour while not paying them enough or allowing them to settle permanently in urban areas. As a result, migrant workers had to depend on the rural areas for part of their subsistence and for family life. In this way capital would not be 'wasted' on the provision of wages and social services (family housing in town and on the mines, a full service of water and sewerage, schools, hospitals, etc.) required to reproduce another generation of labour.[7] The South African capitalists have received other benefits from enforcing a system of oscillating migrant labour. Not least among these benefits has been greater political control over the workers (and their families). Since the workers are constantly on the move between home and town and find it difficult to overcome barriers of geography, nationality and language, they are less able to organize against their employers or the government. In addition, employers benefit from the maintenance of a pool of rural labour which they can draw on to meet fluctuations in demand for labour at a minimal economic and political cost.

As South Africa itself did not have a population large enough for the kind of labour reserve needed, people from neighboring countries such as Botswana were drawn into the South African system. Since the end of the last century Batswana have gone to work in the mines, factories, kitchens and farms of white South Africa. However, in the period since independence in 1966, the Botswana economy has undergone several major changes which have affected the size and direction of labour migration. With the discovery of copper, nickel and diamonds and the establishment of an administrative infrastructure to foster development, there has been a significant increase in demand for labour inside the country. As a result, the direction of the labour flow shifted so that by 1976 two times as many migrant workers from rural areas were headed for Botswana's towns and mines as to South Africa.[8] The pattern of

7. See, *inter alia*, Bernard Magubane, *The Political Economy of Race and Class in South Africa*, (New York: Monthly Review Press, 1979); Carmen Diana Deere, 'Rural Women's Subsistence Production in the Capitalist Periphery', *Review of Radical Political Economies*, 8, (1967).
8. Government of Botswana, *National Development Plan, 1976–81.* (Gaborone: Government Printer, 1977) table 1–2.

oscillating migration to South Africa has been replicated inside Botswana due to the low wages paid to urban workers.   As a result, the rural areas have been maintained as labour reserves, now supplying both South Africa and urban Botswana.[9]   The net effect has been a substantial increase in the number of migrant wage earners: in 1976 23 per cent of the national population were migrants.[10]

The case of Botswana

With its long history and high rate of labour migration, Botswana provides a valuable case study of the impact of migration on women.   The outmigration of a large proportion of the adult population has altered economic and social relations.   Subsistence agriculture, once the basis of the economy, has been largely replaced by working for wages.   Today, household income derives in large part from the activities of individuals who work away from the family and are paid wages on an individual basis.   Such separation of workers from the ownership of the major means of production (the mines, factories and big farms) is characteristic of the process of capitalist development.   According to the Rural Income Distribution Survey of 1974, the poorer 50 per cent of households counted on money transfers and employment as their primary source of income, despite the fact that the 1974 harvest was very good and in some parts of the country a record.[11]

In Botswana, as in much of southern Africa, labour migration has been the dominant form of capitalist penetration.   People's lives and livelihood have been integrated into the world economy through labour migration rather than through direct (peasant) production.[12]   Isaac Schapera studied the effects of labour migration in Tswana life in the 1920's—40's.   His research offers a detailed historical base line for longitudinal comparison.   It was in the 1940's that labour migration became a major force in Tswana society.   In 1936 6 per cent of the total population were migrants; by 1943 the percentage had increased to 10 and since then has grown dramatically.   In 1978 I carried out an intensive study of migrancy in Kgatleng district in southeastern Botswana.   This study included the collection of detailed demographic, economic and social data from a sample of 210 households.[13]   A comparison

9.   David Massey, 'The Changing Political Economy of Migrant Labor in Botswana', *South African Labour Bulletin*, 5, (1980), 5, pp. 4–26.
10.   Government of Botswana, *National Development Plan, 1976–81.*
11.   Government of Botswana, *Rural Income Distribution Survey, 1974–75*, (Gaborone: Government Printer, 1976), p. 101.   RIDS was a national random sample survey of 1200 households.   All forms of income, monetary and in kind, were included in the calculations.   Only the top 5 per cent of the households did not rely on transfers or employment as major income sources.
12.   Lionel Cliffe, 'Labour Migration and Peasant Differentiation: Zambian experiences', *Journal of Peasant Studies*, 5, (1978), p. 326.
13.   My colleague David Massey who was conducting similar interviews in Kgatleng in 1978 has kindly allowed me to aggregate some of his data with mine.

THE IMPACT OF MALE LABOUR MIGRATION ON WOMEN IN BOTSWANA   371

of this contemporary material with Schapera's earlier data provides a clear picture of the impact of migration on women's lives.

The impact on women has been profound. The first section will show that marriage and family relations have shifted significantly, placing women in a more isolated position. The following section will demonstrate the effect on women of changes in productive activities. Together, these factors have led to major changes in women's social and economic situation. Drawing on the experience of women in Botswana, the concluding section will address the issue of female dependence, a topic which has generated considerable controversy in studies on women.

Changes in marriage patterns

Isaac Schapera has provided a detailed picture of Tswana marriage in the 1920's and 1930's. He found that men and women married in their twenties, following a long engagement. Schapera was told that 'in the old days' people wed when they were even younger.[14] In the 1920's families selected spouses for their children, although sons and daughters were consulted on their preferences. 'Extremely few people' never married, as marriage offered social status, companionship, economic cooperation and, for men, legal paternity of their children.[15] Cultural convention strongly discouraged sexual relations before becoming formally engaged. While a woman might bear a child after her engagement, she would rarely have more than one until her marriage had been finalized.[16]

By the 1970s marriage patterns had altered dramatically, due primarily to the impact of high levels of outmigration. Marriage is now delayed until a later age. While migrant workers might come home between jobs or on vacation, they generally do not settle down until they reach their thirties. Until then, they prefer to continue working as migrants while they gather the financial resources to set up their own household.[17] Today, men marry when they are over thirty, some ten years later than fifty years ago.[18]

Even though marriage may be delayed, courting relations and love affairs between men and women flourish. Before the final step of marriage takes place and, frequently, even before an engagement has been formalized, most women have borne several children. This pattern is in marked contrast with the pattern of sexual relationships of two previous periods, according to Schapera, in terms both of the frequency with which unmarried women have

---

14. Isaac Schapera, *Married Life in an African Tribe*, (Harmondsworth: Penguin, 1971), pp. 38 and 62–3.
15. Schapera, *Married Life*, p. 32.
16. Schapera, *Married Life* and Schapera and Simon Roberts, 'Rampedi Revisited: another look at a Kgatla Ward', *Africa*, **45**, (1975), pp. 258–279.
17. In the 1978 Kgatleng study 84 per cent of the married men were living at home.
18. Interviews in Kgatleng district, 1978.

children and of community attitudes. In the days before the European intrusion into Tswana life, very few women bore children before marriage. If they did, they faced severe public humiliation.[19] By the 1920s and 1930s, more unmarried women were having children, and community attitudes had modified to the point where women were privately condemned but no longer publicly ridiculed. In 1943 Schapera found that 23 per cent of unmarried women of childbearing age (15 to 54) had borne children in Kgatleng district;[20] by 1978 the figure was up to 54 per cent. Today, the situation of an unmarried mother is generally accepted by her family and community.

Most children today will probably spend their first few years with their mother in her parents' home. Consequently, three generation households are common, with both young men and young women with their children remaining with their parents. As a result, individual households have increased in size. In Kgatleng today, the average number of people in a household is nine, while a study by Schapera in 1929 found five to six people.[21]

If a woman marries, she and her children will move into her husband's home. Until that time, the children are chiefly provided for by her family's income, including any remittances sent by the migrant relatives. The young unmarried father usually offers only a small portion of his earnings to the mother of his children, as a token of his continued commitment to marry. Those men who do not intend to marry the mother of their children usually give nothing as support. In either case, the bulk of a man's earnings goes to his parents. Out of a sample of 58 people collecting remittances at the [South African] Mine Labour Organisation office in Kgatleng, 49 were close blood relatives of the miner (mainly his mother but sometimes his sister), 14 were wives and 2 were fiancées.[22]

Not all relationships can withstand the frequent separation required by migrancy. Love affairs and engagements break off. Some women remain unmarried mothers, even though they would prefer to marry.[23] This situation occurs due both to a gap in the number of women and men of marriage age and to the decline of polygamy which could have permitted otherwise single women to marry.[24] The population gap is itself the result of two factors. First,

19. Isaac Schapera, 'Premarital Pregnancy and Native Opinion: a note on social change', *Africa*, 6, (1933), pp. 59–89.
20. Isaac Schapera, *Migrant Labour and Tribal Life*, (London: Oxford University, 1947), p. 173.
21. Schapera, *Married Life*, p. 86. A 1972 study in another district of Botswana obtained figures on household size similar to those from Kgatleng in 1978. D. F. Eding, A. A. J. Udo and M. S. P. Sekgomo, *Report on Village Studies*, (Gaborone: Ministry of Agriculture, 1972).
22. Author's interviews at people's homes and with people collecting remittances at the Mine Labour Organisation's office in October 1977.
23. Most women interviewed by the author wished to marry. The few women I knew who preferred to remain single (though not necessarily childless) were all financially self-supporting and secure.
24. Schapera presented the following figures on the incidence of polygamous marriages in Kgatleng district: 1850–43 per cent, 1880–30 per cent, 1932–4 per cent. *Married Life*, p. 87. In 1978 there were no polygamous marriages in the sample.

THE IMPACT OF MALE LABOUR MIGRATION ON WOMEN IN BOTSWANA 373

a number of male migrants are 'lost' to South Africa and never return home. Second, cultural norms and the delayed marriage age mean that men marry in their thirties women who are still in their twenties. Thus, the pool of available women is greater than the pool of men, even when men who are only temporarily absent in South Africa are included. According to the population census of 1971, in the 20–39 age group, there were 89 men per 100 women. If only the men and women currently residing at home are counted, there were 63 men per 100 women in this age group.[25]

When a relationship ends, women have a legal right to obtain child support for any children a man fathered. As divorce and marital separation are relatively uncommon in Botswana, the laws chiefly affect unmarried mothers. Customary law has for a long time recognized the right of a woman's family to a 'seduction payment' (*marebana*) for a woman's first child. However, new laws have been implemented to expand women's (and children's) rights both in the customary and, more recently, in the magisterial courts in response to the increased need for child support.[26] With this assistance, women are increasingly availing themselves of the opportunity to go to court.

However, field work in one district showed that most unmarried mothers have not received support through these channels.[27] There are many obstacles to obtaining assistance in these ways. First, a woman or her guardian may decide against asking for *marebana*, because they 'do not believe in it' (an explanation which often covers several other reasons), or because it is the woman's second child and many people consider a woman undeserving of support for more than one child, or because a woman has no immediate male guardian and she is unwilling to face the man's family alone. Second, even if a woman is promised payment by a court ruling, the man may successfully avoid paying. In cases at the main traditional court (*kgotla*) in Kgatleng in 1976 and 1977, only 21 out of 72 men who were sentenced to make *marebana* payments in fact paid the full amount required. Most paid a tiny portion of the amount. Before 1974 the payment was $96 in Kgatleng. Then it was increased to $216 or four head of cattle, though no man had ever been so financially foolish as to pay cattle which would be worth considerably more than $216. Moreover, even if a woman does ask for *marebana* payment and does get paid, the sum of $216 is hardly sufficient for raising a child to adulthood.

---

25. Government of Botswana, *1971 Population Census*, (Gaborone: Government Printer, 1972), table 14.1.
26. On customary law, see John Comaroff and Simon Roberts, Marriage and Extra-Marital Sexuality: the dialectics of legal change among the Kgatla', *Journal of African Law*, **1**, (1977) pp. 97–123; on magisterial law, see the Affiliation Proceedings Act of 1970 and the Amendment Bill of 1977.
27. Author's field work in Kgatleng, 1978. Kgatleng's customary courts have a reputation for being more sympathetic to women. See Comaroff and Roberts, 'Marriage and Extra-Marital Sexuality'.

As an alternative, a woman may take her case to the District Commissioner's Office instead of the *kgotla*. However, this procedure is apparently not a viable alternative for women. An average of only 13 cases a year were heard at the District Commissioner's Office in Kgatleng between 1971 and 1976. One reason that women prefer to go to the *kgotla* is that the lump sum settlements assessed at the *kgotla* under customary law are easier to collect than the monthly payments stipulated for in the Affiliation Proceedings Act.

In sum, *marebana* laws and the affiliation act do not provide a financial solution for unmarried mothers, though these laws can be of some assistance.[28] They can foster an atmosphere of greater responsibility on the part of men. However, community attitudes have not consolidated around the liberalized laws. While social institutions are undergoing change, as evidenced by the new laws, so attitudes also are in flux and conflict. A number of public figures have made scathing attacks on the women who use the law, and the issue has been debated in letters to the newspaper and in people's homes.[29]

When fathers do not support their children, there is evidence that the children may suffer nutritionally. The Ministry of Health conducted a small study of young children who were nutritionally at risk, defined as below 80 per cent of normal weight for age. Of these children, 42 per cent received no support from their fathers. The study also found a strong correlation between a family's lack of livestock (both cattle and small stock) and nutritional deficiencies and concluded that socio-economic factors were more important than lack of knowledge of good nutritional practices in explaining this health problem.[30]

Moreover, female children were found to be more likely nutritionally at risk than male children. In 1978 the Ministry of Health collected information on 1693 children under age of five who were nutritionally at risk. These children represented all those who were reported by clinics throughout the country to be at risk in January and February 1978. The results showed that significantly more girls than boys were below the normal weight for age. Of those at risk, 60·1 per cent were girls and 39·8 per cent boys. This ratio was roughly consistent from clinic to clinic across the country.[31]

While the men who father these children can be considered financially irresponsible for not supporting them, the problem should be seen in its proper

28. Thus, this author does not share the enthusiasm of Comaroff and Roberts about recent improvements in the regulations concerning the bringing of *marebana* cases to court. Improvements, yes, but ones which have still to help women significantly.
29. See, for example, the Botswana *Daily News* of 4 July 1978 and 15 February 1979. In the 1978 article, the then leader of the Opposition, Philip Matante, stated that 'Girls nowadays misuse the law to make more money to make their lives more comfortable'.
30. J. Kreysler, 'Some Aspects of Women, Health and Nutrition, with Special Reference to Kgatleng District and Serowe Village', (Gaborone: Ministry of Health, 1978), unpublished paper.
31. Figures tabulated by the author from a national survey of clinics conducted by the Ministry of Health in 1978.

socioeconomic context. Decades of oscillating migration have led to a decline of authority in the family which might otherwise have brought pressure to bear on its irresponsible members. South Africa's political economy in particular has led to problems of this nature. South Africa needed a large labour reserve not just so that the reserve could bear part of the cost of subsistence, but also so that it would serve as a place for the social reproduction of the labour force: a place where women go into confinement, give birth and then raise the children at no cost to *apartheid*, while the men return to the mines and factories, leaving the women behind. Though migrant men are victims of this system, the women bear a greater burden.

For the survival of themselves and their children, most unwed mothers must rely on support from their own immediate family—parents and brothers in particular. Within their own family, however, women are able to contribute relatively little to the household's economic security. Though women perform vital economic and social functions (growing crops, raising children, caring for the sick and old, and seeing after the small stock) these activities offer few financial rewards. Yet while women's financial security is provided by family ties, these ties are undergoing major changes. Reciprocal obligations and cooperation are no longer as strong as in the past. The family, under its male head, is no longer the key production unit. People earn money and earn it separately from their families. This process of individualization increases the vulnerability of those with limited resources, such as women.

The situation of female-headed households

Changes in household structure have occurred as a result of new patterns of marriage. A significant number of women never marry. According to the data from Kgatleng district, if a single mother does not marry by the time she reaches her late thirties, she will probably move out of her parents' home and establish her own household.[32] The existence of households headed by single women represents a major change in the social and economic structure of rural Botswana. Isaac Schapera noted the emergence of this new type of household on the final page of his 1930s study of married life in Botswana.[33]

Today, 7 per cent of all households are headed by single women.[34] (This number includes the few women who state they are separated, divorced or engaged to be married.) In addition, a further 16 per cent of all households are headed by widows, bringing the total of female-headed households to 23

32. In the 1978 Kgatleng sample, 77 per cent of the single mothers over forty had established their own homes and more were in the process of doing so.
33. Schapera, *Married Life*, p. 321.
34. Wendy Izzard, 'Preliminary Ideas on the Rural-Urban Migration of Female-Headed Households within Botswana', in Carol Kerven (ed.) *Workshop on Migration Research*, (Gaborone: Central Statistics Office, 1979), p. 74, citing preliminary figures from the National Migration Study, a national random sample survey of 3000 households.

per cent.[35] There are indications that the number of single women heading households is closely related to labour migration: Kgatleng district has the highest percentage of such households (15 per cent) and also the highest rate of outmigration. Moreover, within Kgatleng, the study of three different villages showed that the village with the highest level of migration also had the highest number of single women heading households (22 per cent).

Under customary Tswana law all women regardless of their age were defined as legal and political minors requiring male guardians. Since national independence women have gained legal recognition as adults responsible for themselves in many areas. These changes have resulted from the democratic ethos of the national government and perhaps in response to the appearance of female-headed households. Thus, women can now vote, undertake legal proceedings in magisterial courts and request land from the district land board. However, such changes occur haltingly; by custom women still often find themselves excluded from exercising their rights fully. In 1968, when the government took control of land allocation from the chiefs and placed it in the hands of land boards, women became free to apply for land. Nevertheless, it is not clear to what extent land boards treat women equally with men, regarding the size and especially the quality of the land allocated. Several cases have come to my attention where women were harshly treated by land boards. As population (and cattle) pressure increase on land, the danger of discrimination against women in the allocation of this resource will grow.

Legal changes regarding women's rights have not provided for women the economic support they need. While women have gained *de jure*, for the most part they lack the economic capacity to take full advantage of these rights. For example, single women may now have the right to land, but they often lack the resources to make farming worthwhile. They tend to have limited means of ploughing and little labour to hoe the fields. In court, women have won increased rights in the crucial area of child support, yet too often they are unable to get favourable decisions enforced. In the past, the families of the women and of the man would both come to the court hearing and would help guarantee that child support would be paid. Today, young men follow their own way and are not easily disciplined either by family pressure or the court. In the past, the chief had the authority to require family involvement in the court decision. Today, the political power of the chieftainship has diminished in matters of community welfare, land and cattle.

The data from Kgatleng district show that households headed by single mothers are significantly poorer than male-headed households. Table 1 demonstrates that women are severely disadvantaged as farmers, lacking equal access to the necessary assets of land and cattle.

35. Izzard, (Preliminary Ideas on the Rural-Urban Migration'.

THE IMPACT OF MALE LABOUR MIGRATION ON WOMEN IN BOTSWANA 377

TABLE 1
Agriculture According to Type of Household Head

	Single Women	Widowed Women	Men
Access to the means of production:			
percentage without fields	28	21	15
percentage not owning cattle	69	64	35
Agricultural activity, 1976/77 season:			
percentage ploughing	38	36	79
percentage providing for own ploughing (as opposed to purchasing ploughing services)	12	47	45
average harvest	8 bags	6 bags	29 bags

Source: field work in Kgatleng district, 1978.

Robert Lucas has shown in his study of arable agriculture that, because women have fewer resources for crop farming, they farm smaller pieces of land, at higher cost and with smaller harvests than men.[36] A major constraint on successful farming in Botswana is the lack of draft power in the form of cattle. Table 1 shows that few single women who head households own (or hold) enough cattle for ploughing. Even when they do, they often face other difficulties. There may not be an adult present with the skills to inspan the oxen.[37] Thus, the family will either have to join with others to share a plough and labour or else hire a tractor or oxen. Either way of coping may entail a delay in ploughing a crucial factor in dry land farming in a semi-arid country such as Botswana. Furthermore, paying for ploughing is expensive and heightens the risk of taking substantial loss due to the high cost of hiring and the possibility that the harvest may be small.

Even when a family is able to plough at the right time, other obstacles to good farming remain. The family must be able to gather sufficient labour to hoe and to scare birds properly. This task is not necessarily easy when well over a third of the men over fifteen are away and most of the children are in school.[38]

The shortage of cattle among female-headed households affects more than crop farming. Cattle provide financial security as they can be sold in time of need, and they offer nourishment in the form of milk or, more rarely, meat. In

36. Robert E. B. Lucas, 'The Distribution and Efficiency of Crop Production in Tribal Areas of Botswana', *Working Papers*, no. 44, (African Studies Center, Boston University, 1981). Lucas's findings are based on data from the Rural Income Distribution Survey. He lumps together households headed by widows with those headed by single women.
37. Louise Fortmann, *Women's Agriculture in a Cattle Economy*, (Gaborone: Ministry of Agriculture, 1981), p. 7.
38. Government of Botswana, *1971 Population Census*, (Gaborone: Government Printer, 1972) and *National Development Plan*.

addition, they provide a basis for capital accumulation through herd development. They are used to make various exchanges in kind between kin (e.g. milk or use for ploughing) and between families whose children marry (i.e. as bridewealth). Thus, the possession of cattle is key to many aspects of economic and social relations in Botswana.

Widows, who account for 16 per cent of all households face difficulties similar to those of single women. Referring again to Table 1, it can be seen that they also have limited resources for farming and obtain small harvests. Both types of female-headed households could benefit from kinship cooperation. In the past, many redistributive mechanisms existed and the extended family was expected to assist those in need. Obligations toward widows were carefully specified in Tswana customary law. While families continue to share responsibilities today (for example, people still do help relatives to plough and old women often look after the children of their working daughters) the frequency and extent of cooperation has diminished significantly. People share less and within a narrower family circle.

These changes have resulted principally from the commoditization of the economy. While wage employment has grown, so also has the need for cash to buy goods and services. Services such as education and goods such as school uniforms, radios, tea and sugar are in increasing demand. The penetration of capitalist relations of production has altered old forms of cooperation and exchange. Goods formerly exchanged for use on the basis of kinship or need are now bought and sold for cash. Resource-poor households, both male as well as female-headed, have been hurt as a result. In the past a family group orientation made economic sense. There were few opportunities to earn a living beyond the village and few ways to store wealth. Sharing made the efficient use of resources possible and provided a form of social security, whereby people could rely on relatives if they met with misfortune (or the group could turn to their chief who customarily made provisions for hard times). This economic system should, however, not be mistaken for a system of 'primitive socialism', but one where having wealth carried the onus of generosity.

While some of the economic rationale for sharing still holds today, there are countervailing pressures of individualism which weaken cooperative relations.[39] Income generating activity is dispersed geographically and provides rewards to individuals, basically through wages. Cash has become a primary means of exchange. Assistance is offered increasingly on the basis of narrow contractual or reciprocal relations, rather than on the basis of cooperation without consideration of pay-off.

39. B. C. Thema, 'The Changing Patters of Tswana Social and Family Relations', *Botswana Notes and Records*, **4**, (1972), pp. 39–43.

THE IMPACT OF MALE LABOUR MIGRATION ON WOMEN IN BOTSWANA   379

For example, in the key areas of agricultural production, the practice of cooperative ploughing and herding has declined. Case studies carried out in two areas of southeastern Botswana provide evidence of the problem with ploughing.[40] In his study, Donald Curtis found that a high percentage of people hire cattle and that even when cooperative ploughing occurred between relatives, the arrangements were beset with difficulties: the resource-poor household got lands ploughed late in the season or only a portion of the field got done. Of the fifteen widows in his sample, none had their fields ploughed for them by their husband's brother, as required by custom. Curtis also noted a trend in his survey area for social relationships to shift 'away from the several generation family group in which the sons of a man form a close knit group of households ... toward a situation where social relationships centre around the individual household'.[41]

Both Donald Curtis and Kunnie Kooijman show that cooperative cattle herding between grown children of the same parents has become difficult.[42] In the past, fathers and children customarily herded their cattle together, sharing in both the responsibilities of herding and the benefits of draft power and milk. This joint effort occurred even when the father's herd was too small to permit ultimate allocation of cattle to each child. Families today are less willing to herd together. If the herd is small, a man may not willingly lend his son to take of his brother's cattle. The opportunities for school and wage labour outweigh the benefits of milk and ploughing services. While each part of the family separately pursues its own immediate income, future cooperation based on a past of mutual assistance is discouraged.

Furthermore, as cattle become more valuable commercially, customary obligations become more onerous for the man who holds cattle. Cattle production has become a major commercial venture, with the opening of an abbatoir in 1954 and with the preferential access guaranteed for Botswana beef in the European community market since 1975. Owners of large herds are less likely to plough using their own cattle, due to a desire to preserve their value for market. Consequently, cattle owners are increasingly reluctant to plough for relatives, though they may be willing to help in some other smaller way. Likewise, the increased value of cattle means heightened tensions over their control. Widows seem to face particular difficulties. When a cattle owner dies, his brothers may try to keep his cattle from his widow. This is by no means impossible to do, since the cattle may be herded with those of the brothers

40. Donald Curtis, 'The Social Organization of Ploughing'; Kunnie Kooijman, *Social and Economic Change in a Tswana Village'*, (Ph.D. dissertation, University of Leiden, 1978). In her study, Kooijman provides one beautifully detailed case history of one family's changing ploughing arrangements over three generations.
41. Curtis, 'The Social Organization of Ploughing'.
42. Curtis, 'The Social Organization of Ploughing', Kooijman, *Social and Economic Change*, pp. 19–20.

(especially if she has no son to herd) and the widow may not be aware of the exact number her husband had. In the Kgatleng study, a number of widows complained that their cattle had suddenly disappeared or had reportedly died while in the care of their husbands' families.[43]

Female-headed households, whether they be headed by widows or by women who never married, are increasingly insecure economically. They find it difficult to farm and assistance from their extended family is less likely than in the past. As cooperation between resource-rich households and related poor ones declines, the division between rich and poor becomes wider and more rigid. This pattern is developing on a broader scale, with other resource-poor households also affected. Minority groups in Botswana, such as the San people, for example, who have traditionally lacked access to land and cattle and have served as a client group providing labour to Tswana 'masters', also suffer as a result of these changes. This process of polarization in wealth is being fostered at the national level by new laws privatizing resources which had previously been held communally, such as land, and by government policies which direct development funds towards population groups and economic sectors which are already relatively wealthy. The increased right of legal redress for women (and the existence of advocacy programmes for the San and other remote area dwellers) has done little to mitigate the wider social and economic disruption which is occurring.

The impact of economic development programmes

In Botswana rural women work mainly in the least productive and most neglected economic sector: arable agriculture. Crop farming accounts for a mere 4 per cent of the country's Gross Domestic Product.[44] According to a study by the UN Food and Agricultural Organization, 91 per cent of the households in the country infrequently or never produce enough food to meet family consumption needs.[45] Yet 75 per cent of rural households regularly engage in crop farming, according to this study.[46] The work involved in this farming is done by both men and women (and children), but the bulk of the responsibility rests with the women. While men clear the fields as needed and do the ploughing (or at least arrange for it to be done), women generally do the weeding, bird scaring, harvesting, threshing and finally the storing of the food. In this work women often receive assistance from children and occasionally also from men.[47]

43. Author's interviews. Other scholars have made brief reference to this problem. See Kooijman, *Social and Economic Change*, p. 185; David Cooper, 'Rural-Urban Migration of Female-Headed Households in Botswana Towns', in Kerven (ed.), *Workshop on Migration*, p. 123.
44. Lucas, 'The Distribution and Efficiency of Crop Production', p. 1.
45. Republic of Botswana and United Nations Food and Agricultural Organization, *A Study of Constraints on Agricultural Development in the Republic of Botswana*, (Rome, 1974), p. 4.
46. *Ibid.*
47. Carol Bond, *Women's Involvement in Agriculture in Botswana*, (Gaborone: Ministry of Agriculture, 1974), *passim*.

THE IMPACT OF MALE LABOUR MIGRATION ON WOMEN IN BOTSWANA   381

In the period prior to independence in 1966, the colonial government had ignored crop agriculture. (The colonial authorities also paid scant attention to cattle husbandry.)[48] Since independence the government has developed new projects in several economic sectors (especially in cattle ranching, mining and infrastructure) but it has continued to neglect arable agriculture. As of today, there is no integrated package of policies, seed development, marketing, pricing, and extension work, to assist crop farmers. By the late 1970s the Ministry of Agriculture had gone only as far as carrying out a pilot project to test an integrated farming system suitable for small farmers. Ironically, this project was initially restricted to male participants only.

Until recently, the major effort at increasing crop yields has been through extension work. However, this programme has had limited success. Until 1973 the programme was confined to a 'pupil farmer' scheme which in effect restricted its efforts to a tiny number of families who had ample resources in cash, cattle and land to develop. This programme was later abandoned in favour of an effort to reach a wider group of farmers. Despite this effort, agricultural extension still helps very few women farmers. Whether a woman is married or not, she makes decisions on crop agriculture. Married couples today make decisions jointly, though it is not clear whose opinion carries greater weight,[49] although there is some evidence that in the past women had less of a decision-making role. In female-headed households women are, not surprisingly, the primary decision-makers, though they may consult a male relative before carrying out a major decision.

The failure of agricultural extension toward women stems from at least two causes. First, the lack of an integrated farming system, tailored to the needs of small farmers, means that the extension worker actually has little to offer most women, who are usually small farmers.[50] Second, the almost entirely male extension staff has hesitated to approach women farmers, citing as reasons a variety of cultural inhibitions as well as the women's general lack of resources.[51]

Today the development of the economy has propelled productive activities other than crop farming to the forefront. At the household level, the new income earning opportunities that have been created are restricted chiefly to

48. S. J. Ettinger, 'South Africa's Weight Restrictions on Cattle Exports from Bechuanaland, 1924–41', *Botswana Notes and Records*, 4, (1972) pp. 21–29; Christopher Colclough and Stephen McCarthy, *The Political Economy of Botswana*, (New York: Oxford University Press, 1980), ch. 1.

49. Bond, *Women's Involvement*, p. 135ff.

50. One extension worker told the author of a class he attended at the agricultural college where students had to devise a programme for a woman who headed her own household, had land and a little cash and no cattle. The students, only half-jokingly, suggested that the woman should grow marijuana illegally for sale.

51. See F. M. Bettles, *Women's Access to Agricultural Extension Services in Botswana*, (Gaborone: Ministry of Agriculture, 1980). According to Bettles, 15 out of 185 'agricultural demonstrators' are women; of these women, 10 are currently engaged in extension work, with the others working at office jobs. p. 18.

men. Commercial cattle ranching has grown rapidly and the wage sector has provided new jobs. Because these changes are advantageous mainly to men, they have in turn meant a reduction in women's proportional contribution to household income.

The only significant development in rural production in the last thirty years has been in cattle raising. However, cattle ownership is highly concentrated. Only 55 per cent of households own cattle, and half of the national herd is owned by 10 per cent of the population.[52] Cattle production has increased steadily since independence, fostered both by a succession of years of relatively good rain and by government development programmes. (See Table 2) The Ministry of Agriculture has devoted most of its efforts to cattle and has particularly focused on that small group of families who own large herds. Private rights to grazing lands and cattle management training are being offered primarily to this group. The government prefers to assist in large cattle programmes which will increase GNP (and export earnings) and help the big cattle owners who dominate the government service.

TABLE 2
Cattle Production

	National herd (million head)	Throughput at abbatoir (thousand head)	Value of abbatoir sales (million pula)*
1968	1·7	104	11·6
1972	2·2	157	22·6
1976	2·9	212	53·4

*1 Pula = $1·13
Source: Christopher Colclough and Stephen McCarthy, *The Political Economy of Botswana*, (New York: Oxford University Press, 1980, p. 122).

By contrast, in the area of small stock development, almost nothing has been done. Yet a small stock programme would assist more people than a cattle programme. Small stock ownership is much less skewed than cattle ownership. The United Nations Food and Agricultural Organization found that 70 per cent of households own some small stock.[53] A small stock programme would particularly benefit women, as the management of poultry, goats, sheep and pigs tends to be their responsibility.

The only area of major government assistance to women has been in community services. Since independence the government has carried out a programme which has provided health clinics to most villages in the country, dramatically increased the availability of primary schools and reticulated water

52. Government of Botswana, *Rural Income*, p. 111.
53. Government of Botswana, *A Study of Constraints*, p. 5.

THE IMPACT OF MALE LABOUR MIGRATION ON WOMEN IN BOTSWANA 383

to many communities.[54] While these programmes have not particularly increased economic productivity, they have improved women's (and men's) lives.

The increase in wage work in Botswana and in informal market activity has provided more people with larger incomes and with a more secure return on labour than crop farming or managing a small cattle herd can offer.[55] However, the labour market is heavily biased in favour of men: most job categories are restricted to men and male workers are more highly remunerated than female workers.[56] The needs of the South African and Botswana economies, plus the views of what is acceptable work for each sex, insure that men find jobs where women cannot.

Many women have sought work in South Africa. In the Kgatleng district study, one-fourth of the women in wage employment were across the border, working primarily as domestics. Yet these jobs were becoming increasingly difficult to find, and then to keep, in the face of rising unemployment and a security crackdown on those migrating illegally. The 1971 Census showed that 26 per cent of all adult men in Botswana were migrants to South Africa and 5 per cent of all adult women. Almost all of these women were working illegally, while men were able to obtain some work legally through the Chamber of Mines.[57] In interviews, women expressed grave reservations about working (or returning to work) in South Africa. Thus, there will be a growing unemployment problem for those who have in the past relied heavily on employment in South Africa. As a popular folk song goes:

Ramatlabama, go senka dipasa.
Ga o sena boela gae.

[At Ramatlabama (border post), passes are needed.
If you don't have a pass, go back home.]

Not that going home is a solution. The singer continues, now referring to the poverty at home:

Ko morakeng re disa pudi, re gana
kgomo ga ena botshelo.

[At the cattle post we herd (only) goats;
we refuse cattle because they have no life
(i.e., they are dead.)]

54. Richard Chambers, *Botswana's Accelerated Rural Development Programme, 1974–76* (Gaborone: Government Printer, 1977).
55. Michael Lipton, *Employment and Labour Use in Botswana*, (Gaborone: Government Printer, 1978), vol. II, pp. 187–88. Lipton calculates that, to earn the equivalent of the wages of an unskilled new government employee, a farmer would need to own 55 cattle or farm over 33 hectares of cereal (a very large farm by Botswana standards) and receive a high yield per hectare.
56. Robert E. B. Lucas, 'The Distribution of Wages and Employment in Botswana', paper presented at the Conference on the Rural Income Distribution Survey, Gaborone, July 1979, *passim*.
57. Government of Botswana, *1971 Population Census*, table 13.11.

Within Botswana itself, the labour market is heavily biased in favour of men.   Robert Lucas found that women receive significantly lower wages than men.[58]   Women start at a lower wage level and their earnings peak earlier in life than men, meaning that the wage gap between the two groups widens with age.   In 1974 a typical forty-year-old man with primary schooling received 40 pula a month, while a woman in a similar situation received 19 pula or half the man's wage.   In addition, education increases men's earning potential at a greater rate than women's: each year of school raises a man's monthly wage by almost 7 pula, while a woman benefits from only a 5 pula increase.   Much of the difference in wages may be ascribed to sex-based segregation in occupations; most women work as domestics and shop assistants, while men are able to find employment in the more highly paid public sector.   However, the wage gap persists even in salaries received by male and female university graduates who work at similar occupations.

In a survey conducted by the author of secondary school students in Botswana, a marked difference was found in the career and educational aspirations of boys and girls.[59]   While boys aspired to be university graduates and sought a full range of careers, girls tended to want jobs traditional to women, such as teaching and nursing, and to seek only the minimal qualifications necessary for these positions, the junior certificate.   This attitudinal difference is at least in part based on the reality of sex discrimination in the job market: fewer jobs and lower pay for women and the 'double burden' of wage labour and household work.

Despite the difficulties they face in the labour market, women find themselves under increasing pressure to obtain employment.   They are pushed out of the subsistence sector by their responsibility to provide for their children and by the low productivity of arable agriculture.   Labour outmigration of rural women is a recent phenomenon and represents a change in attitude toward women and migration.   Female outmigration only got under way after World War I, some twenty years after men began leaving for South Africa.   There were strong cultural and legal sanctions against female migration.   Continuing at least through the 1940s, women's movements were restricted by customary law.   The chiefs prohibited women from leaving the 'Reserve' by rail unless they had their chief's permission.[60]   Some women left anyway, sometimes sneaking away with a female friend to go to Johannesburg to see the life there and look for work.[61]   Conventional wisdom on southern Africa has largely

58.   The data in this paragraph come from Lucas, 'Distribution of Wages', *passim.*
59.   A detailed analysis of this survey is included in the author's paper, 'Women, Migrant Labor and Social Change in Botswana', *Working Papers*, no. 41, (African Studies Center, Boston University, 1980).
60.   Schapera, *Migrant Labour*, p. 90.
61.   Author's interviews with older women who recounted with relish their secret departure from their parents' homes.

TABLE 3
Female Labour Migration: Kgatleng District, 1943 and 1978

	1943	1978
Percentage of women working away from home	13	25
Percentage of these women who are less than 30 years old	49	58
Percentage of women working away who are single (incl. divorced and widowed)	73	92

Sources: author's Kgatleng sample; Isaac Schapera, *Migrant Labour and Tribal Life,* (London: Oxford University Press, 1947, pp. 61 and 67)

ignored the existence of female labour migration, assuming that men migrate and women remain in the reserve.[62]

Table 3 shows that in comparison with the 1940s, more women are working today; they are younger; and they are more likely to be single.

Further breakdown of the 1978 data reveals that the majority (60 per cent) of the women who were migrant workers were unmarried mothers with children under fifteen years of age.[63] These unmarried mothers are likely to be working than single women without children. The mothers generally leave their children at home in the care of their own mothers. This relationship carries a number of benefits for both the urban woman and her rural family. The working woman is relieved of the problem of day care. With her child (or children) at home, she is likely to send money and goods regularly to her parents, thus helping them to manage. The grandparents benefit from this assistance and also from the children's help around the house. The children themselves are being brought up in the environment preferred by all: a rural home with its Tswana values.[64] Of course, there are instances where the mutuality breaks down, where, for example, the young mother neglects her rural family and the grandmother feels overburdened with child care.

Conclusion
While the economy of independent Botswana has provided new opportunities for advancement, few of these have gone to women. Women engage in a variety of economic activities in order to care for themselves and their families. They farm; they raise children and care for their parents; they work for wages and in the informal sector. Yet despite these efforts, women's work produces

62. See, *inter alia*, Wolpe, 'Capitalism and Cheap Labour-Power', Magubane, *Political Economy.*
63. In Lesotho the situation is parallel, with migrant women being chiefly women with dependents but no husband. Colin Murray, *'Keeping House in Lesotho'*, (unpublished Ph.D. dissertation, Cambridge University, 1976), p. 160.
64. See Hoyt Alverson, *Mind in the Heart of Darkness*, (New Haven: Yale University Press, 1978).

less than the work that men do, partly as result of a culturally derived division of labour and partly due to government policies.

Many scholars have argued that this situation of economic inequality puts women in a position of economic and social dependence on men.[65] This view has generated considerable controversy. Several scholars have counter-hypothesized that women actually gain greater economic and social freedom through male labour outmigration.[66] Still others make a more discriminating argument, holding that greater independence depends on the existence of opportunities for women to earn a reasonable income through their work (agricultural or other).[67] Two scholars of southern Africa who have addressed this question in detail incorporate a sociological component in their analysis. Martha Mueller and Colin Murray contend that, in a situation of oscillating migration, the migrant and his wife are mutually dependent, with each partner needing the other: the man needs a home to which he can return and children who will be recognized as his so that they can support him in his old age, while the woman relies on the man to supplement her farming income.[68] This argument of 'mutual dependence' also underlies much of the southern African literature on economic development, where the rural reserve and the urban wage sector are seen as a complementary whole.

However, none of these arguments deals with the complex interaction between women and men: taking into account both their relative economic resources, their separate economic needs and also the different time frames in which they make decisions. Because women bear the primary responsibility for feeding their children, a woman's need for a family is more immediate than a man's. Moreover, her needs and his needs occur in different time frames. She needs financial support during the long period of years when she is raising her children. The man, on the other hand, may be relatively independent during this time; he may find a job and only feel the need to establish a home and claim his children when he is in his thirties.

65. See, *inter alia*, Achola Pala and Ann Seidman, 'A Proposed Model on the Status of Women in Africa', paper presented at the Conference on Women and Development, Welleseley College, 1976; Anna Rubbo, 'The Spread of Capitalism in Rural Colombia: effects on poor women', in Raynee Reiter (ed.) *Toward a New Anthropology of Women*, (New York: Monthly Review Press, 1975); Karen Sacks, 'Engels Revisited: Women, the organization of production and private property', in *ibid*; Ester Boserup, *Women's Role in Economic Development*, (New York: St. Martin's Press, 1970).
66. For example, Elizabeth Colson, 'Family Change in Contemporary Africa', in J. Middleton (ed.), *Black Africa*, (Toronto: Macmillan, 1970).
67. Monica Hunter (Wilson), 'The Effects of Contact with Europeans on the Status of Pondo Women', *Africa*, **6**, (1933) pp. 259–76; Marjorie Mbilinyi, 'The "New Woman" and Traditional Norms in Tanzania', *Journal of Modern African Studies*, **10**, (1972), pp. 57–72.
68. Martha Mueller, 'Women and Men, Power and Powerlessness in Lesotho', in *Women and National Development*, ed., the Wellesley Editorial Committee, (Chicago: University of Chicago Press, 1977); Murray, *Keeping House*. See also Amy Mariotti for a similar view, though this question is a secondary aspect of her work: '*The Incorporation of African Women into Wage Employment in South Africa, 1920–70*, (unpublished Ph.D. dissertation, University of Connecticut, 1979).

THE IMPACT OF MALE LABOUR MIGRATION ON WOMEN IN BOTSWANA   387

The relative insignificance of women's economic contribution is itself an important factor in understanding delayed marriage and the increase in female-headed households. Besides the fact that oscillating migration itself discourages men from settling down, marriage may also be delayed in Botswana because it does not offer any major economic rewards. In other countries, marriage offers immediate and important assets and rights to a man. In Lesotho, for example, land is a very scarce commodity, and no man can apply for land unless he is married. In Botswana, however, land shortage is not yet serious and young unmarried men may acquire cattle and herd them with their fathers'. Nevertheless, marriage is still attractive but mainly in the long run. As a man grows older, he will need to rely increasingly on his own children to earn wages and to contribute to household income. Marriage gives a man legal paternity of his children and is also important in cultural terms. It confers social status, designating a man as a member of the community who can take care of his own. A husband builds his own home separate from his parents; he and his wife plough a field together; and he makes an effort to build up a herd of cattle. In sum, marriage is still an important institution for men, but its economic return is less intense and occurs later in life than for women.

Thus, the argument of 'mutual dependence' fails to perceive the reality of different levels of dependence. Both women and men depend on labour migration for survival. Yet most women in turn depend on men who are the primary income earners. The ties of support and cooperation between men and women and within families have weakened. Some women raise their children without help from the children's fathers. Assistance within families has declined. As capitalism penetrated Botswana, the whole society became distorted by and dependent on migrant labour. Migration became a necessity to insure the economic survival of the family, even while it undermined the family. Consequently, both women's and men's lives became structured by migrancy patterns. However, what the 'mutual dependence' view ignores is the fact that family ties and economic relationships have been so profoundly altered that it is no longer possible simply to consider the women and the migrant men as a unit. Women's relationship to migrant labour is largely mediated through men, and women's social and economic position has become less secure and more isolated, as their ties to these men have become more tenuous.

One striking manifestation of the process of decline in women's position is the feminization of poverty. An increasing percentage of the poor in Botswana are women. This change is due to the decline in sharing and to the increased privatization of the means of production. Women's earlier access to income and wealth was guaranteed to them as productive members of a kin group headed by men. As land and cattle (and mineral wealth) became privatized, women have been unable to maintain access to these resources. This feminization of poverty which is now underway seems to be occurring at the international level as well, arising out of pressures causing a dissolution of family ties (though counterpressures exist for family members to stick together to establish a joint strategy for survival) and out of a concentration in the ownership of the means of production.

[6]

Part IV: From Household to Workplace: Theories and Survey Research on Migrant Women in the Labor Market

Notes on the Incorporation of Third World Women into Wage-Labor Through Immigration and Off-Shore Production[1]

Saskia Sassen-Koob
Queens College and The Graduate School
City University of New York

The focus is on the growth of export-production in Third World countries and on the massive increase in Third World immigration to the
U.S. Both have taken place over the last fifteen years and both contain
as one constitutive trait the incorporation of Third World women into
waged employment on a scale that can be seen as representing a new
phase in the history of women. The article posits that there is a systemic
relation between this globalization and feminization of wage-labor.

Immigration and off-shore production have evolved into mechanisms for
the massive incorporation of Third World women into wage-labor. While there
is excellent scholarship on both the employment of women in off-shore production in less developed countries and the employment of immigrant women
in developed countries, these two trends have rarely been seen as related. Yet
there are a number of systemic links. Immigration and off-shore production

---

[1]This is derived from the author's forthcoming book *The Foreign Investment Connection: Rethinking
Immigration* (Cambridge University Press). Neither the larger project nor this paper could have
been carried out without the outstanding research assistance of Soon Kyoung Cho.

are ways of securing a low-wage labor force and of fighting the demands of organized workers in developed countries. They also represent a sort of functional equivalence: that is, productive facilities that cannot be shifted off-shore and have to be performed where the demand is, *e.g.*, restaurants and hospitals, can use immigrant labor while facilities that can be shifted abroad can use low-wage labor in less developed countries. There is yet another, more basic connection, and one more difficult to describe. The same set of processes that have promoted the location of plants and offices abroad also have contributed to a large supply of low wage jobs in the U.S. for which immigrant workers are a desirable labor supply.

INDUSTRIALIZATION AND FEMALE MIGRATION

The expansion of export manufacturing and export agriculture in LDCs, both of which are inseparably related with direct foreign investment from the highly industrialized countries (Burbach and Flynn, 1979; UNIDO, 1980), has mobilized new segments of the population into regional and long distance migrations. The mechanisms inducing migration are quite different in the case of export manufacturing from those in commercial agriculture. In the latter there is a direct displacement of small farmers who are left without, or with severely reduced, means of subsistence (George, 1977; NACLA, 1978; Burbach and Flynn, 1979). In export manufacturing, the fragmentary evidence suggests that the disruption of traditional work structures and the corresponding migration inducements are mediated by a massive recruitment of young women into the new industrial zones (*see* Sassen-Koob, 1985). What has made this recruitment effect significant is the locational concentration of export manufacturing in a few countries or regions of countries (UNIDO, 1980; OECD, 1980; ILO, 1980; Lim, 1980; Safa, 1981; Grossman, 1981; Fernandez Kelly, 1983).

Women have a distinct place in each of these developments. Export agriculture has led, in certain areas, to male emigration and to what Elsa Chaney (1980) has called the feminization of small-holder farming; in others, to the proletarianization of women who were once independent producers (Boserup, 1970; Nelson, 1974; Dauber and Cain, 1981; Petritsch, 1981). The particular socioeconomic and cultural configurations that contribute to these diverse patterns have received considerable attention in the anthropological and general development literature but space limitations make it impossible to cite the numerous case studies. Overall, the data for the 1950s and 1960s show the prevalence of female rural to urban migration in Latin America and of male rural-to-rural and rural-to-urban migration in Asia and Africa (Chaney, 1984; Nelson, 1974; Herrick, 1971; Byerlee, 1972; Orlansky and Dubrovsky, 1978;

1146   INTERNATIONAL MIGRATION REVIEW

Petritsch, 1981). This divergent pattern has been explained in part by the lesser role of women in agriculture in Latin America as compared with Africa and Asia (Boserup, 1970). There is disagreement on this aspect. Several recent studies suggest that the contribution of women to agriculture in Latin America has been underestimated due to deficiencies in data gathering (Recchini de Lattes and Wainerman, 1981). The absence of opportunities for paid employment in rural areas is probably a key factor inducing the greater female rural to urban migration (Orlansky and Dubrovsky, 1978).

The large-scale development of export manufacturing in certain regions introduces a new variable into the inquiry. The available evidence strongly documents the overwhelming presence of women among production workers in export manufacturing (Lim, 1980; Safa, 1981; Grossman, 1981; Fernandez Kelly, 1983; Multinational Monitor, 1982; UNIDO, 1980; Pacific Resource Center, 1979; Salaff, 1981; Wong, 1980; Cho, 1983; Arrigo, 1980). Furthermore, there is a high incidence of manufacturing jobs among women in countries or regions within countries where export manufacturing is a key sector of the economy. In these cases we can see a growing incidence of manufacturing jobs and, frequently, a declining share of service jobs among women, a trend that diverges from what has been typical in highly industrialized countries and from what has been the case in Third World countries over the last two decades. For example, in Taiwan, only 13.2 percent of women held manufacturing jobs (including Transport) in 1965; by 1977, this share had risen to 34 percent (Arrigo, 1980: 26).

It is worth noting, for example, that in a rather developed state such as Singapore, the largest single concentration of women workers in the late 1950s was in services. By 1978, it was in production and related jobs. Though in absolute numbers the service sector has increased, its percentage of all jobs declined from 34.7 percent in 1957 to 14.9 percent in 1978, a function of the quintupling of production jobs which accounted for almost 36 percent of all jobs in 1978 (Wong, 1980: 9). This is clearly a result of the expansion of export production. The conjunction of the weight of this type of production and the distinct employment patterns it promotes have generated an additional pattern that contrasts with what is typical in highly developed countries: there is no bimodality in the age composition of women workers. The labor force participation rates of women 20 to 24 years of age is very high yet there is no resurgence in participation among women aged 40 and over (Wong, 1980: 8).

This new pattern diverges significantly from what most of the literature on female migration in the Third World found to be the case in the 1950s, 1960s and well into the 1970s. The general pattern found was that most women migrants to cities became employed in domestic service and in informal sector activities (Boserup, 1970; Schmink, 1982; Delaunoy, 1975; Shah and Smith, 1981; Orlansky and Dubrovsky, 1978; Recchini de Lattes and Wainerman,

1982; Youssef, 1974; Jelin, 1979). Furthermore, the evidence points to a dis-placement of women from manufacturing as the branches typically employing women become modernized, more capital intensive and operate on larger scales of production (Petritsch, 1981; Dauber and Cain, 1981; Tinker and Bramsen, 1976; Boulding, 1980; Parra Sandoval, 1975; Institute of Social Studies, 1980; Ahmad and Jenkins, 1980; Caughman and Thiam, 1980). The same pattern is evident in the development of heavy industry: as the latter becomes an increasingly significant component of a given region's or country's manufacturing sector, the share of jobs held by women in this sector declines; for example, the share of women in manufacturing in Brazil declined from 18.6 percent to 11 percent from 1950 to 1970 (Schmink, 1982: 6).

The prevalence of women in export manufacturing and the high incidence of manufacturing jobs among women in countries where this type of produc-tion is prominent raises a number of questions as to the nature of this devel-opment. One element in the explanation is the marked concentration of elec-tronics, garments, textiles, toys and footwear in export manufacturing — that is, industries that have traditionally employed women. Indeed, the expansion of these industries is beginning to result in changes in the sex composition of rural to urban migration streams in areas of Asia and the Caribbean where males used to be prevalent (World Bank Staff, 1975; Standing, 1975; Arrigo, 1980; Kelly, 1984). For example, Standing (1975) notes a tendency to substitu-tion of male labor within the non-agricultural sector in Jamaica over the last two decades, with the share of women in manufacturing going from 23–24 percent in the early 1950s to 35 percent in 1973 (Standing, 1975: 1).

These trends point to the need for certain distinctions. First, the distinc-tion between so-called traditional and modern forms of manufacturing, shows women to have experienced declines in their shares of jobs as an industry modernizes. However, if we consider the developments in the new industrial zones, perhaps a better formulation would be one that distinguishes between labor-intensive and capital-intensive forms of production. This would allow for the incorporation of both the earlier instances of female employment in certain industries and contemporary cases as diverse as electronics and gar-ments. Furthermore, it overcomes the inadequacy of conceiving of certain industries, notably garments, and certain forms of organization of work, no-tably sweatshops and industrial homework, as pertaining to the traditional, non-modern sector, a notion that can easily be read to mean that these forms will become increasingly insignificant as modernization takes place. The growth of labor intensive manufacturing plants in several Third World coun-tries, as well as the growing use of sweatshops and industrial homework via sub-contracting both in the Third World and in highly industrialized coun-tries, all point to the viability of these forms in "modern" contexts. In some instances they would seem to be integral to the functioning of advanced capitalism in the current historical phase (Sassen-Koob, 1985). This reading of current developments carries considerable implications for an analysis of women's participation in waged employment. While earlier trends suggested both a tendency toward "modernization" in industry and a corresponding displacement of women from manufacturing, these new trends point to growing participation.

However, this growing participation is posited on certain forms of organization of the work process, forms which generate low-wage jobs where workers' empowerment is often difficult. This raises a question about female migrants as a social category and at this point a second set of distinctions needs to be considered. As Orlansky and Dubrovsky (1978: 6) posit, female migrants are characterized by a double disadvantage, one of sex and one of class. Certainly the little evidence available on remuneration shows women migrants to have the lowest wage expectations (Standing, 1975) and actual pay. To this we should add the evidence described earlier on the absence of opportunities for women migrants to be employed in the "modern" sector and their prevalence in domestic service and in informal activities. What emerges clearly is that a large share of women migrants constitute a certain kind of labor. Singer (1974) argues that the employment of women migrants in domestic service in the Third World represents a vehicle for the reproduction of a labor reserve that can be seen as the equivalent of the welfare state in highly industrialized societies. The evidence points to women's exits and re-entries into this type of employment and supports this argument. Domestic service can be seen as providing a livelihood and means for integration into an urban situation. The movement out of domestic service employment and the magnitude of this movement will depend on the characteristics of the job supply (Marshall, 1976). It would seem that in the case of export manufacturing the reserve-status stage becomes unnecessary due to the accelerated growth in labor demand. At the same time, we need more empirical studies examining what the employment options are for the women who are fired or resign from manufacturing jobs. Does domestic service — at least in certain locations — become one of the few alternatives and does it, then, function, as a privatized mechanism for social reproduction and maintenance of a labor reserve?

The category of female migrants consists, thus, of several concrete components ranging from reserve status conditions to full participation in waged employment. The key is the systemic link between the formation of various components of this category in particular historico-geographic configurations and broader processes of social change, such as the development of commercial agriculture or the new export-led industrialization. Migrations do not just happen: they are one outcome or one systemic tendency in a more general dynamic of change. The internal transformation of the category is similarly linked, with broader processes of social change.

WAGE LABOR THROUGH IMMIGRATION   1149

The migrations of young women into the new industrial zones are linked with basic economic transformations in the world economy that assume concrete forms in particular locations. Some aspects of this articulation are quite evident, such as the massive redeployment of labor-intensive segments of production to Third World locations, which has generated a large demand for workers. Others are much less so and require further empirical and conceptual elaboration. One of these aspects is the question as to a possible systemic link between this accelerated growth of export manufacturing and the new immigration to the U.S., much of it consisting of women orginating in countries that have been the central sites for export manufacturing. This kind of analytic effort would further develop the category of female migrant and incorporate it into a theoretical space that seeks to capture central features of the current phase of world capitalist development.

The coexistence of high employment growth and high emigration in the main countries of origin of the new immigration to the U.S. is theoretically unsettling. The push factors traditionally used to explain domestic or international migration, most importantly lack of economic growth, are insufficient. In fact, according to most of these there should have been a decline, if anything, in the levels of emigration. Export industries tend to be highly labor-intensive, this being precisely one of the rationales for locating factories in low-wage countries. The job creation impact is further accentuated by high concentrations of export manufacturing in certain areas, due to the need for access to transportation abroad and the more cost-effective development of necessary infrastructure and servicing.[2]

Thus the question is, how did a situation of general employment growth contain conditions for promoting emigration? Answering such a question requires a detailed examination of the characteristics of this type of industrial growth, its employment effects, and the cultural-ideological impact on the people it touches. We need to specify the links between the objective conditions represented by rapid, mostly export-led industrialization and emigration, particularly migration to the U.S. The evidence clearly documents the existence of industrialization and of immigration into the U.S. What is necessary is a conceptual and empirical elaboration of the linkages between these two processes. Because the analysis from which this article is derived is complex, is based on several distinct bodies of data, and at times must rely on inference, there follows a brief description of the main steps involved in the conceptual and empirical elaboration of the links between industrialization and emigration. For each of these steps there is brief mention of the main findings relevant to an analysis of migration in the major Asian and Caribbean sending countries. These findings represent, in principle, one of several possible out-

---

[2]An earlier version of Pp. 10–12 appeared in Sassen-Koob, 1984a.

comes in an examination of the relation between industrialization and migration (for a full exposition of the analytical framework and a re-elaboration of the available evidence see Sassen-Koob, 1985).

First, it is necessary to examine the characteristics of the new industrial growth in less developed countries and to place it in the context of the overall economic organization of a country. A good part of the growth in these countries can only be accounted for by the growth in exports. Access to the world market is a must given fairly limited internal markets. The development of a world market for these countries is intimately linked to a significant growth in direct foreign investment (UNIDO, 1980; ILO, 1980; OECD, 1980). One distinctive trait about industrial growth in the major new immigrant sending countries is the weight of export production. While this is a particularly strong trend in the Asian and Caribbean countries, it is also present in Mexico and Colombia, two countries with rather developed industrial economies and large internal markets.

Second, it is necessary to examine the employment effects of these patterns of growth. Export agriculture requires a large supply of low-wage workers at crucial periods of the production cycle. Export-oriented plants are often concentrated for reasons having to do with servicing and transportation, a fact which may tend to accentuate the labor-demand impact. Finally, large agglomerations of firms producing for export generate a range of additional jobs, from the packaging for shipment abroad to the construction and operation of airports and harbors.

Third, it is necessary to examine how these labor needs are met. Both export agriculture and export manufacturing have mobilized large numbers of people into wage-labor. The large-scale development of commercial agriculture in Latin America and the Caribbean contributed to the creation of a rural wage-labor supply through the displacement of subsistence farmers and small producers. This displacement was also central in promoting rural unemployment and migrations to the cities. On the other hand, because it is highly labor intensive, export manufacturing could conceivably have contributed to solve the unemployment problem, particularly among prime aged males. Instead, the evidence overwhelmingly shows that it has drawn new segments of the population into the labor force: mostly young women who under conditions of more gradual industrialization would not have entered the labor force in so massive and sudden a way (Lim, 1980; Safa, 1981; Grossman, 1981; Fernandez Kelly, 1983).

Fourth, it is necessary to examine the migration impact, if any, associated with this job creation and labor recruitment. Precisely because of the significant job-creation effect of export-manufacturing and its concentration in a few areas, the extent of the mobilization of young women into the labor force has been considerable. This effect has been further accentuated by the high turnover rates resulting from the employment practices in the plants and the mental and physical fatigue associated with these jobs. A hypothesis that emerges from these patterns is that in areas where there has been a large development of new industrial zones, the large mobilization of women into the labor force has contributed to the disruption of unwaged work structures in communities of origin: the young men are left without mates and partners, the households are left without a key labor factor (*but see also*, Salaff on the case of Hong Kong, 1981).

One could further posit that the disruption of unwaged work structures resulting from an extremely high incidence of young female emigration has increased the pool of unemployed. It may have stimulated the departure of men and women who may not have planned on doing so. At the same time, the high turnover rates in the new industrial zones and the pronounced preference by employers for young women has contributed to growing unemployment among women. Incipient westernization among zone workers and the disruption of traditional work structures combine to minimize the possibilities of returning to communities of origin. In sum, these developments can be seen as having induced the formation of a pool of migrant workers. We need research on each one of these aspects.

Fifth, it is necessary to examine whether these conditions could promote the emergence of emigration as an option actually felt by individuals, particularly migration to the U.S. At this point the fact of a strong foreign presence becomes significant. It is not only the concentration of foreign investment in a few areas. It is also the fact that it dominates the new industrial zones objectively and culturally, thereby creating linkages to the countries where the capital originates. Of interest here is the evidence showing that recent migrants have a higher propensity to move again (Morrison, 1967; Land, 1969) which would suggest that migrants to the new industrial zones will tend to be available subjectively for yet another move. Also of interest is the evidence pointing to the weight of economic incentives in migration (Brigg, 1973 reviews the literature on this subject; Standing, 1975; Harris and Todaro, 1970; Cohen and Sassen-Koob, 1982). The familiar image of the U.S. as a land of opportunities can operate as a strong pull factor, possibly strengthened by the aura of dynamic growth in the new industrial zones populated with U.S. firms and producing for export to the U.S. market.

Finally, the strong presence of foreign firms facilitates access to information and a sense of familiarity with the potential destination, both aspects found to be important in migration studies (World Bank Staff, 1975:22–23). Indeed, distance is found to be a major deterrent in many studies on migration. Contacts and information about the destination location can overcome it partly. Thus, the migration from South Asian and Caribbean Basin countries to the U.S. over the last two decades can be seen as a case where the powerful deterrent effect of distance is overcome by the various factors discussed here, from the imagery about the land of promise to the objective linkages represented by employment in U.S. firms located in the Third World. In this context, the liberalization of U.S. immigration policy after 1965 can be seen as the other side of the processes that have built the structural and subjective linkages with several Third World countries. In brief, I am positing that the distinctive traits of export manufacturing—notably its locational concentration, labor intensity and use of young, mostly first-time entrants into waged employment—makes it into one of these processes for structural and subjective linking (Sassen-Koob, 1985; 1984a).

THE NEW LABOR DEMAND: CONDITIONS FOR THE ABSORPTION OF IMMIGRANT WOMEN

The technical transformation of the work process underlying the redeployment of manufacturing and office jobs to less developed areas has also reshaped the job supply in the developed areas. Furthermore, the spatial dispersion of plants and offices has created a need for an expanded, centralized management and servicing apparatus located mostly in highly developed areas. Both of these processes together with the overall shift to a service economy have directly and indirectly, created a significant increase in the supply of low wage jobs, particularly female-typed jobs, in highly developed countries.

Today, as in the past, the immigration of women is not simply a function of kinship. There are objective conditions that create a demand for female workers given the sex-typing of jobs and the lower wages paid to women. The shift to services and the technically induced downgrading of many jobs have generated an expansion in types of jobs associated with women workers. Taking some liberty with the term, one could argue that there has been not only a growing female labor force participation, but also a feminization of the job supply. The feminization of the job supply in conjunction with the growing politicization of native women may well create a growing demand for immigrant women.

Here I will focus on the general increase in the supply of low-wage jobs and on the particular configuration these trends assume in major cities, these being the main recipient areas of the new immigration.

At the national level the general trends shaping the job supply have brought about a greater inequality in the income distribution of workers over the last decade. The shift to a service economy is generally recognized to result in a greater share of low-wage jobs than is the case with an economy dominated by a strong manufacturing sector (Singelmann, 1978; Bluestone, Harrison, Gorham, 1984). Second, some of the fastest growing service industries are characterized by a larger than average concentration of low-wage and high-income jobs, which means we can expect an even stronger polarization (Stanback and Noyelle, 1982; Applebaum, 1984). Third, there has been what I call a downgrading of the manufacturing sector: major new industries, notably in high-technology, have large shares of low-wage jobs in production and assembly while several of the older industries have undergone a social reorganization of the work process characterized by a growth in non-union plants and rapid growth of sweatshops and industrial homework (NY State Department of Labor, 1982a; 1982b; Sassen-Koob, 1981; 1981b; Balmori, 1983; Morales, 1983; Marshall, 1983; Benamou, 1985). Fourth, the technological transformation of the work process, in part underlying the above trends, has further added to polarization by either upgrading or downgrading a vast array of middle-income jobs: mechanization and computerization have transferred skills to machines and have shifted certain operations from the workplace to the computer room or designer's studio.

This polarization is evident when we compare 1970 and 1980 census data on earnings. The two highest earnings classes increased their total share from 32 percent to 37 percent while the two lowest classes increased their share from 32 to 38.5 percent. Correspondingly the two middle earnings classes reduced their share by 11 percent. When we control for sex these trends are even more pronounced in the case of women. Thus while 42 percent of all women as compared to 34.4 percent of all men held jobs in the two lowest earnings classes in 1970, this share had increased to 52 percent for women and only to 35.7 percent for the men by 1980. Men and women lost about equal shares in the two middle income strata. And all the gains in the two highest income strata were obtained by men, while women actually lost some representation (*see,* Table 1).

All these trends are operating in the major cities that have received most of the immigrants. Indeed, for several reasons I should expect these trends to be even more intense in such cities (Sassen-Koob, 1984). First, the locational concentration of major new growth sectors in such cities entails a disproportionate concentration of industries with highly polarized income distributions. The data on earnings classes show that almost half of all workers in the producer services are in the next to lowest earnings class compared with 17 percent in manufacturing (Stanback *et al.,* 1981). The producer services are the economic core of such cities as New York and Los Angeles, and one of the most dynamic sectors in the economy as a whole.

There also is an indirect creation of low-wage jobs associated with a polarized income distribution. It takes place in the sphere of social reproduction as indicated by consumption. The expansion of the high-income workforce in conjunction with the emergence of new cultural forms has led to a process of high-income gentrification that rests, in the last analysis, on the availability of

TABLE 1
DISTRIBUTION OF TOTAL U.S. LABOR FORCE* AMONG EARNINGS CLASSES, 1970 AND 1980

Earning Classes[a]	Distribution of Total U.S. Labor Force %							
	1970				1980			
	Total		Female	Male	Total		Female	Male
1.60 and above	11.3	32.2	7.5	9.4	12.9	37.0	4.8	11.0
1.59 to 1.30	20.9		18.6	18.9	24.2		14.5	20.7
1.29 to 1.00	18.9	35.8	21.5	23.1	12.8	24.5	12.8	15.6
.99 to .70	16.9		10.5	14.3	11.7		15.8	17.0
.69 to .40	22.8	32.0	13.5	15.4	25.2	38.5	16.7	11.8
.39 and below	9.2		28.4	19.0	13.3		35.4	23.9

Source: Based on U.S. Bureau of the Census, 1982. *Money Income of Households, Families and Persons in the United States: 1980.* (Current Population Reports: Series P-60, No. 132); and U.S. Bureau of the Census, 1972, *Money Income of Households, Families and Persons in the United States: 1970.*

Notes: *Civilian workers 14 years and over by total money earnings.

[a] Earnings classes are derived from the application of 1975 average earnings for each major occupation within each industry group. A basic assumption is that the relative income at 1975 levels for each occupational-industrial subgroup is constant — in this case from 1970 to 1980. I followed the method used by Stanback and Noyelle (1982) in their comparison of 1960 and 1975 earnings for industry-occupational cells (see chapter 3). The total earnings distribution obtained is then divided into quintiles. The major industry groups are Manufacturing, Construction, Distributive Services, Retail, Producer Services, Consumer Services, Nonprofit Services (Health and Education), Public Administration. Not included are Agriculture, Fisheries and Mining. The major occupational groups are Professional, Technical, Manager, Office Clerical, Nonoffice Clerical, Sales, Craft Workers, Operatives, Service Workers, Laborers.

a vast supply of low-wage workers. As I have argued at greater length else-where (Sassen-Koob, 1981) high income gentrification is labor-intensive, in contrast to the typical middle class suburb that represents a capital intensive process—tract-housing, road and highway construction, dependence on pri-vate automobile or commuter trains, heavy reliance on appliances and house-hold equipment of all sorts, large shopping malls with self-service operations. High-income gentrification replaces much of this capital intensity with work-ers directly and indirectly. Behind the gourmet food stores and specialty bou-tiques that have replaced the self-service super-market and deparment store lies a very different organization of work. Similarly, high-income residences in the city depend to a much larger extent on hired maintenance staff than the middle class suburban home with its heavy input of family labor and of ma-chinery, epitomized by the ever-running lawnmower.

A different type of organization of work is present both in the retail and in the production phase. High-income gentrification generates a demand for goods and services that are typically not mass-produced or sold through mass outlets. Customized production, small runs, specialty items, fine food dishes are generally produced through labor intensive methods and sold through small, full-service outlets. Subcontracting part of this production to low-cost operations, be they sweatshops or households, is common.

Second, there is a proliferation of small, low-cost service operations made possible by the massive concentration of people in such cities in addition to a large daily inflow of non-resident workers and of tourists. The ratio between the number of these service operations and the resident population is most probably significantly higher than in an average city or town. Furthermore, the large concentration of people in major cities will tend to create intense inducements to open up such operations as well as intense competition and marginal returns. Under such conditions the cost of labor is crucial and hence the likelihood of a high concentration of low-wage jobs. The overall outcome for the job supply and the range of firms involved in this production and delivery is rather different from that characterizing the large department stores and supermarkets which tend to buy from mass producers often located at great distances from the retail outlets. Mass production and mass distribution outlets facilitate unionization both in production and in sales. The changing organization of work creates conditions that make immigrants a desirable la-bor supply.

Third, for these same reasons together with other components of demand, the relative size of the downgraded manufacturing sector will tend to be larger in larger cities (although such a downgraded manufacturing sector may not necessarily be present in *every* urban environment). The expansion of a down-graded manufacturing sector in major cities is the result of several concrete developments besides the more general processes of social and technical transformation cited above. First, labor intensive industries were affected differentially by capital flight from the cities. In the case of New York's garment industry, the largest employer in the city's manufacturing sector, the bigger shops with mechanized branches, specialized shops and the industry's marketing and design operations have remained in the city. It is worth noting that the garment industry in Los Angeles added 80,000 jobs from 1970 to 1980, a fact often overlooked in analyses of that region as a high-tech center. Furthermore, the changing structure of consumption has also affected the garment industry (Sassen-Koob, 1984); the greater demand for specialty items and limited edition garments has promoted the expansion of small shops and industrial homework in cities because small runs and vicinity to design centers are important locational constraints. A parallel argument can be made for other industries, notably furniture, furs and footwear. Also immigrant-owned plants have grown in number rapidly in view of easy access to cheap labor and, most importantly, a growing demand for their products in the immigrant communities and in cities at large.

The expansion of the low-wage job supply contains conditions for the absorption of immigrants. It coincides with a pronounced increase in the overall numbers of immigrants, both women and men. Slightly over half of all immigrants legally admitted during the 1960s and 1970s were women. While the share of women in total immigration remained constant, their numbers increased markedly, going from one million in the decade of the 1950s, to over 2 million in the 1970s (*see,* Table 2).

The regional concentration of immigrants makes their labor impact much stronger than these figures would suggest. About 40 percent of all immigrants counted by the 1980 Census lived in only two states, California and New York, and then largely concentrated in a few major cities. Furthermore, the labor market impact of immigrants is also magnified by the tendency for undocumented immigrants to be located in the same areas as legal immigrants of a given nationality. One study (Warren and Passell, 1984) estimated that almost half of all the illegal aliens counted by the 1980 Census that had entered since 1960 were women (*see,* Table 3 & 4). This may or may not contradict the common view that most undocumented workers are men insofar as the Census would inevitably fail to count those who may have been in the country in the intercensal periods and left before 1980.

While the labor force participation rate of immigrant women is generally lower than that of immigrant men and native women, their occupational concentration is far more pronounced. If we consider the five states in which most immigrants are living (New York, California, Texas, Florida and Illinois) the sharpest difference in occupational distribution is between native and immigrant women in operative jobs: only about 8 percent of native compared with 20–25 percent of immigrant women held operative jobs according to the 1980

TABLE 2

LOW WAGE, UNSKILLED JOBS LIKELY TO EMPLOY IMMIGRANTS:
SELECT SERVICE INDUSTRIES, NEW YORK CITY, 1978[a]

	Employment in Select Service Industries			
	Finance, Insurance Real Estate[b]	Business Sevices[c]	Other Service Industries[d]	Total
Managers, Professionals and Technical	104,460	65,800	140,600	310,860
Services				
Low-Wage Jobs	30,520	52,430	40,900	123,850
Total	36,980	54,950	83,520	175,450
Maintenance				
Low-Wage Jobs	9,150	1,980	19,590	30,720
Total	12,700	15,880	45,510	74,090
Clerical				
Low-Wage Jobs	1,420	5,020	3,450	3,890
Total	201,630	102,140	80,710	384,480
Sales	23,890	10,180	4,490	38,560
Total all Occupations	379,660	248,950	354,830	983,440
Total Low-Wage Jobs[e] (N)	41,090	59,430	63,940	164,460
% of Total	10.8%	23.9%	18.9%	16.7%

Source: Based on New York State Department of Labor, Division of Research and Statistics, *Occupational Employment Statistics: Services, New York State, April–June, 1978,* 1980, and New York State Department of Labor, Division of Research and Statistics, *Occupational Employment Statistics: Finance, Insurance, and Real Estate, New York State, May–June, 1978,* 1979.

Notes: [a]This is derived from a survey by the New York State Department of Labor (1980, 1979). The sample was drawn from establishments (only those covered by New York State Unemployment Insurance Law) in select service industries. Excluded from the sample were the following service industries: educational services (SIC 82), private households (SIC 88), and the hospitals industry sub-group (SIC 806). Private households and hospitals contain significant numbers of low-wage jobs known to be held by immigrants. Excluded from the sample were establishments and activities which include significant numbers of low-wage jobs known to employ immigrants, notably, restaurants.
[b]SIC codes 61–65.
[c]SIC codes 73, 81.
[d]SIC codes 70, 72, 75–80, 83, 84, 86, 89.
[e]The jobs identified as low-wage are only a segment of all low-wage jobs. They are those that lack language proficiency requirements, are not part of a well-defined advancement ladder and are not usually part of a highly unionized occupation.

TABLE 3

IMMIGRANTS ADMITTED BY SEX

	1951 1960	1961 1970	1971	1972	1973	1974	1975	1976	1977	1978	1979	1971 1979
Number Admitted	2,515	3,322	370.5	384.7	400.1	394.9	386.2	398.6	462.3	601.4	460.3	3,962
Men	859	1,488	172.5	179.7	186.3	184.5	180.7	184.9	216.4	286.4	219.5	1,859
Women	1,014	1,834	197.9	204.9	213.7	210.3	205.5	213.8	245.9	315.1	240.8	2,103

Source: Immigration and Naturalization Service, *Annual Report* (various years).

TABLE 4

ESTIMATES OF ILLEGAL ALIENS COUNTED IN THE 1980 CENSUS BY SEX AND PERIOD OF ENTRY FOR
ALL FOREIGN-BORN PERSONS AND PERSONS BORN IN MEXICO
(Population in thousands)

Period of Entry	All countries			Mexico			All other countries		
	Both sexes	Male	Female	Both sexes	Male	Female	Both sexes	Male	Female
Entered since 1960*	2,047	1,097	950	931	531	400	1,116	566	549
Entered 1975–1980	890	494	396	476	278	198	413	216	197
Entered 1970–1974	551	297	254	280	159	121	270	138	132
Entered 1960–1969	570	290	281	138	77	61	432	212	220

Source: Warren and Passel (1983).

Census (Bach and Tienda, 1984). Nowhere does the occupational distribution of men contain this large a divergence between natives and immigrants. Probably the second largest difference is in clerical jobs: 37 to 40 percent of native women held such jobs in 1980, compared with 25–30 percent of immigrant women.

About half of all immigrant women are concentrated in two occupations, operatives and services. There are variations by nationality. Nearly 70 percent of all Hispanics in the five states that accounted for most immigrants, held operative, service or laborer jobs. The figure for Asians who arrived during the 1970s was 40 percent (Bach and Tienda, 1984: 13–14). The figure for all women workers in the U.S. holding these types of jobs was 29 percent (U.S. Department of Commerce, 1983). The incidence of low-wage jobs among Asians may be growing, pointing to the possibility of a new phase in Asian migration after the earlier phase dominated by middle class origins and high levels of education. At the other extreme, fewer immigrant women than native women hold professional jobs: the share among the first was 9–10 percent, among the second, 14 to 16 percent.

The evidence by industry shows a similarly high concentration in certain sectors. The share of immigrant women in transformative industries (garment, textiles and food, principally) ranged from 24 to 34 percent, which was about 10 to 15 percent higher than that of native women. The second largest single concentration was in social services, where from 22 to 27 percent of all immigrant women in the five main states can be found. A significantly higher share of native women are in this grouping, ranging from 32 to 37 percent. The differences between native and immigrant women are less pronounced in the other industry groups. From 23 to 30 percent of immigrant women are in the producer and distributive services, a share slightly lower than that of native women. These services are a key component in the economies of large cities (Stanback and Noyelle, 1982; Sassen-Koob, 1984), suggesting the possibility of an interaction effect between demand and supply factors—that is, a growing demand for low-wage female workers in these expanding sectors alongside a growing supply of immigrant women workers.

These trends tend to be confirmed by localized studies. For example, using the data from the Fordham University Survey of Colombians and Dominicans in New York City, Castro (1982) found that the incidence of blue-collar jobs among Colombian women in New York City was significantly higher than that among native women in the U.S. and than that among women in Colombia. Cohen and Sassen-Koob (1982) similarly found a very high incidence of women in blue-collar jobs: of all Hispanics in the survey holding blue collar jobs, almost 41 percent were women. This is a high figure compared with that for the U.S. as a whole, where women are one-sixth of all blue collar workers. (U.S. Department of Commerce, 1983) (*see,* Table 5).

TABLE 5
OCCUPATIONAL DISTRIBUTION BY NATIONAL ORIGIN AND SEX,
QUEENS (NYC), 1980
(percentages)

	Colombian	Puerto Rican	Other Hispanics	All Hispanics
White Collar, Total	100.0	100.0	100.0	100.0
Male	44.4	28.6	41.7	37.0
Female	55.6	71.4	58.3	63.0
Blue Collar, Total	100.0	100.0	100.0	100.0
Male	62.5	66.7	55.2	59.2
Female	37.5	33.4	44.8	40.8
Services, Total	100.0	100.0	100.0	100.0
Male	44.4	25.0	43.5	36.5
Female	55.6	75.0	56.5	63.5

Source: Cohen and Sassen-Koob (1982).

The expansion of a downgraded manufacturing sector, be it the garment sweatshops in New York City or the high-tech production plants in the Los Angeles region, can be seen to generate a demand for low-wage women workers. Immigrant women have clearly emerged as a labor supply for these kinds of jobs. It is well-known that the garment, furs, and footwear sweatshops rely heavily on immigrant women. The high share of immigrant women in California's high-tech production and assembly operations has been well documented (Solorzano, 1982).

Similarly, the expansion of low-wage service jobs, particularly pronounced in major cities for reasons discussed above, generates a demand for low-wage workers. Also in this case immigrant women can be seen as a desirable labor supply. Even more so than in the case of the downgraded manufacturing sector, many of these jobs have been historically and/or culturally typed as women's jobs.

There is, then, a correspondence between the kinds of jobs that are growing in the economy generally, and in major cities particularly, and the composition of immigration — largely from low-wage countries and with a majority of women. This correspondence does not necessarily entail the actual employment of immigrant women in such jobs. However the available evidence on immigrant women shows them to be disproportionately concentrated in operative and service jobs and disproportionately located in certain states, notably New York and California, and then especially in major cities.

CONCLUSION

The expanded incorporation of Third World women into wage labor is a global process that assumes specific forms in different locations. These forms and locations may seem unrelated and disparate. I examined two instances of this incorporation and the possibility of a systemic relation between them. The two instances are: a) the recruitment of women into the new manufacturing and service jobs generated by export-led manufacturing in several Caribbean and Asian countries; for a number of reasons this type of industrialization has drawn mostly young women without much prior wage-laboring experience; b) the employment of immigrant women in highly industrialized countries, particularly in major cities which have undergone basic economic restructuring; waged employment represents for many immigrant women a first labor market experience, but it is increasingly becoming the continuation of patterns already initiated in countries of origin, among which, possibly, the recruitment of women into export manufacturing in the main immigrant sending countries.

The study of women migrants has typically focused on their family situation and responsibilities and on how gender is affected by the migration to a highly industrialized country. I sought to add another variable by linking female migration to basic processes in the current phase of the capitalist world economy. Global processes of economic restructuring are one element in the current phase of Third World women's domestic and international migration. While many of these women may have become domestic or international migrants as a function of their husbands or families' migration, the more fundamental processes are the ones promoting the formation of a supply of women migrants and a demand for this type of labor. Some of the conditions that have promoted the formation of a supply of migrant women in Third World countries are one expression of the broader process of economic restructuring occurring at the global level. The particular expression in this case is the shift of plants and offices to Third World countries. Similarly with conditions that have promoted a demand for immigrant women in large cities within the United States. The particular expression in this case is the general shift to a service economy, the downgrading of manufacturing—partly to keep it competitive with overseas plants—and the direct and indirect demand for low-wage labor generated by the expansion of management and control functions centered in these large cities and necessary for the regulation of the global economy. All of these are contributing towards informalization in various sectors of the economy. The associated feminization of the job supply and the need to secure a politically adequate labor supply combine to create a demand for the type of worker represented by immigrant women. This suggests that gender cannot be considered in isolation of these structural arrangements and that gender alone is insufficient to specify the conditions of migrant women whether within their countries of origin or outside.

REFERENCES

Balmori, D.
1983 "Hispanic Immigrants in the Construction Industry: New York City, 1960–1982". Center for Latin American and Caribbean Studies, New York University, *Occasional Papers*, No. 38.

Beckford, G.
1972 "Persistent Poverty". London: Oxford University Press.

Benamou, C.
1985 " 'La Aguja': Labor Union Participation among Hispanic Immigrant Women in the New York Garment Industry". Center for Latin American and Caribbean Studies, *Occasional Papers*. New York University.

Bluestone, B.B. Harrison and L. Gorham
1984 "Storm Clouds on the Horizon: Labor Market Crisis and Industrial Policy". Boston: Economics Education Project.

Bonilla, A.F. and R. Campos
1982 "Imperialist Initiatives and the Puerto Rican Worker: From Foraker to Reagan", *Contemporary Marxism*, 5:1–18.

Boserup, E.
1970 *Woman's Role in Economic Development*. New York: St. Martin's Press.

Boulding, E.
1980 *Women: The Fifth World*. Washington, DC: Foreign Policy Association, Headline Series 248. Feb.

Brigg, P.
1973 "Some Economic Interpretations of Case Studies of Urban Migration in Developing Countries". Washington, DC: International Bank for Reconstruction and Development, Staff Working Paper 10. 151. March.

Burbach, G. and S. Flynn
1980 *Agribusiness in the Americas*. New York: Monthly Review Press and NACLA.

Byerlee, D.
1972 "Research on Migration in Africa: Past, Present and Future". Department of Agricultural Economics, African Rural Employment Paper No. 2. Michigan State University. Sept.

Castro, M.G.
1982 "Mary and Eve's Social Reproduction in the Big Apple: Colombian Voices". Center for Latin American and Caribbean Studies, New York University: *Occasional Papers*, No. 35.

Caughman, S. and M. N'diaye Thiam
1980   "Soap-making: The Experiences of a Woman's Co-operative in Mali", *Appropriate Technology*, 7(3):4–6. Dec. London.

Chaney, E.M.
1984   *Women of the World: Latin America and the Caribbean*. Washington, DC: Office for Women in Development, U.S. Agency for International Development. May.

Chaney, E.M. and M.W. Lewis
1980   "Women, Migration and the Decline of Small Holder Agriculture". Washington, DC: United States Agency for International Development, Office of Women in Development. Oct.

Oho, S.K.
1984   "The Feminization of the Labor Movement in South Korea". Department of Sociology, University of California, Berkeley. Unpublished.

Cohen, S.M. and S. Sassen-Koob
1982   *Survey of Six Immigrant Groups in Queens, New York City*. Queens College, City University of New York.

Dauber, R. and M.L. Cain, eds.
1981   *Women and Technological Change in Developing Countries*. Boulder, CO: Westview Press.

Delaunoy, I.V.
1975   Formacion, Empleo y Seguridad Social de la Mujer en America Latina y el Caribe". In *Participation de la Mujer en el Desarrollo de America Latina y el Caribe*. Edited by Henriques de Paredes, P. Izaguirre and I.V. Delaunoy. Santiago, Chile: UNICEF Regional Office. Pp. 59–114.

Fernandez-Kelly, M.P.
1983   *For We Are Sold, I and My People: Women and Industrialization in Mexico's Frontier*. Albany: SUNY Press.

George, S.
1977   *How the Other Half Dies: The Real Reasons for World Hunger*. Montclair, NJ: Allanheld, Osmun.

Grasmuck, S.
1982   "The Impact of Emigration on National Development: Three Sending Communities in the Dominican Republic". Center for Latin American and Caribbean Studies, New York University: *Occasional Papers*, No. 32.

Gross, R.
1979   "Women's Place in the Integrated Circuit", *Southeast Asia Chronicle*, 66:2–17.

Harris, J. and M. Todaro
1970   "Migration, Unemployment, and Development: A Two-Sector Analysis", *American Economic Review*, 60(1):126–142. March.

Herrick, B.
1971   "Urbanization and Urban Migration in Latin America: An Economist's View". In *Latin American Urban Research*, Vol. 1. Edited by F. Rabinovitz and F. Trueblood. Beverly Hills, CA: Sage Publications.

1164 INTERNATIONAL MIGRATION REVIEW

Institute of Social Studies, New Delhi
1979 "A Case Study on the Modernization of the Traditional Handloom Weaving Industry in the Kashmir Valley: The Integrated Development Project for the Woolen Handloom Weaving Industry in Jammu and Kashmir". Bangkok: Asian and Pacific Centre for Women and Development. May.

International Labor Office
1982 *Yearbook of Labor Statistics, 1981.* Geneva: ILO.

_____
1981 *Employment Effects of Multinational Enterprises in Developing Countries.* Geneva: ILO.

Jelin, E.
1979 "Women and the Urban Labor Market". International Labor Office, World Employment Programme Research. Working Paper No. 77 of the Population and Labor Policies Programme. Sept.

Kelly, D.
1984 "Hard Work, Hard Choices: A Survey of Women in St. Lucia's Export Oriented Electronics Factories". Unpublished Research Report.

Land, K.
1969 "Duration of Residence and Prospective Migration: Further Evidence", *Demography*, 6(2):133-140.

Lim, L.Y.C.
1980 "Women Workers in Multinational Corporations: The Case of the Electronics Industry in Malaysia and Singapore". In *Transnational Enterprises: Their Impact on Third World Societies and Cultures*. Edited by Krishna Kumar.

_____
1978 "Women in Export Processing Zones". New York: UNIDO.

Marshall, A.
1983 "Immigration in a Surplus-worker Labor Market: The Case of New York". Center for Latin American and Caribbean Studies, New York University, *Occasional Papers*, No. 39.

_____
1976 *Inmigracion, demanda de fuerza de trabajo y estructura ocupacional en el area metropolitana.* Buenos Aires: Facultad Latinoamericana de Ciencias Sociales.

Morales, R.
1983 "Undocumented Workers in a Changing Automobile Industry: Case Studies in Wheels, Headers and Batteries", *Proceedings of the Conference on Contemporary Production: Capital Mobility and Labor Migration*. Center for U.S.-Mexican Studies, University of California, San Diego.

Morrison, P.
1967 "Duration of Residence and Prospective Migration: The Evaluation of a Stochastic Model", *Demography*, 4:553-561.

Multinational Monitor
1982 *Focus: Women and Multinationals.* Washington, D.C. Summer.

Nelson, J.
1974 "Sojourners vs. New Urbanites: Causes and Consequences of Temporary vs. Permanent Cityward Migration in Developing Countries". Center for International Affairs, Harvard University.

New York State Department of Labor
1982a   *Report to the Governor and the Legislature on the Garment Manufacturing Industry and Industrial Homework.* New York: New York State Department of Labor.

1982b   *Study of State-Federal Employment Standards for Industrial Homeworkers in New York City.* Albany: New York State Department of Labor, Division of Labor Standards.

1980   *Occupational Employment Statistics: Services, New York State, April–June 1978.* Albany: New York State Department of Labor.

1979   *Occupational Employment Statistics: Finance, Insurance and Real Estate, New York State, May–June 1978.* Albany: New York State Department of Labor.

North American Congress on Latin America
1978   "Capital's Flight: The Apparel Industry Moves South", *Latin America and Empire Report*, 11:3.

1977   "Electronics: The Global Industry", *Latin America and Empire Report*, 11(4). July/Aug.

Organization for Economic Co-Operation and Development
1981   *International Investment and Multinational Enterprises: Recent International Direct Investment Trends.* Paris: OECD.

1980   "International Subcontracting: A New Form of Investment". Paris: OECD, Development Centre.

Orlansky, D. and S. Dubrovsky
1978   "The Effects of Rural-Urban Migration on Women's Role and Status in Latin America". Paris: UNICEF, *Reports and Papers in the Social Sciences*, No. 41.

Parra Sandoval, R.
1975   "La desnacionalizacion de la industria y los cambios en la estructura ocupacional colombiana 1920-1970". Bogota: CIDE.

Petritsch, M.
1981   "The Impact of Industrialization on Women's Traditional Fields of Economic Activity in Developing Countries". New York: UNIDO.

Pineda-Ofreneo, R.
1982   "Philippine Domestic Outwork: Subcontracting for Export Oriented Industries", *Journal of Contemporary Asia*, 12(3):281-293.

Port Authority of New York and New Jersey
1982   *Regional Perspectives: The Regional Economy, 1981 Review, 1982 Outlook.* New York: Planning and Development Department, Regional Research Section.

Portes, A.
1979   "Illegal Immigration and the International System: Lessons from Recent Legal Mexican Immigrants to the United States", *Social Problems*, 26. April.

1166 INTERNATIONAL MIGRATION REVIEW

Recchini de Lattes, Z. and C.H. Wainerman
1979 "Data from Household Surveys for the Analysis of Female Labor in Latin America and the Caribbean: Appraisal of Deficiencies and Recommendations for Dealing with Tehm. Santiago: CEPAL.

Safa, H.I.
1981 "Sunway Shops and Female Employment: The Search for Cheap Labor", *Signs*, 7(2):418–433. Winter.

Salaff, J.
1981 *Working Daughters of Hong Kong*. New York: Cambridge University Press, ASA Rose Monograph Series.

Sassen-Koob, S.
1985 "The Foreign Investment Connection: Rethinking Immigration". Cambridge University Press. Forthcoming.

———
1984a "Direct Foreign Investment: A Migration Push Factor?", *Government and Policy*, 2:399–416. London: Pion. Nov.

———
1984a "The New Labor Demand in Global Cities". In *Cities in Transformation*. Edited by Smith. Beverly Hills: Sage.

———
1984b "Foreign Investment: A Migration Push Factor?". In *Government and Policy*, Special Issue on International Migration. Edited by Bennett and Muller. London: Pion. Nov.

———
1981a "Towards a Conceptualization of Immigrant Labor", *Social Problems*, 29. Oct.

———
1981b "Exporting Capital and Importing Labor". Center for Latin American and Caribbean Studies, New York University: *Occasional Papers*, No. 28.

Schmink, M.
1982 "La mujer en la economia en America Latina". Mexico: The Population Council, Latin America and Caribbean Regional Office, Working Papers No. 11. June.

Shah, N.M. and P.C. Smith
1981 "Issues in the Labor Force Participation of Migrant Women in Five Asian Countries". East-West Population Institute, East-West Center: Working Papers No. 19. Sept.

Singelmann, J.
1978 *From Agriculture to Services: The Transformation of Industrial Employment*. Beverly Hills and London: Sage.

Singer, P.
1974 "Migraciones internas: consideraciones teoricas sobre su estudio". *Las migraciones internas en America Latina*. Fichas No. 38, Nueva Vision. Argentina.

Solorzano Torres, R.
1983 "Female Mexican Immigrants in San Diego County". Center for U.S.-Mexican Studies, University of California, San Diego. Research in Progress.

WAGE LABOR THROUGH IMMIGRATION   1167

Stanback, Jr., T.M. and T.J. Noyelle
1982   *Cities in Transition: Changing Job Structures in Atlanta, Denver, Buffalo, Phoenix, Columbus (Ohio), Nashville, Charlotte.* New Jersey: Allanheld, Osmun.

Standing, G.
1975   "Aspiration Wages, Migration and Female Employment". ILO: World Employment Programme, Working Paper No. 23 of the Population and Employment Project. Nov.

Tinker, I. and M. Bo Bramsen, eds.
1976   *Women and World Development.* Washington, DC: Overseas Development Council.

United Nations Industrial Development Organization
1982   *Changing Patterns of Trade in World Industry: An Empirical Study on Revealed Comparative Advantage.* (ID/281). Vienna: UNIDO.

_____
1980   *Export Processing Zones in Developing Countries.* New York: UNIDO.

_____
1979   *World Industry Since 1960: Progress and Prospects.* (ID/229). Vienna: UNIDO.

U.S. Department of Commerce Bureau of Census
1983   Census of Population 1980. Characteristics of the Population. General and Social Characteristics U.S. Summary. Washington D.C.

Warren, R. and J.S. Passel
1983   "Estimates of Illegal Aliens from Mexico Counted in the 1980 U.S. Census. Washington, DC: Bureau of the Census, Population Division.

Wong, A.K.
1980   *Economic Development and Women's Place: Women in Singapore. International Reports: Women and Society.* London: Change.

World Bank Staff
1975   "Internal Migration in Less Developed Countries". Washington, DC: International Bank for Reconstruction and Development, Bank Staff Working Paper No. 215. Prepared by L.Y.L. Yap. Sept.

Youssef, N.H.
1974   "Women and Work in Developing Societies". University of California, Berkeley, Institute of International Studies.

Part IV
Enclaves and Labour Markets

[7]

Immigrant Enclaves: An Analysis of the Labor Market Experiences of Cubans in Miami[1]

Kenneth L. Wilson
Florida Atlantic University

Alejandro Portes
Duke University

Data from a longitudinal sample of Cuban émigrés are used to test competing hypotheses about the mode of incorporation of new immigrants into the U.S. labor market. Classic theories of assimilation assumed a unified economy in which immigrants started at the bottom and gradually moved up occupationally, while they gained social acceptance. Recent dual labor market theories define new immigrants mainly as additions to the secondary labor market linked with small peripheral firms. Multivariate analyses confirm the existence of the primary/secondary dichotomy but add to it a third alternative condition. This is the enclave economy associated with immigrant-owned firms. While most immigrant enterprises are small, competitive ones, enclave workers show distinct characteristics, including a significant return to past human capital investments. Such a return is absent among immigrant workers in the secondary labor market. Causes and implications of these findings are discussed.

The purpose of this study is to examine the extent to which the phenomenon of self-enclosed minorities modifies general labor processes in the U.S. economy. Empirical data with which to address this question come from a sample of recently arrived Cuban émigrés.

The classic sociological literature on immigrant minorities uniformly portrayed the adaptation process as one in which initial economic hardships and discrimination gave way to gradual acceptance by members of the dominant groups and eventual assimilation. With minor variations, different authors identified the culmination of the process as the entrance of immigrants, or their descendants, into the mainstream of the economy and their cultural fusion with the majority (Handlin 1951; Warner and Srole 1945; Wittke 1952). More recently, Gordon (1961, 1964) distinguished

---

[1] Data on which this paper is based were collected as part of the ongoing study, "Latin American Immigrant Minorities in the United States," at Duke University. Data collection and analysis were supported by grants MH 23262-02 from the National Institute of Mental Health and SOC75-16151 from the National Science Foundation.

the ideal types of cultural pluralism and Anglo-conformity, but still the overriding theme was that of blending in and contributing to national welfare. Thus the major goal of immigration research was to document the barriers to assimilation confronted by various minorities and to orient policy decisions at the national and local levels toward their removal.

During the 1960s and in the wake of militant protests by urban ethnic minorities, a new critical literature arose. Spearheaded by the writings of black authors (Carmichael and Hamilton 1967; Malcolm X 1967), this literature documented the tenacity of barriers against entrance of blacks and other "unmeltable" ethnics into the better-paid and more prestigious occupations. Such scholars as Robert Blauner (1972) took up the theme and went on to explore the historical role played by the exploitation of these groups in the development of the American economy. Borrowing a concept developed by González Casanova (1965) in Mexico, the exploitation of nonwhite minorities was termed "internal colonialism."

The assimilationist and internal colonialist perspectives offered diametrically opposite predictions about the fate of racial and ethnic minorities in the United States. According to the first, gradual learning of the culture and acquisition of occupational skills would open the way for entrance into "middle-class" society; according to the other, cultural assimilation of these groups was irrelevant since their subjection and exploitation in the labor market were preconditions for the continuing growth of U.S. capitalism.

Later research has advanced our knowledge of the role of race and ethnicity in the American class structure. It has, by and large, confirmed the persistence of racial differences in status and income even when cultural skills and past individual attainments are taken into account (Duncan 1969; Jencks 1972; Portes and Wilson 1976; Gordon 1971). Other recent studies have tended to concentrate on the specific manner in which blacks, Chicanos, and other minorities have become inserted into the U.S. labor market and on the historical evolution of their condition. As a consequence, the earlier and broader concepts of internal colonialism and colonized minorities have become progressively abandoned in favor of those of segmented class structure and its variants in the industrial economy: "split" and dual labor markets (Bonacich 1972; Gordon 1972).

Since all these perspectives have been concerned with phenomena at the center of the American political economy, they have neglected others taking place at the fringes but having definite theoretical implications. These pertain to immigrant minorities which remain spatially concentrated in a particular city or region. The distinctive characteristics of these groups are that they are less culturally assimilated than native ethnic minorities, tend to cling to their languages and customs, and frequently do better economically than minorities in the mainstream economy. The resilience and economic

Labor Experiences of Cubans

achievements of these enclaves do not fit well the predictions of either assimilation theory or internal colonialism. Nor, as we will see, is their case satisfactorily explained by dual labor market theories, as currently developed.

Some recent studies have significantly advanced our understanding of self-enclosed immigrant minorities. Most of these have had, as empirical base, the situation of Asian immigrants (Bonacich, Light, and Wong 1977; Sung 1967). To our knowledge, however, the existence of an enclave labor market distinct from those in the general economy and the factors leading immigrants to remain thus confined have not been systematically explored.

The purpose of the following sections is twofold: first, to describe the historical origins of a different immigrant enclave—Cuban émigrés in Miami; second, to examine whether the members of an enclave labor force can be distinguished empirically from immigrants who have taken jobs in the general economy. Before proceeding to description and analysis, however, we discuss recent theories of the evolution of the U.S. economy and the dual labor market as an appropriate framework for the subsequent analysis.

DUAL LABOR MARKETS AND IMMIGRATION

The Dual Economy

Analyses of the dual economy (Averitt 1968; Galbraith 1971) are based on the recognition that monopolistic tendencies in industry are no longer a statistical anomaly but constitute perhaps *the* defining feature of advanced capitalism. Monopoly firms are governed by principles different from those employed to describe firm behavior under competitive conditions. Averitt refers to the monopolistic sector as the "center economy"; Galbraith terms it the "industrial state."

With attention concentrated on long-run stability, center firms tend to gain gradual control of the many contingencies which make the existence of peripheral firms problematic. Center firms are able to make full use of economies of scale and to structure productive organizations which are both geographically dispersed and vertically integrated. These firms have moved in recent years to control their sources of supply in technology and raw materials and their markets. Market control is effected through oligopolistic pricing and through the molding of consumer tastes by mass advertising (O'Connor 1973). To insulate themselves further from market contingencies, monopoly firms develop large cash reserves and stabilize their labor force through training programs and promotional ladders or "internal markets" (Edwards 1975).

American Journal of Sociology

The notions of dual or segmented labor markets were originally developed independently of the theory of the dual economy. These notions began inconspicuously as a series of empirical observations about ghetto employment (see Doeringer et al. 1969; Baron and Hymer 1968; Ferman 1968). Some of the most consistent findings were that there seemed to be little relationship between investment in human capital—either formal education or job-training programs—and employment. There was a remarkably high level of job instability. For those who averaged 35–40 hours per week, wages were low, often below the poverty line; the discipline in their jobs was often harsh and arbitrary; there appeared to be an absence of ladders to success, most jobs usually providing almost no opportunity for promotion.[2]

In short, central city jobs appeared to be cut off from the rest of the economic system. Individuals, usually minority members, who were caught in these labor markets had little hope for escape. Thus, various investigators were led to postulate the existence of a dual labor market. The primary labor market has the positive characteristics of stability, chances for promotion, high wages, and good working conditions, while the secondary labor market has the negative traits outlined above (Wachtel 1972). Gordon (1971) pursued the implications of this division and found that the predominant proportion of occupational mobility (measured as job changes) was within these labor markets with very little mobility between them.

Over time, it became clear that these findings converged with the emerging theory of the dual economy. The primary labor market corresponds to the center economy, the secondary labor market resides in the periphery. The market power of monopoly firms enables them to pass on increases in costs to consumers and, hence, finance the advantageous condition of their workers. The periphery, being subject to the constraints of competition, must maintain low wages, otherwise firms may be forced into bankruptcy. Low wages and absence of internal ladders of promotion encourage rapid turnover of workers. For some economists, job instability is the defining characteristic of the secondary labor market (Piore 1975).

[2] Doeringer and Piore (1971) add the following hypothesis: not only does the secondary labor market possess negative characteristics; it also encourages the development of negative psychological characteristics in the labor force that services the secondary market. Particularly, over time there is a gradual rapprochement between poor working conditions in the secondary labor market and poor work habits of minority workers, such as arriving at work late and general task irresponsibility. The main problem with this hypothesis is that of separating contextual labor market effects from those due to individual work habits. To avoid such overlap, the hypothesis must specify psychological characteristics that endure even when the worker has found a job in the primary labor market. Such a hypothesis would require special data and analysis and is beyond the scope of this paper.

Labor Experiences of Cubans

Immigrant Workers and Economic Dualism

The contemporary literature on international migration deals primarily with movements sharing two characteristics. First, they are displacements of *labor*, that is, of individuals who migrate with the intention of selling their labor power in places of destination. Second, they tend to occur from less economically developed areas to economically developed centers. Recent historical studies of immigration to the United States and Western Europe have emphasized the increasing importance of immigrant labor in the development of these advanced economies (Rosenblum 1973; Burawoy 1976; Castles and Kosack 1973; Sassen-Koob 1978).

Contemporary immigration to the United States has become fragmented in ways that parallel the situation described by dual labor market theories. On the one hand, immigration laws have moved toward encouraging migration of highly skilled foreign workers and professionals; on the other hand, they have formally barred the less skilled from entry into the country (Keely 1979). Thus, for example, the amended 1965 Immigration Act reserves the third and sixth preference categories for professional, technical, and skilled workers in short supply in the country.

Further, the U.S. Department of Labor maintains a Schedule A of occupations for which there is "a shortage of workers willing, able, qualified, and available." Individuals in these occupations receive special privileges when applying for an immigrant's visa. In recent years, Schedule A occupations have included physicians and surgeons, nurses, speech therapists, pharmacists, and dietitians.

The effect of these regulations has been to encourage a flow of immigration directed to the primary labor market. Highly qualified immigrants find employment in large-scale firms, research institutions, public and private hospitals, universities, and the like (Stevens, Goodman, and Mick 1978). The numerical extent of this flow is not insignificant. In 1977, 62,400 foreign professionals, managers, and technicians were admitted to the United States for permanent residence (U.S. Bureau of the Census 1978, p. 86).

Given existing regulations, it is not surprising that the occupational distribution of *legal* immigrant cohorts in recent years compares favorably with that of the domestic labor force. For example, during the 1970s the percentage of professional and technical workers among occupationally active immigrants has consistently exceeded that in the U.S. civilian labor force (Portes 1978). Nor is it surprising that studies focusing on legal immigration report significant upward occupational mobility after several years (North 1978), absence of discrimination in pay and work conditions (Stevens, Goodman, and Mick 1978; North 1978), and an economic situation equal to or better than that of domestic workers (Chiswick 1978).

American Journal of Sociology

On the other hand, a numerically larger flow of immigrants is composed of individuals with few skills who find employment in the low-wage menial occupations identified with the secondary labor market. Low-wage labor immigration bypasses occupational selection procedures of the immigration law through several channels. First, workers in less developed territories under U.S. jurisdiction can generally travel without restrictions to the mainland. The most important case is Puerto Rican migration. Though formally a domestic movement, migration from Puerto Rico has many of the same characteristics as international labor flows from Third World countries (Maldonado 1979).

Second, an immigrant group already in the United States can avail itself of family reunification provisions and other clauses of the present immigration law to continue the movement from the source country. A substantial proportion of Asian immigration, from countries such as Korea, and of legal Mexican immigration appears to be of this type (Bonacich 1978; Alba-Hernandez 1978).

Third, and most important, illegal or undocumented immigration into the United States currently brings in hundreds of thousands of low-skill workers. Though no reliable figures on the magnitude of illegal immigration exist, even the most conservative estimates place it significantly above that of *total* legal immigration. Apprehensions by the U.S. Immigration and Naturalization Service, used as a very rough indicator of the magnitude of the illegal flow, exceeded one million in 1976 and again in 1977 (U.S. Immigration and Naturalization Service 1978). The main source of illegal immigration is Mexico, but increasing flows from the Dominican Republic, the British Caribbean, Colombia, and Central America have also been detected (Cornelius 1977).

Dual labor market writings dealing with recent immigration have focused primarily on the flow directed to the secondary labor market. These studies have dealt, for example, with the situation of Puerto Rican migrants in Boston (Piore 1973), Korean and other Asian immigrants on the West Coast (Bonacich 1978), and undocumented Mexican immigrants throughout the Southwest and Midwest (Barrera 1977; Bustamante 1975). Along with domestic minorities, new immigrant workers are defined as additions to the more vulnerable labor pool destined to the low-wage, unstable occupations of the peripheral economy. Past occupational experience and other investments in human capital count very little for these immigrants because, unlike workers in the primary sector, they are hired primarily because of their vulnerability rather than their skills (Galarza 1977; Bach 1978; Bustamante 1975).

A recent paper by Bonacich (1978) has argued that immigrant entrepreneurs fulfill "middleman" functions by exploiting their own national group in the interest of larger firms in the center economy. With this sole

Labor Experiences of Cubans

exception, however, the dual labor market literature has not regarded immigrant labor and immigrant economy activity as phenomena deserving special attention. If only by default, these theories define immigrant enterprises as just one more segment of the peripheral economy. The logical derivation from this perspective can be formalized as follows:

1. *New immigrant workers will concentrate in the secondary labor market. With the exception of those who gain access to the primary sector, immigrants will share all the characteristics of peripheral employment, including low prestige, low income, job dissatisfaction, and the absence of return to past human capital investments. The situation of workers employed by immigrant enterprises will not differ from those in the larger secondary labor market.*

This prediction and the general characterization of "entrapment" in the peripheral economy are contradicted by the experience of at least some immigrant groups. The case of the Japanese (Boyd 1971; Daniels 1971; Petersen 1971) is well known, but other studies have highlighted similar experiences among other national groups such as the Chinese (Sung 1967; Light 1972). For the Koreans, Bonacich notes the proliferation of immigrant businesses and the mobility opportunities that they make available (Bonacich, Light, and Wong 1977).

It should be noted also that the situation of these minorities is not adequately portrayed by aggregate studies of legal immigration. As seen above, the positive characterization of immigrant mobility in these studies is based largely on the arrival of professional, managerial, and skilled talent encouraged by current immigration provisions. The aggregate statistics reflect insertion of these immigrants into the primary labor market, but they fail to capture the distinct phenomenon of immigrant enclaves.

For these last groups, it appears that although new arrivals are forced to work hard for low wages, they do not find upward mobility channels blocked. Many immigrants manage to move up either within existing enterprises or by setting up new businesses. A charted path seems to exist in several of these instances leading from hard labor in the firm of another immigrant to gradual promotion culminating in another business concern.

Some social psychological explanations have been advanced for the economic success of some immigrant minorities (Hagen 1962; Kurokawa 1970; Eisenstadt 1970). A more compelling structural reason, however, appears to be the existence of advantages for enclave enterprises which those in the open competitive sector do not have. Put succinctly, immigrant enterprises might manage to create a workable form of vertical integration by developing ethnically sympathetic sources of supply and consumer outlets. They can organize unorthodox but effective forms of financial and human capital reserves by pooling savings and requiring new immigrants to spell a tour of duty at the worst jobs. These advantages may enable enclave firms to reproduce, albeit imperfectly, some of the characteristics of monopolistic control accounting for the success of enterprises in the center economy.

A necessary condition for the emergence of an economic enclave is the presence of immigrants with sufficient capital. Capital might be brought from the original country, as is often the case with political exiles (Fagen, Brody, and O'Leary 1968), or accumulated through savings. Individuals with the requisite entrepreneurial skills might be drawn into the immigrant flow to escape economic and political conditions in the source country or to profit by the opportunities offered by a preexisting immigrant "colony" abroad.

Although the data presented below do not permit direct analysis of immigrant firms, they allow a test of an important additional hypothesis, which directly contradicts conventional predictions as stated in hypothesis 1:

2. *Immigrant workers are not restricted to the secondary labor market. In particular, those inserted into an immigrant enclave can be empirically distinguished from workers in both the primary and secondary labor markets. Enclave workers will share with those in the primary sector a significant economic return to past human capital investments. Such a return will be absent among those in the "open" secondary labor market.*

A review of the recent history of Cuban immigration and the development of the Cuban enclave in Miami is presented next as an introduction to the empirical analysis.

CUBAN IMMIGRATION AND THE DEVELOPMENT OF THE CUBAN ENCLAVE

The immigrant flow giving rise to the Cuban enclave in Miami has political rather than economic roots. Massive Cuban immigration to the United States began with the advent of Fidel Castro to power in January 1959. The first émigrés, members of the overthrown Batista regime, represented a small minority. As the revolution consolidated, however, it began to implement a populist program contrary to the interest of the dominant classes. Immigration increased as landowners, industrialists, and former Cuban managers of U.S.-owned enterprises left. Others left in anticipation of new measures as the revolution accelerated the transformation of the Cuban class structure; many came to Miami to organize a military force with which to overthrow the Castro government. From mid-1959 to October 1960, approximately 37,000 émigrés came, most of them well to do and many bringing to the United States considerable assets (Thomas and Huyck 1967).

After the defeat of the exile force in the Bay of Pigs in April 1961, the

Labor Experiences of Cubans

flow of refugees accelerated further and its composition began to diversify, reaching down to the middle classes and even sectors of the urban working class (Clark 1977). By the end of 1962, official figures reported 215,323 Cuban émigrés in the United States.

To process this massive flow, the Kennedy administration established the Cuban Refugee Program (CRP) under the secretary of Health, Education, and Welfare. The arrival of Cuban refugees in Miami was viewed at the time as a source of strain aggravating the depressed economy of the area. Thus, efforts of the Cuban Refugee Emergency Center, established by the CRP in Miami, concentrated on relocating the émigrés throughout communities in the United States. Cuban lawyers were transformed into language teachers and sent to high schools and colleges in the North. Others found widely varied occupations, often with the support of private charity organizations. To insure that relocation proceeded smoothly, the center made emergency welfare aid contingent on acceptance of job offers when available. By 1967, 251,000 Cuban émigrés had registered with the CRP, and 153,000 had been relocated away from Miami. The program was widely regarded in federal circles as a complete success (Thomas and Huyck 1967).

With many ups and downs, which included the establishment of a "family reunification" airlift by agreement of the two governments, the inflow of Cuban émigrés continued during the next decade. At the end of 1976, official figures for Cuban refugee arrivals in the United States totaled 661,934 (U.S. Immigration and Naturalization Service 1977). During this entire period, the relocation program conducted by the Cuban Refugee Center continued. By the early 1970s, there was evidence, however, of a significant return migration to Miami. In 1973, a survey estimated that over 25% of Cubans residing in Miami were returnees from other U.S. locations (Clark 1973). The proportion at present should be, if anything, higher.

Cultural and climatic reasons have obviously much to do with return decisions. More important, however, there is evidence that relocated émigrés used their period in northern areas much as other migrants have used their stay in high-wage industrial regions: as an opportunity for accumulating capital. Small-scale investments by returnees from the North were added to those made with capital brought from Cuba to consolidate an immigrant economic enclave.

Cuban-owned enterprises in the Miami area increased from 919 in 1967 to about 8,000 in 1976. While most of them are small scale, some employ hundreds of workers. Enclave firms tend to concentrate on textiles, leather, furniture, cigar making, construction, and finance. An estimated 40% of the construction companies are Cuban owned, and émigrés control roughly 20% of the local commercial banks (*Time* 1978; Clark 1977). There are

American Journal of Sociology

also some investments in agriculture, especially sugar cane plantations and sugar mills.

Enclave firms in the service sector include restaurants (a favorite investment for small entrepreneurs), supermarkets, private clinics, legal firms, funeral parlors, and private schools. In 1976, the population of Spanish origin in Dade County (Miami) was estimated at 488,500 or 33% of the total. About 82% of this population is Cuban. Over half of the population in the municipalities of Miami and Hialeah is Cuban (Clark 1977). Numerical concentration and diversity of economic activities allow many immigrants to lead lives restricted almost completely to the enclave. This is especially true among those employed in Cuban-owned firms.

More important, newly arrived émigrés in Miami have an option of economic incorporation not available to other immigrant minorities. It remains to be seen, however, whether their participation in the enclave economy possesses empirically distinct characteristics or whether competitive immigrant-owned enterprises merely reproduce those labor processes associated with the broader peripheral economy.

METHOD

Data Collection

Data for this study come from a sample of Cuban immigrants interviewed at the point of arrival in the United States during the fall of 1973 and spring of 1974. The sample was reinterviewed three years later during 1976–77. Unlike more established groups of émigrés, recent immigrants usually lack the capital to go into business by themselves and, hence, must join the labor market. They are employed by firms in the primary and secondary markets as well as by enclave enterprises. It is this characteristic which makes the sample suitable for testing the hypotheses above. In all, 590 new immigrants were interviewed during the original survey. All had arrived in the United States via Miami and had stayed in that city.

The first survey met with considerable initial obstacles. The two daily flights or "airlifts" between Cuba and Miami had been suspended just before the beginning of data collection, thus closing the only major source of new immigrants. While Cubans continued to leave via Spain, few could come to the United States since they required a permanent resident's visa. In October 1973, however, Secretary of State Kissinger signed an executive resolution authorizing Cuban exiles in Spain to come to the United States as parolees. Flights were organized to transport those wishing to come. These "family reunion" flights had Miami as their major point of destination.

Labor Experiences of Cubans

Through the cooperation of agencies organizing these flights, newly arrived émigrés were contacted and interviewed at their place of residence. No available data on the population of Cuban émigrés exist against which to compare sample results. The U.S. Immigration Service data on Cuban immigrants pertain to those who adjusted their status to that of permanent residents. It takes a minimum of two years before new émigrés can effect this adjustment. Hence, official figures for "new" Cuban immigrants do not pertain to those who actually arrive in the country during a given year. Excluding refusals (6%), the sample is, however, coterminous with the universe of exiles during the survey period since most new arrivals were contacted.

The original sample was limited to males aged 18–60 and not dependent on others. This excludes women, children, and the aged. Restriction of the sample to males in the productive ages was dictated by the many complexities of an exploratory study and the impossibility of dealing adequately with all categories of immigrants. Priority was given to family heads and economically independent individuals who, in this immigrant group, are overwhelmingly adult males.

In 1976–77, three years after the first survey, a follow-up was conducted. Difficulties of tracing respondents are well known and have been the subject of a growing methodological literature (Eckland 1968; McAllister, Butler, and Goe 1973). Difficulties were compounded in this case by the unique characteristics of the sample. On the basis of a series of field techniques and the efforts of a number of people, a total of 427 cases were located and reinterviewed. This represents 72% of the original sample or 76% if respondents who died or left the United States are discounted. Practically all follow-up respondents had stayed in Miami.

A high attrition rate presents a serious challenge to any attempt to correlate U.S. experiences with the characteristics of the original sample as a whole. We assessed the extent of this bias by comparing means for the original and follow-up samples and correlating a "Missing" dummy variable with a series of first-wave variables. Following Astin and Panos (1969), we also entered major first-wave predictors of income into a stepwise procedure with "Missing" as the dependent variable.

None of these results indicate the presence of a significant bias. Table 1 presents correlation and regression coefficients linking first-wave predictors with "Missing." Not a single correlation differs significantly from zero. All β weights are small, and the joint amount of variance explained in the "Missing" variable is 2%. While it is still an inferential leap to assume the absence of bias among second-wave variables, these results provide some assurance about the validity of generalizing the findings to the original sample. We interpret results accordingly.

American Journal of Sociology

TABLE 1

CORRELATIONS AND REGRESSIONS OF FIRST-WAVE VARIABLES
WITH SECOND-WAVE ATTRITION VARIABLE,
CUBAN IMMIGRANTS (1973–77)

| | "MISSING" | |
INDEPENDENT VARIABLES	r	β
Father's occupation....................	−.081	−.093
Father's education....................	0	.066
Mother's education....................	−.023	−.019
Size-place of early community of residence	−.055	−.045
Age................................	.097	.084
Education...........................	−.024	−.029
Main occupation at arrival............	−.014	−.007
Knowledge of English at arrival........	.015	.055
Income aspirations at arrival...........	.037	.041
R^2................................	...	.022

NOTE.—For dependent variable: missing = 1, nonmissing = 0.

Data Analysis

The ensuing analysis is conducted in two parts. First, we assess the extent
to which a range of variables differentiates immigrants in the three labor
markets: primary, secondary, and enclave. The set of variables selected
for this analysis pertains to the work situation and the quality of life the
immigrant has experienced in the United States. According to the theoretical discussion above, we expect to find systematic differences in occupational prestige, economic stability, occupational and income satisfaction,
perception and experiences of discrimination, interaction with Anglo-Americans, and other related variables between immigrants employed in center
and peripheral firms. If hypothesis 2 holds, we would also expect enclave
workers to emerge as an empirically distinct group, but approaching some
of the characteristics of workers in the primary sector.

For this part of the analysis, we employ discriminant analysis (Van de
Geer 1971, pp. 243–72; Klecka 1975). Discriminant analysis allows the
specification of a nominal reference variable which is used to extract whatever significant discriminant functions exist in a set of independent variables. The maximum number of functions is one fewer than the number of
subpopulations. If fewer than the maximum possible number of discriminant functions are significant, then some of the subpopulations are not
empirically distinguishable from each other, at least in regard to the variables included in the analysis.

Second, we examine processes of occupational and income attainment
within each labor market. Independent variables for this analysis are

Labor Experiences of Cubans

those conventionally included in human capital and status-attainment models of income (Mincer 1970; Sewell and Hauser 1975), plus those representing skills specifically relevant to immigrant populations. If hypothesis 2 holds, immigrants in the secondary labor market will show the least return to prior attainments and human capital, while those in the primary and enclave labor markets will exhibit similar, and higher, levels of return for their past investments. Different processes of attainment will be reflected in significant variations in metric regression coefficients across the three labor markets.

The major problem for the two parts of the analysis is the establishment of criteria for assignment of immigrants to one or another labor market. Identification of those in the enclave is the most straightforward. All immigrants indicating employment in firms owned by Cubans were assigned to the enclave. A total of 143 cases, or 33% of the follow-up sample, were classified as enclave workers.

The division of the rest of the sample into primary and secondary sector is more problematic. Economists have used as criteria both the structural characteristics of occupations and industries and the demographic characteristics of their respective workers (Edwards 1975). Since part of our purpose is to test for differences in the characteristics of immigrant workers, we have used only the first type of criteria for our definition of primary and secondary sectors. Three criteria were employed: (1) The presence of an "internal labor market" or promotional ladder within the industry (Doeringer and Piore 1971); particularly, occupation/industry classifications wherein at least 25% of the workers had "considerable" opportunities for advancement were considered as candidates for the primary labor market (for more detailed information on this criterion see Freedman [1976], appendix C). (2) The median establishment size: occupation/industry classifications within which more than 10% of the workers were employed in firms with more than 1,000 workers were candidates for the primary labor market. (3) Occupation/industry classifications with average wages higher than $6,000 per year were candidates for the primary labor market.

Only those occupation/industry categories that were high on all three criteria were classified in the primary labor market. In the general U.S. population, this classification would result in 54% of the workers being assigned to the primary labor market (Freedman 1976, p. 21). In our immigrant sample, the corresponding figure is 36% of the follow-up sample.

These criteria represent necessary approximations to the primary/secondary division. Given the characteristics of the labor market in Miami, an area dominated by tourism and small industry (Fagen, Brody, and O'Leary 1968), the likely direction of bias is toward assignment to the primary sector of immigrants actually employed in competitive enterprises.

American Journal of Sociology

The effect of this error is conservative, since it would attenuate actual differences across labor markets, thus reducing the chances for statistical differences.

RESULTS

1. We first test the hypothesis that immigrants in the dual and enclave labor markets can be empirically distinguished on the basis of their experiences and socioeconomic situation in the United States. For this analysis, a set of the 12 most pertinent independent variables was selected. Four of these are objective indicators: present occupational prestige, measured in Duncan SEI scores; home ownership, an indirect measure of economic stability; number of relatives living in the United States; and objective information about U.S. society. The fourth is a composite index formed by the unit-weighted sum of six items measuring knowledge of political and economic facts. Factor analysis indicated a clear unidimensional structure and a high level of internal consistency.[3]

The rest of the variables are subjective indicators measuring such attitudes as income satisfaction, desire to change occupations, desire to return to Cuba, and willingness to come to the United States if the experience had to be repeated. Three additional subjective variables are self-reports: opportunities for relating with Anglo-Americans, perceived discrimination against Cubans in the United States, and personal experiences of discrimination. In the subsequent analysis, all variables are coded in agreement with their labels. Variable means and standard deviations are presented in the Appendix.

Results of this analysis are presented in table 2. Included are standardized discriminant function coefficients, relative percentages for each eigenvalue, canonical correlations, and group centroids. Wilks's λ's have been transformed into χ^2s and probability levels are also presented. The analysis yields two significant discriminant functions. Canonical correlations in each case represent the association between the discriminant function and the $m - 1$ set of dummy variables representing the m different subgroups. Canonical coefficients for both are modest but not insignificant.

[3] The U.S. information index is constructed by the sum of correct responses to six factual questions: (1) name of the current vice-president of the United States, (2) name of the governor of the state, (3) knowledge of the meaning of social security, (4) knowledge of the effect of home mortgage interest on personal income tax, (5) knowledge of the annual interest rate charged by common credit cards (e.g., "Master Charge"), and (6) knowledge of the approximate interest rates charged by commercial banks on personal loans. These items were entered into a principal components factor analysis. All loadings exceed .45 and the first factor explains 65% of the common variance. Successive factors produce eigenvalues lower than 1.0. Internal consistency, as measured by Cronbach's α, is .691.

Labor Experiences of Cubans

TABLE 2

DISCRIMINANT ANALYSIS OF CHARACTERISTICS OF CUBAN
IMMIGRANTS IN THREE LABOR MARKETS

Variables	First Function	Second Function
Occupational prestige....................	.14	−.27
Home ownership........................	.22	−.13
Relatives in United States (N)...........	.31	.13
Information about U.S. society...........	.02	−.32
Income satisfaction.....................	−.07	−.57
Desire to change occupations............	−.40	−.12
Plans to move to another country........	.02	−.35
Would not come to United States if he had to do it over.........................	.10	.25
Would return to Cuba if things changed there...............................	.27	−.04
Opportunities for relating with Anglos....	−.70	−.02
Perceived discrimination against Cubans in United States.......................	.33	.07
Personal experiences of discrimination.....	.13	−.55
Eigenvalue-relative percentage...........	60.8	39.2
Canonical correlation...................	.38	.32
χ^2...................................	90.00	36.00
$P<$...................................	0	0
Group centroids:		
"Enclave"...........................	.49	−.02
Primary labor market.................	−.32	−.30
Secondary labor market...............	−.25	.52

The nature of the two discriminant functions can be gleaned from the standardized coefficients. Disregarding signs for the moment, the first and most important function is defined by opportunities for relating with Anglos, desire to change occupations, perceived discrimination against Cubans, and number of relatives living in the United States. The second discriminant function is defined by income satisfaction, personal experiences of discrimination, plans to move to another country, information about U.S. society, and occupational prestige.

The most important results, however, are the group centroids, for they bear directly on the hypotheses above. These are the average discriminant scores for each group on the two functions. The significant χ^2 for the first function is mostly due to distance in the reduced function space between the enclave group and the other two. In other words, immigrants in the primary and secondary markets are undistinguishable in this function, but both are empirically distinct from immigrants in the enclave. This result clearly supports hypothesis 2 and disconfirms the view of enclave workers as only one segment of the secondary sector.

Looking now at the direction of coefficients, enclave membership appears ʼssociated with more relatives living in the United States, lesser opportuni-

American Journal of Sociology

ties for relating with Anglo-Americans, and stronger inclinations to return to Cuba if political conditions were to change. These results appear predictable. Less predictable, perhaps, membership in the enclave economy is also linked with lesser interest in changing occupations and with higher perceptions of discrimination against Cubans in the United States.

The second discriminant function rearranges the groups differently. In this case, the significant difference in the reduced function space is that between the enclave and primary sector, on the one hand, and the secondary sector, on the other. The difference between the first two groups is insignificant. Thus, in this second dimension, which is closely defined by variables reflecting occupational and economic conditions, immigrants in the enclave are nearer those in the primary sector. This result again supports hypothesis 2. Predictably, membership in the secondary labor market is associated with lesser income satisfaction, lesser occupational prestige, lesser information about U.S. society, and less willingness to come to the United States if the decision had to be taken again. Surprisingly, however, secondary sector membership is also related to lesser reported experiences of discrimination in the United States.[4]

Taken as a whole, these findings challenge the view that workers confined to an immigrant enclave share in the disadvantages of those in the secondary labor market and are undistinguishable from the latter. The variables available in these data at least suggest that the experiences and economic situation of immigrants can separate those in the enclave economy from those in the "open" labor market along a major axis and bring together enclave and primary workers, in opposition to those in the secondary labor market, along a second.[5]

2. Having established systematic differences in terms of current experiences and situations among the three labor markets, we must examine whether the economic effects of background variables, in particular, past investments in human capital, also differ across them. In this part of the analysis, we compare the effects of predictors conventionally included in

---

[4] A possible explanation is that the low positions occupied by secondary sector workers shield them from confronting barriers in the dominant society which are experienced by immigrants in higher-status occupations, especially those in the center economy.

[5] Another way to display these results is with regression analysis, which has the advantage of being more readily understood. Unfortunately, regression analysis is not suitable for our purposes at this stage. It affords no easy way to assess the empirical distinctiveness among three categories of a nominal variable with reference to a list of dependent variables. However, in order to get a rough assessment of the comparability of our findings with regression results, we turned our hypotheses around and estimated the multiple correlations between the list of variables as independent variables and the three labor markets as three dummy dependent variables. The multiple correlations range from .28 to .37 and are roughly similar to the canonical correlations we report for the discriminant analysis.

Labor Experiences of Cubans

human capital and status-attainment models on three dependent variables in each labor market. These dependent variables are principal occupation in Cuba, present occupation in the United States, and present income. Independent variables include father's and mother's education, father's occupation, respondent's education in Cuba, education since arrival in the United States, and age. Occupational variables are coded in Duncan's SEI scores, education in Cuba is coded in years completed and in the United States in completed months, and income is the respondent's present monthly earnings in dollars.

In addition, we include as predictors two variables not generally found in human capital models but indicative of important skills for newly arrived immigrants. One is the index of information about U.S. society described above. The other is an objective test of knowledge of English. This is an index constructed by the sum of correct answers to eight items, each asking the respondent to translate a word or sentence from English into Spanish. As with the U.S. information index, the knowledge-of-English index was constructed after factor analysis had indicated a clear unidimensional structure and high reliability.[6]

All parental variables, education, principal occupation in Cuba, and age were measured during the first interview. All other variables, including items in the information and knowledge-of-English indices, were measured during the second. Income is regressed on independent variables in its natural form since skewness in the distribution does not justify a log transformation. Conclusions would not be altered by such transformation, but it would obscure the substantive interpretation of coefficients. Means and standard deviations of all the variables are presented in the Appendix.

Regressions of income and occupation on independent variables are presented in table 3. Figures in the table are metric coefficients; those which meet the standard criterion of exceeding twice their standard errors are enclosed in parentheses. If hypothesis 1 is correct, the pattern of regression results for immigrants in enclave firms should be similar to that of immigrants in the secondary sector. For both groups, effects of human capital and past attainments on occupation and income should be significantly weaker than among immigrants in the primary sector. If hypothesis 2 is correct, on the other hand, enclave and primary sector workers should be similar and register greater returns to their past attainment and skills than those in peripheral firms.

In addition to present occupation and income, we have included occu-

[6] The test is designed to measure English comprehension at elementary and junior high school levels and includes sentences like "There is a horse near the church" and words like "guilt" and "surplus." All item loadings exceed .65 in a principal components factor analysis. The first unrotated factor accounts for 70% of common variance, with no secondary factor having an eigenvalue of 1.0 or higher. Internal consistency (α) for this index is .94.

TABLE 3

HUMAN CAPITAL DETERMINANTS OF INCOME IN THREE LABOR MARKETS

DEPENDENT VARIABLES	INDEPENDENT VARIABLES										R^2
	Father's Occupation	Father's Education	Mother's Education	Education in Cuba	Education in United States	Knowledge of English	Information about U.S. Society	Age	Occupation in Cuba	Present Occupation	
Enclave											
Occupation in Cuba	−.017	.305	.405	(3.446)				(.550)			.394
Occupation in United States	−.216	−.677	1.600	(3.296)	.146	−.988	.742	.176	(.183)		.333
Present income	1.683	.256	−13.027	−3.212	−.059	−14.462	(51.667)	−2.414	.041	(3.746)	.208
Primary Labor Market											
Occupation in Cuba	.131	(1.474)	−1.571	(3.158)				.294			.359
Occupation in United States	.120	.132	−.129	(1.883)	−.154	(1.676)	−.094	.557	(.272)		.307
Income	1.178	2.070	−1.803	−2.671	−5.544	9.448	(47.417)	−3.803	1.909	(3.111)	.255
Secondary Labor Market											
Occupation in Cuba	.100	.483	−.791	(3.237)				.110			.334
Occupation in United States	−.115	−.543	1.792	.211	.256	−.796	−.712	−.440	(.338)		.210
Income	−.977	−3.530	19.575	−9.186	−1.296	.604	6.616	−5.357	1.628	.955	.143

NOTE.—Numbers are metric regression coefficients. Coefficients exceeding twice their SEs are enclosed in parentheses.

Labor Experiences of Cubans

pation in Cuba as a dependent variable to check the possibility that contemporary differences across labor markets are not a result of structural market characteristics in the United States but of individual traits. It is conceivable that systematic differences in the causal relationships among variables predated the arrival of immigrants in the United States and account for those found at present. This would run contrary to dual labor market theory, according to which such differences are due to structural characteristics of the firms where immigrants become employed.

Results in table 3 show a fundamental similarity in determinants of principal occupation in Cuba across the three labor markets. While modest reliable effects are associated with age in one subsample and father's education in another, the major determinant of occupation in all three groups is education. Each year of completed education yields a reliable gain of roughly three SEI prestige points in each subsample. These coefficients are so strong that they quadruple their respective standard errors in all three groups.

Although in Cuba education resulted in a clear occupational return for all immigrants, the same is not true in the United States. Education has sizable positive effects on present occupation for immigrants in the primary and enclave labor markets but not for those in the secondary sector. In terms of the overall pattern of results, past individual attainment and background variables explain roughly one-third of the variance of present occupation in the primary and enclave subsamples but only one-fifth in the secondary sample. The latter figure is due only to the inertial effect of principal occupation in Cuba on present occupation. These results lend clear support to relationships predicted by hypothesis 2.

Stronger evidence against the definition of enclave enterprises as an extension of the peripheral economy is provided by the regressions of income. Only two individual attainment variables—present occupation and the index of information about U.S. society—have significant effects on income. These effects, however, are quite strong *and* they are limited to the primary and enclave subsamples. Net of other variables, each additional point of occupational prestige represents a reliable gain of over $3.00 per month in both subsamples. More important, each unit change in the six-point information index yields a net gain of $47 per month in the primary sector and $52 in the enclave. Metric coefficients corresponding to information about the United States triple their respective standard errors in both subsamples. In contrast, not a single significant effect of past attainment or human capital indicators on income is found in the secondary labor market. While total explained income variance is modest in all cases, the figure for the secondary subsample is the lowest.

These results reinforce those in the first part of the analysis in showing the similarity of immigrant workers employed in center and enclave firms

American Journal of Sociology

and their common and systematic differences from those confined to the peripheral sector. Taken as a whole, these findings support dual labor market predictions concerning the different yield of human capital investments in different sectors of the economy but correct their routine assignment of immigrant workers to the secondary labor market. For Cuban immigrants at least, the payoff of education, occupational status, and objective information appears as great among those employed in enclave enterprises as for those working in the mainstream center economy.

CONCLUSION

The data analysis above has shown the impossibility of automatically merging enclave workers into the peripheral economy and the fact that they reproduce, in a number of ways, the characteristics of those in the primary labor market. Strictly speaking, these results cannot be generalized beyond the universe of Cuban émigrés from which they were drawn. Nonetheless, although the Cuban political exodus clearly possesses many unique characteristics, these results are in general agreement with past qualitative and historical analyses of other immigrant groups. The significance of our findings is that they provide, for the first time, quantitative evidence of the empirical distinctness of an enclave labor force and the limitation of dual labor market theories for understanding its character. Additional research is required, however, to test the possibility of generalizing these results to other immigrant minorities.

The literature available in this area seems to agree that the development of immigrant enclaves requires two conditions: first, the presence of immigrants with sufficient capital and initial entrepreneurial skills; second, the renewal of the enclave labor force through sustained immigration (Sung 1967; Bonacich, Light, and Wong 1977). Our hypothesis that the findings above can be replicated for other immigrant minorities is based on the fact that these conditions are not unique to the Cuban case, nor do they appear to require the unique circumstances of a political exodus. Other charted paths seem to exist through which other immigrant groups have fulfilled them, as the case of the Japanese and the more recent one of the Koreans indicate.

Future research in this area must consider not only the situation of individual workers but also the structural characteristics of immigrant enterprises. Such research would help elucidate a contradiction in the existing literature. On the one hand, the economic success of such groups as the Japanese, the Cuban, and the Korean has been noted repeatedly; on the other, the exploitation which immigrant workers suffer at the hand of immigrant entrepreneurs has been stressed.

Bonacich (1973, 1978), for example, analyzes with insight the functions

Labor Experiences of Cubans

that immigrant entrepreneurs play with respect to larger firms in the center economy. As "middleman minorities," they enact economic directives from above and channel upward profits extracted from the exploitation of their respective groups. Enclave entrepreneurs can help cheapen labor costs for larger firms by the exploitation of the more vulnerable immigrant labor force. This might take the form of either intermediate input production for larger enterprises or a modern "put-out" system in which finished consumer goods, such as clothing, are produced in the enclave under contract for larger manufacturers.

Though speculative at this point, we hypothesize that the contradiction between the image of success and the image of exploitation of immigrant enclaves is more apparent than real. The line of reasoning pursued in the foregoing analysis suggests that the low-wage labor of immigrant workers is what permits survival and expansion of enclave enterprises which, in turn, open new opportunities for economic advancement.

Immigrant entrepreneurs make use of language and cultural barriers and of ethnic affinities to gain privileged access to markets and sources of labor. These conditions might give them an edge over similar peripheral firms in the open economy. The necessary counterpart to these ethnic ties of solidarity is the principle of ethnic preference in hiring and of support of other immigrants in their economic ventures.

The economic expansion of an immigrant enclave, combined with the reciprocal obligations attached to a common ethnicity, creates new mobility opportunities for immigrant workers and permits utilization of their past investments in human capital. Not incidentally, such opportunities may help explain why many immigrants choose to stay in or return to the enclave, forgoing higher short-term gains in the open economy.

Additional research is required to test this interpretation and examine possible differences across immigrant groups. At this point, we note only that this interpretation is in line with the results above insofar as they indicate that enclave workers are not better off initially, but that they are subsequently rewarded for skills and past investments in human capital.

Findings presented in this paper reintroduce a topic not adequately accounted for by theories of immigrant assimilation or internal colonialism, or by recent writings on the dual economy and dual labor markets. While often described in journalistic and qualitative terms, the phenomenon of immigrant enclaves and its theoretical implications have not received sufficient attention in the sociological literature. The results presented above raise perhaps more questions than they answer. Still, the remarkable geographic concentration of this sample and the differences detected for immigrants employed in center, peripheral, and enclave enterprises suggest the significance of the phenomenon and the need for additional research on the topic.

American Journal of Sociology

APPENDIX

VARIABLE MEANS AND STANDARD DEVIATIONS

Variable	Mean	SD
Father's occupation (SEI scores)	28.51	20.38
Father's education (years)	6.10	3.21
Mother's education (years)	5.59	2.45
Education in Cuba (years)	8.57	3.67
Education in United States (months)	2.99	5.89
Knowledge of English (correct answers)	2.69	2.74
Information about U.S. society (correct answers)	3.26	1.76
Age (years)	42.20	7.64
Occupation in Cuba (SEI scores)	39.76	24.46
Present occupation (SEI scores)	30.58	21.48
Present income (dollars per month)	647.05	293.71
Home ownership (yes = 1, no = 0)	.14	.35
Relatives in United States (N)	4.39	5.26
Income satisfaction (low = 1 to high = 3)	2.09	.96
Plans to move to another country (yes = 1, no = 0)	.05	.22
Would not come to the United States if he had to do it over (yes = 1, no = 0)	.04	.20
Would return to Cuba if things changed (yes = 1, no = 0)	.72	.45
Opportunities for relating with Anglos (very few = 1 to many = 4)	1.40	1.02
Perceived discrimination against Cubans (yes = 1, no = 0)	.30	.46
Personal experiences of discrimination (never = 0 to frequently = 3)	.76	.96

REFERENCES

Alba-Hernandez, Francisco. 1978. "Mexico's International Migration as a Manifestation of Its Development Pattern." *International Migration Review* 12 (Winter): 502–13.
Astin, A., and R. J. Panos. 1969. "The Educational and Vocational Development of College Students." Washington, D.C.: American Council on Education.
Averitt, Robert T. 1968. *The Dual Economy: The Dynamics of American Industry Structure.* New York: Norton.
Bach, Robert L. 1978. "Mexican Immigration and the American State." *International Migration Review* 12 (Winter): 536–58.
Baron, Harold M., and Bennett Hymer. 1968. "The Negro Worker in the Chicago Labor Movement." Pp. 232–85 in *The Negro and the American Labor Movement,* edited by J. Jacobson. Garden City, N.Y.: Doubleday.
Barrera, Mario. 1977. "Class Segmentation and Internal Colonialism: A Theory of Racial Inequality Based on the Chicano Experience." Mimeographed. San Diego: University of California, San Diego.
Blauner, Robert. 1972. *Racial Oppression in America.* New York: Harper & Row.
Bonacich, Edna. 1972. "A Theory of Ethnic Antagonism: The Split Labor Market." *American Sociological Review* 37:547–49.
———. 1973. "A Theory of Middleman Minorities." *American Sociological Review* 38 (October): 583–94.
———. 1978. "U.S. Capitalism and Korean Immigrant Small Business." Mimeographed. Riverside: University of California, Riverside.
Bonacich, Edna, Ivan H. Light, and Charles Choy Wong. 1977. "Koreans in Business." *Society* 14 (September/October): 54–59.
Boyd, Monica. 1971. "Oriental Immigration: The Experience of the Chinese, Japanese, and Filipino Population in the U.S." *International Migration Review* 5 (Spring): 48–61.

Labor Experiences of Cubans

Burawoy, Michael. 1976. "The Functions and Reproduction of Migrant Labor: Comparative Material from Southern Africa and the United States." *American Journal of Sociology* 81 (March): 1050–87.

Bustamante, Jorge A. 1975. "Espaldas mojadas: Materia prima para la expansión del capital norteamericano." *Cuadernos del Centro de Estudios Sociologicos*, no. 9 (Mexico, D.F.).

Carmichael, Stokely, and Charles V. Hamilton. 1967. *Black Power: The Politics of Liberation in America.* New York: Vintage.

Castles, S., and G. Kosack. 1973. *Immigrant Workers and Class Structure in Western Europe.* London: Oxford University Press.

Chiswick, Barry R. 1978. "The Effect of Americanization on the Earnings of Foreign-born Men." *Journal of Political Economy* 86:897–921.

Clark, Juan M. 1973. "Los Cubanos de Miami: Cuántos son y de dónde provienen." *Ideal* 2 (January): 17–19.

———. 1977. "The Cuban Exodus: Why?" Mimeographed. Miami: Cuban Exile Union.

Cornelius, Wayne A. 1977. "Undocumented Immigration: A Critique of the Carter Administration's Policy Proposals." *Migration Today* 5 (October): 5–8, 16–20.

Daniels, Roger. 1971. *Concentration Camps USA: Japanese-Americans and World War II.* New York: Holt, Rinehart & Winston.

Doeringer, Peter B., Penny Geldman, David M. Gordon, Michael J. Piore, and Michael Reich. 1969. "Urban Manpower Programs and Low-Income Labor Markets: A Critical Assessment." Mimeographed. Washington, D.C.: Manpower Administration, Department of Labor.

Doeringer, Peter B., and Michael J. Piore. 1971. *Internal Labor Markets and Manpower Analysis.* Lexington, Mass.: Heath.

Duncan, Otis Dudley. 1969. "Inheritance of Poverty or Inheritance of Race?" Pp. 85–110 in *On Understanding Poverty: Perspectives from the Social Sciences*, edited by Daniel P. Moynihan. New York: Basic.

Eckland, Bruce K. 1968. "Retrieving Mobile Cases in Longitudinal Surveys." *Public Opinion Quarterly* 32:51–64.

Edwards, Richard C. 1975. "The Social Relations of Production in the Firm and Labor Market Structure." Pp. 3–26 in *Labor Market Segmentation*, edited by R. C. Edwards, M. Reich, and D. M. Gordon. Lexington, Mass.: Heath.

Eisenstadt, S. N. 1970. "The Process of Absorbing New Immigrants in Israel." Pp. 341–67 in *Integration and Development in Israel*, edited by S. N. Eisenstadt. Jerusalem: Israel University Press.

Fagen, Richard R., Richard A. Brody, and Thomas O'Leary. 1968. *Cubans in Exile.* Stanford, Calif.: Stanford University Press.

Ferman, Louis A. 1968. "The Irregular Economy: Informal Work Patterns in the Ghetto." Mimeographed. Ann Arbor: University of Michigan.

Freedman, Marcia. 1976. *Labor Markets: Segments and Shelters.* New York: Universe.

Galarza, Ernesto. 1977. *Farm Workers and Agri-Business in California, 1947–1960.* Notre Dame, Ind.: University of Notre Dame Press.

Galbraith, John Kenneth. 1971. *The New Industrial State.* New York: Mentor.

González Casanova, Pablo. 1965. *Le democracia en México.* Mexico, D.F.: Era.

Gordon, David M. 1971. *Class, Productivity and the Ghetto.* Ph.D. dissertation, Harvard University.

———. 1972. *Theories of Poverty and Underemployment: Orthodox, Radical, and Dual Labor Market Perspectives.* Lexington, Mass.: Lexington.

Gordon, Milton M. 1961. "Assimilation in America: Theory and Reality." *Daedalus* 90, no. 2 (Spring): 263–85.

———. 1964. *Assimilation in American Life: The Role of Race, Religion, and National Origins.* New York: Oxford University Press.

Hagen, Everett E. 1962. *On the Theory of Social Change: How Economic Growth Begins.* Homewood, Ill.: Dorsey.

American Journal of Sociology

Handlin, Oscar. 1951. *The Uprooted: The Epic Story of the Great Migrations That Made the American People.* Boston: Little, Brown.

Jencks, Christopher. 1972. *Inequality: A Reassessment of the Effects of Family and Schooling in America.* New York: Harper & Row.

Keely, Charles B. 1979. *U.S. Immigration: A Policy Analysis.* New York: Population Council.

Klecka, William R. 1975. "Discriminant Analysis." Pp. 515–27 in *Statistical Package for the Social Sciences,* edited by N. H. Nie, C. H. Hull, J. G. Jenckins, K. Steinbrenner, and D. H. Bent. 2d ed. New York: McGraw-Hill.

Kurokawa, Minako, ed. 1970. *Minority Responses.* New York: Random House.

Light, Ivan H. 1972. *Ethnic Enterprise in America: Business and Welfare among Chinese, Japanese, and Blacks.* Berkeley: University of California Press.

McAllister, Ronald J., Edgar W. Butler, and Steven J. Goe. 1973. "Evolution of a Strategy for the Retrieval of Cases in Longitudinal Research." *Social Science Research* 58:37–47.

Malcolm X. 1967. *Malcolm X on Afro-American History.* Introduction by George Breitman. New York: Merit.

Maldonado, Edwin. 1979. "Contract Labor and the Origins of Puerto Rican Communities in the United States." *International Migration Review* 13 (Spring): 103–21.

Mincer, Jacob. 1970. "The Distribution of Labor Incomes: A Survey with Special Reference to the Human Capital Approach." *Journal of Economic Literature* 8:1–26.

North, David S. 1978. "Seven Years Later: The Experiences of the 1970 Cohort of Immigrants in the U.S. Labor Market." Mimeographed. Report to the Employment and Training Administration. Washington, D.C.: Department of Labor.

O'Connor, James. 1973. *The Fiscal Crisis of the State.* New York: St. Martin's.

Petersen, William. 1971. *Japanese Americans: Oppression and Success.* New York: Random House.

Piore, Michael J. 1973. "The Role of Immigration in Industrial Growth: A Case Study of the Origins and Character of Puerto Rican Migration to Boston." Mimeographed. Cambridge, Mass.: Massachusetts Institute of Technology.

———. 1975. "Notes for a Theory of Labor Market Stratification." Pp. 125–50 in *Labor Market Segmentation,* edited by R. C. Edwards, M. Reich, and D. M. Gordon. Lexington, Mass.: Heath.

Portes, Alejandro. 1978. "Illegal Immigration and the International System." Pp. 179–88 in *Undocumented Workers: Implications for U.S. Policy in the Western Hemisphere: Hearings before the Sub-Committee on Inter-American Affairs,* U.S. Congress, House, Committee on International Relations. Washington, D.C.: Government Printing Office.

Portes, Alejandro, and Kenneth L. Wilson. 1976. "Black-White Differences in Education Attainment." *American Sociological Review* 41 (June): 414–31.

Rosenblum, Gerald. 1973. *Immigrant Workers: Their Impact on American Labor Radicalism.* New York: Basic.

Sassen-Koob, Saskia. 1978. "The International Circulation of Resources and Development: The Case of Migrant Labour." *Development and Change* 9:509–45.

Sewell, William H., and Robert M. Hauser. 1975. *Education, Occupation, and Earnings: Achievement in the Early Career.* New York: Academic Press.

Stevens, Rosemary, Louis W. Goodman, and Stephen S. Mick. 1978. *The Alien Doctors: Foreign Medical Graduates in American Hospitals.* New York: Wiley.

Sung, Betty Lee. 1967. *Mountain of Gold: The Story of the Chinese in America.* New York: Macmillan.

Thomas, John F., and Earl E. Huyck. 1967. "Resettlement of Cuban Refugees in the United States." Paper presented at the annual meeting of the American Sociological Association, San Francisco.

Time. 1978. "Hispanic Americans: Soon the Biggest Minority." Special Report (October 16), pp. 48–61.

Labor Experiences of Cubans

U.S. Bureau of the Census. 1978. *Statistical Abstract of the United States*. Washington, D.C.: Government Printing Office.

U.S. Immigration and Naturalization Service. 1977. *Cubans Arrived in the United States by Class of Admission, January 1, 1959–September 30, 1976*. Special Reports. Washington, D.C.: INS Statistics Branch.

———. 1978. *Annual Report 1977*. Washington, D.C.: Government Printing Office.

Van de Geer, John P. 1971. *Introduction to Multivariate Analysis for the Social Sciences*. San Francisco: W. H. Freeman.

Wachtel, Howard M. 1972. "Capitalism and Poverty in America: Paradox or Contradiction?" *American Economic Review* 62:187–94.

Warner, W. Lloyd, and Leo Srole. 1945. *The Social Systems of American Ethnic Groups*. New Haven, Conn.: Yale University Press.

Wittke, Carl. 1952. *Refugees of Revolution: The German Forty-eighters in America*. Philadelphia: University of Pennsylvania Press.

[8]

UNWELCOME IMMIGRANTS: THE LABOR MARKET EXPERIENCES OF 1980 (MARIEL) CUBAN AND HAITIAN REFUGEES IN SOUTH FLORIDA*

ALEJANDRO PORTES
Johns Hopkins University

ALEX STEPICK
Florida International University

This article examines the situation of two recently arrived and disadvantaged immigrant groups in the context of two competing theoretical traditions: classical assimilation and recent labor market segmentation theories. Predictions of both concerning U.S. labor market entry of foreign minorities and determinants of subsequent mobility are tested on the basis of representative surveys. Most are disconfirmed. The analysis supports the hypothesis of heterogeneous modes of incorporation into the labor market, including substantial numbers of refugees who remain outside of it. Sizable proportions have only managed to find fringe employment in an emerging informal economy in South Florida. Among Cubans, employment in the ethnic enclave is associated with positive returns comparable to those of entry into the "primary" labor market. Haitians lack an enclave option and thus cluster into secondary and informal employment, although most remain without work. Determinants of these various situations are examined on the basis of multivariate logistic regressions. Implications of results for immigration theory and policy are discussed.

This paper examines the extent of differentiation in labor market situations of two recent immigrant groups: 1980 Cuban refugees, the so-called Mariel exodus, and Haitian refugees arriving at the same time. Both groups represent recent trends in U.S.-bound immigration and can be fruitfully compared with the experiences of earlier groups as well as with general theories of the role of immigrants in the American labor market. Until recently, the common image of recent immigrants among social scientists as well as among the public at large was one of a fairly homogenous group. Contributing to that image was an abundant literature on the history and adaptation experiences of turn-of-the-century immigrants. Although scholarly and journalistic accounts of the Italians, the Poles, the Irish, the Greeks, and others obviously differed in detail, they sounded a similar underlying theme.

Turn-of-the-century immigrants arriving in U.S. shores in search of work were described as finding it in menial, low-paid occupations in industry, canal and railroad building, and the like. They formed tightly knit communities for

* Direct all correspondence to: Alejandro Portes, Department of Sociology, Johns Hopkins University, Baltimore, MD 21218.

The data on which this paper is based were collected with the support of grant #SES-8215567 from the National Science Foundation. The analysis was conducted while the senior author was a visiting research fellow at the University of California-San Diego. We thank Karl Alexander and anonymous referees for their comments on an earlier version.

self-protection and support and then gradually started moving into the mainstream of society, a painful process completed only after several generations (Handlin, 1951; Warner and Srole, 1945; Child, 1943). The basic contours of these histories were so similar as to enable later writers to portray immigrant adaptation as a uniform charted path in which newcomers took their place at the end of the labor market queue and proceeded to improve slowly, but predictably, their employment and social situations (Sowell, 1981).

Recent structuralist theories of immigration and ethnicity also support the notion of a uniform entry point and labor market position among recent arrivals. Differences between classic assimilationist and current structural theorists center on whether there is indeed "queuing" and thus eventual mobility of foreign minorities (Petersen, 1971; Lieberson, 1980; Sowell, 1981; Alba, 1985), or whether they remain confined to the bottom jobs or the lower tier of a segmented labor market (Bonacich and Cheng, 1984; Piore, 1979). Both positions agree, however, that at entry, immigrants tend to have three characteristics in common: first, they are channeled into menial low-paid jobs; second, they represent a pliable and frequently exploited labor pool; third, their chances for mobility are restricted and dependent on language acquisition and learning of the host culture.

The basic notion of a uniform entry point stands alongside a rapidly accumulating research literature which points exactly in the opposite direction. Several studies have documented the existence of "entrepreneurial" minorities and of economic-enclave construction among recent immigrant groups (Light, 1979, 1980; Kim, 1981; Wilson and Martin, 1982; Wilson and Portes, 1980). Although many of these immigrants may spell a tour of duty at the worst jobs, they often move quickly into self-employment through the support of preexisting ethnic networks. A second and perhaps more significant instance is provided by studies of professional and technical immigration. Although the literature on the "brain drain" is sparse, it documents the presence in the United States of thousands of immigrants whose entry-point positions were neither menial nor lowly paid and who attain even more desirable jobs in a relatively short period of time (Glasser and Habers, 1974; Stevens et al., 1978).[1]

A third example is provided by the increasing number of political refugees and asylees arriving in recent years. The status of refugee is not associated with a uniform mode of entry into the American labor market. Occupational entry points of political refugees may range from the conventional low-wage menial jobs depicted in the assimilation literature to self-employment or high professional occupations. More importantly, recent refugees have the option *not* to enter the labor market at all, remaining dependent instead on federal and state assistance. This option is made possible by provisions of the 1980 Refugee Act, which conferred distinct benefits to individuals admitted to the United States under this status.[2]

Immigration thus seems to be moving away from the uniform flow of unskilled menial labor posited by theorists of multiple and opposite persuasions. Instead, it appears to be turning into an increasingly diversified process with immigrants found at many levels of the occupational structure, including a significant number outside of it. The groups which are the subject of this study are, however, among those who because of a uniquely disadvantaged position may be expected to follow a uniform adaptation path—one starting at the very bottom of the labor market. Examining the extent to which there is internal differentiation within them provides a test of the alternative views of basic occupational homogeneity versus different modes of labor market entry. The background to immigration of each group and their subsequent precarious occupational situation are described in the next sections, following details of data collection.

SAMPLES

Data for this study come from samples of Cubans arriving in the United States from the port of Mariel in 1980 and of Haitians coming by boat about the same time. Surveys of both refugee groups living in South Florida in late

---

[1] A case in point is Indian immigration. Seventy-seven percent of the 206,000 first-generation Indians counted by the 1980 Census had been in the country less than 10 years. Despite their recency, median Indian household income in 1980 was $25,644, well

---

above the national figure and approximately $11,000 above the median for the entire foreign-born population. This position of privilege is closely associated with the fact that 66 percent of the Indian-born population had completed four or more years of college and that 43 percent were employed in professional specialty occupations in the United States (U.S. Bureau of the Census, 1984).

[2] Results of a survey conducted by the U.S. Office of Refugee Resettlement in 1982 indicated that 24.1 percent of Indochinese refugees were unemployed, twice the national figure, and that 47 percent of refugee households received cash assistance at the time, the figure increasing with household size and number of children (Bach et al., 1984).

1983 and 1984 were conducted on the basis of stratified multi-stage area samples. The sampling strata for the Cuban survey are political divisions within Dade County—the cities of Miami, Miami Beach, Hialeah, and unincorporated Dade County divisions. Strata in the Haitian survey are localities in three adjacent counties known to contain the majority of this group in the region—the cities of Miami and Ft. Lauderdale and the town of Belle Glade.

Within each stratum, areas of high concentration of the respective groups were delimited and blocks within them were designated as primary sampling units. For Cubans, delimited areas are census tracts where 50 percent or more of the population is of Cuban origin, except Miami Beach, where the universe includes the three census tracts with the highest Cuban concentration, none of which exceeds 50 percent. Recent Haitian refugees cluster even more than Cubans, and several prior studies had already defined their primary areas of concentration (BSRI, 1983; Stepick, 1984). In Miami, this area is known as Little Haiti and encompasses seven census tracts in the northeast quadrant of the city; in Ft. Lauderdale, the Haitian neighborhood comprises 28 adjacent city blocks; in Belle Glade, it clusters in the town's two poorest tracts.

Within each delimited area, blocks were assigned unique four-digit identifiers and selected through a simple random-sample procedure. Within blocks, the probability of selection was fixed at one, making all eligible households in selected blocks fall into the sample. The universes were defined as households containing at least one eligible respondent, that is, a Cuban or Haitian immigrant between the ages of 18 and 60 who arrived in the United States in 1980 or after.[3] Within each selected unit, an eligible individual was interviewed and was asked to furnish information about him- or herself and about other household members.

Samples are not self-weighting since a fixed number of interviews were assigned a priori to each stratum to insure sufficient representation. Original target samples were 500 from each universe; weighted samples, adjusting for unequal probabilities of selection, are 499 Haitians and 520 Cubans. Parameter estimates presented below are computed on the basis of these weighted samples. Data from these samples are statistically representative of the universe of households containing at least one adult refugee in the areas of concentration of the respective populations in South Florida.

Excluded are the estimated one-fourth of Mariel refugees who were resettled and remain outside of the Miami SMSA (Clark et al., 1981; Boswell and Curtis, 1984: Ch. 3) and an unknown number of post–1980 Haitian refugees who settled elsewhere. There is agreement, however, among researchers familiar with this group that Little Haiti is the principal point of concentration of recent Haitian refugees and that Belle Glade and Ft. Lauderdale are the main secondary concentrations in the immediate vicinity of the Miami SMSA (Stepick, 1985; BSRI, 1983).

BACKGROUND TO IMMIGRATION

Together the Cuban and Haitian inflows of 1980 added approximately 140,000 people to immigration to the United States. Although this number probably represents no more than 10 percent of the combined total of legal and undocumented immigrants during that year (U.S. Immigration and Naturalization Service, 1984), it had an enormous impact because of the manner of its arrival and the publicity surrounding it. The image of thousands of ragged refugees arriving in overloaded boats from Mariel and of desperately poor Haitians coming aboard barely seaworthy craft had a profound effect on the American public mind. A reluctant U.S. government refused to grant the new arrivals political asylum, admitting them only on a temporary basis as "entrants, status pending."

The histories and general characteristics of each immigration have been described in detail elsewhere (Bach, 1984; Pedraza-Bailey, 1985; Miller, 1984). For our purposes, what is important are those aspects which made their reception and settlement so difficult and which lead to the expectation of a common and disadvantaged employment situation. Between the months of April and October of 1980, 124,779 Cubans arrived in the United States, more than in the preceding eight years. During May 1980 alone, more refugees arrived than in 1962, the previous record year of Cuban immigration. This unexpected exodus had its origin in the decision of the Cuban government to permit the departure of disaffected and other "undesirable" elements from the Island. Calling the departees "scum," the Cuban government proceeded to insure that the label would stick by deliberately placing aboard the boats hundreds of individuals with criminal records, mental patients, and social deviants (Clark et al., 1981). Haitian emigration was not a government-sponsored initiative, but one promoted by private entrepreneurs offering sea transport for profit. Haitian boat arrivals had been detected by the Immigration and Natu-

---

[3] All Cuban respondents arrived during the Mariel exodus of 1980; Haitian respondents arrived in 1980, 1981 or 1982, the majority during the first year.

496

ralization Service (INS) previously, but they did not exceed an average of 3000 per year. In 1980, however, the number swelled to over 15,000. Although still a manageable flow, it took place closely after the Mariel boatlift, the two becoming one in the public mind.

Coming in the midst of an economic recession, Mariel Cubans and Haitian boatpeople found employment opportunities highly restricted, and confronted widespread hostility among domestic minorities with whom they were to compete in the labor market. The very negative images diffused by the press and the media aggravated their situation. In particular, wide publicity was given to the undesirables arriving aboard the Mariel flotilla, despite the fact that subsequent research showed that hardened criminals, mental patients, and other deviants did not exceed 5 percent of this population (Bach et al., 1981; Boswell and Curtis, 1984). Although never mentioned explicitly, the fact that Haitian arrivals were uniformly black and that the proportion of blacks among Mariel entrants was several times greater than among earlier Cuban cohorts also seemed to contribute significantly to a less-than-favorable reception (Bach et al., 1981; Portes et al., 1981).

Policies of the federal government toward the two new immigrant groups concentrated on stopping the inflows and easing the situation in the most heavily impacted communities. The Carter administration pressured the Cuban government to close Mariel and finally succeeded in October 1980. Simultaneously, a maritime interdiction program was initiated to turn back Haitian refugees at sea. At about the same time, the Federal Emergency Management Agency removed processing of new Cuban entrants from Miami and reorganized it in military camps in the North. Harsh conditions in the camps gave rise to a series of riots during the Spring of 1981. In Miami, INS kept a substantial number of Haitians in detention and concentrated on demonstrating the economic motives of their migration and, hence, their ineligibility for political asylum. Several hundred Haitians were repatriated until litigation before the courts slowed the process (Stepick, 1982).

The federal government's refusal to grant either group political asylum deprived them of benefits under the new 1980 Refugee Act. Although subsequent congressional action alleviated this situation, emergency aid was limited and most of it lapsed by 1983. Lacking either jobs or government assistance, many refugees were compelled to rely on private charity or to invent jobs in a burgeoning "informal" economy in Miami.

The events of 1980 represented not only a remarkable episode in American immigration history, but they also left behind thousands of newcomers whose social and economic adaptation was most problematic. These were unwelcome immigrants, wanted apparently by no one and often lacking even families to receive them. Unlike Indochinese refugees arriving at the same time and whose resettlement was sponsored and guided from the start by the federal government, 1980 entrants had little access to any of the set paths of early adaptation. This situation did not augur well for their future. The next sections report on the actual events that followed these 1980 migrations and on the situation of both refugee groups after four years in the United States.

PRELIMINARY FINDINGS

The beginning of the Mariel exodus dovetailed with the end of field work for the 1980 Census. As a result, figures reported by the census on the foreign-born Cuban and Haitian population exclude the more recent arrivals. Although this has been a cause of concern for state and local agencies, it has the fortuitous consequence of permitting a clear-cut comparison between the pre-1980 refugee communities and those arriving in 1980.

Table 1 presents comparisons of our two refugee samples with state and national figures over the range of variables available for the foreign-born in the census. Although national data offer an informative point of reference, the more pertinent comparison is with Florida because of the concentration of both groups in that state. The pattern of results in Table 1 is not identical for both refugee groups, but there are significant similarities.[4] They both have

---

[4] Means and standard deviations are computed on the basis of weighted samples adjusted for unequal probabilities of selection within strata. A stratified cluster sample design renders the usual formula for the variance of the mean inappropriate since stratification reduces between-group variance among strata and clustering reduces the number of independent sampling units. The latter effect is the more serious since it can lead to an underestimation of the variance computed on the assumption of simple random sampling. In this case, the appropriate formula for the variance of the mean within each stratum is:

$$\text{Est } \sigma_{\bar{x}_c} = (1\text{-}f) \, \frac{1}{m} \left[\frac{1}{m\text{-}1} \, \sum^m (\frac{Ni}{N})^2 \, (X_1 - \bar{X}_c)^2 \right]$$

Where: (1-f) is the correction for a finite population;
    m is the number of clusters;

    $(\frac{Ni}{N})^2$ is the square of the relative weight of N each unequal cluster;

    $(X_1 - \bar{X}_c)^2$ is the covariation within each cluster, c. (Kish, 1967: Ch. 6).

Table 1. Cuban and Haitian Immigrants in the United States and Florida, 1980

Variables	Cubans			Haitians		
	U.S.[a]	Florida[a]	1980[b] Entrants	U.S.[a]	Florida[a]	1980[b] Entrants
Median Age	40.3	41.2	37.0*	28.9	29.4	29.0
Average Persons per Household	3.04	3.07	3.07	3.49	3.51	3.09*
Percent High School Graduates (Persons 25 years of age or over)	40.2	38.6	24.8*	55.9	27.2	4.9*
Percent with Four Years of College or More (Persons 25 years of age or over)	10.3	10.0	7.6	9.5	4.5	0.0*
Percent who Report Speaking English Well or Very Well (Persons 18 years of age or over)	36.1	32.1	10.6*	66.5	51.2	17.8*
Percent Black	2.3	1.4	11.8*	96.6	95.4	90.2*
Mean Number of Workers per Family	1.7	1.8	1.7	1.7	1.5	2.1
Percent Unemployed (Persons 16 years of age or over)	8.4	7.9	26.8*	13.3	13.4	58.5*
Percent Unemployed, Males (16 years of age or over)	6.8	6.3	25.8*	12.3	11.7	38.8*
Mean Weeks of Unemployment in the Preceding Year (Persons 16 years of age or over)	14.3	13.8	21.7*	18.0	16.9	25.0*
Percent Managers and Professional Specialty Occupations (Civilian Labor Force)	10.7	11.1	10.0	7.5	3.9	1.1*
Median Household Income (1979 dollars)	15,161	11,786	9,433*	13,243	8,223	5,521*
Percent of Families below Poverty Level[c]	20.5	22.0	26.0	25.6	39.2	61.0*

[a] Foreign born, arrived between 1970 and 1980.
[b] Significance tests compare entrant sample with Florida 1980 Census.
[c] Percent of households below the federal poverty level for a household of three, 1983.
* $p < .01$.
Sources: U.S. Bureau of the Census, *Detailed Population Characteristics, United States Summary,* Series PC80-1-D1-A, Washington, D.C.: U.S. Government Printing Office, March 1984. Table 255.
U.S. Bueau of the Census, *Detailed Population Characteristics, Florida,* Series PC80-DO11, Washington, D.C.: U.S. Government Printing Office, October 1983. Table 196.

much lower levels of education on the average and report much less knowledge of English than the respective pre–1980 resident populations. Although pre–1980 Haitians in Florida had much lower proportions of high school and college graduates than the same group

---

It is not possible with the data at hand to estimate variances in this manner because individual cases were coded into unique strata but not clusters (city blocks). The effect of clustering, however, is directly proportional to the average size of the clusters. In our case, average cluster sizes (N/m) are small; 2.7 in the Cuban sample and 2.84 in the Haitian. To minimize the probability of a type II error, however, we assumed a positive intraclass correlation (rho) of 4. Estimated variances are computed as:

Est. $\sigma = [1 + rho\ (m\text{-}1)]\ \sigma sr$,

where σsr is the variance computed on the assumption of simple random sampling. Under this conservative assumption, estimated variances are thus: 1.68 σsr for the Cuban sample and 1.74 σsr for the Haitian. Tests of significance reported in Table 1 are based on these figures.

---

nation-wide, the proportion among post–1980 refugees is still lower. In 1984, the rate of unemployment among our respondents was three to four times greater than comparable state figures in 1980, whether total or male unemployment rates are considered. Average weeks of unemployment in the preceding year for the refugees came close to doubling the 1980 figures. Not surprisingly, median household incomes in constant dollars are significantly lower among 1980–81 refugees than among earlier arrivals.

On the average, Cubans are much older than Haitians, both before and after 1980, but within the Cuban population the 1980 refugees are much younger. In agreement with prior studies (Bach et al., 1981; Clark et al., 1981), the proportion of blacks and mulattoes among Cuban respondents is approximately eight times the figure reported for the pre–1980 Cuban population, although it still hovers at about one-tenth of the sample. Without significant exception, these results confirm the characterization

Table 2. Labor Market Characteristics of Cuban and Haitian Entrants, 1983

	Cubans		Haitians	
	Self (N = 520) %	Spouse (N = 304) %	Self (N = 499) %	Spouse (N = 250) %
Total Samples [a]				
Out of the Job Market	13.1	14.9	4.5	3.0
Unemployed, Looking for Work	26.8	19.0	58.5	32.9
Employed Subsamples				
Underemployed [b]	7.8	12.0	17.5	13.2
Self-employed	15.2	12.9	0.5	1.3
Occupation, Employed Subsamples				
Managers, Professional Specialty, Technicians	12.9	10.0	1.1	0.0
White Collar and Sales	16.7	18.5	5.5	3.3
Craftsmen and Repair Workers	28.3	28.3	9.8	17.2
Operatives and Laborers, except Farm	22.6	25.9	42.2	43.3
Farm Laborers	4.1	4.8	22.7	20.0
Servants and Unskilled Service Workers	15.4	12.4	18.7	16.2

[a] Percentages do not add to 100 because categories are not mutually exclusive.
[b] Thirty hours per week of work or less.

of recent Cuban and Haitian refugees as heavily disadvantaged groups even relative to their respective immigrant communities.

To begin the analysis of possible differences within this apparently hopeless situation, we examined the distribution of respondents and their spouses over a series of employment characteristics. Results are presented in Table 2. The main finding here is that the modal form of incorporation of these groups to the American labor market is no incorporation at all. Thirty-nine percent of Cuban respondents and fully 63 percent of Haitians are without work; among their spouses, the figures are somewhat lower but still sizable. These data also show that their situation is, for the most part, involuntary: in each group, those looking for work exceed those who have voluntarily withdrawn from the labor market. This pattern is considerably more marked among Haitians than Cubans.

The next row of Table 2 adds to this picture the proportion of the underemployed, defined as those working less than thirty hours per week.[5] With the addition of this category, the proportion of those whose employment situation is problematic (unemployed and underemployed) comes to about one-third of economically active Cubans, one-half of Haitian spouses, and two-thirds of Haitian respondents.

The bottom rows of Table 2 begin to introduce some variation in this dismal landscape.

[5] Although no data are available on this point, we assume that to a large extent underemployment is also involuntary. This follows from the low reported proportions of voluntary unemployment, especially among Haitians, and the low income levels in both samples.

Three years after arrival, about 15 percent of employed Cuban respondents and their spouses had started their own businesses. Although the meaning of "self-employment" among these groups is somewhat problematic, as will be seen below, the figures at least suggest the start of some independent entrepreneurship. In this respect, as well as in the occupational distributions of the employed, the two refugee groups differ sharply. There are hardly any self-employed among the Haitians, and the occupations of those who have found jobs concentrate in the bottom categories: servants and unskilled service laborers, farm workers, and semi-skilled operatives. In contrast, there are sizable proportions of Cuban refugees in the top three occupational categories, particularly craftsmen and skilled workers. The 13 percent of Cuban respondents in professional and technical occupations is actually higher than among the pre-1980 Cuban-born population. A closer examination of this group reveals, however, that it concentrates in lower-level professional occupations, such as school teachers and draftsmen.

Although these results begin to show some occupational differentiation, they do not suffice to dispel the image of groups who, if different from the popular view of immigrants, are so only by being in a still more precarious situation. If patterned differences in labor market entrance exist within these groups, we must probe for them further. For this, it will be necessary to seek guidance from theories in this area.

LABOR MARKET SECTORS

A central debate in the field of stratification focuses on whether the labor market should be

UNWELCOME IMMIGRANTS

conceived as a single, unified entity or whether it should be seen as segmented into various sectors (Edwards, 1975; Tolbert et al., 1980; Hodson and Kaufman, 1982; Baron and Bielby, 1984). Although the debate continues and evidence accumulates on both sides of the issue, there is little doubt that the weight of empirical results leans in the direction of some form of market segmentation (Kalleberg et al., 1981; Hodson, 1984). Our purpose here is not to test this theory anew with immigrant samples, but rather to draw from it and from related sources, ideas relevant to our research problem.

Recent studies have attempted to break down the configurations characterizing discrete labor markets and examine the latter's continuous components and their consequences (Wallace and Kalleberg, 1981). Despite these efforts, the principal thrust of the segmentation perspective continues to be the assertion of a dual labor market, each sector separated from the other by a coherent set of characteristics. The descriptions of primary and secondary labor markets are quite familiar by now and require no repetition. As far as immigrant workers are concerned, the general expectation stemming from this theory is that those who manage to gain access to the primary sector will enjoy better working conditions and remunerations than those confined to jobs in the secondary sector. The latter should comprise, however, the vast majority of these groups (Piore, 1979; Edwards, 1979: Ch. 10).

An unsolved debate within this general perspective is whether labor markets should be conceptualized and measured at the level of entire industries (Tolbert et al., 1980) or individual firms (Hodson, 1984). For our purposes, however, it would make little sense to rely on an industry-wide classification for two reasons. First, the local labor market in South Florida is characterized by a predominance of relatively small firms, and there is likely to be considerable error in assigning local firms to sectors on the basis of national averages. Second, we have data on individual firms, provided directly by respondents and hence do not need to rely on approximations.

For reasons to be explained below, the primary and secondary sectors are defined as composed of firms outside the Miami ethnic economy, that is, companies whose owners or top executives are native whites, plus public-sector agenceis. Size of firms will be employed as the primary stratifying variable. Around 1980, the 32,000 companies with paid employees in Dade County (Miami SMSA) averaged 14 workers per firm (Jorge and Moncarz, 1982). Relative to this average, firms with over 100 employees can be considered quite large

and hence more likely to reproduce the characteristics associated with primary markets.

The primary–secondary division does not exhaust, however, the potential modes of labor market entry available to new immigrants. The same segmentation literature has branched out into distinctions of "tiers" within the primary sector (Piore, 1975) and a division between occupational and firm labor markets within the same upper segment (Althauser and Kalleberg, 1981). For immigrant workers, however, a more pertinent literature is that which identifies ethnic economies or "enclaves" as a distinct labor market sector. Enclaves are formed by clusters of immigrant-owned enterprises which tend to hire recent arrivals from the same nationality. Although similar in outward appearance to other small firms, they possess certain characteristics which open significant mobility opportunities for immigrant workers.

As described in several recent studies (Wilson and Martin, 1982; Wilson and Portes, 1980; Waldinger, 1985; Bonacich and Modell, 1980), the primary characteristic of ethnic economies is the use of a common cultural bond for economic survival and advancement. The principle of ethnic solidarity requires that recent arrivals spell a tour of duty at menial low-wage jobs. The cheapness of their labor is a central factor allowing fledgling immigrant enterprises to compete and survive (Grasmuck, 1984; Nee and Nee, 1973). The same principle requires, however, that employers promote their workers as new positions become open within their firms or support their eventual move into self-employment.

In Miami, the possibility of entry into an enclave labor market is limited to Cuban-owned firms. In 1983 there were almost no known Haitian enterprises in the area, but Cuban firms with paid employees exceeded an estimated three thousand (Diaz-Briquets, 1984; Jorge and Moncarz, 1982). For our analysis, participation in the enclave sector will be operationally defined as employment in Cuban-owned firms plus self-employment, with exceptions to be indicated below. Almost no Haitian respondent was self-employed or employed by a co-national. Those working for Cuban firms were tentatively classified as enclave participants, leaving for the analysis to clarify their actual situation.

Hypothesizing that primary, secondary, and enclave sectors are potentially distinct modes of labor market entry is justified by a prior research literature which has documented their existence as well as the position of ethnic minorities in them (Edwards, 1975; Bonacich, 1972; Waldinger, 1985; Wilson and Martin, 1982). In our case, however, the picture is rendered more complex by the apparent

500

emergence of an "informal sector" in Miami. Informal activities are those which employ labor on a noncontractual basis and in terms which generally violate tax, wage, and fair labor laws. Payment of subminimum wages and nonpayment of taxes and benefits confer on these activities a distinct competitive advantage, reinforced in turn by the absence of covenants protecting employees from arbitrary dismissal.

Although relatively absent from the sociological literature, several recent studies have documented the proliferation of informal activities in metropolitan areas like New York (Sassen-Koob, 1984), San Diego (Fernandez-Kelly and Garcia, 1985), and the San Francisco Bay Area (Castells, 1984). Examples of these activities include sweatshop production of apparel and electronics components (Morales, 1983; Marshall, 1983; Saxenian, 1983); unregulated piece-rate homework in the garment and footwear industries (NACLA, 1979; Mazur, 1979) and off-the-books labor in restaurants, hotels, and cleaning services (Morales and Mines, 1985; Sassen-Koob, 1984). Also included are unprotected domestic servants and itinerant self-employed workers such as odd-jobbers and street vendors.

The largely illegal labor practices in the informal sector are different from those that prevail in the secondary and enclave labor markets. The latter are composed of small, but established and state-regulated enterprises that pay low, but still legal wages. A major difference among the three sectors appears to be the sources of their labor force. The secondary sector is described as dominated by blacks, women, and other domestic minorities (Edwards, 1979: Ch. 10; Berrera, 1980; Doeringer and Piore, 1971); the enclave sector employs mostly legal immigrants; the informal economy, on the other hand, seems to draw primarily from recent undocumented immigrants (Wells, 1984; Grasmuck, 1984; Sassen-Koob, 1984).

Although not undocumented, the tenuous legal status of post–1980 Cuban and Haitian refugees and their consequent lack of government protection makes it likely that many would seek employment in the informal sector, if such an alternative were available. Consequently, we hypothesize the existence of four distinct labor market situations among employed respondents in our samples. Although the first three can be readily identified, the very illegality of much informal employment renders it difficult to tap on the basis of direct survey questions. For this reason, we must approach its definition indirectly through several indicators. In our data, labor market sectors can be empirically defined as follows:

Secondary: all employed workers, except those below.

Primary: public-sector employees and workers in firms employing more than 100 workers, minus those below.

Enclave: workers in Cuban-owned firms, regardless of size, plus the self-employed who meet at least one of these criteria: (a) having paid employees; (b) being engaged in professional practice; (c) having a regular, established place of business.

Informal: (a) workers paid in cash or without tax deductions; (b) domestic servants and kindred; (c) the itinerant self-employed, such as odd-jobbers and street vendors; (d) workers whose hourly wages are below 80 percent of the legal minimum.[6]

Table 3 presents the distribution of employed respondents and their spouses over these four sectors. As shown in the table, rates of participation in the primary sector, as defined, are uniformly the lowest at about one-tenth for all four groups. At the opposite extreme, the informal sector comprises about one-third of every group. Two additional results of this initial classification deserve mention: (1) excluding the primary sector, Cuban workers distribute themselves about evenly among the other three labor markets, while Haitians concentrate overwhelmingly in the secondary; (2) enclave firms predictably hire many more Cubans than Haitians, but the number of the latter employed in this sector is not insignificant.

Identifying these four sectors on the basis of arbitrary indicators does not prove that significant differences exist among them. Although the distribution by sectors appears reasonable, this division may be artifactual and does not disprove the hypothesis of a single labor market and an homogenous mode of entry. The next logical step is to examine whether significant differences exist and whether they accord with theoretical expectations. The literature on dual labor markets, as well as those on ethnic enclaves and the informal economy, lead us to expect systematic variation in the sexual and racial compositon of the various sectors, as well as in such variables as knowledge of English, information about the host society, income, length of unemployment, satisfaction and opportunities in the current job, and welfare dependence.

To test this hypothesis, we employ discriminant analysis (Van de Geer, 1971:243–72). This procedure allows the specification of a

---

[6] The hourly wage cutting point is arbitrary. It is more strict than the legal minimum wage itself to insure that only flagrant violations are included.

UNWELCOME IMMIGRANTS

Table 3. Labor Market Sectors, Employed Cuban and Haitian Entrants, 1983

	Cubans		Haitians	
Labor Market Sector[a]	Self (N = 331)	Spouse (N = 218)	Self (N = 186)	Spouse (N = 123)
A. Primary	12.8	11.5	10.6	8.3
B. Secondary	24.9	29.7	47.7	53.7
C. Enclave	30.9	28.1	8.3	7.5
D. Informal	31.4	30.7	33.4	30.5

[a] See text for definitions.

nominal reference variable which is used to extract whatever significant functions exist in a set of independent variables. The maximum number of functions is one fewer than the number of subpopulations. If fewer than the maximum possible number of discriminant functions are significant, then some of the populations are not empirically distinguishable from each other, at least in regard to the variables included in the analysis. A shortcoming of discriminant analysis is the assumption of a multivariate normal distribution (M.N.D.), seldom met by sociological data (Fienberg, 1980:106–109). In the absence of a fully satisfactory solution, we replicated the analysis through a series of maximum-likelihood logistic regressions which do not depend on M.N.D.

The number of sub-groups and the broad range of possible differences among them suggest that we cast our net fairly wide. Our original analysis included a set of twenty-five variables, but results presented below include only those which yielded at least one significant discriminant-function coefficient. Six of these variables are background characteristics or indicators of early reception in the United States: age; sex; education; number of relatives in the United States and help received from them; and confinement to a detention camp upon arrival. A second set taps various contemporary social characteristics, including marital status, knowledge of English, ethnic social relations, opportunities to meet Anglo-Americans, and experiences of discrimination by them. The rest of the variables are indicators of present occupational and economic situation, including objective variables such as length of U.S. unemployment, time in current job, monthly household income, and length of welfare aid and subjective self-reports, such as perceived opportunities in the present job.[7]

Results of this analysis are presented in Table 4. Included are standardized discriminant-function coefficients and group centroids. Wilks λ is transformed into χ^2 and probability levels are presented. The complementary maximum likelihood analysis was performed by fitting equations to binomial dependent variables corresponding to each of the significant discriminant functions. With some exceptions, results replicated those of the previous analysis, including a close fit between logit and unstandardized canonical discriminant-function coefficients. Since, for our purposes, relative rather than absolute order of magnitude is most important, the table presents standardized canonical-function coefficients. Those flagged as significant, however, are restricted to variables meeting minimum statistical criteria in both analyses.[8]

and *0* otherwise. ENGLISH is the score on an 8-point scale of English comprehension developed for use with immigrant samples (Portes and Bach, 1985: Ch. 3); standardized item alpha reliability is .94 for the Cuban sample and .90 for the Haitian.

The following social and economic characteristics are dummy variables coded in agreement with their labels: predominantly intraethnic social relations (ETHSOC); opportunities to meet with Anglo-Americans (ANGLO); discrimination by Anglos experienced by respondent or his family (EXPDIS); current employment in manufacturing (MANUF); opportunities to advance in present job (OPPORT); and employment in more than one occupation (TWOJOB). The remaining variables are indicators of employment and economic situation: UNEMPL is length of past unemployment in the United States in months; JOBTIME is tenure in the present job, also in months; HINCOME is household income in dollars per month; TIMEAID is total number of months of private or public welfare aid since arrival.

[8] Significant standardized coefficients are those exceeding 1.65 of their respective standard errors in both the discriminant and logistic regression analyses. Binomial dependent variables for the latter were as follows:

Function I: Primary and Enclave (Cubans) over Informal; Secondary excluded.

Function II (Cubans only); Enclave over Primary and Secondary; Informal excluded;

Function III: Primary over Secondary; Enclave (Cubans) and Informal excluded.

These results are available upon request.

[7] AGE and education (EDUC) are coded in years. KIN is the number of respondent's relatives living in the United States, and KINHELP is the aid received from them at the moment of arrival, coded as a dichotomy and in agreement with its label. CAMP is *1* if the respondent was interned in a detention camp at arrival and *0* if released directly into the community. MARSTAT is the respondent's marital status, coded *1* if married, including common-law unions,

Table 4. Discriminant Analysis of Labor Market Sectors: Cuban and Haitian Entrants

Variables[a]	Cubans (N = 331)			Haitians (N = 186)	
	I	II	III	I	II
AGE	.026*	−.204	.067	.009	−.131
SEX	−.104	.047	−.225*	−.046	−.251*
EDUC	−.061	−.400*	−.235*	.131	.116
CAMP	.290*	.527*	.134	.430*	−.181
KIN	−.125	.250	−.315*	.441*	.149
KINHELP	.157	.035	.131	−.007	−.441*
MARSTAT	.245*	.281*	−.082	.147	.415*
ENGLISH	−.030	.008	−.473*	.252	−.472*
ETHSOC	.046	.305*	.073	.038	.102
ANGLO	.067	−.410*	.077	−.138	−.088
EXPDIS	−.225*	.093	−.210	−.157	.077
UNEMPL	.106	.051	.602*	.132	.311*
MANUF	.317*	−.364*	.055	.009	.049
JOBTIME	.114**	.036	−.257*	.187	−.018
OPPORT	.486*	−.038	−.033	.056	−.094
TWOJOB	.071	.349*	−.084	−.406*	.107
WORKERS	.236*	−.036	−.062	.092	−.236
HINCOME	.357*	.030	.268	.725*	−.043
TIMEAID	−.228**	−.203	.004	−.223*	−.030
Eigenvalue	.409	.175	.119	.427	.288
Percent of Variance	58.25	24.86	16.86	59.68	40.32
Canonical Correlation[b]	.539	.387	.326	.547	.473
χ^2	191.25	85.08	34.93	101.97	42.44
	p<.001	p<.02	p<.07	p<.001	p<.03
Group Centroids					
Primary	.728	−.659	−.586	1.098	−1.236
Secondary	.025	−.381	.499	.280	.398
Enclave	.547	.499	.016	—	—
Informal	−.892	.079	−.181	−.876	−.297

* p< .05. ** p< .01.

[a] See footnote 7 for definition of variables.

[b] Figures are standardized canonical discriminant function coefficients.

The analysis yields three significant discriminant functions in the Cuban sample. Canonical correlations represent the association between each discriminant function and the $m-1$ set of dummy variables representing the m different subgroups. The first canonical correlation is of moderate size and the second and third are modest, but not insignificant. The nature of the three discriminant functions can be gleaned from the standardized canonical coefficients. Disregarding signs for the moment, the first and most important function is defined by age, marital status, camp internment at arrival, experiences of discrimination, and a set of economic variables including employment in manufacture, opportunities in current employment, number of household workers, household income, and welfare dependence. The second discriminant function is defined by education, camp internment at arrival, marital status, ethnicity of social relations, opportunities to interact with Anglos, number of jobs, and industrial employment. The third

function is defined by sex, number of kin in the United States, knowledge of English, length of unemployment, and time in present job.

For our purposes, the most telling results are the group centroids, for they bear directly on the hypothesis above. The significant χ^2 for the first function is due mostly to distance in the reduced function space between the primary and the informal sectors. The secondary group falls almost in the middle, while the enclave group is close to the primary sector. This result clearly supports the distinctness of the informal sector as one mode of labor market incorporation and its position at the opposite extreme of those employment situations which appear most desirable. The latter are defined by the primary and enclave groups which converge on the positive side of the function space.

Looking now at the direction of coefficients, informal-sector membership is associated with a greater presence of younger and single individuals, more frequent experiences of discrimination, and less time spent in camps at arrival. Economic variables may be used to describe the opposite situation exemplified by the primary and enclave sectors. These variables are associated with industrial employment, greater opportunities in the present job, higher income, greater number of household workers, and less welfare dependence. Clearly, this first function is indicative of aspects and correlates of successful economic adaptation, at least during the first years in the United States.

The second discriminant function rearranges the groups differently. In this case, the significant difference in the reduced-function space is that between the enclave on the one hand, and the primary and secondary sectors on the other. The fact that the enclave and primary groups occupy opposite extremes indicates that, although sharing in the characteristics of relatively favorable economic adaptation reflected in the first function, they are still distinct in terms of the social aspects of their respective employment situations. Predictably, enclave-sector membership is associated with greater in-group social relations and lesser opportunities to interact with Anglos. Relative to participants in the two-tiered open labor market, enclave-group members are also less educated and less likely to be employed in industry; they are, however, more likely to be married, to have spent time in camps, and to hold more than one job.

The third function shows another facet of the differences between these groups. In this instance, it is the opposition between the primary and the secondary sectors which defines the principal polarity. This result supports the assertion of different employment situations among these refugees along the upper and lower tiers of the open (nonethnic) labor market. Predictably, secondary-sector membership is associated with a predominance of females, longer spells of unemployment, and less stable job tenure; it is also related to lesser knowledge of English and a weaker network of kin in the United States.

Taken as a whole, this analysis challenges the view that recent refugees are confined to a homogeneous niche in the American labor market. Despite a common unfavorable reception and a difficult early resettlement period, significant differences developed in their employment situation and its correlates. The analysis indicates that the background, social experiences, and economic situation of Cuban refugees can separate those in each tier of the open segmented labor market along one axis, both groups from participants in the enclave economy along a second, and each from confinement into the informal sector in a third.

These conclusions must be modified immediately, however, in the light of results obtained for the Haitian sample. An initial analysis which reproduced the one just described yielded only two significant discriminant functions. Inspection of the group centroids indicated that the sectors which failed to differentiate were the enclave and the secondary. Results in Table 4 are based on reclassifying the Haitan sample, eliminating the enclave sector, and redistributing its members to the remaining criteria. As expected, the bulk of this group fell in the secondary sector.

It is unnecessary to discuss Haitian results in detail since they reproduce those already described among Cubans for the first and third discriminant functions. Although the cluster of significant canonical coefficeints varies somewhat, the pattern of group centroids is unmistakably the same. The primary and informal sectors are again at opposite extremes of the first function. In this instance, the informal group is characterized by a weaker network of kin and, as in the case of Cubans, briefer camp internment at arrival. Economic variables also define the opposite extreme of the function space: primary-sector membership is again associated with higher household income and less welfare dependence, as well as with less propensity to rely on more than one job. The second discriminant function again rearranges groups in a way that highlights the contrast between primary and secondary sectors. As among Cubans, the secondary sector is associated with a predominance of females, longer unemployment, and lesser knowledge of English. Among Haitians, singles predominate in this sector, as well as those who received little help from kin at arrival.

The fact that similar discriminant functions are identifiable in the two samples provides clear evidence of the differences that they reflect. The missing discriminant function in the Haitian sample is precisely that which separated the enclave from both segments of the open labor market among Cubans. This absence indicates that employment in an ethnic-enclave economy does not have the same consequences for all groups. The distinct characteristics associated with participation in the enclave sector do not appear to extend beyond those of the same nationality as the firm owners. For Haitian refugees, employment in the Cuban enclave is no different, at least in terms of these variables, from participation in the secondary labor market.[9]

---

[9] Our findings are subject to the objection that one of the exogenous variables, monthly household income, is partially contaminated by the use of subminimum wages as a criterion for classification of the

504   AMERICAN SOCIOLOGICAL REVIEW

This analysis has demonstrated the existence of significant differences across labor market sectors, but it has failed to clarify what these differences mean in terms of either the refugees' backgrounds or their present situation. Having established that different modes of labor market entry exist, we must also clarify how immigrants get into them and with what consequences. Table 5 presents a preliminary overview of the relevant data, reserving for the next section a systematic analysis of causal determinants.

Reading across rows, age, sex, race, and marital status all vary significantly in the Cuban sample. The unemployed are younger, on the average, and more often single than others. Blacks and women are also overrepresented in this category, but both are underrepresented in the enclave. Informal workers are also more likely to be black and single, although the percentage of females in this sector is not higher than in the secondary sector. Among Haitians, race is too homogenous a trait to register significant differences, and so is age, given the youth of the entire sample. Females are again overrepresented among the unemployed and underrepresented in the primary sector.

Education in the home country, education acquired in the United States, and knowledge of English do not vary much across labor market sectors, nor between the employed and the unemployed in the Cuban sample. This result suggests that entry into better employment situations is more dependent on ascriptive factors and social networks than on individual qualifications in this group. Among Haitians, however, both education at arrival and knowledge of English are significantly related to employment in general and to primary-sector entry, in particular.

The bottom rows of Table 5 reveal the most poignant differences among sectors in terms of average economic condition. The general pattern for both samples is that respondents who gained access to the primary sector have experienced the least unemployment, are least likely to receive welfare assistance, and have the highest individual and household incomes. Among Cubans, those working in the enclave come next in terms of favorable economic circumstances, surpassing, albeit by an insignificant margin, average income in the primary sector. The obverse of this picture is the condition of the unemployed and the informally

---

informal sector. We replicated the analysis after eliminating respondents whose *only* reason for inclusion in the informal sector was very low wages. Since these represent a small group in both samples, it is not surprising that results did not differ significantly from those reported above.

employed, who show consistently the longest periods of unemployment, higher levels of welfare dependence, and lowest incomes. Their dire economic straits are illustrated by the fact that average *household* incomes for the unemployed in both samples were below the 1983 federal poverty level for individuals.

DETERMINANTS OF UNEMPLOYMENT AND INFORMAL EMPLOYMENT

The preceding analysis has established two facts: first, that significant differences in modes of incorporation exist within immigrant groups who, in all appearance, should be confined to a uniform position at the bottom of the labor market. Second, that the major cleavage in employment situations in terms of their consequences is between refugees who have entered one or another sector of the legal, contractually regulated labor market and those who find themselves outside of it, either because they cannot find jobs or because the only ones available to them are in the informal economy. In this section, we turn to the issue of causal determinants of this major cleavage, drawing potential explanantions from three different theoretical perspectives.

As dependent variables for this analysis, we selected three dummy variables constructed by dividing successively narrower segments of each sample. The total samples were first divided into employed and unemployed; the same was done with economically active respondents, after eliminating the voluntarily unemployed; the employed subsamples were divided, in turn, into formally and informally employed. In every case, the category of interest—unemployed or informal—was coded *1*.

Among possible explanations of these situations, perhaps the most generally accepted is that stemming from the human capital perspective (Mincer, 1974). As applied to ethnic minorities' labor force participation, this perspective predicts differential outcomes essentially as a function of individual skills and abilities (Borjas, 1982). The latter make individuals more or less desirable to employers which, in turn, conditions their opportunities in the labor market. Although human capital analyses often leave marginal room for contextual variables such as "employer discrimination," their basic thrust is to model labor market outcomes as functions of the workers' own abilities (Chiswick, 1978). As indicators of this perspective, we selected the following variables: education at arrival (EDUC); occupational background in the home country (OCCUP); work experience (WORKEXP);

Table 5. Breakdown of Background and Economic Variables by Labor Market Sectors

Variables	Cubans						Haitians				
	Primary (N=42)	Secondary (N=83)	Enclave (N=104)	Informal (N=102)	Unemployed (N=189)	p	Primary (N=20)	Secondary (N=105)	Informal (N=61)	Unemployed (N=312)	p
Mean Age	40.6	39.9	38.4	38.8	35.4	.001	30.2	32.9	33.8	31.3	n.s.
Percent Female	38.1	30.6	20.0	30.3	53.4	.001	8.3	30.1	37.7	77.4	.00
Percent Black	7.1	10.3	5.2	15.7	15.1	.07	95.0	86.0	89.0	85.2	n.s.
Percent Married	71.4	65.6	79.2	54.6	46.3	.001	25.0	61.1	35.7	49.8	.001
Education at Arrival (Years)	10.1	9.5	8.9	8.7	8.6	n.s.	6.2	5.1	5.0	4.2	.03
Education in U.S. (Months)	3.4	6.3	4.6	4.2	5.4	n.s.	5.3	4.6	4.2	4.2	n.s.
Average Knowledge of English[a]	2.0	2.6	2.0	1.8	2.0	n.s.	4.7	2.2	2.4	1.6	.001
Average Months of Unemployment	2.8	8.1	5.5	5.7	18.8	.001	8.8	9.2	11.0	22.2	.001
Percent Employed in Industry	53.0	36.3	33.2	19.0	—	.01	19.1	17.9	16.3	—	n.s.
Percent Receiving Welfare[b]	3.5	17.2	8.9	23.0	51.0	.001	10.2	9.5	16.6	39.5	.001
Average Monthly Income	872	780	883	580	—	.001	692	602	430	—	.01
Average Household Income	1411	1195	1392	872	401	.001	1052	860	689	310	.001

[a] Scores in the Knowledge of English scale. See footnote 7.
[b] See footnote 7 for definition of WELFARE.

size of place of birth (URBAN) as an indicator of urban origins and experience; knowledge of ENGLISH; information about U.S. society (KNOWUS); and education in the United States (USEDUC).[10]

Other theorists of labor force participation have repeatedly called attention to ascriptive differences in participation and related outcomes which persist even after controlling for all relevant human capital variables. Such is the case, for example, with significant differences between sexes and between races, each documented by an extensive research literature (Duncan, 1968; Lieberson, 1980; Rosenfeld, 1980; Treiman and Roos, 1984). A third perspective has focused primarily on immigrant minorities, emphasizing the importance of contextual variables as determinants of employment situation, net of individual-level characteristics (Piore, 1979; Marshall, 1983; Wilson and Portes, 1980). Although these last two perspectives do not deny the significance of human capital, they focus on other factors which like gender and skin color and, in the case of immigrants, their mode of reception in the host society can decisively affect labor market outcomes. To test these hypotheses, we selected the following variables: SEX; RACE; marital status (MARSTAT); help received from relatives after arrival (KINHELP); internment in a detention camp at arrival (CAMP); and predominant ethnicity of the U.S. neighborhood where respondents have mostly lived (NEIGHBOR).[11]

Each dependent variable was regressed on all predictors. Since endogenous variables are dichotomies, OLS will not do because their measure violates by definition the assumption of homoscedasticity and would probably misspecify the true probability function. Probit and logistic regression obviate the difficulties

created by OLS in this situation, although each presents other difficulties, such as the assumption that individual probabilities can be derived exactly from the maximum likelihood function (Hanushek and Jackson, 1977:203). Despite these problems, we opted for logistic regression.

The first column of each panel of Table 6 presents full regressions of each dependent variable in both samples. In each, the logarithm of the probability of being unemployed or informally employed is expressed as a linear function of a constant and the set of human capital, ascriptive, and contextual factors listed above. Our interest in this analysis is to identify the most significant predictors. The magnitude of coefficients and, in particular, the associated t-values must be interpreted, however, with caution. Inspection of the correlation matrix in both samples reveals sizable intercorrelations, especially in the subset of education and knowledge variables. These correlations suggest multicollinearity. A summary indicator of multicollinearity is provided by the determinant of the correlation matrix among exogenous variables. This statistic is bounded by 0 (perfect linear relationship between two or more variables) and 1 (perfect independence) (Farrar and Glauber, 1967). The determinants in this case are .089 in the Cuban sample and .134 in the Haitian, figures which again support the hypothesis of multicollinearity.

If this is the case, it is not possible to arrive at a parsimonious model of significant effects based on the t-values alone since the latter may be negatively affected by high intercorrelations among predictors. In the absence of a standard solution to this problem, we proceeded to fit a series of models, checking for suppression effects and drastic changes in the magnitudes of coefficients as variables were added or subtracted. With a few exceptions, this analysis confirmed the overall pattern of the full models, showing a few variables to have reliable effects and most to be unstable predictors. Final models with insignificant effects deleted are presented in columns 2 of each panel of Table 6.

Logit coefficients express the incremental effect of exogenous variables on the logarithm of the probability ratio corresponding to each endogenous variable. To facilitate their interpretation, we also computed net changes in actual probabilities, ΔP, associated with effects of each exogenous variable:

$$\Delta P = \exp(L_1)/[1 + \exp(L_1)] - \exp(L_0)/[1 + \exp(L_0)],$$

where $L_0 = \text{Log}[P/(1-P)]$, the logit of the odds-ratio at the sample mean; $L_1 = L_0 + B_j$, the logit after the unit change in X_j (Petersen,

---

[10] URBAN is a 7-point scale ranging from "less than 10,000" to "1 million or more." OCCUP are scores in Treiman's (1977) occupational prestige scale, selected because of its cross-national comparability. WORKEXP is defined as age minus education minus 6. KNOWUS is an 8-point scale of information about U.S. society developed for use with immigrant groups; items range from knowledge of political figures to various tax and credit matters (Portes and Bach, 1985: Ch. 3); standardized alpha reliability is the same for both samples (.73). USEDUC is total months of courses of education taken since arrival.

[11] RACE is coded 1 for whites, 0 for blacks and mulattoes. NEIGHBOR is 1 if most residents in the neighborhood where respondent has lived are of the same group (Cubans or Haitians) and 0 otherwise. All other variables were defined previously.

Table 6. Regressions Describing Effects of Various Characteristics on the Log-Odds of Unemployment and Informal Employment

	A. Cubans								
Exogenous Variables	I[b] (Unemployed, Total Sample) Logit Coefficients[d]			II[b] (Unemployed, Labor Force) Logit Coefficients			III[c] (Informally Employed) Logit Coefficients		
	1.	2.	3. ΔP	1.	2.	3. ΔP	1.	2.	3. ΔP
ASCRIPTIVE									
SEX	−.463	−.454	−.103	296	−.259	−.051	−.011		
	(4.16)	(4.30)		(2.12)	(2.15)		(.074)		
RACE	.026			−.084			−.246		
	(.17)			(.53)			(1.17)		
HUMAN CAPITAL									
EDUC	−.033			−.028			−.020		
	(1.71)			(1.33)			(.81)		
WORKEXP	−.013	−.013	−.004	−.015	−.012	−.004	−.009		
	(2.44)	(2.56)		(2.47)	(2.48)		(1.22)		
URBAN	.043			.070	.070	.014	.006		
	(1.44)			(2.01)	(2.02)		(.16)		
OCCUP	.001			.001			−.005		
	(.55)			(.71)			(.92)		
USEDUC	.004			−.001			−.001		
	(.49)			(.08)			(.10)		
ENGLISH	.006			.017			−.014		
	(.24)			(.61)			(.42)		
KNOWUS	−.074	−.068	−.020	−.060	−.062	−.011	−.082	−.107	−.024
	(2.51)	(2.60)		(1.82)	(2.18)		(2.21)	(3.28)	
CONTEXTUAL									
MARSTAT	−.368	−.370	−.083	−.444	−.450	−.083	−.301	−.319	−.063
	(3.60)	(3.72)		(3.87)	(4.06)		(2.21)	(2.39)	
CAMP	.027			.038			−.182		
	(.25)			(.31)			(1.25)		
KINHELP	−.329	−.355	−.081	−.321	−.357	−.072	−.130		
	(3.11)	(3.48)		(2.68)	(3.13)		(.96)		
NEIGHBOR	−.130			−.053			−.515	−.479	−.091
	(.78)			(.28)			(2.48)	(2.39)	
P	.399			.293			.314		
N	520			468			331		

	B. Haitians								
Exogenous Variables	I[b] (Unemployed, Total Sample) Logit Coefficients[d]			II[b] (Unemployed, Labor Force) Logit Coefficients			III[c] (Informally Employed) Logit Coefficients		
	1.	2.	3. ΔP	1.	2.	3. ΔP	1.	2.	3. ΔP
ASCRIPTIVE									
SEX	−1.070	−1.101	.271	−1.060	−1.806	−.262	−.083		
	(9.15)	(10.09)		(8.94)	(9.84)		(.39)		
RACE	.006			−.011			.005		
	(.04)			(.07)			(.02)		
HUMAN CAPITAL									
EDUC	−.015			−.021			.008		
	(.77)			(1.02)			(.26)		
WORKEXP	−.007			−.009			.015		
	(1.14)			(1.36)			(1.41)		
URBAN	.106	.102	.023	.112	.103	.024	.070		
	(2.57)	(2.56)		(2.64)	(2.58)		(.97)		
OCCUP	−.015			−.011			−.016	−.103	−.004
	(1.40)			(1.56)			(2.40)	(2.33)	
USEDUC	.001			.001			−.013		
	(.05)			(.05)			(.74)		
ENGLISH	−.026			−.023			−.020		
	(.81)			(.71)			(.41)		
KNOWUS	.011			.019			.031		
	(.26)			(.43)			(.46)		

Table 6. *Continued*

EXOGENOUS VARIABLES[a]	B. Haitians I[b] (Unemployed, Total Sample) Logit Coefficients[d]			II[b] (Unemployed, Labor Force) Logit Coefficients			III[c] (Informally Employed) Logit Coefficients		
	1.	2.	3. ΔP	1.	2.	3. ΔP	1.	2.	3. ΔP
CONTEXTUAL									
MARSTAT	−.062			−.042			−.430	−.361	−.073
	(.56)			(.38)			(2.35)	(2.17)	
CAMP	.001			.019			.096		
	(.01)			(.16)			(1.45)		
KINHELP	−.102			−.120			.312		
	(.93)			(1.07)			(1.54)		
NEIGHBOR	−.050			−.048			−.330	−.252	−.053
	(.45)			(.42)			(1.83)	(1.77)	
P	.630			.611			.334		
N	499			478			186		

[a] See footnotes 7, 10, 11 for definition of variables.
[b] Unemployed coded 1, others 0.
[c] Informally coded 1, others 0.
[d] t-values in parentheses.

1985). Probability changes are presented in columns 3 of the respective panels of Table 6.

Unemployment, whether total or among the economically active, is dependent on almost the same set of variables in each sample. This result reflects the fact that unemployment in both groups is mostly involuntary. The set of predictors varies significantly, however, between samples. Comparing Cuban and Haitian regressions, the single most significant finding is the very strong effect of sex on employment status. This result cannot be attributed to gender differences in education and other human capital variables, since the latter are controlled. Net of them, the disadvantage of women with respect to men is reflected in a 10 percent greater probability of unemployment in the Cuban sample and a full 27 percent in the Haitian.

When only those in the labor force are considered, the gender effect in the Cuban sample is halved while in the Haitian it remains essentially the same. This finding indicates that the substantial rates of unemployment found in both groups but especially among Haitians are due, to a large extent, to the difficulties of refugee women in gaining access to even the most modest jobs, regardless of their qualifications.

The human capital hypothesis is supported in the Cuban, but not the Haitian sample by the significant effects of work experience and knowledge of U.S. society. However, neither is very sizable in absolute terms. Next to sex, the two strongest effects on unemployment among Cubans correspond to contextual variables. Aid from relatives at the time of arrival reduces the likelihood of unemployment four years later by 8 percent on the average; being married has a similar absolute effect.

Net of sex, the only reliable effect in the Haitian sample is that of place of birth and it is counterintuitive. Urban origin, instead of reducing the likelihood of unemployment, increases it. A unit change in the 7-point scale for size of place of birth reduces the probability of finding employment by 2 percent. The fact that this is not a random effect is demonstrated by its persistence in multiple models fitted to the Haitian data. In addition, it is also present in the Cuban sample, where a unit increase in urban origin decreases the probability of employment by 1.4 percent among the economically active.

Additional analyses did not provide evidence of significant interaction effects in either sample. There are several results in these regressions, however, which require elucidation, and perhaps none as much as the urban-origin effect. Reasons why urban-born refugees should find themselves at a disadvantage relative to those born in small towns and rural places are not readily apparent. A possible explanation lies in the higher occupational and income aspirations among those coming from the larger cities. Finding that they cannot meet these aspirations, they may opt to remain unemployed until better opportunities come along. A second explanation is based on different levels of social support. Urban life is more "anomic" and less conducive to organized migration, which relies on established networks in places of destination. If this is the case, we may have misspecified the equation by including help from relatives as a predictor, but not their number or that of close friends.

UNWELCOME IMMIGRANTS   509

Table 7. Regressions Describing Effects of Urban Origin and Places of Settlement on Unemployment[a]

Exogenous Variables	Cubans			Haitians		
	1. Logit Coefficient	2. t-value	3. ΔP	1. Logit Coefficient	2. t-value	3. ΔP
SEX	−.291	2.34	−.063	−1.032	9.14	−.205
WORKEXP	−.012	2.33	−.003			
URBAN	.062	1.66	—	.074	1.69	—
KNOWUS	−.068	2.32	−.012			
MARSTAT	−.446	3.96	−.013			
KINHELP	−.343	2.93	−.080			
BEACH[b]	.236	1.42	—			
HIALEAH	−.121	.79	—			
DADE[c]	−.805	2.48	−.192			
LAUD[d]				−.686	4.70	−.158
BELLE[e]				−.498	3.64	−.110
P	.293			.611		
N	468			478		

[a] Unemployed coded 1, employed 0. Economically active samples.
[b] Miami Beach coded 1, others 0.
[c] Unincorporated Dade County coded 1, others 0.
[d] Fort Lauderdale coded 1, others 0.
[e] Town of Belle Glade coded 1, others 0.

We tested each of these interpretations by adding the relevant independent variables, but found support for neither. Introduction of these predictors leaves the effects of urban origins essentially unaltered.

The above explanations would seem to exhaust possible ones, except that we also found a high correlation between places of birth and places of destination. Urban refugees, particularly those coming from the capital cities, evince a clear preference for settling in the city of Miami and, among Cubans, in Miami Beach. It is possible that the clear preference of urbanites to remain in core urban settings decreases their chances for employment since economic competition in these areas is greatest. Table 7 presents results of introducing in the unemployment equations dummy variables representing respondents' principal places of settlement since arrival. To avoid redundancy, only results for the involuntarily unemployed are presented. In both samples, city of Miami is the omitted category. Relative to it, residence in three out of four outlying areas significantly decreases the probability of unemployment, while residence in Miami Beach is not statistically different from residence in the core city. Effects of urban origin drop to insignificance in both samples. Based on these results, these puzzling effects can be attributed to a combination of preferences among individuals born in the larger cities for resettling in central urban places plus an unanticipated contextual effect, namely, apparent differences in employment opportunities for refugees in various areas of settlement. Judging by the size of the coefficients,

places of settlement can have a strong impact on immigrants' employment situation.

The third panel of Table 6 shows that entry in the informal sector as opposed to more regular forms of employment is a function of a different set of predictors. There are three reliable effects in each regression, and two are common to both samples. Marriage increases the probability of regular employment by approximately 6 percent on the average in each sample. Settling in neighborhoods where most residents are of the same nationality also increases significantly the probability of regular employment in both groups. The third effect corresponds to a human capital variable, but it is not the same across samples. Among Haitians, a unit change in background occupational status reduces the probability of informal employment by approximately half a percent. Among Cubans, a unit increase in the knowledge-of-U.S. scale reduces that probability by 2.5 percent.[12]

[12] This last result may be challenged, however, on the grounds that the causal effect actually runs in the opposite direction. Since variables were measured at the same time, it is possible that level of information does not reduce the probability of informal employment but that the latter reduces information. As seen above, KNOWUS is also a significant predictor of unemployment and the same argument may be applied to that effect. If the argument is correct, however, there should be a negative relationship between length of unemployment or length of informal employment and level of information. The argument posits essentially a "negative" socialization effect (Hyman, 1967): the longer the respondent has experienced either situation, the lower should be his/her level of information. We tested this alterna-

510   AMERICAN SOCIOLOGICAL REVIEW

Effects of marital status and neighborhood of residence require clarification. It is not immediately obvious, for example, why marriage should reduce the probability of informal employment. This effect can be interperted as a contextual one, due to the intervening influence of other omitted variables. It can also be interpreted as an irreducible ascriptive effect which is due to employer preferences and other intangible advantages in the labor market. The neighborhood effect is clearly a contextual one, but it is not obvious why co-ethnic neigh-·borhoods should decrease rather than increase the probability of informal employment.

An initial interpretation of both effects is based on differential levels of social support. Married refugees tend to have large networks of kin and friends since they can add to their own those of their spouses. The same is true for refugees living in mostly ethnic neighborhoods. Larger and more supportive networks may facilitate entry into regular employment, avoiding bottom jobs in the informal sector. To test this interpretation, we selected three variables: total number of relatives, constructed as the sum of relatives of self and spouse living in the same city; total number of friends in the city; and help received after arrival (MOSHELP), coded *1* if most came from relatives and friends and *0* if most came from other sources.

A second interpretation of the marriage effect is based on the objective need of married refugees to find better-paid jobs in order to support their families. This need would spur them to avoid the informal sector and seek regular employment. If this interpretation is correct, number of children living with the respondent should increase the need for regular employment, while number of other family workers contributing to the household budget should decrease it.

A final explanation of both the marriage and neighborhood effects is a residential one. Married refugees may settle more frequently in areas where employment opportunities are better, while singles may tend to prefer the central city, where they are more restricted. The ethnic-neighborhood effect may also be due to concentration in areas where opportunities for regular employment are more favorable. If this interpretation is correct, the neigh-

borhood effect would be spurious. To test this last interpretation, we employ the same set of residential dummy variables introduced above.

Table 8 presents results of this final analysis. For brevity, insignificant effects are deleted although results are based on all predictors. As figures show, none of the above interpretations receives support in either sample. The original marriage and neighborhood effects remain intact in both instances. Among Haitians none of the variables representing social support, economic need, or place of settlement has a reliable effect on informal employment. Among Cubans, the analysis uncovers two additional significant effects. Contrary to the economic-need argument, number of other family workers *decreases* the probability of informal employment by about 7 percent; early help from kin and friends has a similar effect. Both of these are contextual effects which provide some additional support for the importance of such variables in determining employment situation, although they fail to account for the original effects.

Marital status and ethnic-neighborhood effects are thus neither spurious nor interpretable as a consequence of the above set of intervening variables.[13] Based on these results, we conclude that marriage represents in this instance a quasi-ascriptive characteristic, akin to sex, whose effects probably inhere in employer preferences and other external factors and not in personal need or social networks. Similarly, ethnicity of neighborhood is interpretable as a broad contextual variable whose effects are irreducible to the immediate circle of kin and friends or the help they may provide.

SUMMARY AND CONCLUSIONS

This paper started with the common view of immigrants as a fairly homogeneous category and the presumption that newcomers arriving under unfavorable circumstances would be channeled to low-paid jobs at the bottom of the labor market. This view, based on the histories of earlier European immigrations, is applied by extension to those occurring at present. Contrary to it, our analysis uncovered significant differences in labor market situations among groups who, because of their modest background and unfavorable reception, could be expected to best fulfill that prediction. The very difficult conditions confronted by recent Cuban and Haitian refugees are reflected less

tive interpretation and found no support for it. Relationships are not negatively monotonic as predicted, but follow an erratic pattern. Regardless of whether each employment situation is of recent date or goes back to the time of arrival, levels of information are uniformly low and do not change predictably with time. Based on these results, we conclude that the knowledge effects on both dependent variables are not mispecified.

[13] A similar analysis of the effect of marital status on unemployment in the Cuban sample yielded identical results. As in the case of informal employment, other potential explanatory factors failed to reduce the original effect.

UNWELCOME IMMIGRANTS												511

Table 8. Logistic Regressions Describing Effects of Original Predictors and Additional Variables on Informal Employment

Exogenous Variables[a]	Cubans[b]			Haitians[b]		
	1. Logit Coefficient	2. t-value	3. ΔP	1. Logit Coefficient	2. t-value	3. ΔP
OCCUP	—	—	—	−.012	2.10	−.003
KNOWUS	−.100	2.81	−.024	—	—	—
MARSTAT	−.549	2.59	−.104	−.332	1.97	−.072
NEIGHBOR	−.542	2.59	−.100	−.259	1.82	−.054
WORKERS	−.285	2.03	−.062	—	—	—
MOSHELP	−.332	2.39	−.071	—	—	—
P	.314			.334		
N	331			186		

[a] See footnotes 7, 10, 11 and text for definition of variables.
[b] Informal employment coded 1, regular employment, 0.

in their uniform entry into minimally paid jobs than in the absence of any entry at all. The large numbers of both groups who were unemployed in 1983 faced one of the most precarious situations of any minority in the country since they also lacked sustained government assistance, due to their irregular legal status.

These alarming circumstances are not the entire story, however, because a substantial number of both groups managed to find some form of employment. Theories of labor market segmentation would predict the wholesale entry of such immigrants into the lower tier or secondary labor market. Contrary to this prediction, we found considerable heterogeneity in labor market situations. Refugees employed in the secondary sector are flanked, on one side, by those who gained access to more favorable employment circumstances in the primary labor market and, among Cubans, in the ethnic enclave; on the other side, are those relegated to the informal economy.

The empical identification of an enclave sector which employs approximately a third of working Cuban refugees and the favorable circumstances surrounding their employment only confirm results of prior research. What is unanticipated in these results is that an enclave mode of incorporation is available only to immigrants of the same nationality as the firm owners. For others, in this case Haitian refugees, employment in the enclave is indistinct from entry into the secondary labor market.

The existence of an unregulated sector of the South Florida economy is confirmed by other independent evidence. Although research on the informal economy is difficult because of the illegal character of many of these activities, individuals familiar with local labor conditions confirmed their widespread character. During the summer of 1983, we conducted a series of open-ended interviews with labor leaders, labor researchers, and entrepreneurs in Miami in conjunction with the beginning of the sur-

veys. Several of these informants were able to confirm independently facts which point toward an expanding informal sector.[14] Informants indicated that recent Cuban and Haitian refugees did not enter a well-established informal economy, but that their presence stimulated its development. Their precarious situation, often approaching destitution, compelled many to avail themselves of any income-earning opportunities. Entrepreneurs, especially owners of highly competitive firms, took advantage of the opportunity. These reports coincide with the survey findings in pointing toward a substantial number of recent refugees employed in this manner and to the highly unfavorable wage and work conditions attached to this mode of employment.

Given the very difficult initial situation of these refugees, an appropriate question is why more of them did not find themselves unemployed or employed in the informal sector. The analysis of this question produced two major findings. First, certain human capital variables significantly affect employment opportunities in both samples. Occupational-status background, work experience, and knowledge of U.S. society all reduced the probability of unemployment or informal employment. The latter variable, in particular, consistently improved labor market prospects among Cubans. Second, major factors affecting employment in both groups are related less

---

[14] Among these facts is the drop of unionized labor from 90 to less than 10 percent of construction starts in the Miami SMSA because of the proliferation of firms hiring nonunion labor, often on an informal basis. Similarly, the garment industry, centered in Hialeah, has been rapidly decentralized through a putting-out system which distributes cloth to immigrant seamstresses working at home for a piece rate. Under-the-counter hiring practices, without employee benefits or tax deductions, have also become common in other small businesses such as restaurants and motels.

512

to human capital than to certain ascriptive and contextual characteristics. Among them, sex differences and marital status are major ones whose effects proved irreducible to individual abilities or to the support of social networks. Help from relatives improved employment possibilities among Cubans, while residence in a predominantly ethnic neighborhood reduced the probability of informal employment among both groups. Finally, an analysis of the anomalous effect of urban origins indicated that places of settlement in the United States can also condition the probability of escaping unemployment. In synthesis, results showed that it is not how much education Cuban and Haitian refugees brought or how much English they learned, but where they settled, whether they were male and married, and how much support they extracted from their kin networks which determined their chances for entry into some form of regular employment.

Once stated, the fact that there are significant labor market differences even among the most downtrodden groups seems obvious. Yet the thrust of popular and scholarly rhetoric has generally gone in the opposite direction. As a noted scholar in this field states:

As one moves from one country to another and reads through historical descriptions, one even begins to believe that there is something in common among jobs held by migrants . . . The jobs tend to be unskilled, generally but not always low paying, and to carry or connote inferior social status; they often involve hard or unpleasant working conditions and considerable insecurity; they seldom offer chances of advancement toward better paying, more attractive job opportunities. (Piore, 1979:17)

There is much truth to this description, but it is by no means the whole story. Results presented above show that even among the most unfortunate new immigrants, there can be significant differences in modes of incorporation into the American labor market and that such differences do not occur at random, but are explainable through a patterned set of factors. Our results do not warrant much optimism as to the collective future of recent Cuban and Haitian refugees, but indicate that, in their case as well as others, research should move beyond blanket generalizations to understand the plurality of situations confronted by each foreign minority.

REFERENCES

Alba, Richard D.
1985 Italian Americans: Into the Twilight of Ethnicity. Englewood Cliffs, NJ: Prentice-Hall.

Althauser, Robert P. and Arne L. Kalleberg
1981 "Firms, occupations, and the structure of labor markets: a conceptual analysis." Pp. 119–49 in Ivar Berg (ed.), Sociological Perspectives on Labor Markets. New York: Academic.

Bach, Robert L.
1984 "Socialist construction and Cuban emigration: explorations into Mariel." Paper presented at the Conference on Cuban-American Studies: Status and Future. Cambridge, MA, May (mimeo).

Bach, Robert L., Jennifer B. Bach and Timothy Triplett
1981 "The flotilla 'entrants': latest and most controversial." Cuban Studies 11:29–48.

Bach, Robert L., Linda W. Gordon, David W. Haines and David R. Howell
1984 "The economic adjustment of Southeast Asian refugees in the U.S." Pp. 51–56 in United Nations Commission for Refugees, World Refugee Survey 1983. Geneva: United Nations.

Baron, James N. and William T. Bielby
1984 "The organization of work in a segmented economy." American Sociological Review 49:454–73.

Barrera, Mario
1980 Race and Class in the Southwest: A Theory of Racial Inequality. Notre Dame: Notre Dame University Press.

Bonacich, Edna
1972 "A theory of ethnic antagonism: the split labor market." American Sociological Review 37:547–49.

Bonacich, Edna and Lucie Cheng
1984 "A theoretical orientation to international labor migration." Pp. 1–56 in Lucie Cheng and Edna Bonacich (eds.), Labor Immigration under Capitalism. Berkeley: University of California Press.

Bonacich, Edna and John Modell
1980 The Economic Basis of Ethnic Solidarity, Small Business in the Japanese-American Community. Berkeley: University of California Press.

Borjas, George P.
1982 "The earnings of male Hispanic immigrants in the United States." Industrial and Labor Relations Review 35:343–53.

Boswell, Thomas D. and James R. Curtis
1984 The Cuban-American Experience. Totowa, NJ: Rowman & Allanheld.

BSRI
1983 Demography, Social Status, Housing, and Social Needs of the Haitian Population of Edison-Little River. Report prepared for the Metro-Dade Government and the City of Miami by the Behavioral Science Research Institute. Miami (mimeo).

Castells, Manuel
1984 "Towards the informational city? High technology, economic change, and spatial structure." Working Paper #430, Institute of Urban and Regional Development, University of California, Berkeley.

Child, Irving L.
    1943 Italian or American? The Second Genera-
          tion in Conflict. New Haven: Yale Univer-
          sity Press.
Chiswick, Barry R.
    1978 "The effect of Americanization on the
          earnings of foreign-born men." Journal of
          Political Economy 86:897–921.
Clark, Juan M., Jose I. Lasaga and Rose S. Reque
    1981 The 1980 Mariel Exodus: An Assessment
          and Prospect. Washington, D.C.: Council
          for Inter-American Security.
Diaz-Briquets, Sergio
    1984 "Cuban-owned businesses in the United
          States." Cuban Studies 14:57–64.
Doeringer, Peter and Michael Piore
    1971 Internal Labor Markets and Manpower
          Analysis. Lexington, MA: D.C. Heath.
Duncan, Otis D.
    1968 "Inheritance of poverty or inheritance of
          race?" Pp. 85–110 in Daniel P. Moynihan
          (ed.), On Understanding Poverty: Perspec-
          tives from the Social Sciences. New York:
          Basic Books.
Edwards, Richard C.
    1975 "The social relations of production in the
          firm and labor market structure." Pp. 3–26
          in Richard C. Edwards, Michael Reich, and
          David M. Gordon (eds.), Labor Market
          Segmentation, Lexington, MA: D.C.
          Heath.
    1979 Contested Terrain: The Transformation of
          the Workplace in the Twentieth Century.
          New York: Basic Books.
Farrar, D. E. and R. R. Glauber
    1967 "Multicollinearity in regression analysis:
          the problem revisited." Review of Eco-
          nomics and Statistics 49:92–107.
Fernandez-Kelly, Maria Patricia and Ana Garcia
    1985 "Advanced technology, regional develop-
          ment, and women's employment in South-
          ern California." Discussion paper, Center
          for U.S.-Mexico Studies, University of
          California, San Diego.
Fienberg, Stephen E.
    1980 The Analysis of Cross-Classified Categori-
          cal Data. Cambridge, MA: MIT Press.
Glasser, William A. and Christopher Habers
    1974 "The migration and return of profession-
          als." International Migration Review
          8:227–44.
Grasmuck, Sherri
    1984 "Immigration, ethnic stratification, and na-
          tive working class discipline: comparisons
          of documented and undocumented Domini-
          cans." International Migration Review
          18:692–713.
Handlin, Oscar
    1951 The Uprooted: The Epic Story of the Great
          Migrations that Made the American People.
          Boston: Little, Brown.
Hanushek, Eric and John E. Jackson
    1977 Statistical Methods for Social Scientists.
          New York: Academic Press.
Hodson, Randy
    1984 "Companies, industries, and the measure-
          ment of economic segmentation." Ameri-
          can Sociological Review 49:335–48.

Hodson, Randy and Robert L. Kaufman
    1982 "Economic dualism: a critical review."
          American Sociological Review 47:729–39.
Hyman, Herbert
    1967 Survey Design and Analysis. New York:
          Free Press.
Jorge, Antonio and Raul Moncarz
    1982 "The future of Hispanic market: the Cuban
          entrepreneur and the economic develop-
          ment of the Miami SMSA." Discussion
          paper in Economics and Banking, Interna-
          tional Banking Center, Florida Interna-
          tional University.
Kalleberg, Arne L., Michael Wallace and Robert P.
    Althauser
    1981 "Economic segmentation, worker power,
          and income attainment." American Journal
          of Sociology 87:651–83.
Kim, Illsoo
    1981 New Urban Immigrants: The Korean
          Community in New York. Princeton:
          Princeton University Press.
Kish, Leslie
    1967 Survey Sampling. New York: Wiley.
Lieberson, Stanley
    1980 A Piece of the Pie: Blacks and White Immi-
          grants Since 1880. Berkeley: University of
          California Press.
Light, H. Ivan
    1979 "Disadvantaged minorities in self-employ-
          ment." International Journal of Compara-
          tive Sociology 20:31–45.
    1980 "Asian enterprise in America: Chinese,
          Japanese, and Koreans in small business."
          Pp. 33–57 in Scott Cummings (ed.), Self-
          Help in Urban America. New York: Ken-
          nikat.
Marshall, Adriana
    1983 "Immigration in a surplus-worker labor
          market: the case of New York." Occasional
          Papers Series #39, Center for Latin Ameri-
          can and Caribbean Studies, New York Uni-
          versity.
Mazur, Jan
    1979 "The return of the sweatshop." The New
          Leader (August):7–10.
Mincer, Jacob
    1974 Schooling, Experience, and Earnings. New
          York: Columbia University Press.
Miller, Jake C.
    1984 The Plight of Haitian Refugees. New York:
          Praeger.
Morales, Rick
    1983 "Undocumented workers in a changing
          automobile industry." Proceedings of the
          Conference on Contemporary Production:
          Capital Mobility and Labor Migration.
          Center for U.S.-Mexico Studies, University
          of California, San Diego.
Morales, Rick and Richard Mines
    1985 "San Diego's full-service restaurants: a
          view from the back-of-the-house." Re-
          search Report, Center for U.S.-Mexico
          Studies, University of California, San
          Diego.
Nee, Victor and Brett de Bary Nee
    1973 Longtime Californ': A Documentary His-

tory of an American Chinatown. New York: Pantheon.

NACLA
1979 "Undocumented immigrant workers in New York City." NACLA Report on the Americas 13:2–46.

Pedraza-Bailey, Silvia
1985 Political and Economic Migrants in America: Cubans and Mexicans. Austin: University of Texas Press.

Petersen, Trond
1985 "A comment on presenting results from logit and probit models." American Sociological Review 50:130–31.

Petersen, William
1971 Japanese Americans, Oppression and Success. New York: Random House.

Piore, Michael J.
1975 "Notes for a theory of labor market stratification." Pp. 125–71 in Richard C. Edwards, Michael Reich and David M. Gordon (eds.), Labor Market Segmentation. Lexington, MA: D.C. Heath.
1979 Birds of Passage: Migrant Labor and Industrial Societies. New York: Cambridge University Press.

Portes, Alejandro and Robert L. Bach
1985 Latin Journey: Cuban and Mexican Immigrants in the United States. Berkeley: University of California Press.

Portes, Alejandro, Juan M. Clark and Manuel M. Lopez
1981 "Six years later, a profile of the process of incorporation of Cuban exiles in the United States: 1973–1979." Cuban Studies 11:1–24.

Rosenfeld, Rachel
1980 "Race and sex differences in career dynamics." American Sociological Review 45:583–609.

Sassen-Koob, Saskia
1984 "The new labor demand in global cities." Pp. 139–71 in Michael P. Smith (ed.), Cities in Transformation. Beverly Hills: Sage.

Saxenian, Annalee
1983 "The urban contradictions of Silicon Valley: regional growth and the restructuring of the semiconductor industry." International Journal of Urban and Regional Research 7:237–62.

Sowell, Thomas
1981 Ethnic America: A History. New York: Basic Books.

Stepick, Alex
1982 "Haitian refugees in the U.S." Minority Rights Group Report #52, London: MRG.
1984 "Haitians released from Krome: their prospects for adaptation and integration in South Florida." Occasional Papers Series, Dialogue #24, Latin American and Caribbean Center, Florida International University.

1985 "Haitians in Miami, an assessment of their background and potential." Research Report, Department of Sociology and Anthropology, Florida International University.

Stevens, Rosemary, Louis W. Goodman and Stephen Mick
1978 The Alien Doctors, Foreign Medical Graduates in American Hospitals. New York: Wiley.

Tolbert, Charles M., II, Patrick M. Horan and E. M. Beck
1980 "The structure of economic segmentation: a dual economy approach." American Journal of Sociology 85:1095–1116.

Treiman, Donald J.
1977 Occupational Prestige in Comparative Perspective. New York: Academic Press.

Treiman, Donald J. and Patricia A. Roos
1984 "Sex and earnings in industrial society: a nine-nation comparison." American Journal of Sociology 89:612–50.

U.S. Bureau of the Census
1984 "Socio-economic characteristics of U.S. foreign-born population." Release #CB84-179, Washington, D.C.: U.S. Department of Commerce (mimeo).

U.S. Immigration and Naturalization Service
1984 1980 Annual Report, Washington, D.C.: U.S. Government Printing Office.

Van de Geer, John P.
1971 Introduction to Multivariate Analysis for the Social Sciences. San Francisco: W. H. Freeman.

Waldinger, Roger
1985 "Immigration and industrial change in New York City's apparel industry." Pp. 323–49 in Marta Tienda and George Borjas (eds.), Hispanics in the U.S. Economy. New York: Academic Press.

Wallace, Michael and Arne L. Kalleberg
1981 "Economic organization of firms and labor market consequences: toward a specification of dual economy theory." Pp. 77–117 in Ivar Berg (ed.), Sociological Perspectives on Labor Markets. New York: Academic Press.

Warner, W. Lloyd and Leo Srole
1945 The Social Systems of American Ethnic Groups. New Haven: Yale University Press.

Wells, Miriam
1984 "The resurgence of sharecropping." American Journal of Sociology 90:1–19.

Wilson, Kenneth and W. Allen Martin
1982 "Ethnic enclaves: a comparison of the Cuban and black economies in Miami." American Journal of Sociology 88:135–60.

Wilson, Kenneth L. and Alejandro Portes
1980 "Immigrant enclaves: an analysis of the labor market experiences of Cubans in Miami." American Journal of Sociology 86:295–319.

Part V
The Effects of Return Migration and Remittances

[9]

World Development, Vol. 14, No. 6, pp. 677–696, 1986.
Printed in Great Britain.

0305–750X/86 $3.00 + 0.00
Pergamon Journals Ltd.

Remittances from International Migration:
A Review in Perspective

SHARON STANTON RUSSELL*
Massachusetts Institute of Technology, Cambridge

Summary. — Remittances — the portion of international migrant workers' earnings sent back from the country of employment to the country of origin — have come to play a central role in the economics of labor-sending countries. Recent research has tended to focus on enumerating the costs and benefits of remittances. This paper proposes an alternative perspective and delineates the "Remittances System" as a heuristic to clarify intermediate relationships between determinants and effects of remittances. Using the heuristic as a framework for review of recent literature concerning remittances, the paper identifies gaps in currently available research and argues for greater focus upon the social and political consequences of remittance flows.

1. INTRODUCTION

The shift in the pattern of international migration over the past two decades, from permanent migrations for resettlement to "temporary" migration of workers for employment, together with growth in the numbers of these migrants, has brought with it international transfers of financial resources acknowledged to be "on an historically unprecedented scale."[1] Remittances — the portion of migrant workers' earnings sent back from the country of employment to the country of origin — have come to play a central role in the economies of the labor-sending countries and have become a focal point in the ongoing debate concerning the costs and benefits of international migration for employment. Particularly over the past decade, and especially with reference to the major European and Middle Eastern migrations, the growing importance of remittances has generated a number of studies designed to explore the dimensions, determinants, uses, and effects of remittances and the governmental policies introduced to manipulate them. A decade of accumulated investigation probably warrants a reflective review in its own right; but recent evidence that remittances are leveling off or even declining, coupled with the prospect that the downturn in oil prices may be associated with a sharper reduction in the flow of both workers and remittances in the Middle East, makes it even more timely to review what has been learned, to identify gaps in our understanding of remittances and to weigh the evidence

concerning prospects for the future. The purpose of this paper is to undertake both a retrospective and a prospective assessment of remittances; in the process, a conceptual framework is proposed to sharpen the focus of future investigation and debate.

Section 2, below, provides an overview of the issues in the central debate regarding the costs and benefits of remittances and introduces the alternative heuristic for organizing the examination of remittances. Sections 3 through 5 review the findings and issues concerning some of the key questions about remittances: what is the volume of remittance flows? What are the mechanisms by which remittances are made? What factors determine the flows of remittances? What are the uses of remittances in the labor-sending countries — and their effects? What policy measures have countries introduced — first to attract remittances, then to influence their domestic uses — and how successful have these been? Finally, Section 6 undertakes to assess the prospects for the future flow of remittances in light of evidence concerning the dynamics of remittances and emerging changes in the world economy. Where appropriate and feasible, contrasts or comparisons are drawn between the European and Middle Eastern experiences.

---

*The author thanks Myron Weiner and Nazli Choucri of the Department of Political Science, Massachusetts Institute of Technology for their comments on earlier drafts of this paper, and Gurushri Swamy of the World Bank for our several discussions of remittance issues.

2. THE DEBATE AND AN ALTERNATIVE PERSPECTIVE

Few discussions of remittances, no matter what their central purpose, fail to make at least summary reference to the potential benefits and costs of remittances for the labor-sending countries. Kritz *et al.* (1981) illustrate the point and summarize the debate as follows:

> At the heart of the question of the impacts on the (sending) countries are the twin issues of labor and remittances . . . . Can remittances be channeled into productive investment, or are they, because of their dispersion, doomed to underwrite expanded imports of newly desired consumer goods, to finance food imports due to decline in agricultural production, and thus fuel inflation in land and home construction? Despite the foreign exchange and balance of payments advantages, do remittances help the development process or, like drug dependency, do their existence and current uses primarily feed the need for more foreign exchange and exacerbate the balance of payments process, thus increasing the need for ever more remittances and the accompanying dependency on receiving countries?[2]

So prevalent is the tendency to couch discussions of remittances in benefit–cost terms, that it would appear useful to catalogue, more or less exhaustively, the principle arguments on both sides. Table 1 does so, drawing upon a review of

some of the major contributions to the debate. Some of the research concerning remittances has focused centrally upon extracting and assessing in a comprehensive way the evidence regarding these largely macroeconomic effects (see Gilani, 1981; Oberai and Singh, 1980). Much of the discussion, however, has focused on identifying and/or reiterating the benefits and costs, either for purposes of stressing the importance of these issues *per se*, or less frequently as a means of setting the context for a more selective empirical investigation. The weighing of costs and benefits has formed part of the conceptual framework within which investigation of remittances has taken place, and is, to varying degrees, explicit or implicit in much of the work discussed below.

In adhering to the cost–benefit framework, however, many discussions of remittances appear to have emerged without a clear vision of the "Remittance System" or of the locus and focus of the investigation within that system. As a consequence, the cost–benefit approach often fails to delineate clearly the complex set of relationships which mediate between determinants and effects and does little to suggest how these relationships might be explored in future research. The use of an economic framework for analysis of remittances has also helped to discourage indentification and investigation of the *noneconomic* effects of remittances. Figure 1 and Table 2 seek to

Table 1. *Benefits and costs of remittances from international worker migration*

Benefits	Costs
1. Ease foreign exchange constraints and improve balance of payments	1. Are unpredictable
2. Permit imports of capital goods and raw materials for industrial development	2. Are spent on consumer goods which increases demand, increases inflation, and pushes up wage levels
3. Are potential source of savings and investment capital formation for development	3. Result in little or *no* investment in capital generating activities
4. Cushion effects of oil price increase	4. High import content of consumption demand increases dependency on imports and exacerbates BOP problems
5. Net addition to resources	5. Replace other sources of income, thereby increasing dependency, eroding good work habits and heightening potential negative effects of return migration
6. Raise the immediate standard of living of recipients	6. Are spent on "unproductive" or "personal" investment (e.g. real estate, housing)
7. Improve income distribution (if poorer/less skilled migrate)	7. Create envy and resentment and induce consumption spending among non-migrants

Source: Some, if not all these considerations are mentioned by each of the following: Chandavarkar (1980), Birks and Sinclair (1979), Bohning (1979), Burki (1984), Ecevit and Zachariah (1978), Gilani *et al.* (1981), Kritz *et al.* (1981), Newland (1979), Oberai and Singh (1980), Serageldin (1981).

REMITTANCES FROM INTERNATIONAL MIGRATION 679

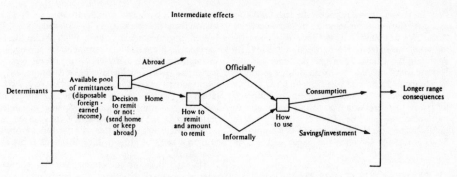

Figure 1. *The remittance system: a decision model.*

Table 2. *The remittance system: Determinants and intermediate effects*

Potential determinants of remittances	Expected direction of relationship	Intermediate effects				
		Available pool of remittances	Decision to remit or not	How to remit	Amount to remit	Uses
Number of workers	+	×				
Wage rates	±	×				
Economic activity in host country	+	×				
Economic activity in sending country	+	×				
Exchange rate	±		×	×		
Relative interest rate between labor-sending and receiving countries	±		×	×		
Political risk factors in sending country	−		×			
Facility of transfering funds	+	?	×	×		
Ratio of females in population in host country	−		×		×	
Years since outmigration	±		×		×	×
Household income level	−		×		×	×
Employment of other household members	−		×		×	×
Marital status	+		×		×	?
Level of education	−		×	?	×	×
Occupational level of migrants	−		×		×	×

clarify the intermediate relationships between determinants and effects of remittances and thereby to provide a model of the Remittance System which is implicit but unspecified in much of the currently available research. Table 2 identifies the range of determinants considered in the literature and specifies the expected direction of the relationship between these determinants and five major "intermediate effects" of remittance flows. Because four of the five intermediate effects involve direct decisions on the part of migrants, Figure 1 depicts a decision model which highlights the key decision points and choice variables facing migrants.

This model of the components of the Remittance System is put forward as a "perspective" to sharpen understanding of the location and focus of past research on remittances and to highlight those decision variables which have been the subject of governmental efforts to influence the flow and uses of remittances. In the following sections, the model is used as a framework for organizing a review of recent literature concerning remittances from international migration. By depicting what have been the elements and the "boundaries" of that system to date, the model also helps to illuminate ways in which the system is incomplete as presently defined, and thereby to point the direction for future research. In particular, the notable absence of attention to political and social consequences of remittance flows is a point to which the paper will return.

3. REMITTANCE FLOWS: DATA ISSUES, DETERMINANTS, AND EFFECTS

(a) Data issues

Efforts to document the volume of remittance flows have been characterized by estimates of their gross total value, growth over time, and scale in relationship to key economic indicators. These estimates have been indicative or illustrative, rather than systematic — in large part because the data problems discussed later are so great as to make the exercise of organizing them more systematically appear to be hardly worth the effort. The illustrative approach, despite its obvious limitations, gives a consistent picture of the growing importance of remittances.

The estimate of gross total value was US $23 billion for 1978, based on Swamy's (1981) aggregation of International Monetary Fund (IMF) balance-of-payments (BOP) data for a sample of 32 developing countries of Europe, the Middle East, Asia, South and Western Africa, and Central and South America.[3] Burki (1984) has estimated the value of remittances for all developing countries in 1982 at US $28 billion.[4] Other observers place the total value of remittances somewhere between US $15 billion and US $30 billion annually. It has been estimated that the total number of migrants for employment worldwide is approximately 20 million,[5] which would suggest an average annual remittance of US $1,000 — a figure which is not only plausible but, given the empirical evidence, probably an underestimate.

The growth in volume of remittances over time has been different for different countries, but in the aggregate there is little question about the trend toward increase through the 1970s: for a sample of 13 labor-exporting countries in the Mediterranean, Middle East and South Asian regions, Ecevit and Zachariah (1978) calculated an increase from US $4.6 billion in 1972 to US $8.1 billion in 1975 (in current prices). The 32

countries in Swamy's sample to which US $23 billion was remitted in 1978 had only US $3 billion in remittance inflows in 1968. While these spectacular increases held strong in the aggregate through the 1970s, there has been general agreement (see Birks and Sinclair, 1979; Swamy, 1981) over the past several years that the rate of growth is slowing across the board; that the absolute level of remittances began to decline in some countries (e.g., Yugoslavia and Korea) as early as the late 1970s; and that the period of phenomenal rates of growth in remittances is probably over.

The fact that the fireworks have died down does *not* suggest, however, that remittances are no longer of central concern. The fact remains that the current level of remittances is in the order of 8 –10 times what it was a decade ago and remittances have, by all accounts, come to play a major role in the economies of the labor-sending countries. The significance of that role is frequently underscored by calculation of remittances as a percentage of the macroeconomic indicators such as gross national product (GNP), gross domestic product (GDP), or government expenditures. The most frequent and probably most meaningful comparison, however, is with exports and imports, a comparison which stresses the relative contribution of remittances to foreign exchange earnings, the importance of the "labor-export industry" and the role of remittances in a country's ability to pay the import bill. As can be seen in Table 3, the significance of remittances is considerable: for six out of the 12 labor-exporting countries, remittances are more than 50% of exports in 1977 and are between 20 and 50% of imports. For individual countries like Egypt, Jordan, Pakistan and the Yemens, the degree of dependency upon remittances is considerable.

Having given some flavor for the scale and relative importance of remittances, it is necessary to return to the factors that shape the underlying quality of the data: without a clear understanding of these factors, investigation into the determinants of remittance flows is confounded. The estimates of remittances given above reflect the *officially* recorded flows in balance-of-payments data reported by countries and compiled by the IMF. There are a number of problems with these data.[6] First, data are not available for some labor-exporting countries. Second, different countries record and report remittances in different places in the BOP statistics: some have a separate line item for workers' remittances, others lump remittances with private transfers; some include only cash remittances, others have included or plan to include the value of in-kind transfers (discussed below). A third set of prob-

Table 3. *Flow of workers' remittances and its share in total imports and exports of goods in selected labor-exporting countries*

Country	1974			1975			1976			1977		
	Remittances*	As percent of Exports	Imports	Remittances*	As percent of Exports	Imports	Remittances	As percent of Exports	Imports	Remittances	As percent of Exports	Imports
Algeria	390	9	9	466	11	7	245	5	4	246	4	3
Bangladesh‡	36	13	2	35	9	1	36	10	1	83	18	9
Egypt	189	11	5	367	23	7	754	47	18	1,425	66	27
India‡	276	8	5	490	12	8	750†	17	12	1,400†	22	20
Jordan	75	48	12	167	109	18	396	198	34	425	186	38
Morocco	356	21	17	533	35	18	548	43	16	577	44	18
Pakistan‡	151	15	6	230	22	8	353	31	12	1,118	88	40
Syrian Arab Republic	62	8	4	55	6	3	51	5	2	91	9	7
Tunisia	118	13	9	146	17	8	135	17	8	142	16	8
Turkey	1,425	93	33	1,312	94	25	982	50	17	982	56	17
Yemen Arab Republic‡	159	1,325	69	221	1,556	72	525	4,269	137	1,013	5,449	139
Yemen P.D.R.	41	410	23	56	373	32	115	261	40	198§	352	49

Source: International Monetary Fund consolidated balance of payments reports, restricted. As reprinted in Ecevit in Kritz *et al.* (1981), pp. 270–271.
*In current prices, million US dollars, gross figures.
†Estimates.
‡Fiscal year.
§Preliminary.

lems is associated with differences in reporting requirements. For example, in India, reporting of remittances below 10,000 rupees has not been required; some remittances made by corporations flow through the national accounts but not necessarily through the balance of payments. There is a fourth set of definitional reasons why caution also needs to be exercised in the use and interpretation of IMF balance-of-payments data: only one of three relevant categories of financial flows is called "workers' remittances" — this includes the value of transfers from workers abroad for more than a year. However, the category called "labor-income" — which refers to factor income accruing to laborers working abroad for less than 12 months, and the category "migrant transfers" (intended to reflect the flow of goods and changes in financial assets resulting from migration) are also of relevance for study of the aggregate financial flows associated with international migration. In the World Bank's study of remittances (Swamy, 1981) these categories are aggregated, not only to conform to the Bank's definition of worker remittances, but because few labor-sending countries distinguish clearly or consistently among the categories.

Probably the greatest source of bias in the BOP data results from the fact that only a portion of total remittances flows through official channels. Empirical evidence as to the nature of alternative mechanisms and the extent of their use is skimpy, often anecdotal, but the very lack of information, together with the potential magnitude of the unofficial flows and the fact that many of the policy measures to be discussed later are attempts to influence these flows, suggests the usefulness of summarizing at this point what little is known about transfer mechanisms and their use. Figure 1, presented earlier, depicts graphically the sequential decision points to which this discussion relates: depending upon the strength and direction of the factors which determine remittance flows (to be discussed later in this section) the migrant chooses, first, whether to retain the funds abroad or to send them home. If the migrant chooses to remit, the decision must then be made to use either official or informal channels.

Assuming the migrant does remit, the most classic (if not the most prevalent) pattern may be summarized as follows: a worker takes that portion of his earnings which he or she desires to send home to a bank in the country of employment and initiates a foreign transfer — usually in a "hard" currency such as US dollars — for which the worker pays a service fee. The foreign currency transfer is received by a corresponding bank in the home country and converted through the central bank to local currency for deposit in the migrant's account. The central bank keeps the foreign currency and it is recorded as a receipt on the balance of payments. This pattern and its near-variants, i.e. those characterized by the flow of finances through regular domestic, private and central banks, are the "official channels" whose transactions will be reflected in the BOP. It should be noted that foreign and "offshore" banks may *not* necessarily report to the balance of payments in the labor-sending countries.

The unofficial, or informal channels are myriad: the mechanisms used for the transfer of *cash* include postal money orders, private money changers or other agents, transfers through foreign corporate employers, and various mechanisms by which funds are hand-carried back to the country of origin — by the migrant during visits or upon repatriation, by friends or trusted agents.

The little empirical evidence available suggests there is considerable variation, both among and within countries, concerning the use of official versus informal channels. For Pakistan, it has been estimated that 85.5% of migrants studied used formal banking channels; the figure is even higher if the calculation excludes the North West Frontier Province (NWFP) where there is an active informal money market and 48% of migrants report using informal channels.[7] In the Sudan, only 24% of a sample of migrants surveyed reported that they transferred monies through banks and only a small percentage of Omanis reported using banks.[8] In the Yemen Arab Republic (YAR), the principal mechanism for transfer of funds has been private agents, who make their profit on the difference between the buying and selling rates of the currency, although there is some evidence to suggest Yemeni migrants are tending more recently to use the services of newly opened branch banks.[9] As a number of observers note, however, the fact that remittances are transferred through private agents does not necessarily mean that funds will not flow through the BOP: unofficial agents may well use the official banking system themselves.

The portion of cash remittances hand-carried by migrants is difficult to assess but in Pakistan, it has been estimated that 27% of the average inflow of remittances is carried by the migrants themselves)[10] while in Samoa, it is reported that a significant proportion of remittances is hand-carried by the migrant rather than sent by postal money order. Restrictions on the size of money orders, combined with the facts that the names of money-order recipients are announced on the radio and that migrants are expected to distribute gifts upon their return all contribute to the preference for hand-carrying funds. The portion of remittances repatriated in-kind, in the form of consumer durables and other goods has proven equally difficult to measure and is influenced by some of the governmental policies discussed later. In-kind transfers are thought to be in the range of 9% of cash remittances for Pakistan[11] and between 8 and 10% for Yemen.[12]

This brief review of the official and informal mechanisms for the transfer of remittances helps to underscore the difficulties associated with using official balance-of-payments data as presently recorded for purposes of analyzing actual remittance flows. To construct a better data base, it would be necessary (albeit difficult if not nearly impossible) to build up estimates on a country-by-country basis, using numbers and occupational distribution of workers and wage rate data, and to attempt to construct a matrix which would give some idea of the distribution of flows between labor-receiving and labor-sending countries.

The foregoing overview of the channels and mechanisms through which remittances flow also provides a backdrop against which to examine the complexities of and interactions among the factors which determine remittance flows and their uses. Table 2 lists the major determinants which have been identified and indicates the expected direction of their effect on the levels remitted. As is the case with other aspects of remittance research, empirical studies are few, though growing in number; nevertheless, it is worth summarizing what is hypothesized and known about the effects of each determinant upon gross remittance flows and the channels by which they are likely to be sent.

(b) *The available pool of remittances (disposable foreign-earned income)*

Birks and Sinclair (1979) have pointed out that the variations in the number of migrants departing are considerably less than the variations in the levels of remittances,[13] suggesting that the number of migrants alone is not sufficient to explain the volume of remittance flows. Nevertheless, this factor has been widely recognized as one of the most important determinants of the volume of flows. In the one study which focuses most systematically upon identifying and measuring the determinants of remittances, Swamy found that for Greece, Yugoslavia and Turkey, the number of migrants abroad and their wages explain over 90% of the variation in remittance inflows, with the number of workers

accounting for most of the variation. Both the numbers of workers in the host country and wage rates are closely tied to the levels and changes in economic activity, not only the country of employment, but in the labor-sending country as well. Indeed, when examining fluctuations in remittances in relation to the trend rates of GDP and deviations from trends, Swamy (1981) found that the level of, and cyclical fluctuations in, economic activity in the host countries explained 70–90% of the variation in remittances, probably because changes in these macroeconomic indicators reflect changes in the demand for, and numbers of, migrant workers and possible changes in their wage rates. Other studies have estimated that the oil price increase in 1973–74 and its effects on the European economies resulted in the outflow of some 600,000 migrant workers,[14] a factor closely associated with an observed downturn in remittances in some labor-sending countries.

While economic recession and the related decrease in demand for labor would appear to explain changes in remittances associated with the European migration, in the case of the Middle East, reductions in the numbers of workers, and a downturn in remittances to specific countries have been observed even in the midst of growth in the country of employment, in part because wage rates were more responsive to international market forces. In Yemen, it has been observed that the rate of increase in remittances has slowed dramatically, from 100% per annum through 1976–77, to 32% in 1977–78 and 6% in 1978–79 (a decline in real terms).[15] In large part, this observed decline appears to be associated with downward shifts in the unskilled wage rate in Saudi Arabia during the 1977–78 period: in June 1978, it was reported that wages in Saudi Arabia were on the order of one half what they had been 6 months or a year before and were more or less comparable to what they were in 1975, a change associated with the increasing competition from Pakistani and Indian workers entering the Saudi labor force at wages from a third to a quarter of those previously commanded by Yemeni workers. A distinct, but related factor has been a narrowing of the wage differential between Saudi Arabia and Yemen, associated with increased demand and inflation in Yemen's "remittance economy."[16]

(c) *Whether and how to remit*

As depicted in Table 2, the levels of and fluctuations in economic activities in host and sending countries, and their consequences for the number of workers and wage rates, affect the gross pool of remittances *available* for return to the labor-sending countries. Another set of factors influences whether remittances will be retained abroad or sent home and, in the latter case, how they will be sent (results represented as the second and third columns under "intermediate effects" in Table 2 and as choice points in Figure 1). Some of these determinants inhere in the political, economic and institutional environment; others have to do with the sociodemographic characteristics of migrants and their families.

The exchange rates and relative interest rates between labor-sending and receiving countries are certainly linked to levels of and fluctuations in economic activity in the two countries,[17] but their effect on remittances is likely to be seen most at the points of decision about *whether* to remit or not and *how* to remit. In the literature, there has been relatively little systematic attention to the influence of exchange rates on remittances. What evidence there is reflects debate on the subject. There are several aspects of exchange rates to be considered: there is, first, the differential between the official exchange rates of labor-sending and receiving countries; second, a potential differential between official rates and "free-market" (or "black-market") rates in the labor-sending country, and; third, if government policy has provided for it, a differential between the official rate and the "premium" rate offered to emigrant workers. In her case study of Yugoslavia, Greece and Turkey, Swamy (1981) found that *neither* the exchange rate differentials between official and "premium" rates, nor those between official and "free-market" rates had any significant effect on total remittances (although they may have contributed to a reallocation of savings among different available accounts). On the other hand, Chandavarkar (1980) has maintained that,

> The most important macroeconomic requisite for inducing remittances through official channels is a realistic unitary (single) rate of exchange for the currency of the labor exporting country . . . . Remittances are notably sensitive to any indications of currency overvaluation and are prone to slow down in such cases, leading to widespread resort to unofficial channels to transfer funds.[18]

Observers have noted anecdotally that in India, remittances went up when the rupee was de-linked from the dollar and the pound sterling. There has been speculation that the decline in official workers' remittances in Egypt's current account between October 1981 and March 1982 was associated with the significant differential (±25%) between the official and free-market

rates. These reports (while yet to be carefully documented or thoroughly studied) together with conflicting findings in the literature, suggest there is room for more investigation into the effects of foreign exchange rates on remittances. There may well be a threshold of difference above which exchange rate diferentials begin to have an effect.[19]

The notion that there are "threshold differentials" may also be important in assessing the effects of relative interest rates between labor-sending and receiving countries. Swamy (1981) again found interest rate differentials to have no effect on total remittances. What she did find was evidence that foreign currency savings accounts in the home country were substituted for domestic currency accounts with less favorable rates. Evidence regarding the efficacy of policy measures to influence this determinant will be assessed below, but presently available findings raise questions about the importance and strength of relative interest rates as a determinant of remittance flows.

Interest rates may or may not fully reflect a migrant's subjective perceptions about the degree of political risk associated with repatriating funds. Chandavarkar (1980) has noted that "the confidence felt in the safety and liquidity of financial assets in the labor-exporting countries" is a determinant of remittance flows, citing evidence that remittances to the Peoples' Democratic Republic of Yemen (PDRY) declined after nationlization but increased again after government provided assurances of stability.[20] The reported drop in official remittances to Egypt is linked by some to political uncertainty in the months following the assassination of President Sadat. Little empirical work has been done, however, to explore or measure the effects of political risk on remittances.

Virtually no research has been done to assess the importance of the availability and quality of institutional transfer mechanisms, such as banks and corporations, nor has there been research into their role(s) in facilitating remittance flows. It was noted earlier that Yemeni migrants appear to be shifting from private agents to banking channels, as branch bank facilities have become established. Gilani *et al.* (1981) have attributed the relatively high proportion of migrants using official channels to "the rapid increase in quality of service and coverage offered by the banking system for this purpose."[21] Filipino workers seeking to repatriate funds from the Middle East reportedly face bank charges ranging from 3 to 18% of the transfer, a factor which has led to heavy reliance on friends and relatives to hand-carry funds or to the use of merchandise transfers. One report concludes, "most workers in fact want to remit their funds, but are thwarted by the lack of banking infrastructure."[22]

The transfer of remittances through corporations is a little-described, but potentially significant mechanism, particularly used where labor-sending country governments are actively involved in the recruitment and contracting process. That is to say, corporations may be the vehicles for transfer when workers have relatively little choice about whether or how to remit, and thus the presence or absence of corporate involvement in remittance transfers may have a significant effect on the volume of official and unofficial remittances and how and in what form they flow. Forty-five percent of Filipino workers overseas are employed by Philippine contractors who automatically deduct between 50 and 70% of the worker's salary and place it, through the contractor's bank, in the Philippine account of the migrant or the beneficiaries. Other labor-sending countries would seem to have similar arrangements with their national corporations. When the arrangement is with a foreign corporation however, the funds remitted for workers' wages may not appear on the balance of payments, particularly if they are held in a foreign bank's branch. While the value of remittances sent worldwide through such channels is not known, it is thought to be potentially quite large.

A number of sociodemographic characteristics of migrants have been linked to the flow of remittances. Swamy (1981) found that, for a pooled sample of three Mediterranean countries over 18 years, the "ratio of females to the total migrant labor population of each nationality has a significant negative coefficient, suggesting that demographic factors may be far more important in determining the changes in the value of per capita remittances than financial variables."[23] Samoan data showing a decline in remittances over time, together with evidence of "chain migration" support the notion that, as dependents join the outmigrant, remittances diminish. The issue is closely linked to length of time since outmigration and to marital status, as the ratio of females in the host country is likely to rise only as temporary migrants marry, settle and become permanent. To the extent that European labor policies are more conducive to settling, these factors may be more important determinants of remittance flows in Europe than in the Middle East where the majority of workers have been single males. However, it is probably too soon to tell how much demographic settling will take place in the Middle East. The qualitatively different nature of migration in the Middle East, together with the short length of time covered by the study, may explain why Gilani *et al.* (1981) found little drop in remittances over time. Oberai and Singh (1980) found an increase in remittances over time, but these results are difficult to compare with those reported above, as their study is of *internal* migration and it is not clear where the spouses are residing. Their finding that married migrants are more likely to remit than unmarried migrants may suggest that at least some spouses in their sample are living separately. It would seem logical to conclude that geographical location of the spouse has more influence on whether and how much migrants remit, than does marital status *per se*. This conclusion is consistent with evidence that an increasing proportion of females in the country of employment is associated with a reduction in remittances.

Not only the location of the primary family unit, but also its economic situation and alternative sources of income are likely to affect remittances. The evidence as to exactly *how* these variables affect remittances is somewhat conflicting. In their study of internal migration, Oberai and Singh (1980) found that lower caste migrants were more likely to remit than those from higher castes; the fewer the number of other household members working, the more likely migrants were to remit; the landless and those in the lowest income groups were significantly more likely to remit than the better-off. Migrants from agricultural households, however, were slightly less likely to remit, probably because of the greater possibility of meeting basic needs, e.g., for food and clothing, from the land. No microeconomic surveys of international migrant's households have as yet come to light to provide data which might be compared with these. But findings regarding those correlates which *have* been examined in the context of international migration suggest the factors Oberai and Singh (1980) explore will prove to be of relevance. Serageldin *et al.* (1981) have observed that the more highly educated and those of higher occupational levels have a lower propensity to remit than the less educated, probably because these migrants are more aware of alternative uses for their money, are more sensitive to exchange rate variations, are apt to take their dependents with them, and are under less pressure to remit for purposes of family support.[24] In contrast, however, Gilani *et al.* (1981) found no *significant* difference in the percentage of earnings remitted by migrants of different occupational levels — all sent back between 41 and 56% of their earnings, albeit the trend was toward lower remittances by those at higher occupational levels. Similarly, while they found class or caste affected propensity to remit, Oberai and Singh (1980) found *education* to have no statistically significant effect on the decision whether or not to remit.

These equivocal and sometimes contradictory findings argue most for greater clarity, consistency, and precision in defining *what* is being measured in studies of the links between class, educational/occupational and income levels and remittances, and only then for further investigation. The evidence reviewed here suggests it is probable that education and occupation (surrogates for income) do not affect the first order decision — i.e. whether or not to remit — as much as they do the second order decision — how much to remit; this probability underscores the importance of distinguishing between these two decisions and of focusing on identifying the *marginal* propensity to remit among different occupational groups. Understanding the character of these relationships is of more than academic interest: in attempting to project the net effect of changes in economic activity and of changes in the occupational composition of migrant populations for future remittance flows, information concerning the marginal propensity to remit by income level will prove to be important. In Oberai and Singh's (1980) sample, the fact remained that the average size of remittances from the wealthier migrants was significantly greater than from poorer migrants. Whether a labor-sending country's total volume of remittances will decline as its unskilled migrant workers are replaced by the more skilled will depend on whether or not the lower marginal propensity to remit is offset by the higher levels of income earned.

4. THE USES OF REMITTANCES AND THEIR EFFECTS ON THE LABOR-SENDING COUNTRY

(a) *The evidence*

The area which has attracted the greatest interest and debate concerns the uses of remittances by migrants (the final intermediate effect identified in Table 2) and the implications of remittances for development in the labor-sending countries. As noted earlier, it is generally acknowledged that the effects of remittances on the balance of payments has been positive; there is, however, no such consensus regarding the value and effects of remittances *within* the domestic economy. Indeed, the general view has tended to be skeptical or frankly negative, stressing the costs identified in Table 1. Empirical, country-

level work which can shed more light on the issue has just begun to emerge in recent years and a number of investigations are still in process.

Ecevit (1978) has highlighted the central issue impeding efforts to direct or control the uses and effects of remittances: they are essentially private monies. Drawing a distinction between remittances and other types of transfers from abroad, he points out,

> Foreign aid and foreign investment are generally earmarked for specific investment projects or are readily available for direct investment by governments. Remittances, on the other hand, are essentially transfers of personal income used partly for consumption — by the immediate family of the worker at home, or by himself upon his return — and partly for savings and investment. At least a portion of the transfers, therefore, has no direct impact on investment and the remaining funds are not necessarily channeled into productive investment in lines with the country's investment priorities.[25]

Chandarvarkar's 1980 review of the uses of remittances in Yugoslavia, Turkey, Portugal, the Yemen Arab Republic, India and Pakistan summarizes the somewhat equivocal but largely negative character of the fragmentary empirical evidence. In Yugoslavia, the centrally planned economy's limited outlets for productive investment resulted in overmechanization of small farms. In Turkey, incentive schemes (discussed below) are credited with having had some positive effect, but the 1970 Abadan Survey emphasized that migrants' savings were being used primarily for housing, with a lesser proportion going into small factories and shops (see Table 4). In Portugal, similar results were found: a survey by Catholic Rural Centers showed 38% of remittances were spent on land and housing,

Table 4. *Turkey: use of migrants' savings, 1970 (percent)*

Housing	49
Small factories and shops	23
Family businesses	6
Land	9
Car or bus	5
Farm machinery	2
Education	5
Shares	1
	100

Source: Abadan as reported in Kayser (1972), p. 43.

32% on domestic appliances and 24% on the education of children. No investment in industry or trade was found. One positive finding was reported, however: "Agencies have begun to proliferate in the Portuguese villages and the workers have adopted the habit of opening accounts with them, generally in the form of short-term deposits."[26]

In the Yemen (YAR), the use of remittances to purchase land, especially in urban areas, has resulted in skyrocketing prices, a result similar to that found in India, where the Commerce Research Bureau's survey of 402 emigrant households in the Malabar subregion of Kerala showed that, once debt commitments and current consumption needs were met, "the assets most preferred by emigrant households were land, buildings, and jewelry. Consequently, land prices in the region doubled or even tripled . . . investment in shares and securities was reported to be almost nil."[27] (Interestingly, however, the survey also observed another effect: a fourfold increase in bank deposits between 1970 and 1976, reflecting, as in the Portuguese case, a growth in "the banking habit" as well as in the means to support it.) Perwaiz's study of remittance use in Pakistan reportedly concludes that cash remittances were "frittered away in personal consumption social ceremonies, real estate and price escalating trading" while in-kind remittances were mostly "status-oriented consumer goods."[28]

In addition to questioning the value of the uses to which remittances have been put, critics have pointed out a number of wider, secondary effects. The nature of their uses has been associated with high levels of inflation: Serageldin et al. (1981) have pointed out that the increase in Yemen's cost of living index has exceeded gains in Gross Domestic Product resulting from remittances and that remittances pose an "extra inflationary problem for planners to face."[29] For Yemen, Korea, Pakistan and elsewhere, it has been observed that inflation, together with specific skill shortages resulting from migration[30] has led to rising wage rates and dramatic changes in the relative price of labor. The availability of foreign exchange, together with growing demand for consumer goods not available in the domestic market has been linked with a rising demand for imported goods. Perhaps most importantly, a number of observers have pointed out that the influx of remittances and the preoccupation with their effects on the balance of payments has deflected governments from attending to the underlying facts of unemployment, inequality and underdevelopment which have led to migration in the first place.[31]

(b) *Judging the evidence*

The predominant view of remittances in the literature of the mid-to-late 1970s was negative. Beginning in the early 1970s, Southern European labor-sending countries started to question the value of remittances, and the effects of the 1973–74 oil price rise only sharpened these questions further. While the effects on countries exporting labor to the Middle East were (and still are) less well documented, concern among these countries also grew to the point that Birks and Sinclair (1979) could report in the late 1970s that, "Official disenchantment over the impact of remittances is widespread amongst governments of labor supplying countries in the Arab world."[32] That disenchantment was reflected in Jordan's Crown Prince Hassan Bin Talal's keynote address to the 1978 International Labour Conference, where he called for financial compensation to labor-sending countries, to rectify the "imbalance in terms of return" to sending and receiving countries.[33]

The few empirical studies which have begun to emerge more recently acknowledge the predominant judgement about remittances; at the same time, they are beginning to add shading and dimension to the rather flat portrait which has been painted, and they raise some new evidence for consideration. Gilani et al. (1981) found that families of Pakistani migrants did indeed use remittances to increase consumption (one-third of households reported increased expenditure on basic staples) and most "investment" was in real estate and housing (migrant households spent a third more on the latter each year than nonmigrant households) while another significant portion of remittances was spent on sons' marriages. Overall, it was found that 62% of remittance expenditure goes into current consumption, 22% into real estate, 11.5% into real physical investments and 1.4% into financial investments.[34] However, when the "lumpy" and nonrecurring consumption expenditures for real estate, consumer durables and marriages were excluded, and migrants' behaviors compared to those of a control group, the consumption propensities of migrants and nonmigrants were not found to differ significantly. The Pakistani data reviewed here are acknowledged to be preliminary, and more refined measures of the marginal propensity to consume are reportedly being undertaken. However, these findings do raise questions as to whether migrants behave differently from nonmigrants, or whether in fact the perceived negative consumption effects of remittances are no different from the results that would have obtained if the poorer members of a

developing society had been made better off by
some other means. Gilani's findings underscore
the point that the relevant focus of analysis is not
simply the consumption and savings behavior of
migrants, but also the behavior of migrants in
comparison with nonmigrants.

In assessing the value of the use of remittances,
most observers acknowledge that the benefits
accrue largely to the individual migrant's family.
The benefits to the economy and the society at
large are viewed as being much more questionable, given the effects of remittances on increasing consumer demands, fueling inflation and
increasing imports. Others point out, however,
that the social benefits have not been fully
assessed. They note that expenditures on land
and housing have multiplier effects in the domestic economy, as landsellers reinvest their proceeds and as construction and renovation provide
new jobs. They also note that the use of
remittances for housing and education can improve health and productivity, thereby resulting
in wider social benefits.[35] Virtually no empirical
attention has been given to systematic explora-
tion of the effects of remittances on such human
capital development.

Gilani *et al.* (1981) point out that "the increased income from remittances does have an
egalitarian aspect, for no other net inflow of
resources to the public at large has historically
been as equally distributed over the national
population as remittances."[36] In his analysis of
the effects of remittances on households in
northwest Pakistan, where migrants have come
from poorer strata of the population, Burki
(1984) estimates that migrants are remitting
amounts equal to three times the pre-migration
family income. He concludes that migration "has
played a decisive role in removing the worst
manifestation of absolute poverty from many
poor regions of Pakistan."[37] Oberai and Singh
(1980), in their study of internal migrants, reach
a similar conclusion and go on to quantify the
effects. Noting that the distribution of remittances is more equal than the distribution of
household income, they calculate that, for their
sample,

> remittances raise the average income of out-migrant
> housholds by 30.7% (and) there is a decline in the
> Gini coefficient of 16.5%, from 0.515 to 0.430. This
> means that the distribution of income tends to
> become more equal when we include remittances,
> which confirms (the) earlier finding that the relative
> effect of remittances is much greater on poorer
> households (and helps to reduce) the relative gap
> between the bottom and the top income groups.[38]

Elsewhere, they point out,

> The over-all pattern of expenditure . . . appears to

be consumption-oriented, but should not be interpreted as being mainly unproductive; in an
economy in which levels of living are low, consumption expenditure may often be functional and may
induce significant improvements in labour productivity . . . (in addition) a much larger percentage of
households could undertake investment because of
remittances.[39]

In judging the body of evidence concerning the
uses and effects of remittances, the fact that
migrants have evidently invested only a small
proportion of remittances should not be surprising, given the expected marginal propensity to
save among those at the socioeconomic levels
from which the vast majority of migrants have
been drawn. More notable is the fact that many
previously unable to save have both the willingness and means to do so at all. Furthermore,
expenditures on land, housing, jewelry and even
marriages can be viewed as forms of investment:
the value of land at least keeps pace with
inflation; housing units can be rented to provide
a continuing source of cash flow; gold and
jewelry have been attractive investments worldwide; and the son whose remitted earnings
enable him to marry into a wealthier family may
well provide a means of economic and social
mobility for his entire family. There is little
evidence that migrants have done other than put
their money where the rates of return are best.

More recent investigations of remittance uses
and effects continue to confirm earlier findings,
but also begin to uncover the determinants of the
consequences of remittances as they introduce
comparisons between different types of migrants
and begin to explore equity considerations. In a
recent example, an economic study of internal
and international migration from two Mexican
villages found an overall positive effect of remittances on income inequality. However, the study
also found that the effects of remittances on the
distribution of rural income depend upon a
number of mediating factors, including the degree to which migration opportunities are diffused through the village population, the length
of village experience with international migration, the levels and distribution of education
embodied in migrants to different destinations,
and the "mix" of internal and international
migrants in the village.[40]

Just as political risk may affect the flow of
remittances at the macro level, so may shifting
power relationships at the family, kinship, and
community levels affect the uses and effects of
remittances. Yet, in considering the longer-range
consequences of remittances, researchers have
only recently begun to address the subject of
political and social consequences. In his study of
Samoa, Shankman (1976) found that remittances

made migrants more responsive to the more immediate family circle and weakened the sense of responsibility to the wider social group, even as they weakened dependence on the landholders and thus altered traditional patterns of authority. A Thai study reports that young migrants use remitted earnings to establish independent households much earlier than has traditionally been feasible,[41] thus altering long-established intergenerational relationships, while a study of villages in Kerala (India) reports increasing independence of women in migrant households.[42] In Pakistan, remittances have enabled migrant families to purchase Japanese-made Suzuki vans which rural women entrepreneurs are using to carry their farm produce to urban markets.[43] A recent review of studies concerning the impact of migration on social structure in Egypt found (as in Thailand) that migration had accelerated the move to independent nuclear families. Evidence as to the effects of husbands' migration on wives' social status was more mixed: some researchers have found more egalitarian relationships between the spouses, while others have argued that these effects are often temporary and depend upon the wife's stage in the life cycle when migration occurs, as well as upon her degree of economic independence.[44] But, as the Egyptian review concludes, studies which permit this level and type of analysis are relatively few.

Studies which address the broader political implications of remittance flows are almost entirely absent. Much remains to be learned about the effects of remittances on class or ethnic group relations, political participation, demand for governmental services, the shape of national development policies, and the international relations between labor-sending and receiving countries.

The debate as to the balance between costs and benefits is by no means over. Whatever their effects, it is clear that the potential impact of remittances is considerable and it is for this reason that governments have actively sought to attract them and influence their use. The next section examines these efforts.

5., POLICY MEASURES TO INFLUENCE THE FLOW AND USE OF REMITTANCES

Over the years, governments have introduced a number of policy measures to affect migrants' decisions at the choice points identified in Figure 1, that is, to induce, first, the flow of remittances back to the labor-sending country, and then their uses domestically. Because remittances are essentially private transfers, these policy measures have been largely in the form of incentives but in some instances they have been imposed as requirements.

For the European migration experience, which has been in effect over a longer period of time than migration to the Middle East, government policy measures instituted by the major labor-sending countries have been relatively well documented and evaluated in the literature. Several recent studies (most notably Swamy, 1981; the UN Survey, 1982; and Rogers in Kritz *et al.*, 1981) provide fuller descriptions of these schemes and they will be only summarized here. In Yugoslavia, citizens have been permitted to hold foreign currency accounts since 1959 and liberalization of these accounts in 1966 and 1971 was associated with an increase in the number of accounts. Interest on these accounts has been paid in foreign exchange, at a rate comparable to that available on local currency accounts because the central bank has compensated commercial banks when the dinar exchange rate has depreciated. The interest rates have also been higher than in Germany as a further inducement for migrants to remit. Foreign currency account holders have enjoyed a number of other benefits, including preference for importing and for obtaining loans for building and investment, and the opportunity to purchase foreign currency bonds.[45] Rogers has reported that "between two and three thousand migrants have extended loans to enterprises . . .; these loans have been used together with credits obtained from other sources to expand existing enterprises or create new branches and some of the newly created jobs have been filled by the migrant creditors or by members of their families."[46] At the same time, she goes on to note, the cost of credit has often proven too high for these enterprises, many of which have been undercapitalized and slow to develop. On balance, Rogers concludes, these schemes have engaged only a small portion of total remittances.

Greece has also permitted migrants to hold foreign currency accounts, as did Turkey for a period of time. In Turkey, the interest rate was the same as for domestic currency accounts but, in 1979 a scheme was introduced whereby a 10–15% bonus was offered on foreign exchange deposits; another scheme in effect introduced premium exchange rates for remittances. Turkish migrants also enjoyed special import privileges for consumer goods and machinery. Turkey is thought to be the first country to attempt to induce investment of migrants' remittances, through the formation of "Village Development Cooperatives" whose subscribers were given preference for migration — a feature which is viewed as having contributed to their lack of success, as a number of cooperatives were reported to have been formed solely to facilitate migration. A modest, but more successful undertaking was the formation of companies owned by Turkish workers abroad and assisted by the German government. There were 27 of these in 1975; the 10 most established firms had 20,000 shareholders and 1,000 employees.[47]

Despite all this effort, and some evidence that for Yugoslavia and Greece at least, the foreign currency account schemes did induce increased deposits, Swamy (1981) found the policy measures to have had no significant impact on the total flow of remittances and reports evidence that the growth of deposits in Yugoslavia and Greece is the result of substitution from domestic accounts.

The policy measures introduced by countries sending labor to the Middle East are far less fully described and there are no known systematic evaluations of their efficacy. Much of what little is known is based upon Birks and Sinclair's (1979) exhaustive study of the Arab labor-sending countries. They have reported that the Yemen Arab Republic, despite the importance of remittances for its balance of payments and their scale in relation to GNP, has done little to establish policies to attract or influence the use of remittances. While, reportedly, "Government's first five year plan (1976–77 to 1980–81) did propose establishment of a general union of emigrants as a means of encouraging the flow of emigrants' savings and channeling the savings to deposits or shares in emigrant-financed companies,"[48] it is not known whether these plans have been implemented.

Egyptians living overseas may subscribe to Egyptian bonds on favorable terms and joint-venture banks have been established in countries of employment. Reportedly, "one half of the US $10 million subscribed to a new trading and investment bank has been contributed by Egyptians working in the United Arab Emirates."[49]

The Sudan has instituted a number of policy measures aimed at attracting and channeling remittances, including devaluations, which have been undertaken for broader economic reasons, but which have had the effect of making legal exchange at official rates more attractive. "Incentive exchange rates" have been introduced from time to time, albeit contrary to IMF obligations, but these are reported to have been abolished.[50] The "Land for Emigrants Programme" has allowed easy exchange of hard currency for building plots and is reported to have contributed to rising land prices but little to attracting

remittances; only 1,000 plots had been sold by early 1979. The "Nil Value Customs Policy" on imported goods allowed for the use of hard currency deposits retained in special accounts over 6 months to be used for customs relief up to US $14,000 but this policy was abolished in 1979.

In Jordan, a "Development Bond" scheme has been used to translate savings into investment and migrants are believed to have invested heavily on the Jordan stock exchange.[51] Opportunities and incentives for migrants to invest at home were a major topic of discussion at the First Conference of Jordanians Abroad, held in Amman during the summer of 1985.[52]

Serageldin (1981) has noted that there are no known mandatory schemes among Arab labor-sending countries. This has not been the case among the Asian labor-sending countries, however. Evidence regarding the details of their policy measures is even more fragmentary than for the Arab countries, but a number of policy measures have been briefly described. The Philippines is well known to require remittance of up to 70% of a migrant's earnings. An executive order, signed by President Marcos in December 1982, sought to tighten this requirement by requiring proof of compliance before annual renewal of the migrant's passport would be granted. However, the high bank charges associated with remittance through banking channels, together with lack of effective government control over nearly 55% of all remittances (noted earlier in this paper) suggest that such an order would be difficult to implement.[53] The Philippines, among other Asian countries, has also used direct government-to-government bilateral discussions to induce a more orderly and regular flow of remittances. Such arrangements have been tried by Mediterranean labor-sending countries as well, without much success, because of the relatively low proportion of migrants being recruited and placed through government assisted agencies.[54]

Korea reportedly "maintains close control over remittances, ensuring that overseas workers for Korean companies remit wages earned abroad by having their employers deposit the money in foreign currency accounts in the Republic of Korea.[55] In this case, the requirement is likely to have had more effect because of the Government's active involvement in the "project package" approach to labor export, whereby Korean contractors are assisted in bidding and winning jobs for which the provision of labor is a major component. Korea also has a policy for the maintenance of family ties which has been observed to be chiefly to ensure the flow of remittances. The effects of these policies appear to have been significant. Korean workers are thought to remit, on average, 80% of their earnings. In 1982, the more than 195,000 workers abroad remitted US $1,600 million ($1.6 billion) or 7% of all Korea's export earnings.

China is a relatively new entrant into the recent wave of labor-exporting, and while results have reportedly fallen below target, there were thought to be 25,000 Chinese abroad in 1983. Eight state-owned enterprises are involved and have earned China US $940 million between 1979 and June 1982. Like the Philippines, China has introduced mandatory remittance requirements: "the average Chinese worker's salary is split three ways. The worker keeps 30% for living expenses overseas; 30% is sent to the family in China; and the remaining 40% goes to the Chinese government."[56]

India's Foreign Currency Accounts Scheme allows Indian migrants to maintain pound sterling and US dollar accounts in India in tax-free, interest-bearing time deposits, while favorable concessions permit importation of goods. Reportedly, these measures have been effective in attracting remittances.[57] There are recent indications that India continues an active program to entice remittances through a variety of incentives: an English-language advertisement placed by the Kuwait India International Exchange Company in a widely distributed Gulf newspaper proclaims,

> Cheerful news for non-resident Indians. Estate Duty abolished. Income tax exemption limit raised to RS. 18,000/- and surcharge on income tax abolished. Wealth tax exemption limit raised to Rs. 2.5 lacs. Tax rates reduced. T.V., Video, Radio license fees scrapped. Interest ceiling on convertible debentures increased from 13.5 to 15%. We are at your service for remitting your savings to India.[58]

Few of the Arab governments' policy measures and virtually none of those introduced by Asian governments have been evaluated systematically. Future empirical work will need to respond to a number of general concerns. Birks and Sinclair (1979) have noted that "attempts at state control of remittances tend to result in an increase in informal exchanges, which also prevents the fiscal authorities from estimating the macroeconomic effect of migrant remittances."[59] The fundamentally private nature of remittances raises serious questions as to the political limits of state intervention, particularly among those countries which have attempted to impose mandatory requirements. Developments in the Philippines illustrate the point: an organization called UNFAIR (United Filipinos Against Forced Remittances) was established in 1984 to overturn that country's law requiring repatriation

of remittances and to allow workers to keep control of their earnings.[60]

There is also a question as to whether or not the volume of remittances which can be influenced by policy measures warrants the administrative and potential political costs. Writing of the Arab governments' policy efforts, Birks and Sinclair (1979) conclude,

> None of these schemes has great impact upon the flows of remittances, only catching small proportions of total funds transferred. The contribution to development funds of government-handled remittances tends to remain small. It is impossible to be empirically or analytically precise, but it is likely that the positive contribution of such schemes is less than the hindrances to development associated with inflation and distortions of the economy engendered by remittances.[61]

Little attention has been paid to the role of labor-*receiving* countries' policies as they affect the flow of remittances. By and large, it appears that the countries of employment have done little to interfere with the free flow of workers' earnings. Although Saudi Arabia prohibits direct payroll deductions, contractors are permitted to remit funds for their workers. Libya reportedly does exercise foreign exchange controls and Iraq has not allowed more than 60% of workers' salary to be converted to foreign exchange.[62] There is potential for change, however, as economic conditions decline for the oil-exporting countries. This prospect raises, once again, questions about the relative balance of power between labor-sending and receiving countries — a factor affecting the future prospects for remittance flows, the issue to which we now turn.

6. PROSPECTS FOR THE FUTURE

Most assessments of the European worker migration conclude that radical changes in the flows of remittances are unlikely to occur in future. The flow of workers has slowed, and emphasis now is upon issues relating to the integration of foreign migrants and, increasingly, their families. The greater potential for volatility in remittance flows exists in association with migration to the Middle East, and it is upon this we shall focus here.

Observers have, for some time, predicted a slowdown, if not a rapid decline, in remittances from the Middle East. Birks and Sinclair (1979) have termed the prospect of this decline "inevitable" and have predicted it will be "a rapid one."[63] Other observers (see Serageldin et al., 1981) concur, for several reasons. First, rates of growth in labor-receiving countries have slowed during the past decade. Second the structure of demand for labor in the countries of employment is expected to alter, as the large infrastructure projects which have employed masses of un-skilled workers reach completion. The emerging demand is expected to be for more skilled and highly educated foreign workers to staff manage-ment, administrative and service positions. The effect of this change on remittances is likely to be interactive and cumulative: fewer workers will be required in the aggregate and, in addition, as was shown earlier, higher income migrants have a lower marginal propensity to remit, in part because they are often permitted to take their families. The net effect on total remittances will depend upon how much the effects of a lower propensity to remit and the reduced numbers are offset by the higher income levels. There is also growing evidence, at least for the Gulf states, that demographic settling of migrants is begin-ning to occur. While the process may be gradual, over time it is likely to reduce remittances as well.

The recent oil-price downturn, together with the economic effects of the Iran–Iraq war, has begun to focus attention on its likely implications for migration to and remittances from the Middle East. While it is too early to assess how dramatic the effects will be, there is some evidence of change in both the levels and patterns of migra-tion, some of which supports the hypothesis that Asian countries may be more seriously affected than Arab labor-sending countries. In Qatar, 700 casual Asian laborers were reported to have lost their jobs as early as March 1983 because "there was not enough money in the bank to pay them," and payments to contractors were delayed up to 5 months.[64] Observers in the Philippines reported in early 1983 that then-existing contracts in the Middle East were being renegotiated, many at 45–50% of their former value, while the govern-ment had to repatriate hundreds of Filippino workers stranded in Libya without pay.[65] In 1984, Philippine construction and manpower suppliers signed $100 million in overseas con-tracts, down 64% from $283 million in 1983. Prospects are thought to be equally grim for Korea, as the "project package" approach proves comparatively easy to turn off. The value of Korea's construction contracts in the Middle East dropped from $11.3 billion in 1982, to $9.023 billion in 1983, and again to $5.9 billion in 1984.[66]

Other factors may contribute to the slow-down's greater effect on Asians.[67] By the early 1980s a growing antipathy was evident toward Filipino workers in Saudi Arabia, who by then comprised 5% of the indigenous population and some of whom had become involved in crimes punishable by death. Regional conferences to consider the effects of migration began to enumerate the political and social "dangers" of "foreign" (that is non-Arab) labor in the Gulf;[68] intellectuals began to point out that nationals of labor-receiving countries were becoming "minor-ities in their own lands;"[69] and, by 1985, terms such as "cultural invasion," "neocolonialism" and "enemy attacks on Arabic" were not uncom-mon in press reports concerning non-Arab work-ers in the Gulf.[70] In addition to these sociocultu-ral factors, a number of other developments have combined to signal a shift back to preference for Arab migrants. These include a decline in the comparative wage advantage formerly offered by East Asians, a shift in the structure of labor demand that favors Arab-speaking workers to staff supervisory and teaching positions, and possibly a greater sense of responsibility toward their Arab brothers from the region. A growing preference for Arab labor is reflected in require-ments such as that UAE hotels increase the proportion of Arabs they employ from 12 to 30%. London-based companies have begun to report a booming business in the recruitment of Arabs working outside the region: "There is a clear preference for Arab executives — or at least Arabic-speaking expatriates — rather than Americans, Europeans or Asians. Proficiency in Arabic is increasingly sought . . . because there is often a need to train local staff."[71]

It is clear that the oil price downturn is having an effect on both the development budgets and the current accounts of the oil-producing coun-tries. Saudi Arabia, the region's largest labor importer, cut both its development and recurrent budgets by 20 and 18% respectively and still recorded a deficit of US $12,741 million in 1984.[72] The Kingdom's Fourth Development Plan, announced in early 1985, spelled out the con-sequences for migration: 600,000 foreign workers would be expected to return home during the five-year plan period and any new employment of expatriates would be limited to the growth sectors (agriculture, manufacturing, financial and business services).[73] Overall, for 1986 oil rev-enues in the region will be substantially below what they were in 1980 and 1981 and some degree of return migration has undoubtedly begun to occur among Arab as well as Asian migrants. Still, a number of factors may mitigate the speed and severity with which these develop-ments affect remittances. Oil-producing coun-tries are clearly drawing down their reserves in order to finance deficits and to keep their economies running at something close to pre-vious levels; they are likely to continue to do so: the domestic and international political, as well as economic, consequences of radical change are likely to bring all efforts to bear on smoothing the readjustment process. Many of the development budgets which are being trimmed have been underspent in the past, leaving some room for reduction without a notable effect on labor import. Finally, there is some hope that oil demand will rise again in the latter part of the 1980s as Western economies adjust to lower oil prices and expand.

As was the case in Europe in the mid-1970s, the net effect of these developments on the labor-sending countries may be less than might at first be anticipated. Whatever the outcome, the recent changes in the economic equation are likely to engender a sober reappraisal of the role of remittances.

7. CONCLUSION

The subject of remittances is, in the final analysis, virtually inseparable from the broader issues of international migration such as the number and characteristics of migrants and the rates at which they return home. Despite these close links, however, the topic warrants focused attention, as remittances have grown to become a central factor in the domestic economies of labor-sending countries. This review of recent literature on remittances has attempted to organize the still fragmentary evidence along a perspective which distinguishes, more sharply than heretofore, among determinants and the various aspects of the remittance system they may be expected to affect.

Research concerning remittances remains impeded by the quality of available data. International organizations such as the IMF may be able to introduce measures to enhance the frequency and consistency of reporting. But the major problems and needed improvements remain at the level of the labor-sending countries. Until and unless they feel the need of better information for policy and planning purposes, little change is likely to occur on this point.

The determinants of remittances, when laid out clearly in relation to the behaviors they affect, can be seen to influence different aspects of the remittance system. There is considerable room for greater clarity in the literature as to which relationship — and which interactive effects — are being examined and as to the strength and direction of those interrelationships.

The picture as to primary uses of remittances within labor-sending countries is consistent: land, housing, basic staples, and consumer durables predominate. The evidence is less clear as to secondary uses, either by migrants, after the first round of expenditures, or by those selling what migrants seek to purchase. Similarly, first-order effects — positive on foreign exchange and balance of payments, negative on inflation, consumption demand, import demand and dependency upon remittances — have been defined more clearly than possible second-order effects such as more equitable distribution of income, social mobility, or changes in power and authority relationships at the family and societal levels. At the national level, much remains to be learned about the consequences of remittances for a host of other political issues: how do remittances affect the shape of national development policies? or the foreign relations between labor-sending and labor-receiving countries? or political organization and activity among former migrants? Until many of these political and social questions can be answered, cost–benefit assessments will be incomplete.

Policy measures to capture and influence the uses of remittances have been considered relatively ineffective when viewed in relation to the total volume of remittances. It is not clear, however, that this is the relevant comparison, nor have the efforts of many Middle Eastern and Asian countries yet been fully assessed. Results of policy intervention would appear to differ from country to country, with factors such as the inherent strength of the determinants and tolerance for state control having an effect. The question remains whether the volume of remittances which can be directed is sufficiently large as to offset the costs of remittances *per se* and of the institutional and administrative mechanisms needed to direct them. The greatest benefit may be gained from attention to developing alternative domestic investment options which offer rates of return competitive with those migrants have, quite rationally, sought from their expenditures so far.

The prospect of a downturn in the demand for labor in the countries of employment raises the spectre of a drop in remittances, accompanied by massive return migration. It is not clear that labor-sending countries have developed contingency plans to cope with the economic readjustments which a drop in remittances would entail, nor with the reintegration of their overseas workers. If efforts of labor-receiving countries to slow the downturn are successful and if labor-sending countries experience a drop in their import bill, as the price of oil drops, the gross economic effects may be minimal. But if these efforts are not successful, the possibilities of significant unemployment in a climate of economic austerity introduce new political dimensions. The judgement as to the balance between ben-

694   WORLD DEVELOPMENT

efits and costs of remittances is by no means final   for continued vigorous and focused attention to
as yet. The renewed salience of the issue argues   the debate

NOTES

1. Bohning (1979), Foreword.

2. Kritz *et al.* (1981), p. xxv.

3. Swamy (1981), pp. 1,6.

4. Burki (1984), p. 672.

5. Martin and Richards (1980), p. 4.

6. Swamy (1981, pp. 4 –7) provides one of the most
comprehensive discussions in the literature on data
issues and their importance to the study of remittances,
particularly of their determinants. She raises many of
the points discussed in this section.

7. Gilani *et al.* (1981), p. 110.

8. Serageldin *et al.* (1981), p. 216.

9. McClelland (1978), Annex A, p. 3.

10. Gilani *et al.* (1981), p. 101.

11. *Ibid.*

12. McClelland (1978), Annex B, p. 2.

13. Birks and Sinclair (1979), p. 299.

14. United Nations (1982), p. 20.

15. McClelland (1980), p. x.

16. McClelland (1978), p. 2. A similar set of interactions among relative wage rates has been reported
recently for Korea, where the Korea Overseas Development Corporation notes that demand for Korean
workers peaked in the mid and late 1970s: "as Korean
labor became more expensive, clients began looking for
cheaper sources" (*MEED*, 18 February 1983, p. 58).

17. For the sake of simplicity, we are leaving aside the
fact that third-country rates may also be of significance,
although the potential influence of this fact should be
noted and may be of some importance for more
sophisticated migrants.

18. Chandavarkar (1980), p. 37.

19. A closer examination of Swamy's statistical
appendices reveals that the size of the exchange rate
differential is, indeed, relatively small.

20. Chandavarkar (1980), p. 37.

21. Gilani *et al.* (1981), p. 110.

22. Sacerdoti (1983), p. 67.

23. Swamy (1981), p. 36.

24. Serageldin *et al.* (1981), p. 255.

25. Ecevit and Zachariah (1978), p. 36.

26. Kayser (1972), p. 49.

27. Reported in Chandavarkar (1980). p. 39.

28. *Ibid.*

29. Serageldin *et al.* (1981), p. 211.

30. Bottlenecks resulting from migration of selected
portions of the labor force have been noted for a
number of labor-sending countries, and their role in
inducing replacement migration has also been stressed.
However, since these effects are more a consequence of
the movement of *people* than the flows of money, these
points are not elaborated further here.

31. See Ecevit and Zachariah (1978), p. 37.

32. Birks and Sinclair (1979), p. 301.

33. Bohning (1979), p. 194.

34. Gilani *et al.* (1981), p. 43.

35. See, for example, Chandevarkar (1980), p. 39.

36. Gilani *et al.* (1981), p. 40.

37. Burki (1984), pp. 680, 682.

38. Oberai and Singh (1980), p. 239.

39. *Ibid.*, pp. 236–237.

40. Stark *et al.* (1986).

41. Singhanetra-Renard (1983).

42. Gulati (1983).

43. Burki (1984), p. 683.

44. Amin and Awny (1985), pp. 155–199.

45. Swamy (1981) pp. 22–23.

46. Rogers in Kritz *et al.* (1981), p. 354.

47. Swamy (1981), pp. 24–25.

48. Birks and Sinclair, cited in United Nations (1982), pp. 56–57.

49. Serageldin *et al.* (1981), p. 219.

50. Chandavarkar (1980), p. 37.

51. Pennisi in Serageldin *et al.* (1981), p. 221.

52. Hashemite Kingdom of Jordan (1985).

53. Sacerdoti (1983), p. 66.

54. United Nations (1982), p. 25.

55. *Ibid.*, p. 50.

56. *MEED* (18 February 1983), p. 69.

57. Chandavarkar (1980), p. 37.

58. *Arab Times* (28–29 March 1985).

59. Birks and Sinclair (1979), p. 300.

60. *Kuwait Times* (11 April 1985), p. 4.

61. Birks and Sinclair (1979), p. 301.

62. Sacerdoti (1983), p. 67.

63. Birks and Sinclair (1979), pp. 302, 308.

64. *MEED* (8 April 1983), p. 30.

65. Sacerdoti (1983), p. 66.

66. *Jerusalem Star* (7 March 1985), p. 12.

67. Such a result would be consistent with Swamy's finding that, after the 1973 –74 recession in Europe, the effects were greater (more negative) for the newer labor exporters than for the traditional suppliers.

68. See, for example, El-Tamimy (1983), pp. 287–310.

69. Ibrahim (1982), p. 59.

70. *Arab Times* (23–24 May 1985), p. 6.

71. *MEED* (18 February 1983), pp. 57–69.

72. *MEED* (22 March 1985), p. 29.

73. Kingdom of Saudi Arabia (1985), pp. 16–17.

REFERENCES

Amin, B. A., and E. Awny, "International migration of Egyptian labour: A review of the state of the art," manuscript report (Ottawa: International Development Research Center, May 1985).

Arab Times, Kuwait India International Exchange Company advertisement (28–29 March 1985).

Arab Times, "Gulf intellectuals fear 'cultural invasion'" (23–24 May 1985), p. 6.

Birks, J. S., and C. A. Sinclair, "Migration and development: The changing perspective of the poor Arab countries," *Journal of International Affairs*, Vol. 33, No. 2 (1979) pp. 285–309.

Bohning, W. R., "International migration and the international economic order," *Journal of International Affairs*, Vol. 33 (1979) pp. 187–200.

Bonn, J. M., *The Crumbling of Empire: The Disintegration of World Economy* (London: G. Allen & Unwin, 1938).

Burki, S. J., "International migration: Implications for labor exporting countries," *The Middle East Journal*, Vol. 38, No. 4 (Autumn 1984), pp. 668–684.

Chandavarkar, A. B., "Use of migrants' remittances in labor-exporting countries," *Finance and Development* (June 1980), pp. 36–39.

Chandrasekhar, S., *Hungry People and Empty Lands: An Essay on Population Problems and International Tensions* (London: G. Allen & Unwin, 1954).

Ecevit, Z., and K. C. Zachariah, "International labor migration," *Finance and Development*, Vol. 15, No. 4 (December 1978) pp. 32–37.

El-Tamimy, A. M. K., "Political consequences of foreign migration," in N. Fergany (ed.), *General Summary of Seminar on Foreign Labor in the Arab Gulf Countries* (Beirut: Center for Arab Unity Studies, 1983) pp. 287–310. (Arabic).

Gilani, I., M. F. Khan and M. Iqbal, "Labour migration from Pakistan to the Middle East and its impact on the domestic economy," Final Report, Research Project on Export of Manpower from Pakistan to the Middle East (Washington, D.C.: The World Bank, June–July 1981).

Gulati, L., "Impacts of male migration to the Middle East on the family: Some evidence from Kerala," Paper presented at the Conference on Asian Labor Migration to the Middle East (Honolulu: East–West Population Institute, September 1983).

Hashemite Kingdom of Jordan, "First Conference of Jordanians Abroad," Conference papers (Amman, Jordan: Ministry of Labor and Social Development, July 1985). (Arabic)

Huq, A., "Perspectives on migration research: A review of theory, evidence, methodology and research priorities," *Pakistan Economic and Social Review* Vol. 17, Nos. 1–2 (1979), pp. 66–81.

Ibrahim, S. E., *The New Arab Social Order: A Study of the Social Impact of Oil Wealth* (Boulder: Westview Press, 1982).

Jerusalem Star, "Falling oil revenue having its impact on Korea and the Philippines" (7 March 1985), p. 12.

Kayser, B., *Cyclically-determined Homeward Flows of Migrant Workers* (Paris: OECD, 1972).

Kingdom of Saudi Arabia, "Summary of the Fourth

Development Plan — preliminary draft" (Riyadh: Rajab 1405 A. H., April 1985).

Knowles, J. C., and R. Anker, "An analysis of income transfers in a developing country: The case of Kenya," *Journal of Development Economics*, Vol. 8, No. 2 (April 1981). pp. 205–226.

Krauss, M. B., and W. J. Baumol, "Guest workers and income-transfer programs financed by host governments," *Kyklos* Vol. 32, Nos, 1–2 (1979), pp. 36–46.

Kritz, M. M., C. B. Keely, and S. M. Tomasi, (Eds.), *Global Trends in Migration: Theory and Research on International Population Movements* (Staten Island, NY: Center for Migration Studies, 1981).

Kuwait Times, "Filipinos seek prosperity abroad" (11 April 1985), p. 4.

Martin, P. L., and M. F. Houstoun "The future of international labor migration," *Journal of International Affairs*, Vol. 33, No. 2 (1979) pp. 311–333.

Martin, P. L., and A. Richards, "International migration of labor: Boon or bane?" *Monthly Labor Review*, Vol. 103 (October 1980), pp. 4–9.

Middle East Economic Digest (MEED)
Vol. 27, No. 11 (18–24 March 1983), pp. 3–4.
Vol. 27, No. 14 (8 April 1983), pp. 30–31.
Vol. 27, No. 7 (18 February 1983).
Vol. 27, No. 15 (15 April 1983), pp. 52–53.
Vol. 27, No. 12 (22 March 1983), p. 29.

McClelland, D. H., "Yemeni worker emigration and remittances," Mimeo (Sana'a, Yemen, June 1978).

McClelland, D. H., "Some major aspects of the economy of the Yemen Arab Republic," Mimeo (Washington, D.C.: Bureau for the Near East, Agency for Inernational Development, March 1980).

Newland, K., *International Migration: The Search for Work* (Washington, D.C.: Worldwatch Institute, 1979).

Oberai, A. S., and H. K. M. Singh, "Migration, remittances and rural development: Findings of a case study in the Indian Punjab," *International Labor Review*, Vol. 119, No. 2 (March–April 1980), pp. 229–241.

Papademetriou, D., "The effects of labor migration in and to Europe on the countries of worker origin," Paper presented at the International Studies Association Annual Meeting (Toronto, Canada: 25–29 February 1976).

Papademetriou, D., "European labor migration: Consequences for the countries of worker origin," *International Studies Quarterly*, Vol. 22, No. 3 (1978), pp. 377–408.

Sacerdoti, G., "A Gulf well runs dry," *Far Eastern Economic Review* (3 March 1983), pp. 66–67.

Serageldin, I., J. Socknat, S. Birks, B. Li, and C. Sinclair, "Manpower and international labor migration in the Middle East and North Africa," Final Report, Research Project on International Labor Migration and Manpower in the Middle East and North Africa (Washington, D.C.: The World Bank, June 1981).

Shankman, P., *Migration and Underdevelopment: The Case of Western Samoa* (Boulder, CO: Westview Press, 1976).

Singhanetra-Renard, A., "Going abroad: Thai labor movement to the Middle East from the village standpoint," Paper presented at the Conference on Asian Labor Migration to the Middle East (Honolulu: East–West Population Institute, September 1983).

Stark, O., J. E. Taylor, and S. Yitzhaki, "Remittances and inequality," *Discussion Paper* No. 1212 (Cambridge, MA: Harvard Institute of Economic Research, February 1986).

Swamy, G., "International migrant worker's remittances: Issues and Prospects," *World Bank Staff Working Paper* No. 481 (August 1981).

United Nations, *International Migration Policies and Programmes: A World Survey*, Department of International Economic and Social Affairs, Population Studies, Monograph No. 80 (New York: United Nations, 1982).

[10]

Nermin Abadan-Unat

The Socio-Economic Aspects of Return Migration in Turkey

The Socio-Economic Aspects of Return Migration in Turkey [1]

This paper examines the various aspects of return migration from Europe to Turkey between 1973 and 1985. Inspite of the recruitment stop of 1973, the size of the Turkish migrant population in Europe has increased, as a result of family reunion and the growing number of political asylum seekers following the military intervention of 1980.

Return movements have been realized in two forms:

a. Officially encouraged definite return of migrants and all of their families,
b. Individual return due to personal preference and timing.

In 1983 the Federal Republic of Germany and France adopted special policies providing financial incentives for return and enabling the restitution of the employer's contribution to social security funds. Although roughly 300,000 Turkish citizens took advantage of these incentives between 1983 and 1985, high unemployment and rising inflation in the home country constantly reduced the attractiveness of induced organized return.

The essence of the paper is devoted to the non-organized return of Turkish migrants, representing two types, the early and the late returning migrants. The first category represents predominantly the return due to failure. These migrants settle down in rural regions, they do not opt for active farming, but make their living through land leasing. The late returnees choose either a middle-sized town or large city in which to spend their retirement years, or in the case of younger returnees, to re-enter the labour-market as self-employed or as an industrial worker. The second group also comprises a significant number of second generation migrants who were in part obliged by their parents to return.

Comparing the reasons for return in the 70's and 80's, it becomes evident that the education and schooling problems of migrant children, the growing xenophobia and the increasing legal insecurity in prolonging their stay abroad, have been instrumental in the return decision of the 80's.

Those setting up an independent small business have generally not applied for additional credits. Their size remains small, with 40 percent employing not more than one to three persons. The continuity and change of values and attitudes of women migrants is also touched upon. The overwhelming majority of these women who were unemployed housewifes prior to their departure became gainfully employed abroad. Only four percent re-entered the job market after their return. Reasons for non-integration in the host country, the impact of migration upon the decision-making process within the family and the place of the traditional role-model for women are also discussed.

The paper briefly evaluates the various governmental policies in Turkey such as low custom duties for returnees, financial support for weak enterprises, housing credit, and the creation of special German schools for migrant children.

By briefly touching on the political behavior of returning migrants, the low percentage of voting at frontier gates and the inability to participate in local administration in the host countries - except in Sweden and the Netherlands - the dominant attitudes of depoliticisation can be explained.

The paper concludes by stating that while the return process of the 60's and 70's represents a return of failure or conservatism, the 80's reflect a return for retirement and innovation. The second generation, who in many cases was compelled to return through parental authority, represents the group facing the greatest amount of difficulty in readjustment and re-integration.

Türkiye'ye Geridönüş'ün Sosyo-Ekonomik Yönleri

Makale, 1973-1985 yılları arasında Türkiye'ye yapılan dönüş göçünü ele almaktadır. Gerçi Avrupa ülkeleri 1973 ten sonra yeni işgücü istihdamına son vermişlerse de, Avrupadaki Türk göcmen işçi ve ailelerinin sayısı, ailelerin birleşmesi ve 1980 den sonra artan siyasal iltica talepleri nedeni ile artmıştir.

Dönüş göç hareketi iki biçimde ele alınabilir:

a.   *Resmi yollardan özendirilen toplu dönüş hareketleri olarak; bu yoldan göçmen işçi ve ailesi kesin dönüşe yöneltilmektedir.*

b.   *Kişisel tercih ve zamanlamaya dayalı, bireysel dönüş hareketleri olarak; 1983 de Federal Almanya ve Fransa özel tazminatlar ödemek, ayrıca işverenin sosyal sigortaya aktarmış olduğu parasal ödentilerin iadesi yolu ile genis çaplı bir özendirme politikası gütmüştür. Gerçi 1982-1985 yılları arasında toplam 300.000 Türk işçisi bu olanaklardan yararlanma yoluna gitmişse de anayurtda devam eden yüksek işsizlik ve enflasyon oranı, bu dönüş hareketlerinin hızını duyulur biçimde azaltmıştır.*

Makalenin özünü, bireysel dönüş hareketleri oluşturmaktadir. Bu alanda iki tip dönen işçi göze çarpmaktadır: "erken" ve "geç" dönenler. Birinci türe girenler, genellikle endüstri yaşamına uyum gösterememiş kişileri kapsamaktadir. Bunlar, daha çok kırsal bölgelere yerleşmekte, tarımla fiilen uğraşmamakla beraber, daha çok toprak rantından geçinen kişilerdir.

"Geç" dönenler farklı bir kategoriyi oluşturmaktadır. Bunların bir kısmı, başarılı bir uyum göstermiş, emeklilik haklarını almış kişilerdir. Daha genç kuşağa mensub olanlar, Türk iş hayatına bağımsız bir iş kurmak veya endüstride çalışmak suretiyle dönmek isteyenleri kapsamaktadir. Aralarında ana babaları ile kesin dönüş yapma zorunluluğu karşısında bırakılan ikinci kuşak mensupları da bulunmaktadir. Bu ikinci grupta yer alanların önemli bir kısmı endüstrileşmiş bölge ve kent kesimlerinde uyumlu bir kaynaşma başarmışlardır.

Makalede 70 li ve 80 li yıllarda dönüşe neden olan başlıca etkenlere de değinilmektedir. 80 li yıllarda çocuklara eğitim olanakları sağlamak, artan yabancı düşmanlığından uzaklaşmak ve sürekli olarak yurt dışında yaşama isteğine rağmen karsılaşılan hukuki güvensizlik basit dönüş nedenleri arasında yer almaktadır.

Makalede dönen kadın işçilerin tutum ve değerlerinde gözlemlenen süreklilik ve değişme de ele alınmaktadır. Bu kadınların büyük çoğunluğu yurt dışına gitmezden önce ev kadını oldukları halde, yurt dışında bulundukları sürede hep ücretli olarak çalışmışlar, ancak döndükten sonra sadece % 4 ü yeni bir çalışma düzenine girmiş bulunmaktadir. Ayrıca gözlemlenen durumlardan hareketle dış göçün aile içi karar verme sürecine etki yaptığı ancak geleneksel rol modelinde bir farklılık yaratmadığı hususlar da saptanmış bulunmaktadır. Yazıda dönen işçilere hükümet uygulamaları yolu ile gösterilen kolaylıklar - gümrük indirimi, işçi şirketlerine parasal destek, ev kredisi, çocuklar için Almanca dilinde öğretim yapan özel okulların kurulması gibi önlemler de ele alınmaktadır.

1987 genel seçimlerinde sınır kapılarında verilen toplam oyların sınırlılığı-sadece 49.800 oy - ve yurtdışında yasayan işçilerin Isveç ve Hollanda hariç, hiç bir ülkede yerel yönetime faal olarak katılamamaları dönen ve kalan göçmen işçilerin yoğun bir depoliticizasyon süreci içinde bulunduklarını açıklamaktadır.

Sonuç olarak görülyor ki 60 lı ve 70 lı yıllarda yapılan dönüşler genelde bir başarısızlık ya da tutucu değerlere bağlı kalma özelliğini yansıtmasına karşın, 80 li yıllarda yapılan dönüşler başarılı biçimde emeklilik yıllarını geçirme ya da yenilikçi girişimleri gerçekleştirme gibi istekler içeren nitelikler taşımaktadır. Ayrı iki kültür çevresinde yetişen ve kendilerine farklı iki kural ve değer sistemi benimsetilmeğe çalışılan ikinci kuşak mensuplarının, bu dönüş sürecinde en büyük sorunlarla karşılaşan grup olduğu bu irdelemede ortaya çıkmaktadır.

Soziale und wirtschaftliche Aspekte der Remigration in die Türkei

In diesem Beitrag werden verschiedene Aspekte der Remigration zwischen 1973 und 1985 in die Türkei untersucht. Trotz des Anwerbestops seit 1973 hat die türkische Migrantenbevölkerung Europas durch die Familienzusammenführung und die wachsende Zahl derer, die nach der Intervention der Militärs 1980 politisches Asyl suchten, zugenommen.

Der Rückkehrprozeß vollzieht sich auf zweierlei Weise. Erstens gibt es die offiziell unterstützte endgültige Rückkehr der Migranten mit ihren Familien. Zweitens bleibt die Rückkehr oft ein individueller Entschluß, abhängig von persönlichen Vorlieben und Zeitplanungen.

1973 haben die Bundesrepublik Deutschland und Frankreich zeitgebundene Rückkehr-förderungsmaßnahmen inkraftgesetzt, und die Rückzahlbarkeit der von den Arbeit-nehmern geleisteten Sozialversicherungsbeiträge ermöglicht. Zwischen 1983 und 1985 haben fast 300.000 Türken diese Maßnahmen in Anspruch genommen. Trotzdem hat die so geförderte organisierte Rückkehr ihre Attraktivität aufgrund der zunehmenden Inflation und der hohen Arbeitslosigkeitsrate im Heimatland verloren.

Im wesentlichen beschäftigt sich dieser Beitrag mit der nicht organsisierten Rückkehr türkischer Migranten, die als frühe und späte Rückkehrer in zwei Gruppen gefaßt werden. Unter den frühen Rückkehrern sind viele, die in der industriellen Arbeitswelt nur schwer Fuß fassen konnten, und sich nach der Rückkehr in ländlichen Gebieten niederlassen - aber ohne den Wunsch, das Land zu bestellen. Sie

The Socio-Economic Aspects of Return Migration in Turkey 33

---

versuchen, als Landverpächter zu leben. Die späten Rückkehrer gehen in die mittelgroßen oder großen Städte, und leben dort von ihrer Rente. Die jüngeren unter ihnen arbeiten als Kleinunternehmer oder als Industriearbeiter. Zu dieser Gruppe zählen viele Jugendliche, die zum Teil mit ihren Eltern gemeinsam zurückkehren mußten.

Ein Vergleich der Gründe, die zur Rückkehr in den siebziger oder achtziger Jahren führten, macht deutlich, daß in den achtziger Jahren vor allem die Erziehungs- und Ausbildungsproblematik der Migrantenkinder, die wachsende Fremdenfeindlichkeit und die zunehmende Rechtsunsicherheit bezüglich der Aufenthaltsdauer für den Entschluß zur Rückkehr ausschlaggebend waren.

Diejenigen, die sich mit kleinen Betrieben selbständig gemacht haben, haben im allgemeinen keine zusätzlichen Kredite aufgenommen. Die Betriebe bleiben klein; bei 40 Prozent liegt die Zahl der Beschäftigten zwischen ein und drei Personen.

Auch die Kontinuität und der Wandel von Verhaltensweisen und Wertvorstellungen der Migrantinnen wird behandelt. In der Zeit vor der Arbeitsmigration waren die meisten von ihnen Hausfrauen, haben aber im Zuwanderungsland eine Erwerbstätigkeit aufgenommen. Nach der Rückkehr in die Türkei bleiben nur vier Prozent von ihnen erwerbstätig. Die Ursachen für die fehlende Integration im Zuwanderungsland, die Einwirkungen der Migration auf den Entscheidungsprozeß in der Familie und der Stellenwert des traditionellen Rollenverständnisses der Frauen werden erörtert.

Der Artikel evaluiert die verschiedenen Regierungsmaßnahmen der Türkei für die Rückkehrer, wie niedrige Zollsätze, finanzielle Unterstützung für Kleingewerbebetriebe, Kredite für den Hausbau und die Einrichtung von Schulen mit deutschem Sprachunterricht für die Kinder der Rückkehrer.

Das vorherrschend unpolitische Verhalten der Rückkehrer, ersichtlich an der geringen Wahlbeteiligung an den Grenzübergängen, wird damit erklärt, daß eine Beteiligung der Migranten an kommunalen politischen Entscheidungen in den Zuwanderungsländern bisher unmöglich war - eine Ausnahme bilden hier Schweden und die Niederlande.

Der Aufsatz schließt mit der Feststellung, daß die Rückkehrbewegung in die Türkei in den sechziger und siebziger Jahren in Anpassungsschwierigkeiten und Konservatismen begründet liegt. Die Rückkehrbewegungen der achtziger Jahre zeichnen sich eher durch das Phänomen des Ruhestands oder durch innovatives Verhalten aus. Die zweite Generation mußte in vielen Fällen mit den Eltern zurückkehren und wird möglicherweise erhebliche Anpassungsschwierigkeiten zu bewältigen haben.

****

Introduction

Among the sending countries of the Mediterranean, Turkey, a late-comer on the scene of international migration, is no doubt confronted with substantial returns of first-generation migrants who went to look for better wages and new chances in the early 60's, as well as an ongoing out-migration due to family reunion and limited job opportunities. In the space of fifteen years, from 1970 to 1985, the intensity, content and geography of migration from the Southern countries to the more industrialized countries in the North have undergone very substantial changes. These may be summed up as follows: a massive reduction in the transfers of permanent labour, an increase in flows of non-working population, a reduction in Greek, Spanish and to a lesser extent Italian emigration to North-West Europe.

In this respect, three types of regional migration can be identified:

a.   Countries with a falling migratory potential: Greece, Spain, Italy;
b.   Countries with an existing high migratory potential: Portugal and Yugoslavia;
c.   Country with a very high migratory potential: Turkey.

As *G. Simon* rightly points out, of all countries in OECD Europe, Turkey has experienced the greatest surge of emigration to Western Europe since 1970-1973 and has the highest departure potential of anywhere on the southern coast of Europe. The migratory thrust may be summed up in two figures: about 660,000 Turks in Europe in 1971-1972, over two millions in 1985. This threefold increase occurred against a theoretically discouraging background for migration and inspite of the return of over 400,000 migrants since the beginning of the 1980's. It reflects both the extent of family reunification and the high fertility of Turkish families abroad and also the ability of this new working-class emigration to adapt to an economic situation that had become difficult (*G. Simon:* 1987, p. 268).

Another proof of adaptability is provided by the development of other second-choice settlement centers. The increase in the Turkish population is noticeable in France (53,000 in 1975, 123,000 in 1982), where Turks are both the youngest community (one out of every two Turks is under 30) and the most recent arrivals (41 percent lived outside of France in 1975). Their dependency ratio 3.34 is the highest of all alien groups. Large increases were found in Belgium (80,000 in 1982) and the Netherlands (71,000 in 1975; 155,000 in 1983) as well as in Austria, Switzerland and Sweden. The numbers recorded in these countries increased by over 300,000 from 1975 to 1983. The extension and diversification of Turkish migration, which in 1970 was highly concentrated in the Federal Republic of Germany, are among the striking features of the new migratory trend. The spreading out of Turkish migration has partly been caused by the military intervention of 1980 and explains the relative high number of political asylum seekers. According to the official figures published by the Turkish Ministry of Labour in 1980, 57,913 Turks representing 53 percent of the total number of asylum seekers, applied to the German authorities for asylum. Ultimately, this situation produced changes in the procedure of legal asylum seeking in the Federal Republic of Germany. It can be assumed that a substantial number of these asylum seekers used this method to secure employment, and thus, represent pseudo-asylum requests. Nevertheless, the radical changes which took place after the military intervention of September 12, 1980 in Turkey induced a significant number of political activists to apply for asylum abroad.

The major factors which make Turkey the main reservoir for potential migration can be summed up as follows: a high rate of natural population increase (average annual increase over ten years: 2.2 million), the saturation of the employment market (16.5 percent of unemployment and 58 percent of the working population being located in agriculture), an escalating inflation and the great discrepancy in the standard of living between Turkey and the host European countries.

This potential is depicted by the relative high presence of Turkish workers in oil-producing countries in 1984 (see Figure 1).

Figure 1

Number of Workers from Southern Europe
in Oil-Producing Countries in 1984

Turkey	250,000
Yugoslavia	40,000
Italy	30,000
Spain	30,000
Greece	10,000
Portugal	10,000
Total	370,000

Source: J. Widgren, International Migration - New Challenges to Europe, Strasbourg, 1987, p. 10

Presently, there is a considerable outflow of returning migrant workers from the oil-producing countries, indirectly caused by the fall in oil prices and new restrictions in regard to immigration. As regards Turkey, migration to oil-producing countries reached a peak in 1981, and is now diminishing (see Figure 2).

Figure 2

Emigration from Turkey to oil-producing countries

1979	1981	1984
21,000	55,000	45,000

Source: *J. Widgren*, op. cit., p. 10

1.   Return: Myth or Reality?

Considering only the diversified character of out-migration from Turkey, the nature of the return movement must be carefully assessed. According to German statistics, homeward flows surged in 1975 and 1976 (148,000 and 130,000 departures), then fell, levelled off in 1979 and 1980 (66,000 and 70,000) and picked up sharply again two years ago (86,000 in 1982, 100,000 in 1983, 90,000 in the first six months of 1985) (*Widgren:* 1987, p. 33).

However, even statistics like these hide the truth. Most returns are cyclical in their nature, and many of those who have returned, re-enter the country of immigration again after some time. Many enter the independent economic sector. This re-entry movement into the tertiary sectors of immigration countries also indicates a process of settling down permanently in Western Europe. Family reunification over the last ten years, childbearing in the host country, and the growth of new generations raised and educated in the host country have firmly settled these populations, making the idea of returning for good even more remote.

Thus, return movements have to be evaluated in view of present conditions, which are summarized by *J. Widgren* as follows:

-        the family reunion process of the guest workers of the 1960s and early 1970s was completed around 1980 and these guest workers and their children are gradually becoming permanent settlers; this is happening during a period of declining population growth in northern Europe;

-        the idea of permanent return to southern Europe has been replaced by life-long short-term commuting between countries of settlement and countries of origin;

- the situation of ex-guest workers is characterized by higher living standards but also by high unemployment, considerable difficulties experienced by the 'second generation' in entering the labour market, and rising tendencies towards xenophobia; all this is occurring in spite of the recent economic recovery;

- immigration to the most-industrialized European countries remains at a high level due to the general internationalization of European societies and to third world pressure, for example by asylum seekers;

- the process of European integration has been reinforced and so the common labour market of the European community will gradually encompass large parts of southern Europe;

- southern Europe is now increasingly experiencing immigration pressures from non-European countries to the same extent as northern European countries, and the classical dichotomy between receiving and sending countries in Europe no longer exists;

- the 'employment safety-valve', which the expanding middle East oil-producing economies have provided for Mediterranean emigrants since the mid-1970s, is now being drastically reduced due to falling oil prices;

- the whole OECD-area is increasingly experiencing third world migratory pressures in the long-term perspective, and immigration control measures have recently been reinforced in several countries (*Widgren:* 1987, p. 6).

2. Organized and Individually-Determined Return

With the sudden stop of recruitment on behalf of the European major industrial countries the problem of return, coined 're-integration' by administrators of host countries, became an extensively discussed, analyzed and, from politicians, an encouraged, alternative policy model. This trend obliges us to first distinguish between:

a. Officially-encouraged, public policy related incentives for the definite return of the migrant worker and his family. These incentives have been implemented due to the closing of major industrial firms and have created an almost obligatory return situation;

b. Individual or family scale returns as a result of personal preferences and timing.

In both cases, the most relevant role exercised during the decision-making phase is the evaluation and visualization of the economy of the home country. Although a significant number of personally motivated reasons might have induced the migrant to opt for a drastic change of his working and living place, the major push factor still remains the lack of available jobs; that is unemployment in the receiving country. The dream to achieve a major improvement in one's own standard of living, the hopes attached to owning a lucrative business after the return, have been the major motivations to go abroad. These economically oriented reflections, which dominate the working and savings attitudes of the migrants while abroad, logically play a determining role in regard to their intention to return.

During the very early stages of Turkish migration, the expectations of easily finding a proper job were relatively very high - 65 percent in 1963 (*Abadan:* 1964, p. 89), they declined however soon after the recession of 1966/1967 and have continued to be low, particularly in comparison with the other migrants in Europe. Investigating the degree of preference of the influx of foreigners, *Böhning* has drawn attention to the intriguing differences between migrant nationalities. In the Federal Republic of Germany nine out of ten Italian, eight out of ten Spanish, seven out of ten Greek, five out of ten Yugoslav and only three out of ten Turkish workers did return in the early 80's (*Böhning:* 1984, pp. 123-162).

2.1 Organized Return

The ongoing flow of remittances, although tending to diminish, reflect a potential return, since they are the result of decisions by individuals to put their money in the banks of the sending rather than the receiving countries. They also represent the attention and care devoted to the well-being of those left behind. The large sums sent to the home country for other purposes than to meet immediate needs did not by any means create new employment opportunities. This is why Turkey, with its constitutionally-anchored economic, social and cultural development plans, each covering a five year period, was the first country to attempt to channel remittances into productive projects.

A scheme for village development co-operatives was established as early as 1963, and in 1972 Turkey and the Federal Republic of Germany signed an agreement on assistance to the 'Arbeitnehmergesellschaften' (workers enterprises) of Turkish workers living in the Federal Republic of Germany and investing in Turkey. In 1975 Turkey founded the State Industry and Worker Investment Bank (DESIYAB), aiming at delivering credit loans to firms established by Turkish workers abroad. Up to now, more than 4,900 jobs have been created in this way, and a further 2,400 jobs as a result of loan-giving systems.

The development of measures of this kind in Turkey runs parallel to those undertaken in the Federal Republic of Germany. A new agreement between the two countries provides for a special fund, which will make loans to former migrant workers. Moreover, in 1983 the Federal Republic of Germany enacted a law to promote the willingness of foreigners to return to their countries of origin. This law was unique in that it was intended to expire very quickly and did so on June 30, 1984. It provided for assistance for the return of foreigners who were either unemployed or threatened with unemployment. Each returnee recieved 10,500 DM plus 1,500 DM for each child. Altogether, 13,700 foreigners took advantage of this provision. In addition, Turkish (and Portuguese) workers were able to collect their employer's contribution to the social security fund: 120,000 foreigners (including 93,000 Turks and 14,000 Portuguese) took advantage of this. Repatriation assistance was also granted to those who had had part-time work for six or more months, some 16,833 foreign workers, of which 14,459 (86 percent) were Turks, applied for assistance under the scheme. Altogether, nearly 300,000 foreigners, mostly Turks, left the Federal Republic of Germany, taking advantage of the financial inducement policy.

France also tried to implement policies to encourage migrants to return, but these attempts have made little or no impact. The low amount of financial support offered was the major reason for its lack of popularity. The incentives adopted in 1977 took the form of a 10,000 FF grant to every migrant worker having resided more than five years in France, and 5,000 FF per member of the family. In 1984 a more substantial inducement to return was offered between 700,000 and 100,000 FF (*Seccombe* et al: 1986, p. 39).

Finally, international organizations such as the Council of Europe have also attempted, with the European Resettlement Fund, to reduce regional disparities by extending loans aiming at regional development and job creation. So far, the Fund has contributed to the creation of 40,000 jobs in sending countries, including 25,000 in Spain, 9,000 in Italy and 4,000 in Turkey.

With its low standard of living and its high unemployment rate, Turkey, more than other northern Mediterranean labour exporting countries, offers little incentive to return home. The percentage reduction in the number of Turkish workers employed in the EEC was only nine percent of the total employed in 1973, whereas the comparable percentage for Italian immigrant workers was 18 percent for Greeks 17 percent, for Yugoslavs 19 percent, Spaniards 12 percent.

In recent years, there has been an increase in the rate of return from the Federal Republic of Germany. In 1982, about 70,000 Turks returned home, 100,000 in 1983 and 120,000 in 1984. The increase in return migration reflects the continuing recession in Western Europe. By March of 1984 due to the growing unemployment in the Federal Republic of Germany, policy was centered upon the encouragement of return migration (*SOPEMI:* 1984, pp. 34-35).

However, it seems imperative to recall that the huge network of human and material
bonds that has been established between receiving and sending countries has
changed the guest workers of yesterday into the life-long short-term commuters of
tomorrow; the first generation and to some extend the second too, *will live with
one foot in both countries.* This tendency reduces the attractiveness of massive,
induced, organized returns.

2.2   The Non-Organized, Individual Return

Although the percentage of returning Turks appears to be lower than the other
foreign migrants working in Europe, there has been a continuing stream of returning migrants in recent years. Who are they? Do they represent different characteristics than the earlier returnees? What has been the choice of settlement, investment, mode of life?

At this point it should be recalled that at the very beginning of Turkey's planned
'export of excessive manpower', the assumption was centered around the hypothesis,
that a temporary entrance into the world of highly organized industrial production
would enable the Turkish worker to acquire new skills and knowledge and thus
provide the Turkish economy, upon their return, with the necessary trained labour
force. This assumption proved, to a very large extent, to be an unrealized myth.
Neither the workers who went abroad and whose first ambition was to secure fast
accumulations of savings, nor the type of employment offered within the European
job market, could have secured the expected educational gains. Furthermore, the
dream of almost every migrant worker to set up his own independent business upon
his return was much stronger than the alternative to re-enter the industrial sector.
A study carried out as early as 1967 (*Kayser:* 1967) following the recession in the
Federal Republic of Germany, shows that during a sudden and massive economic
crisis, Turkish workers preferred to take up refuge with their countrymen employed
in sectors untouched by the recession, rather than return to the home country.
They displayed a lack of trust toward the labour market in the home country and
refused to identify themselves with the Turkish wage-earning class. This tendency
towards a refusal to take up industrial occupation in the home country has been
defined by *Abadan-Unat* as the 'proletarian/boss' role model. A model in which the
migrant worker tries to overcome his frustrations and inferiority complex caused by
his obligation to perform dirty, risky and prestigeless work abroad, by switching
over to the role of land, real estate, or small-scale business ownership and renter
at home (*Abadan:* 1972, p. 293).

Next to this psychological predisposition, the spatial background and the age group
he belongs to play a decisive role in shaping his attitudes and orientation towards
his own society. In reality, and this point should be stressed, returning migrants resettle in a much more flexible and complex way than is generally realized within

what we may call the 'composite' Mediterranean economy, in which the individual, often of rural origin, simultaneously combines earnings from a small agricultural holding or a small business, with less-readily admitted earnings from undeclared work in a community where families have several forms of employment. Returning migrants prefer, it seems, to combine part-time farming and land-leasing with rural industry and commerce.

3. Two Types of Returnees: The Early and the Late Returning Migrants

3.1 The Early Returnees

The process of return, although a constant, elementary feature of the international migratory flow, demands a sharp distinction in regard to timing. There is a relevant difference between the relatively low, sporadic return of migrants, who went abroad in the early 60's and 70's, and the relative high number of returnees in the 80's. While the first wave was predominantly male, married but housed abroad in dormitories by themselves, the second group chose to return after family reunification had taken place. The first category represents the *early*, the second the *late* returnees.

In the case of the first category, as reflected in the various surveys (*Tuna:* 1966 *State Planning Organization S.P.O.:* 1971; *Abadan-Unat* et al.: 1975; *Yasa:* 1979; *Gitmez:* 1979), the migrants' dominant common trait appears to be an inability to adjust to industrial life and, for those of rural origin, to return to their original villages. Most of the *early* returning migrants declared to have returned for family reasons - but in reality, individual disillusionment, and an inability to master the requirements of a rigid division of labour and time schedule, seem to have played decisive roles in their decision to give up the much-desired job abroad. Although a substantial majority wanted to set up a business of some sort, most have failed to do so. Those who put their savings in industrial joint ventures with a goal to set up a factory (and work in it) upon their return were mostly defrauded of their money while abroad. Those who went abroad through the agricultural cooperative scheme often failed to keep up their dues and few imported machinery under the concession scheme (*Abadan-Unat*). Without generalizing too much, one may say that this group bears the greatest resemblance to the return of failure or conservatism as described in detail by *F. Cerase* (1984).

The *early* returnees generally represent an unsuccessful attempt made by individuals born, raised and socialized in rural areas, who were unable to adjust themselves to an alien industrial urban environment, and thus preferred to return to where their roots lay - to the villages. This return enables some of them to regain prestige and respect among their peers and gain social status. However, this upward mobility creates also envy and jealousy so that quite a few or these returnees finally opt to reside in some small towns in the same region, in order to escape intensive gossip and social-group pressure from the peers in the village of their origin. The survey of *Gitmez* of 1979 indicates that among returnees from the three central provinces of Anatolia, namely Afyon, Kirsehir and Bursa, 35 percent chose to live in a provincial center, 15 percent in provincial district town and 50 percent in villages (*Gitmez*: 1979, p. 175).

However, the relevant feature of this return to rural areas lies in the fact that these returnees are not interested in increasing agricultural production or mechanization, they are not desirous of working as farmers on the land they acquired. They prefer to lease their land. There is a clear-cut increase in regard to land ownership on behalf of returnees, but a decline in the numbers of active farmers.

A study on the impact of international migration on a district - Bogazliyan in the province of Yozgat, Central Anatolia, and its surrounding 38 villages (*Abadan-Unat* et al.: 1975) - indicated that return migrants have made no tangible contribution to the economic development of Bogazliyan by using training and experience acquired abroad; the majority of them departed from Turkey as unskilled workers in the agrarian sector and most come back without any new skills. The intensive flow of money into the district produced a significant improvement in the standard of living in migrants' households, manifested especially in a greater variety of better-quality foods, clothing and household furnishings. However, increased consumer demand, arising from additional purchasing power, had been particularly profitable for the old group of businessmen and only secondarily to return migrants (*R. Penninx*: 1983, p. 801).

Finally, almost three-quarters of all respondents in the above cited surveys were thinking of going abroad again, inspite of their first frustrating experiences.

3.2   The Late Returnees

Systematic efforts to encourage return migration as well as growing xenophobia in Europe resulted in a much larger return movement in the 80's. This movement has also been influenced by the anxiety of some very conservative families, who opted for a return in order to prevent the second generation, particularly their daughters, from entering into a mixed marriage or getting too settled down abroad. For this group, almost all of the seven categories mentioned by *Rogers*, such as positive changes in the country of origin, events at home requiring the presence of the migrant, dissatisfaction in the country of residence, family needs, realization that sacrifices made so far are too great, and the conviction that needs can be better satisfied at home, apply in order to explain their motivation for return (*Rogers*, 1969).

The Socio-Economic Aspects of Return Migration in Turkey 43

A very recent survey carried out by the University of Bursa in Bursa, a province representing Turkey's fastest-developing industrial center, indicated that among the new returnees one finds a relatively high percentage of migrants qualified for pension rights, representatives of the second generation who came back due to parental decision and authority - often against their will - and a significant group of persons belonging to the age category of 31 to 40 (24 percent), desirous to re-enter the job market in Turkey. The distinctive characteristic of this last group is a long stay abroad (42 percent over 10 years), a high skill-level (73 percent) and industrial work experience initially acquired in the home country (75 percent). These returnees have opted for very different alternatives upon their return, 44.26 percent have returned to industry and are at present wage-earning workers, 34.33 percent have founded an independent business of their own and 21.31 percent are benefitting from a retirement pension (*Bursa Survey:* 1986, Table 38).

Table 1

Status of Returnees and Willingness to Re-Emigrate (in Percent)

Do you want to become a migrant worker once more? Status	Yes	No	Total
Worker in home industry	23.0	21.1	44.1
Enterprise owner	10.5	24.0	34.5
Unemployed or retired	13.5	7.9	21.4
Total	47.0	53.0	100.00

Source: *Bursa Survey,* 1986, Table 48

3.2.1   The Occupational Status or Late Returnees

The survey of Bursa of 1986 reflects the big change, which parallels the fast-developing trend of regional industrialization taking place in the Bursa area, where Turkey's automobile, spare parts and textile industries are concentrated. The degree of satisfaction, as compared to the alternative of re-emigrating, reveals an interesting split. The relatively high satisfaction lies in the fact that about 57 percent consider their savings as sufficient and 40 percent feel satisfied with their ability to make full use of their skills which they acquired abroad.

3.2.2   Reasons for Return

While the majority of the returnees in the 70's explained their return with personal reasons such as inability or unwillingness to adjust, illegal status, illness or accident, the *late* returnees of the 80's have been more affected by the structural factors pertinent to the receiving countries, as well as the concern with regard to the education and future of their children.

Table 2

Major Reason for Return in Bursa Survey 1986 (in Percent)

Unemployment in the receiving country	10.8
Xenophobia, hostile social climate	10.5
Collective decision of all family members	7.5
Nostalgia	8.9
Education and schooling of the children	23.0
Health and occupational illness	5.9
Setting up of personal business in Turkey	8.9
Return encouraging policies, acquisition of pension rights	4.3
Refuse of prolongation of work and/or permit	11.5
Total	100.0

Source: *Bursa Survey*, 1986, Table 32

The above cited reasons indicate that 38 percent is related to the host countries policies and attitudes affecting migrants. Analyzing the cited reasons further, it should not surprise that the education and schooling of children occupies such a relevant place (23 percent). The various difficulties faced by the second generation in Europe, in terms of achieving an upward mobility through the educational ladder and acquiring professional skills, are increasingly more understood by the parents, who themselves have created and lived in a kind of subculture, but do not want their children to remain in the enclave of the ghetto mentality or particularly, to belong to the working class.

The second relevant factor, unemployment, gains a different importance when measured with the time spend abroad, accordingly

a.   a prolonged stay abroad diminishes the impact of unemployment, whereas

b.   migrants with a short stay abroad or second generation migrants who want to enter the job market but not by exercising manual work, are more affected by unemployment. The younger generation especially has a very hard time when they are faced with the competition of indigenous teenagers.

The major reasons for returnees *for not wanting to re-enter* the labour market on a wage-earning contract basis are as follows:

a.   The determination to realize a change in social status;
b.   the image they will project on their peer groups;
c.   the acquisition of pension rights (at home or abroad) thus stepping outside of the job market;
d.   deteriorated health conditions due to hard working conditions abroad;
e.   high unemployment at home, low wages, insufficient accident - and professional illness - prevention and heavy working conditions in the home country;
f.   the unwillingness of women with work experience abroad to re-enter the job market due to family obligations and a discouraging social climate.

3.2.3   Re-Entering Industry at Home

The reasons for a group of *late* returnees to function as industrial workers in their home country is reflected in the Bursa survey as follows:

a.   Insufficient savings (34.3 percent)
b.   Failure in setting up an independent business (7.4 percent)
c.   Obligation to take up wage work (41 percent)
d.   Desire to make use of the acquired professional skills and experiences (5.2 percent)
e.   Desire to work (9.7 percent)

Comparing the age groups with occupational status, we see that the bulk of the self-employed remains with the 41 and over group, while re-entering industry is divided equally among the 31 to 40 and the 40 and over group.

For those desirous to re-enter Turkish industry, the questions, how long of a stay abroad contributed to the acquisition of new skills and did this group contribute to the general development of Turkey's economy, were answered as follows: 60.5 percent were not able to use their professional skills and experiences in Turkey; 64.2 percent of the returnees were employed in similar institutions as before their departure. This means that the skill drain in boom periods in Europe led to a high drain of the skilled labour force, which consequently has not been utilized in occupations other than their first occupation at home.

Table 3

Distribution of Returnees According to Age and Occupational Status (in Percent)

Distribution of age	Status: Worker	Self-employed	Retired or job seeking	Total
20 or less	0.3	0.3	0.3	1.0
21 – 30	8.9	4.6	4.3	17.7
31 – 40	14.4	7.2	2.9	24.6
41 – 50	15.4	18.0	9.5	43.0
50 and over	5.2	4.3	4.2	13.8
Total	44.3	34.4	21.3	100.0

Source: *Bursa Survey*, 1986, Table 40

An additional obstacle for re-entering into the Turkish industry lies in the weak structure of the governmental job-recruitment institutions. The Turkish Labour Office spent most of its efforts in placing unqualified job-seekers in state economic enterprises and did not establish connections with the private sector. Thus, only persons with determination, manifold connections and personal contacts have been able to find satisfactory employment on their own.

3.2.4   Self-Employed Returnees

Setting up an independent business has been a predominant choice for returnees at large. This tendency has been reinforced over the years due to the failure of the workers enterprises and the collapse of village development co-operatives (*Abadan-Unat*: 1986, p. 389). Particularly returnees with a long stay abroad and sufficient savings have adopted this alternative (34.3 percent). The size of these enterprises reveals their relatively limited impact in terms of creating new job opportunities.

Table 4

Channels of Job-Placement for Returnees

Turkish Labor Office	10.3%
Friends	28.1%
Personal efforts	40.7%
Personal relationship with employer	11.8%
Relative of employer	3.7%
Other	5.1%
Total	100.0%

Source: *Bursa Survey*, 1986, Table 58

These enterprises are concentrated in small industry; 21.4 percent are producing consumer items, 36.9 percent working with industrial part production; 7.7 percent investment commodities; the remaining 34.5 percent offer services. The major difficulties encountered by this group are as follows: obtaining credit 27.8 percent; securing a qualified labour force 27 percent; finding a suitable location 5.7 percent; primary material 4.8 percent; management 5.7 percent; marketing 12.5 percent; machine, equipment 2.8 percent; inflation 29.8 percent.

An interesting feature is the fact that almost two thirds of these enterprises have not applied for any credit (61.4 percent). This situation can be explained by the returnees' attitude of self-reliance and belief in being able to master the situation

without getting indebted. It also reflects a choice for labour-intensive projects and
actually serves as a symbol of upward mobility. There are also other reasons such
as a preference for small size, a negative attitude, actually a reticence for enlarging
the enterprise, lack of information about the market situation due to a prolonged
stay abroad and a lack of knowledge about the necessary amount of capital needed
for the building up of a lucrative business.

Table 5

Size of Enterprises Set Up by Returnees in Regard to Personnel

No employees	22.1%
1 - 3 "	40.3%
4 - 6 "	19.2%
7 - 10 "	11.5%
10 or more "	6.7%
Total	100%

Another important problem resides with the problem of the scarcity of qualified
labour. On the one hand, employers are unable to hire additional labour because the
potential workers are asking too-high wages (27.8 percent) or dislike the working
conditions (12 percent), on the other hand, qualified workers are not available (41.0
percent).

3.2.5   Job-Seeking Retired or Unemployed Returnees

The Bursa survey showed that within their sample about 10 percent were retired, 11
percent unemployed, both desirous to re-enter the job market. This group faced
great difficulties; 57 percent had been searching over one year for a suitable job,
17 percent for 7 to 12 months and 25 percent around 0 to 6 months. Only 30
percent would be willing to take an unskilled job, around 61 percent were looking
for a qualified job, preferably as a foreman. The most important obstacle for this
group lay in the fact that about 73 percent of all open job ads indicate a maximum
age of 35. Another relevant factor seems to be the tendency for joint ventures
founded with foreign capital, high technology and know-how, to recruit their
qualified labour force directly among migrants employed abroad. The interesting

point of this group of returnees, is that unlike the classical model of retirement, in which the persons are satisfied with a peaceful life chosen for their old age, these *late* comers, being too young for an inactive life style, are trying very hard to compete with their younger cohorts, while residing in a very fast developing urban setting. This group of persons, who have lived with great deprivations abroad in order to accumulate some savings and who find upon their return that they are not able to build up the imagined stressless existence they were hoping to achieve, represents the most disillusioned group.

4. Women Returnees

The majority of the literature dealing with women migrants has focussed on those female migrants leading the life of a housewife as well as those family members left behind (*Abadan-Unat:* 1984, pp. 111-131). Specific studies dealing with returned women migrants are just beginning to be undertaken. So far, an unpublished small survey carried out in two districts of the Turkish capital, Ankara, namely Demetevler and Yenimahalle, may shed some light on this topic. One of the distinctive characteristics of these women lies in the fact that over 80 percent of the returnees have selected the capital Ankara as their place of residence, a metropolitan city and often a city which was not their place of origin. This indicates that their families had specific reasons for selecting their new home. Indeed the major reasons of preference were the existence of a large number of relatives and friends, a more diversified job market and better educational opportunities for their children. About 68 percent of the respondents were under the age of 40, 86 percent were married, 52 percent had only completed primary school, 16 percent secondary school and 10 percent high school. The overwhelming majority of these women (90 percent) were unemployed housewives or students prior to their departure, had all been gainfully employed abroad, but only 4 percent had taken up a paid job following their return. The reasons for retiring from active work participation are health reasons (18.7 percent), no need to work (31 percent), dislike of work (18.7 percent), old-age retirement (2 percent) and childcare obligation (8.3 percent). The attitude toward work indicates that for the overwhelming majority of the women their stay abroad was seen as a transitional phase, comparable to a kind of compulsory military service, which enabled them to accumulate savings and permit them an ascendance in their social status.

Looking at the family structure of the respondents, 48 percent were living as a nuclear family prior to their departure, only 8 percent were members of an extended family. About 64 percent of these women went to the Federal Republic of Germany between 1967 and 1974, 32 percent, mostly second generation migrants, joined their family while staying abroad. In the Federal Republic of Germany 68 percent of these women were employed in industry, 28 percent in the service sector.

During their stay abroad these women led a rather isolated, segregated life. Their interest in regards to events happening in German society remained distant. Only 52 percent read Turkish newspapers, 34 percent watched TV programs. The mass consumption in regard to the media was that of Turkish video films, these programs were watched by 86.4 percent of the sample. The data indicates that in terms of developing ideas and values, the impact of mass media in the host society remained at an almost unnoticeable level, while reinforcement of the values of the home country continued to be infused in an uninterrupted way.

In regard to integration, 72 percent declared to have deliberately remained uninvolved with the German society. Among those who answered this question positively, fluency in speaking and reading German occupied the first place. Among the reasons given to explain the refusal to integrate into the host society, 35 percent indicated their unwillingness to change their habits and behavior, 54 percent confessed they had been unable to establish friendly relations with Germans and to accept the norms of German society. It seems relevant to emphasize that almost all respondents stressed the fact that all their efforts were directed to uphold their bonds to Turkish society and to resist efforts tending to 'Germanize' them. Yet the same group responded very positively on their experience abroad (90 percent); for 40 percent it was the opportunity to accumulate savings, for 51 percent it was the possibility to enlarge one's horizons, to get a new perspective on the world and new knowledge. The contradictory character of these answers can be explained by the anxiousness on behalf of these women not to give the impression that they had adopted lax and permissive heterosexual habits abroad, thus losing their reputation as faithful and devoted spouses and mothers.

In spite of the above cited contradicting responses and although the level of integration has remained at its low level, the impact of the migratory process seems to have created certain changes. Accordingly, 58 percent of the respondents want to share the decision-making process with their husbands, 62 percent are in favor of women working outside the home. Nevertheless, the traditional role model for women, namely, to be a mother and a homemaker, remains placed on a high pedestal. For 32 percent this status appears to be the primary way to achieve a full personality. Another dimension related to equality among spouses is reflected in the negative attitude of 94 percent about tolerating polygamy - a form of marriage outlawed in Turkey since 1926. Changing attitudes in regard to child education seems also to have taken root; 86 percent are in favor of asking the opinion of their children when intra-family matters are to be decided. The great value and importance attached to education is also reflected in an almost egalitarian preference for university education for boys (68 percent) and girls (66 percent).

In sum, it can be stated that the emancipatory impact of migration on women appears to be of limited scope, particularly in those cases where women joined their husbands later, remained under a strict marital control while abroad and did not re-enter the labour market upon return. Their position appears to be more conservative than those left behind wives of migrants, who during their long periods of separation acquired a certain degree of independence in conducting their own affairs.

The majority of the married migrant women who returned have shown no strong motivation to develop their abilities and make use of the new knowledge and experience acquired abroad. Although women are showing a determination to shed certain traditional attitudes, the prevailing social control forces them to repress these changing attitudes.

The most important change seems to have taken place within the relationship among spouses and the decision-making process. The strong demand for upward mobility appears to lie predominantly in the sphere of conspicuous consumption, displaying expensive furniture, and owning little- or seldom-used electrical equipment.

5. The Re-Integration of the Turkish Second Generation

With an increasing number of returning migrant families, the problem of a succesful insertion of Turkish migrant children who started their education abroad constitutes at present one of the most pressing problems in Turkey. The new type of '*Alamanyalı*' family, similar to traditional families living in rural or '*gecekondu*' (squatter-houses) environments, are adamantly determined to secure for their children the chance of upward mobility. This explains why these parents are less inclined to place their children in vocational schools as often encouraged in the Federal Republic of Germany, but prefer to take them back to Turkey, and enroll them in lycées, which assure the transfer into the universities, provided they are able to pass the entrance examinations. At present, the Turkish government has set aside three German and Turkish teaching lycées in Istanbul, one in Ankara and another in Izmir, in order to grant a preferential treatment for the enrollment of children of returning migrants. The scarcity of Turkish teachers being able to teach in German has led to a bilateral agreement according to which the German government provided 90 German teachers, paid by German authorities, to teach in these schools and thus enabling the students to preserve and develop their acquired linguistic capacities. It is not an exaggeration to say that in the near future the graduates of these lycées, and those graduates who pursue higher education will be sought after by joint ventures established with German capital. Tourism establishments in Turkey dealing predominantly with foreigners will no doubt grant these youngsters better opportunities than establishments in the Federal Republic of Germany, where the demands of the German school system are very high, hard to satisfy and where the competition with young Germans is very tough.

Turkish parents are particularly aware that unless they return to their home country, the future of their children lies nowhere else than in vocational work-this being the best solution since the majority of Turkish teenagers leave comprehensive schools abroad without a diploma (62 percent). This awareness induces them either to return collectively or to opt for a fragmented family. A significant group of Turkish parents want to compensate for all of the frustrations and deprivations they have experienced abroad by preparing a better life for their children, a life which is not that of an industrial worker.

Yet, the choice for a split return - mother and children in school age going back home, father and adult children remaining abroad - gives way to a number of new problems. The socialization process which started in Europe creates a noticeable cultural distance between parents and children, paired with a clash of values. Young migrants, who share the identity crisis of youth as a whole and the difficulties in communicating with adults, also suffer very often from a state of malaise created by the ambivalent relationship between the culture of their country of origin and their host country's culture. This relationship sometimes takes the form of cultural conflict due to the host country's attempts at passive assimilation and the active resistance on the part of the immigrant families, whose attachment to the culture of origin is often somewhat ritualistic.

One of the most frequent subjects of generational conflict is related to the relationship between the sexes and its evaluation. While according to Western standards teenagers have a right to establish close friendships, meet each other and spend vacations together, the traditional Turkish families, faithful to the social context of Islamic values related to chastity, attempt to exercise harsh control over all types of relationships, including even the breaking off of correspondence. This situation becomes even more dramatic when traditional families forge prearranged marriages resulting in the dropping-out of gifted young girls from school. After their return, they are bound to lead a very frustrated existence.

This firm parental control frustrates the second generation very much. In school, these teenage returnees feel isolated. They have a greater degree of self-confidence compared to their peers, they dress differently and the dominant feature of their character is imbued with strong individualism. Because of their distinct otherness they build networks among themselves. Their choice in regard to literature and music also differs. It is not exaggerated to state that growing up 'between two cultures' demands from the second generation greater sacrifices than it had from their parents. They are forced to internalize a partly unknown set of norms and value systems. In addition they have to familiarize themselves with new subject matters in school - history, geography, religion. Youngsters are accomplishing this process of integration in two opposed ways: either in the form of high adjustment based on strong identification with the Turkish nation or in the form of a simulated conformism paired with a rejection of the values of the home country. In the second case, the stay abroad is only positively looked upon and mostly idealized. In school, second generation returnees - unless they have been able to achieve a succesful entrance in mainstream Turkish society - have an extremely high desire to return to Europe.

6. Governmental Policies for Returned Migrants

Although Turkish politicians and administrators are repeatedly advising their compatriots to maintin strong effective ties with the home country while keeping their present jobs abroad, a series of measures for re-integration has been put into action over the years. The major facilitation migrant resettlement measures are:

- lower custom duties and facilities for the import of household goods and imports of equipment for resettlement,

- support and bailing out of workers enterprises, created by the migrants with the purpose of preparing work places for them upon their return,

- fiscal and monetary incentives to invest in the country: sale of bond shares in privatized state economic enterprises or public institutions such as toll bridges and roads, accounts in foreign currencies, transferable interest-bearing accounts,

- better material and family environment: housing aid, special credits in the buying of second homes in vacation areas, easier entrance in housing cooperatives, recognition of diplomas, creation of bilingual classes in schools giving priority admission to returning migrant children, facilitated re-admission of migrant children in normal schools.

Among the above cited measures the most comonly applied are:

a. the utilization of accounts in foreign currency in Turkish banks, as interest rates in home country banks are almost double in comparison to European rates,

b. acquisition of flats and summer houses built through governmental credit, to be bought in foreign currency.

According to a recent survey, 38.9 percent of returned migrants have foreign exchange deposit accounts with the Turkish Central Bank, another 42.9 percent have similar accounts in other Turkish banks. 85.2 percent have bought real estate such as houses and plots of land (*Central Bank Survey:* 1986, p. 5). The impact of this extensive wave of real estate investment has had a direct effect on rents which escalated very fast parallel to Turkey's undiminished rate of inflation in recent years. Thus the investment pattern of migrants can be looked upon as positive in regard to boosting construction industry, while negative in regard to the raise of average rents and house prices.

7.   Political Behavior of Returning Migrants

This is a vast topic, to broad to be discussed in this paper in detail. Nevertheless, it should be underlined that residency abroad encourages a foreign worker's political expression to be oblique and unorthodox. Unless they naturalize, migrant workers remain at least formal members of their native political systems. In the web of governmental and social institutions from the mother country and those native political, cultural and social practices that accompany foreign labour migration, is to be found a fertile environment nourishing continued migrant political identification with the mother country and interest in political affairs there.
Sociological studies of migrant workers have indicated that migrant workers interact frequently with compatriots, thereby encouraging continued identification with their native country. The language barrier is another factor encouraging their interaction. The maintenance of identification with the native land lies in the creation of overlapping social, cultural and economic microcosmos of their native country. Their major reference points continue to be friends, the cuisine, culture, and associations from their native country and political development there (*M. J. Miller:* 1981, p. 43).

The great majority of returned Turks formerly living in the Federal Republic of Germany were subject to a deliberate policy of depoliticisation. So far, only Sweden, in 1975, and the Netherlands, three years ago, have granted foreigners the right to vote in communal elections. This explains why over time a significant number of Turkish migrants became involved with Turkish associations in the Federal Republic of Germany, which at the beginning served as surrogate trade unions, but later acquired clear cut political colors. These associations started to recruit members from cities and towns with a large Turkish concentration and became satellites of extremist rightist and leftist, and fanatically religious political parties in the home country. Thus, on the one side the fascist-leaning National Action Party, on the other side the ultra-conservative pro-Islamic National Salvation Party (today represented by the Welfare Party) did establish sections and private schools in the Federal Republic of Germany. While the branches of the rightist party were eventually dissolved, the schools remained. To what degree these small parties - at present not represented in parliament - as well as the government and major opposition parties in Turkey continue to cultivate special links with returned migrants has not been assessed. Observations may lead to the conclusion that for the majority of returning migrants the present government party, ANAP (Motherland Party) which promotes a liberal, market-oriented program and strongly defends the merits of entrepreneurship, meets their political aspirations. Returning migrants living in a rather scattered way in Turkey's urban and rural settings, have so far not organized themselves into some kind of pressure group. Their existence passes unnoticed during electoral campaigns at home - the real target for political parties is the financial and moral support of the migrant groups abroad in view of influencing the left behind family members. Turkish citizens residing six months and longer abroad have been given the right to vote at any border crossing since November 1987. The political participation of this group has been very low - a total of 49,800 cast votes - although six weeks prior to the general election voting booths were set up at all airport entries and frontier gates.

8.   Re-emigration and Turkish Public Opinion

Return migration does not occupy a central place in Turkish public opinion. This attitude might be partly explained by the fact that returned migrants are usually better off and more highly regarded in the community than their compatriots who have remained at home. The majority of average Turkish citizens believes problems related to return should be solved on an individual level by rapid and unquestioning adjustment. Given the urgent priorities of the needs of Turkey's population, special privileges accorded to returnees seem to be out of place. A survey carried out in 1985 on behalf of the Friedrich-Ebert-Foundation by SIAR involving 528 returnees indicates that this opinion is also shared by the migrants themselves. 77 percent of the respondents felt that all the problems which had emerged since their return could be handled personally. 73 percent of the respondents thought that a major part of these problems stemmed from the negative attitude displayed by their direct environment. 61 percent believe that all problems related to reintegration can be solved in the long run, 26 percent consider these problems as unsolvable (PIAR/SIAR, 1985).

9.   Informal Networks Abroad: Their Impact on the Home Entry

The rural, family-centered, regional or religious socialization expresses itself through informal social networks and keeps up the migratory chain, particularly through matrimonial bonds. Turks of the Black Sea region or Kurdish, Arcassian origin marry exclusively within their own group. They do not permit their daughters to marry outside of their own group. The practice of endogamy is still the prevailing custom.

Thus, the participation in chain migration, by reconstructing a part of the family network abroad, keeps the migrant and his family in a close interaction with the country of origin. This enables the village community, although geographically distant, to exercise a certain degree, of remote social control on its members abroad and reinforces ethnicity ties (*Wilpert* and *Gitmez:* 1987, p. 181).

Summing Up

Turkish migration has no doubt led to the emergence of a new social stratum. Those living in Europe, regardless of their place of employment, are called *alamanyalı* ("those from Germany"). Those who migrated to Middle Eastern countries are labelled *migrating citizens*. Both types are rooted in two countries. Predominantly employed in Europe, they tend to behave as a privileged group at home. Their preference to live from rental income or small business produces a type one might call *the proletarian bourgeois*.

Returned migrants feel relatively secure due to their savings, purchasing power, life experience and pension. Their attitude toward the state, meaning the bureaucratic apparatus of various kinds, has changed. Instead of considering themselves subjects, they have learned abroad to become citizens. Although many of them were treated in a discriminatory way abroad, reduced to second class citizenship, they learned to insist on their rights and ask for fair treatment. This feeling of self-reliance becomes much more evident once they have returned to the home country, where lack of attention on behalf of public services quickly becomes a topic of grievance. Bitter experiences abroad have produced more-demanding citizens upon return.

The return process of the 60's and 70's represents rather a return of failure or conservatism, comprising legal or illegal migrants who failed to adjust to the highly industrialized world they entered. This first wave of returnees, unable to realize their primary aim, have mostly returned to the rural areas from which they came. Life since is slightly different from what it used to be before they left. The return movement of the 80's however represents both return for retirement and return of innovation. It also means a much better way of re-entering into Turkey's main-stream society. For a significant number of returnees who spent 15 or more years abroad, return means the beginning of the last stage of their life in more comfort and security than they ever possessed. For those who still feel themselves suf-ficiently vigorous, full of enterprising spirit and physically able, returning home means a new challenge, which might yield success and high prestige.

Assumptions which were strongly asserted at the beginning of the migratory process, such as migration will serve to train skilled industrial manpower, appears to be partly valid in regions with fast industrialization. However, a lack of foresight, adequate planning and efficient organization has led to a substantial waste of human and financial resources mainly triggered by local patriotism. The great willingness of Turkish migrants to contribute with their savings to the development of their own country in form of workers enterprises and village development co-operatives has not been sufficiently supported. Thus, direct benefits of their return accrues more in metropolitan areas and so far has created only a limited positive impact in rural areas.

The second generation returnees, who in many cases were forced to comply with the decision of their parents, represents the group facing the greatest amount of difficulties of readjustment. Most of them are confronted with a dilemma in terms of their cultural identity. The self-imposed isolation from the culture and even more, from the host country which they adopted created a counter-culture for those who were born and who grew up abroad and were socialized in the dominant culture. Their return implies such frustration and disillusionment, nevertheless for many it represents a less stressful, sometimes even superior entrance to higher education institutions. For those who are able to pass the hurdles of admission to the university, the input of their linguistic skills paired with a determination to excel might in the near future produce some key elements within the elites of tomorrow.

The first and second generation of *alamanyalı* represent a new generation in Turkey, those who dared to look for a future outside the national boundaries. Even if some of the returnees of today want to retain traditional values and customs and thus re-import the ethnic boundaries they have self-imposed during their stay abroad, a significant part represents a new synthesis. In this capacity they are exercising an increasingly, felt permanent impact on Turkey's economic life and political choices.

Note

1) Paper presented at the conference of the "International Migration of Middle Easterners and North Africans: Comparative Perspectives", May 19-21, 1988. Von-Grunebaum-Center for Near Eastern Studies, UCLA.

Literature

Abadan, Nermin: 1964, Bati Almanya'daki Türk iscileri ve Sorunlari (Turkish workers in the Federal Republic of Germany and their problems). State Planning Organization. Ankara.

Abadan-Unat, Nermin: 1971, La Récession de 1966/67 en Allemagne Fédérale et ses répercussions sur les ouvriers turcs, in: The Turkish Yearbook of International Relations, S. 39-61.

Abadan-Unat, Nermin: 1972, Le non-retour à l'industrie, trait dominant de la chaine migratoire turque, in: Sociologie de Travail 3, Special Edition: Les Travailleurs immigés, S. 278-293.

Abadan-Unat, Nermin: 1974, Turkish external migration and social mobility, in: Benedict, P./Tümertekin, E./Mansur, F. (Hg.), Turkey. Geographic and social perspectives. Leiden, S. 362-402.

Abadan-Unat, Nermin: 1975, Educational Problems of Turkish Migrants' Children, in: International Review of Education XXI/3, S. 311-322.

Abadan-Unat, Nermin: 1976a, Turkish Migration to Europe and the Middle East: Its Impact on Social Structure and Social Legislation, in: Michalak, L. O./Salacuse, J. W. (Hg.), Social Legislation in the Contemporary Middle East IIS. University of California, Berkeley, S. 325-369.

Abadan-Unat, Nermin: 1976b, Turkish Migration to Europe, 1960-1975. A Balance Sheet of Achievements and Failures, in: dies. (Hg.), Turkish Workers in Europe, 1960-1975. A Socio-Economic Reappraisal. Leiden, S. 1-44.

Abadan-Unat, Nermin: 1977, Implications of migration on emancipation and pseu-do-emancipation of Turkish women, in: International Migration Review 11, S. 31-57.

Abadan-Unat, Nermin: 1979, Die politischen Auswirkungen der türkischen Migration im In- und Ausland, in: Orient 20, S. 17ff.

Abadan-Unat, Nermin: 1981, Social Change and Turkish Women, in: dies/u.a. (Hg.), Women in Turkish Society. Social, Economic and Political Studies of the Middle East XXX. Leiden, S. 5-31.

Abadan-Unat, Nermin: 1982, The Effect of International Labor Migration in Women's Role. The Turkish Case, in: Kagitcibasi, C. (Hg.), Sex Roles: Family and Community in Turkey. Bloomington, S. 207-234.

Abadan-Unat, Nermin: 1984, International Labor Migration and its Effect upon Women's Occupational and Family Roles: A Turkish View, in: UNESCO (Hg.), Women on the Move: Contemporary Changes in Family and Society, S. 133-158.

Abadan-Unat, Nermin/Keles, R./Penninx, R./Renselaar, H. van/Velzen, L. van/Yeni-sey, L.: 1976, Migration and Development. A Study of the Effects of International Labor Migration on Bogazliyan District. Den Haag.

Abadan-Unat, Nermin/Ünsal, A.: 1976, Migration through the Eyes of Political Parties, Trade Unions, Employers' Associations and Bureaucracy, in: Abadan-Unat, N./et al. (Hg.), Migration and Development, A Study of the Effects of International Labor Migration on Bogazliyan District. Ankara, S. 43-99.

Akcali, N./Genc, M. (Hg.): 1967, Bursa Survey. Unpublished report. Bursa.

Böhning, W. R.: 1984, ohne Titel, in: Studies in International Migration. London, S. 123-162.

Central Bank of the Turkish Republic: 1986, Saving tendencies of Turkish citizens working in Western Germany and on those already returned home permanently. Ankara.

Cerase, Francesco P.: 1974, Migration and Social Change. Expectations and Reality. A Case Study of Return Migration from the United States to Southern Italy, in: International Migration Review 8/2, S. 245-262.

Gitmez, A. S.: 1983, Yurt disina isci göcü ve geri dönüsler (External and Return Migration). Istanbul.

Güven, S. H.: 1986, Yurda dönen iscilerin mesleki uyumlari (Occupational adjustment of returning migrants), in: Akcayli, N. (Hg.), Ikinci Kusak Türklerin Mesleki uyumlari. Bursa, S. 87-103.

Kayser, B.: 1972, Cyclically-determined homeward flows of migrant workers. OECD. Paris.

Miller, M. J.: 1981, Foreign Workers in Western Europe. An Emerging Political Force. New York.

OECD (Hg.): 1981ff., SOPEMI. Continous reporting system on migraton. Paris.

Penninx, R.: 1982, A Critical Review of Theory and Practice. The Case of Turkey, in: International Migration Review 16/4, S. 7ff.

Rogers, T. W.: 1969, Migration Prediction on the Basis of Prior Migratory Behavior: A Methodological note, in: International Migration 7, S. 13-22.

Seccombe, I. J./Lawless, R. I.: 1986, Between Western Europe and the Middle East: Changing Patterns of Turkish Labor Migration, in: Revue Europeenne des Migrations Internationales 2/1, S. 37-41.

Simon, G.: 1987, Migration in Southern Europe: An Overview, in: OECD (Hg.), The Future of Migration. Paris, S. 258-291.

State Planning Organzisation (Hg.): 1974, The S.P.O. Survey of 1971 of Migrant Workers who had returned to Turkey. Ankara.

Tuna, O.: 1967, Yurda Dönen Iscilerin Intibaki Sorunlari (An inquiry onto the reintegration of workers who have returned from abroad). State Planning Organizsation.

Widgren, J.: 1987, International Migration - New Challenges to Europe, in: Council of Europe (Hg.), Migrants in Western Europe: present situation and future prospects. Straßbourg, S. 1-43.

Wilpert, C./Gitmez, A.: 1987, La microsociété des Turcs à Berlin, in: Revue Européenne des Migrations Internationales 3/1-2, S. 178-196.

Yasa, I.: 1979, Yurda Dönen Isciler ve Toplumsal Degisme (Returning migrants and social change). Ankara.

Nermin Abadan-Unat
Ankara University
Visiting Professor
at UCLA 1988

Part VI
Migration and Social Structure

[11]

Migration and Social Structure: Analytic Issues and Comparative Perspectives In Developing Nations

Calvin Goldscheider
Brown University

There are profound relationships between migration and social structure, reflecting the varieties of migration types, the complexities of social structure, and the reciprocal ways migration and social structure are interrelated over time, in different societies, for different communities and social groups. Almost every thread of social structure may be linked to migration patterns at macro- and micro-levels of analysis, cross-sectionally and longitudinally, with variation over the life cycle, connections to levels of socioeconomic development, and relationships to social class and subject to political control. This paper focuses on several propositions that identify and illustrate the complexities of these linkages in developing nations and suggests some of the ways in which our understanding of social structure enhances the analysis of migration processes and vice versa.[*]

Whereas in the historical experience of Western nations, migration has been associated with industrialization and economic development, concern has been expressed that migration to the cities of Third World countries results from the "pushes" of rapid population growth and economic stagnation in rural areas. Far from being associated with economic growth and development in the Third World, it has been suggested that migration there causes poverty and unemployment in urban places. Moreover, it is often argued that out-migration from rural areas of developing nations exacerbates the population growth of cities in distinctive ways compared to the past patterns in industrialized countries. In the European past, the net flow of rural migration was to cities where the natural increase of population was low or negative; currently in developing countries, rural migration is to cities already growing in

[*] This paper builds on ongoing research being carried out at the Population Studies and Training Center, Brown University. Some of the detailed findings are presented in Goldscheider, 1983a, 1984a, 1984b. Comments on earlier versions of this paper by Frances K. Goldscheider and Sidney Goldstein, Brown University, and two anonymous reviewers are gratefully acknowledged.

Migration and Social Structure

population size from the excess of birth over death rates—cities with high levels of natural increase.

This assessment of the negatives and problems associated with rural out-migration in less developed nations has led the majority of governments there during the last decade to express increasing concern over issues of population distribution. Many have considered policies to stem the flow of rural persons to urban places and have attempted to control such movements directly, through the imposition of migration restrictions on new permanent urban residence, or indirectly, through proposed investments in rural development (cf. Findley, 1987).

The concern over the problems of rural-urban migration in developing countries and the proposed policies to limit this migration are not fully justified by the conclusions of social science research. In particular, an examination of three central issues linking migration and social structure illustrates the need to reconsider the oversimplified conclusion associating rural-urban migration with negative features of socioeconomic development in both the cities and rural areas of developing nations. These issues may be phrased generally as questions: (1) What are the relationships between migration and other demographic processes, and how are these relationships linked to changes in the social structure? (2) What have been the social and economic adjustments of migrants in the cities of developing nations? (3) What are the conditions generating rural out-migration? Are there alternatives to viewing migration in the context of rural pushes on individuals who calculate the costs, benefits, and risks of their moves relative to their mobility aspirations? A consideration of the research on each of these issues raises a series of questions about the complex linkages between migration and social structure in developing countries and suggests, in turn, methodological and theoretical strategies for new research questions. Where appropriate we shall emphasize some of the commonalities rather than differences among Third World countries. Our focus is on these developing nations but we should also note that there are many parallels emerging from research on more developed countries. After considering each of these sets of issues, we conclude with selected methodological considerations in the sociological analysis of migration.

MIGRATION AND DEMOGRAPHIC CHANGE

On the surface, the relationship between migration and population processes in the urban and rural sectors of developing countries seems straightforward: People move out of rural areas to the cities and contribute to the population growth of those places of destination by their numbers and by the concentration of migrants in the age categories most associated with family formation and reproduction. Since population continues to grow rapidly in the rural areas of these countries, this urbanward movement does not relieve pressures of population on rural resources. An examination of several short- and long-term complexities in the relationship between migration and demographic processes, however, challenges this oversimplified view.

Demographic Effects Through Population Size and Composition

Migration has a direct impact on the population size of areas of origin and destination and hence is indirectly linked to social structure. Economic production, consumption patterns, labor markets, household and family networks, political power and authority structures, and other social, economic, and political aspects of society that are linked to population size will all be affected by migration.

These indirect demographic linkages are complicated by the selectivity of migration (by age, sex, marital status, for example) and the relationships between these sociodemographic characteristics and the social organization of places of origin and destination. Thus, for example, to the extent that migration is selective of young adults (and it usually is), not only the population size but also the age structures of places of origin and destination may change dramatically. Such changes in population composition have further effects on population growth and therefore on social organization. Thus, migration is linked to social structure through its effects on both the changing size and the composition of populations and through the fundamental relationships between demographic size-composition and social structure.

Demographic Behavioral Responses to Migration

The demographic effects of migration we have just noted are "mechanical," that is, they do not require changes in motivation, norms, or values in order to result in significant shifts in social structure. In contrast, there are demographic connections that are behavioral, involving choices and goals. One major context is to treat these behavioral connections within the theory of "multiphasic responses" and its extensions (Davis, 1963; Friedlander, 1969, 1983; Mosher, 1980a, 1980b; Zelinsky, 1983). In broad outline, the argument is that in the process of the transition to low and controlled population growth, populations respond in a variety of ways and with every means to population pressure and relative socioeconomic deprivation. These multiphasic responses include the range of intermediate variables (or proximate determinants) determining control over marital fertility (e.g., contraceptive usage and abortion) as well as delayed marriage and celibacy. They also include internal and external migrations. Multiphasic demographic response theory is a modified Malthusian framework that treats migration, in addition to

Migration and Social Structure

the "checks" of fertility and mortality control, as one potential population response to the pressures on the economic well-being of families—pressures often brought about by population growth through rapid and sustained mortality reduction. Internal and international movements reduce the pressures of population growth by transferring people out of places, just as the decline in fertility reduces population growth rates by reducing natural increase. In rural areas, migration responds to the combined pushes of population growth and diminishing economic opportunity. Movement out of rural places provides an outlet for "excess" natural increase and fits "the interests and structure for peasant families in the evolving economy" (Davis, 1963:355).

In the original formulation of this theory, rural out-migration was treated only as one of the multiple responses of the rural population in industrializing nations. Migration may, however, be viewed as a substitute or a delay mechanism for fertility reduction or for alternative demographic or non-demographic responses (Friedlander, 1969, 1983). In this extension and elaboration of the argument, migration is treated as a safety valve relieving population pressure and thereby resulting in a delay of fertility change.

This pattern is not the result of compositional effects or the selectivity of migration; it is not the result of social structural changes as migrants are exposed to new social situations in places of destination. Rather, migration is a behavioral response, a relief from population pressure. When the rates of migration are relatively high and when the movement is permanent, the fertility level of the residual rural population is likely to remain high. Research in various developing nations and historical illustrations demonstrate the utility of this approach as a theoretical map in studying demographic transitions (Mosher, 1980a, 1980b; Friedlander, 1983).

Migration as a Vehicle of Diffusion

Migration may be linked to social structural changes through the diffusion of new ideas, attitudes, and behavior. Migration may be viewed as a vehicle or mechanism of moving "traditional" people into contact with "modernity." When the focus is on the urban area, the issues tend to be these: How "traditional" are rural in-migrants to the city and how "modern" are city residents? Migration tends to select those with particular socioeconomic characteristics, often the least traditional segment of the population in places of origin. When this is the case, we ask, Does this selectivity facilitate the integration of migrants in new places? How much residential contact and occupational interaction actually occur between migrants and urban natives? What are the social, economic, and cultural mechanisms that link migration to social changes through exposure of migrants to modern urban places? Does this dif-

fusion process result in changed fertility of the migrants as they integrate into the cities?

These questions revolve around when the nonurban population
will become urbanlike in behavior and characteristics. A broader set of
questions can extend these issues to include the diffusion of modernity
to rural areas through rural out-migration. Return migration to rural areas,
like migrations that are temporary and seasonal, may lead to the direct
diffusion of urban patterns to the rural population at places of origin.
Other more direct effects are brought about through remittances from
migrants to places of origin, visits to places of origin, urban visits of
rural friends and kinspeople, and other forms of communication linking
the social and economic structure of places of origin and destination.
The transferal of goods and money from out-migrants back to rural areas
may change the standard of living and the consumption aspirations of
the households from which persons migrated. Changes may also result
from the flow of information about social, economic, and educational
opportunities in places of destination and of "modern" ideas about consumption, production, values, and family loyalty. Still more changes may
occur through alterations in the control kinship network exercises over
economic resources and over the status of family members.

Unlike the effects of migration on social structure through demographic size and composition changes, these linkages of migration
and social change are not mechanical or automatic. The process of diffusion may change over time for different units (individuals, households,
communities) and may operate through kinship-ethnic-occupational
networks. It is also clear that diffusion is not the same for all types of
migration. The effects are more powerful when the migration is to primate cities from rural areas; moves to centers of social and economic
development contrast with moves to urban or rural places where social,
economic, and cultural changes have been less extensive. When migration is linked to other demographic changes by way of diffusion processes, the longer-term impact on population change will be different
than when the linkages between migration and population processes are
mechanical and demographic.

Uprooting and Social Organizational Linkages

Another sociologically grounded framework for examining the
linkages between migration and social structure focuses on the relationship between migration, on the one hand, and structural differentiation and the changing opportunity structure, on the other. Moving
out of a rural area may directly involve a break with kinship dominance
over economic resources and with the control the family exercises over
the status of its members. The nature and extent of the potential break

Migration and Social Structure

with kin and community depend on the type, permanence, and distance of the migration and on the whole complex of ties migrants retain with their family and place of origin. Whatever the form of these ties, however, migration alters in one way or another the control exercised by the family over resources and status. Over time, these changed systems of control generate the likelihood of additional migration.

In this context, changes in the family and fertility of persons not migrating may result from the migration of others. The impact of migration is not solely on places (of origin and destination), on the migrants themselves, and on people in places of destination. Migration may also have a profound impact on the *nonmigrants* at places of origin. This impact may be on the community at large; migration may affect population size, family and political patterns, intergenerational relationships, and economic activities. There is another set of migration consequences that is more subtle; it involves the impact of migration on members of the household who do not move. Migration may involve changes in the economic and other social roles associated with family members, changes in the broader kin control over resources, and changes in the status and the role of persons in the broader kinship-community network. The movement of select members of households may increase the income disparities among household members, even when resources flow from the migrant back to the household. When migration alters the exercise of control over resources, migration may contribute to the process of structural differentiation. In turn, the processes of structural differentiation (in this example, the separation of economic control from family dominance) and inequalities within kinship groups tend to be associated with changes in patterns of reproduction.

In pointing to the potential relationship between migration and developmental processes that are associated with uprooting and differentiation, this framework does not imply that kinship groups do not facilitate migration or that all kinship bonds are ruptured in the migration process. Kinship groups clearly play an important role in the migration of selected household members and often assist in the integration of migrants in places of destination (Hugo, 1981; Goldscheider, 1984b). There is substantial evidence identifying the extensive and continuous ties between migrants and their place of origin (Findley, 1977, 1982; Simmons et al., 1977; Goldstein and Goldstein, 1981). These continuing linkages and bonds to places of origin should not be misinterpreted, however, to imply that kinship dominance and control remain unchanged.

Migration may free individuals from some of the constraints and obligations of traditional rural social structure and from the ascriptive role of place and family of birth. This process may characterize long-term, permanent movers more than seasonal and local migrants. However, even return migrants to rural areas do not easily fit back into the social, economic, and political structures of their places of origin.

These different emphases and frameworks suggest alternative views of the migration-social structure relationship. The compositional effects of migration on social structure, for example, are indeterminate in terms of the predicted direction of change, since those effects depend on specific forms of selectivity. Diffusion and the uprooting effects of migration are likely to result in changes in family relationships, kinship control, and social and economic changes within the rural community. In contrast, the demographic behavioral framework hypothesizes that migration will relieve population pressure and reduce the likelihood of changing family and fertility patterns in rural areas. Thus, these frameworks vary in their predictions about the impact of migration on social change and provide interesting challenges for research to specify the conditions under which the various outcomes are more likely to emerge.

The social changes these frameworks associate with migration are hardly ever national. They are sometimes regional but are most striking at the community level or for particular subgroups within communities. These subgroups may be defined differently for each community along class (e.g., farmers, owners, the landless, service workers) or ethnic-racial-tribal lines. These more homogeneous units need to be examined to disentangle the contexts under which migration and changes in the social structure are linked.

Emerging clearly from these considerations is the conclusion that the links between migration and population processes operate directly in a demographic context and in more complex and indirect ways through the relationships between migration and social structure. Most importantly, the available evidence linking migration and demographic change does not point unequivocally to the negative demographic consequences of migration for the population growth of less developed nations or to the urban sectors within these countries. In some cases, and under some conditions, rural out-migration may have a long term positive impact on the reduction of population growth rates.

THE ADJUSTMENT OF MIGRANTS IN URBAN PLACES

A second set of issues relates to the association of migration with high rates of urban unemployment and poverty. Often, because of the impact of migrants on urban population but also because of the lack of social and economic adjustment of migrants, migration is described as hindering the economic development of cities in Third World countries. It has been argued that the movement of unskilled, uneducated rural workers who cannot be accommodated in the available housing and who work largely in the informal sectors of the urban economy may

Migration and Social Structure

also have negative economic effects on the native urban population. Since cities cannot provide jobs and housing for the excess rural population, continuous migration to the city from the countryside, it is argued, may be counterproductive, economically and socially.

Research on migrant adjustment in developing countries has been carried out in recent years in several cities, mostly in the largest urban centers. The primary question of these studies has been this: How do migrants in urban places adjust to their new place of residence? Most of this research focuses on economic and housing adjustments; some have included measures associated with social and social-psychological aspects of adjustment. We highlight some of the research findings for Seoul, Korea; Surabaya and Semerang, Indonesia; Teheran, Iran; and Bogota, Colombia. (Four of these studies have been included in Goldscheider, 1983a; on Semerang, Indonesia, see Lerman, 1987.) These studies qualify the oversimplified view that migrants to urban places of developing countries are not integrated economically or socially.

At one level, the relationship between migration and economic opportunities is simple and straightforward. Job searches and better employment possibilities are among the basic reasons for migration from rural to urban areas. Several migration models posit that the relative absence of employment possibilities in places of origin and the greater job opportunities in places of destination are the most important factors in understanding migration patterns. Whatever other factors are involved in the analysis of migration, the economic motive looms very large.

At the macro level as well, ruban-urban migration is connected to economic expansion and opportunities. Particular sectors of the economy within large cities draw on the supply of rural surplus labor. Migration thus becomes one mechanism for national economic integration. The relative supply of labor in areas of origin and the relative demand for labor in places of destination link economic opportunities and migration rates. In turn, intergenerational and intragenerational occupational mobility become the pivot around which migration and economic development revolve.

And yet, migration to large cities of developing nations has in the policy literature been more often linked to the push of rural economic stagnation than to the pull of urban opportunities. It has been associated with unemployment, underemployment, and poverty in the city. If economic competition between migrants and urban natives results in depressed wage levels and high rates of urban unemployment, if few jobs are available and competition for these jobs is fierce, why do rural persons continue to move to cities in search of jobs and opportunities? The reconciliation of this paradox lies in several directions. Although jobs may be scarce in urban places, there are fewer in places of origin, or at least fewer with the relative economic potential of those in urban places. Moreover, people may move to cities not because of actual job opportunities but for *potential* employment; hence, the issue becomes one of relative opportunities and of aspirations for jobs, not the job market per se (Todaro, 1976). These aspirations may be not only for the sake of the migrants themselves but for their families and particularly their children. In addition, migration is selective of the more skilled and the highly motivated; these migrants do well in the urban labor market in competition with others for scarce resources. Often they become self-employed, working in the tertiary sector of traditional segmented labor markets. Then, indeed, not all migrants find employment and hence are either unemployed in the cities or return to places of origin.

Some evidence has been organized to document these various alternatives in different countries and contexts. A recent study of Semerang, Indonesia (Lerman, 1987) concluded that while many of the migrants in this city cluster in informal sector occupations, most have attained white-collar or skilled blue-collar positions. Despite some evidence that a dual labor market has emerged there, the evidence points unmistakably to the role of education as the most important factor determining occupational attainment in both the formal and informal sectors, among migrants and those born in the city.

Similar findings characterize other urban locations in the Third World. Few employment differences emerge between migrants and the native urbanites in Seoul, Surabaya, Teheran, and Bogota in the late 1970s, after background characteristics such as education are taken into account and after migrants have spent several years in the city. An examination of the concentration of migrants and lifetime urban residents in various economic sectors reveals that migrants tend toward the traditional sectors of the economy, e.g., self-employed traders and street vendors. Recent migrants have lower employment levels in more productive enterprises because of their socioeconomic backgrounds, particularly their low levels of education. But neither recency of migration nor movement per se accounts for the relative concentration of migrants in particular sectors of the economy. Rather, educational background and skill level are the critical factors.

Thus there appears to be no structural feature that inhibits migrants from participating in the urban occupational system relative to their skill level and after a short settling-in period. The quality and extent of contact with the modern sector that usually, but not always, occur in the city and rarely within rural areas are the keys to understanding this process, not mere residence in urban places. This contact is probably more significant for those who remain in the city and less

Migration and Social Structure

significant for those who return to their rural areas after a short urban stay.

Migration and employment are, therefore, intertwined in complex ways with the fundamentals of social organization and economic development. The evidence appears to point to unexpectedly high levels of migrant employment in urban places and to an association between geographic and occupational mobility. These findings at the individual level point to the economic benefits of migration for the migrants. The data suggest further that migrants push some of the lifetime urban residents toward greater upward mobility. It is not clear from the evidence whether these relationships hold at the community or regional levels.

Migration is also associated with housing demands and migrants are often located within poor housing or in areas of conspicuous housing problems. Clearly, acquiring housing in new places takes time as job, income availability and cost of housing interact in complex ways.

Often migrants are concentrated in particular areas of a city, forming alliances with family friends who preceded them. These initial contacts assist the newcomer in finding housing and getting a job. The impression is often conveyed that migrants primarily live in the sections of the city that are poor and unhealthy, reflecting the chaos of rapid, unregulated urban growth. Is the poverty of cities the consequence of urban growth or of migration? Evidence from the urban surveys in less developed nations suggests that many of the features of thse poverty areas are not the simple or direct results of migration. While some migrants are concentrated in these poor areas, patterns of concentration tend to be for short periods of time, in the early stages of urban adjustment. Most importantly, migrants are disadvantaged in this way because they are poor; they along with the poor long-term residents of cities occupy inadequate, substandard housing. It is the broader sources of poverty, not the factors of migration, that need to be addressed in the housing issues of Third World nations (see Linn, 1984).

One overall conclusion from these studies of migrant adjustment in urban places is that migrants (at least those that remain in the urban area) are not conspicuously disadvantaged relative to the urban population, except for the initial period subsequent to their arrival in the city. Research findings show surprisingly few systematic differences between migrants and native urban residents in terms of social and personal adjustments, when some basic background characteristics are taken into account. Education, not urban exposure, is more directly associated with shaping modern attitudes. School contact appears to be critical, since that usually involves contact with modern sectors in urban places. The sources of what disadvantage there is appear to be embedded in the background baggage migrants bring with them—their educational level, prior urban exposure, and type of community of origin. These sources tend be structural rather than cultural or attitudinal. After short durations in the city, the migrants converge with the urban-born in socioeconomic characteristics and access to opportunities. After longer exposure to the modern sectors of the city, migrants tend to approximate the urban lifetime population. These studies show that individual migrants adjust well and benefit economically and socially from their migration.

INDIVIDUAL AND HOUSEHOLD PERSPECTIVES IN RURAL AREAS

Does the stagnation of rural economies push individuals to migrate out of rural areas? Will economic and social changes in rural areas free persons from the constraints of family and community, reduce the need for agricultural labor, generate aspirations for new opportunities, and result in out-migration? Or will rural development result in greater local opportunities, expanding jobs and creating new industries? Will changes in rural areas alter the motivation for moving away and cause rural residents to decide to remain, not to be uprooted from families, friends, and local networks? Both sequences have characterized rural places in Third World countries (cf. Connell et al., 1976).

The view of rural areas as pushing out migrants often assumes that the decision whether or not to move is one individuals make based on calculations of costs and benefits; it fails to link individual to the groups of which they are a part or to specify which groups within rural communities are more and less responsive to changing opportunities in rural and other places. To address some of these concerns we shift our focus to comparative research in rural areas and alter the level of analysis to focus on the community of origin. We now ask a series of questions about rural areas: What impact does migration have on rural areas? How does the urban experience influence those returning to rural areas? What are the effects of moving from one rural area to another? Do these consequences vary when migration is sponsored by governments or when it is voluntary? How is migration from rural areas linked to social class, household contexts, and the social and economic development of communities? These questions are addressed by a series of research studies of rural areas of Korea, Sri Lanka, Mali, and the Philippines. (The details are presented in Goldscheider, 1984a; Lee, 1985; and Findley, 1987.) The comparative results are highlighted below.

First, the determinants of migration are not uniform or universal but vary with the type of migration involved. Return migration to rural places and cityward migration in Korea are associated with different sets of social and economic factors; short- and long-term rural migration in

Migration and Social Structure

Mali are characterized by different sets of determinants; voluntary and state-sponsored migration are linked to different socioeconomic correlates in rural Sri Lanka.

What have we learned comparatively about the determinants of rural migration? In Korea, most of the return migrants were responding to new opportunities in rural areas. Attractive jobs in rural places were developed in large part through government investments and the policy to "close" the largest urban areas to new migrants and redirect industries to alternative centers. Those previously resident in rural areas were more likely to know of these opportunities, through family and friends and through regular return visits, and responded to them when they represented better jobs than their current urban occupations. These return migrants could not be considered failures in the city. Indeed, they tended to be more educated than the in-migrants who remained in the city. They also were less likely to have jobs tied to urban occupational networks or to be tied to the city by home ownership or urban organizational affiliation. They were more likely to be self-employed and had more links to the rural area through more frequent visits to family. They were drawn back to their rural areas of origin in response to nonagricultural opportunities opening up for more educated, urban skilled persons. Hence, it is not lack of success or "imperfect information" about urban opportunities that resulted in return migration but "location specific capital" (see DaVanzo, 1981) plus new economic opportunities. Social, not primordial, ties were critical. These patterns qualify the tendency to generalize about the association of rural return migration with urban failures, even if this finding is particular to rural migrants in one part of Korea.

Many return migrants in Korea moved to the city originally to respond to educational opportunities and those who returned to their places of origin tended to have higher levels of education than those who remained in the city; they used their educational level as a means to obtain good jobs opening in places of origin. But the relationship between education and migration operates in a social context. Thus, for example, formal educational level has little role in the agricultural sector of Sri Lanka and hence is unrelated to return migration there.

What factors may be associated with migration to rural areas if not educational attainment? The answer lies in the social ties linked to the economic viability of farming. In Sri Lanka, for example, agricultural laborers tend to migrate less while, somewhat surprisingly, peasant proprieters are more mobile. No simple relationship between migration and social class emerges. The stratification patterns of rural communities, particularly patron-client relationships, are of primary importance. Laborers are clients who are more tied in economically to patron control than are peasant proprieters who cultivate small plots of land with low

685

levels of economic productivity. Rural migration becomes an integral part of this stratification picture, since some of the landowners (i.e., peasant proprieters) are the rural migrants. The government policy to select particular types of rural persons to move to new rural areas involved the powerful system of social and economic relationships. Potential migrants to new rural areas were screened by the local patrons who encouraged the peasant proprieters to move while encouraging agricultural laborers, their clients, to remain. Out-migration was highest among those who were less economically viable in places of origin and had fewer social ties. In Sri Lanka, lower levels of integration of selected segments of the rural community facilitated their response to new opportunities. Economic opportunities in and of themselves did not determine migration, since there was variation in response to those opportunities. The variation was tied to position within the social structure by class and social-family-community linkages (cf. Connell et al., 1976).

How these linkages operate is further clarified by research in Mali, the least developed country of those considered in this review (see Mazur, 1984). There the decision-making unit is not the individual but the household. Households, not individuals, control resources in local rural areas. These resources include land, credit, capital, technical knowledge, social contacts, and social networks. The central question then becomes, How do households allocate these resources among opportunities known and accessible? Part of this decision might be mobility or migration. Migration then becomes one strategy of social and economic survival of rural households. In Mali, the individuals most likely to be sent out of the household are young males, many moving across national boundaries (for a similar observation see Arnold and Shah, 1986). Clearly heads of households and older persons are less likely to migrate. Those with no land to cultivate have higher out-migration rates, while those with some land may combine agricultural labor with other cash-earning activities for which they may sometimes migrate for short periods. The absence of land or the possession of nonviable agricultural holdings makes cash-earning opportunities elsewhere more attractive. Thus not all migration from rural areas is permanent; there are short- and long-term migrants from households that retain their locations and positions within the community. (On households see DaVanzo, 1981; Harbison, 1981; Stark, 1982; Wood, 1981; Mazur, 1984; Lee, 1985; Smith et al., 1984; McNetting et al., 1984; Findley, 1987.)

These substantive findings and the conceptual shift away from individual levels of analysis toward households and families direct our attention as well to contextual analysis that focuses on the community level. For example, it has been documented that including the unemployment rates of rural origin areas have significant effects on migration

Migration and Social Structure

patterns (in more developed countries) in addition to individual employment and other characteristics (DaVanzo, 1978). In more recent studies of migration intentions and rural out-migration in the Philippines the contextual and individual effects are addressed directly and also linked to households (Lee, 1985; Findley, 1987). Local socioeconomic conditions significantly affected the probability of migration intentions for farmers but not for nonfarmers there; land ownership was the most decisive factor in the migration probabilities of non-farmers but had a negative effect on the migration of farmers. Local community characteristics more strongly influenced the migration intentions of farmers and older persons who had a high level of commitment. Local socioeconomic characteristics were significant determinants of the probability of moving for those with no prior migration experience but not for those with migration experience (Lee, 1985). The community perspective is therefore an important corrective to migration research focused solely on individual characteristics. And household-family issues take on particular significance in the broader context of community.

The distinction between family and community levels is parallel to the distinction between the situation and setting of migration (Findley, 1987; Mitchell, 1985). The "situation" refers to a particular set of family and economic circumstances in which persons find themselves; the "setting" refers to the overall social and economic conditions of the broader community or society. The two levels need of course to be integrated to identify why persons in similar environments adopt different migration strategies. Examining only the characteristics of individuals clearly does not get at this. Similarly, while the broader community-societal features alone are helpful in identifying opportunity structures, when examined together with family characteristics these community factors take us much farther toward understanding the complexities of migration decisions. The integration of family and community levels is therefore critical. Sociologists have articulated that position since Durkheim and Weber; it clearly needs to be applied and reinforced in sociological studies of migration. Individuals are embedded in families and families are embedded in communities, linking individuals to the broader society.

Families make decisions in ways different from individuals, and migration is a household- or family-level decision even when the specific decision is made by one person. Many migration options are available to families: whether to move or to stay; who among the family members should move; when; for how long; and of course where to move. Families also make decisions in relation to their economic circumstances and goals. Since migration is connected to social mobility or aspirations for mobility, it is likely to become part of the family's strategy for mo-

Sociological Forum

bility or economic survival. These family decisions and considerations may coincide with those of the individuals within families, but not necessarily.

A review of the literature on the relationship between social class and migration in developing countries reveals a series of inconsistent and inconclusive findings. In part this reflects the lack of comparability among studies. Thus, an examination of the relationship between social class and migration includes issues of patronage (see the study on Sri Lanka in Goldscheider, 1984a) as well as complex community-household interactions as documented for the Philippines (Findley, 1987). Families in different production sectors have different ways of exchanging labor and resources (Standing, 1985), and there is a general relationship between modes of production and migration (Balan, 1983; Connell, 1976). Some have suggested that the relationship between social class and migration may be curvilinear, i.e., both those at the upper level and those at the lower levels of the social class hierarchy are more likely to be risk takers (Findley, 1987, for a review and evaluation). This particularly appears to be the case when the focus is on the movement of one person from the family unit to a new place of residence for at least a period of time (See Findley, 1987; Mazur, 1984; Goldscheider, 1984a).

The level of prior migration characteristic of a community may also affect the relationship between social class and migration. As documented for the Philippines (Findley, 1987), middle-class families are less likely than upper- or lower-class families to migrate where there is minimal migration experience in the community. But in communities with a more widespread and larger migrant reference group, even middle-class risk-averse families adopt migration as a strategy and are more likely to migrate than families at the extreme ends of the stratification system.

Similarly, there are important relationships between community levels of economic development and the probability of family migration. Not surprisingly, the higher the socioeconomic development of the community, the lower the migration out of the community. In large part, this reflects the extent of local economic opportunity; it also reflects the nature of these opportunities. The availability of nonfarm jobs, for example, reduces the probability of out-migration; creating opportunities for supplemental farm earnings does not reduce the probability of migration. Local opportunities to expand farm production tend to raise the probability of migration; agricultural development or commercialization has no effect on the probability of out-migration. A complicating factor is the accessibility of other communities: where there is a high degree of accessibility, rising levels of living are associated with

Migration and Social Structure

more out-migration; in less accessible communities, the level of living has no effect on migration propensities (Findley, 1987).

Findley (1987) also reports that large family size precipitates and facilitates migration because of demographic pressure within the family and because of labor supply. More adults within the family mean that there are enough adults left behind to carry out economic activities, even if one family member migrates. This pattern suggests long-term effects of high fertility on migration propensities—an important connection in light of the earlier discussion of multiphasic demographic response theory.

These findings on place-to-place variation in migration fit into models of migration focusing on temporal changes. Just as the relationship between social class and migration may vary over time (Brown and Sanders, 1981), social class and migration varies among communities (see Findley, 1987).

EMERGING RESEARCH AND METHODOLOGICAL ISSUES IN THE SOCIOLOGY OF MIGRATION

A review of recent research in migration in less developed nations reemphasizes the need to integrate the study of all types of movements from place to place with an understanding of emerging social systems and the community contexts. There is no basis for limiting the migration framework to demographic parameters. It has been documented that careful comparative research yields much in the way of generalization and specification at the macro and micro levels. Three important guidelines should shape our research efforts as we investigate the specific community, societal, comparative, and historical contexts of internal migration. These are (1) the new analytic questions that are associated with a household focus; (2) a dynamic view of migration, its determinants and consequences, in generational perspective; and (3) a reexamination of the adjustment of migrants in a framework of competition and conflict. While the analysis of households, the focus on generations, and an emphasis on conflict and competition are common concerns in a wide range of sociological research, they have rarely been applied systematically to the study of migration.

It has been repeatedly observed that migration varies with changes in the community as well as with the life cycle and socioeconomic characteristics of persons. We have emphasized that the household context weaves together community and individual characteristics. This context also raises new and important analytic questions. When, for example, do children leave the household to establish an independent residence? Which household members are more likely to move? How are economic

Sociological Forum

activities in the household managed when family members are absent? When are outside laborers brought in to substitute for absent household members? How long can a household be viable as a social and economic unit when sons and daughters are absent to earn money and obtain an education? How are ties among migrants and nonmigrants maintained at the household level? How do households facilitate the selective movement of their members?

Some other issues need reformulation when we focus on households. For example, the definition of migration and migrant have been continuing problems of research. At the household level, the question becomes, When is someone who has been absent for a period of time defined by the household as a migrant? When does return migration become repeat migration? How are short-term and circular migration defined by members of the household? A fundamental question is of course how households are defined. These issues of definition are particularly problematic in rural areas of developing nations where short-term and seasonal migration are common and where household membership and residential units are more amorphous.

Another set of questions emerges when we focus on the household as a decision-making unit. How, for example, are the costs and benefits for households calculated? How are these decisions made and who makes them? The costs and benefits for individuals are clearly not necessarily synonymous with those for households. Hence, a focus solely on the individual decision maker, on individual choices whether and where to move, and on individual calculations of costs and benefits is an inadequate basis for understanding the relationship between migration and social structure.

As frameworks for understanding migration, the economic argument about decision making and the analysis of the costs and benefits of migration have particular difficulties as currently formulated. (See Todaro, 1976, for an excellent summary of the micro-economic argument.) First, there is a range of issues that are noneconomic; at best, the economic aspects must be understood in the context of the social structure to address variation and change. Then, while migration may be determined by economic factors, these factors differentially affect segments of the community, subgroups, and households. Relative economic opportunities and access to those opportunities are critical in the understanding of migration, but migration processes cannot be understood without attention to the social context.

The major problem with the economic framework is the emphasis on *individual* decision making and the *individual* migrant rather than the household. As a result, there is a misplaced focus on the calculus of individual costs and benefits rather than the costs and benefits of units larger and more complex than the single person. The balance of

Migration and Social Structure

consideration of whether to migrate depends on the internal structure or composition of the household, its location within the community (in particular, its economic resources, its need for labor, and alternative sources of labor that are available), and the location of the community within the broader region (in particular, the opportunities available within the region and access to them).

At the same time we need to shift our focus away from studying the migration only of men in search of opportunities to include the study of women and children. The inclusion of women in the analysis of migration should not be, however, solely as appendages to male migrants; our questions should go beyond why women migrate, whether they differ from male migrants, and whether they accompany men in search of jobs. Nor do we want to confine our focus to the reproductive roles of women and only examine the effects of migration on fertility. We need as well to look at the distribution of economic, family, and cultural roles within households where women are migrants.

What happens to women who remain in rural areas while their husbands or children work for periods of time elsewhere? Do their economic roles expand? Is their status as workers and producers altered by the out-migration of others? How are their household obligations and authority affected? Do new networks of relationships emerge for wives and daughters—migrants and stayers? Even the fertility questions should be altered. We need to ask, What is the impact of migration on the changing roles and statuses of women within the family and household? How does migration change the power and control others have over their lives? What are the resultant changes in family formation, reproduction, and the tempo of childbearing? Here, as always, the household level of analysis places emphasis on the relationships between individuals in a social and economic network.

A second perspective that needs to be incorporated more directly into our theories and research on migration is intergenerational: the recognition that the dynamics of migration extend beyond the life cycles of persons and communities to generations. In some places, for example in Sri Lanka, research has shown that government distribution of land resulted in migration to rural areas, greater equalities of landholding, and improved living standards. What is likely to happen to the children of these migrants? An equal division of land among surviving offspring will reduce landholdings and may reduce standards of living as well. If there are differential patterns of fertility among migrants or differential survivorship, greater inequalities are likely to emerge in the next generation. Moreover, if there are differential inheritance patterns by birth order or by gender among the offspring of these migrants, some children will be more likely to move than others, either in search of better opportunities or to obtain an education so as to use other means besides family resources to secure nonagricultural employment. The migrant family is more likely to encourage, facilitate, and subsidize the out-migration of selected children either as part of their economic mobility strategy or as the basis for the continuous employment of those children who will inherit the land and those who will not.

In this context, the examination of social class and migration focuses on the how migration affects the generational transfer of wealth and the impact on traditional sources of power of the selective movement of children away from family and kin. The separation of family continuity from particular geographic locations sets the stage for the emergence of new sources of power and new bases of social class formation. Migration allows for the restructuring of social and economic networks that are not solely family based. These broader issues connect migration, family, and class formation to households and communities and place the analysis of migration at the core of the study of social structure and social change.

The dynamic, intergenerational view of migration generates new questions that require new research orientations. The issues raised for the relationship between migration and social structure in the late twentieth century developing nations parallel the classic demographic problems of European countries in the nineteenth century. Parallels do not imply similarities, for it is clearly understood that many social, demographic, economic, political, and cultural patterns and alliances distinguish Western countries in their demographic transformation from the hetergeneous group of countries lumped together under the rubric "developing" or "Third World" countries. But the analysis of the linkages between migration and social structure requires frameworks or theories that are general enough to allow comparisons across nations and time periods, to identify the general and isolate the unique.

The centrality of households and families in understanding the relationships between migration and social structure and the focus on cohorts, generations, and intergenerational transfers place the sociological analysis of migration in less developed nations at the core of demographic theory as well as within the major sociological intellectual traditions of Weber, Durkheim, and Marx.

A final item on the research agenda for migration studies is to reorient the examination of migrant "adjustment" in urban places to focus on relationships between groups and, hence, to investigate patterns of conflict and competition among migrants and between migrants and natives. Studies of migrant "adjustment" have tended to have an urban bias, taking the urban-born as the standard and asking, When and in what ways will the new migrants from rural places become urbanlike? While more recent research has corrected some of the urban bias, there

Migration and Social Structure

remains a consistent orientation toward assimilation and integration. Issues of competition and conflict have been de-emphasized, if not ignored completely. Yet clearly contact between migrants and natives (however each is defined) is as likely to result in competition, conflict, and tension as in assimilation, adjustment, and integration. When the migrant stream originates primarily from one region or one particular location, when migrants tend to develop their own social and economic networks, and when the migrants are from an ethnic-racial-tribal group different from the natives, migration is likely to exacerbate conflict and competition. Studies by political scientists of international movements and of some patterns of internal migration have emphasized the conflicts associated with migration. Recent research in the Middle East and in African countries and new research among minority populations in China point to the importance of studying ethnic conflict generated by migration as well as the adjustment of migrants (Weiner, 1978, 1982; Atemie, 1987; Ma, 1987; Al-Haj, 1987).

Movements of people from one rural area to another or from urban areas back to rural places of origin and short-term seasonal movements of workers (circulation migration) do not fit into the conventional modes of analysis associated with adjustment. There are no simple standards of comparison, no obvious group to adjust to, and no permanent adjustment to occur. A more fruitful framework of analysis would emphasize the many layers of economic competition and conflict among communities, households, and groups, in different places and at different times.

A focus on sociologically salient units of analysis such as ethnic-tribal groups, social classes, or local communities adds to our understanding of the determinants and consequences of migration. Migrant settlement patterns are often based on social class and ethnic affiliation. Access to opportunity and to resources vary by class and ethnic factors and differs among regions. These social, economic, and geographic contexts are connected to the probability of migration and to the direction of movement. Access to economic and migration opportunities implies, therefore, not only geographic proximity but also social networks that are supportive and provide information.

This raises directly the issue of state intervention. Often we assume free market access to opportunities without political constraints. But clearly political intervention is becoming more, rather than less, common in developing nations. It is unlikely that governments, local and national, distribute opportunities equally among places and among groups. Investments vary, and patronage systems are major and continuing forms of political control. In turn, these patronage systems regulate migration directly through control over who can move and indirectly through differential influence and investment power. When political considerations are taken into account, it becomes even more important to attend to community-level effects on migration.

Parts of the puzzle in the relationships between migration and social structure are beginning to take shape. A fully developed theory is unlikely to appear until we have an accepted theory of social structure and social change. In the meantime, however, we search for theoretical maps so that the growing number of empirical studies can be compared, evaluated, and organized. Emerging from recent research are critical new ways to study and interpret migration and social structure. These orientations fit solidly within a broader understanding of comparative development, community contexts, household and family analysis, stratification, and ethnic conflict in comparative-historical perspectives. In turn, the study of migration patterns may provide a critical handle for the systematic analysis of the social transformations occurring in Third World nations.

The oversimplified association of rural out-migration with negative consequences in urban areas that call for policy remedies to prevent further movement from the countryside seems to be based less on social science research than on political considerations. Much more comparative research on the costs and benefits of nonmigration (as well as on migration) needs to be done before we can assess the determinants and consequences of migration in development processes.

REFERENCES

Al-Haj, Majid
1987 Social Change and Family Processes: Arab Communities in Shefar A'm. Boulder, CO: Westview Press.

Arnold, F. and N. Shah
1986 Asian Labor Migration: Pipeline to the Middle East. Boulder, CO: Westview Press.

Atemie, Josiah
1987 "Ethnicity and social adaptation: A study of status change among migrants to Port Harcourt, Nigeria." Ph.D. dissertation, Brown University.

Balan, Jorge
1983 "Agrarian structures and internal migration in historical perspective; Latin American case studies." In Peter Morrison (ed.), Population Movements: Their Forms and Functions in Urbanization and Development. Liege: Ordina Editions.

Brown, Lawrence and R. Sanders.
1981 "Toward a development paradigm of migration with particular reference to the Third World." In Gordon De Jong and Robert Gardner (eds.), Migration Decision Making: Multi-Disciplinary Approaches to Microlevel Studies in Developed and Developing Countries. New York: Pergamon Press.

Connell, J. et al.
1976 Migration from Rural Areas: The Evidence from Village Studies. Delhi: Oxford University Press.

DaVanzo, Julie
1978 "Does unemployment affect migration? Evidence from micro data." Review of Economics and Statistics 60:504–514.
1981 "Microeconomic approaches to studying migration decisions." In G. De Jong and R. Gardner (eds.),

Migration Decision Making. New York: Pergamon Press.

Davis, Kingsley
1963   "The theory of change and response in modern demographic history." Population Index 29:345–366.

Findley, Sally
1977   Planning for Internal Migration: A Review of Issues and Policies in Developing Countries. Washington, DC: U.S. Bureau of the Census.
1982   Migration Survey Methodologies. Liege: IUSSP Papers No. 20.
1987   Rural Development and Migration: A Study of Family Choices in The Philippines. Boulder, CO: Westview Press.

Friedlander, Dov
1969   "Demographic responses and population change." Demography 6:359–381.
1983   "Demographic responses and socioeconomic structure." Demography 20:249–272.

Goldscheider, Calvin
1983b   "Modernization, migration, and urbanization." In Peter Morrison (ed.), Population Movements: Their Forms and Functions in Urbanization and Development. Liege: Ordina Editions.
1984b   "Migration and rural fertility in less developed countries." In W. Schutjer and S. Stokes (eds.), Rural Development and Human Fertility. New York: McGraw-Hill.

Goldscheider, Calvin, ed.
1983a   Urban Migrants in Developing Nations: Patterns and Problems of Adjustment. Boulder, CO: Westview Press.
1984a   Rural Migration in Developing Nations: Comparative Studies of Korea, Sri Lanka, and Mali. Boulder, CO: Westview Press.

Goldstein, Sidney and Alice Goldstein
1981   Surveys of Migration in Less Developed Countries. Paper no. 71, East-West Population Institute, Honolulu, HI.

Harbison, Sarah
1981   "Family structure and family strat-egy in migration decision making." In G. De Jong and R. Gardner (eds.), Migration Decision Making. New York: Pergamon Press.

Hugo, Graeme
1981   "Village-community ties, village norms and ethnic and social networks: A review of evidence from the Third World." In G. De Jong and R. Gardner (eds.), Migration Decision Making. New York: Pergamon Press.

Lee, Sun-Hee
1985   Why People Intend to Move: Individual and Community Level Factors of Out-Migration in the Philippines. Boulder, CO: Westview Press.

Lerman, Charles
1987   "Workers in transition: Patterns of occupational attainment and migration in Semarang, Indonesia." Ph.D. dissertation, Brown University.

Linn, Johannes
1984   Cities in the Developing World. New York: Oxford University Press.

Ma, Rong
1987   "The integration of migrants in rural areas of Chifeng, the Inner Mongolia autonomous region, China." Ph.D. dissertation, Brown University.

McNetting, R. et al.
1984   Households: Comparative Studies of the Domestic Group. Berkeley: University of California Press.

Mazur, Robert
1984   "Rural out-migration and labor allocation in Mali." In C. Goldscheider (ed.), Rural Migration in Developing Nations: Comparative Studies of Korea, Sri Lanka, and Mali. Boulder, CO: Westview Press.

Mitchell, J. Clyde
1985   "Toward a situational sociology of wage labour circulation." In R. Prothero and M. Chapman (eds.), Circulation in Third World Countries. London: Routledge and Kegan Paul.

Mosher, William
1980a   "The theory of change and response: An application to Puerto

Sociological Forum

Rico, 1940–1970." Population Studies 34:45–58.

1980b "Demographic responses and demographic transitions." Demography 17:395–412.

Simmons, Alan, S. Diaz-Briquets, and A. Laquian
1977 Societal Change and Internal Migration. Ottawa: International Development and Research Centre.

Smith, Joan et al.
1984 Households and the World-Economy. Beverly Hills: Sage Publications.

Standing, Guy, ed.
1985 Labour Circulation and the Labour Process. London: Croom Helm.

Stark, Oded
1982 "Rural to urban migration and intrafamilial risk-taking agreements in LDCs." Paper presented at the Annual Meetings of the Population Association of America.

Todaro, Michael
1976 Internal Migration in Developing Countries. Geneva: ILO.

Weiner, Myron
1978 Sons of the Soil: Migration and Ethnic Conflict in India. Princeton, NJ: Princeton University Press.

1982 "Migration and development in the Gulf." Population and Development Review 8:1–36.

Wood, C.
1981 "Structural changes and household strategies: A conceptual framework for the study of rural migration." Human Organization 40:338–344.

Zelinsky, Wilbur
1983 "The impasse in migration theory." In Peter Morrison (ed.), Population Movements: Their Forms and Functions in Urbanization and Development. Liege: Ordina Editions.

[12]

Family And Personal Networks In International Migration: Recent Developments And New Agendas[1]

Monica Boyd
Carleton University, Ottawa

Family, friendship and community networks underlie much of the recent migration to industrial nations. Current interest in these networks accompany the development of a migration system perspective and the growing awareness of the macro and micro determinants of migration. This article presents an overview of research findings on the determinants and consequences of personal networks. In addition, it calls for greater specification of the role of networks in migration research and for the inclusion of women in future research.

Twenty-five years ago, labor migration was a major component of immigration flows to industrial nations. Australia, Canada and the United States admitted a substantial proportion of migrants based on their economic contributions. Many Northern European countries encouraged and received labor migrants admitted ostensibly for short periods of time. These labor based migrations offered apparent confirmation of Ravenstein's law that males predominated in long distance migration. Such movement also was consistent with the prevailing theoretical approaches which stressed the movements of people as responses to push and pull forces in places of origin and destination.

Labor migration and the migration of young unaccompanied males still characterize migration into areas such as Singapore, parts of Latin America and the oil rich Middle Eastern nations. Elsewhere such characterizations are less accurate. In major settlement countries, family based migration predominates, and women are as prevalent as men in legal migration flows. Similarly in Europe, the migration of family members, the majority being women and children, augments the earlier flows of male "guestworkers".

The changing composition of migrant flows to industrialized nations accompanied the economic downturns of the 1970s and 1980s in many

---

[1] The author thanks Gordon DeJong for perceptive comments in the initial stages of this project, Jared Keil for loaning me his library on women and development and James Fawcett for his patience.

countries. However, attributing such shifts solely to depressed labor demand is facile. The trends also reflect the maturation of migration streams, stimulated by social networks based on family/household, friendship and community ties and relationships.[2] Existing across time and space, social networks are highly relevant for studies of international migration. By binding migrants and nonmigrants together in a complex web of social roles and interpersonal relationships (Massey *et al.*, 1987:138), these personal networks are conduits of information and social and financial assistance. They also shape migration outcomes, ranging from no migration, immigration, return migration or the continuation of migration flows.

By the late 1980s, a growing body of research existed regarding the role of social networks in the etiology, composition, direction and persistence of migration flows, and in the settlement and integration of migrant populations in receiving societies. There now exist many ways of conceptualizing and studying family, friendship and community ties as key ingredients in international migration. Not surprisingly, there is no one orthodox treatment of personal networks, and not surprisingly a number of empirical and theoretical challenges remain. The remainder of this article examines more thoroughly these characterizations of the field. First the current interest in social networks is linked to other developments in international migration. Research areas which consider and/or emphasize the role of personal networks, particularly those based on family ties, in explaining the origin, composition, adjustment and dynamics of migration are then reviewed. Finally, two types of agenda which would enhance the explanatory powers of social network related research in the 1990s are discussed.

CONCEPTUALIZING MIGRATION: THE EVOLVING CENTRALITY OF NETWORKS AND FAMILY

Despite its current popularity, the subject of social networks is not new in international migration research. Analysts in the 1960s and 1970s studied the process of chain migration and the role played by kin and friends in providing information and facilitating migration (*e.g.*, Anderson,1974; Mac-Donald and MacDonald, 1964; Ritchey, 1976; *See*, also, Hugo, 1981:195-205). However, current migration patterns and new conceptualizations of migration underlie more recent interest in the role of family,

[2] Immigration networks exist through family and friendship, community practices such as festivals, membership in associations and as "intermediaries" such as labor recruiters, immigration consultants, travel agents, smugglers and other forms (Gilliespie and Browning, 1979:513; Lim, 1987b:4). To date, considerable attention is focused on the operation and implications of networks based on family, friendship and community ties. These networks may be considered "personal" networks to distinguish them from networks based on social ties based on distant or organizationally defined social relations (such as those associated with "intermediaries"). However, sociologists and anthropologists generally use the term social networks to refer to networks of personal relations. In this paper I use "social" networks and "personal" networks interchangeably.

friendship and community based networks.

Today, contemporary treatments of migration theory often begin with the almost *de rigueur* reference to the demise of push-pull theory. According to this theory, people moved either because social and economic forces in the place of destination impelled them to do so or because they were attracted to places of destination by one or more social and economic factors there. Reviews of push-pull theory note its implicit assumption of immobility, its limited ability to predict the origin of flows and changes therein, and the emphasis on the movement of people as a result of rational calculations performed by individual actors (Fernandez-Kelly, 1983b:205; Pedraza-Bailey, 1985:5; Portes and Bach, 1985:4-5).

The origins and legitimacy of these criticisms lie in the vastly changing nature of migration from the 1960s on. Four migration trends augmented pre-existing legal settlement flows to countries such as Canada, Australia, New Zealand and the United States: 1) temporary labor migration to Europe, characterized by eventual settlement (Castles, 1984); 2) clandestine or irregular migration to traditional settlement areas as well as to European countries; 3) the migration of workers from Third World areas such as Korean and Pakistan to countries such as Saudi Arabia and Kuwait where industrialization programs were underway; and 4) the movement of workers to newly industrializing areas of the Third World countries (Castles, 1986:776-777). These trends revealed a heretofore unacknowledged dynamic character to migration. The origins of these flows, their regularization, their reversals and cessation were not always well understood and, in the European guestworker migration, certainly underestimated.

Immigration research in the 1970s and 1980s was stimulated by these changing migration flows in Europe and the Middle East, as well as by the movement of capital from core industrialized economies to the less developed nation, and by issues of race, class and labor market segmentation in receiving societies. Such research increasingly viewed international migration as conditioned by structural factors. Important structural factors included bilateral agreements regarding labor migration, foreign investment patterns, devolution and change in local economies — particularly agrarian economies — and the distinction between policies of migrant settlement and those of immigrant integration.

The migration trends of the 1970s and 1980s also challenged existing explanatory frameworks, and they stimulated the development of alternative theories to account for origins, stability, uses of immigrant labor and immigrant social and economic adaptation (Papademetriou, 1988a; Portes and Bach, 1985: Chapters 1 and 10). Influenced by marxist theory (Burawoy, 1976; Castles and Kosack, 1973), dependency and world systems schools (Petras, 1981; Portes and Walton, 1981) and labor market segmentation theory (Piore, 1975; 1979), these theoretical developments interpreted migration phenomena from a structural perspective with an emphasis on understanding labor migration (Portes, 1987; Portes and Bach, 1985: Chapters 1 and 10). Such approaches permitted the understanding of international labor migration within the context of a global economic system which not only linked less developed countries to industrial ones, but also restructured domestic economies (Castles, 1986; Sassen-Koob, 1980; 1981; 1984; 1988).

Structural approaches to migration emphasize linkages between societies as fundamental for the understanding of migration flows, their size, direction and persistence. These emphases call attention to existence of migration systems, in which places are linked by the flows and counterflow of people, as well as by economic and political relations between countries or areas. Approaching migration from a systems perspective offers several advantages. First, it departs from a static conceptualization of migration as a one time event from place A to place B. Second, it emphasizes interdependence and reciprocity (Papademetriou, 1988a). For these two reasons, systems approaches offer three advances in the conceptualization of migration. Such approaches force attention on stability and movement in both sending and receiving areas, examine flows within the context of other flows, and emphasize that flows of people are part of, and often influenced by, flows of goods, services and information (Fawcett and Arnold, 1987:456).

In sum, by the 1980s, researchers increasingly considered migration as representing and evolving from linkages between sending and receiving countries (Lim, 1987a; 1987b; Salt, 1987). Social networks represented one such link in these migration systems. Networks connect migrants and nonmigrants across time and space. Once begun, migration flows often become self-sustaining, reflecting the establishment of networks of information, assistance and obligations which develop between migrants in the host society and friends and relatives in the sending area. These networks link populations in origin and receiving countries and ensure that movements are not necessarily limited in time, unidirectional or permanent.

A migration system approach also illuminates the connections between macro and micro approaches to the study of migration. This connection is another reason for examining social networks in migration. Researchers increasingly invoked structural explanations for migration while measuring migration as the movement of individuals or groups of individuals. A real danger also was the replacement of an undersocialized view of migration in which all action reflected individual wishes and preferences with an oversocialized view in which people were passive agents in the migratory process, projected through time and space by social forces. Introducing social networks in migration partly alleviated these dilemmas in migration research.

Social relations both transmit and shape the effect of social and economic structures on individuals, families and households. Additionally, social ties transmit information about places of destination (including places of return migration) and sources of settlement assistance. Thus, studying networks, particularly those linked to family and households, permits understanding migration as a social product — not as the sole result of individual decisions made by individual actors, not as the sole result of economic or political parameters, but rather as an outcome of all these factors in interaction. This approach also permits conceptualizing migration as a contingency. Whether migration occurs or not, and what shapes its direction, composition and persistence is conditioned by historically generated social, political and economic structures of both sending and receiving societies. These structures are channeled through social relationships and social roles which impact on individuals and groups.

The domestic unit is an important component in social network based migration. Households and families are common representations of this domestic unit.[3] The importance of this unit in migration research is fourfold. First, domestic units are sustenance units. As sustenance units, they have their own structural characteristics which condition the propensity to migrate and the pattern of migration. A number of studies show that the motivation and ability to migrate as well as the pattern of migration are influenced by the resource levels of households, the age and sex structure of the family/household and the stages of the family life cycle (Harbison, 1981; Schmink, 1984). Households with middling levels of financial resources may be more likely to sponsor migration of one or more members than households with few resources (Dinerman, 1978; Pessar, 1982). Households with few adults or conversely many dependent children may be less likely to participate in migration in part because no household members are likely candidates (Harbison, 1981; Root and De Jong, 1986) and because the income generating capacity is low for household members left behind (Escobar *et al.*, 1987). However, studies of select Mexican communities find that men with young children are more likely than recently married men to migrate to the United States, because of increased economic needs of the family (Massey *et al.*, 1987; *See*, also, Escobar *et al.*, 1987). These studies indicate that migration is not a haphazard movement of poor people. Instead, it is a calculated movement, designed to relieve economic pressures at various stages of the life cycle. Also, the type of migration (settlement, temporary and recurrent) varies with the stage of the life cycle (Escobar *et al.*, 1987; Massey *et al.*, 1987:207-215).

In addition to acting as sustenance units, domestic units are socializing

[3] Households may contain nonfamily members. Families usually include only those members related by blood, marriage or adoption and even here definitions may include or exclude multiple generation or may vary according to political considerations (Hune, 1985; 1987:124).

agents and are the foundation for family and household based networks (Harbison, 1981). As socializing agents, families transmit cultural values and norms which influence who migrates and why. Families also transmit norms about the meaning of migration and the maintenance of familial based obligations over time and space.

Equally important, families represent a social group geographically dispersed. They create kinship networks which exist across space and are the conduits for information and assistance which in turn influence migration decisions (Harbison, 1981). Shadow households in the place of destination consist of persons whose commitments and obligations are to households in the sending area. Such persons may be especially likely to assist in the migration of other household or family members or to remit funds to the family members remaining behind (Caces *et al.*, 1985).

Finally, families are migratory units. Families may migrate together or individuals can be sent out with the clear expectation that other members will be sent for (Boutang and Garson, 1984:586; Harbison, 1981; Mac-Donald and MacDonald, 1964). Both types characterize migration to North America, Europe and Oceania, and family migration *in toto* represents a large share of migration flows to these regions.

RESEARCH AGENDAS AND FINDINGS

Numerous diagrams emphasize the family migration and social networks as central ingredients of systems approaches involving both macro and micro variables (Fawcett and Arnold, 1987: Figure 19.1; Salt, this volume: Figures 1-4). Such diagrams also capture various research agendas. To date, most research that examines family migration and the role of social networks falls within the following topics: 1) economic, political and social structural factors in sending and receiving countries; 2) bilateral treaties between countries regarding labor migration; 3) government policies governing the admission of international migrants; 4) linkages to sending areas, often analyzed through remittances and returns; and 5) the settlement and/or integration of migrant populations. Although this classification of research indicates major research findings and initiatives, the classification is admittedly heuristic and oversimplistic. Many of these areas overlap substantively. A migration system perspective also conceptually links many areas of research.

Structural Conditions in Sending and Receiving Areas

Classic push-pull approaches sought to understand migration as the result of social, economic and political factors in sending and receiving areas. However, two more recent approaches use social psychological and political economy frameworks to link migration to structural conditions.

One development rests on a social psychological approach to understanding migration. Here, researchers link macrolevel influences to the migration decisionmaking process of individuals using a variety of conceptual and analytical models (De Jong and Gardner, 1981; Fawcett, 1985-1986a). A major premise of the value expectancy model is that some motivations for migration have counterparts in environmental and structural factors. The model emphasizes the processes through which such macro stimuli convert into individual decisionmaking processes (De Jong and Fawcett, 1981; Gardner, 1981). Background and personal aspects are linked conceptually and analytically to migration intentions/behaviors by their impact on the individual/family expectancy that migration will be followed by a given consequence and by the value of that consequence (De Jong and Fawcett, 1981). Such perceptions in turn affect migration intentions and actual migratory behavior (De Jong *et al.*, 1983; Simmons, 1985-1986). Social contacts with relatives and friends are central to this model. Social contacts represent networks of information and social and economic assistance between areas, and they are important influences in international migration decisionmaking processes (De Jong, Root and Abad, 1986; De Jong, *et al.*, 1985-1986; Fuller *et al.*, 1985-1986).

In addition to social psychological frameworks, the gradual incorporation of marxist and world systems approaches into migration research also emphasize links between the family unit, personal networks and structural features of sending and receiving areas (Eades, 1987). The marxist and world systems approaches call attention to demand in receiving industrial nations for the reproduction of cheap labor, the subsequent movement of capital to less developed regions with cheap labor, the bifurcation of industrialized economies into skilled and unskilled sectors, and the intensification of export oriented production instead of import substitution activities in less developed countries.

Governments often develop economic, social and political policies alongside these developments. For example, the recruitment of guestworkers by European countries and the development of the United States *bracero* program represent formal agreements which ensured a supply of cheap labor (Burawoy, 1976; Sassen-Koob, 1980). After the mid 1960s, changes in United States tariff laws stimulated the movement of textile and electronics work to less developed countries, coinciding with the development of free trade zones, the establishment of run-away shops of which the Mexican *maquiladora* are a form, and the general reliance on export diversification as opposed to import substitution in small countries (Safa, 1986). At the same time, the inability of services to be exported meant a growing demand for cheap (immigrant) labor in core economies (Sassen-Koob, 1980; 1981; 1983; 1984; 1988).

FAMILY AND PERSONAL NETWORKS IN MIGRATION 645

The development of a world economic system links national economies and governments, changes domestic economies and alters the employment structures of receiving and sending countries. Other dimensions of economic and political interrelationships also exist between countries including agreements of economic and technical assistance, political alliances and trade and tariff agreements (See, Fawcett and Arnold, 1987; Weintraub and Stolp, 1987). These all are preconditions for economic and refugee migration. However, two mechanisms connect these interrelationships to migration: social networks and household survival strategies.

A starting point for research on social networks is that structural factors provide the context within which migration decisions are made by individuals or groups. However, at this microlevel analysis, the decision to migrate is influenced by the existence and participation in social networks, which connect people across space. As noted previously, networks provide resources in the form of information and assistance. Once these networks develop, they support and encourage additional migration. Thus they explain the persistence of migration long after changes in the original migration inducing structural conditions (Massey et al., 1987; Portes, 1985; 1987; Yücel, 1987). Various Mexican communities (Escobar et al., 1987; Massey et al., 1987) and the post-guestworker migration to European countries (Buechler and Buechler, 1987) are based on the institutionalization of migration through social networks.

Because households are units which mediate between individuals and the larger structural setting, they are an important component in the relationship between structural conditions and migration (Crummett, 1987: 247-248; Pedraza-Bailey, 1985). Much migration research which incorporates household/family strategies emphasizes the reorganization of local and national economies within the context of a world economy. The household unit is a co-resident group which ensures its maintenance and reproduction by generating and allocating a common pool of resources including labor and monetary income (Schmink, 1984; 1986; Wood, 1981; 1982). Household strategies are actions directed at balancing the household resources, the consumption needs and the alternatives for productive activity (Pessar, 1982). Migration of individual members or the entire household unit represents a strategy at the household level to achieve a fit between resources such as land or capital, the consumption needs of its members and the alternatives for generating monetary and nonmonetary income (Pessar, 1982:348; Wood, 1982:313). Migration can be an important strategy for generating income in the form of remittances.

Households survival mechanisms also show why migration does not always occur, the existence of linkages between households at origin and destination, and the consequences of outmigration for nonmigrant members (Briody, 1987; Pessar, 1982). In her analysis of Mexican illegal migration, Dinerman (1978) argues that migration as a household strategy is conditioned by social ties at the community level as well as by the local economy. Under certain circumstances migration can be an economic alternative to producing cash by selling household production goods in the local market. Further, generation of cash through migration ensures household economic viability and the meeting of social obligations. However, migration also requires cash for transportation, food and documents as well as clothing and possibly the need to replace the lost free labor. As a result, most immigrants come from extended households with secure income (Dinerman, 1978). Pessar's (1982) analysis of Dominican migration to the United States also illuminates the use of migration as a strategy for reducing the process of land fragmentation and downward mobility which occurs as a result of economic transformations. Such migration reduces the operating capacity of family farms, thereby creating additional incentives for the migration of more household members to the United States. The ensuing kin based chain migration of employable household members means the creation of new households in the United States and in the Dominican Republic. Marked differences exist in the structure of such households with dependents remaining in the Dominican Republic and connected to those in the United States through remittances.

Bilateral Treaties and Labor Recruitment

Agreements between governments regarding labor migration represent specific examples of economic based policies which stimulate migration flows. The emergence of labor brokers also represents a mechanism, often officially sanctioned, for the recruitment of labor. Well known examples of both are those of the United States-Mexican Bracero Accord (1942-1962), the role of government visa granting agencies in the flow of guestworkers to European EEC countries; and more recently the contract recruitment of Asian workers to the oil rich areas of the Middle East. The perception of migration as temporary and a one time event is basic to such agreements. In reality, these agreements establish a bridgehead of migrants who represent one end of a migratory chain. Kinship and personal ties across space are created with the potential for inducing more migration and/or for creating dynamic processes of migration, emigration and remigration.

Temporal trends as well as indepth studies provide evidence for these generalizations. In Europe, declining guestworker recruitment after the early 1970s did not stop migration. Clandestine migration has increased alongside the legal admittance immigration of women and children (OECD, 1988). These changes also exist elsewhere. In two of the four Mexican communities studied by Massey *et al.* (1987), the bracero years not only created an history of legal and clandestine migration but also established contacts in the United States. Over time networks based on family, friendship and community ties developed and expanded. Their availability shaped household survival strategies, thereby stimulating more migration and legitimating and regularizing its occurrence.

In short, two fundamental tenets in migration research are that 1) social relationships across distances create social ties which in turn are the basis for the continuation of migration over time as well as for its changed composition; and 2) through these networks, labor migration has the strong potentiality for changing into family migration. To be sure, these tenets do not have universal applicability. But the existing exceptions offer the opportunity to further specify the roles of social networks. For example, in Asian migration to the Middle East, contract migration dominates, labor rotation appears high and accommodation is in segregated compounds. These arrangements appear to have circumvented the establishment of a "bridgehead" migratory population, at least among unskilled laborers. Whether such arrangements are the necessary and sufficient conditions to prevent the maturation of migration streams through the development of social networks and family reunification remains a topic for future study.

Immigration Policies

In addition to or as part of bilateral treaties and agreements, major receiving countries in the industrial world have rules and procedures regarding the border crossing of persons who are not foreign born and/or who are not citizens of the designated country, but who seek employment and/or residence in that country. These selection criteria can be viewed from macro and micro perspectives. Following Jasso and Rosenzweig (1987:1215), at a macro level, criteria for admission are determinants of the size and characteristics of legal immigrant flows. But, from a micro perspective, the selection criteria provide the foundation for the process by which a person or group of persons become resident in a given country. And the criteria may play a part in the strategies devised by potential migrants, leading to no migration, immigration or illegal entry. Such strategies, shaped by immigration rules and regulations, show how immigration laws can illicit unintended consequences and in turn create new laws.[4] These strategies exist within the broader context of the social, economic and political conditions in the sending and receiving countries, and they involve the decisions of both individuals and families or households.

Where immigration policies include provisions for family reunification and permit admission on the basis of family relationships, chain migration

[4] For example, the perception that laws permitting migrants to sponsor new brides or grooms are abused is the basis for regulations which grant permanent residency to newly wed sponsored spouses only after a period of time (before the two year anniversary in the United States and up to two years in Sweden).

of family members often results. In many European countries, migration of spouses and children now is permitted (OECD, 1987; Papademetriou, 1988b). Family migration currently predominates in the United States. The requirement of U.S. citizenship to sponsor relatives stimulates its acquisition by resident family members and in turn fosters family migration (Jasso and Rosenzweig, 1986; 1987). The time lag between entry and subsequent sponsorship may be even less in countries such as Canada where citizenship is not a requirement for most categories of family migration and the level of sponsorship may be higher (Samuel, 1988).

Two overlapping approaches at present dominate research on the role of personal networks in meeting or circumventing immigration policy. The first emphasizes the decisionmaking process of potential migrants as informed and guided by existing immigration law. For example, research into the migration intentions of persons residing in the Ilocas Norte area of the Philippines shows that close family ties between potential migrants and United States residences are associated with intentions to migrate, with U.S. relatives acting as petitioners and with the timing of other events such as receiving a passport. From the immigrants' perspective, family migration provisions in United States immigration law are important explanations for legal immigration (De Jong, Root and Abad, 1986). The second area of research quantifies the stimulative effect of family ties on immigration flows. The groundbreaking work by Jasso and Rosenzweig (1986; 1987) permits estimating the rates at which naturalized citizens of the United States sponsor the immigration of various relatives. Such work reveals a decay curve whereby depletion occurs over time in the stock of relatives abroad who are eligible to migrate. Their study of naturalization pattern by the foreign born also shows that migrants are very responsive to immigration regulations and to changes therein (Jasso and Rosenzweig, 1987).

These two research perspectives generate at least three future research agenda. One challenge is to specify further the process of chain migration in relation to immigration law. Definitions of family adopted in immigration policies influence what family members migrate and over what phase of the chain migration. These definitions vary considerably by receiving country (Hune, 1987), but tend to emphasize eligibility based on nuclear families formed by legal marriage. This definition of family may not fully reflect the kin group that is the unit of adaptive strategies. This discrepancy is likely in areas where extended family structures and consensual marriages exist (Garrison and Weiss, 1979). What is the relationship of such discrepancies to legal versus illegal migration? If personal networks provide information and resources to legal migrants along with fulfilling formal requirements, such information and resources may be similarly available to others in the household.

In fact, family networks are central features of illegal migration. In the United States, legal migration is associated with the illegal migration of Mexicans. Reichert and Massey (1980) observe that when a majority of family members possess the U.S. resident visa, the family often migrates as a unit. If they are old enough to work, family and household members who lack proper documentation frequently accompany other members. Similar observations characterize migration into European countries, Australia (Boutang and Garson, 1984) and Canada, where a study of the 1983-1985 Illegal Migrant program found that over 80 percent of the applicants for permanent resident status had close relatives (spouses, brothers and sisters) in Canada. Once in a host country, illegal migrants can develop social and economic connections which assist in regularizing their status (Massey, 1987).

Further research also is needed on the structure of family induced chain migration. When labor migration occurs, spouses, usually wives, and children immigrate later. If regulations permit, adult offspring, siblings and parents are later participants in the migration process. Do these linkages occur sequentially or is the pattern one of mass family migration. If return migration occurs, does it disrupt the pattern, and under what conditions? These are useful questions, for the pattern of family chain migration affects the tempo of the multiplier effect. It may also influence the decisionmaking process of potential migrants.

The nature of sponsorship and its effects are two additional areas of research for the 1990s. In North America, the term "sponsor" refers to the person or group who desires the presence of the would-be migrant and who undertakes various actions to substantiate the application. The procedures differ slightly in the United States and in Canada (Canada Employment and Immigration, 1986; Jasso and Rosenzweig, 1988). However, petitioners can be persons, groups of persons, the federal government in the case of refugees, or businesses. Most research today emphasizes sponsorship by persons who are connected to the applicants by family ties. In such research, being sponsored is synonymous with the evoking of family networks for the purpose of migration. However, other types of sponsorship may evoke different types of networks.

To what extent do personal networks, represented not just by family but also by friendship and community of origin ties, play a role in corporate sponsorship in which immigration requires arranged and government approved employment? Are persons who enter as refugees or as economic migrants under occupational demand based criteria devoid of personal networks? Or, do such networks influence the migration process but elude capture by bureaucratically defined categories of admission? And to what extent do these migrants embody social ties which stimulate subsequent migration?

Finally, attention should be given to the consequences of sponsorship ties. United States research assumes the value and usefulness of sponsorship, and little information exists on the functions of sponsorship (Yu and Liu, 1986). At least for refugees where sponsorship can be undertaken by individuals or by groups, the type of sponsorship appears to matter for economic adjustment. Bach and Carroll-Sequin (1986) observe a lower labor force participation for refugee women who are sponsored by their relatives rather than by other American families or church groups. Such rates appear to reflect the greater incorporation of these women into ethnic communities where women are either under greater constraints to remain in the home or else lack the connections necessary for locating employment. Other examples show negative as well as positive consequences of sponsorship. In Canada, the family sponsored migrants are ineligible for training allowances associated with language training programs. This feature may depress the participation of sponsored migrants, many of whom are women (*See,* Boyd, 1987). In many European countries where residence permits are distinct from work permits, the admission of spouses and children is not always synonymous with legal permission to enter the labor force.

Return Migration and Remittances: Maintaining Networks

In part because of the distinctions embedded in host country's regulations, family migration is often labeled as "noneconomic". It also usually is equated with residential permanency. But such characterizations are facile if not inaccurate. In North America, migrant women often have labor participation rates which are as high or higher than native born women. Their economic participation contrasts with perceptions of migrant women as accompaniments — if not dependents — of their male sponsors. For migrants in Europe, family related migration often represents a household strategy of accumulating as much money in as short a period possible through the wage earning activities of multiple household members. Return to the sending area is one desired outcome of this family migration.

Return migration involves the movement back to the country or area of origin, either temporarily or for long periods. Because return migrants embody information and resources about receiving areas, such migration links sending and receiving areas and preserves the use of social networks in the migratory process. Social networks also are maintained in three other ways: 1) by the visits of migrants who have settled in the receiving country; 2) by the reliance on activities such as sports associations or village fetes which link the sending and receiving areas (Hily and Poinard, 1987; Massey *et al.*, 1987; and 3) by marriages which sustain kinship obligations across time and space (Ballard, 1987) and which encourage capital mobilization and success in the receiving country (Rex and Josephides, 1987).

Household migration strategies often include remittances, or the sending of money from the receiving area to the sending area. These remittances can take the form of money transfers to families in the sending areas, payments to schools in the home country where children are educated, and investments in the land, and businesses of the sending areas (H.C. Buechler, 1987: 3). Remittances are noteworthy for four reasons: 1) they indicate the existence of social networks across space (Caces *et al.*, 1985); 2) they have economic effects in the sending area; 3) they may maintain the use of migration as a household strategy; and 4) they send back important messages about comparative opportunities and standards of living, thereby stimulating future migration flows (Fawcett and Arnold, 1987).

Much has been written about the economic impact of such flows to Mexico and Europe. Most remittances are used for the purchase of consumer goods or family support rather than productive investment. However, such spending patterns must be analyzed within the context of the larger socioeconomic setting of the sending community, including employment and investment opportunities, national development trends and policies and the interest of national governments in the foreign exchange value of such remittances (Ballard, 1987). As well, immigration induced income also can increase dependency on migration wage labor, particularly under conditions of agricultural restructuring and export oriented industrialization in Third World areas (Ballard, 1987; Gonzalez, 1979; Pessar, 1982). Such dependency ensures the persistence of migration flows and the continued utilization of social networks.

Adjustment in the Receiving Country

Family migration and networks are part of immigrant settlement and integration in the receiving countries. Settlement refers to the intention and decision to settle in receiving countries. It does not preclude an eventual return to the sending areas or subsequent migration elsewhere. Integration involves the adaptation, acculturation and assimilation of individuals and groups in the receiving society (Kritz and Keely, 1981: xxvii), and it connotes (but does not guarantee) greater residential permanency in the host society.

Settlement and integration processes are influenced by kin and friendship ties, village based networks and customs (such as festivals), membership in ethnic associations and shared cultural and ethnic origins. These personal networks provide money to finance moves. They also provide food, shelter, job information and contacts, information on health care and social services, recreation and emotional support (*See*, Cornelius, 1982: 392; DaVanzo, 1981: 110; Massey *et al.*, 1987: Chapters 6 and 9; Tienda, 1980; Yücel, 1987). These network resources change with length of residency. As the period of settlement grows, family reunification is more likely, increasing the existence of family based networks in the receiving society. The volume and amount of remittances may decline, and membership in ethnic and non-ethnic based voluntary associations may increase (Portes and Bach, 1985: Chapter 9; Massey *et al.*, 1987). These "period" effects in turn affect subsequent cohorts of migrants. Recent migrants also enter an area with many more relatives, friends and contacts than did earlier migrants (Massey *et al.*, 1987). They also may find social and economic situations substantially modified by their predecessors (J.M. Buechler, 1987: 258).

To be sure, the operation of networks and their temporal developments are shaped by policies of receiving countries regarding integration and settlement. A distinction can be made between countries which stress immigration and immigrant settlement and those which do not (OECD, 1987). The preceding generalizations are relevant for countries which conceptualize migration as permanent and immigrant integration as a desired outcome. In countries which view migrants as marginal and temporary, other characterizations regarding the content and development of networks may exist. For example, as a correlate of Germany's alien policy, the achievements of Turkish workers in Germany depend very much on their personal relationships (Yücel, 1987). The intense utilization of networks based on kin and ethnicity results in the "colonization" of certain factories and towns or villages by Turks related through kinship or village origins.

Legal and illegal status also conditions the use and development of networks and the incidence of family migration. Illegals from Mexico frequently migrate without their wives and children. They also have fewer family and friendship ties than do legal migrants from Mexico (Massey *et al.*, 1987). Again, such patterns vary according to the migration and settlement policies of the receiving countries. In Germany (FRG) where legal labor recruitment was organized initially through authorized institutions in Germany and in several major sending countries (Yugoslavia, Turkey), family and village networks alone did not ensure that relatives and fellow villagers would be in close proximity in terms of work or residence. In fact, during the first year, many workers were isolated from previous networks and forced to rebuild social relationships in new environments. In contrast, for the illegal migrants there was almost no severance of social networks, for the operation of networks was crucial for all aspects of the migratory process, ranging from the decision to migrate to the obtaining of employment (Yücel, 1987).

In addition to kin networks, ethnic associations and ethnic enclaves have multiple roles in the migratory/settlement/integrative process. Ethnic based associations which focus around some activity such as sports, religion or recreation act as conduits for information and help. To the extent their activities involve contact with the origin community, they also may link migrant members to the communities of origin and facilitate reintegration upon return to the origin community (Massey *et al.*, 1987). However, the role they play in the integration of their members in the receiving society is deserving of more research. In her study of German associations, Schoenberg (1985) shows that it is over simplistic to see participation in ethnic organizations as an indication of ethnic cohesion and social segregation vis-à-vis the larger society. An equally simplistic assumption is that such associations integrate members in the host society by providing networks of contacts and information. Much depends on the activities and the goals of the ethnic association (Schoenberg, 1985; Sassen-Koob, 1979). Such goals and objectives are shaped by the structural differences between the origin and destination societies, which influence the mediating role of associations (Sassen-Koob, 1979). Other factors are national policies of integration and settlement and the class composition of migrants.

Much is written about the impact of ethnic enclaves on the economic status of individuals, families and migrant communities. Ethnic enclaves can be defined in several ways, but generally the term refers to small enterprises that are owned by (self-employed) members of an ethnic community. Here, the labor force is drawn extensively from the same ethnic community using kin, friendship and ethnic ties. Networks are an integral part of such enclaves. They provide essential information on the setting up of businesses, the economic inputs required, the problems encountered and the labor requirements (Werbner, 1987: 220). They also link employers and potential employees through personal ties. Ethnic businesses extensively use family ties, often relying on the participation of women in the operation of family businesses (Model, 1985; Kim and Hurh, 1985; Rex and Josephides, 1987; Werbner, 1987).

In the United States, participation in an ethnic enclave depends on the interaction of ethnicity, entry status and family ties. Mexicans and Haitians who lack ethnically defined economic enclaves do not do as well as Cubans who are in ethnic enclaves. The economic disadvantage arises in part because of the absence of family ties (Haitian refugees) and because previous migration experience as illegals (Mexicans) allocates them into the secondary labor market (Portes and Bach, 1980; 1985; Portes and Stepick, 1985; Stepick and Portes, 1986). Employment in the primary labor market is more likely for other migrants (particularly those from Asia) who do not enter the United States on the basis of family ties (Portes, 1981). However, they tend to be in subordinate positions within that sector (Portes and Bach, 1985: Chapter 10).

Considerable debate exists about the consequences of participation in an enclave economy for recent migrants (*See,* Portes and Bach, 1985; Portes and Jensen, 1988; Model, 1985). One view holds that ethnic enclaves help economic adjustment because ethnic ties provide networks of social support and facilitate the learning of new skills (Perez, 1986; Portes and Bach, 1985; Yücel, 1987). The positive implications of the ethnic enclave result from the reciprocal relations embedded in ethnically based social networks. If employers profit from the hiring of fellow immigrants, they also are obligated to train them, hold open supervisory positions and support their movement into self-employment (Portes and Bach, 1985:343; See, also, Model, 1985). This view contrasts with the argument that ethnic firms exploit the more recently arrived migrants by paying low wages and hiring migrants for jobs which are menial, dead end and have poor working conditions. From this perspective, employment in an ethnic enclave shares considerable similarity with employment in the secondary labor market.

Additional research is needed to refine and further this debate. A recent FRG study (Yücel, 1987) shows that impact of enclave employment depends on the life cycle of the business enterprise and the legal status of migrant workers. If ethnic entrepreneurs attempt to break into self-employment through the establishment of small industrial workshops, they may employ illegal migrants if available. Such employment minimizes costs to employers and provides contacts, jobs and some job training to such migrants. However, as such enterprises become more successful and as state policing of hiring illegals increases, entrepreneurs shift their employment to legal migrants. Such practices both support and maintain illegal migrants as an underclass in an ethnic enclave (Yücel, 1987).

ISSUES FOR THE 1990s

Although it provides insights in the character and continuation of migration flows, current research on family and personal networks also generate questions requiring future consideration. Some of these questions evolve from specific research topics, discussed in the preceding sections. However, two general issues shape research agenda for the 1990s. These issues are 1) greater specification of the role of networks in migration; and 2) the inclusion of women in models which currently are gender blind.

Development Regarding Networks in Migration

Three types of research agenda exist for migration networks. One centers on greater refinement of the concept "network". Most migration studies which examine networks do not incorporate the distinctions provided from the sociological field of network analysis. As a result, some potential refinements in the study of networks and their role in migration are absent. For example, Granovetter's (1973) pioneering research showed that under certain conditions, weak ties — those involving relationships between ac-

FAMILY AND PERSONAL NETWORKS IN MIGRATION   655

quaintances — as opposed to strong ties — those reflecting relationships between close friends and relatives — can maximize information flows and social mobility opportunities, in part because they provide bridges between two or more cliques. The distinction between weak and strong ties appears useful in studies of ethnic enclaves (*See*, Werbner, 1987) and may be relevant in other areas of migration research.

The second agenda calls for a more comprehensive look at the dynamics of networks. Most studies of personal networks in international migration emphasize their existence, operation and persistence across time and space. In addition, most studies examine networks within the context of movement from less developed areas to more developed areas, and most studies focus on networks which are associated with or derive from labor migration, as opposed to refugee or "forced" migrations.

These foci are understandable given the fixation of researchers and policymakers on the persistent and almost uncontrollable nature of current migration to industrialized countries. To better understand the dynamics of migration networks, two questions require answers: 1) why and when do personal networks fail to emerge; and 2) under what conditions do networks weaken and/or disappear.

To answer these questions, the conditioning effects of micro and macro variables across time and space must be considered. Thus, the study of the dynamics of personal networks in migration is closely associated with a third research agenda which calls for further empirical and conceptual refinements in the study of migration systems. These refinements require continued, new and sustained efforts at linking together the component parts and understanding changes in such linkages. The specific questions to be addressed in this exercise are numerous (Fawcett and Arnold, 1987; Lim 1987a, 1987b; Salt, 1987). Personal networks, or ties between people, represent only one out of many kinds of networks, such as political (military, foreign relations) or economic (trade, foreign investment) ties between sending and receiving nations. However, refinements in the conceptualization of migration systems will provide a broad generalized framework from which to study the origins, persistence and decline of networks, and to compare the dynamics of personal networks vis-à-vis other networks.

Bringing in Gender

In addition to the empirical and theoretical challenges associated with studying networks from a migration systems perspective, another challenge is that of understanding the relationship between gender and networks in migration. To date much of the recent research on networks is indifferent to gender. Some studies emphasize the experiences of male migrants or all migrants undifferentiated by sex, while others emphasize group behavior as represented in household decisionmaking strategies. Such emphasis is consistent with a general research orientation which assumes that women migrate as part of family migration (Morokvasic, 1983; 1984; Ranney and Koussoudji, 1984). As a consequence, little systematic attention is paid to gender in the development and persistence of networks across time and space.

Does a complete understanding of the role of personal networks in international migration require specific attention to gender? Answering this question requires some reflection on the meaning of the term "a complete understanding". A methodological approach would be to show that the pattern and strength of relationships between "independent" and "dependent" variables are the same or are different for females and males with respect to a given model. For example, this could be done in the value-expectancy decisionmaking research or in research on the multiplier effects of family migration. However, such approaches risk assuming *a priori* the basic parameters of the model against which to undertake female-male comparisons. A conceptual approach asks if existing models can be enriched or extended by explicit analyses of women in network and family migration research. Using this standard requires ascertaining that the inclusion of women requires additional conceptualization or adds new research topics.

The impetus for the latter approach arises from feminist perspectives on the relations between gender and social and economic institutions (for examples, *See*, Jaggar, 1983; Sokoloff, 1980). Although unresolved debates and differences exist among feminist schools (Jaggar, 1983; Sargent, 1981), a major tenet is that the gender division of labor must be included in any account of the social relations of production in a society. That is to say, the division of labor — the structured activities in a society — are gendered. Further, not only do men and women undertake different tasks, but women are responsible for activities in the domestic sphere. These different tasks are the basis for the social construction of gender in which women are excluded from some activities, confined to others, dependent on males, docile, subservient and assigned secondary status in the labor market (Arizpe and Aranda, 1986; Elson and Pearson, 1981; Lim, 1983).

Feminist perspectives call for analyses which conceptually include a gender division of labor as a key ingredient of theoretical paradigms. Although the field of migration research has not been immune to such calls, such inclusions are limited largely to research on women and development (Beneria, 1985; Fernandez-Kelly, 1983a; 1983b; 1986; Leacock and Safa, 1986; Nash and Fernandez-Kelly, 1983; Nash and Safa, 1986) and to migration research which emphasizes the female migration within the context of the new international division of labor (Sassen-Koob, 1984) or capitalist modes of production (Phizacklea, 1983a).

Does the inclusion of women or the issue of a gender division of labor require additional conceptualization efforts or add new research topics to the field of migration? Selected areas of research on family migration and personal networks indicate an affirmative answer. Review of material presented previously in this article shows that gender differences in social and economic roles influence migration decisionmaking processes, modify the conceptualization of household strategies, influence the sex composition of labor migration, are often incorporated into immigration policies and are embedded in the organization of ethnic enclaves.

In models of migration decisionmaking, the sex of the person exerting pressure or serving as a source of aid or information may influence the effect of such pressure or information. In a male dominated society, for example, female approval for migration may carry little weight in decisionmaking processes (Trager, 1984:1274; Young, 1985:167). Where social norms demand attachment of women to a family structure, resulting family pressures may prevent any migration of unattached women (Shah, 1983; Thandi and Todaro, 1979; 1984). In other circumstances, gender differences in the division of labor may favor migration of women more than men. For example, not only is the migration of young women from rural to urban areas in the Philippines, and particularly to Manila, substantial, but also it represents a family strategy for obtaining short term remittances (Lauby and Stark, 1988; Trager, 1984). However, family strategies regarding remittances are linked to gender roles and cultural values. Families expect daughters to be obedient, less likely to spend money on themselves and more likely to remit money to the family unit (Trager, 1984). Offers of assistance by female friends and relatives to prospective female migrants may evoke powerful images of protection and chaperoning, thereby facilitating migration intention or behavior (Huang, 1984:253). In short, migration decisionmaking processes are shaped by sex-specific family and friendship sources of approval, disapproval, assistance and information.

In addition, male hierarchies of power and authority which exist in households call for refining approaches which treat the household as a monolithic unit, focus on total income and emphasize the pursuit of rational economic behavior (Bach and Schraml, 1982; Schmink, 1986:143, 149-150). In discussing household strategies, the same question asked of family strategies can be posed: whose strategies are we observing (Hareven, 1987: xvi)? Families and households are not always harmonious decisionmaking units and collective strategies are not always identical to those of individuals (Fawcett and Arnold, 1987; Hareven, 1987; Schmink, 1986:150). Do household/family units develop strategies on the basis of rational economic behavior (Schmink, 1986)? In patriarchal societies, household strategies which involve males but not females migrating may not be predicated on the basis of economic rationality (Schmink, 1986:150). Also, who benefits or pays the costs for these collective strategies in which individual needs or interests may be suppressed (Crummett, 1987; Fernandez-Kelly, 1983a)? Mexican women employed in maquiladora work are there because of a dependency of the family on their wages, a dependency often elicited by high male unemployment. Faced with low wages and the need to reconcile domestic responsibilities with employment requirements, these migrant women and their families have not experienced improvements, and they must rely on the informal sector for meeting additional living requirements (Fernandez-Kelly, 1983a).

Recognizing the gender division of labor also refines analyses which emphasize the structural conditions of sending countries as powerful stimulants of migration streams. The existing gender division of labor is predicted on the subordinate position of women to men. It influences whether males or females become a "surplus" population and hence more subject to outmigration during periods of economic transformation. For example, female rather than male migration is likely to occur under the following circumstances: 1) where men control agricultural ownership and production; 2) where reorganization of agriculture polarizes the peasants into large land holdings versus smaller or landless holdings; and 3) where nonagricultural domestic manufacturing, undertaken by women, is destroyed by the introduction of externally manufactured goods (Beneria and Sen, 1986; Sassen-Koob, 1984; Young, 1985). Thus, in Latin America, the internal and international migration of women is considerable, in contrast to areas of Africa where the involvement of women in agriculture fosters the migration of males.

The introduction or expansion of export oriented manufacturing often requires a labor force characterized by cheapness, docility, obedience and ease of control. While such characteristics are not innately female as opposed to male, they are implicit in most systems of gender differentiation (*See*, Elson and Pearson, 1981; Hancock, 1983; Lim 1983). As a result, women represent labor for micro-electronic, toy making, textile and component assembling industries. In combination with the structural changes in local economies, such employment opportunities condition and encourage female migration (Arizpe and Aranda, 1986; Fernandez-Kelly, 1983a, 1983b; Safa, 1986; Sassen-Koob, 1984). Much of this migration is rural to urban migration within Latin American and Asian countries (Khoo, Smith and Fawcett, 1984). However, from an international migration perspective, such migration is noteworthy for two reasons.

First, some international migration of women also exists between Asian countries and between Latin American countries (Fong and Lim, 1982; Hancock, 1983; Marshall, 1979). International migration flows among Third

FAMILY AND PERSONAL NETWORKS IN MIGRATION   659

World countries most likely will increase in the decades ahead (Salt, 1987). If immigration rises, the patterns may be more readily interpreted by a framework which recognizes the role of gender differentiation in conditioning migration from sending areas and in establishing desired labor pools.

Second, from the perspective of the new international division of labor, the movement of capital to peripheral areas coincides with the increasing demand for low wage labor in the core (Sassen-Koob, 1984; 1988). Economic transformation in core does not innately require female labor, but it creates a low skill, low wage service economy which is consistent with the perceived characteristics of female labor. The growth in Third World immigration, particularly under family reunification policies, is associated with a female immigrant supply for such jobs and the growing demand for this type of labor (Castles, 1987; Sassen-Koob, 1984). According to this perspective, the use of family networks and increased family migration does not indicate the demise of labor migration as much as its transformation. Yet this transformation has not been central to much research on networks.

Government agreements are integral to the creations of free trade zones, where intensive female employment exists in certain types of industries. Governments also may use gender related criteria in the implementation of gender blind international agreements. For example, during the early stages of the European guestworker movement, would-be migrant Portuguese women faced hurdles in obtaining visas from Portuguese officials for official emigration. This appears to have been a deliberate policy, based on a gender division of labor in which women remained, literally and figuratively, in the home. Such location, and the resulting economic dependency, ensured remittances and from the government's viewpoint, the continued flow of foreign exchange to Portugal (*See,* Leeds, 1987).

The gender division of labor also influences the formulation and implementation of immigration policy and regulations. The presumption of males as breadwinners and females as dependent spouses can be built explicitly into immigration policy. Thus it can shape the use of family networks in migration. In the early 1980s, women without British citizenship in Britain faced greater difficulty in sponsoring the immigration of their fiances than did their male counterparts (WING, 1985). Even when gender is not used as an explicit criteria, outcomes associated with a gender division of labor may dampen the use of family networks which connect to women migrants. For example, lower wages is one well known correlate of the secondary status of women in the labor force. But in Canada, when family income is below the low income cutoffs, immigrants may be ineligible to sponsor the migration of family members. This ruling is gender blind. However, female earnings are approximately 60 percent those of men. Thus women who are single or single parents may be less eligible to sponsor relatives.

An important tenet in the feminist literature on women and capitalism is that changing modes of production do not do away with a gender division of labor and a subordinate status of women. Rather, changing modes of production often intensify as well as decompose old forms and recreate new expressions. Examining the use of family ties in the operation of ethnic enclaves indicates that the persistence of a gender division of labor and its new expressions are crucial for the success of enclave businesses. But the success is built on a paradox, not yet incorporated fully in the existing research on ethnic enclaves.

The paradox arises because the involvement of women in ethnic enclaves has the appearance of growing equality. Actually it may reflect no change or new expressions of sexual inequality. On the one hand, ethnic enclaves appear to facilitate the employment of ethnic women through the existence of particularistic hiring criteria and family firms as well as through child care arrangements resulting from social arrangements within the enclave and often the presence of elderly relatives. Women often view such employment as furthering the family's economic status and thus achieving family objectives (Anthias, 1983; Perez; 1986; Prieto, 1986)

But, in fact, these patterns of female employment can simply recast patriarchal gender relations in a new setting. Two separate studies of Greek-Cypriot women in London and Cuban women in the United States note that women view their economic role as subservient to that of males in their families, work with the permission of their husbands, and maintain full responsibility for child care and domestic work (Anthias, 1983; Fernandez Kelly and Garcia, quoted in Portes and Jensen, 1988).

Female employment in enclaves also generates two issues for future research. First, in the enclave economy women represent a flexible cheap source of labor in unwaged or low paid work and personalistic settings, all of which increase the viability of entrepreneurs (Anthias, 1983; Kim and Hurh, 1985; Model, 1985; Perez, 1986). Phizacklea (1983:110) argues that much of the literature on ethnic economies ignores the fact that the *petit bourgeois* class position, represented by self-employment and small factory ownership, can only be achieved through the labor of other migrants particularly female relatives (*See*, also, Anthias, 1983; Portes and Jensen, 1988). Second, most studies which document the positive effects of enclave employment examine the experiences of males. Women's employment calls for refining ethnic enclave research to include female specific segmentation, quite possibly approximating secondary labor markets as traditionally defined (Piore, 1975).

CONCLUSION

To date, the study of networks has stimulated considerable research and

FAMILY AND PERSONAL NETWORKS IN MIGRATION   661

developed new insights into international migration flows and settlements. Social networks based on kinship, friendship and community ties are central components in migration systems analysis. They mediate between individual actors and larger structural forces. They link sending and receiving countries. And they explain the continuation of migration long after the original impetus for migration has ended.

Because kinship ties are a major source of personal networks in migration, the interest in personal networks also directs attention to the role of families and households in migration and in family migration per se. The study of personal networks and family related migration includes many perspectives and emphasizes many areas. This article reviews five domains of research. Economic and social conditions in the place of origin as well as in the place of destination influence the activation of personal networks in mobilizing migration and the way in which such networks are utilized. Immigration policies and the legacy of bilateral treaties regarding labor recruitment also structure the settings within which individuals make migration decisions, and they stimulate family migration through kinship ties. Personal networks and their stimulative effects on migration also are maintained and transformed through remittances, return migration and by the settlement and integration of migrants.

The study of personal networks in migration reveals the importance of social relations in migratory behavior. It provides insight into the origins, composition, direction and persistence of migration flows. At the same time, a large research agenda remains. In addition to the specific issues raised in various parts of the overview section, greater attention could be given to the nondevelopment and cessation of personal networks and to the incorporation of personal networks in a broader migration systems approach. The near absence of women in many studies also indicates an insensitivity to the ways in which the gender division of labor shapes the determinants and consequences of personal networks in migration. Responding to these gaps are the research challenges for the 1990s.

REFERENCES

Anderson, G.
1974   *Networks of Contacts: The Portuguese in Toronto.* Waterloo, Ontario: University of Waterloo Press.

Anthias, F.
1983   "Sexual Divisions and Ethnic Adaptation: The Case of the Greek-Cypriot Women". In *One Way Ticket: Migration and Female Labour.* Edited by A. Phizacklea. London: Routledge and Kegan Paul. Pp. 73-94.

Arizpe, L. and J. Aranda
1986   "Women Workers in the Strawberry Agribusiness in Mexico". In *Women's Work: Development and the Division of Labor by Sex.* Edited by E. Leacock and H.I. Safa. South Hadley, MA: Bergin and Garvey Publishers, Inc. Pp. 174-193.

Bach, R. and R. Carroll-Seguin
1986   "Labor Force Participation, Household Composition and Sponsorship Among
       Southeast Asian Refugees", *International Migration Review*, 20(2):381-404. Summer.

Bach, R. and L.A. Schraml
1982   "Migration, Crisis and Theoretical Conflict", *International Migration Review*, 16(2):320-
       341. Summer.

Ballard, R.
1987   "The Political Economy of Migration: Pakistan, Britain and the Middle East". In *Migrant
       Workers and the Social Order*. Edited by J. Eades. London: Tavistock Publications.
       Pp. 17-41.

Beneria, L., ed.
1985   *Women and Development: The Sexual Division of Labor in Rural Societies*. New York:
       Praeger Publishers.

Beneria, L. and G. Sen
1986   "Accumulation, Reproduction and Women's Role in Economic Development: Boserup
       Revisited". In *Women's Work: Development and the Division of Labor by Sex*. Edited by E.
       Leacock and H.I. Safa. South Hadley, MA: Bergin and Garvey Publishers, Inc.
       Pp. 141-157.

Boutang, Y.M. and J.P. Garson
1984   "Major Obstacles to Control of Irregular Migrations: Prerequisites to Policy",
       International Migration Review, 18(3):579-592. Fall.

Boyd, M.
1987   *Migrant Women in Canada: Profiles and Policies*. Report prepared for the OECD
       Monitoring Panel on Migrant Women. Ottawa: Employment and Immigration Canada,
       Immigration Research Division.

Briody, E.
1987   "Patterns of Household Immigration into South Texas", *International Migration Review*,
       21(1):27-47. Spring.

Buechler, H.C.
1987   "Introduction". In *Migrants in Europe: The Role of Family, Labor and Politics*. Edited by
       H.C. Buechler and J.M. Buechler. New York: Greenwood Press. Pp.1-7.

Buechler, J.M.
1987   "A Review - Guest, Intruder, Settler, Ethnic Minority or Citizen: The Sense and
       Nonsense of Borders". In *Migrant in Europe: The Role of Family, Labor and Politics*. Edited
       by H.C. Buechler and J.M. Buechler. New York: Greenwood Press. Pp. 283-304.

Buechler, H.C.and J.M. Buechler, eds.
1987   *Migrants in Europe: The Role of Family, Labor and Politics*. New York: Greenwood Press.

Burawoy, M.
1976   "The Functions and Reproduction of Migrant Labor: Comparative Material from
       Southern Africa and the United States", *American Journal of Sociology*, 8(5):1050-1092.
       March.

Caces, F., *et al.*
1985   "Shadow Households and Competing Auspices: Migration Behavior in the
       Philippines", *Journal of Development Economics*, 17(1):5-25.

Canada. Employment and Immigration
1986   *Your Rights and Canada's Immigration Law*. Catalogue MP23-65/1986. Ottawa: Minister
       of Supply and Services.

Castles, S.
1987 "Migratory Process, Ethnic Relations and Labour Market Segregation". Paper No. 6. Wollongong: University of Wollogong, Centre for Multicultural Studies. Dec.

1986 "The Guest Worker in Western Europe: An Obituary", *International Migration Review,* 22(4):761-778. Winter.

1984 *Here For Good: Western Europe's New Ethnic Minorities.* London: Pluto Press.

Castles, S. and G. Kosack
1973 *Immigrant Workers and Class Structure in Western Europe.* London: Oxford University Press.

Cornelius, W.
1982 "Interviewing Undocumented Immigrants: Methodological Reflections Based on Fieldwork in Mexico and the U.S.", *International Migration Review,* 16(2):378-411. Summer.

Crummett, M.
1987 "Rural Women and Migration in Latin America". In *Rural Women and State Policy: Feminist Perspectives on Latin American Agricultural Development.* Edited by C.D. Deere and M. Leon. Boulder, CO: Westview Press. Pp. 239-260.

DaVanzo, J.
1981 "Microeconomic Approaches to Studying Migration Decisions". In *Migration Decision Making: Multidisciplinary Approaches to Microlevel Studies in Developed and Developing Countries.* Edited by G.F. De Jong and R.W. Gardner. New York: Pergamon Press. Pp. 90-129.

DeJong, G.F. and J.T. Fawcett
1981 "Motivations for Migration: An Assessment and a Value Expectancy Research Model". In *Migration Decision Making: Multidisciplinary Approaches to Microlevel Studies in Developed and Developing Countries.* Edited by G.F. DeJong and R.W. Gardner. New York: Pergamon Press. Pp. 13-58.

DeJong, G.F. and R.W. Gardner
1981 "Introduction and Overview". In *Migration Decision Making: Multidisciplinary Approaches to Microlevel Studies in Developed and Developing Countries.* Edited by G.F. DeJong and R.W. Gardner. New York: Pergamon Press. Pp. 1-12.

DeJong, G.F., *et al.*
1983 "International and Internal Migration Decision Making: A Value-Expectancy Based on Analytical Framework of Intentions to Move from a Rural Philippine Province", *International Migration Review,* 17(3):470-484. Fall.

DeJong, G., B.D. Root and R.G. Abad
1986 "Family Reunification and Philippine Migration to the United States: The Immigrants Perspective", *International Migration Review,* 22(3):598-612. Fall.

DeJong, G., *et al.*
1985-86 "Migration Intentions and Behavior: Decision Making in a Rural Philippine Province", *Population and Environment,* 8(1/2):41-62. Spring/Summer.

Dinerman, I.R.
1978 "Patterns of Adaptation Among Households of U.S. Bound Migrants from Michoacan, Mexico", *International Migration Review,* 12(4):485-501. Winter.

Eades, J.
1987 "Anthropologists and Migrants: Changing Models and Realities". In *Migrants, Workers and the Social Order*. Edited by Jeremy Eades. London: Tavistock Publications. Pp. 1-16.

Elson, D. and R. Pearson
1981 "'Nimble Fingers Make Cheap Workers': An Analysis of Women's Employment in Third World Export Manufacturing", *Feminist Review*, 7:87-107. Spring.

Escobar, A., M. Gonzalez and B. Roberts
1987 "Migration, Labour Markets and the International Economy: Jalisco, Mexico and the United States". In *Migrants, Workers and the Social Order*. Edited by J. Eades. London: Tavistock Publications. Pp. 42-64.

Fawcett, J.
1985-86 "Migration Psychology: New Behavioral Models", *Population and Environment*, 8(1/2):5-14. Spring/Summer.

Fawcett, J.T. and F. Arnold
1987 "Explaining Diversity: Asian and Pacific Immigration Systems". In *Pacific Bridges: The New Immigration from Asia and the Pacific Islands*. Edited by J.T. Fawcett and B.V. Carino. Staten Island: Center for Migration Studies. Pp. 453-474.

Fernandez-Kelly, M.P.
1986 "Introduction". In *Women's Work: Development and the Division of Labor by Sex*. Edited by E. Leacock and H.I. Safa. South Hadley, MA: Bergin and Garvey Publishers, Inc. Pp. 1-10.

1983a *For We are Sold, I and My People*. Albany: State University of New York Press.

1983b "Mexican Border Industrialization, Female Labor Force Participation and Migration". In *Women, Men and the International Division of Labor*. Edited by J. Nash and M.P. Fernandez-Kelly. Albany: State University of New York Press. Pp. 205-223.

Fong, P.E. and L. Lim
1982 "Foreign Labor and Economic Development in Singapore", *International Migration Review*, 16(3):548-575. Fall.

Fuller, T., P. Lightfoot and P. Kamnuansilpa
1985-86 "Mobility Plans and Mobility Behavior: Convergences and Divergences in Thailand", *Population and Environment*, 8(1/2):15-40. Spring/Summer.

Gardner, R.W.
1981 "Macrolevel Influences on the Migration Decision Process". In *Migration Decision Making: Multidisciplinary Approaches to Microlevel Studies in Developed and Developing Countries*. Edited by G.F. DeJong and R.W. Gardner. New York: Pergamon Press. Pp. 59-89.

Garrison, V. and C.I. Weiss
1979 "Dominican Family Networks and United States Immigration: A Case Study", *International Migration Review*, 13(2):264-283. Summer.

Gillespie, F. and H. Browning
1979 "The Effect of Emigration upon Socioeconomic Structure: The Case of Paraguay", *International Migration Review*, 13(3):502-518. Fall.

Gonzalez, N.L.
1979 "Garfuna Settlement in New York: A New Frontier", *International Migration Review*, 13(2):255-263. Summer.

Granovetter, M.S.
1973   "The Strength of Weak Ties", *American Journal of Sociology*, 78(6):1360-1380. May.

Hancock, M.
1983   "Transnational Production and Women Workers". In *One Way Ticket: Migration and Female Labour*. Edited by A. Phizacklea. London: Routledge and Kegan Paul. Pp. 131-145.

Harbison, S.F.
1981   "Family Structure and Family Strategy in Migration Decision Making". In *Migration Decision Making: Multidisciplinary Approaches to Microlevel Studies in Developed and Developing Countries*. Edited by G.F. DeJong and R.W. Gardner. New York: Pergamon Press. Pp. 225-251.

Hareven, T.K.
1987   "Family History at the Crossroads", *Journal of Family History*, 12(1-3):ix-xxiii.

Hily, M.A. and M. Poinard
1987   "Portuguese Associations in France". In *Immigrant Associations in Europe*. Edited by J. Rex, D. Joly and C. Wilpert. Aldershot, England: Gower Publishing Company. Pp. 126-165.

Huang, N.C.
1984   "The Migration of Rural Women to Taipei". In *Women in the Cities of Asia: Migration and Urban Adaptation*. Edited by J.T. Fawcett, S.E. Khoo and P.C. Smith. Boulder, CO: Westview Press. Pp. 247-268.

Hugo, G.J.
1981   "Village-Community Ties, Village Norms and Ethnic and Social Networks: A Review of Evidence from the Third World". In *Migration Decision Making: Multidisciplinary Approaches to Microlevel Studies in Developed and Developing Countries*. Edited by G.F. DeJong and R.W. Gardner. New York: Pergamon Press. Pp. 186-224.

Hune, S.
1987   "Drafting an International Convention on the Protection of the Rights of All Migrant Workers and Their Families", *International Migration Review*, 21(1):123-127. Spring.

_____
1985   "The Articles of the International Convention on the Protection of the Rights of All Migrant Workers and Their Families", *International Migration Review*, 19(3):573-615. Fall.

Jaggar, A.
1983   *Feminist Politics and Human Nature*. Totowa, NJ: Rowman and Allanheld.

Jasso, G. and M.R. Rosenzweig
1987   "Using National Recording Systems for the Measurement and Analysis of Immigration to the United States", *International Migration Review*, 21:1212-1244. Winter.

_____
1986   "Family Reunification and the Immigration Multiplier: U.S. Immigration Law, Origin Country Conditions and the Reproduction of Immigrants", *Demography*, 23:291-311.

Khoo, S.E., P.C. Smith and J.T. Fawcett
1984   "Migration of Women to Cities: The Asian Situation in Comparative Perspective", *International Migration Review*, 18(4):1247-1263. Winter.

Kim, K.C. and W.M. Hurh
1985   "Ethnic Resources Utilization of Korean Immigrant Entrepreneurs in the Chicago Minority Area", *International Migration Review*, 19(1):82-111. Spring.

Kritz, M. and C.B. Keely
1981   "Introduction". In *Global Trends in Migration: Theory and Research in International Population Movements*. Edited by M.M. Kritz, C.B. Keely and S.M. Tomasi. Staten Island: Center for Migration Studies.

Lauby, J. and O. Stark
1988   "Individual Migration as Family Strategy: Young Women in the Philippines". Cambridge, MA: Harvard University Migration and Development Program.

Leacock, E. and H. Safa, eds.
1986   *Women's Work*. South Hadley, MA: Bergin and Garvey Publishers.

Leeds, A.
1987   "Work, Labor and Their Recompenses: Portuguese Life Strategies Involving Migration". In *Migrants in Europe: The Role of Family, Labor and Politics*. Edited by H.C. Buechler and J.M. Buechler. New York: Greenwood Press. Pp. 9-59.

Lim, L.L.
1987a "IUSSP Committee on International Migration, Workshop on International Migration Systems and Workshops", *International Migration Review*, 21(2):416-423. Summer.

1987b "IUSSP Committee on International Migration: Work Shop on International Migration Systems and Networks". Unpublished document. March.

Lim, L.
1983   "Capitalism, Imperialism and Patriarchy: The Dilemma of Third World Women Workers in Multinational Factories". In *Women, Men and the International Division of Labor*. Edited by J. Nash and M.P. Fernandez-Kelly. Albany, NY: State University of New York Press. Pp. 70-91.

MacDonald, J.S. and L.D. MacDonald
1964   "Chain Migration, Ethnic Neighbourhood Formation and Social Networks", *Milbank Memorial Fund Quarterly*, 42:82-97.

Marshall, A.
1979   "Immigrant Workers in the Buenos Aires Labor Market", *International Migration Review*, 13(3):488-501. Fall.

Massey, D.S.
1987   "Do Undocumented Migrants Earn Lower Wages than Legal Immigrants? New Evidence from Mexico", *International Migration Review*, 21(2):236-274. Summer.

Massey, D.S., *et al.*
1987   *Return to Aztlan: The Social Process of International Migration from Western Mexico*. Berkeley: University of California Press.

Model, S.
1985   "A Comparative Perspective on the Ethnic Enclave: Blacks, Italians and Jews in New York City", *International Migration Review*, 19(1):64-81. Spring.

Morokvasic, M.
1984   "Birds of Passage are Also Women", *International Migration Review*, 18(4):886-907. Winter.

1983   "Women in Migration: Beyond the Reductionist Outlook". In *One Way Ticket: Migration and Female Labour*. Edited by A. Phizacklea. London: Routledge and Kegan Paul. Pp. 13-32.

Nash, J. and M.P. Fernandez-Kelly, eds.
1983   *Women, Men and the International Division of Labour.* Albany: State University of
       New York Press.

Nash, J. and H. Safa, eds.
1986   *Women and Change in Latin America.* South Hadley, MA: Bergin and Garvey Publishers.

OECD (Organization for Economic Co-operation and Development)
1988   Continuous Reporting System on Migration, SOPEMI, 1987. Paris: Organization for
       Economic Co-operation and Development, Directorate for Social Affairs, Manpower
       and Education.

_____
1987   "Annex B: National Policies and Practices of Entry Control in OECD Member
       Countries". In *Continuous Reporting System on Migration, SOPEMI, 1986.* Paris: Or-
       ganization for Economic Co-operation and Development, Directorate for Social Affairs,
       Manpower and Education. Pp. 96-128.

Papademetriou, D.
1988a "International Migration in a Changing World". In *International Migration Today,*
       Volume 2: Emerging Issues. Edited by C.W. Stahl. Paris: UNESCO. Pp. 237-250.

_____
1988b "International Migration in North America and Western Europe: Trends and
       Consequences". In *International Migration Today.* Volume 1: Trends and Prospects.
       Edited by R.T. Appleyard. Paris: UNESCO. Pp. 311-380.

Pedraza-Bailey, S.
1985   "Cuba's Exiles: Portrait of a Refugee Migration", *International Migration Review,*
       19(1):4-34. Spring.

Perez, L.
1986   "Immigrant Economic Adjustment and Family Organization: The Cuban Success Story
       Reexamined", *International Migration Review,* 20(1):4-20. Spring.

Pessar, P.A.
1986   "The Role of Gender in Dominican Settlement in the United States". In *Women and
       Change in Latin America.* Edited by J. Nash and H. Safa. South Hadley, MA: Bergin
       and Garvey Publishers, Inc. Pp. 273-294.

_____
1982   "The Role of Households in International Migration and the Case of the U.S. Bound
       Migration from the Dominican Republic", *International Migration Review,*
       16(2):342-364. Summer.

Petras, E.M.
1981   "The Global Labor Market in the Modern World Economy". In *Global Trends in
       Migration.* Edited by M.M. Kritz and C.B. Keely. Staten Island: Center for Migration
       Studies.

Phizacklea, A.
1983a "In the Front Line". In *One Way Ticket: Migration and Female Labour.* Edited by
       A. Phizacklea. London: Routledge and Kegan Paul. Pp. 95-112.

_____
1983b "Introduction". In *One Way Ticket: Migration and Female Labour.* Edited by
       A. Phizacklea. London: Routledge and Kegan Paul. Pp. 1-12.

Piore, M.J.
1979   *Birds of Passage: Migrant Labor and Industrial Societies.* Cambridge:
       Cambridge University Press.

Portes, A.
1987   "One Field, Many Views: Competing Theories of International Migration". In *Pacific Bridges: The New Immigration from Asia and the Pacific Islands*. Edited by J.T. Fawcett and B.V. Carino. Staten Island: Center for Migration Studies. Pp. 53-70.

1985   "Urbanization, Migration and Models of Development in Latin America". In *Capital and Labour in the Urbanized World*. Edited by J. Walton. London: Sage Publications Ltd. Pp. 109-125.

1981   "Modes of Structural Incorporation and Present Theories of Labour Immigration". In *Global Trends in Migration*. Edited by M.M. Kritz, C.B. Keely and S.M. Tomasi. Staten Island: Center for Migration Studies.

Portes, A. and R.L. Bach
1985   *Latin Journey: Cuban and Mexican Immigrants in the United States*. Berkeley, CA: University of California Press.

1980   "Immigrant Earnings: Cuban and Mexican Immigrants in the United States", *International Migration Review*, 14(3):315-341. Fall.

Portes, A. and L. Jensen
1988   "The Enclave and the Entrants". Unpublished paper. Department of Sociology, Johns Hopkins University. May.

Portes, A. and A. Stepick
1985   "Unwelcome Immigrants", *American Sociological Review*, 50(4):515-529. August.

Portes, A. and J. Walton
1981   *Labor, Class and the International System*. New York: Academic Press.

Prieto, Y.
1986   "Cuban Women and Work in the United States: A New Jersey Case Study". In *International Migration: The Female Experience*. Edited by R.J. Simon and C.B. Brettell. Totowa, NJ: Rowman and Allanheld. Pp. 95-113.

Ranney, S. and S.A. Koussoudji
1984   "The Labor Market Experiences of Female Migrants: The Case of Temporary Mexican Migration to the U.S.". *International Migration Review*, 18(4):1120-1143. Winter.

Reichert, J. and D.S. Massey
1980   "History and Trends in U.S. Bound Migration from a Mexican Town", *International Migration Review*, 14(4):475-491. Winter.

Rex, J. and S. Josephides
1987   "Asian and Greek Cypriot Associations and Identity". In *Immigrant Associations in Europe*. Edited by J. Rex, D. Joly and C. Wilpert. Aldershot, England: Gower Publishing Company. Pp. 11-41.

Ritchie, P.N.
1976   "Explanations of Migration". In *Annual Review of Sociology, Volume 2*. Edited by A. Inkeles. Palo Alto, CA: Annual Reviews Inc. Pp. 363-404.

Root, B.D. and G.F. DeJong
1986   "Family Migration: Conceptualizing the Migrating Unit in a Developing Country". Revision of a paper presented at the annual meeting of the American Sociological Association meeting. New York.

FAMILY AND PERSONAL NETWORKS IN MIGRATION   669

Safa, H.I.
1986   "Runaway Shops and Female Employment: The Search for Cheap Labor". In *Women's Work: Development and the Division of Labor by Sex*. Edited by E. Leacock and H.I. Safa. South Hadley, MA: Bergin and Garvey Publishers, Inc. Pp. 58-71.

Salt, J.
1987   "Contemporary Trends in International Migration Study", *International Migration*, 25(3):241-265. September.

Samuel, T.J.
1988   "Family Class Immigrants to Canada, 1981-1984: Some Aspects of Social Adaptation", *International Migration*.

Sargent, L. ed.
1981   *Women and Revolution: The Unhappy Marriage of Marxism and Feminism*. London: Pluto Press.

Sassen-Koob, S.
1988   "The New Labor Demand: Conditions for the Absorption of Immigrant Workers in the United States". In *International Migration Today*. Volume 2: Emerging Issues. Edited by C.W. Stahl. Paris: UNESCO. Pp. 81-105.

1984   "Notes on the Incorporation of Third World Women into Wage Labor through Immigration and Off-shore Production", *International Migration Review*, 18(4):1144-1167. Winter.

1983   "Labor Migration and the New Industrial Division of Labor". In *Women, Men and the International Division of Labor*. Edited by J. Nash and M.P. Fernandez-Kelly. Albany: State University of New York Press. Pp. 175-204.

1981   "Toward a Conceptualization of Immigrant Labour", *Social Problems*, 29:65-85. October.

1980   "The Internationalization of the Labor Force", *Studies in Comparative International Development*, 15:3-25. Winter.

1979   "Formal and Informal Associations: Dominicans and Colombians in New York", *International Migration Review*, 13(2):314-332. Summer.

Schmink, M.
1986   "Women and Urban Industrial Development in Brazil". In *Women and Change in Latin America*. Edited by J. Nash and H. Safa. South Hadley, MA: Bergin and Garvey Publishers, Inc. Pp. 136-164.

1984   "Household Economic Strategies: A Review and Research Agenda", *Latin American Research Review*, 19(3):87-101.

Schoeneberg, U.
1985   "Participation in Ethnic Associations: The Case of Immigrants in West Germany", *International Migration Review*, 19(3):416-437. Fall.

Shah, N.M.
1984   "The Female Migrant in Pakistan". In *Women in the Cities of Asia: Migration and Urban Adaptation*. Edited by J.T. Fawcett, S.E. Khoo and P.C. Smith. Boulder, CO: Westview Press. Pp. 108-124.

Simmons, A.B.
1985-86 "Recent Studies on Place-Utility and Intention toMigrate: An International
        Comparison", *Population and Environment*, 8(1/2):120-139. Spring/Summer.

Sokoloff, N.
1980   *Between Money and Love: The Dialectics of Women's Home and Market Work*. New York:
        Praeger Press.

Stepick, A. and A. Portes
1986   "Flight into Despair: A Profile of Recent Haitian Refugees in South Florida",
        International Migration Review, 20(2):329-350. Summer.

Thadani, V.N. and M.P. Todaro
1984   "Female Migration: A Conceptual Framework". In *Women in the Cities of Asia: Migration
        and Urban Adaptation*. Edited by J.T. Fawcett, S.E. Khoo and P.C. Smith. Boulder: CO:
        Westview Press. Pp. 36-59.

1979   *Female Migration in Developing Countries: A Framework for Analysis*. Center for Policy
        Studies Working Paper. New York: Population Council.

Tienda, M.
1980   "Familism and Structural Assimilation of Mexican Immigrants in the United States",
        International Migration Review, 14(3):383-408. Fall.

Trager, L.
1984   "Family Strategies and the Migration of Women: Migrants to Dagupan City,
        Philippines", *International Migration Review*, 18(4):1264-1277. Winter.

Weintraub, S. and C. Stolp
1987   "The Implications of Growing Economic Interdependence". In *The Future of Migration*.
        Paris: Organization for Economic Co-operation and Development. Pp. 137-169.

Werbner, P.
1987   "Enclave Economies and Family Firms: Pakistani Traders in a British City". In *Migrants,
        Workers and the Social Order*. Edited by J. Eades. London: Tavistock Publishers.Pp. 213-233.

WING (Women, Immigration and Nationality Group)
1985   *Worlds Apart: Women Under Immigration and Nationality Law*. London: Pluto Press.

Wood, C.H.
1982   "Equilibrium and Historical Structural Perspectives on Migration",
        International Migration Review, 16(2):298-319. Summer.

1981   "Structural Changes and Household Strategies: A Conceptual Framework for the Study
        of Rural Migration", *Human Organization*, 40:338-44. Winter.

Young, K.
1985   "The Creation of a Relative Surplus Population: A Case Study from Mexico". In *Women
        and Development: The Sexual Division of Labor in Rural Societies*. Edited by L. Beneria.
        New York: Praeger. Pp. 149-178.

Yu, E.S.H. and W.T. Liu
1986   "Methodological Problems and Policy Implications in Vietnamese Refugee Research",
        International Migration Research, 20(2):483-501. Summer.

Yücel, A.E.
1987   "Turkish Migrant Workers in the Federal Republic of Germany: A Case Study".
        Migrants in Europe: The Role of Family, Labor and Politics. Edited by H.C. Buechler and
        J.M. Buechler. New York: Greenwood Press. Pp. 91-115.

Part VII
Refugees and Displaced Persons

[13]

Sociological Theories of International Migration: The Case of Refugees[1]
Anthony H. Richmond

Sociological theories of international migration (including refugees) should be capable of explaining the scale, direction and composition of population movements that cross state boundaries, the factors which determine the decision to move and the choice of destination, the characteristic modes of social integration in the receiving country and the eventual outcome, including remigration and return movements. Studies of international migration have not attempted such an ambitious agenda. Research has generally focused on specific aspects, such as the demographic characteristics of immigrants, migration decision-making, economic and social adaptation in receiving countries, the policies of sending and receiving countries, or global trends in population movement. Empirical studies have been conducted on an ad hoc basis, largely uninformed by developments in general sociological theory.

Typologies

Early writers utilized simple typologies to classify migratory movements. Fairchild (1925) distinguished invasion, conquest and colonization from immigration as such. He classified societies as 'peaceful or warlike' and 'low or high culture'. He endeavoured to show that the types of migration and their consequences were influenced by this distinction. Later writers emphasized the difference between *voluntary* and *involuntary* movements. Included in the former were seasonal, nomadic and other temporary moves as well as more permanent migrations which were largely economic in nature. Involuntary movements included slaves and those impelled by war and other political pressures (Price, 1969).

Petersen (1958) developed a more elaborate typology using several dimensions. The first involved the relation of 'man' to nature, the state, norms and other men. The second concerned the migratory force linked to each of the former, i.e. ecological push (nature), migration policy (state), aspirations (norms) and what he called 'social momentum'. These elements generated different classes of migration which he labelled (i) primitive, (ii) forced/impelled, (iii) free and (iv) mass. Petersen introduced a

8　　　　　　　　　　　　*The Sociology of Involuntary Migration*

further classification, based on the consequences of the movement, into 'conservative' and 'innovating' types. For example, group settlements were essentially conservative, enabling the migrants to preserve a traditional life-style in varying degrees. In contrast, individuals choosing to migrate on their own led to 'pioneer' situations and larger-scale voluntary movements to urbanization and social change.

Typologies of this kind fail to go beyond the descriptive level and have little explanatory or predictive value. Advances in the sociological analysis of developmental processes throw doubt upon the validity of distinguishing evolutionary stages or postulating essential correlations between technology, economic growth, political systems, social institutions and demographic behaviour. To the extent that there are causal relations between these variables, they are more complex than such simple typologies would suggest. Furthermore, as is shown below, the distinction between movements of population that are 'voluntary' and 'involuntary', or 'forced' and 'free', is of doubtful validity.

Theories of Migration

Theories of international migration can be broadly classified as *macro* and *micro* in their level of analysis. In the former category are those which focus on migration streams, identifying those conditions under which large-scale movements occur and describing the demographic, economic and social characteristics of the migrants in aggregate terms. The macro level also includes most theories concerning the immigrant adaptation process, economic and social integration, assimilation, etc., when regarded from a structural or cultural perspective. The micro level includes studies of sociopsychological factors differentiating migrants from non-migrants, together with theories concerning motivation, decision-making, satisfaction and identification. It may also include some aspects of immigrant adaptation, when regarded from a strictly individualistic perspective as distinct from the broader societal consequences.

Space does not permit a comprehensive review of all theories concerning migration. Reference may be made to a number of texts, cited in the bibliography, which examine various approaches e.g. Eisenstadt (1954), Rossi (1955), Mangalam (1968), Jackson (1969), Jansen (1970), Kosinsky (1975), Simmons (1977), de Jong

Sociological Theories of Migration   9

and Gardner (1981), Kubat and Hoffman-Nowotny (1981) and Kritz et al. (1981). However, a brief summary of the more important contributions is appropriate. It should be noted that almost all the theories are addressed to the phenomenon of 'voluntary' migration. In most cases economic factors are assumed to be predominant, both in determining the out-flow and in interpreting the experience after migration. Often the writers explicitly state that they are not concerned with refugees or politically motivated migrants. Whereas it is taken for granted that some regularity can be detected in the flows of economic migrants, it is generally assumed that refugee movements are spontaneous and unpredictable, although there is growing evidence that this is not the case. When questions of absorption in receiving countries are considered, the experiences of refugees are rarely distinguished from those of economic migrants.

Macro-theories

Ravenstein (1885, 1889) put forward so-called 'laws of migration', based on empirical observation of internal migration in the nineteenth century. Some of his generalizations have stood the test of time, such as the fact that most migrations are over short distances, that they generate counter-streams and that they are related to technological development. Others have been contradicted, including the suggestion that urban populations are less migratory than rural, that females predominate among short-distance movers or that migration proceeds by stages from rural areas to small towns, and from the latter to larger cities and metropolitan areas.

Stouffer (1940, 1960), also considering internal migration, related mobility and distance, while introducing the concept of 'intervening opportunities'. Lee (1966), building on Ravenstein's observations, offered a model of migration which linked positive and negative factors at the areas of origin and destination with the decision to migrate, taking into account intervening obstacles and personal factors. He related the volume of migration to the diversity of the territory and the composition of its population, to fluctuations in the economy and to difficulties in surmounting intervening obstacles.

Mabogunje (1970) developed a 'systems model', recognizing an interdependence between sending and receiving areas. He identified four components in migration movements: economic,

10   *The Sociology of Involuntary Migration*

social, technological and environmental. He described migration as a 'circular, interdependent, progressively complex and self-modifying system'. A 'systems' approach was used also by Tos and Klinar (1976), in examining the experience of Yugoslavian temporary workers, including the return migration question. A theory of societal systems was applied by Hoffman-Nowotny (1981) to generate a general theory of migration based on the relation between power and prestige in a society. It emphasized the importance of 'structural tensions' derived from inequalities and status inconsistencies in the sending country, which generated anomic tendencies. The tensions may be resolved by emigration to a country where status aspirations can be attained. He uses the term 'under-casting' to describe a process where structural tensions in the sending country are relieved by emigration but may be transferred instead to the receiving country, which must find ways of integrating the newcomers. Although the model was developed with economic migration largely in mind, Ferris (1985: 17) suggests that it may be applicable also to the movement of refugees.

The question of immigrant adaptation has generated a variety of theoretical perspectives at the macro level. Richmond and Zubrzycki (1984) identified six different models of migration and occupational status, each derived from alternative theoretical premises. The classical approach focused on assimilation and was 'functionalist' in orientation. It contrasted with a Marxian, or 'conflict', model which emphasized class differences between immigrants and indigenous populations. Colonial situations gave rise to a form of elite migration, whereas the more common experience in the twentieth century has been cross-sectional in terms of occupational status, and pluralistic from a cultural point of view. Recent theories have focused upon the phenomenon of stratification and segmentation of labour markets, leading to ethnic enclaves. Finally, the importance of structural changes generated by technological innovation and postindustrial developments have also influenced the flow of migrants and their modes of integration in advanced societies. Comparative studies of Canada and Australia suggested that none of these models, by itself, was sufficient to account for the experience of post-Second World War immigrants in these countries, although each throws some light on particular aspects of adaptation. (Burnley and Kalbach, 1985; Rao et al., 1984; Richmond and Zubrzycki, 1984). Studies of the labour market and other experiences of Cuban and Haitian refugees in the United States also demonstrated the heterogeneity of the

Sociological Theories of Migration 11

experience. They pointed to the need for alternative theoretical models to account for different modes of incorporation, which were not always disadvantageous to the newcomers, despite an initially unfavourable economic and social climate (Pedraza-Bailey, 1985; Portes and Mozo, 1985; Portes and Stepick, 1985).

Global Systems

It is generally recognized that in the study of international migration the reality of a global economy, polity and social system must be recognized, however much conflict and contradiction there may be in the interface between quasi-sovereign states (Richmond, 1988). Wallerstein (1974) traced the origins of the present world system to the mercantilist period in the seventeenth century. Contemporary economists and sociologists have shown that there is a global labour market in the modern world economy (Amin, 1974; Petras, 1981; Portes, 1983). They distinguish 'core', 'semi-peripheral' and 'peripheral' areas and relate the flow of labour to capital investment and resource development. Drawing on Marxist theory, they identify a 'reserve army' of labour in developing countries which may be exploited by wealthier imperialist powers. Richmond and Verma (1978) suggested a 'global system of international migration' with four sub-systems, each of which may also be internally differentiated according to level of development. The most advanced postindustrial societies have high rates of 'exchange' migration, particularly of highly qualified people, but they note that tremendous pressures towards emigration have built up in less-developed areas of the world. They predicted that 'this process will only be contained by increasingly restrictive immigration policies in the more advanced countries which will be compelled to adopt punitive measures to combat illegal immigration' (Richmond and Verma, 1978: 32).

Political Economy

A central issue in the study of refugee movements is the relation between economic and political determinants of population movement. The theories considered so far have been generally applicable to movements of people from poorer to richer areas, from regions of economic underdevelopment to those experiencing

12   *The Sociology of Involuntary Migration*

growth, or to the exchanges of skilled and highly qualified migrants between advanced societies to which the term *transilience* has been applied (Richmond, 1969). Although the de jure definition of refugee status (a 'Convention refugee'), used by the United Nations[2] and adopted by various countries in determining eligibility for admission, emphasizes 'a well-founded fear of persecution', it is no longer possible to treat 'refugee' movements as completely independent of the state of the global economy.[3] Complex questions of sovereignty, perceived interests, international relations and ideological considerations are also involved (Weiner, 1985).

The situations which most commonly give rise to large refugee movements and requests for asylum include external and civil wars, political unrest and revolution, terrorism, the expulsion of ethnic minorities, ethnoreligious and communal conflict, displacement of populations through technological developments such as mechanization of agriculture and hydroelectric schemes, land reforms and resettlement programmes, famines and other 'natural' disasters, as well as a wide variety of human rights violations and oppressive state regimes.[4] In all these cases economic, social and political factors are interdependent. It is not necessary to invoke Marxist assumptions concerning the ultimate determining influence of modes of production on state formations, or to attribute all forms of political oppression to the interests of 'bourgeois capitalism', to recognize that the crises which have occurred in the Middle East, Central America and Asia are not unrelated to the ideological and military confrontation of the superpowers, the competing interests of multinational companies and the problems of development facing Third World countries (World Bank, 1984; Sivard, 1985).

Zolberg (1986) has pointed out that refugee movements 'do not constitute a collection of random events' but form distinct patterns which are related to political transformations, such as the break-up of former colonial empires. The formation of new states and nation building are rendered more difficult by economic underdevelopment. Even the economic aid and refugee policies of the wealthier and more powerful countries are dictated by the narrowly defined interests of the countries 'imposing aid' (Harrell-Bond, 1986). Dowty (1987: 183) notes that 'so-called economic migrants are often responding as much to political repression as to material deprivation'. He gives, as examples, refugees from Ethiopia where political pressures and war combine with famine to cause massive flight; Haiti where political repression and economic underdevelopment go together; and El

Sociological Theories of Migration   13

Salvador where would-be refugees have been returned because they are regarded as 'victims of generalized violence', rather than individual persecution. Dowty (1987: 236) states that 'in such circumstances, the distinction between "economic" and "political" refugees becomes meaningless'. From a sociological point of view this is true. However, it does not prevent governments from making a de jure distinction between 'Convention' refugees and others, refusing asylum to those who do not meet the strict criteria of the UN Convention.

Micro-theories

Social psychologists have addressed themselves to questions of motivation and the decision to move. In the last resort, migration is an individual choice although such decisions may be made in consultation with family members or others in a close-knit community or religious group. Most micro-level studies of migration decision making have been conducted among those whose main motivation has been economic or family related. An assumption of 'rational choice', following a considered evaluation of options available, is implicit in most theories of motivation. A distinction is generally made between 'push' and 'pull' factors, which must be taken into account and weighed in the balance. Human needs and aspirations are generally represented in terms of economic benefits, social mobility or family reunion. 'Costs' and 'benefits' of migration are then calculated according to the individual's own hierarchy of values and presumed net advantage. So-called 'place-utility' theories endeavour to explain why individuals decide to move, or to choose particular locations, in terms of their perception of the advantages they offer and anticipated satisfaction. Empirical studies using this concept have lent only partial support to it and suggest that a more generalized 'value-expectancy' model which relates goals to expectations in terms of subjective probabilities of achievement. It is a cognitive model which assumes the availability of adequate information on which to base decisions. More complex psychological explanations take into account the influence of 'significant others' in the decision-making process, the role of cognitive dissonance and the tendency to adhere to a decision once made despite negative feedback (de Jong and Gardner, 1981). Although theoretically elegant, such explanations are only weakly supported by empirical evidence and tend to overlook

14   *The Sociology of Involuntary Migration*

the multiple cognitive and conative influences which prevail in a media-saturated information environment.

Although refugee movements are usually represented as 'forced', they are only an extreme case of the constraints that are placed upon the choices available to an individual in particular circumstances. The choices facing a landless peasant displaced by a multinational company producing for export, may be unemployment, begging, stealing, sickness, starvation and death for him and his family. Choices facing an ethnic or political minority may be to join a dissident army, face political imprisonment, torture or death. In either case the limited options available involve excruciating choices. Flight is one of these options. Kunz (1973, 1981) put forward an explanation of refugee behaviour in terms of what he called 'kinetic models'. He distinguished 'anticipatory' from 'acute' movements and further categorized 'majority identified', 'alienated' refugees and 'reactive-fate groups', from those with a clearer purpose. The common denominator is a sense of loss of control over one's own fate. 'The borderline between political refugees and those dissatisfied economically,' he noted, 'can indeed be blurred when displacement occurs in reaction to events. Yet, the magnitude of the decision should be kept in mind as well as the pressures of the social forces which finally result in the seeking of exile' (Kunz, 1981: 50–1).

Keller (1975: Ch. 3) described the trauma of becoming a refugee, with illustrations from the experience of the fifteen million people displaced by the partition of India and Pakistan in 1947, when a million people died. The author suggested stages in the refugee generating process, starting with a rejection of the idea that disaster is imminent and a determination to carry on as normal a life as possible, followed by the trauma of flight, which in turn leads to long-term effects, including feelings of guilt, invulnerability and aggressiveness. A study of Vietnamese-Chinese refugees in Canada showed that the resettlement process often involved downward occupational mobility, fatalistic attitudes, a preoccupation with family reunification, and a profound desire to escape dependency (Lam, 1983).

Various studies have examined the psychological aspects of immigrant adaptation, emphasizing the more serious trauma faced by refugees and the mental health problems experienced (Cohon, 1981). A 'social displacement syndrome' can be identified. An incubation period may be followed by paranoid symptoms, hypochondria, anxiety and depression (Tyhurst, 1977). However

Sociological Theories of Migration   15

unrealistic, some may cling to the 'myth of return' or work politically for the 'liberation' of the former country (Zwingmann and Pfister-Ammende, 1973; Anwar, 1979; Stein, 1981; Luciuc, 1986).

Structuration and Voluntaristic Action

The relation between structural constraints and individual choice is a central problem in sociological theory. It involves fundamental questions of free will and agency, over against theories which imply behavioural determination by forces over which we have little or no control. The nature of the problem was expressed in oversimplified form by Marx when he wrote that 'men make history, but not in circumstances of their own choosing'. Almost all social theorists have recognized the paradox which this reflects. Is the recognition of structural constraint compatible with a voluntaristic theory of action?

Talcott Parsons addressed this issue throughout his work, commencing with his synthesis of the writings of classical theorists in *The Structure of Social Action* (1937). Recently, Sciulli (1986) noted that the term 'voluntaristic action', as used by Parsons and others, has several different meanings. First, it can refer to the actor's free will, or capacity to make choices despite constraints. Second, it can mean a capacity for self-initiated action, whether or not this capacity is realized. Third, it can refer to the concept of individual autonomy despite the limitations of ideal or material conditions. Fourth, it may represent individual autonomy as an unstable element in the social order. Fifth, voluntaristic action may be understood as the residual 'normative' elements not subsumed under 'behavioural', 'conditional' or 'material' categories. Sciulli himself prefers a reformulated distinction which Parsons implicitly developed when he distinguished 'purposeful rational action toward quantifiable ends' from 'non-rational action, directed toward transcendental ends', as in the case of religious rituals. This left a third type of social action which involved 'normative practices'. Although within the sphere of non-rational action the latter cannot be regarded as ultimate or transcendental. 'Voluntaristic action is comprised, therefore, of qualitative worldly ends as well as the shared symbols and norms which allow actors to simply maintain a shared recognition of these ends' (Sciulli, 1986: 748). It is the recognition of these shared values which provides a bulwark against an arbitrary exercise of power. Without

16   *The Sociology of Involuntary Migration*

voluntaristic action, and the institutionalized values which support
it, direct coercion, or the manipulation of belief by a dominant
minority, is likely to occur.

In somewhat different terms the same point is made by Giddens
(1984: 174) when he distinguishes various forms of constraint,
which may be material, associated with sanctions or structural in
form. The latter are derived from the 'given' nature of structural
properties which the individual is unable to change and which
limit the range of options. Giddens's concept of 'structuration',
however, replaces a static view of social structures as completely
external to the individual, with one which emphasizes the process
by which social structures are created and changed through the
exercise of 'freedom of action'. It is necessary to explore this
idea further if we are to develop a satisfactory sociological theory
of motivation that will account for the behaviour of migrants
and refugees.

Turner (1987) reviewed various sociological theories of motivation, including that of Giddens which he sees as having a psycho-
analytic basis in that it identifies both conscious and unconscious
determinants of social action. Key elements are unconscious
needs for security and trust in relations with others. Practical
consciousness and reflective monitoring lead to routinization
and social integration. Unconscious needs increase in salience
when these established institutions break down (Turner, 1987:
20–1; Giddens, 1984: 4–7, 281–4). Turner incorporates several
other social psychological traditions into his synthetic model,
including those of social exchange, interactionist theories, and
ethnomethodology. He postulates a hierarchy of 'needs'. These go
beyond the primordial requirements of biological survival. They
are socially determined and include needs for group inclusion,
trust, security, symbolic and material gratification, self-conception
and 'facticity', i.e. the shared understanding of inter-subjective and
external worlds, which in turn is linked to power and the ability
to achieve goals through negotiation and exchange with others.
Turner's model involves complex 'feedback' loops and assumes
that failure to achieve these goals leads to diffuse anxiety and
strategies to avoid such feelings. One of these strategies may
be exit from a situation which persistently fails to satisfy needs
(Turner, 1987: 24).

The implications of this sociological theory of motivation for a
studies of migration and refugee movements need more detailed
explication than is possible here — a few key points are

Sociological Theories of Migration 17

highlighted. First, migratory decisions, even those taken under conditions of extreme stress, do not differ from other kinds of decision governing social behaviour. The same sociological model of motivation is applicable. Second, the distinction between 'free' and 'forced' or 'voluntary' and 'involuntary', is a misleading one. All human behaviour is constrained. Choices are not unlimited but are determined by the structuration process. However, 'degrees of freedom' may vary. Individual and group autonomy and potency are situationally determined. It would be more appropriate to recognize a continuum at one end of which individuals and collectivities are *proactive* and at the other *reactive*. Under certain conditions, the decision to move may be made after due consideration of all relevant information, rationally calculated to maximize net advantage, including both material and symbolic rewards. At the other extreme, the decision to move may be made in a state of panic facing a crisis situation which leaves few alternatives but escape from intolerable threats. Between these two extremes, many of the decisions made by both 'economic' and 'political' migrants are a response to diffuse anxiety generated by a failure of the social system to provide for the fundamental needs of the individual, biological, economic and social. Third, a reasonable hypothesis would be that when societal institutions disintegrate, or are weakened to the point that they are unable to provide a substantial section of the population with an adequate sense of group inclusion, trust and ontological security, a refugee situation is created.[5]

Structural Constraints and Facilitators

I have argued elsewhere (Richmond, 1988: 38) that an adequate sociological theory of migration must incorporate an understanding of social action and human agency, the question of conflict, contradiction and opposition in social systems, the meaning of structure and change, and the importance of power. A key element in structuration theory is the recognition that social structures not only constrain but they also enable. Constraint involves an asymmetrical distribution of power, which may involve naked force and physical coercion, material rewards, threats of deprivation or various forms of persuasion and inducement. However, Giddens (1984: 173) points out that sources of constraint are also means of enablement: 'They open up certain possibilities of action at the

18   *The Sociology of Involuntary Migration*

same time as they restrict or deny others'. Parsons' use of the concepts of 'power' and 'influence' is relevant here. Power is not necessarily a zero sum concept (Parsons, 1960, 1963; Giddens, 1968). Its unequal distribution may lead to conflict but it must also be understood as a resource which facilitates the achievement of collective goals. It is notable that, in his review of the studies of 'place-utility' and intention to migrate, Simmons (1985–6) concluded that background variables (constraints and facilitators) had a stronger association with actual migration than expressed intentions.

Based on her experiences in an African refugee camp, Harrell-Bond (1986: 283–329) discussed the 'oversocialized concept of Man' which fails to recognize the extent to which, in critical situations, individual survival undermines social values including those which normally induce humane responses. Following Bettelheim's account of life in a concentration camp, Giddens (1984: 63) makes the same point when he notes that any sustained attack on the routines of social life produces a high level of anxiety and a stripping away of socialized responses. It takes time to rebuild social structures, and attempts to impose order often fail for lack of grassroots co-operation. Psychological stress and accompanying levels of depression and anxiety may reach pathological levels. Bereavement exacerbates the problem but crises can be perceived as a threat, a loss or a challenge. Adaptive and coping mechanisms can be generated, although outside help may be needed to do so.

Harrell–Bond goes on to point out that, in order to answer the question of how refugees survive, their relationship with the host society must be considered. Refugees are generally perceived as a 'problem' or a 'threat' to those countries whose borders they cross. However, they may also generate opportunities and become a source of positive social change. As in the case of other immigrants, they may bring human capital, skills or experience that benefit the receiving society. International agencies may become involved, attracting investment in transportation or new industries. Markets may be created, marginal land cultivated, schools started or health services established. Short-sighted interference by outside agencies pursuing policies dictated by the interests of foreign powers or private corporations, whether represented as well meaning or not, may have the opposite of the desired effect. Harrell-Bond (1986: 366) argues that humanitarians and researchers alike should become *facilitators*, using their resources to enable refugees to help themselves. Either way, the outsiders are necessarily agents of social change, as are the refugees themselves.

Sociological Theories of Migration 19

Conflicts and Contradictions

No society is without conflicts arising from the unequal distribution of resources, competing interests, opposing values and internal contradictions. Giddens (1984: 193–4) distinguishes 'existential contradiction' and 'structural contradiction'. The former concerns human existence in relation to the natural world. It comes to the forefront when people are faced with the question of absolute survival and must make choices that could mean sacrificing their own lives for the sake of others, a not unreal conflict in disaster situations and under oppressive regimes. More familiar are the structural contradictions which arise out of changing social systems. Giddens (1984: 196) notes that 'the emergence of state-based societies also alters the scope and pace of "history" by stimulating secondary contradictions. States bring into being, or at least greatly accentuate, social relations across considerable reaches of time and space'. One example of structural contradiction in this context is the provision of international law and the UN Convention on Human Rights (not observed in practice by all states), which provides the right to leave a country without any complementary right of admission elsewhere. The result is the creation of 'stateless persons' and 'refugees in orbit', i.e. reactive migrants who have escaped intolerable conditions in one place but can find no state willing to offer asylum or resettlement opportunities. Dowty (1987) has chronicled the 'contemporary assault on freedom of movement' which has led to the closing of borders and increasingly restrictive immigration and refugee policies in many countries. A further contradiction following from this is that it is mainly the poorest countries in Africa and Asia that presently shoulder the burden of providing shelter and aid for the millions of people displaced by wars that are fuelled by superpower confrontation and the arms bazaar (Myrdal, 1976; Sampson, 1977; Ferris, 1985; Sivard, 1985).

Refugee Movements: A New Paradigm

The above review of sociological and social psychological theories pertaining to international migration leads to two key conclusions. First, an absolutely clear distinction between the economic and the sociopolitical determinants of population movement is not

20   *The Sociology of Involuntary Migration*

appropriate. A multivariate approach is necessary. There may
be exceptional cases where both the underlying and precipitating
causes can be identified as 'purely' economic or political. However,
in the modern world where states, religious leaders, multinational
corporations and supra-state agencies (such as the IMF and the
World Bank) are involved in decisions which affect the lives of
millions of people, the majority of population movements are
a complex response to the reality of a global society in which
ethnoreligious, social, economic and political determinants are
inextricably bound together.

Second, a distinction between voluntary and involuntary
movements is also untenable. All human behaviour is constrained
and enabled by the structuration process within which degrees of
freedom of choice are limited. Individual autonomy is relative to
opportunity structures which are themselves determined by social
forces. The distribution of economic and political power is central
to the decision-making process at the individual and collective
level. 'Rational choice' within a means–end schema, in which
individuals maximize net advantage, is a special case rarely found
in isolation from decisions which are influenced by direct coercion,
manipulated opinion and value systems, the non-rational pursuit
of transcendental goals and normatively oriented voluntaristic
action. In this context, decisions regarding migration are more
appropriately designated *proactive* or *reactive*, according to the
degree of autonomy exhibited by the actors involved.

The resulting paradigm of international migration is diagram-
matically represented in Figure 1, in the form of a matrix.[6]
The vertical axis represents decision-making on a continuum
from maximum to minimum autonomy. The horizontal axis
represents the interaction of economic and sociopolitical forces,
reflecting that they come full circle as internal and external state
powers converge. Proactive migrants include retirees, transilients,
returnees, reunited families and ordinary 'emigrants'. UN Convention refugees, stateless persons, slaves and forced labourers are
clear examples of reactive migrants. Between these two extremes,
a large proportion of the people crossing state boundaries combine
characteristics, responding to economic, social and political
pressures over which they have little control, but exercising a
limited degree of choice in the selection of destinations and the
timing of their movements. The nearer the category falls to the
vertical axis the more important are the economic determinants,
while those closer to the horizontal periphery are more in the

Sociological Theories of Migration 21

FIGURE 1
Paradigm of International Population Movements

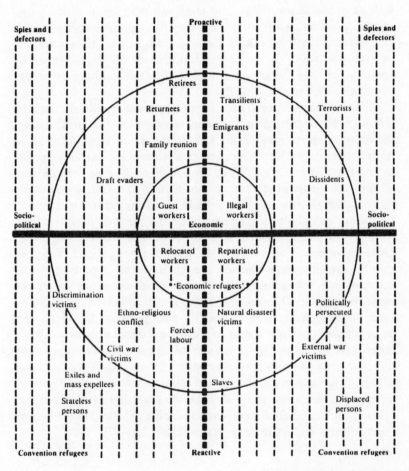

Copyright © 1987 A.H. Richmond

political domain, although no clear-cut boundary between these factors can be drawn.

The central core of international migration consists of those responding to the uneven development of the global economy, to the demands for labour in oil-rich and economically advanced societies, and to the displacement consequent upon urbanization in

22   *The Sociology of Involuntary Migration*

the Third World. These economic determinants are not independent of the sociopolitical context in which they occur. Such migrants are vulnerable to cyclical fluctuations of the global economy as well as political instability and changing policies in sending and receiving countries alike. At times they find opportunities available as contract or 'guestworkers', but they are subject to repatriation or exclusion when the perceived interests of traditional receiving countries change. Many are treated as 'illegals' and are subject to deportation when discovered.

'Convention refugees' are the prototypical political migrants, although the historical circumstances in which the precise legal definition of a 'refugee' in the UN protocol was formulated limits its applicability to the contemporary world system. At the opposite extreme to those who qualify as 'Convention refugees', on the basis of their demonstrated fear of persecution, are those politically motivated proactive migrants who fall into the category of 'spies', 'terrorists' or defectors'. In some cases they may deliberately infiltrate genuine refugee movements. Furthermore, there is growing evidence of collusion between the intelligence agencies in various countries which have allowed actual or former agents, political activists and 'war criminals', to enter other countries under the guise of refugees (Deschenes, 1986; Rodal, 1987; Wright, 1987). Intermediate cases, also combining sociopolitical and economic determinants, include American draft evaders (Kasinsky, 1976), other political dissidents, victims of ethnic discrimination and those who may be persecuted because of their religious or political beliefs, together with a growing class of so-called 'economic refugees'. The extent to which they are regarded as admissible in other countries often depends upon ideological considerations and cross-cultural understanding (Kalin, 1986: 230–40).

Conclusion

Sociologists are still a long way from being able to explain all aspects of international migration within a single theoretical framework. The paradigm outlined above brings together certain key elements in structuration and social psychological theory, in order to explain certain broad features of contemporary international migration, particularly that of refugees. At the risk of gross over-simplification it may be stated that:

Sociological Theories of Migration 23

$$M = P + R$$

where: M is the total number of international migrants, P is the number of proactive migrants, and R is the number of reactive migrants.

In turn, $P_{a\,b\,t}$ is the number of proactive migrants from place a seeking entry to place b in time period t. It is likely to be a function of distance, intervening opportunities and obstacles, rationally calculated net advantages (not exclusively economic in nature), qualified by a variety of non-rational considerations derived from the voluntaristic nature of social action. The number actually admitted to country b will depend upon a variety of policy considerations, themselves combining rational and non-rational elements. Similarly, $R_{a\,b\,t}$ is the number of reactive migrants from place a seeking entry to place b in time period t. This is likely to be a function of the degree to which societal institutions in place a have disintegrated to the point that they are unable to provide a substantial section of the population with an adequate sense of group inclusion, trust and ontological security, qualified by the perception of place b as capable of reducing the anxiety thus created. The receptivity of those in place a to R will depend upon the same considerations applied to P, with additional non-rational elements, likely to be invoked as a consequence of a conflict between humanitarian values and strictly self-interested motives.

Certain policy conclusions can be drawn from the above analysis. First, the present UN definition of a 'Convention refugee' is inadequate in the face of the contemporary demographic realities. Even the adoption of a 'B' category, or designated class of persons who do not meet the de jure requirements, but are admissible on other grounds, does not do justice to the scale or complexity of the global situation facing reactive migrants. Attention needs to be given to a reformulation of the concept of 'refugee' to take into account a variety of crisis and disaster generating situations, which warrant international collaborative relief effort. It raises issues of sovereignty and international law which only jurists are qualified to address. Sociological theory can only point to the inadequacy of existing international codes.

Second, the right to leave must be matched by the right of asylum. Wealthy countries should not close their borders or adopt more restrictive immigration policies merely because the scale of reactive migration has increased or the racial and cultural

24 *The Sociology of Involuntary Migration*

characteristics of those seeking refuge has changed. Finally, it is evident that, in the last resort, the 'refugee problem' is only a symptom of much more profound conflicts and contradictions within our global system. Ultimately, the flow of international migrants, both proactive and reactive, will be responsive to a more egalitarian economic order and to the creation of a more peaceful, demilitarized society.

Notes

1. I am indebted to the Research Grants and Scholarships Committee of the Faculty of Arts, York University for a minor research grant to assist in the preparation of this paper and to Fernando Mata for research assistance. I wish also to thank my colleagues, Professor Fred Elkin, Clifford Jansen, Michael Lanphier, John O'Neill and Alan Simmons, for their helpful comments on an earlier draft of the paper.

2. The United Nations Convention on Refugees, 1951, and the Protocol of 1967, define a refugee as one who 'by reason of a well-founded fear of persecution for reasons of race, religion, nationality, membership in a particular social group or political opinion: (a) is outside the country of his nationality and is unable or, by reason of such fear, unwilling to avail himself of the protection of that country; or (b) not having a country of nationality, is outside the country of his former habitual residence and is unable or, by reason of such fear, is unwilling to return to that country'.

3. Although quite evident in the contemporary world, the connection between economic conditions and political persecution is not new. Marrus (1985: 31) notes that, in the case of the Jewish exodus from Eastern Europe in the nineteenth century, 'neither in the persecution policy nor in the motivation for emigration do we find forcible uprooting in the usual sense. Jews from the tsarist empire seem to represent an intermediate case...neither entirely refugees nor entirely voluntary emigrants, they included elements of both, sometimes to the confusion of outside observers'. He goes on to give other more recent examples of economic and political factors combining to induce migration.

4. Even 'natural' disasters involve a large element of human responsibility, to the extent that such events as earthquakes and volcanic eruptions can be predicted with some degree of probability, and appropriate building and other codes enforced. Floods, famines and fires are all preventable and in many cases are actually the result of human intervention. It goes without saying that chemical spills, mining disasters and nuclear 'accidents' are all man-made. Once the disaster has occurred, the speed and efficiency of remedial action is closely related to the economic and political context of the relief operations, and the degree of co-operation between government and non-governmental agencies.

5. By 'ontological security' in this context is meant confidence in the social world and one's ability to survive in it, physically, and in terms of social identity.

6. The figure is drawn in the form of a 'mercator' projection of a sphere, although no geographic connotation is intended. The distribution of types of

Sociological Theories of Migration 25

migrant within the quadrants is intended to indicate relative degrees of autonomy in decision-making, together with the relative importance of economic and sociopolitical determinants. Empirical research is needed, using reliable measures of these variables, in order to place a particular movement of population into its appropriate location within the matrix.

For references to accompany this chapter please see page 532.

[14]

Palestinians:
Exiles at Home and Abroad
Janet L. Abu-Lughod

It was a non-sociologist, Edward Said, who perhaps captured most accurately the social psychological condition of Palestinians today when he described it as a state of 'exile', which he defined as the 'unhealable rift forced between a human being and a native place, between the self and its true home'. He characterized exile existentially as a 'condition of terminal loss' caused by 'a discontinuous state of being' (Said, 1984: 49, 51).

I know of no concept in the field of migration studies that comes close to this sensitive perception of the distinction between 'migrant' and 'exile'. All movement *from* 'a native place'[1] (in the sense of a physical *and* social place in which one was formed) to some other physical and/or social place causes some rift, some loss, some discontinuity in the state of one's being. All migration from one culture to another creates some marginality and involves an often painful adjustment process whenever the migrant attempts, with greater or lesser success, to combine identities that do not necessarily fit together. Migrant strategies may range from re-encapsulation[2] to almost wilful passing;[3] but since the move has been at least to some extent voluntary,[4] it is assumed that options existed for the mover, not only with reference to the move itself, but to the modality of adaptation.

Forced migration has a different character, although admittedly it is difficult to draw a neat line between the 'pushes' of exit and the 'pulls' of entrance. Today we take for granted enormous mobility of populations — whether for work, for immigration, to 'better' oneself or give one's children advantages. And we often consider such moves as at least partially 'forced', in the sense that they are need-driven; if some push forces were not involved, most people would not move. But there is a real break between a voluntary need-pushed migration (whether 'forced' by economic circumstances, political oppression or some other distasteful characteristic of 'home') and a sudden, involuntary severance from one's 'native place'. This is why the situation of refugees is particularly poignant, since the severance is always abrupt and forced.

62   *The Sociology of Involuntary Migration*

Interestingly enough, the term 'refugee' is seldom applied to a single individual; it is a collective or group condition, even when only one representative of the group is being discussed. Single individuals forced to leave their 'native place' for idiosyncratic reasons are not usually referred to as refugees. Classification as a refugee requires collective status; it not only requires that there be many dislocated persons but that their displacement results from a common cause not of their own making.[5]

Hidden in the concept of refugee, however, is also an option, albeit in the future. Whereas it often turns out that 'return' is an empty and unattractive option, it is nevertheless considered a potentially achievable one for the forced migrant. Only forced exile lacks that option, although it does not necessarily also destroy the hope. Only forced exile creates that unhealable rift between the 'self and its true home' which leaves the mover in limbo, unable and unwilling to become fully part of his life in exile for fear that in doing so he will forfeit his life in his 'native place'.

Because of these differences, it is difficult to apply many of the concepts usually employed by sociologists when they discuss migration or even the situation of being a 'refugee' to the condition of being an exile. That is why, for the purpose of this article, we have to add some new concepts if we are to evaluate the state of Palestinians who are, I contend, exiles at home and abroad, rather than refugees.

What existing sociological concepts fail to describe is not only the psychological sense of exile Edward Said so sensitively portrays, but also another part of the Palestinian experience, namely, that one can become an exile even while remaining on one's own soil. For a people rooted in a native land and in a native social milieu, exiles, in the sense of an 'unhealable rift between past and present', can occur when the entire ground has been transformed underfoot. This dislocation and discontinuity may occur almost independently of whether one has been physically relocated.

It is strange that sociology has no concept to describe the phenomenon of 'exile' without moving. It may be that the cases do come to mind: aboriginal people in Australia and other countries; Amerindians who became exiles in their 'native lands', regardless of whether they remained in place or were herded to another location; various peoples colonized by others. By far the most recent and with arguably the highest profile is the case of the Palestinians who in the span of a single lifetime have been subjected to the same wrenching discontinuity in self, irrespective of whether they were

Palestinians – Exiles   63

officially counted as refugees or whether they remained to become
strangers in their own country.

Nor does sociology have any concept adequately to describe
inherited exile status. Our theories assume that refugee status is
both a temporary transition state between one place of settlement
and another and a temporary phenomenon affecting only the
cohort that actually experiences the 'act' of displacement. Exile to
the Palestinians, however, is neither transitional nor transitory; it
is an inherited state.

Consider the fact that the first wave of Palestinian Arab refugees,
some 780,000 persons out of a total of 1.4 million, was created
some forty years ago. Only a small proportion of the Palestinians
alive today, therefore, actually experienced that trauma. Another
130,000 Palestinians experienced exile at home when, in 1948, they
became unwanted residual residents in Israel. Only a small proportion of the 600,000 Palestinians who now hold Israeli citizenship
actually witnessed that disruption between past and future since
the overwhelming majority of Palestinians in Israel today were
born after 1948. In 1967, when Israel occupied the remainder of
Palestine (the so-called West Bank and Gaza), another 1.35 million
Palestinians became exiles — perhaps 300,000–400,000 through
moving, the rest by remaining in place but having the very basis
of their existence transformed. At least half or more of today's
residents in the West Bank and Gaza were born after that event.
The same is true for the rest of the population which lives outside
the soil of Palestine; most of them were born in physical exile.

Thus, most of the Palestinians alive today were born in exile;
theirs is an inherited status. Given the high rates of demographic
increase and therefore the great youthfulness of the population
(some 50 percent is under the age of 18), an overwhelming majority
(possibly as much as 80 percent) of the persons who identify
themselves as Arab Palestinians have never directly known their
'native place' (soil and full-functioning society), that is, they have
never experienced a physical and/or social environment to which
they belonged naturally and without rift. Sociological theories do
not prepare us for this inheritance of exilehood, just as they do not
prepare us to comprehend exile while staying in place.

In this report on the present condition of Palestinians, then,
we include all descendants of the population which in 1948 began
a process of exile which has, to date, lasted some forty years.

64   *The Sociology of Involuntary Migration*

Estimating the Total Population of Palestinian Exiles

Although it is virtually impossible to determine exactly how many persons of Palestinian birth or ancestry exist today, our best estimate, based upon some fairly complex demographic projections and triangulations made by the author in 1980 and projected from that point,[6] is that at least 5.2 million people now claim descent from the 1.4 million Arabs who were residing in Palestine in 1948. This was the year the state of Israel was declared and Jewish forces greatly expanded the boundaries which had been recommended in the partition plan, taking all of Palestine except the hilly regions later annexed to Jordan (the so-called West Bank) and the narrow strip of land in the south (the Gaza Strip) which until 1967 was administered by Egypt. As we have argued above, all five million now exist in a state of physical and/or cultural exile, even those who never became refugees in the official sense of that term as defined by UN conventions. One must distinguish between the various types of Palestinian exiles, however, if one is to understand not only what they have in common but the ways in which their different circumstances have created special problems. Today, five major groups can be identified:

1. Arabs in Israel

Over 600,000 Palestinian Arabs now reside within the pre-1967 provisional borders of Israel. These are remnants of or are descended from the war of 1948 and were thus counted as 'legal residents' in the Israeli Defence Census of November 1948. After an interim period during which they were the victims of considerable displacement and very harsh military control, they received partial rights as Israeli citizens. While they remain on their native soil (although not necessarily in their ancestral homes or villages, some of which have been destroyed or taken over by new Jewish immigrants), they experience exclusion from the general society and suffer discrimination in education, employment and the right to buy land. They constitute an anomaly in a political system that recognizes only Jews as full members of the social and political community. They are the 'exiles at home' par excellence. Although at first this community was psychologically crushed and passively fearful, many have been radicalized since 1967, largely because they have re-established contact with the

second group of Palestinian Arabs from which they were cut off
for two decades.

2. *Palestinians in the West Bank and Gaza*

In 1948, approximately 780,000 Palestinians became 'refugees'
from the zones occupied by Israel. Most joined their compatriots
(who numbered approximately 350,000) in the residual areas of
Palestine, those areas later called the West Bank (including East
Jerusalem) and the Gaza Strip. From the former zone, however,
many continued their search for refuge, crossing the borders into
Syria, Lebanon and especially Jordan.

By the eve of the 1967 war, there were approximately 1.35 million Palestinian Arabs in unoccupied Palestine, some 900,000 living
in East Jerusalem and the hill areas to the north and south of it (i.e.
the West Bank) in the zone which had been annexed to Jordan,
and perhaps another 450,000 living in the Gaza Strip, an area that
had come under Egyptian administration after 1948. After the war
of June 1967 in which Israel invaded and conquered these residual
areas of Palestine, only about 950,000 of these residents were left,
which suggests that perhaps another 300,000–400,000 Palestinians
had been driven from the area by the war (or had been temporarily
absent from their homes to which they were not allowed to return).
Some of these became refugees for the second time in their lives.

At the present time, some two decades since the West Bank
and the Gaza Strip came under Israeli military rule, the number
of Palestinian Arabs in these occupied zones has barely recovered
to the pre-war level, which suggests that in fact there has been
significant and steady attrition in their ranks.[7] Some of this
attrition has come directly through expulsion, incarceration and
violent death, perpetrated by a harsh military government and
vigilante Jewish settlers. Much, however, has been forced by
economic necessity.

Life on the West Bank has been very difficult and survival in
the now grossly overpopulated Gaza Strip even harder. Those who
have managed to remain are known as the 'steadfast' (*samed*) and
continue to resist expulsion and try to survive under a harsh military occupation, having neither citizenship rights nor the protection
of the state which, on the contrary, enforces systematic confiscation
of their land and water rights, destruction of their property, and
harassment and imprisonment under Draconian regulations.

66 *The Sociology of Involuntary Migration*

Although they are neither physical nor juridical exiles (except those who were displaced in 1948), they are subject to extremely harsh assaults on their existence. But, unlike their compatriots in Israel, they have managed under difficult circumstances to maintain much of their kin and social structure. What they have not been able to maintain is their self-sufficiency. Deprived of land and water and prevented from setting up their own institutions and economic enterprises, many former peasants, businessmen and professionals have joined a proletarianized labour force in Israel; to sustain their families, the majority of them have taken low-paid and unprotected (irregular and un-unionized) employment within Israel, the lowness of their wages unavoidably subsidizing the economy of their occupiers. Their alienation and distress have taken a heavy toll on many, although these exiles at home have spearheaded a dogged and increasingly firm resistance.

3. *Palestinians in the Arab States adjacent to Israel*

Living outside Palestine today are another two million Palestinians who reside in the Arab countries just beyond the borders of Palestine: over 600,000 in Lebanon and Syria where most are non-citizens, and perhaps 1.3 to 1.4 million in Jordan where they were granted citizenship in 1949, along with residents on the so-called West Bank. Since, unlike Syria and Lebanon, the Jordanian government has discouraged Palestinians from maintaining their separate identity, there is no way to determine exactly how many Jordanians living on the East Bank or working abroad (largely in the Arab countries of the Gulf) are of Palestinian origin. Our estimate is therefore highly provisional.

In Jordan, Palestinians have perhaps achieved the greatest degree of 'home' in exile. Whereas initially the cultural differences between Jordanians and Palestinians were quite great, and despite the fact that former Palestinian peasants have never been able to re-establish themselves on the land, the sheer magnitude of the Palestinian infusion and the length of time during which they have lived in Jordan have led to the creation of a common culture which, at least in the cities, has bridged the gap between the two peoples. However, despite this, Palestinians retain a poignant sense of exile, the political expression of which has been severely repressed.

Palestinians – Exiles   67

4. Palestinians in the Gulf States

From these points of second settlement, Palestinians seeking a livelihood established temporary communities of third settlement in other Arab countries, especially in countries of the Gulf area where their labour was in demand – primarily Kuwait but also Saudi Arabia and the United Arab Emirates. At the peak of employment opportunities in these areas, the number of Palestinians living and working in the Gulf (and in a few other non-contiguous Arab countries) may have reached as high as three-quarters of a million, but recent years have seen drops in these levels as the oil states retrench in response to the worldwide economic climate and their own social realities.

Palestinians in these places have tended to reconstitute social communities in exile, but their hold on their new homes is precarious. With few exceptions they have not been granted citizenship and their right to remain as residents is conditional on their labour contributions. Upon retirement they must leave and their children, even those born and brought up in the country of temporary residence, have no guaranteed right to remain behind. As the economies of the oil states undergo contraction and as natives of these countries are trained to replace foreign workers, Palestinians without citizenship will no longer be welcomed. Thus, whereas the 'strangeness' of exiles is modified in these countries of common language and heritage, the underlying anxiety of impermanence is pervasive. Many have already been forced to leave; the rest are weighing their options.

5. Palestinians Abroad

Finally, a growing number of Palestinians now live in non-Arab countries where Palestinian identity continues to be kept alive, sometimes through the transplanting of local communities via chain migration and/or sometimes by political mobilization and ethnic organizations. As many as half a million Palestinians may now be living under these conditions — a phenomenon which has become increasingly common since the early 1970s. Some among them have detached themselves from the ethnic community and assimilated; however, the remarkable fact is that the overwhelming majority of them have not, and even the most assimilated among them who have established themselves professionally in their lands

68   *The Sociology of Involuntary Migration*

of adoption, still retain (as Edward Said himself) a gnawing
sense of exile.

A Look to the Future

Given the persistence of what has been called 'The Palestinian
Problem', which is often erroneously attributed to the intransi-
gence and irrational refusal of the Palestinian Arabs to behave
as temporary refugees seeking resettlement rather than as exiles
who are suffering from an unhealable rift in their souls, what
can be done?

In this article I have argued that a long-term process has evolved
which has been basically misdiagnosed, even by well-meaning
persons seeking a humane solution to the 'Palestinian Refugee
Problem'. Until the situation of the 5.2 million Palestinian Arabs
is properly conceptualized and understood, solutions will continue
to evade us.

To reverse the conditions described above, two complementary
approaches are needed. First, a place must be provided for the
restoration of Palestinian society on Palestinian soil, if those
exiles who find themselves 'strangers at home' are not only to
escape their status as a conquered people but to make progress
in healing the rift in their very being. Second, Palestinian exiles
'abroad' must be offered the option of returning to their native
soil and society.

Were these two options available, Palestinians who, in the
past forty years, have not only fiercely guarded their status
as exiles but have passed it on to their children, leaving the
entire community in a psychological limbo which prevents its
members from moving in any viable direction, might once again
be regarded as refugees rather than exiles. As I have argued in
the introduction, the difference between a refugee and an exile
is just this option of return. Until Palestinians can exercise an
option either to return or to relinquish that right voluntarily
and individually (and there is no reason to believe that all
would choose to return), it is unlikely that the 'problem' can be
resolved peacefully. Certainly, proper sociological diagnosis is a
prerequisite to a solution, but only the will to political action can
translate understanding into policy.

Palestinians – Exiles   69

Notes

1. To a sociologist it is clear that 'native place' is not a mere physical place, although in peasant culture 'soil' has been endowed with a mystique that glosses 'known life-space'. Place is a shorthand for the social order in that place, its culture, its meaning.

2. I use the term 're-encapsulation' intentionally. No matter how brief and fleeting the view of the new society, before an immigrant retreats to the protection of an ethnic enclave, the status of encapsulation is irreversibly altered by the awareness of being inside vis a vis an outside.

3. Passing, in race, means concealment of origin and extirpation of 'native place'. The attendant angst has been well described in a number of novels by black writers of an earlier period. It is important to see this as a more general phenomenon found among almost all movers from one culture to another, including from one class to another. All social movers 'pass' to some extent.

4. I do not deny that even in so-called voluntary household moves, powerless family members move involuntarily, but this is not the same as exile.

5. Britishers who had been accused of individually committed crimes and subsequently banished to Australia, for example, were never considered refugees.

6. I have been unable, in the space allotted for this article, to do a new demographic analysis. Many of the figures used in this report, therefore, have been adapted from the detailed estimates developed for my Unesco report, *The Demographic Characteristics of the Palestinian Population* (Abu-Lughod, 1980), which contains full details on methodology and sources. These estimates, duly updated, have been incorporated into the present work. A survey of earlier population changes, based upon careful demographic estimates, appears in 'The demographic transformation of Palestine' (Abu-Lughod, 1971, 1987).

The methodological problems are immense. The last actual census taken in Palestine was conducted by the British Mandate in 1931. At that time, the entire country (the territory that was later claimed by Israel in 1948, plus those areas that became known as the West Bank and Gaza) contained close to 850,000 Arabs and under 175,000 Jews, perhaps a third of whom were indigenous residents of the country and the remainder Zionist immigrants and their offspring. Subsequent estimates were made by British demographers up to 1946, from which I was able to project the number of Palestinian Arabs who would have been living in the country at the end of 1948, had no war occurred. Given the rate of natural increase, a total of 1.4 million Palestinian Arabs by December 1948 is a likely figure. British estimates also allow us to estimate the distribution of that population by region within the country as of 1948. My own analysis (Abu-Lughod, 1971) suggests that the normal place of residence of about 900,000 of these was in the territories that became part of post-1948 Israel while another 500,000 resided normally in the zones later called the West Bank and Gaza. In the entire analysis I ignore Palestinians who had voluntarily migrated abroad before the 1948 war since they are, strictly speaking, neither refugees nor exiles.

7. Since the rate of natural increase for this population has held quite steady at about 3.0 to 3.5 percent per year, this original population would have doubled to some 1.9 million in the intervening period, had there been no attrition.

For references to accompany this chapter please see page 532.

Part VIII
The 'Brain Drain'

[15]

India: 'Brain Drain' or the Migration of Talent?

T. K. OOMMEN *

THE ISSUE

For many years there has been some concern about the migration of skilled people from the Less Developed Countries (LDCs) to the developed and rich countries of Western Europe, North America, and Australia. Much of the views expressed in the past were based on ill-defined concepts and inadequate quantitative data. But more recently, there have been some studies which have contributed towards a clearer perception of this phenomenon.

Two contrasting views appear to be prominent in the debate on 'brain drain'. The first assumes that the enormous investment of scarce resources on higher education in the LDCs is lost through the migration of skilled people from their countries, and this problem (migration) is reaching crisis proportions. The other view suggests that the LDCs are exaggerating the problem of the migration of the skilled, and only a few of their professionals are actually migrating at any point of time. Thus there is not much of an impact on their economies specially when they cannot even employ all the skilled manpower that they generate through their educational institutions.

The main concern with 'brain drain' is that an inordinate number of professionals, including scientists,[1] engineers and allopathic doctors are seen to migrate from LDCs. These skills can be utilized in any country, unlike professions such as law which calls for knowledge of specific societies, cultures and norms, in addition to technical expertise. Lawyers, thus, cannot easily practice their profession in an alien cultural milieu. This essay concentrates on the migration of scientists, engineers and allopathic medical doctors from India to the countries of the West.

Only a relatively small number of scientists, engineers and medical doctors migrated immediately before and after Indian independence, i. e. in the 1940s and 1950s (Misra, 1985:1-10). An important reason for this was the racial proclivities of the host countries, which discouraged, and to a large extent prevented, immigration from Asian countries. For instance, Australia followed a 'whites only' policy till 1958 which encouraged

---

* Jawaharlal Nehru University, New Delhi (India).

immigration from countries such as Britain but discouraged immigration from Asia (London, 1970). There were quotas to restrict the number of Asian migrants who would be admitted into the United States of America, Canada and other countries. These quotas were relaxed in the U.S.A. in 1965 (see Gujral and Gupta, 1983:1-6); in 1958 and 1966 in Australia; in 1967 in Canada; and in 1962 and 1965 in Britain (Bhagwati, 1976:3-27). Till 1962, Britain had allowed relatively large numbers of migrants from the Commonwealth countries (see Misra, 1985:1-10). The new immigration laws that these countries introduced removed the racist restriction on immigration, but the focus was shifted to the skills that immigrants could bring with them. Thus, highly skilled professionals were preferred, who would meet the requirement of specific skills which may be in short supply in the host countries. The largest migrations since then from India were to the U.S.A., Canada and Britain (Bhagwati, 1976:3-27).

In the literature on 'brain drain' from India, frequent references are made to the cost of education, incurred by the country, which is lost through the migration of professionals. For instance, the cost of training an engineer to graduate level in the Indian Institutes of Technology (IIT) is roughly computed at US$ 14,000, most of which is borne by the Indian Government. The IIT graduates are considered the cream of Indian engineers and the loss to India through their migration is not only seen in monetary terms, but also in terms of their possible contribution to the development of the Indian economy. Very often, Indian authors tend to stress the loss to India, but they do not consider the cost that host countries incur when these migrants study at their institutions and at their cost. For instance, the cost borne by the United States of America (the preferred country for advanced study) when Indian students study at U. S. universities at U.S. expense (see Bayer, 1968:465-77), is ignored. Many of these students return to India, and this constitutes a loss to the U. S. (Baldwin, 1970:358-72). Trying to figure out who pays for what and how much each country gains or loses when professionals migrate, will lead to endless argument with no firm conclusions being reached. India does not totally lose its investment in education when professionals migrate, since they contribute to knowledge even when they are based in other countries and they also send remittances to their family members and relatives still in India (see Grubel, 1968:541-58). Some of these migrants do return to India after a few years in the foreign countries, and thus can make direct contributions through the use of their skills in India. 'Brain drain' is thus not an issue that can be considered a 'problem' without various qualifications. Certainly India would benefit from the skills of professionals who remain in the country but, perhaps, when professionals return to India after advanced training they would be of even more benefit to the country. The problem, therefore, would be in devising ways to attract the highly skilled professionals who are now based in other countries to return and settle down in India.

A point to be considered in any debate on the migration of professionals is about what they would be doing in India when they do not choose to migrate. If these professionals were just to join the considerable number of unemployed in the country, it will be a greater drain on the country's resources since they are virtually unproductive, and they have to be fed. Thus the migration of professionals has to be seen from various angles, from the point of view of the costs involved in their training, to the possible employment of their skills, the foreign exchange that they can remit if they were abroad, the fact that a democratic country cannot prevent professionals leaving if they wanted to, and so on. It cannot be said that there is no problem at all when professionals migrate, but a more pragmatic approach would be to consider the ways and means of having professionals get the best of advanced training in other countries (if such training is not available in India itself) and then return to India.

THE CONCEPT OF 'BRAIN DRAIN'

The concept of 'brain drain' has been used rather indiscriminately by many, and to refer to all migration of people who are of a high educational level. But it carries some emotive and pejorative connotations, and therefore needs to be carefully qualified (see Adams, 1968:1-8). In recent years the concept is more circumspectly used and has also gained some clarity. However, for our purpose, the phrase 'migration of talent' or 'migration of professionals' will be used rather than 'brain drain'. This is to take note of the fact that when professionals migrate from India, not all of them remain permanently in those countries. Some do, but many return. 'Migration of talent' indicates both migration from India as well as return to India, a two-way movement of professionals. 'Brain drain' on the other hand does not indicate this two-way movement adequately, but rather emphasizes only a one-way movement of professionals out of India (Ahmad, 1970:215-22). We need to consider also the return of professionals since they are a benefit to their own country; also that they may not have been able to acquire an advanced training and experience if they had remained in their own country.

Studies on the migration of professionals suggest different perspectives from which the problem can be considered. The 'Internationalist' model proposed by Johnson (1968:69-91) suggests that the migration of professionals only reflects the operation of an international market for specialised human capital. The model considers the transfer of talent as mutually advantageous to both the sending as well as the host countries, and that a laissez-faire policy, i. e. non-interference with migration, should be followed. Opposed to this, is the 'Nationalist' model (Patinkin, 1968:92-108) which regards human capital, or at least a minimum level of human capital, as indispensable to a country's economic development. A loss of skilled persons will ultimately result in the economy being gravely affected and development programmes being jeopardised (Adams, 1968:1-8).

Baldwin (1970:358-72) makes the distinction between society's 'human needs' and the economy's 'effective demand' which is useful in placing the two models (Internationalist and Nationalist) in a proper perspective. The Internationalist model gives more importance to the 'effective demand' of the economy while the Nationalist model places more importance on the society's 'human needs'.

WHO MIGRATES? WHERE TO? AND WHY?

Most of the migrants from the LDCs are students (Ahmad, 1970:215-22). Through migrating, they hope or intend to avail themselves of the best possible facilities, get trained under professors of better standing and repute than are found in their countries, learn the latest developments in their fields, and use better equipment than that available in their own countries. In the more prestigious and better universities, particularly, the facilities are likely to be far superior to those available in their own countries (cf. Klaw, 1969). Moreover, outstanding scientists tend to be concentrated in a few institutions and laboratories, and these concentrations make it more likely that a small number of organizations provide evocative environments and are thus the sites of major scientific achievements. A further reason for students and scientists to migrate to advanced countries is that through studying and working with outstanding scientists and in prestigious institutions, they not only acquire superior training, but also gain some prestige through working in these institutions. This prestige could be converted into better jobs at home, when they return, or in the case of medical doctors, a more lucrative private practice in their home country. An added incentive to migrate is also the much higher scales of remuneration than in their own country.

413

A review of the available data shows that the students who had been awarded post-graduate and doctoral degrees and are now settled in India acquired them from a few preferred countries. From the United States there had been 40% of all overseas doctorates and masters and in all the fields that Indians had studied abroad and returned. Thirty-five to forty per cent of the doctorates and masters degrees were acquired from British universities, and the remaining 20-25% were awarded these degrees from other countries.

TABLE 1

Country bias in acquiring foreign qualifications (1971)

Country of qualification	All fields				
	Total	Doctorate	Master	Bachelor	Others
U.K.	33.4	35.2	39.5	23.7	38.8
USA	28.0	40.5	40.7	14.1	7.3
Canada	2.0	4.0	2.0	1.2	1.4
USSR	1.6	3.5	0.9	1.4	1.8
Germany	3.1	6.4	2.0	1.8	6.5
France	1.3	1.8	1.0	1.2	1.7
Other European countries	3.7	4.7	2.9	3.1	6.1
Australia and New Zealand	1.0	1.2	1.0	0.6	1.6
Japan	0.7	0.3	0.3	0.9	1.9
Others	25.2	2.4	9.7	52.0	32.6
Total	100.0	100.0	100.0	100.0	100.0

MAGNITUDE OF MIGRATION FROM INDIA

About 11,000 university graduates, which includes doctors, engineers and scientists, leave the country every year for advanced study and/or work. A conservative estimate suggests that, of this number, about 2,500 will remain abroad permanently, and the rest will return to India. In 1967, the annual migration of the highly educated was about 10% of all university graduates. About 11% of scientists migrated, and also about 20% of the Indian Institutes of Technology (IIT) graduates of 1961-1965. The permanent loss each year is about 2.6% of university graduates, 7% of doctors, 7% of engineers and 2.5% of scientists. Many of the migrants are graduates of prestigious institutions including the IITs and the Indian Institute of Science (IISc, at Bangalore). About 50% of the graduates from the IISc and about 60% of the doctorates from the same institution go abroad every year (Domrese, 1970:215-57).

The largest number of professionals migrate to the U.S.A. and Canada. In the five-year period ending in June 1967 (i.e. 1962-1967) over 10,000 Indians are reported to have migrated to the U.S.A. out of which just over 5,000 were professionals and technical workers. This included 2,141 engineers, 624 physical scientists, 174 physicians and 78 social scientists. In the same five-year period, about 7,000 Indians had migrated to Canada, and just about 2,000 were of the professional category and technical workers. This included 408 engineers, 206 natural scientists and 164 physicians (*Technical Manpower*, April 1970).

Between 1977 and 1979 the total number of professionals who migrated to the United States was 8,035 (scientists, engineers and medical doctors and excluding social scientists). The total number of these three groups in each of the three years was: 3,298 in 1977; 2,673 in 1978; and 2,064 in 1979. The most noticeable trend was that over the years the number of physicians migrating to the U.S.A. has been declining. From a total of 1,984 doctors in 1977 to only 598 migrating in 1979 makes a considerable decline. One of the reasons for such a decline seems to be that there are not more than a few good residencies available to doctors from India. If the trend continues, the 'drain' of doctors to the U.S.A. will automatically 'dry up'.

While it is difficult to say exactly how many Indians among the professionals have left India to settle permanently in a foreign country, there were probably about 30,000 of this category who were abroad in 1971-1972, when in India the unemployed numbered about 110,000 (Banerjea, 1975:190-4). At this time (1971) the total number of Indian physicians working in the U.S.A. was 3,959 (see *Technical Manpower*, August-September, 1973).

FACTORS PROMOTING MIGRATION

Unemployment

One of the most frequently asserted explanations to account for the high rate of migration of professionals is that the Indian economy cannot employ all the professionals produced by Indian universities and institutions of learning. As Usha Nayar (1985:1-13) says, the number of graduates in science and technology produced by Indian universities is fewer than the number of graduates that American universities turn out every year. But the American economy needs even more highly skilled persons, whereas the Indian economy cannot absorb even the small number of graduates from Indian universities.

Grubel (1976:209-24) suggests that India over-invested in education since the end of the second world war. When one considers the available limited opportunities, this may well be the case. Moreover, there are only a few institutions that can employ the scientists that graduate each year. The Government of India has placed more emphasis on a few 'key institutions' to provide the impetus to research and high quality education. Private and public sector industries also employ scientists in their laboratories, but far less than the corresponding employment of scientists in research in the developed countries (see Research and Development Statistics 1982-1983, Government of India, Department of Science and Technology, p. 30). Thus, of the total number of graduates in science produced every year, only a small proportion can be employed in these institutions.

Further, graduates at prestigious institutions prefer to work in high-paying and prestigious occupations and institutions. Thus, of the graduates of the IISc who enter the academic profession, about 10% teach in the IITs (Domrese, 1970:215-57). Higher expectations among these graduates, and possible disappointment when they do not get the kind of high-paying and higher prestige jobs that they want, may be one possible reason for the migration to other countries. However, administrators of the five IITs blame Indian industry for failing to provide IIT graduates with jobs that are sufficiently challenging and also with more opportunities for advancement in their careers (see Neri, 1985:40-57).

Immigration rules

Countries differ in culture, economic development, political systems, and so on, which could influence the migrant. An important condition for migration is the immigration laws that exist in various countries. Countries that favour immigration would obviously be more likely to attract more migrants than those that do not. The countries of the First

World have by and large been in favour of attracting professionals to work in their countries. Socialist countries, on the other hand (the Soviet Union and countries of the Warsaw Pact) do not normally admit immigrants although they allow students to stay in their countries until their studies are completed.

The migration of professionals is to be seen as a temporary stay in any country abroad, and in some instances merely exploratory in nature. Most of them would return to their home country sooner or later. Their return could, however, be expedited if attractive conditions of work and suitable jobs are available in their own country (Glaser and Habers, 1978).

Compared to migrants from some countries such as Brazil and Pakistan, Indians appear to be more prone to emigrate. However, even among the Indians abroad, only a minority are definite in their plans to settle down in the country to which they had migrated. For example, the UNITAR survey found that of the Indians abroad, 34% definitely planned to return to India, 14% thought it was probable that they would return, 22% were uncertain about their future plans, 21% thought it was probable that they would emigrate and only 9% were definite that they would stay abroad permanently (Glaser and Habers, 1978).

Colonial links

Some of the nation-states from which there are much higher rates of migration as also of non-return are former colonies of such countries. For example, the migrants to Britain from India are much more familiar with the educational system of Britain since India closely follows the pattern established by the British. The majority of the professionals (probably all) in India are educated through the English language. Thus, it is likely that migrants prefer to go to countries of former colonial powers in the belief that their problems of adaptation will be much less, compared to another country with a different language and unfamiliar culture. That is why, for example, fewer Indians migrate to Japan compared to those who migrate to Britain (Glaser and Habers, 1978; Johnson, 1968:69-91).

Religious minorities, for example Christians from India, migrate in large numbers not because they face persecution in the country (Christians are rarely discriminated against or persecuted) but because there is a considerable number of schools and colleges, some founded by the British and managed by Christian institutions, to which they had easy accessibility and through which they are educated. These schools follow a system compatible with those countries where English is the dominant language, particularly Britain, which also have predominantly Christian populations. Language and religion thus make it easier for the migrants to interact with the people of those countries, and perhaps the Indian Christians can find the environment more congenial and less foreign than those of other religious groups from India.

Financial incentives and material benefits

In India professionals are not paid enough to be able to maintain what they consider a 'respectable' standard of life. By this is meant better housing, good schools for their children, ownership of a car, a refrigerator, a television, etc. The cost of living has gone up considerably in the country and the inventory of things regarded as essential for a comfortable lifestyle has also increased.

The income that a highly skilled professional can earn in a Western country could be anything like 4-5 times what he would earn in India. By remaining in India many of the material benefits that he could get within a short time would be available to him only by investing all his savings, and probably only a couple of decades after beginning his career. An average middle class family in India would not be able to afford much of the technical gadgets and conveniences that most people in the West take for granted. This would be an attraction for those professionals who are eager to have these items, and could acquire them by migrating (see Chopra, 1985:1-13; Glaser and Habers, 1978). Further, for those professionals who are expected to extend financial assistance to their kin (see Oommen, 1982: 57-93), employment outside the country is a great attraction as they can meet this obligation without sacrificing their own material requirements.

Professionals are an occupational elite in India. The status and prestige that are accorded to professionals such as physicians and engineers, are among the highest. But their income levels are not always commensurate with their high prestige and status. This is particularly true in the government institutions, which have fixed salaries. Private medical practice in urban areas is much more lucrative, and income levels may compare favourably with high ranking business executives of large private sector corporations. But such high incomes are limited only to a few of the professionals. High status and prestige may to some extent compensate for the lack of high salaries, but usually such attributes are achieved by professionals in India only after many years and in the latter years of their careers. Thus, the incongruence between high professional status and low income seems to be an important factor prompting the migration of professionals.

Higher education

One of the most important factors that contributes to the migration of professionals from India is the lack of development in certain branches of knowledge. Much of the latest developments take place in the industrialized countries of the West, even as scientists from the Third World countries contribute to this. Most of the professionals from India travel abroad for higher studies as noted earlier. Some, however, may utilize 'study' as a means of going abroad and perhaps stay there permanently (see Ahmad, 1970:215-22; Fortney, 1970:217-32; Glaser and Habers, 1978).

The possibility of studying under, and working with, 'giants' in the field was an important reason for going abroad. The advantage of working with eminent persons abroad is easy recognition, and higher chance of getting entrenched in the system in the foreign country (see Zuckerman, 1977).

Working conditions

Working conditions for professionals in the Western countries are considered far superior to those in India. Better facilities for research, better equipment and so on, encourage migration and also permanent settlement in foreign countries. Indians consider the professional milieu abroad better. Moreover, they do not feel particularly confident about making a professional contribution within the country (Glaser and Habers 1978).

Spectacular contributions to science in the last 50 years (i.e. between 1920 and 1970) from scientists in India are more likely to be found in the pre-independence days than after independence (Sudarshan 1974:465-67). This, the author attributes to the system which does not discredit mediocrity, and does not have incentives for the exceptionals.

Many complaints are often made about the conditions of work in India. In scientific establishments such as the government laboratories and even within government

417

departments, problems arise between administrators and technical experts. Very often the heads of departments are general administrators who are not likely to have the necessary expertise to make decisions on technical matters. They may not entirely rely on the engineers and scientists to provide recommendations towards policy making as well as in implementation, leading to much frustration among the experts, and to conflict between administrators and the technical experts (see Singh, 1975). The problem of 'protecting their turf' is not confined only to the general administrators but extends also to administrators who are themselves scientists.

Dissatisfaction is caused when directors of institutions, or heads of divisions in research laboratories, have a high degree of power concentrated in them. Lesser degree of professional autonomy, lack of professional recognition, and limited chances of promotion are other reasons for dissatisfaction in government institutions (see Aurora, n.d.). Naturally, the scientists who find the system not to their liking will probably choose to find more congenial surroundings in a foreign country.

It is possible that a 'patriarchal tradition' survives in Indian institutions. As Suri (1967:22-25) describes it, this involves, for instance, a literary tribute to a senior colleague (irrespective of his competence or achievement) who expects his juniors to include his name as author of the article that they write. It has become almost obligatory to pay such tribute. Such a system would give undue credit to persons who are highly placed in the institution's hierarchy and perhaps even deny credit to the person who had done the work. Suri considers this as a practice that would certainly upset a young researcher and may even prompt him to migrate. Writing recently about the Indian academic scene with reference to the social sciences, Oommen, (1983:111-36) found a similar persistence of patron-client ties.

Excessive bureaucratic procedures

A serious problem that scientists in India appear to face is the excessive amount of red-tape involved in the course of their work. Buying new equipment, getting old ones repaired, and even to acquire the barest essential and cheaper materials involve procedures which take up an inordinate amount of time and effort. What makes this worse is that on occasion the researcher has to justify expenses to bureaucrats who are not technically qualified to make such judgements. Homi Bhabha, who is considered as one of the most eminent scientists that India has produced in the 20th century, is said to have complained about this same problem in the 1950s. He had felt that as a consequence his scientific work suffered. When even a scientist of the standing of Bhabha had to put up with such bureaucratic controls, the plight of lesser scientists can well be imagined.

Conditions in other countries, especially the United States of America, are seen to be far better for scientific work, with less bureaucratric interference, and due recognition being given to talent, irrespective of age and status (see Chopra, 1985: 1-13).

Mismatch between Indian education and employment

It has been suggested with reference to the training of allopathic physicians that Indian medical colleges turn out doctors who are more suited to Britain and the United States than to India (Jeffery, 1976:502-7). Jayaram (1977:207-20) goes even further and states that it is almost as if India maintains a certain number of medical colleges specifically for the benefit of other countries. The consumers of health services in Britain and the United States have their parallels in India only among the urban middle classes. The majority of Indians, who live in villages, and a large number of them very poor, do not have the resources to utilise the services of trained, allopathic physicians (see Mathur, 1971:58-96).

Soon after graduating, some of the doctors find themselves unemployed for varying lengths of time. This is because they cannot all be employed by government institutions, and neither can the urban middle classes provide enough work for them. Physicians find their working conditions unattractive in India, and this is specially when they know that they have the necessary skills to find employment in other countries (Jeffery, 1976:502-7), which prompts them to migrate. The receptivity of host countries towards physicians is at least partly conditioned by the high cost and the comparable quality of training.

REASONS FOR RETURNING TO INDIA

Notwithstanding the many adverse conditions that exist in India, quite a few migrants do return. Some of these had returned as soon as they had completed their studies, and some had returned after working for a few years upon completion of their study. All those who return are well aware that the levels of income that they could hope for in India are far below what they were earning abroad or hoped to earn in foreign countries. Income and material benefits, while they are important factors which promote migration to western countries, apparently lost their importance to at least some of the professionals after some time, or other factors took precedence.

Panandikar's study (1971:46-57) found that there was a desire among the migrants to return home after a stay abroad of about 10-12 years. However, he also noticed that some of the returnees decided to return as their wives could not adjust to the foreign way of life.

Merriam's study (1969:52-82) also found that among the faculty of IIT, Kanpur, most of the foreign-trained would have returned to India even if the institution had not been laying down stringent conditions. Contributing to Indian development was a reason that many in that study had mentioned.

One of the reasons for their return was the racial discrimination that the scientists had experienced in the country where they had studied and worked. They felt that their being Indian was a major hurdle in not getting jobs and positions commensurate with their qualifications and experience. Although Indians in Britain considered this a major problem (see Schaefer, 1976:305-27), those in the United States were less concerned about racial discrimination (see Glaser and Habers, 1978).

Those who had been sponsored by the Government of India under various exchange programmes usually returned to India, as required according to the bond signed by them at the time of going abroad. Those who had gone on fellowships from foreign foundations also generally returned.

INFERENCES AND SUGGESTIONS

In a brief essay such as the present one, it is possible to highlight only a few aspects of any problem such as the migration of professionals. We have pointed out the factors that encourage and induce migration, and those that further the return of the professionals. The basic assumption that has underlined our analysis is that any large-scale migration of professionals from a relatively less developed country such as India, with its enormous population, will have a detrimental effect on the total situation prevailing in the country. This detrimental effect is not sought to be gauged in terms of the monetary cost involved in training these professionals, but in terms of the long-term effects on the development of the country including distributive justice.

419

A better life for a majority of India's citizens calls for better health care, better education, better communication for the masses, and so on. While migration of professionals is to a certain extent inevitable - from the perspective of migrating individuals, given the underdeveloped state of the Indian economy, one has to consider the issue of migrating professionals also from the point of view of 'societal needs'. Indian society needs many things, not the least of which are the services of many more physicians, engineers and scientists.

The problem that many have recognized about Third World countries in general, and India in particular, is that there is too large a population in the country. The economy has to grow at a phenomenal rate to ensure any real increase in people's incomes and improvement in their standard of living. However, this has not taken place to any great extent, and one finds that the income differences between those in the advanced countries and those in India are still very large. For the same level of skills, the professional could earn much more in an advanced country of the west. This factor is likely to be influential to a considerable degree in the foreseeable future, and there is no reason to expect that people will suddenly become less interested in their material well-being. Thus, there will always be some people who will find it an attractive idea to migrate to the western countries. It will not be easy to bring them back to India when the primary reason that motivated their leaving India was relatively higher income abroad.

Another category of migrants are those who had left the country with the intention of getting advanced training in their field of specialization; they are expected to return upon completion of their studies. Since they had no intention of remaining indefinitely in the foreign country, this group could be brought back to the country by attractive job offers and other incentives such as new opportunities of using their skills through building up their areas of expertise in the country.

A third group of migrants leave the country because high quality research cannot be carried out in Indian laboratories. For such people ways must be found to bring them back. Indian laboratories do not seem to encourage the bright minds to explore new frontiers of knowledge. India's preoccupation has been to educate the average and not encourage the gifted, leading to the nurturing of mediocrity to the detriment of the exceptionals. 'Not only have we eliminated hereditary royalty, but somehow suppressed intellectual aristocracy' (Sudarshan, 1974: 465). Recognizing that gifted individuals need a special kind of environment and expect preferential treatment, it will be to the advantage of the country to identify such individuals and provide them with as many facilities as possible so that their creative energies may not be wasted, and they do not choose to migrate instead (see Dhar, 1969:404-9).

Obviously the only way to employ more scientists is to increase expenditure on research and development. By investing only 0.85% of the GNP on research and development, not more than a fraction of the annual turnover of science graduates could hope to find employment in scientific institutions and laboratories. On the other hand, the government, which is the major source of research funds, cannot devote more resources than it already does to research and development. However, it may be possible for the private industrial sector to invest more in developing indigenous products for the consumer market in the country. The private sector had spent only Rs. 161.38^2 crores compared to Rs. 997.29 crores spent by the government (Research and Development Statistics 1982-1983). By reducing the protective measures that the Government of India grants to Indian industries, it can make these industries more competitive, resulting in the manufacture of better products. This will be possible only if there is a greater investment in research and development which means a greater possibility of employing a large number of high quality scientists. Moreover, if the research products of the scientists are used in industry there is the greater chance that the scientists will find the work more rewarding and satisfying. This will result in scientists joining research laboratories in India, rather than thinking of leaving the country.

The possibility of travel to other countries to learn of the latest developments in their field, and to contribute to these developments through contacts and working with foreign scientists, should be open to Indian scientists too. This may be for short periods of time, such as in the case of the scientists who are sent to the International Centre for Theoretical Physics at Trieste, Italy (see Salam, 1966: 451-55). This kind of programme could be expanded to encourage a large number of scientists to periodically visit foreign laboratories and institutions for short periods. Such a programme will be beneficial to the country in the long run.

Finally, the conditions of research work should be made more conducive for creative effort. Getting bogged down with matters of procedure, in a typical bureaucratic style of functioning, is something that goes against the spirit of academic quest. Efforts should also be made to give proper and adequate recognition for scientific achievements. It has often been seen in the past that Indian scientists receive recognition in the country only after they have been honoured abroad. This may imply that talent is not intrinsically viewed in India, and there are not many incentives for the professionals to motivate them to do their best while they are in India. They usually produce outstanding results when they are working abroad. There does not seem to be any need or effort to realize one's potential fully in India, as if Indians could be satisfied by second best rather than striving for the best, while working for the country.

The migration of professionals from India in recent years has taken on the form of a collective exodus, and a pattern can be discerned in these migrations. That is, professionals do not migrate out of sheer individual impulse, but are also prompted through various conditions that exist in Indian society. Through the identification of some of these conditions, it is possible that solutions could be found to restrict the number of persons who choose to migrate, and also to bring back those who had already left. However, this involves drastic changes in the official policy towards scientific personnel, considering the fact that government measures already taken have yielded relatively less than impressive results. In this approach, one is required to jointly analyse two sets of factors - socio-economic and psychological attributes of the migrants and structural properties of the situation both at the points of departure and destination - in order to unfold the factors involved in migration and to prescribe remedies to moderate and/or prevent the exodus.

PERSPECTIVES ON THE PROBLEM OF THE MIGRATION OF TALENT

I would like to conclude this essay by suggesting that there are several hidden assumptions in the existing studies; unless one makes them explicit, one cannot unfold the full import and thrust of the conclusions arrived at by these studies. The problem of migration of talent can be viewed from at least three perspectives. These include, first of all, the perspective of the individual concerned, the professional who migrates. Secondly, one could look at the problem from the perspective of the nation-state. Thirdly, the problem can be considered from the point of view of developing a knowledge pool for the whole world.

From the point of view of the migrating individual, the fact of moving has many obvious benefits. The material benefits that an individual derives from working in a more prosperous country may be denied to him if he remains in his own country. Besides the material rewards he may also benefit in terms of working in an atmosphere more favourable for his scientific work. This makes him more cosmopolitan in outlook, and he begins to look at the whole world as his potential field of activity. This cosmopolitanism also fosters in him an individualism which transcends the claims of his country, region, cultural and kin group. This is not to suggest that all migrating professionals take an absolutely individualistic view. They are more likely to carefully consider different factors, weight them up, giving more importance to some and less importance to others. Ultimately it is the overall inference that he derives from these 'pros' and 'cons' that results in his decision to migrate.

A purely individualistic approach would consider migration of talent from the perspective of the benefits that accrue to the producer of knowledge, that is, the scientist. But once it is produced, it should not be constrained by artificial limits imposed on the people who possess knowledge from moving to any place they choose. Moreover, this free market economic orientation would probably go in favour of those with the highest hiring capacity, that is, the affluent countries.

From the point of view of the nation-state, the large-scale migration of professionals is not only a loss in terms of the knowledge that could be utilized in the country, but also that another nation-state that had not invested anything or very little in the development and training of the individual reaps the benefits that legitimately belong to the former. However, the problem of sorting out who benefits and who can automatically claim the loyalty of an individual is not so simple. When a scientist makes a contribution to knowledge in a country other than his native country, inevitably both countries stake the claim to their share of his success.

Besides claiming the loyalty of the scientists, the nation-state also strives to keep the knowledge produced by the scientist in question away from other countries. Knowledge, admittedly, has different values to different people. Scientists consider their contributions to knowledge as the property of the whole world, but the nation-state where they work, or the industrial corporation that sponsors their research, may consider these findings and discoveries as their private property, to be dispersed only at their discretion. This brings us to the third perspective, which is that the knowledge that is contributed by the scientist is considered the property of mankind as a whole. This contribution to knowledge is considered as an important aspect of a scientist's work regardless of his location and citizenship.

There could also be cases where a nation-state is perceived as indifferent to providing the necessary work environment for scientific research. However, that does not prevent it from showing pride in the achievements of its scientists. For instance, though much of the work by S. Chandrasekhar and Har Gobind Khorana was done while they were abroad, India shows a justifiable pride that they are of Indian origin.

Much of the problem of the 'brain drain' is due to a complex of attitudes about the migration of professionals. There is no single consistent view about such migration, and as we noted above, there can be different perspectives from which the 'problem' can be viewed, leading to a different conclusion in each case.

NOTES

1. 'Scientist' refers to specialists in the physical and natural sciences unless otherwise indicated.
2. One crore is ten million. The present exchange rate is (nearly) Rs. 15 to one US dollar.

BIBLIOGRAPHY

Adams, W. (Ed.)
1968   *The Brain Drain.* New York: Macmillan Company.

Ahmad, A.
1970   Gain-Drain Ratio in the Global Exchange of Scientific and Technical Manpower. *Journal of Asian and African Studies.* 5,3.

Aurora, G. S.
n. d.   *Scientific Community in India: the Organisational Context.* Report of a research project sponsored by the Ford Foundation, Hyderabad: Administrative Staff College of India (mimeo.).

Baldwin, G. B.
1970   Brain Drain or Overflow. *Foreign Affairs.* 48,2.

Banerjea, D.
1975   Brain Drain: Its causes and remedies. *Science and Culture.* 41,5.

Bayer, A. E.
1968   The Effect of International Interchange of High-Level Manpower on the United States. *Social Forces.* 46, 4.

Bhagwati, J. N. (Ed.)
1976   *The Brain Drain and Taxation: Theory and Empirical Analysis.* Amsterdam: North Holland Publishing Co.,2

Chopra, S. K.
1985   Bringing them Home - the Problem of Brain Drain in *Seminar on Brain Drain.* New Delhi.

Dhar, M. L.
1969   Creativity in scientific institutions. *Indian Journal of Public Administration.* 15,3.

Domrese, R. J.
1970   The Migration of Talent from India in *International Migration of High-Level Manpower: Its Impact on the Development Process.* New York: Praeger Publishers.

Fortney, J. A.
1970   International Migration of Professionals. *Population Studies.* 24,2.

Glaser, W. A. and C. Habers
1978   *The Brain Drain* (Findings of a UNITAR multinational comparative survey of professional personnel of developing countries who study abroad). New York: Pergamon Press.

Grubel, H. G.
1968   The Reduction of the Brain Drain: Problems and Policies. *Minerva.* 6,4.

Grubel, H. G.
1976   Reflections on the Present State of the Brain Drain and a Suggested Remedy. *Minerva.* 14,2.

Gujral, S. P. and S. S. Gupta
1983   Indian scientific, technical and professional personnel admitted as immigrants to the U.S.A. (1977-1979). *Technical Manpower.* 24,8-9.

Jayaram, N.
    1977   Social Implications of Medical Education in India. *Journal of Higher Education.* 3,2.

Jeffery, R.
    1976   Migration of Doctors from India. *Economic and Political Weekly.* 11,13.

Johnson, H. G.
    1968   An 'Internationalist' Model, in Adams, Walter (Ed.), *The Brain Drain.* New York: Macmillan Co.

Klaw, S.
    1969   *The New Brahmins: Scientific Life in America.* New York: William Morrow and Company, Inc.

London, H. I.
    1970   *Non-white Immigration and the 'White Australia Policy'.* Sydney: Sydney University Press.

Mathur, P. N.
    1971   Demand and Supply of Doctors in India, 1951-1986. *Manpower Journal.* 7,1-2.

Merriam, M. F.
    1969   Brain Drain Study at IIT Kanpur. *Manpower Journal.* 5,1.

Misra, D. N.
    1985   Brain Drain: Consequences and some Related Issues, in *Seminar on Brain Drain.* New Delhi.

Nayar, U.
    1985   Brain Drain: The phenomenon and its causes, in *Seminar on Brain Drain.* New Delhi.

Neri, M.
    1985   The Slow Decline of the IITs. *Business World.* September, 16-29.

Oommen, T. K.
    1982   The Urban Family in Transition, in Augustine, John S. (Ed.), *The Indian Family in Transition.* New Delhi: Vikas Publishing House Pvt. Ltd.

Oommen, T. K.
    1983   Sociology in India: A please for contextualisation. *Sociological Bulletin.* 32,2.

Panandikar, V. A. P.
    1971   Brain Drain - the Indian Myths. *Manpower Journal.* 7,1-2.

Patinkin, D.
    1968   A 'Nationalist' Model', in Adams, Walter (Ed.), *The Brain Drain.* New York: Macmillan Co.

Salam, A.
    1966   The Isolation of the Scientist in Developing Countries. *Minerva.* 4,4.

Schaefer, R. T.
    1976   Indians in Great Britain. *International Review of Modern Sociology.* Autumn, 6.

Singh, B. H.
    1975   *Conflict in a Formal Organisation.* Chandigarh, Department of Sociology, Punjab University, (mimeo.).

424

Sudarshan, E. C. G.
  1974   Science in India. *Economic and Political Weekly*. 9,12.

Suri, S.
  1967   A case study. *Seminar*, April.

Zuckerman, H.
  1977   *Scientific Elite: Nobel Laureates in the United States*. New York: Free Press.

[16]

Migration of Highly Educated Asians and Global Dynamics

Paul M. Ong
Lucie Cheng
Leslie Evans

University of California, Los Angeles

The migration of Asians trained in technical fields is the most important component of the total global migration of scientific, technical and professional workers from developing to developed countries (primarily Australia, Canada and the United States). Though this phenomenon shares common characteristics with the larger international migration of all labor, it is unique in that migration from Asia to the industrialized countries favors the highly educated, and the debate over brain drain remains complex and inconclusive. The far-reaching effects of the movement of Asian high level manpower (HLM) are discussed in light of: 1) the global articulation of higher education; 2) the link to unequal development on a global scale; and 3) the contribution to economic development of the reverse flow of HLM to less developed countries.

Introduction

In recent decades, the movement of Asians trained in the technical fields such as engineering, the sciences, and health professions to the industrialized economies on the Pacific Rim has increased dramatically. Of course, the movement of highly educated labor from Third World countries is not limited to Asians and the developed countries on the Pacific Rim, but this particular pattern is the most important component of the total global migration. In the period from 1961 to 1972, for example, approximately 300,000 scientific, technical and professional workers from all developing countries migrated to Western nations (UNCTAD, 1975). Australia, Canada, and the United States together account for nearly half of the total flow. For the two countries for which we have data, Asians constituted a majority of the total flow from developing nations. The nearly 30,000 Asians who settled in Canada during this period made up 52 percent of all highly educated labor from the Third World to that country, and the 65,000 in the United States comprised 72 percent of flow to that country.[1]

This substantial migration, which commenced in the mid-1960s,[2] has not abated. Between 1972 and 1988, approximately one fifth of a million Asians with training in the science-based professions entered the United States from the four major sending countries. Table 1 provides a detailed breakdown by occupation and country of birth for the years between 1972 and 1985. The data show that an overwhelming proportion of this inflow is comprised of individuals in the pure and applied sciences, with social scientists constituting only a very small proportion. There are also ethnic differences: Indians were the largest ethnic group, with engineers and physicians being prominent components; Filipinos were the second largest group, with health practitioners being particularly important; Koreans had an occupational distribution similar to Filipinos, but were smaller in absolute size; and the Chinese had proportionately a larger number of scientists. Despite this ethnic variation, it is clear that a substantial number of highly educated labor left all four countries.

Equally important, Asians emerged as a dominant group in the immigration of all professionals, from both the developed and developing nations. Asians accounted for less than a tenth of the total inflow into the United States before 1965 but more than a half after 1971. Although not as dramatic as in the American case, workers from developing countries also constituted a large share of the professional migration to Canada. Third World workers were relatively rare prior to the 1960s, but by 1974 they made up over forty percent of all professionally qualified immigrants, with Hong Kong and China, India, and the Philippines being the top three countries of origin (Devoretz and Maki, 1983).

Can we treat this migration merely as an epiphenomenon of the larger international migration of all labor? The answer is partly yes. Many factors that prompt persons with lesser skills to relocate, such as wage differentials and better educational opportunities for their children, also affect the highly educated. These commonalities hold regardless of whether one analyzes migration from a simple push-pull framework or from a world-system framework. One could also argue that the movement of the highly

[1] While the United Kingdom received 28 percent of the global migration of highly educated labor from developing countries, placing it second after the United States, only about a quarter of the immigrants were Asians.

[2] The United States provides an example of the timing of this flow. While there were 14,500 immigrants during the five years between 1961 and 1965, there were nearly 16,000 in 1972 alone.

MIGRATION OF HIGHLY EDUCATED ASIANS   545

TABLE 1
IMMIGRATION OF HIGHLY EDUCATED ASIANS
TO THE UNITED STATES, 1972-85

| Occupation | Country of Birth | | | |
	India	South Korea	Philippines	China
Math and Computer Scientists	1,200	174	599	1,681
Natural Scientists	4,077	547	2,001	2,138
Social Scientists	538	158	447	350
Engineers	15,753	2,964	9,527	9,824
Physicans	15,172	3,002	7.732	3,937
Other Health Diagnosis	2,138	620	2,672	1,184
Nurses	6,858	6,831	20,482	2,811
Other Health Treaters	2,645	2,695	5,372	1,700
Post-Secondary Teachers	2,201	1,343	1,256	2,776

SOURCE: Figures Tabulated from INS Immigrant Tapes. Counts for 1980-81 are incomplete because of lost data. In 1983, Physicians were included in the category of Other Health Diagnosis, and Nurses were included in the category of Other Health Treaters.

educated merely reflects a recomposition of the population in the sending country due to development and an associated rise in the level of education. Among Asian countries, the proportion of the adult population with some college education has increased since the 1960s, as shown in Table 2, which lists statistics on postsecondary schooling for some of Asia's major sending countries. In South Korea, for example, the percentage more than tripled,

TABLE 2
PERCENT WITH POSTSECONDARY EDUCATION

Country	1960	1970	1980
Hong Kong	4.3	4.9 (1971)	7.1 (1981)
India	N/A	1.1 (1971)	2.5 (1981)
South Korea	2.6	5.6	8.4
Philippines	6.2	9.6	15.2
Thailand	0.6	1.1	2.9

DEFINITION AND SOURCE: Statistics are for those 25 years and older and are taken from UNESCO, various years.

from 2.6 percent in 1960 to 8.4 percent in 1980. The Philippines had by far the highest levels among all Asian countries, 15.2 percent by 1980, an astonishing accomplishment for a nation that had not even reached the ranks of the newly industrialized countries (NICs). While data on Taiwan are not readily available, the accessible information also shows a rapid rise in the early 1970s. Whereas only 4.4 percent of the population 12 years or older had a college or university education in 1970, 6.5 percent of the population 15 years or older had attained this status by 1975 (China, 1972 and 1976). As an increasingly larger proportion of the population in developing nations attains a postsecondary education, there should be a tendency for the emigration of labor to include a growing number of highly educated workers.

The migration of the highly educated and that of all other persons from Asia also share a common legislative root. Throughout the first half of the twentieth century, the United States, Canada, and Australia all prohibited large scale Asian immigration, a policy founded largely on racist ideology and a long history of internal anti-Asian hostilities. These nations began dismantling their barriers after World War II, but it took about another two decades before Asians had many of the same rights of entry as whites. The opening of the immigration doors in the 1960s has enabled other Asians to migrate in large numbers. While the laws in the receiving countries offer different preferences and opportunities according to class background and familial ties, both highly educated Asians and all other Asian immigrants benefited from the elimination of racial barriers.

Although the migration of highly-educated Asians cannot be divorced from the larger pattern of migration, the movement of the highly educated is nonetheless unique. Neither the shift in the educational composition of the population nor the common push and pull factors alone or together can account for the flows of highly educated labor because this class of workers is systematically overrepresented by any reasonable measure. The bias in favor of highly educated migration can be seen in the characteristics of recent immigrants to the United States, Canada, and Australia. Although not exactly comparable because of differences in definition, the figures in Table 3 nonetheless show three indisputable facts. First, the percentage of the immigrant population with at least a college education in each of the receiving countries is substantially higher than the levels of educational attainment in the sending countries, as reported in Table 2, which are based on an even less stringent classification, some post-secondary schooling. Second, Asian immigrants are more likely to have a college education than immigrants from the United Kingdom, which is a First World economy with a substantially larger stock of highly educated labor. Third, Asian immigrants are more likely to be highly educated than the native popula-

TABLE 3
PERCENT WITH COLLEGE/UNIVERSITY EDUCATION

Receiving Country	Native Born Population	Recent Asian Immigrants	Recent United Kingdom Immigrants
Australia			
Male	9.0	15.4	10.7
Female	7.7	11.1	7.0
Canada	15.2	37.9	18.6
Male	17.0	43.9	23.4
Female	13.4	32.0	13.8
United States	16.3	37.4	30.5

SOURCES: Australian statistics are from Australian Government, Bureau of Labour Market Research, 1986. Canadian figures are from Basavarajappa and Verma, 1985. United States figures are from United States Government, Bureau of the Census, 1980.

DEFINITIONS: (1) Australian statistics are for working-age population and refer to those with a degree or diploma. Data on immigrants are for all foreign-born of working age.
(2) Canadian statistics are for those 15 years and older with university educational attainment in 1981. Data on immigrants are for those who entered between 1970 and 1979.
(3) United States statistics are for those 25 years and older with four or more years of college. Data on immigrants are for those who entered between 1970 and 1980.

tion in the receiving countries. Thus, regardless of which standard one uses to measure the bias towards the highly educated, the inescapable conclusion is that migration from Asia to the three industrially advanced countries heavily favors the highly educated.

The migration of the highly educated is also unique because it has generated extensive political and policy debates in both the sending and receiving countries, and in international arenas such as the United Nations. The debates go well beyond the right of individuals to resettle in another country, to issues concerning a nation's economic well-being and security. During the 1960s much of the deliberation focused on the charge of "brain drain," the systematic extraction of talents from the developing economies by the industrially advanced economies. The debate stimulated much research sponsored by individual nations and international organizations, but the findings proved to be inconclusive regarding the purported damage to Third World countries. Some intriguing recommendations were generated, such as a tax on migration, but only minor changes occurred in actual practice. Despite continued migration, the brain drain debate subsided in the 1970s. In the 1980s, the People's Republic of China reopened the debate, largely because it has recently joined other Third World countries as sending nations. The current discussions, however, have taken on a new face resulting from the fears in advanced economies of the potential damage caused by reverse or return migration, a trend that is claimed to lead to accelerated technological diffusion. This debate has not yet run its full course.

To make sense of both the relatively high migration flows and the related political and policy concerns, we need to acknowledge that the movement of these people is not merely another undifferentiated component of the larger movements of workers among nations. Our argument that the movement of the highly educated is unique rests on three observations. The first is that this form of migration involves an intermediate process, which we call the global articulation of higher education. The nature of training of highly educated labor in the post-World War II period forces Third World countries to rely on industrially advanced nations for a substantial part of the necessary training. This form of integration, in turn, creates a pool of substitutable labor, which shares common skills, a lingua franca of English and technical terms, and internationalized values, as well as professional networks that cut across national borders. The second observation is that the movement of professional and highly educated workers is tied to unequal development on a global scale, both as an outcome and as a contributing factor. This inequality is reinforced, first, by the net loss of talented individuals to advanced economies from the less developed nations, and second, by the spatial separation of the cost of reproducing labor and the utilization of labor. The third observation, and by no means the least important, is that the reverse flow to less developed countries (LDCs), either in terms of returning students or visiting scholars, though quantitatively smaller, weakens inequality by contributing to economic development in some Asian countries, a process that has accelerated in recent years.

It is through an understanding of the complex and offsetting effects of the movement of highly educated labor that one can understand the motive, and real effects, of existing policies. The potential economic contributions of highly educated labor inevitably make their movement of great concern to national governments. Clearly, developed and developing nations have disparate and often conflicting goals, but the difference is not simply one side wanting brain drain and the other side opposing it. The issues, as we shall see, are more complex and asymmetric, involving not only individual countries attempting to modify the outcomes in the name of national interest but also competing interest groups within each country. Moreover, the issues are not static. Classifying nations as being irrevocably in either one camp or the other is both unrealistic and ahistorical. Singapore, for example, has moved from being a sending nation to a receiving one as it emerges as an industrial city-state with a rapidly growing high tech sector. South Korea and Taiwan may not be far behind. These changes, in turn, redefine the issues because new economic circumstances and accompanying political realities transform the material consequences of the movement of highly educated persons.

The remainder of this paper is organized into two parts. Part One examines the global integration of higher education, which is a precursor to migration. Part Two examines the relationship between highly educated labor and uneven development.

Global Integration of Highly Educated Workers

The creation of a supply of highly educated workers is a social process that requires substantial time and investment, and training that must occur within formal educational institutions; these factors make the highly educated a distinctive form of labor. For discussion purposes, we use three ideal types to draw out important distinctions between highly educated labor, skilled manual labor, and unskilled labor. Our argument, obviously, is an abstraction of reality, for workers in the real world do not fall into just these three discrete categories. The distribution of people by educational achievement is continuous, although it is trimodal in many developing countries. Nonetheless, the abstraction is useful because it helps us understand why the reproduction of highly educated labor possesses unique features and problems.

The regeneration of the supply of unskilled labor in developing countries is tied largely to the expense of rearing children and socializing them to a wage system. Much of the reproduction involves the cost of maintaining the family, a cost that is in part socially determined, and thus varies across economies. In an agrarian setting, the total cost can be minimal, near the subsistence level. Industrialization increases the cost because formal schooling must be established as a secondary institution that socializes individuals to a set of behaviors conducive to industrial modes of production, and to norms needed in an urban, market economy. Schooling, then, is geared towards providing the basic literacy needed for early stages of economic development and to incubate the willingness to accede to the impersonal social relations of production. While this schooling requires public expenditure, the major cost in the reproduction is borne within the family, which is tied to the economy through the labor services sold by the parent or parents and is simultaneously the locus of labor renewal.

The cost of reproduction of skilled manual labor goes beyond the subsistence level and rudimentary socialization. It entails the acquisition of skills that increase workers' productivity. Although training can occur in public institutions, such as vocational education schools, much of the knowledge is transmitted through on-the-job training. In situations where skill levels are high and knowledge is transmitted by older workers, there is a potential for labor to control the training process either through formal apprenticeship programs or informal rules on the shop floor. This enables workers to shelter themselves from competitive market pressures by regulating the supply of new labor, and in doing so, divide the working class either into primary and secondary labor markets, as we see in many advanced economies, or formal and informal sectors in developing countries. Since training, whether controlled by employers or workers, is provided largely through the work place, the final stage in the reproduction of skilled manual labor is intertwined with a nation's ongoing economic activities. In other words, the renewal of labor and its utilization are geographically and temporally coterminous.

The creation of a supply of highly educated labor, however, is very different. It entails the accumulation of basic knowledge that must be acquired almost exclusively in institutions of higher learning, and thus is outside the family and site of production. Training in nearly all of the science-based fields requires at least four years of postsecondary schooling, and in many cases several additional years of graduate studies. This formal education necessitates enormous investments by the individuals in foregone earnings, by their families in monetary and other support, and by society in public expenditures for education. When highly educated labor is utilized in production, defined broadly here to include activities such as research and development, the investments pay off in the form of higher output to firms and society, and higher wages and salaries to the workers.

Beyond the substantial investments and long training period, highly educated labor also differs from the other two categories of labor because of a more decisive separation between the process of reproducing labor and its utilization. Clearly, the separation is temporal, for the accumulation of human capital and its application occur at different times. The separation is also geographic, for the place of training and place of work are physically separated, quite often by great distances. Moreover, after the training, highly educated workers have great latitude to find professional employment in other geographic regions, as we will see later.

One could argue that all investments in the reproduction of labor, even those for resupplying unskilled labor, are forms of human capital. Thus, the cost of rearing a healthy child is an investment to ensure a more productive adult worker. We would not disagree with this point, but we maintain that there is a qualitative difference in investment for physical development and investment in certificated knowledge.

Dependency in Higher Education

The education required to train the highly educated places developing countries in a dependent relationship with Western societies. Although, in the abstract, education of those in the technical fields need not be bound to particular locations, in practice, it has been linked to the advanced economies, which have the advantage of accumulated scientific knowledge and the requisite social infrastructures. The industrialized countries built and have maintained an advanced technological base because of three reasons: (1) an economy large enough to have an intensified division of labor, which is conducive to specialized research and development, and the creation of a cadre of highly specialized professionals; (2) the establishment of an excellent research environment with the most modern equipment, permitting more concentrated research; and (3) massive state support for research and development, particularly for military purposes but which generates spinoffs for industrial applications.

Studying in the advanced economies is the most direct form of the global articulation of higher education. This is not a new phenomenon. During the pre-World War II era, there was a small but not insignificant stream of Asians going to the great European universities to study. Universities such as the University of London developed an unusually large foreign student population, and while Oxford and Cambridge had proportionately fewer Asians, these institutions nonetheless played a central role in training the elite, particularly for the British colonies. The United States had similar ties, with the program between Harvard and Yen-Ching in China being a primary example.

After World War II, the United States emerged as the major place to study for international students. Over the last three decades, the foreign student population from South and East Asia has increased dramatically, from about 10,000 in the mid-1950s, to 30,000 in the mid-1960s, to 60,000 in the mid-1970s, to over 142,000 in 1984-85 (Institute of International Education, various years). Taiwan, India, Japan, Korea, and Hong Kong have been consistently sending large contingents of students, and in recent years, have been joined by the People's Republic of China. While the United States receives the largest absolute number of students, other advanced nations also host large numbers of Asian students relative to their size. For example, Britain, Canada, and Australia continue to receive many students from the Third World countries of the Commonwealth.

The other form of the global integration of higher education is the establishment of schools based on Western educational systems (Watson, 1982; Altbach, 1987). The countries that had been under colonial rule developed these local higher educational systems early. The local British colonial powers, for example, founded several major colleges and universities in South Asia and the Malaysian peninsula, with British universities, and the University of London in particular, serving both as a model and setting academic standards (Pattison, 1984). These local institutions were part of colonial control — training the native bureaucrats needed to run the colonies. The United States played a similar role in its colony, the Philippines, through an expansion of the educational system on the Islands. Although the oldest university was founded when the country was under Spanish rule (Santo Tomas in 1611), the United States introduced state-sponsored higher education in the early 1900s as an instrument "to bring about a thorough socio-cultural, economic and political reorientation" of that society away from Spanish influence and toward American influence (Sanyal, et al, 1981:91). Moreover, American scholars were influential in introducing new disciplines into Asian universities, such as psychology at the University of the Philippines in the early 1920s and engineering at Thailand's Chulalongkorn University in 1913 (McCraig, 1977:101). The early schools in Asia were founded not only by the colonial governments but also by private organizations, particularly the missionary churches, which in some ways were more effective because they penetrated areas not under direct colonial control, such as China.

In the post-colonial time after World War II, reliance on the Western model has continued, particularly on the American model. The wave of nationalism that followed decolonization has brought some limited changes. Departments in the humanities and social sciences have increased the local content of their courses. Even today, there are efforts to "indigenize" higher education through such policies as restricting the medium of instruction to the vernacular language. Despite these nationalistic efforts, technical departments, even in schools founded after the war, have continued to rely on Western standards, using Western textbooks, and hiring faculty trained in Europe, North America, or Australia when possible.

During this period, the United States emerged as the dominant force, shaping higher education in Asia through its foreign aid grants, inter-university programs sponsored by American universities, and efforts funded by private foundations, such as the Ford Foundation and the Rockefeller Foundation (Roy, 1973). The rise of the United States rested not only on the influence wielded by the power of money, which was considerable, but also on the perception of American prowess in scholarship. A survey of Indian scholars who had studied in the United States and Europe

MIGRATION OF HIGHLY EDUCATED ASIANS   553

found that 70 percent of the respondents agreed with the statement that "The world of scholarship has now shifted from the U.K. to the United States and therefore, Indian scholars turn to the United States for knowledge" (Suri, 1977). A similar process occurred in Taiwan, where the professional class moved "toward the American model, with...traditional elements and practices in the profession losing their hold" (Liu, 1977). While Oxford and Cambridge have remained the choice of the elite in many former British colonies, American universities are regarded as the best place for technical training.

This pattern extends to the multinational institutions created in the post-colonial period. The UN Economic and Social Commission for Asia and the Pacific was instrumental in the establishment of the Asian Center for Development Administration in Kuala Lumpur, the Asian Institute of Technology in Bangkok, and the Asian Statistical Institute in Tokyo. In 1976, India, Indonesia, the Republic of Korea, Pakistan, the Philippines, and Thailand jointly established the Asian Center for Training and Research in Social Welfare and Development, located in Manila (Kim, 1976). While these multinational institutions enabled the developing countries to pool their resources and to achieve economies of scale, they nonetheless were still dependent on faculty and training material from Western nations.

Some of the Asian centers of higher learning are quite good, but this does not imply complete autonomy from the Western institutions. Medicine is one area where the developing countries have obtained a high degree of self sufficiency. Many of Asia's medical schools were established during colonial times for both humanitarian reasons and to improve the physical productivity of labor. Today, some, albeit not a majority, of the medical and nursing schools are able to provide training comparable to that provided in Western nations, as indicated by the number of foreign trained health practitioners who are able to obtain licences in the United States and Europe. But even in this field, there is still a tendency to go to Western countries for advanced studies. This tendency is even more prevalent in other technical fields. One indication of continued dependency in the engineering and scientific fields, and even social sciences, is the fact that many Asian academics still send their more talented students to the advanced capitalist countries to be trained. This dependency is inevitable. The cost of independently recreating the institutions and accumulated knowledge is prohibitive, even for smaller Western nations. The international inequality means that less developed countries must continue to depend upon developed countries for training. Like many other systems, higher education reflects larger global uneven development and dependency.

Global Market for the Highly Educated

The very process of reproducing highly educated labor creates an international labor market because of similar training, shared "universal" values, and transnational ties. Of course, not all highly educated Asians, even those who studied abroad, become a part of this labor market or adopt any of the "universal" values. Indeed, some react by becoming ultranationalistic and anti-Western. Nonetheless, the educational process does change enough persons so that an internationalized labor market for the highly trained is more than just a concept. The articulation of the educational system created a lingua franca of the English language and technical terms, international values based on scientific methods, and a global network of information and social connections. These linkages have been facilitated by the development of telecommunications and the advent of air transportation that is fast and affordable.

The training of the highly educated creates values that transcend nationalism. The educational process involves both the acquisition of a shared body of knowledge and a style of thinking. Obviously, the common body of knowledge is rooted in the adoption of Western textbooks and curricula. The training, however, goes beyond acquiring information. Technical education requires the adoption of the scientific method, positivistic thinking that is antithetical to some Eastern cultures. Granted, what passes as creative thinking is largely limited to what Kuhn calls normal science. Nonetheless, there is a qualitative difference in the degree of freedom from culturally bound views. The training of the highly educated, then, contrasts sharply with the parochial orientation in the socializing of unskilled labor or even skilled manual labor, whose education is confined and defined by local cultural and nationalistic goals.

At the same time that traditional values are weakened, Western values are instilled. As stated earlier, the training of the highly educated brings them into contact with Western society, directly as foreign students in advanced countries or indirectly through colleges and universities modeled after Western institutions and staffed by faculty trained abroad. One obvious outcome is the acquisition of English, the language used by the major academic journals and publishers of standard textbooks (Fishman, et al., 1977), and the acquisition of an extensive set of technical terms shared by people within the field. Although the English is frequently far from being perfect, it is professionally functional. Those who study abroad also become acquainted with Western lifestyles and standards of living. This acculturation attenuates nationalistic orientation and eliminates some of the cultural barriers between Asian and Western societies.

MIGRATION OF HIGHLY EDUCATED ASIANS   555

The changes in individuals as they come into contact with Western institutions is not limited to values, language, and style of thinking. There are international societies of learned scholars and other forms of continual contact. Despite long distances, members do have face-to-face contact through numerous international conferences and workshops sponsored by these societies. Modern telecommunication, such as Bitnet, ties the major universities throughout the world into a common electronic network, and facilitates communication, the exchange of information, and even joint work. These linkages enable faculty members in Asian institutions to maintain contact with their former Western mentors through correspondence, conferences, and shared research. The formal societies and informal groups constitute important peer groups through which the highly educated seek recognition and status. Although this form of contact incorporates only a limited number of persons, it includes key individuals who occupy influential academic and administrative positions, who in turn set the tone for their colleagues and students. In fact, membership in these global networks is both a symbol of success and a means of maintaining a privileged position within academies.

Even those who were not educated abroad are affected by the internationalization of the professions. As we have stated earlier, many of the Asian institutions of higher learning, particularly the most prestigious, have been heavily influenced by Western curricula, not a surprising result since Asian alumni from American universities have had a major role in planning and "modernizing" these institutions of higher learning, particularly in Indonesia, Korea, the Philippines and Taiwan (Sloper, 1977:192). Consequently, the education within these universities tends to be internationalized and Westernized. Furthermore, the global networks among the highly educated make it possible for professionals to possess information regarding the existence of jobs or better jobs, abroad as well as at home. Information circulates on openings in industrially advanced countries offering higher wage levels and superior conditions of work. Equally important, these same networks help Western firms to recruit and screen applicants by providing labor intelligence to potential employers.

Of course, the "internationalization" of the highly educated, which is based on Western culture and institutions, does not totally displace all nationalistic values nor does it transform every person with a college education. Nonetheless, it does facilitate the migration of a significant proportion of the highly educated from the developing countries by forming a transnational subculture that serves as a foundation for an integrated labor market. The global integration of higher education and the formation of an international class of labor minimize the cultural and social barriers that would otherwise impede international migration. This integration takes its highest form for those in the technical fields, and to some extent for the more quantitative social scientists, because their skills are least bounded by cultural contents, and because technical terms constitute a large proportion of the new lingua franca. It is this internationalization of professionals, then, that biases global migration towards those with technical and scientific training by breaking down many of the cultural and social barriers between Asian and Western economies.

Uneven Development and Migration Patterns

While the global articulation of higher education and the formation of an international class of labor are preconditions in the movement of the highly educated, it is global inequality that generates the economic incentives for individuals to leave a less developed country for a developed country. Differences in the standard of living between developed and developing countries are in some ultimate sense the underlying cause of migration, when it is not motivated by flight from repression or political disorder. This inequality takes two forms. The first is variation in the overall level of development. Ironically, an increase in development increases the flow by strengthening the preconditions for migration. The level of development, then, acts at the macro or societal level by defining institutions and international linkages. The second form of inequality is wages and career opportunities. The rewards to labor and the ability to practice one's trade do not depend solely on the level of skills (human capital), but also on the capital-to-labor ratio, the relative amount of natural resources, the level of technology, and the forms of organization of the classes, groups, and institutions involved in the production process. Since these factors vary systematically across nations and remain in a state of disequilibrium for relatively long periods, there are corresponding disparities in wages and career opportunities that affect individual decisions to migrate.

There is no simple formula to turn a measure of the level of economic development into a scale that can predict the migration rates of highly educated labor. While per capita income is the most widely used measure of the standard of living, its use in the earlier empirical studies produced ambiguous or conflicting findings regarding the role of this measure (Krugman and Bhagwati, 1976). Certainly, average income levels are important in the case of Asian migration, although not in an expected way. Ballendorf (1972) found a negative correlation between raw per capita income and brain flow to the United States for African countries, and no correlation for Latin American countries, but found a positive correlation for Asian countries. Obviously, the regional variation is related to cultural,

MIGRATION OF HIGHLY EDUCATED ASIANS   557

social, and political differences, even though it is impossible to isolate the relative importance of each factor. But even attempting to interpret the results for the Asian countries alone is not without problems. It would be hard to believe that the positive correlation implies that Asian professionals from wealthier countries are more likely to want to migrate than their counterparts from poorer countries.[3] Instead, the result implies that relatively wealthier developing Asian countries are bigger sources of migration. Within the range of income levels studied, development creates the preconditions necessary for out-migration, such as a high level of integration with Western institutions of higher learning, greater contact and exchange, and imbalances in the labor market, a topic we will discuss later.

International differences in occupational specific earnings rather than aggregate per capita income are the correct independent variables in explaining the propensity rather then the necessary conditions for migration. Advanced economies can and generally do offer higher wages and salaries for highly educated labor, thus providing pecuniary incentive for migration.[4] While per capita income and wages are not perfectly correlated across developing countries because the relative standing of professionals within each country varies widely, the earnings in nearly every Asian country have been substantially lower than that available in the advanced economies. The role of wage differentials is clearly evident in Psacharopoulos' (1971) analysis of 23 countries, which finds that while immigration patterns are not correlated with per capita income or distance, they are strongly correlated with the ratio of United States earnings to earnings in the sending country for specific occupations. Agawal and Winkler's (1984) findings also show strong and positive correlation between the wage ratio and the level of migration. In the Canadian case, Devoretz and Maki (1983) find that professional immigration from developing countries is correlated with the occupational income level in Canada.

Migration is also prompted by international differences in career opportunities. Unlike unskilled and skilled manual labor, highly educated labor is heavily dependent on advanced economies in order to practice their trade. Unskilled labor is not tied to any particular nation because technology is embedded in the machinery that workers use. An extreme example is the operation of automated machinery, where a person is reduced to being a button pusher. The same worker, however, could take jobs that require only little or no rudimentary technology, such as janitorial work.

___

[3] This commonly is known as the ecological fallacy, where results based on aggregate units, in this case countries, are interpreted as individual behavior.

[4] Migration is not a simple process. For students trained abroad, it involves an initial step of deciding to study overseas, and then another step of deciding to remain abroad. Even for those who return, some may decide to emigrate at a later time.

One consequence of what is essentially menial work is that unskilled labor is interchangeable across a wide range of jobs, industries, and national economies. Unskilled labor from less developed nations can be and is utilized by advanced nations, but at the same time, these workers are not dependent upon advanced economies to practice their trades.

Skilled manual labor operates with a technology that is already fully dispersed to the developing countries, eliminating any special linkage to advanced countries. Usually the nature of on-the-job training bestows upon these workers the benefits of being in a sheltered segment of the labor market, thus providing an incentive to remain. Higher wages in the advanced countries have drawn many thousands of such skilled workers every year, but the key elements of presocialization and adaptation for a labor niche unique to the knowledge "industry" and high tech sectors of the advanced economies are missing. Moreover, it is likely that skilled manual workers in advanced nations act politically to prevent the importation of equivalent foreign labor as a means of preserving their own economic niche.

Highly educated labor is only fully empowered for production in advanced economies because their training has two salient characteristics. Firstly, it is narrowly defined, the product of a high degree of specialization. The accumulation of human capital has a "putty-clay" characteristic, relatively flexible during the period of initial investment (educational training) but highly rigid afterwards, making the skills not readily transferable to another field. The second salient characteristic is that human capital is highly complementary to and therefore highly dependent upon very specific types of physical capital. The highly educated must use sophisticated scientific equipment; otherwise, their training would be of relatively little use. Given these two characteristics, the role of highly educated labor varies across jobs, industries, and nations. It is only in advanced economies that highly educated workers can pursue a career in their chosen field, thus providing another incentive to migrate.

Of course, differences in wages and career opportunities are not raw, unmediated forces. Their operation is conditioned by the legal system and hiring policies of both the advanced and less developed nations, and by other factors such as the level of industrial development of the sending country. Nonetheless, both factors create enormous incentives for the highly educated to relocate.

Subordination of Asian Institutions of Higher Education

The receiving country clearly gains from the movement by increasing its pool of talented workers, which enhances its ability to use existing technology, to develop new products and production processes (the source of real per capita growth in advanced countries), and to train the next generation of highly educated labor. Again, nowhere is this more apparent than in the United States. It is estimated that over 10,000 Asian engineers, a large majority of whom are foreign-born, work in Silicon Valley, the core of America's microelectronics industry (Kotkin and Kishimoto, 1988:31). At the same time, over half of the new engineering faculty in American universities are foreign-born (Gillette, 1988), again with Asians constituting a majority. This supply of highly educated labor represents a sizeable net gain to the receiving countries. One source places the imputed human-capital value of the professions who migrated to the United States during the period from 1961 to 1972 at twenty-five billion dollars (UNCTAD, 1975). No doubt, estimations of this type are subject to problems and criticisms; however, unquestionably there was a net loss to the developing countries during much of the 1960s and 1970s. The subordination of Asian countries to the role of supplier of highly educated labor, then, takes on an important feature of Buroway's (1976) migrant labor system, the geographic separation of the reproduction of labor from its utilization in production.

Unequal international standings make it difficult for lesser developed countries to invest in higher education, either locally or for overseas studies, without becoming a supplier of highly educated labor for the developed countries. If these countries worked in closed systems, then there would be no leakage, no loss of manpower to the rest of the world. But, as we have seen, the reproduction of highly educated labor requires integration with advanced nations and inevitably creates a mobile labor force. Worse, the efforts of many LDCs in the capitalist world system to develop their own technological capacity have produced an imbalance between the supply and demand for highly educated labor. Ideally, a developing country should attempt to keep the extent of educational training in line with its ability to absorb that pool of labor. However, it has proven easier to emulate the Western educational infrastructure and expand overseas programs than to develop the necessary industrial base. Although the expansion of higher education is a necessary condition of future industrialization, it is not a sufficient condition. The production of graduates at one point in time can lead either to industrialization later or simply to the loss of most of the graduates, depending on a further set of conditions.

It is important to recognize that the overexpansion of higher education is partially the result of efforts by developing nations to meet the aspirations of its upper and middle classes. Because many of the desirable jobs, particularly in the public sector, have been allocated based on educational credentials, the demand for higher education is high, even though the economy may not be able to absorb the graduates. This mismatch, as Sanderson (1976) has argued, results in an "explosive expansion of secondary and higher education" that fosters "employment expectations that cannot be met." This certainly was a problem in India even before the extensive emigration of the highly educated (Blaug, et al., 1969), and the phenomenon has spread to other developing countries (Blomquvist, 1982). One consequence is a growing class of highly educated labor that is underemployed or unemployed, and that is a potential source of social discontent. One unfortunate outcome of the mounting market and political pressure is an inefficient expansion of the public sector to absorb excess labor. Ironically, migration removes those who may become frustrated, thus functioning as a social safety valve.

A developing nation can become a supplier of highly educated labor to a significant extent. In 1987, there were 1,353 Korean scientists with Ph.D. degrees working in the United States,[5] a number equal to several years of Ph.D. output from all Korean institutions of higher learning. More important, the opportunity to emigrate can distort the local development and can aggravate the local imbalance in the labor market that already exists. In Taiwan, the global integration and movement of highly educated labor have made "the local professional labor market one part of those of the United States and Canada, and less responsive to changes in the local situation" (Liu, 1977:165). The most extreme example of supplying highly educated labor, however, is the link between the United States and the Philippines (Cariño, B., 1987:7-8). There are large numbers of Filipino engineers who emigrated, but the effects within the health fields are without question more profound. Prior to a significant out-migration of highly educated labor, the Philippines was well endowed with health practitioners (Table 4). The much higher numbers of physicians and nurses per 10,000 persons in the Philippines in 1966 than in either South Korea or Indonesia could be explained by the higher per capita income in the Philippines, which was more than twice that of South Korea and nearly three times that of Indonesia. However, the Philippines also had considerably higher ratios than Taiwan, which had roughly the same per capita income. The unusually high levels in the Philippines was due to the fact that health practitioners, and physicians in particular, were considered very prestigious occupations, even though their incomes were low relative to other professionals (Cariño, L., 1977). Since the mid-1960s, the situation has

[5] Based on information provided by Professor Kim Il-Chul, The Population and Development Studies Center, Seoul National University, taken from a directory of Korean scientists and engineers in America published by Korean Institute for Economics and Technology, 1987.

TABLE 4
HEALTH PROVIDERS TO POPULATION RATIOS

Country	Physicians per 10,000 persons		Nurses per 10,000 persons	
	1965	1984	1965	1984
Philippines	7.3	1.5	8.8	2.4
South Korea	3.7	8.6	3.3	17.2
Taiwan	4.0	7.0	1.3	10.5
Indonesia	0.3	1.1	0.8	7.9

SOURCES: World Bank, *World Development Report*, 1990; Republic of China, *Taiwan Statistical Data Book*, 1987. The first ratio for physicians in the Philippines is for 1966.

deteriorated, not only relative to the three other countries but also in absolute terms. The Philippines has fallen behind South Korea and Taiwan, and while Indonesia still lags behind, it is on an upward trajectory while the Philippines is heading downwards.

A massive outflow of doctors and nurses has contributed to the deterioration of health services in the Philippines. Worse, the opportunity to practice in advanced economies has distorted the educational process. There is considerable evidence that training in nursing has expanded in response to the migration. For nurses, "[R]ather than an educational surplus leading to migration, it was the possibility of migration which led to the expansion of nursing education" (Joyce and Hunt, 1982). In general, the production of university graduates in the Philippines increased in the 1970s at a 10-20 percent annual rate while national income grew at only 5-6 percent (turning into an actual decline in the 1980s). It is highly unlikely that Filipinos have pursued a nursing education merely to practice at home because there were few economic incentives. One study found that over a third of the nurses in the Philippines were either underemployed or unemployed, and many, particularly those educated in private colleges, could not recover the cost of their training in terms of local wages (Ongkiko and Suanes, 1984). The main attraction, then, has been the opportunity to work overseas, particularly in the United States. The schools have advertised on the basis of guaranteeing job placements in the United States on graduation, although such promises are not always fulfilled. Although there has been no overproduction in medicine, emigration remains a problem in draining away many physicians.

By the 1970s, the cumulative effects of migration could be seen in the fact that there were nearly as many Filipino health professionals in the United States as in their native country. A 1970 estimate puts the number of Filipino nurses working in the United States at 13,500, or 88 percent of the number working in the Philippines (Joyce and Hunt, 1982). In 1975, there were 10,410 Philippine-trained physicians working in the United States, a number only slightly smaller than the 13,480 employed in the Philippines (Goldfarb, *et al.*, 1984). As the figures in Table 1 indicate, the flow of Filipino nurses and physicians has continued at a high rate. From 1972 to 1985, over 20,000 nurses and nearly 8,000 doctors emigrated to the United States.

One cannot place the total blame for the Philippines' deteriorating health system simply on the pull of opportunities in the United States. After all, the United States has not been the only place where Filipino health practitioners went (Galman, 1981). There are also problems internal to the Islands. The Philippine Medical Association was able to restrict enrollment in pre-medical studies and in medical schools, thus reducing the supply of new physicians (Cariño, L., 1977). Moreover, given the lack of effective domestic demand for nurses, that is, actual employment opportunities at a wage sufficient to clear the market, the Philippines still had a surplus despite the massive out-migration (Rimando, 1984). Finally, President Marcos certainly stimulated emigration by bankrupting the country and suppressing democracy. Nonetheless, the willingness of the United States, and other industrialized nations, to accept Filipino physicians and nurses provide the means for people to leave and the incentive for individuals to increase their demand for education in the health field.

Realignment of the Global Order

While developed nations benefit from migration, developing nations are not necessarily losers in the long run. Despite the dominance of the flows from LDCs to advanced nations, the movement of the highly educated occurs in both directions. While the number of returning students and visiting scholars may be small, they play a crucial role in the transfer of technology. In fact, the ideal carrier is a person who not only completed his or her studies, but also gained practical and on-the-job knowledge by having worked in Western firms or research institutions. Even permanent emigrants play a role. A major difference between earlier labor migration and post-1965 migration of professionals has to do with the fluidity of the flow. After the initial move to the West, many Asian professionals return to their native countries to work, lecture, or conduct research for a period of time before again returning to their Western homes.

The supply of highly educated labor clearly plays a role in an international division of production that is defined in part by the technological level of the countries. One widely cited example is the semiconductor and microcomputer industry. Only the nations with the requisite scientific and engineering manpower, such as the United States and Japan, are involved in the very high value added research and design activities; those countries with more modest manpower resources, such as Korea and Taiwan, can design and produce standardized commodities such as memory chips, micro-computer clones, and peripheries; and those with little more than cheap labor are relegated to low value added activity such as assembling printed circuits and integrated chips that are fabricated elsewhere. This international division of production also extends to more common household goods such as toys. For example, Tomy Kogyo, the third largest toy maker in Japan and a major exporter, has fragmented its business: retaining the research and development at home; locating the production of high tech toys with sophisticated electronics and mechanical devices in Singapore, which has a relatively large number of engineers for a newly industrialized nation; and moving the manufacturing of low value added toys to other Southeast Asian countries which have cheap labor but few engineers (Lim, 1988). This spatial organization of economic activities, then, implies that later stages of economic development require the development of a strong technological base, both in terms of knowledge and manpower.

History shows that backward nations can catch up with leading nations through the development of institutions of higher education. The development of centers of higher learning in the engineering fields helped Germany and Sweden to industrialize rapidly in the nineteenth century and catch up with Great Britain (Ahlstrom, 1982). Indeed, it was this "second industrial revolution," which rested on electricity, the internal combustion engine, and the newly emerging petroleum and chemical industries, that witnessed an exponential growth in the dependency on formal training in the sciences. The United States also developed an educational system that enabled it to absorb technological knowledge needed for its early industrialization, and more importantly, its emergence as a leading power in the twentieth century (Rosenberg, 1972). Japan, both before World War II and then again in the post-World War II period followed a similar path, emerging from backwardness to advanced status based on a sound knowledge base (Holmes, 1977). Today, developing countries pursue a similar path and take advantage of their technological backwardness by bypassing the enormous cost and risk in initially producing the technology. Progress comes not from creating technology anew but through the adoption and integration of knowledge from more advanced nations.

The process of catch-up can be a self-accelerating process for the newly industrializing countries. As a nation successfully integrates technology and expands its economy, it also increases its capacity to absorb highly educated workers, thus retaining a greater proportion of this class of labor. This process can be seen in the case of Taiwan, which has been particularly hard hit by a loss of its exchange students. Taiwan sent 50,000 college graduates overseas for advanced study between 1960 and 1979, with only 6,000 returning home (Kwok and Leland, 1982). Moreover, half of those who did return later left, and those with Ph.D. degrees were less likely to return than those with masters degrees (Wang and Rawls, 1975). But with recent economic growth and an expansion of industries that utilize highly educated engineers, the overall return rate rose from about 8 percent in the 1960s and 1970s to about 20 percent in the mid-1980s (Tsai, 1988). Singapore provides another example. During the early 1970s, when that country was still in its early stages of development, Prime Minister Lee Kuan Yew was one of the more vocal Third World leaders behind the brain drain debate, accusing Australia of stealing Singapore's most talented labor. By the 1980s, Singapore had emerged not only as a NIC but also as a net importer of highly educated labor (Pang, 1990).

The Taiwanese and Singaporean experiences indicate that a developing nation can experience economic growth even when there is a substantial loss in highly educated labor. The numbers who returned and brought back technical skills have proven sufficient for its most recent stage of industrialization. The international diffusion of technology has the potential for altering the world hierarchy. Dependency, then, can be a stage in a process of achieving more equal interdependence with the advanced economies. However, the wide variation in outcomes as demonstrated by the Philippines at one end and Singapore at the other, shows that breaking out of dependency is not an automatic historical process.

REFERENCES

Agawal, Vinold and Donald Winkler
1984   "Migration of Professional Manpower to the United States," *Southern Economic Journal*, 50(3):814-830.

Ahlstrom, Goran
1982   *Engineers and Indusutrial Growth*. London: Croom Helm.

Altbach, Philip
1987   *Higher Education in the Third World*. New York: Advent Books.

Arrow, Kenneth and William Capron
1959   "Dynamic Shortages and Price Rises: The Engineer-Scientist Case," *Quarterly Journal of Economics*, 73(2):302-308.

Ballendorf, Dirk
1972   "A Cause Analysis of the Emigration of Highly Trained Manpower from Poor to Rich Countries," *Journal of Education*, 154(3):79-88.

Basavarajappa, K. G. and Ravi Verma
1985   "Asian Immigrants in Canada: Some Findings from the 1981 Census," *International Migration*, 23(1):97-121.

Blaug, M., P. R. G. Layard, and H. Woodhill
1969   *The Causes of Graduate Unemployment in India*. London: Allen Lane.

Blomquvist, A. G.
1982   "Education, Unemployment and Government Job Creation for Graduates in LDCs." In *Perspectives on Economic Development, Essays in Honour of W. A. Lewis*. Edited by T. E. Barker, A. S. Downes, and J. A. Sackey. Washington, D.C.: University Press of America.

Buroway, Michael
1976   "The Functions and Reproduction of Migrant Labor: Comparative Material from Southern African and the United States," *American Journal of Sociology*, 81(5):1050-1087.

Cariño, Benjamin
1987   "Brain Flow from the Philippines: Facts, Causes and Consequences." Paper presented at the Brain Flow Workship, Center for Pacific Rim Studies, University of California, Los Angeles, June 22-26.

Cariño, Ledivina
1977   "Philippines: Patterns from the United States.." In *Professional Structure in South East Asia*. Edited by T.H. Silcock. Canberra: The Australian National University.

China(Republic of) Census Office
1976   *An Extract Report on the 1975 Sample Census of Population and Housing*. Census Office, December.

_____
1972   *The 1970 Sample Census of Population and Housing*. Census Office, April.

Devoretz, Don, and Dennis Maki
1983   "The Immigration of Third World Professionals to Canada: 1968-1973," *World Development*, 11(1):55-64.

Fishman, Joshua, Robert Cooper, and Conrad Andrews
1977   *The Spread of English*. Rowley, Mass.: Newbury House.

Galman, Cecilia
1981   "The Emigration of Filipino Nurses: An Economic Analysis." Unpublished paper. University of the Philippines.

Gillette, Robert
1988   "Threat to Security Cited in Rise of Foreign Engineers," *Los Angeles Times*, January 20.

Goldfarb, Robert, Oli Havrylyshyn, and Stephen Mangum
1984   "Can Remittances Compensate for Manpower Outflows: The Case of Philippine
        Physicians," *Journal of Development Economics* ,15:1-17.

Holmes, Brian
1977   "Third World University Traditions and Postwar American Influence." In *Professional
        Structure in South East Asia*. Edited by T.H. Silcock. Canberra: The Australian National
        University.

Joyce, Richard, and Chester Hunt
1982   "Philippine Nurses and the Brain Drain," *Social Science Medicine*, 16:1223-1233.

Kim, Ki Hoon
1976   "The Economics of the Brain Drain: Pros, Cons, and Remedies," *Journal of Economic
        Development*, 1(1):55-80.

Kotkin, Joel, and Yoriko Kishimoto
1988   "America's Global Advantage," *California Business*, September:26-53.

Krugman, Paul, and Jagdish N. Bhagwati
1976   "The Decision to Migrate." In *The Brain Drain and Taxation*. Edited by J.N. Bhagwati.
        Amsterdam: North Holland.

Kwok, Viem, and Hayne Leland
1982   "An Economic Model of the Brain Drain," *American Economic Review*, 72(1):91-100.

Lim, Soon Neo
1988   "From Singapore with Love: Local Toy Boys Move into High-tech Gear," *Singapore
        Business*, December:35-43.

Liu, Jen-jen
1977   "Taiwan: Flexible and Mixed Disciplines." In *Professional Structure in South East Asia*.
        Edited by T.H. Silcock. Canberra: The Australian National University.

McCraig, Robert
1977   "American Influence on Higher Education in Asia." In *Professional Structure in South
        East Asia*. Edited by T.H. Silcock. Canberra: The Australian National University.

Ongkiko, Ricardo and Gerard Suanes
1984   *A Rate of Return Analysis of the Nursing Profession in the Philippines*. AB/BS thesis,
        University of the Philippines.

Pang Eng, Fong
1990   "Foreign Workers in Singapore: Policies, Trends and Implications." Paper presented at
        Meeting on Cross-national Labour Migration in the Asian Region: Implications for
        Local and Regional Development, Nagoya, November 5-8.

MIGRATION OF HIGHLY EDUCATED ASIANS   567

Pattison, Bruce
1984   *Special Relations, The University of London and New Universities Overseas, 1947-70.* University of London.

Psacharopoulos, George
1971   "On Some Positive Aspects of the Economics of the Brain Drain," *Minerva,* 9(2):231-42.

Raghaviah, Y., ed.
1981   *Third World Education and Post-war American Influence, India.* Ramakrishna Press.

Rimando, Carlos
1984   "The Migration of Filipino Nurses: Its Implication on the Domestic Market." Unpublished paper. University of the Philippines.

Rosenberg, Nathan
1972   *Technology and American Economic Growth.* New York: Harper and Row.

Roy, Binoy
1973   *United States Infiltration in Indian Education.* New Delhi: Perspective Publications.

Sanderson, George
1976   "Educated Unemployment in Developing Countries," *Labour Gazette,* 76(2):90-94.

Sanyal, Bkas, Waldo Perfecto, and Adriano Arcelo
1981   *Higher Education and the Labour Market in the Philippines.* New Delhi: Wiley Eastern Limited.

Sloper, David
1977   "From Dependency to Autonomy -- An Asian Case Study." In *Professional Structure in South East Asia.* Edited by T.H. Silcock. Canberra: The Australian National University.

Suri, M. Shahnaz
1977   "What Did We Learn from Them?" In *Professional Structure in South East Asia.* Edited by T.H. Silcock. Canberra: The Australian National University.

Tsai, Hong-Chin
1988   "The Return of Students and Scholars from the United States to Taiwan and Its Impact: A Case Study of National Taiwan University." Paper presented at the Center for Pacific Rim Studies, University of California, Los Angeles.

UNCTAD Secretariat
1975   *The Reverse Transfer of Technology: Its Dimensions, Economic Effects and Policy Implications.* United Nations Conference on Trade and Development.

Wang, Lawrence and James Rawls
1975   "The Trans of Training Obtained Abroad to Taiwan," *Industry of Free China,* 43(2).

Watson, Keith
1982   "Educational Neocolonialism, The Continuing Colonial Legacy." In *Education in the Third World.* Edited by K. Watson. London: Croom Helm.

Part IX
Migration in Asia

[17]

International Migration Within and From the East and Southeast Asian Region: A Review Essay

Ronald Skeldon

University of Hong Kong

Five migration systems are described: settler, student, contract labor, skilled labor, and refugee. Settler migration to the U.S., Canada and Australia has consisted primarily of family members; the future may bring a greater emphasis on highly skilled and business categories. Contract labor migration, particularly to the Middle East, has provided jobs, foreign currency through remittances and greater participation of women, but also led to illegal migration, skills drain, and labor abuses. The hierarchy of development has led to intra-regional flows: (1) skilled labor mainly from Japan to other countries in the region, and (2) contract labor and illegal migration from the LDCs to the NIEs and Japan.

Background

Thirty years ago the number of people leaving the countries of East and Southeast Asia for other parts of the world was small. Since then, however, international movements have increased in volume to the extent that they are likely to be one of the major forces for change both within and outside the region well into the twenty-first century.[1] This is not to imply that long-distance migrations from this region are of recent origin; they are not. The southward movement of Chinese peoples into Southeast Asia dates back many hundreds of years, and the systems of labor migration, developed under the aegis of expanding western influence in the nineteenth century, took many thousands of Chinese, as well as Japanese and Koreans,

---

[1] In this essay the East and Southeast Asian region, often referred to as "the region", consists of China, Japan, South Korea, Taiwan, Hong Kong, Singapore, the Philippines, Indonesia, Malaysia, Thailand, Laos, Cambodia and Vietnam.

to North and South America and to Australia, as well as to Southeast Asia. Increasingly restrictive immigration policies in North America and Australia from the 1880s significantly slowed Asian migration to these areas. Although the migration of the Chinese to Southeast Asia continued and increased well into the twentieth century - reaching a peak in the mid-1920s to the Malay peninsula, for example - there too restrictions were gradually introduced and by the late 1930s the movement of Chinese out of China had been reduced to a trickle. Tightly enforced restrictions on emigration were imposed after the founding of the People's Republic of China in 1949. Although there were some local pulses of movement such as to Hong Kong in the early 1960s and some movement into Burma, until the late 1970s China could be considered, demographically at least, as more or less a closed system. Movement out of other Asian countries between the end of the Second World War and the 1960s was also limited, made up essentially of wives of American servicemen who had served in Asian countries, mainly South Korea, Japan and the Philippines.[2]

Since the 1960s, migration from East and Southeast Asian countries has accelerated.[3] The annual numbers of migrants from Asia to the United States increased tenfold from the early 1960s to the late 1980s, from under 20,000 to over 200,000 a year. The situation for Canada and Australia is similar. In the period between 1946 and 1967, only 3.9 percent of the average annual intake of 132,800 immigrants to Canada came from the Asian and Pacific region. By 1990, some 41.8 percent of the annual intake, or 88,675 of 212,166, came from Asia and the Pacific, 68,356 of which came from the East and Southeast Asian region alone. Asians represented slightly less than 7 percent of the 138,481 immigrants to Australia in 1960-61, but by 1988-89 they accounted for 35.8 percent, or 52,128 of the total of 145,316, of which 47,082 came from the countries of East and Southeast Asia.

Several sets of factors since the mid-1960s have occurred to lay the basis for the dramatic upsurge of migration from the countries of East and

[2] The literature on the recent historical migrations of Asian peoples, and particularly the Chinese, is vast. To cite just one key reference to cover each of the major destination areas: V. Purcell, *The Chinese in Southeast Asia* (1965); R. Daniels, *Asian America: Chinese and Japanese in the United States since 1850* (1988); E. Wickberg, ed., *From China to Canada: A History of the Chinese Communities in Canada* (1982); and C.A. Price, *The Great White Walls Are Built: Restrictive Immigration to North America and Australia 1836-1888* (1974).

[3] The most important recent work covering this migration is the collection of essays in Fawcett and Cariño, eds. (1987). A useful overview is found in Appleyard (1988:89-167). Other important general assessments of international migration which cover all or part of the region include: Abella (1990b); Huguet (1991); Gunasekaran and Sullivan (1990); Stahl (1985); and Stahl (1991a), which is updated in Stahl (1991b).

Southeast Asia. The first was the implementation of immigration policies that led to the end of restrictions on Asian immigration to Canada (1962), the United States (1965) and Australia (1966).[4] The elimination of national-origin quotas in restricting immigration to the United States and the introduction of a 20,000 ceiling for those subject to numerical limitations allowed emigration from Asian countries to accelerate.

The second group of factors revolves around the decline of fertility to levels below that of replacement, both within parts of the East Asian region itself and in North America and Australia. This will ultimately affect the growth of the labor force in the absence of immigration, and there is a concern in several parts of the world that future economic expansion may require sustained growth in the labor force through the importation of labor. This perception, in turn, influences the direction of immigration policies in the three major destination countries, Canada, Australia and the United States. The Government of Canada set up a Demographic Review in 1986 to examine, among other things, the implication of slow population growth and the future role of immigration. One of the conclusions of the population forecasts was that a decline in total population after the year 2020 could be prevented only by very high levels of immigration and/or higher levels of fertility. As policymakers considered that the latter solution was unlikely, the country would have to plan for immigration in excess of 200,000 per annum. Australia created the Bureau of Immigration Research in 1989 to review and conduct research into immigration and population issues and held the National Immigration Outlook Conference in November 1990 to focus public debate on the issue of slow population growth and the role of immigration. The United States has so far not attempted to tie in immigration with future manpower requirements in quite the same way as Australia and Canada although in the early 1980s American demographers estimated, based on the fertility and mortality conditions of 1977, that to preserve the United States population at its 1980 level of 226 million over the long term, an annual net immigration of 840,000 would be required. In 1980, the annual intake was around 430,000.[5]

---

[4] For a discussion of the evolution of immigration policy in Canada and Australia, *see* Hawkins (1989), and for the U.S., *see* Bernard (1982).

[5] Some 167 papers on every conceivable aspect of immigration were prepared for the Canadian Demographic Review. A complete list of the papers and a summary of their main conclusions are given in *Charting Canada's Future: A Report of the Demographic Review*, Health and Welfare Canada, 1989. The population forecasts are described in C. Taylor (1988). The United States projections are summarized in Heer (1986).

Immigration policy in both Canada and the United States has been modified recently, perhaps directly or indirectly influenced by the above deliberations. The Canadian 1991-95 Immigration Plan raised the annual intake by a quarter over the period from 200,000 to 250,000 per annum, and the United States Immigration Act of 1990 increased the immigration which is subject to numerical limitations from 534,000 to 738,000 per annum. Bob Hawke, the Australian Prime Minister, stated clearly at the National Immigration Outlook Conference that he was in favor of higher rather than lower immigration and, although the target set for immigration in 1990-91 was lower than that in 1989-90, migration from Asia was still increasing.[6] This apparent paradox can be explained by the recent decline in the importance of trans-Tasman migration from one of the major source countries, New Zealand.

The third set of factors explaining increased migration from the countries of East and Southeast Asia is associated with the demand for labor in the oil-rich countries of the Middle East which has involved not only the countries of East and Southeast Asia but also those of South Asia. From insignificant numbers in the early 1970s, this had grown to over 700,000 in the late 1980s even if there are signs that the numbers are declining as we enter the 1990s.

The combination of these factors has generated the increasing volume and complexity of migration flows both within the region and from the region which has been reinforced by a fourth factor which can be seen as at least partially the result of the recent economic and social change in the region: political pressures which are giving rise to flows of refugees and asylum-seekers. While in no way denying the importance of the historical flows of population in laying the basis for the more recent movements, this review will focus solely on international migration over the last twenty-five years in an attempt to draw out the main trends and characteristics of these movements. In doing so, I hope to point to most of the important recent contributions on the theme and to refer to other materials that might not yet be so widely available. Before going on to examine the specific migration patterns at work in the region, it will be useful briefly to consider the demographic and economic context in which the international population flows are taking place.

---

[6] The best review of recent Australian policy, including targets, is Wooden *et al.* (1990). For an assessment of the most recent policy changes in the United States, *see* Papademetriou (1990); *see also* Samuel (1991) on immigration policies relating to Canada, the United States and Mexico.

The General Demographic and Economic Situation in the Region

Although a decline in fertility has been virtually universal throughout the East and Southeast Asian region and although the majority of countries have achieved significant economic growth over the last twenty-five years, neither the fertility decline nor the economic development has been uniform. There are still great differences in levels of development and in levels of fertility (Table 1). Twenty-five years ago, only Japan could be clearly seen as a highly developed nation which had achieved a low level of fertility. By 1990, South Korea, Taiwan, Singapore and Hong Kong had virtually joined the ranks of the developed economies and, in terms of fertility, were all well below replacement level. Thailand, often cited as the next newly industrializing economy, still has a considerable way to go with a per capita GDP in 1988 just over one tenth of that of Hong Kong. Fertility has, however, declined sharply and, in the early 1990s, was probably just above replacement level. Malaysia, with a much higher GDP per capita than Thailand, has also seen its fertility fall, but the decline has levelled out, or even been reversed, at a level significantly higher than that of Thailand. Indonesia and China, the largest countries in the region, are much lower in terms of their estimated GDP per capita but both have seen their fertility fall significantly, particularly in the case of China.

The economies of all these Asian countries have grown quickly since the mid-1960s, averaging over 4 percent per annum over the twenty-three years from 1965 to 1988. The Philippines, however, has seen much lower economic growth over this period. Its fertility remains moderately high and, in terms of per capita GDP, it ranks above China and Indonesia but well below Thailand. The countries of Indo-China, Vietnam, Laos and Cambodia are at low levels of development and high fertility. In describing levels of economic development and fertility, I do not mean to imply that there is any simplistic relationship between them; there is not. Although those countries with the highest levels of development also tend to have low fertility, the converse is not necessarily the case.

The increasing prosperity of countries around the Pacific Basin since the Second World War, particularly the emergence of Japan as a major economic power together with the four "tigers" of South Korea, Taiwan, Hong Kong and Singapore, has created two important factors for the consideration of international migration: new labor markets and large numbers of people who have the resources to move. The economic development of parts of the Asian region must, however, be seen within the context of the prosperity of the countries of North America and Australia and the increas-

TABLE 1
BASIC DEMOGRAPHIC AND ECONOMIC INDICATORS IN THE REGION

Region	Population (Millions)	Average annual population growth (% per annum)	Total fertility rate		GDP per capita 1988	Average growth rate in GDP, 1965-1988	Proportion of the population urban, 1988
			1965	1988			
Japan	122.6	0.4	2.0	1.7	21,020	4.3	77
South Korea	44.0	1.0	4.9	1.8	3,600	6.8	69
China	1,088.4	1.4	6.4	2.4	330	5.4	26*
Taiwan	20.0	1.1	-	1.7	5,520	9.7	71
Hong Kong	5.7	0.9	4.7	1.6	9,220	6.3	93
Singapore	2.6	1.3	4.7	1.9	9,070	7.2	100
Thailand	54.5	1.5	6.3	2.5	1,000	4.0	21
Malaysia	16.9	2.6	6.3	3.7	1,940	4.0	41
Indonesia	174.8	1.9	5.5	3.4	440	4.3	27
Philippines	59.9	2.5	6.8	3.8	630	1.6	41
Vietnam	64.2	2.1	-	4.0	100-150	n.a.	22
Laos	3.9	2.8	6.1	6.6	180	n.a.	18
Cambodia	6.8	2.5	6.3	-	n.a.	n.a.	12

Source: (a) *World Development Report 1990*, Oxford, Oxford University Press, 1990.
(b) *Asia 1990 Yearbook*, Hong Kong, Review Publishing Company, 1990.
(c) United Nations, *World Population Chart*, 1990.
* From the 1990 population census.

ing trade linkages across the Pacific. The United States is the dominant global economic and political power and, increasingly, the populations of Asian countries are being drawn into the migration fields of the principal urban centers of that power. Political and military factors too, not just economic and demographic issues, are of importance in accounting for the international flows.

This briefest of sketches of the basic economic and demographic indicators of the countries of the region emphasizes the diversity within the region which can be highly simplified into a generalized spatial pattern of a northeast to southwest axis of high development running from Japan and Korea in the northeast, southwestward through Taiwan and Hong Kong, with Thailand, Malaysia and Singapore forming a smaller node of development in the southwest. On either side of this discontinuous "line of development", lie to the north and west the less developed areas of Indochina and the main part of China, and to the east and south the outer islands of Indonesia and the Philippines.

A Typology of Migration Systems in the Region

Typologies of migrants and of migration have to be used with care. It is often difficult to draw firm and clear boundaries between identifiable migrant types or types of migration. Typologies also tend to be time-bound. If different types can be identified for one period, change over time renders the typology invalid for a later period of time. However, in the following discussion of international migration, I feel that a typology of migration systems is indeed a useful heuristic device to examine the different flows which have developed in and from the region over the last two decades. Five different types of migration systems can be identified: (a) *The settler migration system*; (b) *The student migration system*; (c) *The contract labor migration system*; (d) *The skilled labor migration system*; and (e) *Refugee movements*.[7]

The differentiation of these types should not immediately imply that they are mutually exclusive. There is a likely relationship between the first two types, in that many students later become settlers. The fifth category is also becoming increasingly problematic, as the line between a "refugee" and an "economic migrant" is blurred through changes in the nature of asylum-seekers themselves and in shifts in international perceptions as to

[7] For an example of a somewhat different typology, *see* that used to structure Appleyard's (1989) global assessment of international migration: *viz.*, temporary, clandestine, transient professional, permanent, refugee, return.

who refugees are. The difficulties with typologies notwithstanding, there would appear to be clear differences in the nature of these five systems in terms of their permanence. The first and fifth types can be regarded as consisting of more or less permanent movers for the moment, while the other three are theoretically made up of short-term or circular movers. The age, sex and occupational characteristics also vary by type of migration system.

The Settler Migration System

In the 1960-64 period, Japan was the most important source area of Asian immigration into the United States at a time when Asia accounted for only about 8 percent of total immigration to that country. The Japanese were the largest Asian ethnic group in the United States at that time, with some 23,300 immigrants from Japan over the five-year period of 1960-64. The numbers of Japanese immigrants to the United States have stayed more or less constant, with some fluctuations, over subsequent five-year periods to 1985-89, but numbers of migrants from other Asian countries increased dramatically from the second half of the 1960s (Table 2). The five-year migration from China increased tenfold from the early 1960s to the late 1980s while that from the Philippines increased sixteen times and that from South Korea increased eighteen times.

Although the great increase in settler migration to North America is a recent phenomenon, the roots of that migration were developed in the past. The nineteenth-century movements have been referred to already and the communities of Japanese and Chinese in the United States numbered 464,332 and 237,292 respectively in the census of 1960. The 1961 Census of Canada showed that there were 58,197 and 29,157 people of Chinese and Japanese origin respectively in Canada at that time, only a tiny fraction of the total population of 18.2 million. In Australia in 1966, there were 26,700 people of Chinese descent and 2,700 of Japanese descent, an even smaller proportion of the 11.5 million total population at the time. Continued movement between these communities in North America and Australia and the areas of origin, regulated by the immigration laws of origin and destination countries, would have been expected but it was the changing immigration laws of the 1960s which brought about the dramatic increases in Asian immigration.

The patterns of the settler immigration for the period since 1980 for each of the major destination countries are shown in Tables 3, 4 and 5. These data for the United States and Canada include refugees but these are only significant for Vietnam, Laos and Cambodia. Attention can be drawn to

TABLE 2
NUMBER OF IMMIGRANTS TO THE UNITED STATES FROM MAJOR ASIAN SOURCES, BY COUNTRY OR AREA OF BIRTH, BY FIVE-YEAR PERIODS, 1960-89

Country or Area of Birth	1960-64	1965-69	1970-74	1975-79	1980-84	1985-89
Japan	23,327	20,649	26,802	21,993	20,159	21,580
South Korea	9,521	18,469	93,445	155,505	163,088	175,802
China[a]	20,578	65,712	81,202	107,762	168,754	200,617
Hong Kong	3,103	19,088	20,446	27,059	24,299	33,184
Singapore	-	-	635[b]	1,459	1,859	2,467
Thailand	703	2,748	18,740	23,026	25,242	34,396
Malaysia	-	-	1,307[b]	2,471	4,605	5,597
Indonesia	13,261	2,541	2,910[b]	3,426	5,242	6,561
Philippines	15,753	57,563	152,706	196,397	215,504	258,309
Vietnam	603	2,564	14,661	122,987	246,463	149,647
Laos	n.a.	-	166	8,430	102,244	46,994
Cambodia	-	-	166	5,459	58,964	55,229

Source: United States Immigration and Naturalization Service (INS), *Annual Report* (1969 and 1970, Table 14) and *Statistical Yearbook* (1980 and 1981, Table 13), as cited in R.T. Appleyard (ed.), *International Migration Today. Volume I: Trends and Prospects*, Paris, UNESCO, 1988, p. 96.

[a] Includes Taiwan
[b] Data for 1971-74

two features. The first is the decline in the intake of migrants to Canada and Australia during the early 1980s following the recession. The United States immigration policy is much less flexible, based as it is more on family reunification, and no slowdown was observed. The decline in 1989 is artificial as large numbers of people who had entered the country before 1982 and had remained there unlawfully had their status regularized in 1989 by the Immigration Reform and Control Act of 1986. These are excluded from Table 3. Most of the 478,814 regularized during 1989 were from Mexico, although there were almost 7,000 from the Philippines and 2,400 from Taiwan.

The second feature is the growing importance of settler migration from mainland China. Many of those with birthplace "China" in Table 2 moved to the United States from Hong Kong or Taiwan. The place of last residence data in Tables 3, 4 and 5 show the resurgence of the historical pattern of emigration which has been permitted since the reforms in China initiated in 1979. As in the past, the vast majority of the emigrants come from the southern provinces of Guangdong and Fujian.[8]

The principal characteristic of the settler migrant flow, particularly to the United States but also to a large extent to Canada, is that it is dominated by family members. For example, in two of the largest flows into the United States from the region in 1989-90, from the Philippines and South Korea, 76 and 84 percent respectively were made up of immediate relatives, who are not subject to numerical limitation, and relatives who are subject to limitation such as married and unmarried children of United States citizens and their children, as well as brothers and sisters of United States citizens. The movement to Canada is not so family-dominated, yet 43 percent of those who landed in Canada from the region in 1990 (excluding refugees) were family members.

Given this prevalence of family members, the migration flows tend to be biased towards females and to include large numbers of both younger and older migrants. These characteristics are clear not only in the most recent flow data to Canada and the United States (Table 6) but also from the results of large-scale surveys taken amongst migrants to the United States from the region.[9] The large number of females in some of the flows

[8] For an examination of emigration from Guangdong since 1979, *see* Chen and Liao (1989). For a discussion of the movement of the Chinese out of Hong Kong and elsewhere in Asia, *see* Skeldon (1991a).

[9] Two large-scale surveys on Korean and Filipino immigrants coordinated by researchers at the East-West Center in Hawaii will provide much valuable information on Asian migration to the United States. The preliminary results are given in Park *et al.* (1990), and Cariño *et al.* (1990). Kuznets (1987) provides an examination of Korean migration to the United States.

TABLE 3

UNITED STATES: IMMIGRANTS BY COUNTRY OF LAST PERMANENT RESIDENCE, 1981/82 TO 1988/89

	1982	1983	1984	1985	1986	1987	1988	1989*
Japan	4,084	4,234	4,517	4,552	4,444	4,711	5,085	5,044
South Korea	30,697	31,449	32,537	34,791	35,164	35,397	34,151	31,604
China	15,919	14,335	14,425	15,578	16,458	18,589	21,924	20,672
Taiwan	12,099	19,018	14,684	17,517	15,931	14,080	12,376	14,705
Hong Kong	11,908	12,525	12,290	10,795	9,930	8,785	11,817	12,236
Singapore	722	584	1,327	1,389	1,109	926	932	830
Thailand	13,599	13,430	16,034	17,577	19,086	16,489	17,619	29,700
Malaysia	2,758	1,448	2,147	1,636	1,565	1,392	1,881	1,990
Indonesia	2,090	1,581	2,862	2,995	3,420	2,772	2,724	1,637
Philippines	43,600	40,397	46,985	53,137	61,492	58,315	61,017	59,129
Vietnam	65,476	31,678	25,803	20,367	15,010	13,073	12,856	13,145
Laos	31,176	19,285	6,269	4,750	3,654	3,331	4,763	5,748
Cambodia	11,750	14,830	6,045	5,754	4,502	3,979	2,612	1,726
Total	591,131	599,763	543,903	570,009	601,708	601,516	643,025	612,110

Source: United States Department of Justice, *Statistical Yearbooks* of the Immigration and Naturalization Service, Washington.

* Excludes IRCA legalization. When this is included, the total intake is 1,090,924.

TABLE 4
CANADA: LANDED IMMIGRANTS BY COUNTRY OF LAST PERMANENT RESIDENCE, 1980-90

	1980	1981	1982	1983	1984	1985	1986	1987	1988	1989	1990
Japan	737	770	630	333	250	205	273	446	346	541	365
South Korea	957	1,430	1,506	1,017	801	934	1,143	2,276	2,676	2,814	1,853
China	4,936	6,551	3,572	2,217	2,214	1,883	1,902	2,625	2,778	4,430	7,868
Taiwan	827	834	560	570	421	536	695	1,467	2,187	3,388	3,564
Hong Kong	6,309	6,451	6,542	6,710	7,696	7,380	5,893	16,170	23,281	19,908	28,825
Singapore	290	389	435	241	176	166	220	439	1,141	1,634	1,076
Thailand	396	123	201	128	125	73	86	118	154	194	181
Malaysia	702	708	688	399	356	332	418	717	1,676	1,936	1,638
Indonesia	267	214	264	136	131	107	142	219	261	278	249
Philippines	6,051	5,859	5,062	4,454	3,748	3,076	4,102	7,343	8,310	11,393	11,950
Vietnam	25,541	8,251	5,935	6,451	10,950	10,404	6.622	5,668	6,196	9,425	9,048
Laos	6,266	866	375	434	870	379	636	456	842	679	583
Cambodia	3,265	1,337	1,378	1,542	1,727	1,803	1,745	1,612	1,543	2,041	766
Total	143,133	128,618	121,147	89,157	88,239	84,302	99,219	152,098	161,929	192,001	212,166

Source: Employment and Immigration Canada, *Annual Immigration Statistics*, Ottawa.

TABLE 5
AUSTRALIA: SETTLER ARRIVALS BY SELECTED COUNTRY OF LAST PERMANENT RESIDENCE, 1980/81 TO 1989/90

Region or Country of Residence	1980/81	1981/82	1982/83	1983/84	1984/85	1985/86	1986/87	1987/88	1988/89	1989/90
Japan	505	301	331	327	286	358	479	873	843	709
South Korea	n.a.	n.a.	569	564	636	1,201	1,510	1,756	1,627	1,138
China	799	843	375	369	1,439	1,663	1,041	1,014	1,570	1,005
Taiwan	n.a.	n.a.	176	233	344	575	987	1,320	1,884	2,889
Hong Kong	1,690	2,414	2,756	3,691	5,136	4,912	5,140	7,942	9,998	11,538
Singapore	1,467	1,642	1,044	944	1,142	1,215	2,222	2,817	2,806	2,137
Thailand	4,722	4,772	5,519	3,859	2,542	2,549	2,868	3,310	4,054	3,207
Malaysia	7,783	7,835	5,153	4,503	4,762	3,652	5,025	7,295	8,812	8,073
Indonesia	2,740	2,392	2,342	2,410	2,049	2,017	2,067	1,613	1,762	1,610
Philippines	3,123	3,704	3,998	3,650	3,520	4,337	6,431	10,745	9,288	6,233
Vietnam	n.a.	n.a.	582	1,761	2,738	2,389	2,473	1,562	3,128	4,691
Laos	n.a.	n.a.	7	1	3	3	13	13	n.a.	18
Cambodia	n.a.	n.a.	13	1	3	4	1	25	n.a.	10
Total	111,190	118,700	93,177	69,808	78,087	92,410	113,309	143,490	145,316	121,227

Source: Department of Immigration and Ethnic Affairs, Australian Immigration, *Consolidated Statistics*, No. 13, 1982, Canberra; Department of Immigration, Local Government and Ethnic Affairs, *Statistical Note 36: Asian Immigration*, Canberra, 1988; and Bureau of Immigration Research, Australia, *Immigration Update*, December 1989.

TABLE 6

CHARACTERISTICS OF RECENT SETTLER MIGRANTS TO CANADA AND THE UNITED STATES

| | Age structure | | | | | Family class as proportion of total admitted | Sex ratio (males per 100 females) | Total |
	0-14 years	15-19 years	30-44 years	45-59 years	60+ years			
A. Canada, landed immigrants, 1990								
China	6.9	37.9	35.4	10.2	9.5	48.9	103	7,868
Taiwan	25.7	24.2	32.2	12.9	5.2	13.0	101	3,564
Hong Kong	22.4	21.4	39.9	9.7	6.6	27.6	96	28,825
Japan	15.9	28.8	37.3	10.4	7.7	35.6	60	365
Indonesia	15.7	33.7	29.3	11.6	9.6	55.4	95	249
Philippines	16.7	26.8	41.0	7.0	8.5	64.6	67	11,950
Malaysia	19.5	28.3	32.4	11.5	8.2	42.6	91	1,638
Singapore	19.9	23.3	39.0	11.4	6.3	34.9	96	1,076
Cambodia	29.1	39.6	17.1	8.9	5.4	7.2*	102	766
South Korea	17.4	31.7	25.2	16.0	9.8	45.8*	89	1,863
Laos	29.5	46.8	17.9	2.4	3.4	3.1*	157	583
Thailand	29.8	38.1	26.0	3.3	2.8	76.2	41	181
Vietnam	19.5	45.2	23.5	6.7	5.1	41.7	114	9,048

TABLE 6 (continued)
CHARACTERISTICS OF RECENT SETTLER MIGRANTS TO CANADA AND THE UNITED STATES

	Age structure					Family class as proportion of total admitted	Sex ratio (males per 100 females)	Total
	0-14 years	15-19 years	30-44 years	45-59 years	60+ years			
B. United States, immigrants admitted, 1989								
China	8.2	25.0	27.9	20.8	18.2	83	103	32,272
Taiwan	17.5	30.0	38.9	8.4	5.3	56	87	13,974
Hong Kong	20.3	37.3	36.6	4.6	1.3	n.a.	81	9,740
Philippines	16.9	29.3	29.2	14.2	10.5	76	108	57,036
South Korea	24.5	31.9	22.4	13.2	8.0	84	81	34,222
Laos	25.7	40.0	19.8	8.2	6.3	n.a.*	72	12,524
Thailand	51.9	14.7	25.2	5.8	2.3	31	90	9,332
Vietnam	21.3	42.7	20.9	9.9	5.2	19*	102	37,739

* Countries where refugees form the most important component of the intake.

Source: *Immigration 1990, Quarterly Statistics* (final quarter, preliminary), Ottawa, Employment and Immigration Canada and *1989 Statistical Yearbook* of the Immigration and Naturalization Service, Washington, United States Department of Justice, 1990.

Notes:
1. Canadian data are against place of last permanent residence while United States data are against birthplace.
2. The United States figures for "family class" are only approximations. They consist of "immediate relatives" (who are exempt from numerical limitation) and "relative preferences" (who are subject to limitation). As country of chargeability is not necessarily country of birth, there are discrepancies in the totals. These data are indicative rather than exact proportions.
3. The figures for immigrants admitted to the United States do not imply that they arrived in the United States in that year, although the majority did, but that their status was regularized in that year.

- there are only about 80 males for every 100 female migrants to the United States from South Korea, for example - can be explained mainly by two factors. First, there are large numbers of American servicemen who return with a Korean wife, one out of every nine servicemen who are stationed in South Korea, according to one estimate. Secondly, there are significant numbers of baby girls who are given up for adoption to American couples (Kuznets, 1987). These factors are also meaningful in the flow from the Philippines and Thailand.

Apart from family members, there are smaller numbers of settlers who are admitted for their particular occupational skills, entrepreneurial abilities or investment potential. While Canada and Australia have specifically "targeted" these migrants as part of their immigration policies for some considerable time (since 1967 in the case of Canada and 1982 in the case of Australia), the changes introduced by the 1990 United States Immigration Act will also tend to increase the relative importance of the highly skilled and business categories in annual flows. For example, while family reunification remains the bulwark of United States immigration policy, the level for family members was raised only 13 percent to an annual intake of 543,000 from 1995 onwards. The category of independent migrants, however, was virtually tripled with effect from 1992, from 54,000 to 140,000 per annum. Asian migrants can be expected to benefit from these changes if the trends to Canada can be taken as an example. Some 66 percent of the total number of business migrants and entrepreneurs to Canada in 1990 came from the East and Southeast Asian region, 54 percent from Hong Kong and Taiwan alone. Forty-one percent of the self-employed immigrants and other independents were also from the region, even though the total number of immigrants from the region accounted for no more than 32 percent of the global intake of Canada. East and Southeast Asians are thus overrepresented amongst the highly skilled in settler migration. Although ethnicity data are lacking on migrants from Southeast Asia, it is clear that, from the region as a whole, it is primarily Chinese and Chinese-influenced peoples who are participating in these settler movements and setting up regional and global business linkages out of Singapore, Hong Kong and Taipei, and to a lesser extent, Seoul, Kuala Lumpur and Manila.

Although family members dominate the settler migration flows, there is a great range of skills possessed by the migrants. In fact, perhaps one of the few generalizations that can made is that the skills and training of the migrants is characterized by heterogeneity, even if the minority of independent migrants tend to possess higher order skills than the family members (Park *et al.*, 1990; Cariño *et al.*, 1990). The levels of education, even accounting for the family reunification categories, do tend to be higher than those of the populations in the countries of origin. The highly educated group which migrates specifically to continue studying on student visas can be seen as a separate category of movers.

The Student Migration System

The training of students in the United States was not subject to the same ethnic limitation as immigrants, and Asian students figured prominently in the numbers even before the Second World War. Although the number of foreign students in tertiary institutions in the United States in the mid-1950s was only 21,410, those from East and Southeast Asian countries accounted for one fifth of the total. By the mid-1960s, at the time the immigration laws were being reappraised, the number of foreign students had more than doubled to 49,429, with those from East and Southeast Asia accounting for one quarter of this number. By the late 1980s, there were 366,354 foreign students in the United States, and East and Southeast Asian countries dominated as source areas. Seven of the top eight countries of origin of foreign students to the United States, accounting for more than 150,000 students, were in the East and Southeast Asian region (Table 7). The situation for Canada is similar, with seven countries from the East and Southeast Asian region accounting for virtually 45 percent of the 70,891 foreign students there in 1989.[10]

The number of students who choose to remain in the destination country as settlers at the termination of their studies is difficult to ascertain but is likely to be substantial. For example, it has been estimated that about 6,000 students from South Korea adjusted to permanent residence in the United States during the 1970s, although these represented perhaps only about one quarter of the total number of Korean students going to the United States over that period (Kuznets, 1987:60). A study of Chinese students who left Taiwan between 1960 and 1968 showed that only about 5 percent returned to Taiwan and, even among those who returned, the desire to move back to the United States was strong, with almost half seriously considering returning to the United States (Kao, 1971). A more recent study of students from Taiwan has shown that while the number of students going overseas more than doubled from the 1970s to the 1980s, the number returning home also increased. By the 1980s, up to one quarter were estimated to have gone

---

[10] Information on students in the United States can be found in the biennial *Open Doors: Report on International Educational Exchange*, New York, The Institute of International Education, and on students in Canada in the annual *International Student Participation in Canadian Education*, Ottawa, Statistics Canada.

TABLE 7
LEADING COUNTRIES OF ORIGIN OF STUDENTS TO CANADA AND THE UNITED STATES (PERCENTAGES)

	Canada				United States			
	1975	1985	1989	1964/65	1974/75	1984/85	1988/89
China	370	1,285	5,796	-	-	10,100	29,040
Taiwan	223	379	1,831	6,780	10,250	22,590	28,760
Japan	258	1,343	4,016	3,386	5,930	10,290	24,000
India	-	-	-	6,813	9,660	14,610	23,350
South Korea	-	-	-	2,604	3,390	15,370	20,610
Malaysia	947	3,325	2,041	-	-	21,720	16,170
Canada	-	-	-	9,253	8,430	16,430	16,030
Hong Kong	9,076	12,882	11,509	3,279	11,060	10,130	10,560
Iran	-	-	-	3,719	-	16,640	8,950
Indonesia	-	-	-	-	-	-	8,720
Singapore	215	1,455	1,504	-	-	-	-
Philippines	76	1,255	4,921	2,473	-	-	-
Thailand	-	-	-	1,630	6,250	7,220	6,560
United States	7,307	6,001	6,910	-	-	-	-
Total number of foreign students	42,436	53,824	70,891	82,045	154,580	342,113	366,354

Source: United States - *Open Doors 1988/1989.* New York, Institute of International Education, 1989.
Canada - *International Student Participation in Canadian Education, 1989,* Ottawa, Statistics Canada, 1990.

Notes: 1. The United States figures only include those enrolled in degree programs while the Canadian figures include those enrolled in primary/secondary schools and technical colleges as well as degree programs.
2. A dash "-" indicates that that country was not a leading source of students in that year.

back to Taiwan (Hsieh *et al.*, 1989). Whether this loss of trained manpower is indeed a "brain drain" will be considered below after the other systems of migration have been described.

The Contract Labor Migration System

Almost at the same time as these flows of students and emigrants were accelerating to North America and Australia, another important type of population migration was developing from the region: labor migration, primarily to the oil-rich countries of the Middle East. This type of migration can be distinguished from the emigrant flows because systems of labor migration are circulatory, in theory if not entirely in practice. The policies of the destination countries often prohibit permanent settlement and migrants are expected to return home after their contract has been completed. With the exception of the Philippines, which has a longer tradition of contract migration than other countries in the region, the annual numbers leaving during the early 1970s were only in the low thousands. By the early 1980s, the annual numbers from South Korea and the Philippines were in the hundreds of thousands with significant flows from Indonesia, Thailand and, to a lesser extent, China (Table 8). All these countries view contract labor, explicitly or implicitly, as an integral part of their development programs and as a means of generating foreign exchange through remittances sent back by the workers. Such has been the importance of these contract labor flows both in terms of volume and in terms of development issues that they have received considerable attention in the literature.[11]

The labor migration from East and Southeast Asia is but part of a wider system of mobility covering much of the Arab world and the countries of South Asia. This system arose primarily to satisfy the labor demands created by the huge development programs undertaken by a small number of oil-rich countries in the Middle East following the vast capital inflows to these countries after the oil price rises of 1973. The most important destination country was Saudi Arabia where, in the mid-1980s, some 4.5 million foreigners were resident, representing over 60 percent of the total population at that time. The total foreign population in the countries of the Gulf Co-operation Council (Bahrain, Kuwait, Oman, Qatar, Saudi Arabia and the United Arab Emirates) in 1985 was estimated at 7.2 million. Both the

[11] Useful reviews will be found in Gunatilleke, ed. (1986); Arnold and Shah, eds. (1986); Smart (1986); Abella and Atal, eds. (1986); DSE (1987); Stahl and Habib (1991). An interesting summary of contract labor recruitment from China, which had in 1989 some 66,000 laborers in 123 countries, including Australia, will be found in J. Taylor (1991:53-72).

38 ASIAN AND PACIFIC MIGRATION JOURNAL

TABLE 8
AVERAGE ANNUAL NUMBER OF MIGRANT WORKERS REGISTERED IN THE
MAIN LABOR EMIGRATION COUNTRIES OF THE REGION, 1975-1989
(THOUSANDS)

	1975-1979	1980-1984	1985-1989
Indonesia	5.9	24.4	61.4
South Korea	72.3	171.8	96.2
Philippines	75.9	330.9	460.3
Thailand	6.3	60.0	97.0

Source: *International Labour Migration from Asian Labour-sending Countries*, Statistical Report 1989 (RAS/88/029), Bangkok, International Labour Organisation, Regional Office for Asia and the Pacific, 1989, various tables.

estimates of foreigners in the countries of destination of contract labor movement and the estimates of outmigrant laborers from the countries of origin have to be treated with care. There are few exact enumerations of either migrant stock at destinations or flow from origins and, while governments may keep records of those recruited through official channels, there are many unofficial channels in most countries of origin and the figures for flows and stocks are likely to be underestimations.[12]

Many of the contract laborers to the Middle East are unskilled, but the majority of these are from the countries of South Asia. Most of those from Southeast and East Asia possess some kind of skill (Gunatilleke, 1986:17; Stahl and Habib, 1991). Carpenters, mechanics, drivers and skilled construction workers have been much in demand as well as smaller numbers of professionals, particularly medical practitioners and people with technical expertise. Contract migration from the region in question, rather than coming from the armies of the unemployed and the rural or urban poor in labor surplus economies of the countries of origin, tends to come from the ranks of those who are employed and who have a skill. The educational level of contract migrants from both South Korea and the Philippines is significantly higher than that of the workers in these countries as a whole. Rather than relieving population or employment pressures in the home

[12] For assessments of the data, *see* Demery (1986) and Smart (1986).

country, the loss of these workers, albeit temporarily, may have a negative effect on the economy and exacerbate the impact of the loss of skills of the more permanent emigrants to the United States, Canada and Australia discussed earlier. The costs and benefits of the patterns of migration will be considered in more detail below.

The decline in oil prices through the 1980s led to a slowing in the volume of contract labor in the Middle East as some projects had to be postponed or shelved and the Gulf crisis of 1990-91 caused serious disruption, hardship and suffering for many of the workers. Six Filipinos were reported killed in Baghdad and over 15,000 were airlifted home in the first months of the crisis alone.[13] By the end of December 1990, all 60,000 contract laborers from China, all 400 from South Korea, 30,000 of 40,000 from the Philippines, 10,000 of 13,000 from Thailand and 8,000 of 16,000 from Vietnam in the affected areas were reported to have been returned to their countries of origin.[14] Not all, however, wished to return home and many thousands preferred to remain in the Middle East rather than face lower wages or unemployment at home. Saudi Arabia has offered positions to large numbers of those displaced from Kuwait and Iraq. While it is too early to assess the full impact of the recent war on population migration, the number of foreigners required in the short term in Iraq has clearly been reduced but the reconstruction required after the damage wrought by the conflict in Kuwait may rekindle the movement of construction workers.

The recent Gulf crisis aside, one trend appears clear: there is a diversification in the destinations of contract labor, much of it to areas within the region of Southeast and East Asia itself. For example, the proportion of workers leaving Thailand and the Philippines for the Middle East dropped from 97 and 84 percent in 1980 to 77 and 72 percent respectively in 1987-88 even if the absolute numbers increased.[15] The drop for South Korea was even more marked: from 82 percent in 1980 to only 26 percent in 1988. Unlike the other countries in Southeast Asia, the absolute numbers of Korean contract laborers also dropped precipitously from almost 172,000 in 1980-84 to just over 96,000 during 1985-89. Part of the reason for this lies in the cut-backs forced on Middle Eastern nations in the face of declining revenue, but part also lies in the changing nature of the labor market in

[13] See "Exodus from Araby", Far Eastern Economic Review, 4 October 1990, and Connell and Wang (1991).

[14] International Labour Organisation figures cited in Connell and Wang (1991:317).

[15] World Population Monitoring, 1991, draft chapter on "International migration trends and policies", New York, United Nations, p. 14.

these countries themselves. There has been a change from a phase of construction to a phase of maintenance and consolidation. Skilled and unskilled construction workers return home or move on, while the demand for skilled and professional management personnel increases.

There are differences in the nature of the flows of contract labor from one country to another as well as over time. For example, the movement from South Korea has been tightly regulated under the control of Korean companies. When a company won a contract in the Middle East, virtually everything was supplied from South Korea itself. Accommodation was built for the Korean workers and all their daily needs were catered for. As wages were about three times higher than the worker could expect to earn at home, the resultant savings rates were high. Workers were, however, expected to work harder, up to 60 hours a week, their social life was prescribed and breaches of discipline were swiftly dealt with to the point of dismissal and repatriation. Essentially, the contract labor system, as far as South Korea is concerned, is part of the expansion of Korean multinational activity overseas, which is an integral part of its export-oriented industrialization strategy.[16]

Contract labor from the Philippines, Thailand and Indonesia has not been so regulated. Government and private agencies recruit for foreign companies and for individuals, and the rights and protection of the workers have become major issues. Workers may have to make considerable payments to private recruitment agencies in order to secure all the necessary documentation, and the system is liable to abuse. There may be no means of guaranteeing the worker a fair wage or living standard once he or she has arrived at the destination. This has become increasingly important with the participation of women in the contract labor flows. In the late 1970s, only about 15 percent of all the Asian workers to the Middle East were women. By the late 1980s, over one quarter of the estimated one million Asian workers there were thought to be made up of women, particularly from Indonesia, the Philippines and Thailand.[17] In particular, Indonesia, as a comparatively late entrant into the international contract labor market, found it difficult to compete with the more established source countries in the increasingly shrinking market of the Middle East from the early 1980s. Hence, Indonesia's policy was to exploit the niches which were still available, one of which was the expanding demand for housemaids. Some 192,000 Indonesian women were recorded as having gone to Saudi Arabia

---

[16] An excellent account of Korean contract labor is given by Seok (1986).

[17] Abella (1990a). For a discussion of the protection of workers, *see* essays in DSE (1987).

between 1983 and the end of 1988. The majority went to be housemaids to private families. Indonesian women, because they are Muslims, were reputed to receive slightly higher wages than women from other Southeast Asian countries.[18] Because Asian women are working privately, it is difficult to enforce uniform standards of protection. There are many cited cases of virtual imprisonment and other abuses. More highly educated women from the Philippines and South Korea also move to the Middle East as doctors, nurses, salesgirls or clerical workers. For example, 26,589 medical workers left the Philippines in 1985, accounting for 15 percent of all contract laborers during that year; 20,954 of these were nurses (Ball, 1990:100-102).

The flows of contract laborers, unlike the settler flows, are made up of people leaving their families in the places of origin rather than moving to join them at places of destination. Until recently, the flows were dominated by males, although women's participation in contract labor has increased to the extent that they now dominate some of the flows. Migrants tend to be concentrated in the young adult age cohorts, with few in the younger and older age groups. Similarly, the range of skills is much narrower than in the case of the settler migrant flows and concentrated in the manual and technical skills required in the construction industry. However, the evolution from a construction phase of development to one in which services are required has seen changes in the skills and sex composition of the contract labor force, with increasing demand for higher levels of skills and for female-oriented skills such as nursing. At the same time, the changing nature of the origin societies themselves, with the increasing levels of development and educational attainment of their populations, has also contributed to the growing complexity of outmigrant flows. One consequence has been the emergence of a system of highly skilled international migration.

The Skilled Labor Migration System

Included in the contract labor system discussed above are numbers of highly skilled technical migrants which obscure any clear dividing line between that system and the skilled labor migration system. However, the growing importance of the posting of international personnel through multinational companies or government and international organizations identifies a system of movement which is quite different in nature from the

18 Cremer (1988). For an overview of the domestic servant migration system, *see* Asian and Pacific Development Center (1989).

TABLE 9

DEPARTURES, BY PURPOSE, FROM JAPAN AND SOUTH KOREA, 1975 AND 1988/89

	Japan		South Korea	
Purpose	1975	1988	1975	1989
1. Diplomacy	4,266	7,849	1,796	1,148
2. Government	10,027	27,213	4,332	10,191
3. Short stay for business	349,399	1,024,764	23,177	314,418
4. Assignment to overseas branches	13,187	83,017	31,008	87,294
5. Scientific study and research, and conference attendance	5,594	28,924	-	14,070
6. Studying abroad, training and acquiring skills	10,826	84,708	214	50,225
7. Residing permanently	12,445	48,745	35,642	33,066
8. Sightseeing and visits	2,027,191	7,028,001	22,392	572,440
9. Other	33,391	93,616	10,817	129,959
Total	2,466,326	8,426,867	129,378	1,213,111

Sources: *Statistical Yearbooks* of Japan and South Korea, various years.

migrant workers discussed in the previous section.[19] An important component of this system consists of the movement of expatriates from the developed world to East and Southeast Asia to fulfill, usually short-term, financial or commercial assignments.

There is also a movement of highly skilled Asians within the region. Japan, the most developed country in the region, is generally not considered a labor-sending country in the literature on Asian labor migration, yet over the period from the mid-1970s to the late 1980s the numbers of Japanese moving overseas increased dramatically (Table 9). In 1988, over 83,000 were assigned to overseas branches of Japanese companies and a

[19] For a research agenda on this system, *see* Gould, ed. (1988) and Salt and Findlay (1989).

further 29,000 went abroad to engage in scientific study and research (not including students). In 1975, movers in these categories numbered only 13,000 and 5,600 respectively. In 1988, over one million Japanese left Japan for a "short stay for business", although that designation should perhaps not be taken too literally. There is thus significant growth in skilled short-term and medium-term migration that is associated with Japan's rise to the position of an economic superpower, with branches of its companies located around the world. This is a topic that is, as yet, little researched.

The number of annual departures from South Korea for purposes of business in the mid-1970s was between 20,000 and 30,000. Within fifteen years, these had risen tenfold to reach over 300,000 in 1989. The principal destinations of these business trips from South Korea in 1989 were Japan (172,000), the United States (37,000), Hong Kong (28,000) and Taiwan (13,600); only 2,000 to 3,000 went to Middle Eastern countries. These highly skilled flows, from South Korea at least, were also dominated by males. These data show that this highly skilled migration network is quite different from the contract migration discussed earlier.

Few other countries in the region keep such detailed departure statistics as South Korea but the growth of the short-term business linkages is a common feature throughout the region and globally. Singapore's business arrivals, for example, increased by 130 percent from 1979 to 1989, and Hong Kong's total visitor arrivals from Japan, South Korea and Taiwan, including tourists, increased by 150 percent, 270 percent and 816 percent respectively between 1980 and 1989 to a total of over 2.33 million visitors. One estimate of the number of skilled "transients" from Taiwan serving overseas in 1990 is 103,000, mostly in the United States but also in Japan and elsewhere in the region (Lee, 1991).

The creation of the regional networks introduces one of the major new directions of international migration in East and Southeast Asia: the emergence of intra-regional flows. Not all of these flows consist of the highly skilled, although these are the migrants most readily accepted by the countries of the region. With a few exceptions, East and Southeast Asian countries do not allow permanent settlement and immigration is tightly controlled.[20] Because skilled expatriates are entering mainly through the medium of international corporations or other institutions, it is assumed that they will only be resident temporarily and permanent residence is

---

[20] The exceptions would mainly include the movement of Chinese, who might be able to move from Hong Kong to Taiwan, or from Malaysia to Singapore, and become citizens relatively quickly.

rarely granted. However, given the economic and demographic changes outlined earlier in this essay, a demand for labor has arisen that can only be met through the importation of less highly skilled migrants on contract and/or by illegal migration. So important have become these different flows within the East and Southeast Asian region itself that they merit separate attention.

The Emergence of Intra-regional Flows

The high rates of economic growth and the downturn in fertility have created a demand for labor in several parts of the region. This is most acutely felt in Singapore, but Hong Kong, Taiwan, Japan and even South Korea are currently facing the dilemma of how to maintain future high rates of growth in the face of growing demands on a slowly expanding (or even contracting) labor force which is creating labor shortages in key areas and rapidly escalating labor costs. South Korea shifted from a labor surplus to a labor deficit economy in the mid-1970s and Taiwan in the mid-1960s.[21] Three strategies are available to deal with labor shortages: the first is to shift towards capital-intensive high-technology industries, the second is to export capital to areas where labor is still cheap, and the third is to import labor.

Japan and the "four little tigers" of South Korea, Taiwan, Hong Kong and Singapore have pursued these strategies to varying degrees. As far as international migration is concerned, the first strategy increases the volume of the skilled labor transfers discussed earlier. The second strategy also has implications for migration, with the investments abroad setting in motion other chains of population movement. For example, Hong Kong investment in the Special Economic Zone of Shenzhen across the border in China and in adjacent parts of Guangdong Province has created at least two million additional jobs in manufacturing which has contributed to the movement of large numbers of migrants, particularly women, from elsewhere in Guangdong and from further afield.[22] Taiwan is investing heavily in Fujian Province and again migrants are likely to be drawn towards the towns along that part of the China coast.

Singapore and Malaysia. The case of Singapore is perhaps most apposite to our theme. Wages in manufacturing in nearby Johor State are nearly half

---

[21] On South Korea, *see* Kuznets (1987:56), and on Taiwan, *see* Wu and Lan (1991).

[22] For one case study of this movement, *see* Li (1989).

of the equivalent level in Singapore and factory rents and power costs are also considerably lower. It is estimated that the industrial projects that will be established in Johor by the year 2005 will create 276,000 new jobs and Singapore is likely to provide much of the investment required. A large part of this development will be in the "growth triangle" which is planned to link Singapore, Malaysia and Batam Island in Indonesia in a large-scale economic and urban complex. Malaysians will be drawn not only to Singapore, where over 150,000 already are resident, but also to Johor Bahru, the city immediately across the causeway linking the island of Singapore to the Malay peninsula.[23]

Since 1970, the movement of Malaysians to cities in general, not just the area close to Singapore, has caused acute labor shortages in the rural sector, particularly in the oil palm plantations, which is met through illegal migrants from Indonesia. No reliable figures are available, but an estimate of at least half a million illegal migrants is considered reasonable. If correct, this would represent somewhere between 8 and 10 percent of Malaysia's labor force (Hugo, 1991; Guiness, 1990). The number of Indonesian migrants in Johor is about 100,000, one-twelfth of that state's population. Not all Indonesians are in the rural sector, however; others have entered the manufacturing industry. The illegals, whether in rural or urban activities, normally work under contract, often to Chinese middlemen. The situation has reached the point where the Malaysian government can do little to stem the flow and has to accept that large sectors of the economy depend directly upon illegal labor. There have also been significant illegal movements from Indonesia and the Philippines into East Malaysia. For example, it has been estimated that 335,000 Filipinos and 145,000 Indonesians were residing illegally in Sabah in 1988 (Hugo, 1991:7). The illegal migrants throughout Malaysia are temporary, circulating regularly back home, and are primarily male.

Within Singapore itself, the labor shortage has resulted in a stock of between 150,000 and 170,000 foreign workers, which represented at least 11 percent of the total labor force in 1989, up from 72,000 in 1970.[24] About

[23] Relatively little is known yet about the extent of Singapore investment in the "growth triangle". For one earlier and one more recent assessment, see the articles "Twinned hinterlands", *Far Eastern Economic Review*, 18 August 1988, pp. 76-77, and "Search for a hinterland", *Far Eastern Economic Review*, 3 January 1991, pp. 34-38.

[24] See Cheung (1991) for the official figures; the higher estimates are given in Stahl (1991b). For an analysis of the situation to the early 1980s, see Stahl (1985). For a discussion of Singapore's recent migration policies, see Yap (forthcoming). A summary of a recent conference on labor migration in Asia, which contains useful information on Japan, Hong Kong and Malaysia, as well as Hong Kong, is given in Martin (1991).

125,000 of these are unskilled laborers unaccompanied by family members who are tightly controlled by Singapore's immigration policy of worker rotation. There are also some 25,000 professional and skilled workers who are likely to bring their families with them and who, if they fulfill certain conditions, may be granted permanent resident status. In addition, there are a reported 40,000-50,000 domestic servants in Singapore, primarily Filipina women. Despite several amnesties, there are also significant numbers of illegal migrants, mainly males from Malaysia and Thailand. As an estimate of the total number of foreigners in Singapore, 10 percent of the population of 2.7 million would probably be not too far from the real figure. However, the figures are complicated by the number of daily commuter workers who come across the causeway from nearby Johor State.

The whole issue of foreign workers and foreign residents in multicultural Singapore has become very sensitive. Present policy aims to preserve the ethnic "mix" at its current level of 75 percent Chinese, 16 percent Malay and 9 percent Indian. Any immigration that might significantly change this balance is an official cause for concern. One attempt to maintain the balance is to attract skilled and semi-skilled Hong Kong Chinese to counterbalance the need for more lowly skilled Malays. Delayed permanent residence rights are being given to suitably qualified Hong Kong citizens to attract them to Singapore but, as I have shown elsewhere, unless the disaster scenario accompanies the Chinese take-over of the British colony in 1997, relatively few people are likely to move from Hong Kong to Singapore (Skeldon, 1991b). At present, the balance in the population interchange between the two cities is decidedly in favor of Hong Kong.

Hong Kong, Taiwan and Japan too are confronting the problems of labor shortage and illegal migration. In the case of Hong Kong, all illegal migrants from China are repatriated, or imprisoned and then repatriated. Apart from exporting industrialization across the border into China, Hong Kong, like Singapore, has responded by incorporating women into the labor force. In 1989, female labor force participation rates for the age groups 20-24 and 25-29 years were 84 and 76.3 percent respectively. Female participation rates do not drop below 50 percent until the age group 50-54 years. One indirect effect of increased local women's participation in the labor force has been the importation of domestic servants, primarily women from the Philippines. By 1990 there were well over 60,000 in the territory.

Taiwan. In 1987, Taiwan was estimated to have a labor shortage of around 200,000 in the manufacturing sector and 120,000 in the construction industry (Wu and Lan, 1991). Taiwan permits the entry of only highly skilled migrants, who numbered around 20,000 in 1990. However, others enter legally as tourists or trainees on short-term visitor visas of 14 to 60 days and then overstay. Before 1986, the problem of overstayers was negligible but, by 1990, the number of overstayers was estimated to be about 40,000. In a country of over 20 million, this is a small number but one which is likely to increase. The majority are males from, in decreasing order of importance, Malaysia, the Philippines, Thailand and Indonesia. Excluded from these figures are the numbers of Chinese from mainland China who went across the Straits seeking work, mainly in rural areas or small towns. No reliable assessment of their numbers exists, although the estimates range from 10,000 to 100,000, with the best guess being somewhere in the middle. Military officials admit to repatriating some 11,000 between 1987 and 1989. Given the huge differential between wages on the mainland and in Taiwan, this flow can only continue. At present, the government plans to import Southeast Asian laborers on contract to assist in the construction of public works projects that are behind schedule. It is generally accepted, however, that the local private sector will continue to take on illegal migrants for low paying and hazardous jobs.[25]

Japan, a country where international migration has historically, if wrongly, been considered to be of negligible importance, has had to face the need for foreign labor over the last ten years. The importation of labor to cope with labor shortages is not a novel experience for Japan. Between 1921 and 1931, there was a net emigration of over 400,000 Koreans to Japan, with the Korean population in Japan growing from less than 4,000 in 1915 to over one million in 1940.[26]

Leaving aside the important issue of the role of historical immigration in Japan's development, we find that, as in the case of contemporary Taiwan, large numbers of immigrants are entering legally and overstaying their short-term visas. Many enter as students of the Japanese language on short-term courses. These students can legally work for 26 hours a week, but in fact work longer hours. They continue to do so after their visas have expired, a fact to which authorities and employers have been turning a blind eye. It is estimated that there are between 100,000 and 300,000 illegal workers in Japan, a small number given the size of Japan's population. The

[25] For information on migration to Taiwan, *see* C. Tsay (1991); H. Tsay (1991); and the Saturday Review article "Unwanted Cousins", *South China Morning Post*, 5 January 1991.

[26] The whole issue of Koreans in Japan is examined in Lee and de Vos, eds. (1981). The numbers cited are taken from pp. 36-37. A detailed discussion of the process of labor immigration to Japan can be found in Weiner (1989:49-98).

most important sources are the Philippines, Taiwan and China, although Koreans, Thais, Malaysians and South Asians are also thought to number prominently among the illegals. The flows of migrants were, until recently, dominated by women, although the balance is changing with the entry of greater numbers of mainland Chinese and South Asians. The latter are predominantly males who are engaged in the construction industry or "3-D" jobs - demanding, dirty and dangerous.[27] Large numbers of the women enter Japan legally each year as "entertainers" and later disappear into the twilight world of the "water trade". Some 71,000 entered Japan as entertainers in 1988, up from 20,580 in 1980; the majority are Filipina or Thai.

Japan and the newly industrializing economies of East Asia are facing similar problems associated with the very success of their economic development. All have female labor force participation rates similar to those cited for Hong Kong, so the potential for the future expansion of the labor force through the increased participation of women is limited. Nor is the potential for the further transfer of activities to overseas sources of cheap labor likely to be great, as these limits are being reached.[28] Some activities such as construction and most services cannot be transferred. Upward pressure on wage rates will continue in the context of a long-term decline in domestic labor force growth. The rising aspirations of indigenous populations will mean that "3-D" jobs are shunned.

These are forces which have operated in Europe for a considerable time. They were met through the importation of temporary labor which has, over time, proved to lead to permanent migrant and ethnic communities. These conditions are new to post-Second World War Asian societies and clear policy directions have yet to be evolved. Japan's New Immigration Law still bans the importation of unskilled labor "to prevent any influence upon the domestic labor market" (Nagai and Amante, 1991:2). When the law took effect in June 1990, there was an immediate crackdown on illegal foreign workers, with some 25,000 expelled. To replace the workers and attempt to reduce labor shortages, Japan is turning to *nisei*, the overseas Japanese, particularly in Brazil. In the last half of 1990, it has been estimated that 30,000-50,000 Latin Americans of Japanese descent went to Japan under

---

[27] *See* Nagai and Amante (1991) and Abella (1990b). The most detailed assessment of the numbers of illegals available in English is Mori (1990). A shortage of 100,000 workers in the construction industry alone in the late 1980s has been estimated by Inoue, cited in Stahl (1991a:168).

[28] This aspect is developed in Abella (1990b:15).

contract to work.[29] Despite this attempt to preserve the ethnic homogeneity of Japan, it seems unlikely that foreign labor can be excluded indefinitely. The economic slowdown in the Middle East, exacerbated by the recent crisis in the Gulf and the return of thousands of Southeast Asian workers accustomed to high wages, means that there will be a mobile labor force within the region searching for opportunities in an area where there is a persistent and increasing labor shortage. Legal and illegal migration from south to north within the region can only be expected to continue and to expand.

One other demographic factor may bring about international movements of people: the growing sex imbalances in marriageable age groups. In both Japan and South Korea, there will be much greater numbers of men than women in these age groups by the early years of the next century. For example, in South Korea there will be 2 million men aged between 25 and 29 years in 2010 but only 1.5 million women between 20 and 24 years. There are already significant surpluses of men between the ages of 20 and 39 in Japan. While the number of marriages to foreigners in Japan is still small, they increased markedly in the 1980s, from about 4,400 in 1980 to 17,800 in 1989. About 60 percent were to Koreans and Chinese, with the balance to Southeast Asians. Over the long term, there may be a trend towards greater polyethnicity in East Asia too, a trend which has occurred in the other parts of the developed world.

Refugee Movements

The issue of refugees within the East and Southeast Asian region deserves separate treatment in its own right and only a brief summary of the main recent issues can be given here; several comprehensive overviews already exist (Hugo, 1987; Rogge, 1987:237-345; Supang and Reynolds, 1988; Zolberg *et al.*, 1989:155-179; Chan, ed., 1990). Refugees are people under threat: people who cannot return home due to fear of persecution. We could add to this number those who cannot return home if their home areas have been destroyed through some physical disaster. In East and Southeast Asia, most of the latter flee within countries such as the Philippines, Indonesia or China from volcanic eruptions, floods or earthquakes. These are the internally displaced, and national and international relief agencies are deployed to rehabilitate them within their home countries. These internal

---

[29] *See* the articles "For a brighter manana," *Far Eastern Economic Review,* 27 September 1991, and "Latin American 'nisei' fill labor shortage," *Japan Economic Journal,* 8 February 1991.

movements will not be considered further.[30] Those fleeing from their countries because of fears for their safety come primarily from the poorest countries in the region and the countries where foreign interference, in terms of support for particular factions, has been greatest over the last twenty years: Vietnam, Laos and Cambodia.

Since the official end of the Vietnam war in 1975, over two million people have fled from Vietnam, Laos and Cambodia. Some one million have been resettled in the countries of the west, primarily the United States; 300,000 have been resettled in China and over 400,000 remain in camps in countries in the region. The route to the west was often long and dangerous. While the majority fled overland into China or towards Thailand, many tens of thousands made the hazardous boat crossing from Vietnam to Thailand, Malaysia, Singapore, Indonesia or Hong Kong. The numbers who died or were raped or kidnapped en route is not accurately known, but deaths may have been in excess of 100,000. The continuing political instability in Cambodia has meant that some 300,000 "displaced persons" inhabit camps along the Thai-Cambodian border waiting for conditions to improve so that they can go home.

The "high tide" of the refugee movements was from the mid-1970s to the early 1980s, with the greatest outflows around 1979, when some 200,000 left Vietnam. Since then, the flows have fluctuated at lower levels: smaller numbers are leaving their home countries but smaller numbers are also being resettled in the west. The overall trend was downwards until 1986. Since then, there has been a reversal and the numbers of refugees and asylum-seekers have been increasing. A "compassion fatigue" has set in in the developed countries and a virtual stalemate has developed, with thousands caught in limbo in holding camps in countries of first asylum in Southeast Asia and in Hong Kong. In mid-1990 there were 112,800 Vietnamese boat people in countries of first asylum, over 86 percent of whom had arrived after the March 1989 cut-off date when arrivals were no longer automatically considered for resettlement. In Hong Kong alone at the end of 1990, there were some 52,000 Vietnamese still languishing in camps.

A series of contradictions as regards international migration and refugees had developed by the 1990s. The freedom to move is accepted as a basic human right by western democratic systems; yet, in the face of real or potentially massive population transfers, pressures are increasingly being brought by western governments on third world (and ex-socialist bloc)

---

[30] These are listed in Hugo and Chan (1990); *see also* Hugo (1987).

authorities to pursue policies that will encourage their citizens to remain where they are. Voluntary repatriation, and in some cases forced repatriation, is being used as a means to show that the absorptive capacity of wealthier nations is being reached and the returnees should serve as an example to others of the futility of flight. This is particularly the case with the continuing numbers of boat people from Vietnam where it is increasingly perceived that the vast majority of leavers are not under threat but are "economic migrants". The Comprehensive Plan of Action (CPA) of March 1989 was an attempt by resettlement countries, countries of first asylum and the country of origin of refugees to seek an orderly solution to the problem. While countries of origin would attempt "to deter" departures, all those who left would be assumed to be asylum-seekers, unless shown to be otherwise. Those who are "screened out" as economic migrants are then to be repatriated. In Hong Kong, from June 1988, when this procedure was first introduced, to the end of 1990, some 19,969 Vietnamese boat people were interviewed. Of these, only 2,616 were screened in as refugees. The balance were screened out as economic migrants, even after appeal, and were waiting for repatriation or some other action by the international community.

Yet this increasingly restrictive attitude on the part of western developed nations and the closing of borders towards refugees - termed the creation of a form of "global apartheid" by one authority[31] - is occurring at the same time as some countries in the west are increasing their immigration targets and other countries within the region are experiencing the acute labor shortages described earlier. Clearly, the countries that receive wish to select types of migrants, primarily the "best and the brightest", and refugees are not seen to fall into this category.

Information on the composition of refugee flows is scanty. There has been a great ethnic diversity - Chinese, Vietnamese, Laotian or Cambodian, ethnic Vietnamese, hill-tribe groups from Laos and Vietnam. However, there appear to be general demographic characteristics that distinguish them from the settler flows described earlier. The age-sex information on immigrants to Canada in 1990 and the United States in 1989 (Table 6) from the three major refugee-producing countries shows that the flows are younger and biased more towards males when compared with the other "settler" flows. Surveys taken among refugees have shown that the majority fall into the unskilled or semi-skilled categories, which makes the task of training and incorporation into a modern economy more difficult (Dal-

---

[31] Richmond cited in Chan, ed. (1990:2).

glish, 1989:53). Even those who have qualifications experience major problems of adjustment and require additional training (Neuwirth, 1987). Perhaps the most optimistic feature about the refugee situation in East and Southeast Asia is that it is unlikely to get worse over the near future. If Vietnam can indeed be brought back into the regional and global community of nations from its present isolation, then the outflows of boat people may diminish to be replaced by outflows of "settler migrants".

The big unknown within the region is China: if a program of real reform is implemented, large numbers of its citizens may want to leave, just as we have seen in the Soviet Union over the last few years. If there is a return to a period of repression in China, those who benefited during the recent reforms may have to flee as "real" refugees. There are still too many unknowns to make confident statements about the future of refugee flows.

The Consequences of the International Flows

The settlers leaving the region and the students, many of whom also leave permanently, include among their numbers some of the best educated and most highly trained in their age groups. The loss of skills - the brain drain - has been seen as one of the major disadvantages of international movement for the countries of origin. The developed countries are benefiting from the brain drain, while the costs of replacing that group are borne by the developing countries which have lost this manpower at a potentially critical stage in their development. It has been estimated, for example, that over 10 percent of South Korea's supply of high level manpower was lost to the United States during the 1970s and probably more in selected professions (Kuznets, 1987:60). However, the rapid rate of growth of that country during this period hardly suggests that it was significantly adversely affected by the emigration.

The assessment of the impact of emigration has to be set against three other considerations. The first is the return of personnel from the developed countries after they have acquired skills overseas. In South Korea, three-quarters of students sent overseas do return and between 20 and 30 percent of professionals in that country were trained abroad, mainly in the United States but also in Japan. The return of these qualified people is an important element in the transfer of technology, which allows these nations to compete in an interdependent world. Their emigration should be seen as a training of brains as much as a draining of brains.

The second consideration relates to the capacity of the developing country itself to successfully absorb into its labor force the manpower that it does train. It is not too cynical to suggest that the school systems of many developing countries are more developed than the economies that support them. Aspirations are created that cannot be satisfied in the narrowly based local economies, and the problem of the educated unemployed results. The emigration of some of this elite may lessen political pressures and dissatisfactions, while at the same time it permits overseas training to strengthen these elite to play a constructive role in national development should they return in the future.

One cannot be too sanguine, however, about the benefits of overseas training. Regarding contract labor, already shown to involve people of a higher general skill level than the population as a whole, the emigration is not of the unemployed but of those whose skills may be difficult to replace. Their emigration may open up opportunities for others to be promoted or for the unemployed to fill vacancies, but there may also be subsequent falls in productivity from a more poorly qualified labor force. The skills taken by the migrants may not be adequately used at the destination country. This is particularly the case with female migrants entering domestic service who may have teaching or secretarial qualifications, but it also applies to highly skilled settler migrants who may find that the host country will not recognize their medical, legal or other professional qualifications. The result is a de-skilling of the emigrant labor force. Finally, even if emigrants, and in particular contract laborers, do learn skills overseas, these may not be easily applied in the local labor market, resulting in little benefit to either migrant or donor country.[32]

The third consideration relates to the flows of capital back from the host country in the form of remittances. Much has been written on this topic, yet no unequivocal conclusions on their role in international migration and development have emerged.[33] Remittances from migrant workers accounted for over US$1.5 billion to South Korea in 1982, over US$900 million to the Philippines in 1983 and almost US$700 million to Thailand in the same year (Stahl and Habib, 1991:172). These figures are likely to be underestimates, as much is remitted through informal channels. Such a huge volume of money is a significant source of foreign exchange earnings for these countries but it is not clear whether these cash flows are at the same time critical for their development.

[32] An excellent summary of these issues can be found in Stahl and Habib (1991).

[33] One of the best general assessments is still Russell (1986). For a review of the impact of remittances on Asian villages, *see* Rigg (1988). The general issues for Asia are well summarized in Stahl and Arnold (1986).

Remittances are used mainly for consumption rather than investment, a situation that may favor imported goods and dissipate the foreign exchange earned. Remittances may also increase wealth differentials in villages and lead to or exacerbate existing inequalities in land holding. However, expenditure on consumption is likely to improve basic living conditions, nutritional levels and hence welfare levels. It can make an impact on local services and, through the support of community festivals, promote local solidarity. It is virtually impossible to separate the impact of remittances from the impact of other forces of change in origin societies. Nor should remittances be seen simply as a one-way flow, from destination to origin countries; settler migrants have been shown to take considerable capital with them when they emigrate.[34] Emigration and remittances almost certainly produce improvements at individual, family, community and national levels but they are unlikely to be the sole or even the major cause of development. Two authorities conclude from a wide-ranging review of the impact of labor migration on South and Southeast Asia that "labor emigration has, on the whole, provided substantially more benefits than costs to Asian labor-sending countries", although this does not mean that it will stimulate development (Stahl and Habib, 1991:177).

The consequences of emigration must not be seen only from an economic point of view; there are profound social implications too. The physical separation of families during contract labor migration often leads to marital breakdown. The absence of men for prolonged periods on contract throws women into new and unfamiliar roles as family decision-makers, bringing change to societies where men were traditionally seen as heads of family and unquestioned figures of authority. Regardless of type of migrant or level of skills, there are also problems of adaptation to the new country. Women in particular, are subject to exploitation and abuse. The situations vary from group to group depending on the nature of the countries of origin and destination, as shown in the many valuable case studies of these human issues and concerns.[35]

---

[34] *See* Park *et al.* (1990) and Cariño *et al.* (1990). The amount of capital taken by Hong Kong emigrants to Canada is estimated to be somewhere in the region of CDN$2-4 billion per annum. *See* Skeldon (1991a:509) and *The Economist,* 23 March 1991, p. 88.

[35] Some excellent descriptions are given in the country chapters in Gunatilleke (1986) and in Abella and Atal (1986). It could be noted that the evidence for such problems comes primarily from case studies and that broad-based surveys tend to show low rates of these problems (ESCAP, 1986).

Conclusion

Just as there has been an increase in population mobility within the individual countries of East and Southeast Asia over the last twenty-five years, so too has there been a dramatic upsurge in movements from one country to another. Initially, the international movements developed as flows of students but, since 1965, increasingly large numbers of East and Southeast Asians have been moving as settlers, students, highly skilled job transferees and contract laborers. In settler migration, initially there was a dominance of those in occupational categories but this later switched to family members as the original migrants facilitated the movement of their relatives (Appleyard, 1988:97). This trend may change to some extent in the future, given the recent shift in emphasis of United States migration policy. The 1980s have seen the development of important intra-regional labor migration flows, particularly with the Middle East looking less secure as a source of contract labor.

The international migration flows reflect the divisions of wealth in the world: a movement from relatively poor to relatively rich countries. This, however, is too simplistic an explanation for the flows; political factors are also important. Those nations where the United States had the greatest military and political involvement from the 1950s to the early 1970s also have the most pronounced migration to the United States: the Philippines, South Korea, Taiwan and Vietnam. Family networks established through the United States military were an important conduit for subsequent chain migration. American companies too established important linkages with local labor which facilitated subsequent transfers. For example, American companies which were awarded contracts in the Middle East took Thai laborers who had originally worked for these companies on military projects in Thailand. And this was at a time when regional unemployment was rising because of the United States' withdrawal from their air bases in northeast Thailand following the end of the Vietnam war (Sumalee, 1986:259; Witayakorn, 1986:306-307). The anchors for the chain migration networks are often established through the strategies of superpower politics. These caveats aside, migrants are moving towards relatively rich countries and generally, with the exception of the contract movement to the Middle East, from countries of relatively high fertility and labor surplus economies to countries of relatively low fertility and labor deficit economies.

There remain many unknowns. Perhaps one of the most intriguing relates to the number of settlers who may return after acquiring a United States, Canadian or Australian passport. Not all settlers become permanent immigrants but the numbers of returnees and the role they play in their home societies and economies are largely unknown. Another major issue relates to the absorption of return contract migrants: how can these return migrants, accustomed to high wages, be effectively readmitted into low wage, high unemployment economies?[36] The whole issue of the relationship between internal migration and international movements requires investigation, with the evolution of the spatial pattern of mobility within the region at present being little understood.[37] Surveys of Korean and Filipino settler migration to the United States have shown that urban areas, and particularly the primate capital city region, are disproportionately represented amongst the origin areas within the countries (Park *et al.*, 1990; Cariño *et al.*, 1990; Sumalee, 1986; Witayakorn, 1986:313-314). The early contract migration from Thailand to the Middle East was mainly from Bangkok, although the source areas spread relatively quickly into rural areas, particularly in the northeast (Rigg, 1989). The primary cities and areas around American military bases appear to play key roles in linking internal migration systems to international systems. Regional cities such as Singapore and Hong Kong also appear to serve as "sojourning hubs" for onward migration of Filipinos, Malays or Chinese to Canada, the United States or Australia (Gunasekaran and Koh, 1991). Hong Kong may also serve as a conduit for illegal migrants from China to South and Central America who then attempt to enter the United States.

The labor deficit economies of South Korea and Taiwan, as well as Hong Kong and Singapore, are important sources for settler migration to North America and Australia. The Asian countries are also emerging as potential (South Korea) and actual destinations for regional population flows even if much of this is temporary. There are thus important hierarchical systems of movement evolving, with the newly industrializing economics acting not only as "steps" to the more developed countries of the west, but as stages in a mobility sequence. Movement up the development hierarchy accentuates the demographic "vacuum" created by fertility decline and helps to draw in migrants from regional origins lower down the hierar-

[36] A brief program for action is outlined in *Report of the Policy Workshop on International Migration in Asia and the Pacific*, Economic and Social Commission for Asia and the Pacific (1985). The results of one of the studies on return migrants summarized in this report - to Manila in the Philippines - showed levels of unemployment among returnees of almost 50 percent (*see* p. 17). *See also* "Returning migrant workers: exploratory studies" (ESCAP, 1986).

[37] For an analysis of the evolution of mobility systems in Asian countries and elsewhere, *see* Skeldon (1990).

chy.[38] More too needs to be known about the destinations in the host countries. Migrants tend to concentrate in the large urban centers of California or New York rather than in other parts of the United States. Most migrants from Hong Kong to Canada concentrate either in Toronto or in Vancouver.

These urban linkages give substance to that vague notion of the "Pacific Community." It is difficult to foresee future migration between East and Southeast Asia doing anything but increasing. The potential for future movement is great, both within the region and to countries outside. The big cities within the region are likely to pass intra-regional movers and internal migrants on to world cities in North America and Australasia. The trans-Pacific migrations of the twenty-first century may rival the trans-Atlantic movements of early this century. With such large movements of people, the societies of both origin and destination will be irrevocably transformed: in which precise ways we do not yet know, but over the last twenty-five years we have witnessed the beginnings of a new and very different world.

REFERENCES

Abella, M.I.
1990a   "The Sex Selectivity of Migration Regulations Governing International Migration in South and South-East Asia." Paper presented at the UN Expert Group Meeting on International Migration Policies and the Status of Female Migrants, San Miniato, Italy, March 27-30.

_____
1990b   "Structural Change and Labour Migration within the Asian Region." Paper presented at the UN Centre for Regional Development Conference on Cross-National Labour Migration in the Asian Region: Implications for Local and Regional Development, Nagoya, Japan, November 5-8.

Abella, M.I. and Y. Atal, eds.
1986   *Middle East Interlude: Asian Workers Abroad.* Bangkok: UNESCO.

[38] Compare with the hierarchical patterns of internal migration identified by Ravenstein for nineteenth-century England and discussed for developing countries in Skeldon (1990). The idea of hierarchical patterns of movement relates to spatial organization and the new international division of labor as outlined in the "world city" hypothesis of Friedmann (1986) and modified by King (1990). Just how this division of labor relates to patterns of international migration in Asia must await future analyses.

Appleyard, R.T.
1988   "International Migration in Asia and the Pacific." In *International Migration Today.
        Volume I: Trends and Prospects.* Edited by R.T. Appleyard. Paris: UNESCO.

Appleyard, R.T., ed.
1989   *The Impact of International Migration on Developing Countries.* Paris: OECD.

Arnold, F. and N.M. Shah, eds.
1986   *Asian Labor Migration: Pipeline to the Middle East.* Boulder: Westview.

Asian and Pacific Development Center
1989   *The Trade in Domestic Helpers: Causes, Mechanisms and Consequences.* Kuala Lumpur:
        Asian and Pacific Development Centre.

Ball, R.E.
1990   *The Process of International Contract Labour Migration from the Philippines: The Case of
        Filipino Nurses.* Ph.D. dissertation, University of Sydney.

Bernard, W.S.
1982   "A History of U.S. Immigration Policy." In *Immigration.* Edited by R.A. Easterlin, *et al.*
        Cambridge, Mass: Harvard University Press.

Cariño, B.V., *et al.*
1990   *The New Filipino Immigrants to the United States: Increasing Diversity and Change.* Papers
        of the East-West Population Institute, No. 115. Honolulu: East-West Population Insti-
        tute.

Chan, Kwok Bun
1990   "Getting Through Suffering: Indochinese Refugees in Limbo 15 Years Later," *Southeast
        Asian Journal of Social Science,* 18:2.

Chan, Kwok Bun, ed.
1990   "Indochinese Refugees: 15 Years Later," *Southeast Asian Journal of Social Science,*
        18(special issue).

Chen, Yintao and Liao Liqiong
1989   "International Emigration from Guangdong after the Implementation of Economic
        Reform and Opening to the Outside World: Its Characteristics and Trends." Paper
        presented at the International Academic Conference on Population Migration and
        Urbanization in China, Beijing, December 6-8.

Cheung, P.P.L.
1991   "Social and Economic Implications of Singapore's Immigration and Emigration Pat-
        terns." Paper presented at the International Conference on Migration, Centre for
        Advanced Studies, National University of Singapore, February 7-9.

Connell, J. and J. Wang
1991   "Distant Victims? The Impact of the Gulf War on International Migration to the Middle
        East from Asia." In *Gulf War and Environmental Problems.* Edited by K.S.
        Ramachandran. New Delhi.

Cremer, G.
1988   "Deployment of Indonesian Migrants in the Middle East: Present Situation and
        Prospects," *Bulletin of Indonesian Economic Studies,* 24:73-86.

Dalglish, C.
1989   Refugees from Vietnam. London: Macmillan.

Daniels, R.
1988   Asian America: Chinese and Japanese in the United States since 1850. Seattle: University of Washington Press.

Demery, L.
1986   "Asian Labor Migration: An Empirical Assessment." In Asian Labor Migration: Pipeline to the Middle East. Edited by F. Arnold and N.M. Shah. Boulder: Westview.

DSE
1987   International Labour Migration in the Philippines and South East Asia. Manila: German Foundation for International Development (DSE).

Economic and Social Commission for Asia and the Pacific
1986   Returning Migrant Workers: Exploratory Studies. Asian Population Studies Series, No. 79. Bangkok: ESCAP.

———
1985   Report of the Policy Workshop on International Migration in Asia and the Pacific. New York: United Nations.

Fawcett, J.T. and B.V. Cariño, eds.
1987   Pacific Bridges: The New Immigration from Asia and the Pacific Islands. Staten Island, NY: Center for Migration Studies.

Friedmann, J.
1986   "The World City Hypothesis," Development and Change, 17:69-83.

Gould, W.T.S., ed.
1988   "Skilled International Migration," Geoforum, 19:381-445.

Guiness, P.
1990   "Indonesian Migrants in Johor: An Itinerant Labour Force," Bulletin of Indonesian Studies, 26:117-131.

Gunasekaran, S. and T. Koh
1991   "Southeast Asian Migration to Canada, 1981-1988: A Flow Analysis." Paper presented at the International Conference on Migration, Centre for Advanced Studies, National University of Singapore, February 7-9.

Gunasekaran, S. and G. Sullivan
1990   "Cross-border Labour Flows in Southeast Asia," Southeast Asian Affairs 1990.

Gunatilleke, G., ed.
1986   Migration of Asian Workers to the Arab World. Tokyo: The United Nations University.

Hawkins, F.
1989   Critical Years in Immigration: Canada and Australia Compared. Kingston and Montreal: McGill Queen's University Press.

Health and Welfare Canada
1989   Charting Canada's Future: A Report of the Demographic Review. Ottawa: Health and Welfare Canada.

Heer, D.M.
1986   "Immigration as a Counter to Below-Replacement Fertility in the United States." In
        Below Replacement Fertility in Industrial Societies. Edited by K. Davis, *et al. Population
        and Development Review,* 12(supplement):262-269.

Hsieh, Kao-Chiao, *et al.*
1989   *An Investigation of the Current Situation and Problems of Emigration* (in Chinese). Taipei:
        Development Review Council.

Hugo, G.
1991   "Population Movements in Indonesia: Recent Developments and Their Implications."
        Paper presented at the International Conference on Migration, Centre for Advanced
        Studies, National University of Singapore, February 7-9.

_____
1987   "Forgotten Refugees: Postwar Forced Migration within Southeast Asian Countries."
        In *Refugees: A Third World Dilemma.* Edited by J.R. Rogge. Totowa, New Jersey:
        Rowman and Littlefield.

Hugo, G. and Chan Kwok Bun
1990   "Conceptualizing and Defining Refugee and Forced Migrations in Asia," *Southeast
        Asian Journal of Social Science,* 18:28-33.

Huguet, J.
1991   "The Future of International Migration Within Asia." Paper presented at the 17th
        Pacific Science Congress, Honolulu, May 27-June 2.

Kao, C.H.C.
1971   *Brain Drain: A Case Study of China.* Taipei: Mei Ya Publications.

King, A.D.
1990   *Global Cities: Post-Imperialism and the Internationalization of London.* London: Rutledge.

Kuznets, P.W.
1987   "Koreans in America: Recent Migration from South Korea to the United States." In *The
        Economics of Mass Migration in the Twentieth Century.* Edited by S. Klein. New York:
        Paragon.

Lee, C. and G. de Vos, eds.
1981   *Koreans in Japan: Ethnic Conflict and Accommodation.* Berkeley: University of California
        Press.

Lee, J.S.
1991   "Capital and Labor Mobility in Taiwan." Paper presented at the Workshop on Labor
        Flows to Taiwan, Academia Sinica, Taipei, June 6-8.

Li, Si-ming
1989   "Labour Mobility, Migration and Urbanization in the Pearl River Delta Area," *Asian
        Geographer,* 8:35-60.

Martin, P.L.
1991   "Labor Migration in Asia," *International Migration Review,* 25:176-193.

Mori, H.
1990   "An Estimate of the Inflow of Illegal Workers into Japan (1975-1988)," *Journal of International Economic Studies*, 4:63-82.

Nagai, H. and M.S.V. Amante
1991   "Foreign Workers in the Japanese Labour Market: Case Study of Filipino 'Dekasegi Rodosha'." Paper presented at the International Conference on Migration, Centre for Advanced Studies, National University of Singapore, February 7-9.

Neuwirth, G.
1987   "Socioeconomic Adjustment of Southeast Asian Refugees in Canada." In *Refugees: A Third World Dilemma*. Edited by J.R. Rogge. Totowa, New Jersey: Rowman and Littlefield.

Papademetriou, D.G.
1990   "Current Issues in U.S. Immigration Policy." Paper presented at the Conference on National Immigration Outlook, Melbourne, November 14-16.

Park, I.H., *et al.*
1990   *Korean Immigrants and U.S. Immigration Policy: A Predeparture Perspective*. Papers of the East-West Population Institute, No. 114. Honolulu: East-West Population Institute.

Price, C.A.
1974   *The Great White Walls Are Built: Restrictive Immigration to North America and Australia 1836-1888*. Canberra: Australian National University Press.

Purcell, V.
1965   *The Chinese in Southeast Asia*. London: Oxford University Press.

Rigg, J.
1989   *International Contract Labour Migration and the Village Economy: The Case of Tambon Don Han, Northeastern Thailand*. Papers of the East-West Population Institute, No. 112. Honolulu: East West Population Institute.

_____
1988   "Perspectives on Migrant Labouring and the Village Economy in Developing Countries: The Asian Experience in a World Context," *Progress in Human Geography*, 12:66-86.

Rogge, J.R., ed.
1987   *Refugees: A Third World Dilemma*. Totowa, New Jersey: Rowman and Littlefield.

Russell, S.S.
1986   "Remittances from International Migration: A Review in Perspective," *World Development*, 14:677-696.

Salt, J. and A. Findlay
1989   "International Migration of Highly-skilled Manpower: Theoretical and Development Issues." In *The Impact of International Migration on Developing Countries*. Edited by R.T. Appleyard. Paris: OECD.

Samuel, T.S.
1991   "Contemporary Immigration Policies: Canada, the United States and Mexico." Paper
        presented at Multidisciplinary Conference on Contemporary United States-Canadian-
        Mexico Relations, University of Calgary, May 2-5.

Seok, H.
1986   "Republic of Korea." In *Migration of Asian Workers to the Arab World*. Edited by G.
        Gunatilleke. Tokyo: The United Nations University.

Skeldon, R.
1991a   "Emigration and the Future of Hong Kong," *Pacific Affairs*, 63:500-523.

———
1991b   "Hong Kong and Singapore as Nodes in an International Migration System." Paper
        presented at the International Conference on Migration, Centre for Advanced Stud-
        ies, National University of Singapore, February 7-9.

———
1990   *Population Mobility in Developing Countries: A Reinterpretation*. London: Belhaven Press.

Smart, J.E.
1986   "Worker Circulation between Asia and the Middle East," *Pacific Viewpoint*, 27:1-28.

Stahl, C.W.
1991a   "South-North Migration in the Asia-Pacific Region," *International Migration*, 29:163-
        193.

———
1991b   "International Migration in the Asian Region." Paper presented at the Conference on
        International Manpower Flows and Foreign Investment in the Asian Region, Tokyo,
        September 9-12.

———
1985   "Labor Migration amongst the ASEAN Countries." In *Urbanization and Migration in
        ASEAN Development*. Edited by P.M. Hauser, *et al*. Tokyo: National Institute for
        Research Advancement.

Stahl, C.W. and F. Arnold
1986   "Overseas Workers' Remittances in Asian Development," *International Migration Re-
        view*, 20:899-925.

Stahl, C.W. and A. Habib
1991   "Emigration and Development in South and Southeast Asia." In *The Unsettled Rela-
        tionship: Labor Migration and Economic Development*. Edited by D.G. Papademetriou and
        P.L. Martin. Westport, CT: Greenwood Press.

Sumalee, Pitayanon
1986   "Thailand." In *Middle East Interlude: Asian Workers Abroad*. Edited by M.I. Abella and
        Y. Atal. Bangkok: UNESCO.

Supang, Chantavanich and E. Bruce Reynold, eds.
1988   *Indochinese Refugees: Asylum and Resettlement*. Asian Studies Monograph No. 39. Bang-
        kok: Chulalongkorn University.

Taylor, C.
1988   *The Role of Immigration in Determining Canada's Eventual Population Size.* Population
        Working Paper No. 11. Ottawa: Employment and Immigration.

Taylor, J.
1991   *Immigration and Its Labour Market Impact in the Northern Territory.* Canberra: Australian
        Government Publishing Service.

Tsay, Chin-lung
1991   "Labor Flows from Southeast Asia to Taiwan: Size, Characteristics and Impact." Paper
        presented at the Workshop on Labor Flows to Taiwan, Academia Sinica, Taipei, June
        6-8.

Tsay, Hong-chiu
1991   "Foreign Workers in Taiwan: Demographic Characteristics, Related Problems and
        Policy Implications." Paper presented at the International Conference on Migration,
        Centre for Advanced Studies, National University of Singapore, February 7-9.

Weiner, M.
1989   *The Origins of the Korean Community in Japan, 1910-1923.* New Jersey: Humanities Press
        International.

Wickberg, E., ed.
1982   *From China to Canada: A History of the Chinese Communities in Canada.*   Toronto:
        McClelland and Stewart.

Witayakorn, Chiengkul
1986   "Thailand." In *Migration of Asian Workers to the Arab World.* Edited by G. Gunatilleke.
        Tokyo: The United Nations University.

Wooden, M., et al.
1990   *Australian Immigration: A Survey of the Issues.* Canberra: Australian Government Pub-
        lishing Service.

Wu, H.L. and K.J. Lan
1991   "Labor Shortage in Taiwan." Paper presented at the Workshop on Labor Flows to
        Taiwan, Academia Sinica, Taipei, June 6-8.

Yap, Mui Teng
        Singapore's New Immigration Policy, 1989: Benefits and Pitfalls. Occasional Paper. Insti-
        tute of Policy Studies, National University of Singapore. (forthcoming)

Zolberg, A.R., et al.
1989   *Escape from Violence: Conflict and the Refugee Crisis in the Developing World.* New York:
        Oxford University Press.

Part X
The State-System and Migration

SOCIAL PROBLEMS, VOL. 26, NO. 4, April 1979

ILLEGAL IMMIGRATION AND THE INTERNATIONAL SYSTEM, LESSONS FROM RECENT LEGAL MEXICAN IMMIGRANTS TO THE UNITED STATES*

ALEJANDRO PORTES
Duke University

Contrary to conventional views, the process of illegal Mexican immigration does not necessarily originate in the most backward or rural segments of the Mexican population and is not necessarily destined to the agricultural sector of the U.S. economy. Data from a recent sample of formerly undocumented Mexican immigrants indicate that an important segment of this population has nonrural origins, comparatively high levels of education, industrial and service occupational backgrounds, and that most are headed for urban areas and occupations rather than rural areas and agricultural occupations in the United States. These results question the common interpretation that the illegal flow of immigrants is a consequence of economic dualism and rural backwardness in Mexico. They support instead the idea that such immigration is an outgrowth of the accelerating contradictions brought about by capitalist development in Mexico and In other nations in the U.S. periphery. Such international labor transfers are analyzed here as integral components of the progressive articulation of the world economy, a process quite apt to continue linking the U.S. and the Mexican economies. Recently proposed U.S. programs to deal with illegal immigration are reviewed from this perspective. Limitations of using the nation-state as the main unit of analysis and of having an exclusively national perspective on the illegal movement are highlighted.

To assess the foreign policy implications of a new immigration policy, one must first understand its domestic implications for the countries involved. My purpose in this paper is to examine the internal significance of illegal or undocumented immigration for the countries where it originates, as a necessary background against which to evaluate the Carter Administration's proposed policies. For this purpose, I will present data from an ongoing study of Mexican immigration, one addressing at least some of the questions generally asked about the nature of the movement. On the basis of these data and other recent studies, I will analyze (briefly) the Administration's policies for dealing with this illegal flow.

It is important to begin by clarifying what illegal immigration is *not*. It is not, first of all, a flow coming from a single country. The overwhelming representation of Mexico in apprehension statistics is, in part, a function of the deployment practices of the Border Patrol, which tends to concentrate its efforts along the southern border. Although Mexican immigrants are certainly a majority of the illegal or undocumented population, the proportional representation of other countries—especially those from the Caribbean—is not insignificant (Office of the U.S. Attorney General, 1978). A relatively novel twist in Caribbean immigration is furnished by Dominican workers who are reported to enter the United States surreptitiously be crossing the Mona passage into Puerto Rico. Illegal immigration, then, should not be conceived simply as a process involving only Mexico and the United States, but as one originating in several peripheral societies.

Second, illegal immigration is not only caused by "push" forces in the original countries, but by the needs and demands of the receiving economy. The relative stability of the illegal flow, year

* Paper presented at the session on "Undocumented Mexican Workers" meetings of the Society for the Study of Social Problems, San Francisco, September 1978. This is a modified version of a statement originally delivered at the hearings on "Undocumented Workers: Implications for U.S. Policy in the Western Hemisphere" held by the U.S. House Subcommittee on Inter-American Affairs, Washington, D.C., July 26, 1978. The data are part of the project "Latin American Immigrant Minorities in the United States," supported by grants MH 27666-03 from the National Institute of Mental Health and SOC 77-22089 from the National Science Foundation.

after year, cannot be attributed to an impoverished alien population "overwhelming" the U.S. borders; it must be acknowledged that this flow of immigrants fulfills important needs for agricultural and urban industrial firms in the United States. Clearly, the persisting relationship illegal immigration creates is a symbiotic one, simultaneously fulfilling concealed but nonetheless real economic needs—on both sides of the border (see Portes, 1977a, b; Bach 1978b).

Third, illegal immigration is not primarily a movement of economic "refugees" in search of wefare, but one of workers in search of job opportunities. The illegal flow is, above all, a displacement of labor. More specifically, it is a displacement of low-wage labor, advantageous for many enterprises.

Fourth, illegal immigration is not necessarily permanent. Available studies of Mexican immigration at its points of origin, as well as data from this study, suggest that there is a significant proportion of return migration. The dominant stereotype concerning illegal immigration still couples the image of "impoverished masses overwhelming the border" with the idea that those who cross the gates of the land-of-plenty do so never to return. But empirical research suggests that many illegal immigrants do return and that the process is a complex one often involving cyclical entries and departures from the United States (see Cornelius, 1978). Reasons for this pattern are not difficult to understand once one realizes that, although work-opportunities and wages are higher in the United States, the money saved from wages can be used for consumption or reinvestment at much higher rates in the country of origin.

The aspects of illegal immigration just reviewed are not, however, the only commonly-held ideas about the nature of illegal immigration. They are merely the ones most convincingly clarified by past research. The following results begin to address a fifth and so far underresearched aspect—the socioeconomic backgrounds and present characteristics of the immigrants themselves.

THE STUDY

The data presented below come from a study of 822 documented Mexican immigrants interviewed at the point of arrival in the United States during 1972–73. Interviews were conducted in Spanish immediately after completion of immigration formalities. Interviews took place over a nine-month period at border check points in El Paso and Laredo. These are the two major ports of entry along the Texas border, and second and third, respectively, for Mexican immigrants in the nation.

Because of the exploratory nature of the study, the sample was limited to males in the economically productive ages, 18 to 60. Among Mexican immigrants, this group can be assumed to comprise the majority of family heads and self-supporting individuals. Immigrants were interviewed on a first-come basis during regular office hours. A few who crossed at night could not be interviewed. The refusal rate was less than 2 percent.

Statistical comparisons show that this sample is unbiased with respect to the universe of Mexican immigrants during fiscal year 1973 in such characteristics as average age, occupation and education. Because of the geographic location of field sites, the sample does overestimate immigrants originating in central and eastern Mexico and destined for Texas, Arizona, New Mexico and Illinois, and underestimates those originating in western Mexico and destined for California. Except for the latter limitation, the sample appears generally representative of legal Mexican immigration.

The question then is, what relevance does this sample have for illegal immigration? Several past studies have noted the intimate relationship between undocumented and documented Mexican immigration to the United States. The reason is that illegal immigrants can frequently manage to regularize their status through the "family reunification" provision of the 1965 Immigration Law. According to previous studies, legal Mexican immigration differs from most immigrant flows in the past because most of the people involved are not first-comers, but already *de facto* residents of the United States (see Stoddard, 1976).

Results from the present study confirm this impression. Fully 43.7 percent of the sample came outside immigration quota limits as spouses of U.S. citizens (IR-1 visas). An additional 4.7 percent came as children of U.S. citizens (IR-2 visas). The Immigration and Naturalization Service does not break down figures on quota immigrants from the Western Hemisphere (SA-1 visas) by specific categories. Our belief is, however, that most of the 46.5 percent of quota immigrants in the sample received visas as spouses or immediate relatives of U.S. permanent residents.

When asked, 61.5 percent said they had resided previously in the United States. That figure is probably an underestimate, because some respondents might have been reluctant to report prior (illegal) entry: collating responses to a number of other relevant questions, we arrived at an estimate that 69.9 percent of the sample could be reliably regarded as having resided in the United States for extended periods prior to documented entry.

The point of these figures is that the study of legal Mexican immigration is, to a large extent, identical to that of *prior* illegal immigration. No claim is made that former illegal immigrants identified in this manner are representative of the total illegal population. They represent, however, an important and so far unresearched sector of that universe. Their characteristics ideally should be compared with those of illegals identified by other means, such as official apprehensions. Still, the present data offer an initial glimpse of those immigrants who have not only succeeded in remaining in the United States, but have consolidated their position through legal entry.

TABLE 1

Salience of Economic Problems for Recent Mexican Immigrants to the United States 1972-73

Main Reason for Coming to the U.S.	%	Major Problem Confronting Mexico at Present	%
Reunite with family	28.3	No Major Problems	7.5
Work, wages, better living conditions	49.5	*Economic Problems*: Poverty, unemployment, high prices, housing, etc.	61.1
Education for self and children	9.7		
Self-improvement in general, achieve independence	4.3	*Legal and Political Problems*: Corruption, inefficient bureaucracy, antiquated laws, lack of democracy, etc.	13.7
To learn more	1.7		
Likes the U.S.	2.9		
Other reasons	3.7	*Class Inequality*: Indifference of the rich, exploitation of the people, control by those on top	1.8
Total	100.0 (N = 818)[1]		
		Educational Problems: Lack of schools, teachers, illiteracy, etc.	7.0
		Crime Problems: Thieves, alcoholism, prostitution, drugs, etc.	6.3
		Other Problems	2.6
		Total	100.0 (N = 732)[2]

[1]Missing data = 4.
[2]Excludes 90 people who did not know or did not answer.

428   PORTES

RESULTS

Everyone concerned with the process believes that illegal immigration occurs because of economic reasons: immigrants come to take advantage of the superior economic opportunities offered by a developed economy. The usual companion impression is that illegal immigrants must come from the most impoverished and backward sectors of their country of origin. In the specific case of Mexico, undocumented migration to the United States has, for decades, been associated with the plight of a largely illiterate and dispossessed rural population (Briggs, 1978; Santibañez, 1930). The dominant image held of surreptitious border crossers has been that they are peasants, frequently unemployed at home and coming to perform agricultural work in the United States.

Tables 1 to 7, drawn from the present sample, afford the opportunity to test these assertions. First, there is no doubt that immigration from Mexico occurs for economic reasons. Asked for their main reason for coming to the U.S., 49.5 percent of immigrants in the sample responded in terms of work, wages and living conditions. This percentage equals those for all other response categories put together. Further, when asked what they considered was the major problem confronting Mexico, 61.1 percent mentioned poverty, unemployment, high prices and other economic difficulties (Table 1).

The hypothesis that immigrants come predominantly from rural communities is examined in Table 2 by comparing their community of origin (main locality of residence before age 16) with those of the overall population of Mexico. As seen in Table 2 the immigrant sample as a whole and immigrants with prior residence in the United States are more "urban" than the original population. In Mexico, 58 percent of the population lived in communities of less than 10,000 in 1970; so did 37.3 percent of all immigrants and 43.6 percent of immigrants with prior U.S. residence. Forty-eight percent of the formerly undocumented immigrants, however, came from urban communities of 20,000 or more; and the figure for the total Mexican population is only 35 percent.

A related notion is that illegal immigrants are destined primarily to small agricultural communities in the United States. This rural-to-rural migration pattern has figured prominently in most prior descriptions of the flow (Santibañez, 1930; Buroway, 1976). Table 3 presents the size-distribution of communities where immigrants intended to reside. Only 15.5 percent of the total sample and 16.4 percent of immigrants with prior U.S. residence planned to live in communities of 10,000 or less. At the other extreme, fully 73 percent of both formerly undocumented

TABLE 2

*Size-Class of Community of Origin of Mexican Immigrants and Distribution of
Total Mexican Population*

| Population | Immigrant's Community of Origin, 1972–73[1] | | Mexico–1970[2] |
	Prior Residence in the U.S. %	Total Sample %	%
9,999 or less	43.6	37.3	57.7
10,000–19,999	8.3	7.1	7.1
20,000–99,999	20.2	20.5	12.0
100,000 or more	27.9	35.1	23.2
Totals	100.0	100.0	100.0
	(N = 564)	(N = 808)[3]	(N = 48,381,547)

[1]Source: Project data.
[2]Source: U.N., *Demographic yearbook*, 1971–Table 10.
[3]Missing data = 14.

TABLE 3

Size-Class of Community of Destination of Mexican Immigrants, 1972–73

Population of Intended U.S. Community of Residence	Immigrants with Prior U.S. Residence %	Total Sample %
9,999 or less	16.4	15.5
10,000–19,999	1.8	1.8
20,000–99,999	9.0	9.8
100,000–499,999	18.7	26.5
500,000 or more	54.1	46.4
Totals	100.0	100.0
	(N = 567)	(N = 812)[1]

[1]Missing data = 10.

immigrants and of the total sample planned to reside in cities of 100,000 or more; of these, 54 and 46 percent, respectively, planned to live in cities of over half a million. Clearly, these immigrants not only come from cities in Mexico, far more than the majority intend to seek residence in metropolitan areas of the United States.

A third characteristic imputed to illegal Mexican immigrants is that they are either illiterates or come from the least educated sectors of the source population. In one of the best available studies, Samora (1971) found that 28 percent of apprehended *mojados* had never attended school. Similarly, North and Houstoun (1976) reported that 43.5 percent of their sample of apprehended Mexican immigrants had received 4 years of education or less. These conclusions can again be examined on the basis of the present data. Figures in Table 4 compare various indicators of educational attainment for the immigrants studied and for the Mexican population. As seen in Table 4, the proportion of illiterates among such immigrants is much lower than for all adult Mexicans. Similarly, the percentages of immigrants (both the total set and those with prior U.S. residence) who completed primary education or had at least some secondary education is almost twice as high as the corresponding figure for the adult Mexican population. Clearly, while these immigrants by no means belong to the university-trained elite, they are from among those in the working class who have had at least some access to formal schooling and, in the process, acquired modest educational credentials.

TABLE 4

Education of Mexican Immigrants and Comparative Figures for the Mexican Population

Education	Mexican Immigrants–1973		Mexican Population
	Prior Residence in the U.S. %	Total Sample %	15 years of age and older–1970 %
Percent Illiterate (less than 2 years of formal schooling)	3.4	3.0	21.9[1]
Percent Completing Primary School or Higher	58.7	65.4	31.0[1]
Percent with Some Secondary Schooling	26.6	32.4	15.2
Percent Completing Secondary School or Higher	5.3	5.5	4.7
	(N = 563)	(N = 806)[2]	

[1]Male Population only.
[2]Missing data = 16.

TABLE 5

Last and Next-To-Last Sector of Employment of Mexican Immigrants, 1972–73

	Last Occupation		Next-to-last Occupation	
Sector	Immigrants with prior U.S. residence %	Total sample %	Immigrants with prior U.S. residence %	Total sample %
Out of labor market	1.9	6.1	6.7	15.2
Agriculture, Fishing, Mining	12.2	11.2	18.3	16.3
Manufacturing	29.3	24.0	22.7	17.9
Construction	17.3	15.1	15.5	13.0
Transport, Commerce, and Related Services	15.4	18.4	18.2	18.7
Personal Services	23.9	25.2	18.6	18.9
Totals	100.0 (N = 566)	100.0 (N = 808)[1]	100.0 (N = 555)	100.0 (N = 794)[2]

[1]Missing data = 14.
[2]Missing data = 28.

Finally, there is the question of occupational background. Again, the stereotype is that illegal Mexican immigrants are predominantly landless peasants and agricultural workers. In 1970, close to 40 percent of Mexico's economically active population was employed in the agrarian sector, so the proportion among illegal immigrants should if anything, be higher. Table 5 presents data on occupational sector for our immigrant sample. (Last and next-to-last occupations are included because immigrants with prior residence in the United States probably were last employed in *this* country. By asking a question concerning employment prior to the last one, we hoped to approximate their original occupation. Results are, however, similar in both cases.)

Only 12 percent (both of the total sample and of these immigrants with prior U.S. residence) were *last* employed in agriculture and other extractive activities. In contrast, a fourth of both samples were last employed in manufacturing, while transport, commerce and personal services

TABLE 6

Main and Next-To-Last Occupation of Mexican Immigrants, 1972–73

	Main Occupation		Next-to-last Occupation	
Occupational Level	Immigrants with Prior U.S. Residence %	Total Sample %	Prior U.S. Residence %	Total Sample %
Out of labor market	2.5	6.5	6.5	15.1
Agricultural laborer	12.5	11.6	17.7	15.5
Minor urban service laborer and unskilled worker	24.7	21.4	29.6	25.0
Semi-skilled and skilled urban worker	50.5	46.2	34.3	31.1
Intermediate urban service and white-collar worker	8.2	12.5	11.2	12.3
Manager and Professional	1.6	1.8	0.7	1.0
Totals	100.0 (N = 556)	100.0[1] (N = 799)	100.0 (N = 554)	100.0[2] (N = 796)

[1]Missing data = 23.
[2]Missing data = 26.

had employed an additional two-fifths. *Next*-to-last employment was in agriculture and other extractive industries for nearly 20 percent of these formerly undocumented immigrants, but much higher percentages had been in manufacturing and service occupations instead; in fact the latter category was the next-to-last occupation of over a third of the total sample and of those with prior U.S. residence. It should also be noted that rates of reported *un*employment decreased significantly in the period from next-to-last to last occupation, and were especially low among former illegal immigrants (1.9%).

A related question is that of what occupations these immigrants originally had. The relevant data are presented in Table 6. Frequencies for main and next-to-last occupations are presented. (Main occupation refers to the job the immigrant declared he had mostly pursued as an adult.) Results for both variables are again similar. Agricultural labor represents 12 percent of the distribution for main occupations and close to a fifth for next-to-last occupation. But the modal category in both cases is "skilled and semiskilled urban worker," followed by that of "unskilled worker and urban service laborer." Close to half of the immigrants declared skilled and semiskilled trades as their main occupation, and a third had such trades as their next-to-last occupation. Roughly a fourth of the sample, finally, reported unskilled and minor urban service occupations as main and next-to-last occupations.

These results contradict the common impression that illegal Mexican immigrants are mostly rural workers. Most men in the sample are manual workers, but in urban-based occupations. And most of these immigrants, whether formerly undocumented or new arrivals, do not intend to pursue farm occupations in the United States. Table 7 compares the occupational distribution for the total U.S. population with: (a) the universe of immigrants arriving in 1974; (b) the total legal Mexican immigration during that year; and (c) formerly undocumented immigrants in the sample.

Among all legal immigrants to the United States in recent years (i.e., those from all nations),

TABLE 7

Occupational Distribution of Active U.S. Labor Force, Total Fiscal Year 1974 Immigrants, Total Mexican Immigrants, and Immigrants with Prior U.S. Residence

Category	U.S.–1970[1]	Declared First Occupation in the U.S.		
		FY 74[2] Immigrants	FY 74[2] Mexican Immigrants	Mexican Immigrants with Prior U.S. Residence 1972–73[3]
Professional, Technical, and Kindred	14.1	23.5	2.2	0.8
Managers and Proporietors	14.1	6.1	1.4	0.6
Farmers and Farm Managers	3.0	–	–	–
Clerical and Sales	12.7	10.7	3.5	4.9
Craftsmen and Kindred	20.9	13.2	7.7	18.5
Operatives	17.9	11.9	7.9	
Service Workers Including Private Household	8.2	17.8	27.5	11.9
Laborers, except Farm	7.3	12.1	45.4	52.7
Farm Laborers	1.8	4.7	4.4	10.6
Total	100.0	100.0	100.0	100.0

[1]As percentage of the occupationally active population. Source: *U.S. Census, Current Population Report-Persons of Spanish Origin in the U.S.*-Series P-20, No. 280, 1975.
[2]As percentage of occupationally active immigrants. Source: U.S. Immigration and Naturalization Service, *1975 Annual Report.*
[3]Recoded occupational category estimates for comparison with census classification Source: Project data.

the percentage of professionals and technicians has been higher than that among the total U.S. population. This has not been the case, however, for Mexican immigrants, among whom the proportion of highly-trained occupations is insignificant. This trend again confirms the distinct character of Mexican immigration and its ability to bypass occupational certification requirements of the Immigration Law by taking advantage of family reunion provisions.

Farm work is not, however, the modal *intended* occupation for Mexican immigrants. For the total 1974 Mexican immigrant cohort, Table 7 shows that the proportion of farm laborers is 4 percent, essentially the same as for total immigration during the year. Among sample immigrants with prior U.S. residence, the proportion increases to 11 percent, but it is still a minority. The bulk of Mexican immigrants concentrates in the category of nonfarm laborer—unskilled and semiskilled urban workers. Other substantial percentages are found in the categories of service workers and of craftsmen and operatives, all urban-based occupations. This holds true both for the universe of legal Mexican immigrants and for our sample of formerly undocumented ones.

Several caveats are clearly in order at this point. First, these results refer only to Mexican immigration. As seen above, illegal immigration comes at present from several countries. Second, the data for illegal immigrants refer only to a sample of those who have regularized their situation in the United States. Such a group cannot be taken as representative of the total population of illegal Mexican immigrants. Studies based on interviews of apprehended illegals, such as those by Samora (1971) and North and Houstoun (1976), report findings in closer agreement with the generalized image of illegal immigration. The relative numerical significance of the different immigrant profiles emerging from alternative research and sampling strategies remains to be determined.

Nevertheless, it is still remarkable how systematically the present sample differs from the conventional image of illegal immigration. To summarize, most of these immigrants with prior residence in the United States came from cities in Mexico and were bound for metropolitan areas in the United States. Most were literate and, as a whole, exceeded the educational attainment of the source population. Only one-eighth had worked mostly as farm laborers or in related activities; the vast majority were concentrated in urban occupations—manufacturing and service. *Intended* first occupations in the United States were also overwhelmingly urban.

Given the probable importance of the universe represented by these immigrants, one must then ask why results are so different from conventional expectations. To answer, one must entertain a perspective contrasting markedly with that held by most scholars and by the general public.

IMMIGRATION AND DEVELOPMENT

Some reasons why the background of these undocumented immigrants differs from usual expectations can be found in a closer examination of Mexican society itself. Usual "economic dualist" views divide the country into a modern-urban Mexico and a rural-traditional Mexico, and assign illegal immigration to the latter. And the common corollary is that "as modernity overcomes tradition" the sources of the illegal flow will progressively be eliminated.

The above data suggest that a substantial proportion of illegal immigration comes from social groups already modernized, already living in cities and having above-average education. I will argue that the sources of this illegal immigration are not to be found in a backward and traditional rural economy but in the very contradictions accompanying Mexican *development*.

To summarize an argument made before, the process of capitalist industrialization in Mexico has been marked by four major contradictions. First, it mobilized a rural population, cutting traditional ties to the land without offering opportunities for alternative employment. The Mexican revolution, largely fought on the "agrarian question" (Womack, 1968), put many previously isolated peasants in contact with the benefits of modern urban civilization. Neither the triumph of the revolution nor the dominant economic strategy followed afterwards succeded in responding to the new needs for mass employment.

In a country like Mexico, open and declared unemployment is a luxury; few really have access to the system of social security which might subsidize periods of enforced idleness. In 1969, only 20.9 percent of the economically active population (EAP) was covered by Mexican social security (Economic Commission for Latin America, 1974). Thus, it is not surprising that in the 1970 census declared unemployment amounted to only 3.8 percent of the EAP. Much more significant are the figures on disguised unemployment and on underemployment, representing people who must somehow survive with neither minimally remunerated nor stable employment. Twelve percent of the Mexican EAP was estimated to be in conditions of disguised unemployment and an additional 35–40 percent was underemployed in 1970. Together, they amount to almost half of the labor force (Urquidi, 1974; Alba, 1978).

Second, Mexico has experienced the contradiction of a sustained rate of economic growth coupled with an increasingly unequal distribution of national income. During the last three decades, the average annual rate of growth in national GNP has been 6 percent. During the same period, inequality in the distribution of income has not decreased, it has increased—substantially. By 1973, Mexico had a GNP per capita of (U.S.) $774. The top 5 percent of the population had 29 percent of the national income, and the top 20 percent received 57 percent of the national income. At the other extreme, the poorest 20 percent received an income share of only 4 percent (United Nations, 1974). Eighteen percent of the population had annual incomes of less than (U.S.) $75 (cf. Portes and Ferguson, 1977).

Third, Mexico has absorbed an increasingly modern culture and the modern cult of advanced consumption, while denying the mass of the population the means to participate even minimally in it. As in the advanced countries, the mass media have made sure that the attractions of modern consumerism reach the most remote corners of the country. Especially in urban areas, people are literally bombarded with advertising for new products and the presumed benefits that their acquisition would bring. But underemployment and a highly unequal income distribution actually deny access to these goods to the majority of the population (Eckstein, 1977; Alba, 1978).

This situation, which has been labelled the syndrome of "modernity-in-underdevelopment," provides an appropriate background for interpreting some of the findings in this study. It is not surprising that a sizable proportion of undocumented immigrants are neither rural nor illiterate, but come from cities and have above-average education and occupational training. These groups are most susceptible to the emigration alternative for they are most exposed to the contradictions between the desire to consume and the impossibility of doing so. The urban working class, especially its most literate groups, are more closely integrated into modern Mexican society than into the remaining enclaves of subsistence agriculture. For this reason, they are most subject to the contradictions of the system.

Fourth, Mexico faces the contradiction between a formally nationalistic government policy and an international reality of increasing dependence involving control of the Mexican economy by foreign sources. Approximately half of the 400 largest industries in Mexico are foreign-owned, predominantly by U.S. corporations. Over 25 percent of industrial production, especially in the most technologically advanced and dynamic branches, is generated by multinational companies. There are more subsidiaries of major U.S. multinationals in Mexico than in any other Latin American country and these foreign companies are buying up an increasing number of domestic firms (Vaupel and Curhan, 1977).

Mexican foreign trade is entirely dominated by the United States, which accounted, in 1976, for 62 percent of the imports and received 56 percent of the exports. Mexican external public

434   PORTES

debt, which in 1955 represented 54 percent of foreign exchange earnings, had surpassed 160 percent by 1970 (Bach, 1978a).

This extreme external dependence has two major effects on the process of labor emigration. First, Mexican industrialization, carried out under foreign auspices, has been based on importation of capital-intensive technology. The success in productivity of this strategy has been impressive. Manufacturing far outdistances agriculture at present as the most important and most dynamic sector of the economy. Practically all consumer goods now sold in Mexico are produced domestically and the share of manufactured products among total exports is the highest for Latin America. These successes have not been shared, however, by the mass of the population since so few are employed by the industries. Manufacturing absorbs approximately one-fifth of the economically active population, having increased its share by only 5 percent since the early days of the Revolution. The urban *service* sector, not manufacturing, is the one in which employment has increased most rapidly during the last three decades (Cumberland, 1968). The increasing production of domestic goods, coupled with failure to widen the consumer market through employment in the industrial sector, has aggravated, in turn, the other contradictions of the system.

Second, the presence and influence of the United States have accelerated the modernization of Mexican culture and the spread of the cult of consumption. The North has come to appear to be the land where contradictions plaguing Mexico at present can be solved, at least for the individual. Massive emigration to the United States must be regarded as the natural response of part of the Mexican working class to conditions created *for them*, rather than *by them*. Efficient industry coupled with widespread underemployment, diffusion of modern styles of consumption coupled with high concentration of income in higher social classes, both are processes which cannot be understood apart from recognition of the heavy presence in Mexico of foreign, mostly U.S., capital and technology.

In the eyes of the Mexican worker, the United States stands as the place where the benefits of an advanced economy, promised but not delivered by the present national development strategy, can be turned into reality. It is only natural that many trek North in search of the means to acquire what transnational firms and the mass media have so insistently advertised for years. The individual immigrant data presented above and the analysis of the Mexican economic situation in this section have converged and show that illegal immigration has been propelled not by the failure of development strategies, but by their success. The movement does not occur because Mexico is poor and stagnant, but precisely because it has developed rapidly—in one particular direction. The main implication is that we in the United States should not expect that illegal immigration will fade away as Mexico becomes less rural and more developed. Instead, if Mexican development proceeds along the lines it has followed in the past, we must expect more, not less, pressures at the southern border.

POLICY PROPOSALS

Mexican immigration is not only the most sizable component of the illegal flow, but the one for which more information is available. With necessary modifications, I believe that the essentials of the situation just described apply to other countries from which undocumented immigrants come. Caribbean nations, especially the Dominican Republic, have also begun a process of economic development based on import-substitution industrialization, importation of capital-intensive technology, and mobilization of the rural population into urban areas.

The Carter Administration's proposals to deal with illegal immigration consist in essence, of three measures: 1) amnesty for illegal aliens who can prove continuous residence in the U.S. since 1970; 2) five-year work permits without unemployment and social security benefits for those coming after that date; and 3) strict enforcement of the border to prevent continuation of illegal entries. A great deal of attention has been focused on the first two provisions (see Portes, 1978), but it is the third one that is most important to any analysis of the foreign policy implications of these proposals. I will not discuss here the means proposed to close the border, but rather, the purpose. Also, I will not advance an alternative policy, but will only comment on the implications of the existing border enforcement proposal.

There are two ways of looking at the actors or contenders involved in the Administration's proposed policies. The more apparent one is to conceive of two nation-states, the United States and Mexico (or other source country), which have opposite interests. The decision to enforce the border is then taken to defend the interest of one national community even at the expense of the other. A second way of considering the process is to view the different nation-states not as separate entities, but as integral components of the same overarching international system. This world-system contains and indeed depends on the existence of national borders and national states, but both the nation-states and their borders function within the constraints imposed by the international totality.

In the specific case of international labor migration, the fundamental cleavage in the world-system is not between national states, but between social classes. Classes cut across national borders and may have interests contrary to those of the rest of the respective national populations. One could speak of capital and labor as the two relevant classes, but that is too general. Actually, there are four subclasses or class sectors primarily involved in the process: (a) foreign and domestic capital owners in Mexico (and the Mexican *state*); (b) competitive-sector enterprises in the United States; (c) unemployed and underemployed Mexican workers from rural and, as seen above, urban areas; and (d) workers in the United States who serve as an actual or potential labor force to competitive firms. Women and racial and ethnic minorities are disproportionately represented in this labor market.

Owners and managers in Mexico and the Mexican government are placed in the same category here because their interest in labor emigration is ultimately the same. Primarily, this is not an interest in would-be emigrants as an economic resource, but as a political threat. The contradictions of Mexican development and the mass of unemployed and underemployed are serious causes of concern for the future of the social order. This is especially true in a country which not so long ago witnessed popular revolutionary forces bring down an aristocratic regime. Emigration to the North functions in this situation as a welcome and important resource to maintain social peace and meliorate the tensions of economic growth without equality. For the Mexican state, the remittances (savings) sent by emigrants to the United States also represent an increasingly important means of counteracting balance-of-payments difficulties (Cornelius and Diez-Canedo, 1976).

Employers of illegal labor in the United States are not, by and large, major corporations but smaller competitive firms dependent for profits on holding down the costs of labor. In areas where illegals concentrate, many such firms have come to depend on this kind of labor for their very survival (North and Houstoun, 1976; Marshall, 1975). As stated above, illegal immigration thus establishes a symbiotic relationship among owners on both sides of the border, one in which the political legitimation needs of some and the economic labor-saving needs of others are served by the same process.

For the mass of Mexican workers, the best alternative in the long run is obviously a major transformation of the dominant economic order. No one lives in the long run, however, and in the here-and-now emigration to the United States offers many the best chance for fulfillment of their aspirations. As a respondent in Dinerman's recent study of emigrants from a village community in Lake Patzcuaro stated—he did not get too worried when money became scarce because "he could always go North" (Dinerman, 1978).

Illegal immigration does not pose an immediate threat to middle-class nonmanual workers, to artisans and highly skilled workers, and in general to workers organized in strong unions in the

United States. The reason is that illegal labor has neither sought nor gained entry into the mainstream of the American economy. No evidence exists that major corporations have knowingly hired a substantial number of undocumented immigrants. The class of workers in the United States most directly affected by illegal labor competition is precisely the class that is least organized and least able to articulate its interests: the largely female and nonwhite competitive labor sector. In areas where illegal immigrants concentrate, the situation is further confused by the fact that the apparent economic opposition between undocumented and domestic minority workers is tempered by cultural, ethnic and language affinities. To this day, many local unions and ethnic organizations are not certain whether they should oppose and denounce illegal immigrants, embrace them as part of the same community, or adopt some intermediate attitude.

In principle, the Administration's proposals appear progressive for they would strengthen the bargaining hand of domestic workers in the competitive sector, while forcing Mexico and other exporting countries to face their reality without the safety valve of emigration. Out of that situation, presumably, significant structural changes in the direction of equality might result. The configuration of class forces just outlined suggests, however, that the border enforcement clause will be difficult to maintain without a parallel program of regulated access to immigrant labor. On the other hand, border enforcement may be possible in the short run because the amnesty program, also part of the Administration's plan, would turn undocumented workers already in the country into a *de facto* immigrant contract labor force. What we must recognize, however, is that once this group is absorbed the same pressures can be expected to reassert themselves.

Neither the needs of employers of low-wage labor in the United States nor the class structure of Mexican society are likely to change significantly in the near future. The American state, at the center of the contemporary world economy, makes decisions affecting different sectors of American society not only directly but indirectly, through their repercussions in other nations integrated into the same system. It is in this sense that what appears on the surface as "foreign policy" is still domestic policy if we see it from the vantage point of the reality of the international economic system. The U.S. government cannot reasonably ignore the serious threats to political and economic stability that would be posed *in Mexico* by strict enforcement of the border. It can no more do so than ignore the opposition of a politically powerful sector of domestic employers. Despite the apparent intentions of the Administration and the probable eventual support of organized labor, it is not likely that the program as conceived will survive.

International labor migration thus represents a process remarkable for the contradictions between its determinants and the policy measures formulated to control it. The flow of illegal immigration is not an autonomous phenomenon of peripheral countries, but originates in the character of their externally-shaped development. The economic hegemony exercised by the United States over these countries produces patterns of industrialization within them which increase rather than decrease the pressure on their working classes. Conversely, the evolution of the world economy has produced an increasing reliance on foreign sources of cheap labor in the advanced capitalist nations. Precisely because these laborers have been made redundant in their own countries, they can be hired cheaply to counterbalance high wages for the domestic working class. Attempts to prevent such long run structural processes by administrative decisions to "close the border" or reduce the size of the "traditional" rural sector in the nations from which such workers flow are just alternative forms of official fantasy. Policies thus far formulated to deal with illegal immigration highlight the continuing gap between the reality of an internationalized political economy and the national standpoint from which its consequences are interpreted. Flows of capital and of labor are interrelated, international, and influenced by profit and wage levels and by persisting trends in the shares of wealth available to various social classes in the constituent nations of the world economy.

REFERENCES

Alba, Francisco
   1978   "Mexico's international migration as a manifestation of its development pattern." International
           Migration Review 12 (Winter):502–513.
Bach, Robert L.
   1978a   "Foreign policy implications of recent trends in Mexican Immigration." Testimony presented
           before the Committee on International Relations, U.S. House of Representatives, May 24.
   1978b   "Mexican immigration and the American State." International Migration Review 12
           (Winter):536–558.
Briggs, Vernon M.
   1978   "Labor market aspects of Mexican migration to the United States in the 1970s." Pp 204–225 in
           Stanley R. Ross (ed.), Views Across the Border: The United States and Mexico. Albuquerque:
           University of New Mexico Press.
Buroway, Michael
   1976   "The functions and reproduction of migrant labor: Comparative material from Southern Africa
           and the United States." American Journal of Sociology 81 (March):1050–1087.
Cornelius, Wayne A.
   1978   "Mexican migration to the United States: Causes, consequences, and U. S. responses." Center for
           International Studies, Migration and Development Group, Massachusetts Institute of Technology,
           July.
Cornelius, Wayne A. and Juan Diez-Canedo
   1976   "Mexican migration to the United States: The view from rural sending communities." Center for
           International Studies, Migration and Development Group, Massachusetts Institute of Technology,
           June.
Cumberland, Charles
   1968   Mexico: The Stuggle for Modernity. New York: Oxford University Press.
Dinerman, Ina R.
   1978   "Patterns of adaptation among households of U.S.-bound migrants from Michoacán, Mexico."
           International Migration Review 12 (Winter):485–501.
Eckstein, Susan
   1977   The Poverty of Revolution: The State and the Urban Poor in Mexico. Princeton, N.J.: Princeton
           University Press.
Economic Commission for Latin America
   1974   "Economic survey of Latin America, Part 3." United Nations Document E/CN.12/974/Add. 3.
Marshall, Ray
   1975   "Economic factors influencing the international migration of workers." Paper presented at the
           Conference on Contemporary Dilemmas of the Mexican-United States Border. San Antonio: The
           Weatherhead Foundation.
North, David S. and Marion F. Houstoun
   1976   The Characteristics and Role of Illegal Aliens in the U. S. Labor Market: An Exploratory Study.
           Mimeo. Washington, D.C.: Linton and Co.
Office of the U.S. Attorney General
   1978   "Illegal immigration: President's program." Mimeo, Washington D.C., February.
Portes, Alejandro
   1977a   "Why illegal migration? A structural perspective." Latin American Immigration Project Occa-
           sional Papers, Duke University.
   1977b   "Labor functions of illegal aliens." Society 14 (Sept.-Oct.):31–37.
   1978   "Towards a structural analysis of illegal immigration." International Migration Review 12
           (Winter):469–484.
Portes, Alejandro and D. Frances Ferguson
   1977   "Comparative ideologies of poverty and equity: Latin American and the United States." Pp.
           70–105 in Irving L. Horowitz (ed.), Equity, Income, and Policy: Comparative Studies in Three
           Worlds of Development." New York: Praeger.
Samora, Julian
   1971   Los Mojados: The Wetback Story. Notre Dame: Notre Dame University Press.
Santibañez, Enrique
   1930   Ensayo Acerca de la Inmigracion Mexicana a Estados Unidos. San Antonio: The Clegg Co.
Stoddard, Ellwyn R.
   1976   "A conceptual analysis of the 'Alien Invasion': Institutionalized support of illegal Mexican aliens
           in the U.S." International Migration Review 10 (Summer):157–189.
United Nations
   1974   "Report on the world social situation—Social trends in the developing countries, Latin American
           and the Caribbean." U. N. Document E/CN.5/512/Add. 1, 1974.
Urquidi, Victor L.
   1974   "Empleo y explosión demográfica." Demografía y Economía 8(2):141–153.

438   PORTES

Vaupel, James and Joan Curhan
    1973   The World's Multinational Enterprises: A Sourcebook of Tables. Boston: Harvard Business
            School.
Womack, John
    1968   Zapata and the Mexican Revolution. New York: Vintage Books.

[19]

Foreign Labor and Economic Development in Singapore[1]

Pang Eng Fong
Linda Lim
National University of Singapore

This article focuses on foreign labor and economic development in Singapore by reviewing the historical ebb and flow of foreign labor, presenting the prevailing government policy and philosophy on the importation of labor, contrasting the economic benefits and costs of foreign labor, describing common characteristics of foreign workers in Singapore, projecting the implications of such labor in Singapore and discussing policy alternatives.

EBB AND FLOW OF FOREIGN LABOR

The Singapore economy is historically founded on foreign labor. Most Singaporeans are the descendants of immigrants from China, India, Indonesia and Peninsular Maylaysia, accounting for most of the island's population growth from the founding of the city by the British in 1819 until the eve of World War Two. For most of this period, the British colonialists adopted a *laissez faire* policy towards Chinese immigration because it fitted in with their commercial and colonial interests. They were also responsible for bringing in Indian labor from British administered territories on the Indian subcontinent. While there was some free, independent movement of labor, much of the Chinese, Indian and Indonesian immigrant labor was indentured until 1910. Most were transient males. Many only passed through Singapore on their way to plantations, mines and public works sites, mostly in Peninsular Malaysia, and many eventually returned to their home countries after temporary stays there, or in Singapore itself.[2]

---

[1]Revised version of paper read at Department of Economics and Statistics Seminar, National University of Singapore, 17 September 1981.

[2] For a detailed discussion of the history of immigration into Singapore, *See*, P.E. Fong, 1976, "Migration, Public Policy and Social Development in Singapore", mimeographed paper

FOREIGN LABOR AND ECONOMIC DEVELOPMENT   549

The largest immigrant group were the Chinese, of whom six million—two and a half times the present population— landed in Singapore between 1895 and 1927 alone. Their flow was erratic, influenced both by market forces and by occasional colonial immigration regulations. Thus, the number of Chinese immigrants swelled during the rubber boom of the early twentieth century and the prosperous 1920s, but diminished during the 1930s depression and ceased during the two World Wars. In 1933, the British passed an Alien Ordinance, setting quotas on male immigration, but encouraging female immigration to normalize the sex ratio of the settled population. After World War Two, immigrant flows from China and India resumed at a low rate, and in 1953 a comprehensive Immigration Ordinance was enacted which strictly controlled the number and quality of immigrants entering Singapore. But internal immigration from Peninsular Malaysia continued freely until Singapore became an independent nation state in 1965, when it too became subject to controls.

Independent Singapore embarked on an ambitious economic development program. Rapid rates of growth in the late 1960s and early 1970s resulted in domestic labor shortages. As early as 1968, Singapore relaxed its tight immigration policy to let in temporary workers. At the peak of the economic boom in 1973, non-citizen work-permit holders reportedly numbered over 100,000, or about one-eighth of the total Singapore workforce. Most of them were from the southern states of Peninsular Malaysia, particularly Johore.

In addition to unskilled "guest workers" in the manufacturing, shipbuilding and construction industries, Singapore welcomed skilled workers and professionals, and entrepreneurs with industrial experience and capital, on a longer-term basis. In particular, highly qualified and/or wealthy Chinese from Maylasia, Hong Kong, Taiwan, Indonesia, and other Southeast Asian countries were readily granted employment passes and permanent residence.

The world recession of 1974/75 resulted in massive layoffs in Singapore's female-intensive export manufacturing industries which employed large numbers of foreign workers. The government initially requested employers to lay off foreign workers first, but many were reluctant to do so because these were their more senior, more stable

commissioned by Friedrich Ebert-Stiftung for a project on Migration and Social Development in ASEAN Countries.

and productive workers. There was, however, a reduction in new work-permit applications and approvals, and for the next few years, the foreign workforce in Singapore remained stable.

By 1978, the number of foreign workers was on the rise again, particularly in the booming manufacturing sector. In addition to workers from the "traditional" source of supply, Peninsular Maylasia, increasing recruitments were made of workers from "non-traditional" sources, including Indonesia, Thailand, Sri Lanka, India and Bangladesh. In 1979, the government instituted a "corrective" high-wage policy for three years, partly aimed at reducing this dependence on foreign labor. Employers, however, were still allowed to import workers.

Throughout the three years of the "corrective" wage policy, labor shortages have continued to grow as wages have risen, causing supply bottlenecks and delays, especially in the construction sector. It has become more difficult to recruit workers from the traditional source, Peninsular Maylasia, because of high labor demand and rising wages there. In mid-1981, the government decided to liberalize for two years the importation of all, skilled and unskilled foreign workers from both traditional and non-traditional sources, and is now stream-lining work-permit policies to facilitate their recruitment. Official productivity and growth targets for the 1980s project a continued and increasing reliance on foreign workers throughout the decade, despite an aggressive and ambitious economic restructuring program.

PUBLIC POLICY AND PHILOSOPHY

Government policy on the importation of foreign labor reflects primarily the need to fill the growing gap between labor demand and indigenous labor supply. But meeting domestic labor imbalances is only one of the Singapore government's motivations in liberalizing the inflow of foreign labor. While unskilled workers are welcomed so long as they are young, single, do not bring their families with them, and do not marry local citizens (in short, are discouraged and prevented by administrative restrictions from staying permanently), skilled workers, professionals and entrepreneurs are actively recruited and encouraged to make Singapore their home. The rationale is not just to increase the level of skills in a rapidly expanding economy, but to ensure that these skills are imparted to the local

FOREIGN LABOR AND ECONOMIC DEVELOPMENT   551

population and continue to be reproduced in future generations, thereby enhancing population quality.

Singapore planners expect that unskilled migrant workers will be necessary only in the short- to medium-term, whereas the demand for skilled workers and professionals will increase with economic restructuring. Whereas foreign engineers, management and technical personnel have been freely admitted into Singapore since the late 1960s, the 1980s are also seeing the increasingly free admission of other foreign professionals such as lawyers and doctors.

A related reason for encouraging the permanent immigration of skilled, professional and entrepreneurial personnel and the temporary immigration of unskilled foreign workers, is the assumption made by government leaders that immigrants possess and can stimulate in the local population desirable social values and work habits. Government leaders believe that immigrants are able, stable, hardworking and thrifty, and can rouse the competitive spirit of Singporeans. In 1976 Prime Minister Lee Kuan Yew said that immigrants,

> will do many jobs better than the next generation Singaporean would because the next generation Singaporean will have been brought up in an easier environment that has not deprived him of enough basic necessities to make him really want to work so hard.[3]

This sentiment was recently echoed by a "second-generation leader" Goh Chok Tong, former Minister for Trade and Industry, when he said that the importation of foreign labor would "spur" local workers to work harder because,

> There is nothing like the bitter, real-life experience of having to hunt for a job, and finding it difficult to get one, to make Singaporeans take seriously the call to increase productivity.[4]

In short, Singapore needs a "reserve army" of foreign labor to motivate local workers.

Given the government's earlier and continued concern that reliance on foreign labor might slow economic restructuring, the

---

[3] Quoted in P.E. Fong, "Public Policy on Population, Employment and Immigration". In *Public Policy and Population Change in Singapore*. Edited by P.S.J. Chen and J.T. Fawcett. New York: The Population Council, 1979:210.

[4] Quoted in "Spur Effect on Workers", *The Straits Times*, Singapore, June 20, 1981.

decision in mid-1981 to liberalize work-permits seems like a step backward. It takes time for rising wages to curb labor demand, because employers can absorb them in the short-run by organizational improvements, once-and-for-all shedding of surplus labor, and even by accepting temporary losses. The apparent retreat from this policy of curbing labor use seems to be motivated by official concern over the spiralling cost and price inflation of both commercial and residential property, due partly to the persistent shortage of construction labor. In the manufacturing sector, on the other hand, rising wages have restrained employment growth and labor mobility, and stimulated productivity. Easing controls on unskilled foreign labor under these circumstances thus reflects short-run considerations rather than long-run economic imperatives.

In 1982, as the Singapore economy, particularly its export manufacturing sector, began to be affected by worldwide recession, and a slowdown was projected for the hitherto active property development sector, the government reminded employers that "work permit holders from non-traditional countries have been allowed into Singapore only as a temporary measure" and would be phased out by 1984. Therefore,

> they (manufacturers) must further mechanize, automate, computerize and improve management to cut down on workers: or they will have to relocate their factories.[5]

Repatriation would affect particularly employees who have been using women workers from non-traditional sources, especially in manufacturing. These employers were urged instead to employ married Singaporean women in four-hourly work shifts. The long-run aim, then, is to restructure the economy to be entirely dependent on the citizen labor force, except for high-productivity workers who have traditionally been and will continue to be welcomed as permanent immigrants.

THE BENEFITS AND COSTS OF FOREIGN LABOR

The economic benefits of foreign labor to receiving or host countries

[5] Speech by the prime minister, reported in "Tárget: Wholly Singapore Workforce", *The Straits Times*, Singapore, Jan. 1, 1982.

are well known.[6] Imported workers add to the domestic labor supply, and reduce wage costs. In periods of economic boom, they relieve economy-wide or sectoral labor shortages which would otherwise slow down the rate of economic growth. In periods of recession, foreign labor can be readily retrenched and repatriated,[7] reducing the threat of unemployment for citizen workers. Labor imports thus stabilize cyclical fluctuations in the labor market of the receiving nation. To the extent that the availability of foreign labor as a potential or actual substitute for domestic labor also "disciplines" the latter, labor peace and productivity are enhanced. Labor imports increase not only the quantity, but also the range and flexibility of the host nation's human resources. The host country benefits from the employment of foreign skilled, semi-skilled and experienced workers, without having to bear the human capital investment costs of their education and training.

These benefits may be unequally distributed among different sections of the host nation's citizen population. Employers are likely to benefit more from the employment of foreign labor because it reduces their labor costs and increases profits. But citizen workers in competitive employment may find their job opportunities and wages reduced by the increased supply of labor provided by the foreigners. However, citizen workers may also benefit to the extent that the foreigners are employed in low-level jobs which they themselves are unwilling to perform. The employment of foreign labor in the production and delivery of labor-intensive goods and services maintains their low cost to the citizen consumer, whose real income is thereby maintained or improved.

But these short-term economic benefits of importing foreign labor may be offset by long-term costs to the economic development

---

[6] *See*, for example, I.M. Hume, "Some Economic Aspects of Labour Migration in Europe since the Second World War", in *Economic Factors in Population Growth*, edited by A.J. Coale. New York: Macmillan Press for the International Economic Association, 1976:491-518; C.W. Stahl, 1981, "Economic Development and the Export of Labour Services", paper prepared for the ASEAN-Australia Economic Relations Research Project, Workshop on Trade in Services, Australian National University; and Z. Ecevit and K.C. Zachariah, "International Labor Migration", *Finance &Development*, December 1978:32-37.

[7] However, the experience of Western European nations suggests temporary migrants are easier to import than to send home. *See*, Slater, "Migrant Employment, Recessions, and Return Migration: Some Consequences for Migration Policy and Development", *Studies in Comparative International Development*, 1979:3-22, Fall-Winter.

of the receiving nation. The availability and use of cheap foreign labor may encourage the development and maintenance of industries which could never be supported by local manpower supplies and skills.[8] By enabling the importing nation to remain competitive in labor-intensive industries, dependence on low-cost foreign labor may delay, inhibit or prevent frequired upgrading into more capital-intensive technologies in labor-short nations. The availability of skilled and experienced foreign labor may discourage investment in the education and training of citizen workers.[9] Employers of both low-skilled and high-skilled labor would have no incentive to develop ways of increasing the local labor supply, such as part-time, flexible-shift and homework schemes and wage inducements to increase the employment of married women citizens with young children, an important reserve of often educated and experienced domestic labor.

There are also short-run economic costs. Where there is already excess domestic demand for goods and services, the local consumption of foreign workers' wages to their home nations imposes a cost on the host nation's balance of payments through the drain of foreign exchange, and deprives it of savings for investment. The employment of labor intensive techniques, and of unskilled, inexperienced, and sometimes overworked, and undernourished foreign workers, may also lower productivity. In addition to these direct economic benefits and costs, foreign labor has demographic, social and political impacts on the receiving nation.

To the extent that controls on foreign labor restrict their duration of stay, prevent them from bringing their families, from marrying citizens and/or settling permanently in the receiving nation, the demographic effect is limited to a temporary increase in the cohort of young, single population in the host country. Where there are no such restrictions, or they are difficult to enforce, and especially

[8] An extreme case of distorted development based on foreign labor is found in the nations of the Arabian peninsula, who could not operate their vastly increased manufacturing and service industries without foreign labor, as both the absolute number and skill levels of their local workers are inadequate. In these countries, access to cheap imported labor has dissipated capital on ambitious, inefficient and expensive domestic development programs which will remain permanently dependent on supplies of foreign labor.

[9] For example, in the United States access to imported doctors and nurses may have inhibited the expansion of general-practitioner (as compared to specialist) level medical training, and the training of indigenous nursing staff.

FOREIGN LABOR AND ECONOMIC DEVELOPMENT   555

where the foreign workers are ethnically or culturally similar to the local population, many of them are likely to stay permanently, on a legal or illegal basis. They may intermarry or otherwise assimilate with the local population. Skilled and experienced workers are often allowed to settle in the receiving nation, and to bring in their families. The result is an increase in the local population, particularly in the young, fertile age groups, thereby contributing to an increase in fertility. This increases the future domestic labor supply of labor-scarce countries forced by the inadequacy of local population numbers to import foreign workers in the first place. The selective permanent immigration of skilled and professional foreign workers also enhances the quality and skill levels of the local population.

The social and political consequences of foreign labor are less benign. Large numbers of foreign workers can place great pressure on the social infrastructure of the host nation, competing for scarce housing, medical care and other social services. Social problems may arise with the creation of sizeable enclaves of foreign workers, often single males, with an alien language and culture, and no commitment to the host nation and its traditions. Where their wages are low, and working and living conditions poor, the incidence of crime, and the corresponding need for and cost of police and legal services, may increase. If the foreigners are perceived by local workers as reducing their employment opportunities, undercutting their wages, and slowing their training and rate of advancement, social and political unrest may develop, disrupting labor peace and the political stability required for investment. Where the treatment and behavior of foreign workers receive unfavorable publicity, political tensions are created between their home and host nations. In the words of the Prime Minister of Singapore, "...we can see what has happened in Britain, France and even West Germany, because they used immigrants—whether West Indians, Africans, Turks or Yugoslavs—to do those heavy and tough jobs. They have inherited grave social problems.

The Japanese, on the other hand, do all their own heavy and dirty jobs. They have no social problems or riots. Instead, they have high productivity from their homogeneous workforce."

FOREIGN WORKERS IN SINGAPORE

Foreigners who work in Singapore are admitted into the country on one of five types of immigration passes, each with different terms and conditions. At the top end of the occupational scale, skilled and professional workers are admitted on Employment Passes. Visiting professional workers, such as entertainers on short-term tours, receive temporary Professional Visit Passes. A third category of foreign workers, who are resident in Malaysia and commute to Singapore daily for work, are admitted on Day Permits. But the bulk of foreign workers are Work Permit and Block Work Permit holders, concentrated in the low-income occupations. Block Work Permit holders are admitted in groups for specific projects, mostly in the construction and shipbuilding industries. Most low-income foreign workers from non-traditional sources (that is Asian countries other than Malaysia) are admitted on block permits.

In addition, foreigners who invest more than a certain amount of capital in Singapore—originally S$250,000, now raised to S$1 million—can apply for permanent resident status. The permanent resident group also includes other categories of non-citizens, such as the foreign spouses and children of Singapore citizens who have been resident in the country for some time. Permanent residents (known as non-citizen Singapore residents do not need immigration permission to work in jobs that pay more than $1200 a month.

In 1980, Singapore had a labor force of 1.1 million workers, of whom nearly 120,000, or 11 percent, were non-citizens. Of these, one-third, or 40,000 workers, were permanent residents, and the other two-thirds, nearly 80,000, were non-residents (Table 1).

The majority of foreign workers, about 50 percent, are Chinese, but there are proportionately more persons of Malay, Indian, and other ethnic origin among them than there are among citizen workers. Only 8 percent of Chinese workers, but 16 percent of Malay, 20 percent of Indian, and 65 percent of other workers are foreign. Thirty-one percent of the Chinese, 41 percent of the Malay, 56 percent of the Indian, and only 10 percent of the other foreign workers are permanent residents.

Table 1 compares the sex, age, and marital status compositions of foreign and citizen workers. The proportion of males is only slightly higher among non-resident (69%) and non-citizen resident (72%) workers than it is among citizen workers (65%). Non-resident workers are slightly younger (60% under age 30) than citizen workers (53% under age 30), while non-citizen resident workers are older (only 33% under age 30). Proportionately more of the non-resident (56%) than

TABLE 1

Statistics on the Characteristics of
Resident and Non-Resident Workers in Singapore, 1980

	Singapore Residents		Non Residents
	Citizens	Non-Citizens	
Number	957,607	40,208	79,275
a. Female	34.9%	28.2%	31.1%
b. Chinese	79.4	49.7	56.1
c. Malays	13.5	25.5	18.4
d. Aged 30	53.2	32.7	60.1
e. Single	47.5	29.0	55.9
No Qualification/Primary	72.1	77.7	74.7
Tertiary	2.8	8.3	10.7
In Manufacturing	28.6	34.0	46.1
In Construction	5.5	8.4	20.2
In Trade	22.3	22.1	9.4
In Personal and Household Services	3.3	7.0	7.4
Manufacturing Workers in			
a. Textile, Garments and Leather	12.9	19.9	27.8
b. Wood and Wood Products	5.8	10.2	12.8
c. Electrical and Electronics	27.2	23.2	16.6
d. Transport Equipment	11.3	10.8	11.1
Professional and Technical	8.7	9.6	9.9
Administration and Managerial	4.4	7.3	8.6
Clerical and Sales	30.0	19.1	5.3
Production and Related Workers	38.2	45.5	64.5

SOURCE: Compiled from tables in Singapore, Department of Statistics, *Census of Population 1980*, release no. 4. Singapore: Singapore National Printers, 1981.

citizen (48%) workers are single, but proportionately more of the non-citizen resident workers (67%) are married than are citizen workers (50%).

Foreign workers are better-educated than Singapore workers. Eleven percent of non-resident workers and 8 percent of non-citizen resident workers have completed tertiary education, compared with only 3 percent of citizen workers. Foreigners account for nearly a third of all tertiary-educated workers in Singapore.[10]

Compared with Singapore workers, foreign workers are disproportionately represented among production workers. Sixty-five percent of non-resident workers and 46 percent of non-citizen resident workers are production and related workers, compared with 38 percent of citizen workers. Relatively more of the non-resident (9%) and non-citizen resident (7%) than citizen (4%) workers are in administrative and managerial occupations (Table 1). Although foreign workers account for 11 percent of all workers in Singapore, they comprise 19 percent of all administrative and managerial workers and 10 percent of all production and related workers (Table 2).

The sectoral distribution of foreign workers in Singapore (Table 1) shows that they are disproportionately concentrated in manufacturing and construction. In 1980, 29 percent of Singapore citizens, 34 percent of non-citizen residents, and 46 percent of non-resident workers were in the manufacturing sector. Twenty percent of non-resident and 8 percent of non-citizen resident workers were in construction, compared with 6 percent of citizen workers. Although accounting for 11 percent of all workers in Singapore, foreigners comprise 27 percent of all construction, 16 percent of all manufacturing, and 16 percent of all quarrying workers (Table 2). They also account for 21 percent of all personnel and household service workers.[11]

Among workers in manufacturing, 30 percent of the non-resident and 20 percent of the non-citizen resident workers are in the textile, wearing apparel and leather industries, compared with only 13 percent of citizen workers. Thirteen percent of non-resident, 10 percent of non-citizen resident, and only 6 percent of citizen workers are in the wood and wood products industries (Table 1). Large proportions of foreign manufacturing workers are also found in the electrical, electronics, and transport equipment industries. Although accounting for 16 percent of all manufacturing workers, foreigners comprise 27 percent of all workers in the textile, garment and leather

[10]Calculated from Table 40, Singapore, Department of Statistics, *Census of Population 1980*, Release No. 4, Singapore: Singapore National Printers, 1981:72.

[11] Calculated from Table 51, Singapore, Department of Statistics, *Census of Population 1980*, Release No. 4, Singapore: Singapore National Printers, 1981:100-7.

FOREIGN LABOR AND ECONOMIC DEVELOPMENT   559

TABLE 2

Working Persons by Occupational Group
Industry and Residential Status, 1980

	Total		Singapore Residents		% Non-Residents
	Persons	%	Citizens	Non-Citizens	
By Occupational Group					
Total	1,077,090	100.0	88.9	3.7	7.4
Professional and Technical	95,145	100.0	87.7	4.1	8.2
Administrative and Managerial	52,175	100.0	81.4	5.6	13.0
Clerical	167,473	100.0	97.7	1.4	0.9
Sales	131,977	100.0	93.9	4.0	2.1
Services	112,196	100.0	87.4	5.3	7.3
Agricultural Workers and Fishermen	20,954	100.0	92.9	4.2	2.9
Production and Related Workers	434,996	100.0	84.0	4.2	11.8
Not Classifiable	62,174	100.0	98.2	1.0	0.8
By Industry					
Total	1,077,090	100.0	88.9	3.7	7.4
Agriculture and Fishing	16,962	100.0	94.0	3.4	2.7
Quarrying	1,139	100.0	84.0	4.0	11.9
Manufacturing	324,121	100.0	84.5	4.2	11.3
Utilities	8,464	100.0	94.6	4.4	1.0
Construction	72,346	100.0	73.2	4.7	22.1
Trade	229,759	100.0	92.9	3.9	3.3
Transport and Communication	119,917	100.0	93.8	2.7	3.5
Financial and Business Services	79,412	100.0	91.9	3.2	5.0
Other Services	224,554	100.0	92.0	3.3	4.7
Not Classifiable	416	100.0	95.2	2.6	2.2

SOURCE: Singapore, Department of Statistics, *Census of Population 1980*, release no. 4, Singapore: Singapore National Printers, 1981-82, pp. 73-74.

industries, and 28 percent of all workers in the wood and wood products industries. [12]

In summary, in terms of their demographic characteristics (age, sex, and marital status), foreign workers are little different from Singapore workers, with the exception of non-citizen resident workers, with the exception of non-citizen resident workers, who are considerably older, and much more likely to be married, than are non-resident or citizen workers. The ethnic composition of foreign workers is also much less heavily Chinese than that of citizen workers. Where foreign workers differ most from citizen workers is in their educational, occupational and sectoral distribution. They are better educated than Singapore workers, and are disproportionately represented among the tertiary educated. They are also over-represented in administrative and managerial occupations on the one hand, and in production and related work on the other. In the sectoral distribution, they are over-represented in quarrying, construction and in manufacturing—especially in the textile, garment, leather, wood and wood product industries.

Both among employees and the self-employed, non-resident workers have the highest monthly income, followed by non-citizen resident workers, with Singapore citizen workers receiving the lowest income. In other words, foreigners are more well-paid than Singaporeans. The ratio of the mean income of non-resident employees to that of citizen employees is 1.74, and that of the non-resident self-employed to the citizen self-employed is 2.28. [13]

The disparity between male and female incomes is, however, much greater for both categories of foreign workers than it is for citizen workers. Among employees, citizen males receive 1.39 times the mean income of citizen females, while non-citizen resident males receive 2.24 times the mean income of non-citizen resident females, and non-resident males receive 3.62 times the mean income of non-resident females. In absolute terms, non-resident male workers are the most highly paid group, while non-resident female employees are the lowest paid. Foreign female employees receive lower incomes

[12] Figures calculated from Singapore, Department of Statistics, *Census of Population 1980*, Release No. 4, Singapore: Singapore National Printers, 1981.

[13] Figures in this and the following paragraph are calculated from Singapore, Department of Statistics, *Census of Population 1980*, release no. 7 (Singapore National Printers, 1981), pp. 40-41.

than citizen female employees, but citizen female self-employed receive lower incomes than the foreign female self-employed. The foreigner-citizen income disparity is much greater among male workers than among female workers.

These income figures reflect the concentration of foreign female workers in the lowest-income occupations and sectors of the Singapore economy: as production workers in manufacturing, especially in the textile, garment, leather and wood industries, and as personal and household servants. They also reflect the disproportionate representation of foreign, especially non-resident, males in high income administrative and managerial occupations. Whereas foreign male workers, especially the self-employed, constitute an "aristocracy" among the Singapore workforce, foreign female employees belong to its "underclass".

As Table 3 shows, education is an important determinant of income differentials among employees. The more highly-educated receive higher incomes, regardless of nationality. Among workers with no educational qualifications or with only a primary education, the difference in incomes received by non-residents and citizens is relatively small, with non-resident male workers earning slightly more, and non-resident females earning less, than their citizen counterparts. But for those with a secondary or higher education, both male and female non-residents earn much more than their citizen counterparts, with the disparity being much greater for males than for females. A secondary-educated non-resident male earns 2.5 times the income of a similarly educated citizen male, and nearly as much as a tertiary-educated citizen male, who earns only 58 percent of the income of a similarly educated non-resident male. These figures again reflect the "privileged" economic position of non-resident males (especially the highly-educated expatriates) in the occupational distribution.

Table 4 shows that, for both sexes and all nationalities of employees, the highest income is earned in administrative and managerial occupations, followed by professional and technical occupations. Whereas for Singapore residents, clerical occupations pay more than sales, for non-residents the reverse is true. Among all Singapore residents, agricultural workers and fishermen are the lowest paid, while among all non-residents, service workers are the lowest paid. The lowest-paid group are non-resident females in the services sector, followed by non-resident females in production and related work:

TABLE 3

Mean Income of Employees by Education, Residence, Citizenship and Sex Singapore, 1980

Education	Singapore Residents						Non-Singapore Residents		
	Total			Singapore Citizens					
	Persons	Males	Females	Persons	Males	Females	Persons	Males	Females
No Qualification	352 (151,609)	408 (95,942)	255 (55,667)	354 (142,412)	410 (90,237)	256 (52,175)	356 (16,266)	425 (10,274)	257 (5,992)
Primary	426 (409,530)	474 (268,512)	336 (141,018)	426 (394,275)	474 (257,750)	337 (136,525)	415 (38,500)	502 (23,698)	276 (14,802)
Secondary and Upper Secondary	739 (233,112)	866 (128,294)	582 (104,818)	728 (228,297)	848 (125,245)	582 (103,052)	1,855 (10,334)	2,111 (8,573)	626 (1,761)
Tertiary	2,031 (26,128)	2,334 (17,112)	1,456 (9,016)	1,944 (23,713)	2,222 (15,159)	1,451 (8,553)	3,609 (8,221)	3,832 (7,366)	1,678 (855)
Total	552 (820,378)	625 (509,860)	437 (310,519)	546 (788,696)	612 (488,391)	439 (300,305)	949 (73,322)	1,236 (49,911)	341 (23,411)

SOURCE: Singapore. Department of Statistics, *Census of Population 1980*, release no. 7, (Singapore: Singapore National Printers, 1981), pp. 56-58.

NOTES: Figures in parentheses indicate number of persons. Citizens + non-citizens.

TABLE 4

Mean Income of Employees by Occupation, Residence, Citizenship and Sex   Singapore, 1980

Occupation	Singapore Residents						Non-Singapore Residents		
	Total³			Singapore Citizens					
	Persons	Males	Females	Persons	Males	Females	Persons	Males	Females
Professional and Technical	1,125 (81,397)	1,277 (47,662)	911 (33,735)	1,089 (78,197)	1,222 (45,388)	905 (32,809)	2,613 (8,136)	2,903 (6,717)	1,257 (1,419)
Administrative and Managerial	1,917 (31,466)	2,062 (25,479)	1,295 (5,987)	1,844 (29,796)	1,979 (24,015)	1,283 (5,781)	4,057 (5,333)	4,146 (5,117)	1,833 (216)
Clerical	520 (165,802)	589 (65,050)	475 (100,752)	520 (163,433)	590 (63,651)	475 (99,781)	697 (1,278)	770 (800)	572 (478)
Sales	472 (56,150)	539 (37,745)	334 (18,405)	474 (54,147)	544 (36,060)	335 (18,088)	1,061 (1,424)	1,111 (1,293)	569 (131)
Services	375 (94,056)	430 (54,142)	300 (39,914)	378 (89,044)	434 (51,274)	303 (37,770)	313 (7,144)	539 (1,731)	240 (5,414)
Agricultural Workers and Fishermen	325 (7,109)	336 (5,917)	272 (1,192)	324 (6,641)	335 (5,509)	274 (1,132)	338 (392)	339 (367)	322 (25)
Production and Related Workers	401 (323,907)	464 (217,203)	273 (106,704)	400 (307,925)	463 (206,461)	273 (101,135)	426 (49,010)	502 (33,312)	265 (15,698)
Not Classifiable	351 (60,492)	343 (56,663)	474 (3,829)	350 (59,843)	342 (56,034)	475 (3,809)	3,530 (604)	3,560 (574)	2,630 (30)
Total	552 (820,378)	623 (509,860)	437 (310,519)	546 (788,696)	612 (488,391)	439 (300,305)	949 (73,322)	1,236 (49,911)	341 (23,411)

SOURCE: Singapore, Department of Statistics, *Census of Population 1980*, Release No. 7, (Singapore: Singapore National Printers, 1981), pp. 63-68.

NOTES: Figures in parentheses indicate number of persons.

³ Citizens + Non-Citizens.

the bulk of these workers probably comprise domestic servants and production workers in manufacturing, respectively. The highest paid group is non-resident males in administrative and managerial positions, followed by non-resident males in professional and techical occupations. Within every occupational group, non-resident males earn more than citizen males, reflecting their higher educational qualifications.

In general, at the same educational level and within the same occupational group and employment status, non-residents receive higher mean incomes than Singapore residents and citizens, with the exception of non-resident female employees in the lowest educational and occupational groups, who earn less than their citizen counterparts. The high incomes of non-resident males reflect their over-representation in the high educational and occupational groups. The distribution of income is much more unequal among non-residents than it is among citizen workers, reflecting the concentration of non-resident females especially in the lowest educational and occupational groups.

The distribution of foreign workers in Singapore by education, occupation and income all point to a marked "bimodel" distribution. As shown in Figure I, they are heavily represented at the highest and lowest ends of the skill spectrum (measured by educational, occupational or income levels), and under-represented in-between. This "U shaped" curve reflects the intermediate status of Singapore's small and newly-industrializing economy. Singapore has adequate domestic supplies of secondary-educated labor to man a broad range of middle-level jobs, but insufficient highly-skilled and experienced labor for high-level managerial and professional jobs. At the same time, large sectors of the Singapore economy still consist of low-skilled and labor-intensive jobs—for example, in construction and manufacturing—for which there are inadequate supplies of citizen labor. As the Singapore economy grows and restructures itself, the numbers, characteristics and distribution of foreign labor will change, and so will the shape of the curve in Figure I.

IMPLICATIONS OF FOREIGN LABOR FOR SINGAPORE

Singapore's labor force is projected to grow by less than 20,000 a year in the 1980s. Official targets of an 8 percent annual GNP growth rate

FIGURE I
CURRENT DISTRIBUTION OF FOREIGN WORKERS

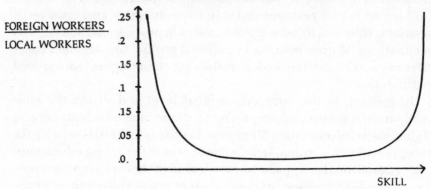

FOREIGN WORKERS
LOCAL WORKERS

and 5½ percent annual productivity growth rate through the 1980s indicate that an additional 5,000 foreign workers a year will need to be imported to make up the domestic labor shortfall. By 1990, if Singapore achieves its economic growth and productivity targets, it will have 170,000 foreign workers in a workforce of 1.37 million, or a foreign worker-labor force ratio of 1 in 8, compared with 1 in 9 today. Under the "high growth" assumption of a 10 percent annual GNP growth and 7 percent to 8 percent annual productivity growth, 10,000 additional foreign workers will be required each year, resulting in at least 220,000 foreign workers. In other words, 1 in 7 (14%) workers in the 1990 labor force of 1.42 million will be foreign if Singapore achieves a sustained growth rate of 10 percent a year in the 1980s.

In both absolute and relative terms, therefore, the population of foreign workers, temporary and permanent, will rise in Singapore in the 1980s. But with economic restructuring, their composition, and representation in different sectors and occupations of the economy, will change. With slow domestic population growth and fast economic growth in high-value activities, there will be increased dependence on high-level foreign professional manpower. At the same time, the upgrading and phasing out of low-value, labor-intensive activities will reduce dependence on low-level, unskilled foreign labor. The positively-sloped curve in Figure II shows the likely changing distribution of foreign labor across the skill spectrum of the economy in the medium term. In the longer run, as more citizens become

INTERNATIONAL MIGRATION REVIEW

trained and experienced in high-skilled occupations and activities, and as more non-citizens are "absorbed" as citizens into the domestic population, the skill profile of foreign workers will flatten out to the line shown on Figure III.

FIGURE II

MEDIUM-TERM PROJECTED DISTRIBUTION OF FOREIGN WORKERS

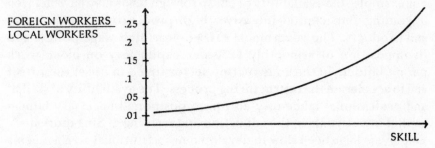

Singapore has in the past benefited greatly from the inflow of foreign labor. Economic expansion has proceeded more rapidly and smoothly than would have been possible with domestic labor supplies alone. Foreign workers have contributed valuable skills, capital and experience to Singapore's development progress. To some extent, their disproportionate retrenchment during the 1974-75 recession minimized domestic unemployment. In key labor-intensive export-oriented sectors of the economy, such as the textiles, garments, electrical, electronics, and shipbuilding industries, foreign labor imports have helped keep wages low and thus to prolong Singapore's

FIGURE III

LONG-TERM PROJECTED DISTRIBUTION OF FOREIGN WORKERS

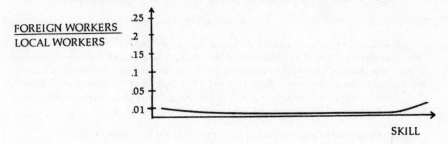

international competitiveness in export markets. They help reduce inflationary bottlenecks in the labor-short construction sector, and by their participation in labor-intensive personal and household services continue to make such services available at reasonable cost to citizen consumers, and to release more highly-educated female citizens for more productive work activities outside the home.

But these benefits have been accompanied by some hidden costs. For example, the availability of cheap foreign labor may have delayed upgrading into capital-intensive, high-productivity technologies and products. The government's three-year high-wage policy, and its imposition of a monthly $230 per capita levy on block work permit holders in the construction sector, tried to offset this effect and to accelerate the restructuring process. The availability of skilled and professional labor may also have postponed necessary human capital investments in the education and training of Singaporeans.[14] Employers have been slow to develop new institutional arrangements to facilitate the employment of married women citizens, even though

> employers know that Singaporean women with children in school are prepared to work four-hour shifts while their children are in school.[15]

Up to now the social costs of absorbing foreign labor have been small. The vast majority of foreign workers have been admitted for stays of limited duration, and are not allowed to bring their families with them, to marry citizens (except under certain restrictive conditions), or to settle permanently in Singapore. In any case, since most of them come from Malaysia, they are ethnically, culturally, religiously and linguistically similar to Singapore citizens, and pose no problems of social integration with the local population. Many of them even have relatives in Singapore. Those who have been admitted permanently, and allowed to marry citizens, are for the most part the more highly-skilled, who are expected to "spur" the local population.

[14] For example, there was a small decline in university student intakes following the 1974/75 recession. Only in 1980 were intakes at tertiary educational institutions sharply incresed; this and subsequent planned increases will take time to come on to the labor market. *See*, Economic Research Center, *Report on the 1980 Survey of University of Singapore Graduates*.May 1981, and Linda Lim and Pang Eng Fong, "Engineers: Facts and Fallacies", *Singapore Business* (May 1981), pp. 61, 63 and (June 1981), pp. 53, 55-57.

[15] Prime Minister of Singapore, quoted in "Target: Wholly Singapore Workforce".

The important question is whether, at this juncture of Singapore's development, when economic restructuring is an urgent priority, the benefits of continued and, indeed, projected increased reliance on foreign labor imports will continue to outweigh the costs. The proximate benefits depend on the supply of foreign labor itself. The traditional source of supply of both skilled and unskilled foreign labor is drying up as Malaysia's own economic growth and labor absorptive capacity increases rapidly.[16] Increasing resort to non-traditional sources of supply in other south and southeast Asian countries may mean a decline in the productivity of foreign labor, because of greater linguistic and educational differences, and in some cases, weaker physical constitutions of manual workers from poor countries. Ethnic and cultural differences may also increase the social costs of absorbing non-traditional foreign workers with no local ties.

Economic restructuring in Singapore means a shift in the composition of foreign labor required, away from the unskilled and towards the skilled and highly qualified professional, technical and managerial workers. The problem here is that such workers, especially in the high-technology manufacturing industries which Singapore is seeking to develop, are in great demand and short supply internationally, including in the advanced industrial nations.[17] Those who are attracted to Singapore may not be the best or even second-rate (both of whom can always obtain superior jobs in their home or third countries), but rather those "close to the bottom of the barrel". In highly competitive world industries employing complex technologies, this does not augur well for the success of industrial upgrading.

At the same time, the indirect economic and social costs of an absolutely and relatively larger foreign worker population are likely to increase. These include the costs of providing housing, public transportation, social services (including health and crime prevention), and recreational facilities for the foreigners. Whether

---

[16] For example, the porportion of non-citizen (mostly Malaysian) graduates from the University of Singapore who remain to work in Singapore has been declining for the last three years. *See,* Economic Research Center, 1981:3, *Report on the 1980 Survey of University of Singapore Graduates.*

[17] One of Singapore's priority industries for the 1980s, electronics, faces a particularly acute worldwide shortage of engineers. Would-be multinational employers and professional "head-hunting" firms have even come to Singapore to recruit foreign and local staff for facilities in the U.S.A.

directly paid for by their employers, by the government, or by the workers themselves, these costs will spill over to the local population, who will have to compete with the foreigners for scarce and increasingly costly housing, and for services like transportation, recreation and public health services. These "congestion costs" will rapidly escalate in Singapore's limited physical area. Local citizens may also have to sibsidize through their tax payments public provision of increased services to accomodate the foreigners. Their dissatisfaction with the declining quality of life may lead to hostility against foreigners, especially the increasing number who will be ethnically and culturally distinct.

Competition between local citizens and foreigners for jobs and for scarce resources may be most serious at the level of skilled and professional labor. To attract and retain such internationally mobile labor from other countries, Singapore has to pay close attention to their conditions of employment and residence (such factors as housing for their families, education for their children, and recreational facilities). But to make foreign professional labor a "privileged class" in Singapore, competing with the rising Singapore professional and middle class for superior employment, housing, education and recreational facilities, will lead to resentment which is socially and economically dysfunctional. It may even lead to a loss of scarce domestic labor and human capital through the increased emigration of skilled and professional citizen workers who can find a better life elsewhere (since their skills and experience are in strong demand in other countries).

In general, the aggregate net benefit of foreign labor to the Singapore economy is likely to be positive. But long-run political as well as economic considerations may argue against a continually increasing dependence on foreign abor. If the distribution of the relative costs and benefits of foreign labor is unequal among different sectors of the population, discontent might develop among citizen groups which suffer, or perceive themselves to suffer, net costs. Differences in the rights, responsibilities and treatment of citizen and foreign workers may become contentions for either or both groups.[18] An increasing proportion of foreign workers may also

---

[18] While foreign workers may consider themselves to be in some cases "exploited" because they do not share in all citizen rights and freedoms, citizen workers may see incentives to attract foreign workers, for example the provision of subsidized housing, as "favoritism" in

dilute national identity and politial cohesion, and call into question the meaning of citizenship itself. The social purpose as well as the economic viability of a development strategy dependent on uncertain supplies of foreign labor may also be questioned.

Six months after announcing a liberalized foreign policy, the Singapore government appears to have had second thoughts, and now plans to restrict foreign labor supply in the 1980s, while restructuring the economy to require only a citizen and permanent resident workforce by 1990. The prime minister believes that "a more homogeneous workforce, working together as a team" will be more productive "because they all feel committed to Singapore".[19]

THE POLICY ALTERNATIVES

First, the government could lower the nation's economic growth targets for the 1980s to a level attainable with a lower rate of foreign and domestic labor force growth. Besides reducing dependence on foreign labor, this will spread and smooth out the dislocations that inevitably accompany any restructuring process. A slower rate of GNP growth with less foreign labor also need not mean a lower rate of real per capita income growth for citizens. Whether the government's growth target for the 1980s can in fact be achieved is questionable. Singapore's open economy is vulnerable to external developments, particularly economic changes in industrial countries. Even so, structural imbalances, for example, the reluctance of Singaporeans to work in constructiont rades, will persist in the labor market and Singapore will continue to need foreign workers in the forseeable future, though not in as large a number as expected in 1981.

Second, the government can revise its short-run labor market policy to reduce the damand and/or increase the supply of labor in one of at least three ways. One way is to continue with the now-abandoned "corrective" high-wage policy without announcing a limited time span, to give employers a sufficiently powerful incentive to save labor in the long run. The danger of this is that it will fuel inflation, as well as force many small local firms out of business, and

---

which they do not share. In certain fields, citizen workers may be preferred for promotions. On the other hand, foreign workers may have a career advantage because they are not liable for national service, including annual reservist training periods.

[19] *Quoted in Target: Wholly Singapore Workforce.*

FOREIGN LABOR AND ECONOMIC DEVELOPMENT   571

discourage new foreign investment. To the extent that large amounts of labor are released for other sectors, however, the inflation may be tempered, and new investments encouraged.

Part of the problem with an across-the-board high wage policy is that it disproportionately affects the services sector, where in some areas restructuring is less technically and economically feasible than it is in manufacturing. A possible compromise policy is to have differential wage increases by sector and by wage level, to compress wage differentials and eliminate low-wage jobs which are disproportionately held by foreign labor, without hampering the development of high-value services employing high-skilled labor. This policy will have the added beneficial side effect of reducing income inequalities.

A second possibility, avoiding the bureaucratic and other inefficiencies associated with a complex wage policy, is to dismantle the National Wages Council and return to market wages immediately. This would hasten market-determined restructuring, but with some dislocation and possibly explosive inflationary consequences if at the same time foreign labor importation were restricted and the domestic labor market continues to be tight.

A third alternative is to return to market forces, but allowing unrestricted access to foreign labor, to cool the domestic labor market. This, however, may retard restructuring and increase the political and social costs of foreign labor.

Short-run labor market policies all involve a combination of wage determination by government recommendation or by market forces) and control of the foreign labor supply. The optimum combination is difficult to determine, since the goal of policy is not merely static adjustment to existing imbalances, but rather adjustment to a dynamic situation of economic restructuring which is yet to take place.

Besides lowering growth targets and enacting short-run labor market policies, there is a structural solution to the problem of labor shortage and foreign labor dependence. This is to shift the long-run sectoral emphasis of Singapore's development strategy away from production-oriented manufacturing towards the more naturally competitive services sector, both of which now compete for inadequate supplies of both skilled and unskilled labor.[20]

[20]For more on this point, *See*, our article, "The Political Economy of a City-State, with

Given the domestic resource constraint, Singapore cannot expect to sustain high rates of growth in all sectors of the economy simultaneously without generating inflationary pressures and bearing the high social and economic costs of increased dependence on foreign labor.

Manufacturing and traded services account for most of the output and employment in the Singapore economy. Next to the much smaller construction and quarrying sectors, manufacturing is most heavily dependent on foreign labor. Although it pays lower wages than any sector except construction, agriculture and fishing, it is losing its competitiveness in labor-intensive exports.[21] Because of its large labor intensive base, and the rigidities imposed by fixed capital investments, restructuring in manufacturing can only take place slowly.[22] It will be an expensive process, in terms of costly manpower training and incentives which have to be offered to induce high-technology investments. Given intense supply-side competition, including for internationally scarce highly-skilled and experienced technical personnel, and given looming demand constraints in world markets for high-technology industries, the success of such restructuring is uncertain.

On the other hand, traded services—including finance, banking, business services, transport, telecommunications and tourism—have grown as or more rapidly than manufacturing over the past decade, and without the incentives that manufacturing enjoys. Productivity and incomes are also much higher in this sector than in manufacturing. With technical and educational upgrading and the spread of computerization, productivity and incomes in traded services can grow at least as fast as those in manufacturing, particularly if enhanced by

Special Reference to Singapore" in *Singapore Business Yearbook 1981/82*.

[21] This, despite the fact that manufacturing has long been effectively subsidized by generous tax incentives, cheap state infrastructural developments such as the provision of industrial estates, and an exchange rate policy which some economists suggest has undervalued the Singapore dollar in order to give export manufacturers an edge in foreign markets. In addition, it has benefited from the liberal immigration policy and, until 1979, a national wages policy to restrain wage increases. Some industries have also enjoyed domestic or international tariff protection.

[22] Whereas new industrial investments may be highly productive, they will take a long time to completely replace the dominant low-productivity, labor-intensive industries, which, themselves, will take time to upgrade, if upgrading is in fact technically and economically feasible in all cases.

appropriate incentive policies. More importantly, Singapore has an established and much stronger international competitive advantage in the export of services, based on its long experience and large human and physical capital investment in this sector, and on its location in a rapidly growing regional economy of which it is the service hub. Even in export manufacturing industries, Singapore's competitiveness is increasingly shifting towards service rather than production-oriented activities—for example, as a regional ware-housing, purchasing, servicing, sales and R and D center serving production facilities in neighboring countries and the world. These commercial, financial and industrial services will become in-creasingly internationalized with the explosion of electronic technology around the world, and with increasing regional and international industrial integration for the regional and world markets.

Both high-value services and high-technology manufacturing will demand more skilled and professional labor as they upgrade. At the same time, as the Singapore population increases and grows more affluent, it will increasingly consume more labor-intensive social and personal services, which have a high income elasticity of demand. This will further increase the domestic demand for unskilled and semi-skilled as well as skilled labor.

In a situation of inadequate domestic supply and uncertain foreign supply of both skilled and unskilled labor, it is economically efficient to concentrate a country's limited resources in the most productive sectors where its natural competitive advantage is greatest. For Singapore, this is the traded service, and not the production-oriented manufacturing sector, whose potential international comparative advantage is problematic. A sectoral shift from low-productivity manufacturing to higher-productivity services will mean a decline in overall labor demand to achieve the same target rate of GNP growth. It will shift labor demand from the sector most heavily dependent on foreign labor—manufacturing—to one which is less dependent.

On the supply side of the labor market, a shift away from labor-intensive manufacturing would release unskilled labor for the nontraded services sector, and skilled labor for professional jobs in the highly competitive traded service sector. In addition, whereas high-technology manufacturing is intensive in the use of male labor, especially in production engineering and technical operations, thereby aggravating the manpower limitations of a small population, high-value services are much more sex-neutral in both the demand for and supply of labor, permitting fuller use of the entire domestic labor force. For example, women already dominate not just clerical jobs in the services sector, but also are well represented in highly-skilled occupations such as systems analysis and computer programming, which are important in high-value service. Within the engineering fields, they are much more inclined towards computer science and electrical and electronics engineering than mechanical, civil and industrial engineering and towards research and design activities rather than production jobs.

Thus a reallocation of scarce resources, particularly labor, from low-productivity, foreign labor-intensive manufacturing to higher-productivity, less foreign labor-intensive services will both reduce overall labor demand and increase domestic labor supply, thereby reducing dependence on both unskilled and skilled foreign labor. Excess demand will probably still exist for skilled and professional personnel, but foreigners of higher quality may be more easily imported for high-value services than for production manufacturing. This is because Singapore is world-competitive in the provision of such services, whereas it is only struggling to establish a foothold in intermediate level high-technology manufacturing.[23]   At the same time, since service activities are less land-intensive than production manufacturing, especially heavy manufacturing activities, they conserve on yet another scarce resource of the island city-state. More land and infrastructural developments can then be shifted from manufacturing to residential and recreational uses, thereby reducing the inflationary housing shortage and other "congestion costs" which constitute part of the costs of hosting large numbers of foreign workers.

A sectoral shift to high-value services will have profound implications not just for infrastructural construction, but also for the structure of government incentives,[24]   and most importantly, for national manpower planning and individual career choices. It will

[23] In other words, Singapore is a more attractive career location for bankers, lawyers, finance and insurance experts, and so on than it is for engineers interested in high-technology manufacturing.

[24] It is the design of appropriate incentives that requires a sectoral specification. Some economists have suggested that the sectoral delineation is irrelevant, and that all that is

require a shift in human capital investments away from fields associated with production-oriented manufacturing—such as production
engineering and certain kinds of vocational and technical training
—and towards fields associated with the skilled professions—such as
law, accountancy, business, finance, scientific and industrial research,
medicine, architecture, computer science and a whole range of
exportable consultancy services and "brain services". It implies an
educational system to train more generalists as well as specialists, to
foster the creative and entrepreneurial skills needed to assure the
vitality of the traded services sector. It suggests reduced emphasis on
developing specific vocational skills required by production-
oriented manufacturing.[25]

In Singapore's current labor market, at least two factors already
point to the need for considering a sectoral shift in long-run development strategy. First, declining cohorts of school-leavers mean
that there are already insufficient qualified candidates for many
industrial training programs. For a manufacturing sector that must
be intentionally competitive to survive in high-technology industries,
there is a limit to the extent to which the quality of student intake can
be reduced to accommodate the need for increased outputs of
technical personnel. To make up for the shortfall in domestic numbers
and talent for male-intensive industrial manpower training programs,
Singapore's planners are diverting talent from other services-oriented
professional fields,[26] and actively recruiting foreign students,[27] who

---

needed is to distinguish between "high-productivity activities" to be encouraged, and
"low-productivity activities" to be discouraged. Apart from the fact that in Singapore the
former are highly correlated with traded services and the latter with production manufacturing
anyway, this distinction is sufficiently precise. It raises questions about the measure of
productivity to be used, the identification of high-productivity activities, the choice of the
appropriate productivity levels for particular activities (for example the Japanese level, the
American level, the South Korean level), the choice between activities with the same high
productivity and so on. This is particularly difficult in a dynamic and fluid situation of
industrial restructuring, when choice has to be made of new activities which have not been
tried or proven competitive in the local context.

[25] This does not, however, necessarily mean a complete move out of manufacturing. As
discussed previously, certain high-value, competitive manufacturing activities would still be
retained and encouraged. But they are more likely to be characterized by service rather than
production functions, for example R and D, quality control, testing, servicing and computerized
warehousing and sales.

[26] For example, medicine is the most popular educational and occupational choice of "top
scholars", reflecting the much higher incomes to be earned in this profession than in most

may not stay on to work in the country.[28]

Second, market signals themselves point to most remunerative employment opportunities for skilled and professional workers in traded services than in the manufacturing sector. For graduates in the private sector, lifetime incomes, and in many cases starting salaries as well, are higher in professional service fields like law, medicine, architecture and accountancy than they are in production engineering. Indeed, a significant proportion of engineering graduates work in higher-paying administrative and managerial positions rather than in engineering itself, representing, at least partly, a waste of expensive human capital investment and a loss of scarce technical personnel to the production-oriented manufacturing sector. Opportunities for entrepreneurship and self-employment, and the higher incomes which frequently come with them, are also greater in traded services than they are in modern manufacturing industries.

In short, manpower training constraints and market signals suggest that Singapore should concentrate more of its increasingly scarce human resources in the traded services sector. By doing so, it will have a more diversified economy, a more balanced investment in education and training than at present, and will also reduce its dependence on foreign labor with minimum cost to Singapore's economy and society.

Singapore's present goal is to have a permanent resident and citizen workforce by 1990. Given its high growth target and strong emphasis on manufacturing as a leading sector, the goal will be difficult to attain. But the government is unlikely to abandon the goal, at least not in the forseeable future. More likely, in keeping with its characteristic pragmatism and flexibility, the government will experiment with new policies to promote growth and curb the need for unskilled foreign workers.

---

others. But the government has imposed a quota on the number of top scoring students who can be admitted to medical studies. Many of the rest are persuaded to accept allocations in engineering.

[27] Already about one third of engineering undergraduates in Singapore are foreigners, and this is likely to increase as student intakes expand. The government has also recently announced that Malaysians will be allowed to enroll in the Economic Development Board's various industrial and vocational training schemes.

[28] For example, 61 percent of non-Singaporean graduates from the University of Singapore in 1980 were from the engineering faculty, but less than one-third of these graduates chose to work in Singapore. *See*, Economic Research Centre, 1981:13, *Report on the 1980 Survey of University of Singapore Graduates.*

[20]

The role of national boundaries in a cross-national labour market

by Elizabeth Petras

I The use of cross-national labour

Export and import of labour, both as free and unfree labour, have been integral to the evolution of inequalities among nations and between regions within a modern world economy. From the purposeful uprooting and massive relocation of populations, to the persistent and often clandestine trickle of labour towards poles of capital growth, both the cause and effect of transnational labour movements are similar; the deepening of the process of combined and uneven development among national units and regional aggregates, and the facilitation of the accumulation of capital by an international capitalist class. When traditional indigenous sources of surplus labour have been numerically inadequate or too expensive, capital has sought similar supplies outside its national boundaries, either through the import of labour, or through the export of capital.

There is a natural tendency for labour to seek out for itself that location where its labour power can be exchanged for the most desirable wages and living conditions; a drive for equalization of the wage scale towards its highest threshold. Within a 'national economy', this process occurs among the various economic sectors and among geographic regions. Within an international capitalist economy, the drive towards equalization of the wage scale occurs through immigration among nations. The pressure towards emigration is a *secular* expression of inequality among nations, and between periphery and core. At times, the core needs more labour from the world market, at times it needs less. During periods of capital expansion and growth, it is beneficial for employers in the core to have easy access to cross-national labour pools. The tendency to import labour is a *cyclical* expression of the uneven expansion of capital accumulation among economic sectors, among nations, and within the world economy. This tendency is operationalized by policies whereby states restrict or encourage access to the labour market located within its designated territories.

But are not exclusionary or restrictive immigration policies which tighten up the requirements for crossing national boundaries primarily designed to protect indigenous core labour from competition from low-wage international labour from the periphery and semi-periphery? Yes and no. The labour market does not 'belong' to labour, any more than it 'belongs' to capital. The term simply designates that relationship of exchange wherein labour power is sold to capital for a wage. Of course, a high degree of competition, with the accompanying tendency to depress wage levels is always disadvantageous to the seller of labour power and advantageous to the buyer. During periods of cyclical contraction, however, too large a surplus of reserve labour can be politically dangerous to capital and a drain on public and private funds. Therefore, it is expedient for the state to reduce the large numbers of low-wage cross-national workers by gradually closing off labour immigration. When national unemployment is high and prolonged, governments typically attempt to protect themselves and their economies through legislation designed to reduce working-class opposition and hostility. Policies which significantly restrict or exclude entrance of alien workers serve such a need. During this century, policies which effectively legislated boundary closure to further immigration have generally appeared within a few years of the particular national economy entering a long downward swing.

The modern world is fragmented into national units, yet the path of capital accumulation moves relatively unfettered by the restrictions of national boundaries. Within the core states, the use of imported workers has allowed capital to extend labour market recruitment beyond its legal national boundaries into poorer and weaker national units. To the degree that international capital is able to move freely among nations seeking the most profitable locations for natural resources, markets and labour supplies, while labour remains governed by state boundaries and policies, a major advantage is derived by capital. Strategies in response to the existence of national boundaries for both capital and labour vary in each instance. In the case of labour import, national boundaries have traditionally been employed by the state in the interests of core capital to regulate the quality and quantity of alien labour, usually with scant interference from the governments of those nations exporting labour. In order to penetrate national boundaries of the periphery in its quest for resources, labour and markets, international capital has at hand a variety of legal, formal and official networks which it can exploit.

For international labour, there is neither a comparable network, nor an international movement which could formulate policies to protect its interests. With the exception of occasional assistance from political groups sympathetic to its plight, this sector of labour, then, is left to improvise on its own. Foreign labour must develop defensive tactics for dealing with the particular form boundary legislation takes at different moments. The way in which migrant labour strategies interact with state policies depends on whether these policies have been designed to facilitate the easy movement of labour across national boundaries, or whether they are intended to deter entry. The greater the motivation to move out of the periphery, and/or the greater the desirability of the jobs available in the core, the more desperate or innovative will be the devices used by workers to penetrate national boundaries.

II National boundary definitions: concepts and functions

Definitions: while it is useful to set down some of the terminology used in the discussion of national boundaries — most of which has been developed and employed in the work of political geographers — it is also important to note that in so doing we are dealing primarily with the form rather than the function of national boundaries.[1]

The idea of a boundary denotes a line, an invisible line, which divides states from one another. Regardless of whether some national boundaries are coincidental with certain natural barriers, e.g., mountain ranges, rivers or international waters, all state borders are social creations, and intricately involved in the process by which states and the social groups they represent have divided up 'global space' of land, air and sea. Prior to the seventeenth century, fixed borders between political communities did not exist (Prescott, 1965, 44–5).

The evolution of modern boundaries was a natural accompaniment to the emergence of modern nation states based as they were on the territorial delimitation of political units, for which specific and defined borders were a requisite (Prescott, 1965, chapter 1).[2] Apart from exceptional instances, wherein demarcation of boundary lines has been established by permanent and relatively impenetrable physical barriers (e.g. Berlin Wall), boundary delimitation consists primarily of treaties, mutually accepted codes and laws, and juridictional areas defined by international law. That is, boundaries are essentially 'paper walls' created by the contractual relations among states.

Regions described as frontiers were the precursors to the modern state boundaries. While they served the function of separating political units from one another, the term refers to zones possessing width as well as length. Frontiers represented space for which there was no dispute over governance. As competition over the allocation of territory and the wealth it contained forced more precise and specific definitions of the powers of states, so too did it force more specific definitions of the locations of boundaries, *as well as their functions*. Whereas in the earlier stages of the development of capitalism on a world scale, resources, both natural and human, were less regulated and

---

[1] Cukwurah (1967, 3) notes that there is an essential juridical difference which exists between a state as an entity and its territorial limits. Consequently, recognition of one state as an international unit by another does not necessarily assume that the recognizing state acknowledges the status of the boundaries of the recognized state.

[2] Prescott fixes the origin of the modern political boundary with the Peace of Westphalia of 1648 and further notes that the demand for fixed and definite boundaries emerged as an effect of the French Revolution, with its emphasis on simplification and formalization of state relations.

160   *The role of national boundaries in a cross-national labour market*

more accessible, as the natural competitive process of capital accumulation accelerated, individual capitalist endeavours and the states which represented them necessarily sought to protect their own claims and resources against rivals by seeking prerogatives through political and juridical devices. The superimposition of formal boundaries so as to fragment territorial control was one such device. Initially, then, the modern state boundary served to enclose national economic systems and protect national economies by artificially restricting 'natural' patterns of production and exchange.

Three features mark the historical evolution of the modern state boundary. First is the fact that no boundary definition is static, but by force of the rivalries among states must be subject to constant redefinition in its role as a political device in that struggle. Second is the trend towards more restrictive control and selectivity which individual states have vested in national boundaries with regard to the crossing of persons, commodities and capital. Third is the increasing inequity of strength or permeability of boundaries characteristic of the relational inequalities between and among the stronger states of the core and the weaker states of the periphery.

In the following sections we shall discuss some of the superordinate facts which have governed the evolution of modern state boundaries, and finally, we shall look at some specific influences of boundary definitions with regard to the cross-national migration of labour.

National boundaries: some historical-political characteristics

1   *Modern boundaries, by their nature, represent political divisions which set forth the authority and autonomy of the individual nation state.* They must exist in order for there to be state sovereignty in what otherwise would be a totally open world economic system, rather than a multitude of partially closed national units which comprise that system. The division and stability of state political units requires real and symbolic walls to section off territorial, political and economic claims. Gibbons, in a generally accepted definition, notes that boundaries, in the strictly political sense, are the limits of governing authority (Gibbons, 1977, 649). Such a definition, however, overlooks the fact of inequality and hierarchy among sovereign units. Secondly, it excludes the possibility that stronger units of the core possess a variety of means — from political to military — whereby they can circumvent or violate the authority of weaker states, at the same time as they maintain protection of their own units from competition from weaker, though rival, states. The political strength or weakness of these borders relative to those of other rival states — that is, their degree of permeability or closedness — generally correspond to the relative economic strength among states, and tends to contribute to the maintenance of that status. Gibbons correctly points out that the delimitation of territory by boundary lines was based on the conception of a political unit which is primarily territorial during the period of the rise of the modern nation state. Boundary lines define the physical

limit of one territorial aspect. But this does not take account of the manner in which the accumulation of capital on a world scale frequently supersedes the regulatory functions of the individual state boundary, i.e., the greater ease with which organizations of international capitalism penetrate the weaker states of the periphery.

2   *International boundaries, created and maintained by the interests of nation states, represent a jurisdictional interface among nations.* They permit the technical application of state policies and economic functions at the border. As regulators of the circulation of goods, people and capital among states, boundaries serve as screens or filters to the actual exchanges which link together the various states. The principles imposed by definitions which individual states succeed in establishing are by no means necessarily harmonious with the needs or welfare of other states which these definitions may affect. The struggle of states to define boundaries so as to derive the greatest advantage within the world system through immigration legislation, tariff laws, trade embargoes, import quotas, etc. is an indicator of the competitive strength among states. Because of their historical position of power, *vis-à-vis* weaker states, core states have more often exercised the prerogative of establishing offensive legal definitions of their borders in expanding their own strength and domination. Such definitions allow for greater legal control, regulation and political techniques for encouraging or discouraging who and what shall pass into their territory. Weaker states have been more likely to resort to defensive legal definitions in attempting to regulate movement across their boundaries. They have sought to deter population (or commodities or capital) from passing out of their territory, or to influence the conditions of work and living for their populations when they are imported as labour by core states. For example, during the period from 1851 to 1914, when about 30 million immigrants swelled the United States' population and labour force, accounts of the deplorable conditions among the immigrant ships were widely circulated (see Abbott, 1924, section 1). The response on the part of the labour exporting countries, at most, was to impose restrictions on who might emigrate and under what circumstances. These regulations were limited primarily to women and minors and young men who had not completed their military obligations, and most had scant means of being enforced. While several of the labour exporting states did establish Emigration Councils or Offices, designed to circulate information about emigration, or facilitate the importation of labour by the United States,[3] they were not apt to enact strong legislation which prevented or controlled penetration of their boundaries by stronger core states or their representatives.

Similarly, the populations of the British Caribbean have been 'open' to labour recruitment by the core without restrictions on the part of the regional

[3] See Abbott, 1924, section II, for a collection of representative legislation and documents.

162   *The role of national boundaries in a cross-national labour market*

governments. In many instances, these governments have assisted in the recruitment, screening and dispatching of their citizens to work abroad. The first and perhaps most extensive case involved the recruitment of British West Indians to work on the construction of the Panama Canal, first under the French and then under the United States' expeditions. Traditional methods of recruiting foreign labour were employed—handbills, contractors, steamer transportation, etc. In the latter instance, the United States Secretary of War, William Taft, personally visited the islands in an attempt to procure 10 000 West Indian labourers. Although the records show that the working conditions and treatment of the workers were brutal and the death tolls from accidents and illness made them a virtually disposable workforce, no protection or intervention on the part of their governments occurred. (One exception during the us phase of canal construction was a demand by Jamaica that the United States pay a head tax and guarantee repatriation costs home. But this was not consistently honoured by the Americans and the West Indian government lacked the power to enforce the agreements after the fact—see McCullough, 1977.)

Similarly, West Indian governments set up procedures to secure and orient labour for British import during the height of the pre-1962 immigration to the United Kingdom. Organizationally, this involvement ranged from informal assistance in Jamaica to government-to-government contracts between Barbados and the United Kingdom.

3   *State boundaries are, by nature, restrictive and negative, no matter what their degree of openness and permeability.* Referring to the endless multiplicity of boundary restrictions in various areas of the world, Boggs (1940, 11) points out that insofar as they restrict the movements of peoples and the exchange of goods, of money, and even of ideas, international boundaries are intended to serve protective functions of various kinds. With respect to the movement of persons, '. . . restriction or even total exclusion of immigrants, visitors, and workingmen from foreign countries, because their competition for work and bread is not desired, because their race, their religion, or their political ideas are unwelcome, or for any other reason . . .' (Boggs, 1940, 10) are both functions of the formal administration and policing of international boundaries. Passports, passbooks, visas, work permits and employment vouchers must be presented, evaluated and approved by authorities of the state. 'If no boundary were there, and if the authority of the state were not manifest, the people would mingle freely . . . and would trade with one another regardless of whether they speak the same language' (p. 10). In Boggs's opinion, 'boundaries rob artisans and labourers of a chance to earn a living; impoverish peoples whose ample capacities are thwarted and instill fear and despair' (p. 106). Prior to 1914, passports or similar documents were not generally required in travelling from one country to another, either in Europe or the Americas. Today passports or similar documents provide

evidence by a 'stranger' of his or her right to be where (s)he is, in establishing identity and the right to travel.

Boundaries, then, serve to keep populations apart, and permit a state to evaluate individuals on the basis of some criterion of 'desirability' or 'undesirability' before permitting their entry across its borders. The determination of 'eligibility' lies with officials at the point of entry— immigration officials, customs inspectors, border patrols. The definition of 'eligibility', however, resides within representative groups of the state and may vary over time according to altering political and economic needs or interests which dominate a particular moment. Correspondingly, the policing functions vested in officials at the point of entry—which we identify today as the consular office (officials) abroad, the immigration and customs checkpoint within, and the men and machines which police the actual borders themselves—also change over time. The border patrol of the United States immigration service, for example, was officially established in 1924, largely to prevent alien smuggling, which became a highly motivated activity after the massive restrictions on immigration imposed by the 1921–24 legislation. Ironically, smuggling of European aliens excluded by the 1924 Act was easier across the Mexican border because the Exclusionary Act had left that boundary comparatively 'open' so as to permit United States agriculturalists easy access to foreign labour from Mexico. Today that patrol, along with their counterparts who police popular points of entry by water and air, have become a massive, well funded, trained and equipped army of wardens charged with maintaining tight closure against the large numbers of individuals seeking to cross national boundaries in search of work. The most efficient methods of protection depend on the channelling of all persons who intend to cross state boundaries through a limited number of state designated access points. In the United States, that function, served for so many years by Ellis Island, has been transferred to operations carried out at the main international airports. Kennedy, O'Hare, Miami International Airport and San Francisco International Airport have become the Ellis Islands of today.

4   *Application of state functions at the border corresponds to specific foreign policies and economic interests and, therefore, is constantly undergoing alteration in selectivity, direction and intensity.* As the contemporary state in capitalist society assumes more and more responsibilities for the functioning of the capitalist economy, its duties have intensified and its roles have multiplied. Many of these functions were unnecessary in an earlier stage of world capitalist development and have been the gradual outgrowth of the greater concentration and centralization of capitalist accumulation, which, it has been argued, necessitates increased planning and rationalization of policies on the part of the state.[4] But to the degree that monopoly capital—

[4] Schonfield (1965, 221) argues that capitalist state planning is 'an activity of very recent origin, belonging to the 1960s, rather than the 1950s'. He offers evidence that the United States and Canada have lagged behind this movement among the capitalist states of western Europe.

164   *The role of national boundaries in a cross-national labour market*

'international' in scale and competition—projects needs at variance with the needs and interests of competitive capital—which is more likely to be 'national' in location and production—friction over specific state policies may arise. What is good for General Motors (whose scale and flexibility permit it to rationalize production and pay higher wages to its relatively smaller workforce, or to move all or part of plant, technology and production across the border to locations of cheaper labour) is not necessarily good for the urban car-wash owner (whose static location, small-scale operation and inefficient technology require that he maintain the highest degree of exploitation of labour through low wages and long hours in order to maintain his margin of profit).

It is difficult to obtain definite confirmation of the aims of states in fixing definitions of their national boundaries, since these aims are often matters of secret policy which can be established only by reference to archives long after the event (Prescott, 1965, 115). While this may hold in most instances, it is possible and useful, nonetheless, to study those debates which are a matter of current public record, specifically in matters of immigration policy. As with all international policies, debates about boundary definitions reflect differences over strategies, tactics and long-term versus short-term interests in the jockeying for positions within a relatively fixed international hierarchy of states. Interpretations as to the most appropriate or efficient strategies may vary among groups, individuals and classes. Immigration legislation in the United States, the United Kingdom and Canada has always been primarily defined by the labour requirements of the individual capital accumulation patterns, and, secondarily, by conjunctural political concerns conducive to the expansion of the accumulation process. It follows, then, that class, race, national-ethnic origin and, in many instances, political allegiance, will form the basis of immigration restrictions. But internal sectoral conflicts have arisen over their specific context.

In Canada, for example, in 1955 the formal reorganization of matters related to immigration under a new Department of Manpower and Immigration reflected the government's matter-of-fact acceptance of its primary motivation in encouraging immigration. Both the new department and the Immigration Act of 1964 were designed to promote immigration of a cross-national workforce, since, in the recommendations of a Senate Committee, '. . . Canada needed more people to maintain and improve her position at home and abroad. . . .' (cited in Hawkins, 1972, 84). Therefore, 'Immigrants should be admitted in substantial numbers, beginning as soon as possible' (Hawkins, p. 83). That '. . . immigration should be geared to the *short and long-term needs of the Canadian economy*' (emphasis added) was the general consensus. A review of the legislation passed during the 1960s, when the Department of Manpower and Immigration was charged with a major immigrant recruitment and training programme (Hawkins, p. 153), and the restrictive legislation of the 1970s, whereby overseas consulates, such as those in the Caribbean which had been a major source of immigration, maintained their operations just to 'close the door',[5] suggests the changing eligibility definitions sought to accomplish just that. Hawkins observes of occupational and educational characteristics of the 1966–67 immigrants, whose eligibility was assessed on the basis of selection criteria involving education, training, occupation and skill, age, language and personal characteristics:

> The great influx of professional and skilled immigrants to Canada in the post-war period has not only met essential manpower needs, but has also constituted an immense saving in national outlay on education and professional and vocational training. The cost of training the highly skilled is substantial . . . (Hawkins, 1972, 46).

On the other hand, some policy-makers questioned whether the planned recruitment of highly educated and trained immigrants, especially where it involved a brain drain from peripheral nations, did not violate 'international obligations' and social responsibilities. The conflict was formulated and responded to in the following statement of the Chairman of the Economic Council of Canada:

> It is a matter of social and political policy whether you want to bring people here and then educate and train them here or whether you want to bring them in educated or trained. I am saying the trend of requirements is in the direction of higher levels of education and higher levels of skills. Now how do you want to get at this? You can bring them in and train and educate them here. But that means you must be prepared from a social and political point of view to do this. In other words, it costs money, it takes time and it requires capital and, at the same time, we have a very heavy job to do in relation to our own population.[6]

In his useful review of the origin and history of international migration law, Richard Plender records the first instance of permanent immigration control as England's Alien Law of 1793. A Francophobic response to the small number of refugees from the French Revolution who were entering England, exaggerated by the fear that Jacobin emissaries might be among the ranks of these refugees, the bill's preamble began with the notation that, 'a great and unusual number of aliens have lately resorted to the kingdom' (see Plender, 1972, 43).[7] Similar bills for the control of immigration, motivated by the same political fears, were passed by the United States and Swiss federations. The American bill was passed in 1798, four years after Canada took measures to 'counteract the danger of the influx of revolutionaries' (Plender, 1972, 44). Based on evaluation of political (or potential political) allegiance and national-ethnic origin of the alien, these

---

[5] Personal interview with Canadian consular official, Kingston, Jamaica, October 1977.

[6] Hawkins, 1972, 46. Dr J. J. Deutsch's statement before the Special Joint Committee of the Senate and the House of Commons on Immigration in December 1966.

[7] The Act called for the submission of a personal history and an account of his status by the alien, the obligation of the alien to surrender any arms, the right of the King to order any alien to live in a specified district, alien registration of name and address, deportation of any alien who had been imprisoned, and the power of the state to put to death 'any alien who had been sentenced to transportation and was subsequently found in the kingdom'.

166   *The role of national boundaries in a cross-national labour market*

laws marked the decline of free movement and the establishment of the right of states to impose direct controls on alien immigration.

In 1875, the United States Congress passed the first restrictive legislation, prohibiting entry to prostitutes, convicts and certain aliens with mental or physical incapacities—'immigrants who were obnoxious' (Plender, 1972, 47). But the Chinese Exclusion Act of 1882 contained requisites for registration and deportation making it the first legislation specifically aimed at selection and importation of international labour (Bennett, 1963, 17). The Exclusion Act and anti-contract labour laws of 1885, 1887 and 1888 also focused on the Chinese and Japanese (Abbott, 1924, 186–88). Passage of these acts was encouraged by organized labour concerned with the competition from low wage, highly exploited Oriental labour, and they were supported by and gave legitimacy to the general racist hostility then sweeping the West Coast.

The first world war marked the sharp rise of immigration legislation everywhere among states, along with the establishment of a passport system for transnational travel. In the context of the rise and growing participation in anticapitalist political groups in the United States, the Alien Anarchist Act of 1918 was passed. As well as imposing a political criterion for entry, this act provided a means of political control to be exercised by the state over the working class by providing for deportation of any aliens falling into any of the named categories of political participants or advocates (see Abbott, 1924, 231–32 for extracts of the Act).

By 1900 the United States had assumed first place among nations in the production and distribution of commodities on the world market, a position which it could never have achieved without having been able to draw freely on a pool of cross-national workers from the world labour market.

> It was during this period also that the manufacturing industries of the country had their marvelous growth. As early as 1880 the products of our manufacturers equalled in amount and value those of Great Britain. The development of these industries created a large demand for common labor, and it was then that the so-called new immigration, coming mainly from eastern and southern Europe, began to arrive in large numbers. In the year 1900 the manufactured products of the United States were greater than those of Great Britain, France, and Germany combined, and between that time and 1910 the value of such products increased from $11 000 000 000 to $20 000 000 000 annually. This increase alone was greater than the whole product of 1890. Without a comparison of this character it is impossible to comprehend the demand that has been created in the United States for European labor, and this expansion in our manufacturing and mining industries explains the vast increase in the immigration from eastern and southern Europe.[8]

But by the period 1915–19 the industrialization had been consolidated and, accordingly, the requirements for surplus labour decreased. In 1921, with the Quota Act which limited the number of immigrants who might enter the United States to not more than three per cent of the number of foreigners of that nationality resident in 1910, closure on further labour importation was

[8] Abbott, 1924, 232–33. Extract from 'Report of Mr Dillingham, the Committee on Immigration, April 23, 1921' us 67th Congress, First Session, *Senate Report no. 17*, pp. 3–8.

effectively legislated (Bennett, 1963, chapter 6). This Act laid the basis for
the system of national quotas which obtained until its replacement in 1965 by
a quota system based on skills, class and education. Formal quotas were
created in 1924 which further favoured northern and western Europeans,
since these constituted the majority of immigrants resident in 1910, the year
on which the quotas were based. (See Tables 1 and 2.)

The following notice, extracted from the Congressional debates on quotas
and closure, expresses the main motivation for redefining eligibility to
immigrate:

> Information having been received that there may be a slackness in the demand for labor
> during the winter months, intending emigrants to America are warned that no passports
> to the United States of America will be issued until further notice.[9]

This advice underscored the fact that labour market conditions within the
importing economy are the primary determinants regulating the flow of
immigration. In a period of economic decline, the state generally moves to
curtail the levels of movement in (Abbott, 1924, 235).

Support and opposition was divided over the redefinition of restrictions.

> In 1923–24, the major defenders of the small quotas provided in what became the 1924
> act were spokesmen for the American Federation of Labor, the American Legion, various
> patriotic societies, and the Immigration Restriction League. Temporary suspension of all
> immigration was recommended by the AFL and American Legion spokesmen. Opposition
> to the extent of quota-based restriction being proposed was expressed by a New York
> taxpayers' association and by industrial and employer organizations interested in the
> continuing availability of certain kinds of labor at 'satisfactory' wage rates—for example,
> National Association of Manufacturers, American Mining Congress, Associated General
> Contractors and National Industrial Conference Board. The NAM, together with the NICB
> and AGC, advocated a flexible policy under which there would be admitted as many
> variously qualified immigrants as the American economy required. The National Grange
> endorsed the 1890 base, but some farm organizations expressed concern lest agriculture
> be deprived of sufficient manpower. Spokesmen for various Jewish, foreign-language and
> sundry other groups, while taking it for granted that restrictions were necessary and/or
> inevitable, advocated a larger aggregate inflow than was contemplated and described a
> 1910 or a 1920 base as less discriminatory than a 1890 base (Spengler, 1958, 49, cited in
> Bennett, 1963, 53).

Nor were all who pressed for special exemption against the closure of their
access to foreign labour denied their requests. For example: '. . . exception in
favor of the states of Texas, Utah, Arizona, Colorado, New Mexico, and
other border states is continued, so as to permit the employment therein of an
unlimited number of Mexicans. The cigar manufacturers of Florida are also
granted an exception so that they can import from Cuba and other adjacent
islands such help as is desired by them. The people of the United States who
are not fortunate enough to reside in the states just mentioned are unable to
obtain any household help, but no exception on their behalf has been made'
(cited in Abbott, 1924, 242).

[9] Communication from the US Secretary of State to the Emigration Committee at Valetta,
Malta, 31 January 1921, in Abbott, 1924, 235.

168   *The role of national boundaries in a cross-national labour market*

Table 1   Immigrants admissible: Quota estimates. Number of natives of countries specified who were resident in the United States in 1910; average number of immigrant aliens who were admitted from such countries during 1910–1914; and the number who would be admissible annually under the 3 Per Cent Plan

| Countries | Population in United States 1910 | Average Annual Immigration 1910–1914 | Approximate number who would be admissible annually under specified per cent limit | | |
			5%	4%	3%
Belgium	49 400	5 590	2 470	1 976	1 482
Denmark	181 649	6 694	9 082	7 266	5 449
France	117 418	8 601	5 871	4 697	3 523
Germany	2 501 333	32 239	125 666	100 053	75 040
Netherlands	123 134	7 147	6 157	4 925	3 694
Norway	403 877	11 416	20 194	16 135	12 116
Sweden	665 207	17 843	33 100	16 668	19 956
Switzerland	124 848	3 762	6 232	4 994	3 745
United Kingdom	2 573 534	89 188	128 677	102 941	77 206
Total northwestern Europe	6 740 400	182 580	337 009	259 615	202 211
Austro-Hungary	1 670 582	225 931	83 529	66 823	50 117
Bulgaria	11 498		575	460	345
Serbia	4 639	4 964	232	186	139
Montenegro	5 374		269	215	161
Greece	101 282	26 442	5 064	4 051	3 038
Italy	1 343 125	220 967	67 156	53 725	40 294
Portugal	59 360	10 380	2 968	2 374	1 781
Rumania	65 923	2 570	3 296	2 637	1 978
Russia	1 732 462	210 922	86 623	69 298	51 974
Spain	22 108	5 722	1 105	884	663
Turkey in Europe	32 230	13 930	1 612	1 289	967
Turkey in Asia	59 729	16 780	2 986	2 389	1 792
Total	6 108 312	738 608	255 416	204 331	153 249

(Cited in Abbot, 1924, 238.)

Table 2   Immigrants admitted by principal races under the 1921 Act

| Race or nationality | Admissions 1923–24 | Admissions 1920–21 | % of Total | |
			1923–24	1920–21
Northern and western Europe	393 342	206 995	55·7	25·7
Southern and eastern Europe and Turkey	192 599	537 144	27·2	66·7
Mexicans	87 648	29 603	12·4	3·7
Everybody else	33 307	31 486	4·7	3·9
Total	706 896	805 228	100·0	100·0

(Cited in Bennett, 1963, 45.)

In the US, allowances for special access still persists in the form of contract labour agreements between the corporate sugar growers of Florida—Gulf and Western, Florida Cane Growers Cooperative and the US Sugar Company—and the large apple growers' associations of New York and New England, and Caribbean governments which allow for seasonal importation of workers through government-to-corporation contracts.

During the Cold War, debates surrounding the McCarren-Walter Act of 1952 focused on the utilization of boundaries as a political tool in the conflict. The Act, which was passed over the veto of President Truman, provided for a continuation of quota allocations among independent countries based on quota levels established in 1924. Non-northern and western European racial and ethnic groups continued to be denied immigrant or resident status in effect. The Act's sponsors justified continuation of the quotas on the basis of arguments made by Senator McCarran: 'We have in the United States today hard-core, indigestible blocs which have not become integrated into the American way of life, but which, on the contrary, are its deadly enemies . . . [I]t is the plan and purpose of the McCarran-Walter bill for us to receive only those aliens who will become integrated, who will become an asset and not a liability to our American society (see Bennett, 1963, 173).

Most of the Caribbean islands were limited to an annual quota of 100 immigrants each. However, Mr Arens, Director of the Senate Immigration Sub-committee, dismissed the possibility that racial considerations were involved with the assertion that, 'It is not the American Negro who claims that the West Indian is discriminated against. This is a false issue straight out of the Communist People's Daily Worker . . . and the Red-front American Committee for the Protection of Foreign Born' (see Bennett, 1963, 191).

Behind the reaffirmation of the quotas was a political philosophy which dominated the Cold War era. Senator McCarran, defended them as strategic in the 'fight against the international Communist conspiracy':

> The truth is . . . that in 1924 this country found itself besieged by millions of people of the world. . . . [I]f we scrap the national origins formula, we will, in the course of a generation or so, change the ethnic and cultural composition of this nation. . . . The times are too perilous for us to tinker blindly with our basic institutions. . . . With the exception of a few on the pink fringe, every authority in the field of immigration agrees with this formula [for quotas]. . . . The cold, hard fact is . . . that this nation is the last hope of western civilization and if this oasis of the world shall be overrun, perverted, contaminated, or destroyed, then the last flickering light of humanity will be extinguished. A solution of the problems of Europe and Asia . . . will come only if America is maintained strong and free; only if our institutions, our way of life, are preserved by those who are part and parcel of that way of life, so that America may lead the world in a way dedicated to the worth and dignity of the human soul (see Bennett, 1963, 173–74).

While they may have been in general accord in their support of the Cold War, policy-makers of the period by no means agreed on the most efficient tactics for strengthening the position of the capitalist states of the core within the world economy. Policies involving boundary redefinitions were no

170   *The role of national boundaries in a cross-national labour market*

exception. In opposing the bill's restrictions, Truman, in his Veto Message, declared that, 'Our immigration policy is equally, if not more, important to the conduct of our foreign relations and to our responsibilities of moral leadership in the struggle for world peace'. Other opponents reiterated the theme that redefinition of the permeability and openness of the United States boundaries might be a useful, rather than detrimental tactic in the Cold War. Secretary of State Dean Acheson advised, 'Immigration . . . is closely linked with our foreign policy and objectives . . . Our immigration policy with respect to particular national or racial groups will inevitably be taken as an indication of our general attitude toward them, especially as an indication of our appraisal of their standing in the world. It will, therefore, shape their attitude toward us and toward many of our other policies.' Averell Harriman, then Director of Mutual Security, stated, 'The kind of immigration policy we adopt is a factor in the world struggle between democracy and totalitarianism.' William H. Draper, United States Special Representative in Europe, elaborated, 'Whether we like it or not, we are part of the world, and we can no longer disassociate ourselves from what happens elsewhere. . . . In endeavoring to strengthen the economic and military defense of the free world, and particularly of the North Atlantic Community, we should recognize immigration policy as one of the elements in achieving economic and political stability as well as social equilibrium (us President's Commission on Immigration and Naturalization, 1953, chapter 3).

'Racial discrimination creates disunity at home and resentment abroad. It interferes with our foreign relations and the role of international leadership which destiny has thrust upon us in recent years. . . . We cannot press for international acceptance of these principles (of human rights for all regardless of race or origin), . . . and at the same time offend nations and races by discriminating against them in our own immigration laws' (*ibid*, p. 50). The dilemma to which the previous statement referred was the serious deterioration of foreign relations in the Caribbean assumed to be the result of the 1952 Act. Close to the Panama Canal and the site of important wartime bases, the British colonies of the West Indies responded to the severe restrictions on their immigration to the us as a matter of racial discrimination. Despite persistent underscription of the British quota, it was not open to the predominantly black population of the eight, then British, territories. The Secretary of State summed it up:

> It is clear that United States immigration policy (towards the West Indies) not only causes resentment weakening the friendship of some of our neighbors, but also causes or emphasizes economic dislocations that weaken those neighbors whom we need as strong partners and who can furnish us with sites for military bases and strategic raw materials (*ibid*, p. 55).

Apart from its usefulness as a political ploy, the opening of the borders was being sought again because of the need to expand the importation of foreign labour to supplement the indigenous labour pool. In the evaluation of the President's Commission on Immigration and Naturalization, '*The American economy still continues to demand some form of immigration to meet the manpower demands of a growing and vigorous nation'* (p. 32). The Report concluded,

> The United States needs more manpower. We need it to meet current labor shortages. We need it to meet the demands of an expanded civilian as well as military economy. And we need it to meet the requirements of national defense and security. *Immigration is a normal and historic source of additional manpower* (p. 32—emphasis added).

The argument for opening national boundaries was tempered by interpretations which would concentrate imported labour in selected occupational and demographic sectors, thus rendering it more 'valuable' to US employers. Nevertheless, the call was essentially being sent out for that group which had always formed the bulk of the cross-national labour force: young, male, adult workers, driven to accept the lower paid, less desirable employment in agriculture and industrial production (US President's Commission on Immigration and Naturalization, 1953, chapter 2). With 'almost full employment and no substantial reserve with which to meet a sudden crisis demanding both military and industrial manpower' (*ibid*, p. 34), and with the slowing of the reproduction of the labour force because of the wartime drop in the birth rates, some government planners were posing a redefinition of the nation's legal-technical labour market boundaries as a solution. Notwithstanding, the Act was passed over the heads of its opponents. The annual quota of any quota area was designated as one-sixth of one per cent of the number of inhabitants in the United States in 1920 attributable to national origin of such quota area, with the guarantee of a minimum annual quota of 100 to every quota area. Entrance of persons from the Caribbean, as well as from Africa or states such as Italy or Greece, continued to be relatively limited. (It is correct to note, however, that despite the retention of the national origins quotas, as it turned out, the intended bias was circumvented between 1952 and 1965 by successive amendments which provided for the admission of relatives and refugees. More than half of these relatives were Italians and a substantial number of others were from Greece, Portugal, Yugoslavia, China and Formosa, all 'non-preference' origins—see Bennett, 1963, chapter 8.)

In 1965, a revision of requirements for immigration replaced the limitations based on nationality (which coincided closely with limitations based on race and ethnicity), with a set of criteria based on 'needed talents and skills' (which coincided more closely with limitations based on class, training and education). Apart from reunification of families, the major criterion was based on the labour certification program designed as a safeguard to 'protect the American economy from undue job competition and from adverse working standards as a consequence of immigrant workers entering the labor market' (Thomasi and Keely, 1975, 10). This was operationalized by the creation of two preference categories for those who entered on the basis of skills: 1) professionals or persons with exceptional ability in the sciences or the arts who were virtually guaranteed free entry and 2) skilled or unskilled workers who could fill specific needs in short

172   *The role of national boundaries in a cross-national labour market*

supply, but who were required to secure a petition from an employer in order to establish eligibility. Numerical limitations previously applied to the Caribbean were also lifted. The 1965 legislation opened the US borders slightly for those seeking work, while maintaining a selective screen which limited the possibilities for general working-class immigration.

Given the prolonged economic recession, with the high unemployment rates which have accompanied it, it was consistent with the history of US immigration legislation that the Labor Certification provision was discontinued with legislation signed by James Carter in 1977. Under its provisions, only under specific circumstances could most working-class individuals from an area such as the Caribbean qualify for immigrant status (e.g. 'reunification of family'). A person from the same area who could show proof of specific assets and capital could immigrate under the category of 'investor' with ease, however.

Canadian government policies were also redefined in 1967 in order to make them more *efficiently* selective and allow for better labour market planning. Canada's new interpretations provided for an 'increasingly well-organized international dimension in the employment and recruitment of highly skilled and skilled labor' (Hawkins, 1972, 15).

England also welcomed immigration from the West Indies and India and Pakistan during this same period. The war, lowered birth rates, and the exhaustion of the agricultural sector as a traditional source of surplus labour created a labour short market at a time when the postwar expansion of British capital required labour surpluses. Recruitment of workers began in the Caribbean. Colonial status as 'British subjects' exempted West Indians from restrictions on the right to enter the United Kingdom. By 1961, the movement had peaked, as had the expansion of the British economy. As the slowing down of the economy lessened the need for supplementary labour, demands for closure of national boundaries began to be heard. In 1962, at the culmination of heated debates, heightened white racism and disputes over statutory restrictions with the Commonwealth Governments, the Commonwealth Immigrants Bill was introduced. Its impact was to restrict entry to those who only a few years earlier had been actively recruited to fill in the labour shortages.

Just as all borders are restrictive, so too are they permeable. The statutory definitions of their degree of restrictiveness or permeability reflect both cyclical and secular economic and political trends in individual states within the contemporary world economy. Within the Caribbean, perhaps nowhere is the selective impact of boundary definitions more evident than with the 1961 political decision of the US to grant 'visa waivers', extended aid, and employment and resettlement assistance to Cubans after the establishment of the present Cuban government. Over 100 000 Cubans moved into the United States between 1959 and 1961. Although most did not qualify under existing restrictions for immigration, they were permitted to remain permanently. Although most were non-immigrants and therefore technically not eligible to take jobs, they were allowed to obtain employment. Reflecting the political mood of assisting 'anti-Communists' throughout the world, the Migration and Refugee Assistance Act sponsored by Francis Walter (who had successfully defended the 1952 legislation 'aimed to secure those immigrants most likely to fit usefully into our economy and our culture') granted dispensation for political immigrants whom the President determined '. . . will contribute to the defense, security or foreign policy interests of the United States'.[10]

5   *While generally governed by the rules of international law, boundary definitions are in fact interpreted according to the needs and legislation of the individual states they represent.* International law has traditionally consisted of the 'body of rules binding on states in their dealings with one another' or, the law which operates between states.[11] Correspondingly, 'the principal link between international law and the individual is nationality'.[12] Plender lists three factors which cause most states to base part of their immigration laws on their nationality laws. The first is the relationship between states which generally determines their attitudes towards admission or non-admission of one another's nationals. Second, they are often bound to do so by treaty obligations. And third, bonds of common interests or regional ties often assume reciprocal immigration privileges (Plender, 1972, 3). These reasons, however, do not account for or explain the economic and political influences, both conjunctural and secular, which motivate states to revise their own legislation or interpretations, even in contradiction to their own superordinate principles, to defy or circumvent international laws, covenants or treaties, or to 'look the other way' where economic or political imperatives are in conflict with legal imperatives with regard to immigration.

As a principle of international law, each state retains the sovereign right to determine who its nationals shall be (Plender, 1972, 30–31). It would seem logical that the massive numbers of cross-national migrants, especially labour migrants, might seek recourse, protection, or intervention through the sanctions of international law. In fact, international covenants are of scant assistance to the international migrant, since they are bound to the principle of the right of jurisdiction of states on these matters. Even though boundary definitions may affect the lives of individuals outside their jurisdiction, they are inaccessible to those individuals in the juridical sense. Individuals have legal recourse in matters involving national boundaries primarily through the limitations and restrictions established by national legal codes. Juridically and politically, 'nationality' is the bond which ties the state to each of its members (Plender, 1972, 30). At the turn of the century, it was the

---

[10] Statement of Representative Francis E. Walter cited in Bennett, 1963, 180, and clause from Migration and Refugee Assistance Act of 1962 cited in Plender, 1972, 235.
[11] Briefly, *The law of nations* (1963), p. 1, cited in Plender, 1972, 2.
[12] Oppenheim, *International law* (1952), p. 508, cited in Plender, 1972, 2.

174   *The role of national boundaries in a cross-national labour market*

opinion of international law that a state might prevent persons who did not belong to it from 'trespassing' on its property (Plender, 1972, 52). Thus, the exclusionary laws of the United States, Canada and the United Kingdom just reviewed were well within the sovereign rights of states with regard to individuals who are not 'its nationals'.

III   Internationalization of labour: some theoretical observations

The idea that the individual 'belongs to the state' is a legal concept which ignores the sociological aspect of the relationship between state and society. The state does not 'belong' to all 'its' members equally, rather, the state, through the government and its policies, operates more in the interests of some classes than others. As a legal-administrative term, 'nationality' has a formal and clearly defined meaning. As a relational term, however, defining the kind and degree of commitment or allegiance between the individual and the state, it is illusive, since all citizens are not served equally by the functioning of 'their' state (Miliband, 1969, 206).[13] In capitalist society, the state is charged with the primary responsibility of defending the interests of the dominant classes: of managing the affairs, of mediating the needs, of capitalism and the capitalist class.[14] These ends are accomplished through the removal or erection of obstacles which benefit or inhibit the functioning of a capitalist economy. The degree of relaxation, selectivity or stringency involved in the formation and enforcement of boundary definitions is illustrative.

Nor does the primary basis of social life rest on the relationship of the individual to the state in modern society, but, rather, it resides in the production of material goods or commodities. Commodity production or production for the market has evolved as a result of the social division of labour. In his discussion of the development of the world economy, Bukharin noted that alongside the classic social division of labour between large subdivisions of the economy (e.g. industry and agriculture), there exists another division of labour between 'national economies' among various countries. There is an international division of labour which oversteps the boundaries of the 'national economy'. Unequal development of productive forces produces a pattern of uneven, irregular development among different countries. Different economic specializations and different economic strength increases the development of an international division of labour—a

[13] From the point of view of the dominant class, nothing could be so obviously advantageous as the assertion which forms one of the basic themes of nationalism, namely, that all citizens, whoever they may be, owe a supreme allegiance to a 'national interest' which requires that men should be ready to subdue all other interests, particularly class interests, for the sake of a larger, more comprehensive concern which unites in a supreme allegiance rich and poor, the comfortable and the deprived, the givers of orders and their recipients.

[14] See Mandel, 1975, especially chapter 15; Miliband, 1969. These are two useful sources on the role of the state.

territorial division of the world (Bukharin, 1966, 20).[15] Here Bukharin had in mind the difference between industrial countries, which tended to import primary materials and agricultural products, and primary producing countries exporting the products of agricultural and mineral production and importing the products of industry.

Countries exporting manufactured goods proved to be the most developed industrial countries of the world and, thus, the main subdivisions of the social division of labour also tend to be expressed on an international scale.

> The social labour of the world as a whole is divided among the various countries; the labour of every individual country becomes part of that world social labour through the exchange (of their labour products) that takes place on a world scale. This interdependence of countries is by no means an accident; it is a necessary condition for continued social growth. International exchange thereby turns into a process of socio-economic life governed by definite laws.
>
> There is a regular market connection, through the process of exchange, between numberless individual economies scattered over the most diverse geographical areas. Thus world *division of labour* and international exchange presuppose the existence of a *world market and world prices* (Bukharin, 1966, 22–23).

Bukharin (1966, 25–26) defined world economy as a system of production relations, and, correspondingly, of exchange relations on a world scale. Pointing out that highly complicated contemporary economic life 'knows a great variety of forms behind which production relations are hidden' (p. 26), he notes that the international movement of capital is also a fact of modern economic life. The growth of the connections of a world market of commodities and capital exchange has tied 'nations' and 'national economies' closer and closer together, creating the basis for production and exchange on a world scale. While the nation remains the basic political unit in this network, much of the production, distribution and investment transcends national boundaries (although, as noted earlier, the weaker states of the periphery are frequently powerless to impose the traditional protective and restrictive functions of their national boundaries on the organizations, enterprises and emissaries of the capitalist world).

What then of the labour market which must exist alongside the commodities and capital markets and what is the role of the sale and exchange of labour in an international division of labour? Normally, 'that commodity which the working class has to sell—its labour power—must by its nature be sold locally and cannot be dealt in across national boundaries (Sweezy, 1942). However, the inequalities among nations and among peoples which have deepened with the expansion of a single world division of labour has assured the capitalist enterprises of the core a gigantic international reservoir of surplus labour at their disposal in whatever

[15] Bukharin's observations of the development of the world economy are introduced here to illustrate the process we are describing, not to serve as a definitive model, since his larger argument on economic planning and the future of the world economy has proved inadequate. Secondly, there are a variety of works which develop related hypotheses about the emergence of an international division of labour which offer additional insights and partial models for us to follow. Among them we would list Wallerstein, 1974; Mandel, 1975; Amin, 1974; Emmanuel, 1972.

176   *The role of national boundaries in a cross-national labour market*

proportions they have needed. A world capitalist labour market allows the core access to cheap labour.

Two techniques permit capital to avail itself of this labour. Either the capital, technology and manager-technicians are exported to countries or regions of labour surplus to establish production there. Or, alternatively, labour reserves are imported across national boundaries to the locations of production within the core. In the latter case, the advantage is that labour can be recruited, refrained or expelled from entry according to sectoral, cyclical and secular demands of capital. The willingness and ability of the core states to define the conditions of crossing or immigrating across national boundaries make it so. The poverty, unemployment, unequal wages and limited opportunities which mark the international division of labour for the working class within the periphery assure a constant pressure to move toward the centres of production within the core when the conditions permit. Labour must naturally seek that labour market where it can sell its labour power to the greatest advantage. Workers recruited from among reserve pools of international labour do not 'belong' to any state, but derive their primary status from 'belonging' to capital, just as capital must 'belong' to labour in order to survive.

Thus the 'internationalization of labour' has two variants. First is that to which we referred before, which occurs because the labour of every individual nation is part of the world social labour through the exchange of their labour products—and, therefore, each of its national labourers, too, is part of that world social labour. Second is that which occurs with immigration when individuals become more directly a part of that international social labour through the sale of their labour power itself.

There is a difference, however. When an individual sells his or her labour power within the nation of which he or she is a citizen, it is done within the network of legal protection and social legislation which that state normally affords its citizens. When an individual crosses national boundaries in order to work, however, they become part of an *international* workforce, but they remain governed or restricted by *national* legislation and policies. Of course, some degree of protection is offered by the legal-social norms of the labour importing country. Nonetheless, the absence of an international set of rules governing the status of the cross-national worker increases his or her susceptibility to exploitation and manipulation.[16]

IV   Immigration and legislation: the current contradiction over national boundaries

Two general categories of immigration to the United States currently predominate: low-wage, highly exploited workers, primarily from the

[16] This observation was originally stimulated by Terence K. Hopkins in his thoughts on the nature of the international working class (see Hopkins, 1977).

Caribbean and Latin America, and a smaller but important group of trained professionals and technicos drawn from throughout the 'developed' and 'underdeveloped' world. During the post-second world war period, but particularly during the expansive war economy of the 1960s, foreign labour of both categories was permitted and even encouraged to move relatively unfettered into the United States. The growing world economic crisis of the 1970s, compounded by the increasing introduction of technology with the associated reduction of the number of work hours required to maintain or expand production, has forced the steady reduction of the flow of the first category, however. This has been accomplished partially by the more efficient and rigorous interpretation and enforcement of existing state policies. Interests concerned with the effective halt and perhaps reversal of the first category of immigration have recently sought extensive legislation from the state which would permit the blocking and efficient policing of the entry of this category of workers.

At the same time, there are other economic interests, particularly the small-scale, less rationalized, competitive industrial and service sector, which still welcome and rely upon the supplies of immigrant workers. Operating on smaller profit margins, or struggling to accelerate and consolidate the process of capital accumulation, these employers find an ideal workforce among the numbers of migrants from the periphery. Urged by the poverty and lack of opportunities generated by regional and national disparities within a world economy, workers from the periphery are willing to work for lower wages and under worse conditions than are indigenous workers, since the level of real and social wages received still represents a relative improvement over that to which they have access at home. In addition, their probably well deserved reputation of being 'hard working' provides an additional attraction to employers. Whether their move is stimulated by hunger or ambition, most immigrants can be seen as having few alternatives in the matter of the wages and conditions they will accept. Indigenous workers, on the other hand, are protected by a threshold of social legislation (welfare coverage, minimum wage laws, food stamps, etc.) which they need not be pushed below in order to survive.

Within this context, the issue of national boundaries takes on special significance. Labour markets associated with industry and services desiring foreign workers effectively bypass national boundaries and penetrate directly into the periphery—Jamaica, Colombia, Mexico, Haiti, the Dominican Republic. Planners, with an eye to reducing political and economic consequences of prolonged unemployment within the core, however, seek to manipulate these boundaries to curtail labour flows from the outermost hinterlands of the market.

Foreign labour, driven from the periphery toward the still available job locations in the core, is often caught in the contradictory position of being informally recruited by some employers, while being legally barred from obtaining these jobs by the imposition of formally inpenetrable national

178   *The role of national boundaries in a cross-national labour market*

barriers. Having no access to traditional organizations of struggle, cross-national labour must resort to alternative measures in its quest for access to jobs. The tactics employed in circumventing or evading legal-national obstacles to desired employment are a side effect of an intracapital conflict in which labour must devise extra-legal means to reach their job destinations.

1   *Boundary definitions: Jamaica and the United States, United Kingdom and Canada*

Within the interstate system the prerogative of establishing strong definitions of boundary permeability and legislating periodic or temporary redefinitions which encourage or disallow legal movement into the labour market within their jurisdiction rests with labour importing states. The effects influence movement patterns within the labour exporting regions. An examination of the history of outmigration in the case of Jamaica will illustrate some specific features of this interaction.

1) The actual volume and direction of emigration corresponds more closely to state policies of the core than to high unemployment levels, high birth rates, or Gross Domestic Product within Jamaica.

While the latter variables create the preconditions for emigration, the movement is set in motion and governed primarily by policies determining who shall be permitted to immigrate to the core states. The figures from Figure 1 and the pattern shown in Table 3 indicate the sharp rises and declines in emigration to the three countries.

a Birth rates: The 1976 birth rate of 29·8 per one thousand persons was the lowest ever recorded in Jamaica. Since 1973 the number of births have remained relatively stable after a downward trend from 1970. While moderately high compared with core countries, it compares favourably with the rest of the Latin American region. Nor could high birth rate alone explain the extremely high emigrations around 1960 and 1970 (see Figure 2), since the birth rates for the years 1943 and 1950 were a relatively low 33 per 1000 (Table 4). (Those cohorts would feed into the outmigration of 1960 and 1970.)

b Unemployment levels: The official unemployment figures are high—and they tell us nothing about underemployment, below subsistence living and penny capitalism. In 1960, the official statistics placed unemployment at about 13% and by 1969 it had 'officially' risen to 18%. By 1972 it had reached 25%, where it has hovered since. Again, while unemployment has been consistently high, its pattern of marked increase does not correspond to patterns of outmigration. On the contrary, when unemployment was lowest during the past 18 years, emigration was highest. At the point where unemployment had peaked—1972—emigration had sharply declined. (Source: Government of Jamaica, Department of Statistics, *1960 Census of the Population*, and 'The Labour Force', 1968, 1969, 1977.)

c Gross Domestic Product: The Jamaican Gross Domestic Product has gradually risen since the second world war, as a consequence of the development and expansion of the bauxite industry and a slight expansion in

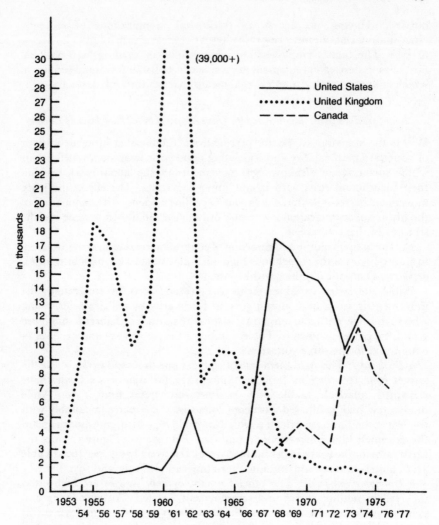

Figure 1   Main streams of Jamaican migration

manufacturing. Ironically, the highest unemployment levels are associated
with those economic sectors which have also shown the fastest economic
growth during the period: mining, refining, public utilities, transportation and
communications, miscellaneous services and financial institutions. Even
allowing for some error in government statistics, it is clear that the national
income growth has been rising faster than population increase. The annual
average growth rate during the 1960–70 period was listed as 4·5%; this rose to

180 *The role of national boundaries in a cross-national labour market*

Table 3 Main streams of Jamaican migration

Year	Ultimate destination: country		
	United States[a]	Canada[b]	United Kingdom[c]
1953	252	202	2 159
1954	798	200	8 039
1955	940	256	18 569
1956	1 168		17 302
1957	1 207		13 087
1958	1 300		9 993
1959	1 732		12 796
1960	1 472		32 060
1961	2 757		39 203
1962	5 619		22 841
1963	2 883		7 494
1964	2 089		9 560
1965	2 175	1 214	9 510
1966	2 743	1 407	7 077
1967	10 483	3 459	8 107
1968	17 470	2 885	4 476
1969	16 947	3 889	2 554
1970	15 033	4 659	2 372
1971	14 571	3 903	1 759
1972	13 427	3 092	1 620
1973	9 963	9 363	1 872
1974	12 408	11 286	1 397
1975	11 076	8 211	1 077
1976	9 026	7 282	880

[a] Total immigrants *admitted*, year ended 30 June, US Immigration and Naturalization reports.
[b] Migrants to Canada, Immigration Statistics Reports, Manpower and Immigration, Canada.
[c] British High Commission, Migration to United Kingdom.

10·4% in 1972 and to over 19% in 1973, according to Jamaican government statistics. (Source: American University, Foreign Area Studies, *Area Handbook for Jamaica*, 1976.)

2) When policies of a state which is the destination of high immigration redefine entrance requirements so as to hinder, limit or halt immigration, that migratory flow tends to move in new directions towards more accessible labour markets in other states. If more 'open' markets do not exist elsewhere, the redirected migration will tend to reemerge as 'extra-legal' movement.

The United Kingdom's Commonwealth Immigrants Act of 1962 virtually halted further immigration of significance from Jamaica (see Figure 1 and Table 3). In December 1965, amendments to the United States' Immigration and Nationality Act came into force. For Jamaicans, entrance requirements

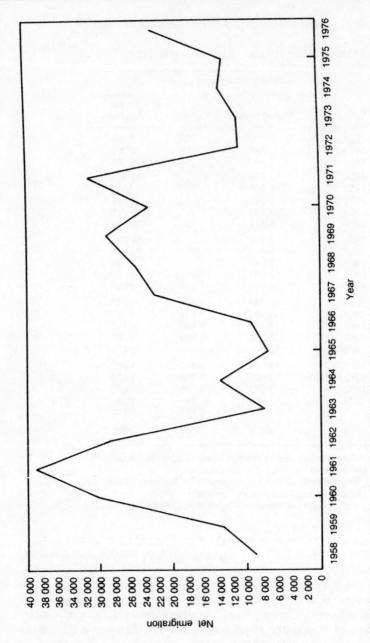

Figure 2 Summary of net emigration from Jamaica, 1958–76

182   *The role of national boundaries in a cross-national labour market*

Table 4   Jamaica, 1861–1976: Live birth rates per 1000 persons

1861	40·0
1871	39·0
1881	38·0
1891	36·7
1911	39·5
1921	27·9
1943	33·2
1953	34·4
1963	39·0
1969	35·1
1970	34·4
1971	34·9
1972	34·3
1973	31·4
1974	30·6
1975	30·1
1976	29·8

Source: Jamaican Registrar General's Department in *Statistical Yearbook of Jamaica,* 1976.

were liberalized. The immediate effect was a very sharp rise in permanent immigrant visas issued (1967: 13 138, as against 5003 in 1966, and 1317 in 1965). Similarly, Canada established a scheme based on a points system in 1967 which is reflected in the gradual rise in Jamaican immigrants. Prior to 1967, immigration was based on sponsorship which essentially meant

Table 5   Summary of net emigration from Jamaica, 1958–76

Year	Net emigration
1958	8 200
1959	13 100
1960	30 400
1961	38 500
1962	28 700
1963	7 300
1964	13 500
1965	6 500
1966	8 900
1967	22 049
1968	24 996
1969	29 000
1970	23 000
1971	31 500
1972	10 200
1973	10 200
1974	13 000
1975	12 100
1976	22 200

Source: Social and Economic Survey, Jamaican National Planning Agency, 1967–1975; Demographic Statistics, Department of Statistics of Jamaica, 1976; Segal (1975).

continued entrance of those national groups already in Canada—a system which had generally excluded Jamaicans before. (See Table 5.)

3) Selective criteria for immigrant status reflect changes within the occupational structure, new technology, and the location and organization of production within the importing economies. Thus the occupational array of Jamaicans who have emigrated to the United States, United Kingdom and Canada corresponds more closely to the occupational structure within the labour importing country than to the Jamaican occupational structure. (See Tables 6 and 7.)

4) In the case of occupational categories for which there is a limited demand within the core but a large supply among the peripheral population, the importing state is apt to regulate entrance more stringently through the use of contract labour schemes, such as those which permit seasonal agricultural workers from the Caribbean to work in the United States only so long as they are actively engaged in harvest or cultivation. The contract specifies a period of employment to commence on the day of the worker's arrival and to terminate on a named date, after which (s)he shall no longer retain the legal right to remain within the United States. The 'Agreement for the Employment of British West Indians in Agricultural Work in the United States' also specifies that the worker shall work and reside at the place of his employer and at no time work for any person other than his employer. This prevents the migrant from entering into competition in the open market and allows both the employer and the importing state to rid themselves of labour surpluses which are not in high demand except for specific tasks. (See Table 8.)

The Canadian Household Service Workers' Scheme offers an example of a less restrictive contract agreement. Thousands of Jamaican women were recruited to Canada to work as domestic servants in private homes for one year after which they were free to work elsewhere and to remain in the country. (See Table 9.) Designed during times of greater affluence and less unemployment, however, the contract contained no stipulation for repatriation if and when the labour of these women was no longer needed. As a result, the Canadian government recently moved to deport a group of Jamaican women, originally recruited through this government-to-government arrangement, on the basis of a technicality involving failure to declare dependent children left at home. The *Toronto Star* observed; 'It's one thing to limit immigration when jobs are scarce, it's another to throw people out when you no longer need them. . . . In the case of these Jamaican mothers, there are special circumstances our government cannot shrug off. Canadian officials were fully aware that most of the women applying to come to Canada had dependent children, whether they admitted it or not. But at the time they preferred to look the other way' (quoted in *The Jamaica Weekly Gleaner*, 27 February 1978).

A higher degree of entrance control is maintained through the use of a device such as a 'work permit' which is employed by Britain. Until 1977, British authorities distinguished between 'work permits' (which were issued to aliens) and 'employment vouchers' (issued to Commonwealth citizens). (See Table

Table 6 Jamaican migration to the United States, Canada, and the United Kingdom, 1966–72

Occupation	1966 US	1966 Can.	1967 US	1967 Can.	1968 US	1968 Can.	1968 UK	1969 US	1969 Can.	1969 UK	1970 US	1970 Can.	1970 UK	1971 US	1971 Can.	1971 UK	1972 US	1972 Can.	1972 UK
Professional, technical and related	346	232	1 357	403	1 777	294	8	1 704	351	—	1 056	334	—	1 078	194	—	810	—	—
Administrative, executive and managerial	45	18	110	37	150	15	—	176	40	—	222	52	—	183	56	—	194	—	—
Clerical	205	223	685	555	1 347	407	—	1 360	571	—	1 061	655	—	783	485	—	797	—	—
Sales	29	16	83	49	146	31	—	161	110	—	128	118	—	121	85	—	105	—	—
Craftsmen	212	146	501	528	1 117	322	—	1 610	453	—	1 798	606	—	1 411	483	—	1 150	—	—
Other skilled	391	21	66	144	2 017	216	—	1 880	330	—	1 803	442	—	1 508	370	—	1 403	—	—
*Semiskilled and unskilled	222	218	4 152	575	6 970	491	—	4 917	604	—	1 967	790	—	2 170	671	—	1 846	—	—
Unclassified	337	16	699	106	—	—	156	—	—	145	—	—	93	—	—	133	—	—	65
Total workers	1 435	890	7 649	2 377	13 524	1 784	—	11 808	2 459	145	8 035	2 997	93	7 254	2 344	133	6 311	—	65
Dependants, no occupation reported	1 308	517	2 834	1 962	3 946	1 102	4 416	5 139	1 430	2 554	6 998	1 662	2 279	7 317	1 554	1 626	7 116	—	1 450
Total migrants	2 743	1 451	10 483	3 457	17 970	2 886	4 640	16 947	3 889	2 699	15 633	4 659	2 372	14 571	3 903	1 759	13 427	2 800	1 515

Source: Annual Social and Economic Surveys, Jamaican National Planning Agency, Kingston, Jamaica, 1968–1972.
ᵃ1966 'Semiskilled and unskilled' includes service workers.
ᵇFigures for UK not broken down by classification.

Table 7 Jamaican migration to US and Canada by occupation, 1972–75

Occupation	United States				Canada			
	1972	1973	1974	1975	1972	1973	1974	1975
Professional, technical and related workers	810	562	566	503	154	267	266	
Farmers, and farm managers	6	—	2	10	—	—	—	
Managers, officials, kindred workers	194	158	175	181	45	223	386	
Clerical and kindred workers	797	595	715	611	280	866	729	
Sales workers	105	82	92	78	61	192	200	
Craftsmen, foremen, kindred workers	1 150	821	1 044	929				
Operatives and kindred workers	976	674	789	774				
Private household	1 617	761	722	810	366	1 236	1 103	
Service workers except private household	436	355	464	395	112	569	657	
Farm labourers and foremen	91	73	136	82				
Labourers except farm and mine	138	124	165	97	17	74	35	
Housewives, children, no occupation reported	7 116	5 758	7 488	6 606				

Source: Economic and Social Survey, 1974, Jamaican National Planning Agency, Kingston, Jamaica. Annual Report, US Immigration and Naturalization Service, 1972.

10.) An alien bearing a work permit had no legal right to enter the United Kingdom, whereas the holder of an employment voucher normally had a right of entry. In practice, an alien who entered with a work permit did not obtain the right to settle there until the completion of his or her fourth year of residence, while a Commonwealth citizen with an employment voucher obtained an immediate right to settle.

Under the 1977 rulings, however, no migrants for employment were allowed to enter without first obtaining work permits. Significant because of their exemption were doctors and dentists coming to take up professional appointments and representatives of foreign firms. In addition, persons seeking seasonal work at agricultural camps are allowed to enter without work permits under special arrangements.

The Department of Employment holds total discretion in issuing work permits. An applicant may appeal to adjudicators against a refusal to grant him a visa or entry certificate, but he *cannot appeal against a refusal to grant him a work permit*. The Department of Employment uses three criteria in deciding whether to issue a permit: 1) employment must be in some manufacturing industry; 2) the vacancy in question must not be capable of being easily filled by a person already in the United Kingdom; and 3) no more vouchers will be issued for unskilled or semi-skilled employment for prospective immigrants.

5) State policies regarding immigration are isomorphic to the hierarchical relations of inequality among nations. Within a global labour market, cross-national labour from the poorer nations frequently moves on to labour markets within the less poor nations within the periphery or semi-periphery, just as labour from the less poor nations seeks to move on to the wealthier and

Table 8 New recruits by islands, June 1951–August 1977

Year	Jamaica	Barbados	Leewards[a]	Windwards[b]	Antigua	St Kitts	Montserrat	Grenada	St Lucia	St Vincent	Dominica	Trinidad	British Guiana	British Honduras	Total
1951	1 285	1 599	500	499								100	96	100	4 179
52	2 601	717	252	504								168	84	84	4 410
53	3 490	954	220	138											4 802
54	1 423	329	218	84								92			2 146
55	2 673	440	199	237								102			3 651
56	3 379	906	7	77											4 369
57	4 313	939	155	225								75			5 707
58	3 722	755	109	419								100	99		5 204
59	4 597	1 128	228	350								212		107	6 622
60	5 897	1 274	219	655								1	105		8 151
61	6 391	1 309				45	45	218	218	164	49	215	5	216	8 875
62	9 727	1 125			166		50	303	200	112	46				11 729
63	9 367	1 925				43	51	143	181	99	47				11 856
64	11 536	1 419						190	197	140	48				13 530
65	9 152	943						67	93	66	40				10 361
66	9 906	882						65	65	66					10 984
67	12 048	1 238						97	98	97					13 578
68	9 464	909						97	126	127					10 723
69	12 084	961							242	243					13 530
70	13 873	910							338	339					15 460
71	10 896	727							520						12 143
72	10 119	702							499	99					11 419
73	10 742	682							200	300					11 924
74	10 032	700							292	292	30				11 346
75	10 263	745							306	306	48				11 668
76	8 657	628							300	309	50				9 944
77	345														345
	197 982	24 846	2 107	3 188	166	88	146	1 180	3 875	2 759	358	1 065	389	507	238 656

[a]The Leeward Islands included Antigua, St Kitts and Monserrat
[b]The Windward Islands included Dominica, Grenada, St Lucia and St Vincent
Source: British West Indies Central Organization, Kingston, Jamaica

Table 9   Female domestic help to Canada

Year	Recruited
1955	75
1956	134
1957	66
1958	100
1959	104
1960	104
1961	104
1962	104
1963	104
1964	104
1965	104
1966	193
1967	130
1968	135

Source: Social And Economic Survey of Jamaica, National Planning Agency, 1968
1959: *Domestic help to Canada*
Under agreement with the Canadian Government, 104 Jamaican women are permitted to enter the Dominion of Canada annually as domestic servants. The contract stipulates that these women work as domestic servants in the country for one year, after which they are free to pursue other activities and are at liberty to remain in the country.
1966: *Domestic help to Canada*
Under an agreement operating with the Canadian Government, 104 Jamaican women were permitted to enter the Dominion of Canada annually as domestic servants. In 1966, the annual quota was increased to 193. The contract stipulates that these women work as domestic servants in the country for one yea, after which they are free to pursue other activities and are a liberty to remain in the country.
Source: *Annual Abstract of Statistics*, nos. 25 and 26, 1966 and 1967, Department of Statistics, Kingston, Jamaica

Table 10   United Kingdom: Number of work vouchers issued to Jamaicans, 1962–67

Year	Male	Female	Total
1962	485	418	903
1963	734	589	1 323
1964	642	610	1 252
1965	647	566	1 213
1966	n.a.	n.a.	294
1967	n.a.	n.a.	287

Source: *Social and Economic Survey of Jamaica*, Jamaican National Planning Agency, 1967, p. 46.
In August 1965 the Government of the United Kingdom restricted the number of Commonwealth immigrant work vouchers to 8 500 per annum. This restriction has resulted in a sharp fall in the number of work vouchers issued to Jamaicans.

188   *The role of national boundaries in a cross-national labour market*

wealthiest nations, suggesting a stratification among international labourers, as well as stratification among national labour markets. Within the Caribbean, this stratification is expressed in the migration of labour from the small islands, whose economies are also weaker, to the large islands whose economies are more affluent within the region. Thus there is a pattern of migration *within* the Caribbean, as well as *from* the Caribbean to the core. But not infrequently, labour movement within the region has been tied directly or indirectly to labour needs created by activity of core capital within this peripheral zone. Jamaicans were imported to supply the Cuban sugar industry when US investment expanded after the turn of the century; Barbados and the Windward Islands (especially St Vincent and Grenada) sent workers to Trinidad during the early period of construction in the Dutch and US oil processing industry; and job seekers who moved freely back and forth from Antigua to the American Virgin Islands during the construction of the tourist facilities are now restricted and being pressured to go back home.

Accordingly, states such as Jamaica have designed legislation to protect their already overloaded labour markets from access to nationals whose employment options are even more limited. Since 1946, aliens seeking to enter employment in Jamaica have been required to produce written work permits issued by Jamaican authorities. These permits are issued by the Minister of Home Affairs 'only when appropriate employment is available and cannot be filled by members of the indigenous labor force' (Plender, 1972, 34). There is a differential application of these restrictions, though. While they are used to keep unskilled labour from the poorer island economies out, they are also relaxed in order to attract professionals and skilled workers in. Ironically, these skilled workers must be recruited in order to replace the Jamaican professionals and technicians who have emigrated to the US, UK and Canada. Despite the limitation of employment of foreigners, in 1973, work permits were held by nearly 3000 aliens occupying professional and technical positions. At the same time, emigration of 1070 professional, managerial and technical workers set against an output of about 2900 new workers in these fields left only a much reduced balance of about 1800 in this category in a country of two million. During the 1960s, only an estimated 23% of the 186 000 workers believed to have emigrated were unskilled. More than 12% of the emigrants were professional, technical and managerial personnel and nearly 50% were craftsmen and skilled and semi-skilled workers (Kaplan *et al.*, 1976).

When partial closure and relaxed policing permit, aliens devise extra-legal strategies for acquiring access to cross-national employment and employers of low-wage aliens similarly 'overlook' formal state requirements. Worker strategies may involve smuggling or other clandestine border crossing, or passage through a port of entry using an ostensibly valid visa which may misrepresent facts pertaining to formal entrance requirements. Tactics such as the outright purchase of fraudulent documents are obvious. Others, such as the double photo file, are more obscure. Some, such as the offering of bribes to consular officers, are time-tested. Others, such as the movement of

Table 11 Comparison of demographic data

Country [sic]	Population	Percent yearly increase	Density	Urban population	Urban percent of total	Life expect-ancy	Infant mortality under 5 yrs/1000	Average persons per room	Labour force (million)	Unemploy-ment (%)	Per capita income ($)
Dominican Rep.	4 497 000	2·9	86	1 319 902	32·8	52	80·4	2+	1·3	—	440
Guatemala	5 809 000	2·8	49	1 441 711	33·6	49	91·5	2+	1·7	15–20	380
Haiti	4 903 000	2·1	179	—	—	47	190·0	—	—	—	100
Jamaica	1 965 000	1·5	173	690 200	37·1	70	35·4	1+2	2·6	23	670
Trinidad/Tobago	993 000	1·3	201	116 972	12·4	64	37·5	2	0·8	—	920
Colombia	24 403 000	3·2	19	9 239 626	52·8	60	80·0	1+2	0·36	—	340
Ecuador	6 839 000	3·4	22	2 332 793	39·3	54	90·4	2+	5·6	—	280
Guyana	782 000	2·5	3	335 482	29·5	51	39·6	—	2·0	21	360
Mexico	55 488 000	3·6	26	28 377 932	58·7	63	63·1	2+	13·1	—	780
Philippines	40 788 000	3·0	127	1 645 459	31·7	—	—	—	11·0	—	220
Korea	33 290 000	2·2	324	12 995 265	41·2	—	—	—	10·2	4·5	300
Hong Kong	4 186 000	1·0	69	4 186 000	—	—	—	—	1·5	—	1 000
Puerto Rico	2 861 000	1·2	310	1 575 490	58·1	—	—	—	0·8	11	1 890
United States	211 228 000	0·7	22	149 324 930	73·5	70	22·1	−1	86·0	—	—

Source: US Immigration (Pamphlet), US Department of State, 1975.
Note: These figures should not be accorded any absolute value but should be evaluated in terms of the trends they represent and the political message they were designed to convey in a discussion sponsored by the US Department of State on the magnitude of 'illegal immigration'.

Table 12 Western hemisphere immigrants to the United States, top ten source countries, fiscal years 1965–73

1965 (FY)		1967 (FY)		1969 (FY)		1971 (FY)		1973 (FY)	
Canada	40 013	Mexico	40 665	Mexico	42 071	Mexico	48 076	Mexico	66 935
Mexico	37 432	Cuba	34 439	Canada	15 722	Cuba	21 403	Cuba	23 690
Cuba	20 086	Canada	24 712	Jamaica	15 252	Jamaica	12 254	Dominican Republic	13 735
Dominican Republic	10 851	Dominican Republic	11 717	Dominican Republic	10 279	Dominican Republic	12 122	Jamaica	9 528
Colombia	9 760	Jamaica	11 204	Cuba	8 952	Canada	11 316	Canada	7 278
Argentina	5 629	Colombia	4 873	Trinidad and Tobago	7 442	Trinidad and Tobago	6 917	Trinidad and Tobago	7 097
Ecuador	4 176	Haiti	3 824	Colombia	6 638	Haiti	6 686	Colombia	5 234
Haiti	3 763	Ecuador	2 623	Haiti	6 407	Colombia	6 208	Haiti	4 865
Costa Rica	2 781	Argentina	2 542	Ecuador	5 173	Ecuador	4 784	Ecuador	4 082
Brazil	2 755	Trinidad and Tobago	2 294	Argentina	3 407	Guyana	2 137	Guyana	2 942

Table 13   Non-immigrant visas granted by United States, top ten source countries, fiscal years 1965–73

1965 (FY)		1967 (FY)		1969 (FY)		1971 (FY)		1973 (FY)	
Colombia	20 107	Brazil	27 965	Colombia	32 772	Colombia	38 095	Venezuela	45 431
Philippines	17 659	Switzerland	25 066	Brazil	31 017	Argentina	37 398	Spain	44 925
Brazil	17 493	Argentina	24 804	Sweden	29 392	Brazil	36 749	India	37 398
Spain	17 220	Philippines	23 851	Argentina	29 319	Peru	30 628	Sweden	37 050
Sweden	16 451	Sweden	22 517	Philippines	28 895	Sweden	29 397	Switzerland	37 049
Peru	15 646	Peru	20 457	Switzerland	23 053	Jamaica	29 394	Greece	32 915
Switzerland	15 504	Colombia	20 029	Spain	22 434	India	28 376	Jamaica	31 846
Israel	15 043	Israel	19 616	India	22 169	Dominican Republic	27 104	Philippines	30 718
Jamaica	13 728	Spain	18 526	Jamaica	21 599	Spain	25 199	Israel	29 704
India	13 302	Norway	17 182	Israel	20 858	Israel	24 965	Norway	28 044

192   *The role of national boundaries in a cross-national labour market*

Table 14   Percentage of United States non-immigrant visa application refusal by country (FY 1972)

35% or higher refusal rate (NIV only)
Guatemala
Ecuador
Guyana
Trinidad and Tobago
Jamaica
Poland
Dominican Republic

25%–35% refusal rate (NIV only)
Colombia
Haiti
Mexico
Bulgaria
Romania
Portugal

15%–25% refusal rate (NIV only)
Panama
Peru
Argentina
Philippines
Korea
Afghanistan
United Arab Emirates
Lebanon
Jordan
Nigeria
Ghana
Czechoslovakia
Yugoslavia

Source: Consular Reports and US Immigration (pamphlet), US Department of State, 1975.

Dominicans into Puerto Rico, and subsequently on to the United States as 'Puerto Ricans', involve more complicated organization. For all methods there is a money and often an emotional price. The worker pays.

Where strict limitation on the issuance of immigrant visas exists, workers often enter on non-immigrant visas (or any visa which does not qualify the bearer to hold employment), obtain work, and remain within the country outside the conditions provided for in the original document. Generally it has been found that US Foreign Service Posts with high rates of visa refusals in the non-immigrant area are located within those countries which are also sources of immigrants who enter under conditions outside those stipulated as permissible by state laws. (See Tables 12, 13, 14.) Jamaica appears for the first time on the list of top ten source countries for non-immigrant visa approval to the US in 1965. This is probably a reaction—both legal and extra-legal—to the 1962 closure on further Jamaican movement into the United Kingdom.

For labour within the periphery, the effect of restrictive boundaries is to shut off an escape route, however illusory, from high unemployment, under-employment, poverty and thwarted aspirations. During periods of inter-national capitalist crisis, closed boundaries confine or throw back a disproportionate amount of unemployment on the labour exporting regions. (At the same time, these economies, depending as they do on export of a single or limited crop(s) or primary product for the world market, are also apt to experience a differential impact from the cutting back on imports by the core as a response to the general slowing down of production.) Imposition and manipulation of boundary definitions of global space are another of the many techniques contributing to the maintenance and deepening of unequal development of national units and regional aggregates within a global economy.

Fernand Braudel Center, State University of New York at Binghamton, New York, USA

V   References

Abbott, E. 1924: *Immigration: selected documents and case records*. Chicago: Chicago University Press.

Amin, S. 1974: *Accumulation on a world scale*. New York: Academic Press.

Bennett, M. T. 1963: *American immigration policies: a history*. Washington DC: Public Affairs Press.

Boggs, S. W. 1940: *International Boundaries: a study of boundary functions and problems*. New York: Columbia University Press.

Bukharin, N. 1966: *Imperialism and world economy*. New York: Howard Fertig.

Cukwurah, A. O. 1967: The settlement of boundary disputes in international law. Manchester: Manchester University Press.

Emmanuel, A. 1972: *Unequal exchange*. New York: Monthly Review Press.

Gibbons, H. A. 1977: Boundaries. *International Encyclopedia of the Social Sciences*. New York: Macmillan.

Hawkins, F. 1972: *Canada and immigration: public policy and public concern*. Montreal and London: McGill-Queen's University Press.

Hopkins, T. K. 1977: Notes on class analysis and the world system. *Review* 1, 67–72.

Kaplan, I. 1976: *Area handbook for Jamaica*. Foreign Area Studies Series, American University.

McCullough D. 1977: *The path between the seas: the creation of the Panama canal, 1870–1914*. New York: Simon and Schuster.

Mandel, E. 1975: *Late capitalism*. London: New Left Books.

Miliband, R. 1969: *The state in capitalist society: an analysis of the western system of power*. New York: Basic Books.

Plender, R. 1972: *International migration law*. Leiden: A. W. Sijthoff.

194   *The role of national boundaries in a cross-national labour market*

Prescott, J. R. V. 1965: *The geography of frontiers and boundaries.* Chicago: Aldine Publishing Company.

Schonfield, A. 1965: *Modern capitalism.* Oxford: Oxford University Press.

Segal, A. 1975: *Population policies in the Caribbean.* Lexington, Massachusetts: Lexington Books.

Spengler, J. J. 1958: Issues in American immigration policy. *Annals of the American Academy of Political and Social Science* 316.

Sweezy, P. 1942: *The theory of capitalist development.* New York: Monthly Review Press.

Tomasi, S. M. and **Keely, C. B.** 1975: *Whom have we welcomed? The adequacy and quality of United States immigration data for policy analysis and evaluation.* Staten Island, NY: Center for Migration Studies.

US President's Commission on Immigration and Naturalization 1953: *Immigration and our foreign policy. Whom shall we welcome?* Washington, DC: US Government Printing Office.

Wallerstein, I. 1974: *The modern world system.* New York: Academic Press.

References to Chapters 13 and 14

ABU-LOGHOD, Ibrahim (ed.) (1971, reissued 1987) *The Transformation of Palestine*. Evanston, IL: Northwestern University Press.

ABU-LUGHOD, Janet (1971, reprinted 1987) 'The demographic transformation of Palestine', in Ibrahim Abu-Lughod, *The Transformation of Palestine*, pp. 139–63.

ABU-LUGHOD, Janet (1980) 'Demographic characteristics of the Palestinian population'. Technical report prepared for Unesco, Paris; mimeo.

AMIN, Samir (1974) 'Modern migrations in Western Africa' in Amin Samir (ed.) *Modern Migration in Western Africa*, pp. 65–124. London: Oxford University Press.

ANWAR, Muhammed (1979) *The Myth of Return: Pakistanis in Britain*. London: Heinemann Educational.

BURNLEY, Ian H. and W.E. KALBACH (1985) *Immigrants in Canada and Australia, Volume 3: Urban and Ecological Aspects*. Toronto: Ethnic Research Programme. Institute for Behavioural Research, York University.

COHON, J.D. (1981) 'Psychological adaptation and dysfunction among refugees', *International Migration Review* 15 (1): 255–75.

DE JONG, G. and R.W. GARDNER (1981) *Migration Decision Making: Multidisciplinary Approaches to Micro-level Studies in Developed and Developing Countries*, New York: Pergamon Press.

DESCHENES, Jules (1986) *Commission of Inquiry into War Criminals Reports*. Ottawa: Canada, The Commission.

DOWTY, Alan (1987) *Closed Borders: The Contemporary Assault on Freedom of Movement*. New Haven and London: Yale University Press.

EISENSTADT, S.N. (1954) *The Absorption of Immigrants*. London: Routledge and Kegan Paul.

FAIRCHILD, H.P.(1925) *Immigration: A World Movement and Its American Significance*. New York: Macmillan.

FERRIS, Elizabeth G. (ed.) (1985) *Refugees and World Politics*. New York: Praeger.

GIDDENS, Anthony (1986) '"Power" in the recent writings of Talcott Parsons', *Sociology* 2(3): 257–72.

GIDDENS, Anthony (1984) *The Constitution of Society: Outline of the Theory of Structuration*. Cambridge: Polity Press.

HARRELL-BOND, B.E. (1986) *Imposing Aid: Emergency Assistance to Refugees*. Oxford and New York: Oxford University Press.

HOFFMAN-NOWOTNY, Hans Joachim (1981) 'A sociological approach towards a general theory of migration', in M.M. Kritz et al (eds), *Global Trends in Migration*.

JACKSON, J.A. (ed.) (1969) *Sociological Studies 2: Migration*. Cambridge: Cambridge University Press.

JANSEN, C.J. (1970) 'Migration: a sociological problem', in C.J. Jansen (ed.) *Readings in the Sociology of Migration*, pp. 3–35. Oxford: Pergamon Press.

KALBACH, Warren E. 'The demographics of settlement', in *D'un continent à un autre: les réfugiés du Sud-Est asiatique*. Ottawa: Association Canadienne des Etudes Asiatiques.

KALIN, Walter (1986) 'Troubled communications: cross-cultural misunderstandings in the asylum hearing', *International Migration Review* 20(2): 230–44.

KASINSKY, Renee G. (1976) *Refugees from Militarism: Draft-age Americans in Canada*. New Brunswick, NJ: Transaction Books.

KELLER, S.L. (1975) *Uprooting and Social Change: The Role of Refugees in Development*. Delhi: Manohar Book Service.

KOSINSKI, Leszek and Prothero R. MANSELL (eds) (1975) *People on the Move*. London: Methuen.

KRITZ, M., C. KEELEY and S.M. TOMASI (eds) (1981) *Global Trends in Migration: Theory and Research on International Population Movements*. Staten Island, New York: Center for Migration Studies.

KUBAT, Daniel and Hans-Joachim HOFFMAN-NOWOTNY (1981) 'Migration: towards a new paradigm', *International Social Science Journal* 33(2): 307–29.

KUNZ, Egon (1973) 'Exile and resettlement: refugee theory', *International Migration Review* 15(1–2): 42–51.

LAM, Lawrence (1983) 'Vietnamese Chinese Refugees in Montreal', unpublished PhD thesis, York University, Toronto.

LEE, Everett A. (1966) 'A theory of migration', *Demography* 3(1): 47–57.

LUCIUK, Lubomyr Y. (1986) 'Unintended consequences in refugee settlement: postwar Ukranian refugee immigration to Canada', *International Migration Review* 20(2): 467–82.

MABOGUNJE, A.L. (1970) 'Systems approach to a theory of rural–urban migration', *Geographical Analysis* 2(1): 1–18.

MANGALAM, J.J. (1968) *Human Migration: A Guide to Migration Literature in English*. Lexington: University of Kentucky Press.

MARRUS, Michael R. (1985) *The Unwanted: European Refugees in the Twentieth Century*. Oxford: Oxford University Press.

MYRDAL, Alva (1976) *The Game of Disarmament: How the United States and Russia Run the Arms Race*. New York: Pantheon Books.

PARSONS, Talcott (1937) *The Structure of Social Action*. New York: McGraw-Hill.

PARSONS, Talcott (1960) 'The distribution of power in American society', in T. Parsons, *Structure and Process in Industrial Societies*, Glencoe, IL: The Free Press.

PEDRAZA-BAILEY, Silvia (1985) 'Cuba's exiles: portrait of a refugee migration', *International Migration Review* 19(1): 4–34.

PEDRAZA-BAILEY, Silvia (1985) *Political and Economic Migrants in America*. Austin, TX: University of Texas Press.

PETERSEN, W. (1958) 'A general typology of migration', *American Sociological Review* 23(3): 256–65.

PETRAS, E. McLean (1981) 'The global market in the modern world economy' in M.M. Kritz et al. (eds) *Global Trends in Migration: Theory and Research on International Movements*, pp. 44–63.

PORTES, Alexandro (1983) 'International labor migration and national development', in M.M. Kritz (ed.) *US Immigration and Refugee Policy: Global and Domestic Issues*, pp. 71–92.

PORTES, Alexandro and Rafael MOZO (1986) 'The political and adaptation process of Cubans and other ethnic minorities in the United States', *International Migration Review* 51(6): 35–63.

PORTES, Alexandro and Alex STEPICK (1985) 'Unwelcome immigrants: the labor market experience of Cuban and Haitian refugees in south Florida', *American Sociological Review* 50(4): 493–514.

PRICE, Charles (1969) 'Assimilation' in J. Jackson (ed.) *Sociological Studies 2: Migration*.

RAO, G. Lakshama, A.H. RICHMOND and J. ZUBRZYCKI (1984) *Immigrants in Canada and Australia*. Volume 1: *Demographic Aspects and Education*. Ethnic Research Programme: Institute for Social Research, York University, Toronto.

RAVENSTEIN, E.G. (1885) 'The laws of migration', *Journal of the Royal Statistical Society* 48: 167–227.

RAVENSTEIN, E.G. (1889) 'The laws of migration', *Journal of the Royal Statistical Society* 52: 242–305.

RICHMOND, A.H. (1969) 'Sociology of migration in industrial and post-industrial societies', in J.A. Jackson (ed.) *Sociological Studies 2: Migration*, pp. 238–81.

RICHMOND, A.H. and R.B.P. VERMA (1978) 'The economic adaptation of immigrants: a new theoretical perspective', *International Migration Review* 17(1): 3–28.

RICHMOND, A.H. and J. ZUBRZYCKI (1984) *Immigrants in Canada and Australia*. Vol. 2: *Economic Adaptation*. Ethnic Research Programme, Institute for Social Research, York University, Toronto.

RICHMOND, A.H. (1988) *Immigration and Ethnic Conflict*. London: Macmillan.

RODAL, Alti (1987) *Nazi War Criminals in Canada: The Historical and Policy Setting from the 1940s to the Present* (unpublished report to the Deschenes Commission). Ottawa: Public Archives of Canada.

ROSSI, Peter H. (1955) *Why Families Move*. Glencoe: The Free Press.

SAID, Edward (1984) 'The winter of the mind: reflections on life in exile', *Harpers* (September 1984): 49–55.

SAMPSON, Anthony (1977) *The Arms Bazaar: the Companies, the Dealers, the Bribes*. London: Hodder and Stoughton.

SCIULLI, David (1986) 'Voluntaristic action as a distinct concept: theoretical foundations of societal constitutionalism', *American Sociological Review* 51(6): 743–66.

SIMMONS, Alan B. (1977) *Social Change and Internal Migration: A Review of Findings from Africa, Asia and Latin America*. Ottawa: International Development Research Centre.

SIMMONS, Alan B. (1985–6) 'Recent studies in place utility and intention to migrate: an international comparison', *Population and Environment* 8(1–2): 120–41.

SIVARD, Ruth Leger (1985) *World Military and Social Expenditures, 1985*, Washington, DC: World Priorities.

STEIN, Barry (1981) 'The refugee experience: defining the parameters of a field of study', *International Migration Review* 15(1): 320–30.

STOUFFER, Samuel A. (1940) 'Intervening opportunities: a theory relating to mobility and distance', *American Sociological Review* 5: 845–67.

STOUFFER, Samuel A. (1960) 'Intervening opportunities and competing migrants', *Journal of Regional Science* 2: 1–26.

TOS, N. and P. KLINAR (1976) 'A system model for migration research: Yugoslav workers in the Federal Republic of Germany', in A.H. Richmond (ed.) *International Migration and Adaptation in the Modern World*, Toronto: ISA, Research Committee on Migration.

TURNER, Jonathan (1987) 'Toward a sociological theory of motivation', *American Sociological Review* 52(1): 15–27.

TYHURST, L. (1977) 'Psychosocial first aid for refugees', *Mental Health and Society* 4: 319–43.

WALLERSTEIN, I. (1974) *The Modern World System: Capitalist Agriculture and the Origins of the European World Economy of the Sixteenth century*. New York: Academic Press.

WEINER, M. (1985) 'On international migration and international relations', *Population and Development Review* 11(3): 441–56.

WORLD BANK (1984) *World Development Report, 1984*. New York: Oxford University Press.

WRIGHT, Peter (1987) *Spycatcher*. Toronto: Stoddart.

ZOLBERG, A.R. (1986) 'International factors in the formation of refugee movements', *International Migration Review* 20(2): 151–69.

ZWINGMANN, C. and M. PFISTER-AMMENDE (eds) (1973) *Uprooting and After*, New York: Springer-Verlag.

Name Index